Machine Learning Using R

With Time Series and Industry-Based Use Cases in R

Second Edition

Karthik Ramasubramanian

Abhishek Singh

Apress®

Machine Learning Using R: With Time Series and Industry-Based Use Cases in R

Karthik Ramasubramanian
New Delhi, Delhi, India

Abhishek Singh
New Delhi, Delhi, India

ISBN-13 (pbk): 978-1-4842-4214-8
ISBN-13 (electronic): 978-1-4842-4215-5
https://doi.org/10.1007/978-1-4842-4215-5

Library of Congress Control Number: 2018965407

Managing Director, Apress Media LLC: Welmoed Spahr
Acquisitions Editor: Celestin Suresh John
Development Editor: Matthew Moodie
Coordinating Editor: Aditee Mirashi

Cover designed by eStudioCalamar

Cover image designed by Freepik (www.freepik.com)

Distributed to the book trade worldwide by Springer Science+Business Media New York, 233 Spring Street, 6th Floor, New York, NY 10013. Phone 1-800-SPRINGER, fax (201) 348-4505, e-mail orders-ny@springer-sbm.com, or visit www.springeronline.com. Apress Media, LLC is a California LLC and the sole member (owner) is Springer Science + Business Media Finance Inc (SSBM Finance Inc). SSBM Finance Inc is a **Delaware** corporation.

For information on translations, please e-mail rights@apress.com, or visit http://www.apress.com/rights-permissions.

Apress titles may be purchased in bulk for academic, corporate, or promotional use. eBook versions and licenses are also available for most titles. For more information, reference our Print and eBook Bulk Sales web page at http://www.apress.com/bulk-sales.

Any source code or other supplementary material referenced by the author in this book is available to readers on GitHub via the book's product page, located at www.apress.com/978-1-4842-4214-8. For more detailed information, please visit http://www.apress.com/source-code.

Printed on acid-free paper

To our parents for being the guiding light and a strong pillar of support.

And to our long friendship.

Table of Contents

About the Authors

Karthik Ramasubramanian has over seven years of practice and leading data science and business analytics in retail, FMCG, eCommerce, information technology, and the hospitality industry with multi-national companies and unicorn startups. Karthik is a researcher and problem solver with a diverse set of experiences in the data science lifecycle, starting from a data problem discovery to creating data science PoCs and products for various industry use cases. In his leadership roles, he has been instrumental in solving many RoI driven business problems through data science solutions. He has mentored and trained hundreds of professionals and students around the world through various online platforms and university engagement programs in data science.

On the descriptive side of data science, he has designed, developed, and spearheaded many A/B experiment frameworks for improving product features, conceptualized funnel analysis for understanding user interactions and identifying the friction points within a product, and designed statistically robust metrics. On the predictive side, he has developed intelligent chatbots based on deep learning models that understand human-like interactions, customer segmentation models, recommendation systems, and many Natural Language Processing models.

His current areas of interest include ROI-driven data product development, advanced machine learning algorithms, data product frameworks, Internet of Things (IoT), scalable data platforms, and model deployment frameworks.

Karthik Completed his M.Sc. in Theoretical Computer Science from PSG College of Technology, Coimbatore (Affiliated to Anna University, Chennai), where he pioneered the application of machine learning, data mining, and fuzzy logic in his research work on computer and network security.

Abhishek Singh is on a mission to profess the de facto language of this millennium, the numbers. He is on a journey to bring machines closer to humans, for a better and more beautiful world by generating opportunities with artificial intelligence and machine learning. He leads a team of data science professionals who are solving pressing problems in food security, cyber security, natural disasters, healthcare, and many more areas, all with the help of data and technology. Abhishek is in the process of bringing smart IoT devices to smaller cities in India so people can leverage technology for the betterment of life.

He has worked with colleagues from many parts of the United States, Europe, and Asia, and strives to work with more people from various backgrounds. In a span of six years at big corporations, he has stress-tested the assets of U.S. banks, solved insurance pricing models, and made telecom experiences easier for customers. He is now creating data science opportunities with his team of young minds.

He actively participates in analytics-related thought leadership, authoring, public speaking, meetups, and training in data science. He is a staunch supporter of responsible use of AI to remove biases and fair use for a better society.

Abhishek completed his MBA from IIM Bangalore, a B.Tech. in Mathematics and Computing from IIT Guwahati, and a PG Diploma in Cyber Law from NALSAR University, Hyderabad.

About the Technical Reviewer

Taweh Beysolow II is a data scientist and author currently based in San Francisco, California. He has a Bachelor's of Science degree in economics from St. Johns University and a Master of Science in applied statistics from Fordham University. His professional experience has included working at Booz Allen Hamilton as a consultant and in various startups as a data scientist, specifically focusing on machine learning. He has applied machine learning to the Federal Consulting, Financial Services, and Agricultural sectors.

Acknowledgments

We are grateful to our teachers, open source communities, and colleagues for enriching us with the knowledge and confidence to write the first edition of this book. Thanks to all our readers. You have made the second edition of the book possible. The knowledge in this book is an accumulation of several years of research work and professional experience gained at our alma mater and industry. We are grateful to Prof R. Nadarajan and Prof R. Anitha, Department of Applied Mathematics and Computational Sciences, PSG College of Technology, Coimbatore, for their continued support and encouragement for our efforts in the field of data science.

In the rapidly changing world, the field of machine learning is evolving very fast and most of the latest developments are driven by the open source platform. We thank all the developers and contributors across the globe who are freely sharing their knowledge. We also want to thank our colleagues our our past and current companies—Snapdeal, Deloitte, Hike, Prudential, Probyto, and Mahindra & Mahindr—for providing opportunities to experiment and create cutting-edge data science solutions.

Karthik especially would like to thank his father, Mr. S Ramasubramanian, for always being a source of inspiration in his life. He is immensely thankful to his supervisor, Mr. Nikhil Dwarakanath, director of the data science team at Snapdeal, for creating the opportunities to bring about the best analytics professional in him and providing the motivation to take up challenging projects.

Abhishek would like to thank his father, Mr. Charan Singh, a senior scientist in the India meteorological department, for introducing him to the power of data in weather forecasting in his formative years. On a personal front, Abhishek would like to thank his mother Jaya, sister Asweta, and brother Avilash, for their continued moral support.

We want to thank our publisher Apress, specifically Celestine, for proving us with this opportunity, Sanchita Prachi for managing the first edition of the book, and Aditee Mirashi for the second edition, Poonam and Piyush for their reviews, and everybody involved in the production team.

—Karthik Ramasubramanian
—Abhishek Singh

Introduction

In the second edition of *Machine Learning Using R,* we added a new chapter on time series modeling (Chapter 9), a traditional topic that has its genesis from statistics. The second newly added chapter is deep learning (Chapter 11), which is fast emerging as a sub-field of machine learning. Apart from these two new chapters, the overall presentation of text and code in the book is put out in a new reader-friendly format.

The new edition continues to focus on building the use cases using R, a popular statistical programming language. For topics like deep learning, it might be advised to adopt Python with frameworks like TensorFlow. However, in this new edition, we will show you how to use the R programming language with TensorFlow, hence avoiding the effort of learning Python if you are only comfortable with R.

Like in the first edition, we have kept the fine balance of theory and application of machine learning through various real-world use cases, which give the readers a truly comprehensive collection of topics in machine leaning in one volume.

What you'll learn:

- Understand machine learning algorithms using R
- Master a machine learning model building a process flow
- Theoretical foundations of machine learning algorithms
- Industry focused real-world use cases
- Time series modeling in R
- Deep learning using Keras and TensorFlow in R

Who This Book is For

This book is for data scientists, data science professionals, and researchers in academia who want to understand the nuances of machine learning approaches/algorithms in practice using R. The book will also benefit readers who want to understand the technology behind implementing a scalable machine learning model using Apache Hadoop, Hive, Pig, and Spark.

This book is a comprehensive guide for anybody who wants to understand the machine learning model building process from end to end, including:

- Practical demonstration of concepts in R
- Machine learning models using Apache Hadoop and Spark
- Time series analysis
- Introduction to deep learning models using Keras and TensorFlow using R

CHAPTER 1

Introduction to Machine Learning and R

Beginners to machine learning are often confused by the plethora of algorithms and techniques being taught in subjects like statistical learning, data mining, artificial intelligence, soft computing, and data science. It's natural to wonder how these subjects are different from one another and which is the best for solving real-world problems. There is substantial overlap in these subjects and it's hard to draw a clear Venn diagram explaining the differences. Primarily, the foundation for these subjects is derived from probability and statistics. However, many statisticians probably won't agree with machine learning giving life to statistics, giving rise to the never-ending chicken and egg conundrum kind of discussions. Fundamentally, without spending much effort in understanding the pros and cons of this discussion, it's wise to believe that the power of statistics needed a pipeline to flow across different industries with some challenging problems to be solved and machine learning simply established that high-speed and frictionless pipeline. The other subjects that evolved from statistics and machine learning are simply trying to broaden the scope of these two subjects and putting it into a bigger banner.

Except for statistical learning, which is generally offered by mathematics or statistics departments in the majority of the universities across the globe, the rest of these subjects—like machine learning, data mining, artificial intelligence, and soft computing—are taught by computer science department.

In the recent years, this separation is disappearing but the collaboration between the two departments is still not complete. Programmers are intimidated by the complex theorems and proofs and statisticians hate *talking* (read as *coding*) to machines all the time. But as more industries are becoming data- and product-driven, the need for getting the two departments to speak a common language is strongly emphasized. Roles in industry are suitably revamped to create openings like machine learning engineers, data engineers, and data scientists into a broad group being called the *data science team*.

K. Ramasubramanian and A. Singh, *Machine Learning Using R*, https://doi.org/10.1007/978-1-4842-4215-5_1

The purpose of this chapter is to take one step back and demystify the terminologies as we travel through the history of machine learning and emphasize that putting the ideas from statistics and machine learning into practice by broadening the scope is critical.

At the same time, we elaborate on the importance of learning the fundamentals of machine learning with an approach inspired by the contemporary techniques from data science. We have simplified all the mathematics to as much extent as possible without compromising the fundamentals and core part of the subject. The right balance of statistics and computer science is always required for understanding machine learning, and we have made every effort for our readers to appreciate the elegance of mathematics, which at times is perceived by many to be hard and full of convoluted definitions, theories, and formulas.

1.1 Understanding the Evolution

The first challenge anybody finds when starting to understand how to build intelligent machines is how to mimic human behavior in many ways or, to put it even more appropriately, how to do things even better and more efficiently than humans. Some examples of these things performed by machines are identifying spam emails, predicting customer churn, classifying documents into respective categories, playing chess, participating in jeopardy, cleaning house, playing football, and much more. Carefully looking at these examples will reveal that humans haven't perfected these tasks to date and rely heavily on machines to help them. So, now the question remains, where do you start learning to build such intelligent machines? Often, depending on which task you want to take up, experts will point you to machine learning, artificial intelligence (AI), or many such subjects, that sound different by name but are intrinsically connected.

In this chapter, we have taken up the task to knit together this evolution and finally put forth the point that machine learning, which is the first block in this evolution, is where you should fundamentally start to later delve deeper into other subjects.

1.1.1 Statistical Learning

The whitepaper, *Discovery with Data: Leveraging Statistics with Computer Science to Transform Science and Society* by American Statistical Association (ASA) [1], published in July 2014, defines *statistics* as "the science of learning from data, and of measuring, controlling, and communicating uncertainty is the most mature of the data sciences".

This discipline has been an essential part of the social, natural, bio-medical, and physical sciences, engineering, and business analytics, among others. Statistical thinking not only helps make scientific discoveries, but it quantifies the reliability, reproducibility, and general uncertainty associated with these discoveries. This excerpt from the whitepaper is very precise and powerful in describing the importance of statistics in data analysis.

Tom Mitchell, in his article, "The Discipline of Machine Learning [2]," appropriately points out, "Over the past 50 years, the study of machine learning has grown from the efforts of a handful of computer engineers exploring whether computers could learn to play games, and a field of statistics that largely ignored computational considerations, to a broad discipline that has produced fundamental statistical-computational theories of learning processes."

This learning process has found its application in a variety of tasks for commercial and profitable systems like computer vision, robotics, speech recognition, and many more. At large, it's when statistics and computational theories are fused together that machine learning emerges as a new discipline.

1.1.2 Machine Learning (ML)

The Samuel Checkers-Playing Program, which is known to be the first computer program that could learn, was developed in 1959 by Arthur Lee Samuel, one of the fathers of machine learning. Followed by Samuel, *Ryszard S. Michalski,* also deemed a father of machine learning, came out with a system for recognizing handwritten alphanumeric characters, working along with Jacek Karpinski in 1962-1970. The subject from then has evolved with many facets and led the way for various applications impacting businesses and society for the good.

Tom Mitchell defined the fundamental question machine learning seeks to answer as, "How can we build computer systems that automatically improve with experience, and what are the fundamental laws that govern all learning processes?" He further explains that the defining question of computer science is, "How can we build machines that solve problems, and which problems are inherently tractable/intractable?", whereas statistics focus on answering "What can be inferred from data plus a set of modeling assumptions, with what reliability?"

This set of questions clearly shows the difference between statistics and machine learning. As mentioned earlier in the chapter, it might not even be necessary to deal with the chicken and egg conundrum, as we clearly see that one simply complements the other and is paving the path for the future. As we dive deep into the concepts of statistics and machine learning, you will see the differences clearly emerging or at times completely disappearing. Another line of thought, in the paper "Statistical Modeling: The Two Cultures" by Leo Breiman in 2001 [3], argued that statisticians rely too heavily on data modeling, and that machine learning techniques are instead focusing on the predictive accuracy of models.

1.1.3 Artificial Intelligence (AI)

The AI world from very beginning was intrigued by games. Whether it be *checkers, chess, Jeopardy,* or the recently very popular *Go,* the AI world strives to build machines that can play against humans to beat them in these games and it has received much accolades for the same. IBM's Watson beat the two best players of Jeopardy, a quiz game show wherein participants compete to come out with their responses as a phrase in the form of questions to some general knowledge clues in the form of answers. Considering the complexity in analyzing natural language phrases in these answers, it was considered to be very hard for machines to compete with humans. A high-level architecture of IBM's DeepQA used in Watson looks something like in Figure 1-1.

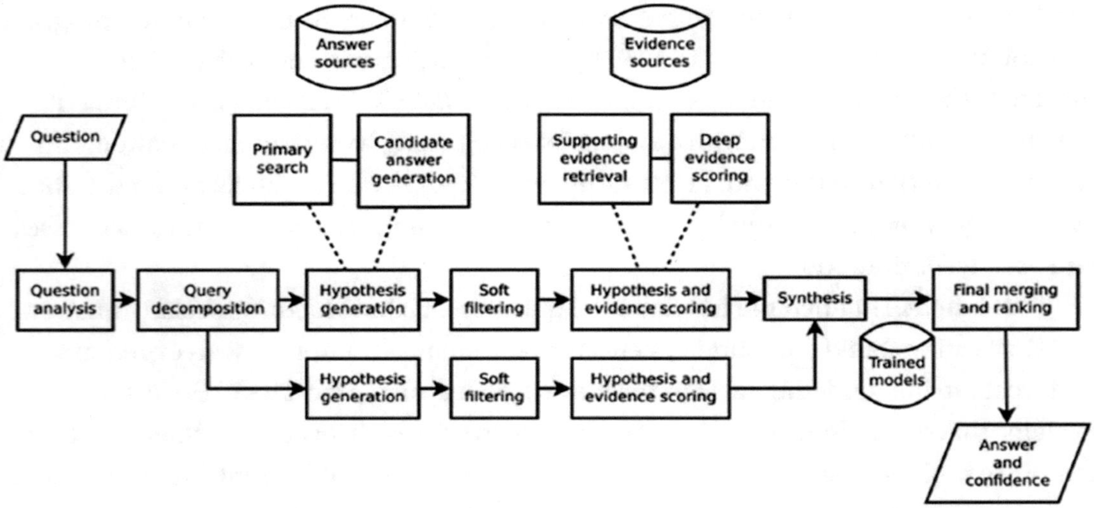

Figure 1-1. *Architecture of IBM's DeepQA*

AI also sits at the core of robotics. The 1971 Turing Award winner, John McCarthy, a well known American computer scientist, was believed to have coined this term and in his article titled, "What Is Artificial Intelligence?" he defined it as "the science and engineering of making intelligent machines [4]". So, if you relate back to what we said about machine learning, we instantly sense a connection between the two, but AI goes the extra mile to congregate a number of sciences and professions, including linguistics, philosophy, psychology, neuroscience, mathematics, and computer science, as well as other specialized fields such as artificial psychology. It should also be pointed out that machine learning is often considered to be a subset of AI.

1.1.4 Data Mining

Knowledge Discovery and Data Mining (KDD), a premier forum for data mining, states its goal to be advancement, education, and adoption of the "science" for knowledge discovery and data mining. Data mining, like ML and AI, has emerged as a interdisciplinary subfield of computer science and for this reason, KDD commonly projects data mining methods, as the intersection of AI, ML, statistics, and database systems. Data mining techniques were integrated into many database systems and business intelligence tools, when adoption of analytic services were starting to explode in many industries.

The research paper, "WEKA Experiences with a Java open-source project"[5] (WEKA is one of the widely adapted tools for doing research and projects using data mining), published in the *Journal of Machine Learning Research,* talked about how the classic book, *Data Mining: Practical Machine Learning Tools and Techniques with Java,[6]* was originally named just *Practical Machine Learning,* and the term data mining was only added for marketing reasons. Eibe Frank and Mark A. Hall, who wrote this research paper, are the two coauthors of the book, so we have a strong rationale to believe this reason for the name change. Once again, we see fundamentally, ML being at the core of data mining.

1.1.5 Data Science

It's not wrong to call data science a big umbrella that brought everything with a potential to show insight from data and build intelligent systems inside it. In the book, *Data Science for Business [7],* Foster Provost and Tom Fawcett introduced the notion of viewing data and data science capability as a strategic asset, which will help businesses think explicitly about the extent to which one should invest in them. In a way, data science has emphasized the importance of data more than the algorithms of learning.

It has established a well defined process flow that says, first think about doing descriptive data analysis and then later start to think about modeling. As a result of this, businesses have started to adopt this new methodology because they were able to relate to it. Another incredible change data science has brought is around creating the synergies between various departments within a company. Every department has its own subject matter experts and data science teams have started to build their expertise in using data as a common language to communicate. This paradigm shift has witnessed the emergence of data-driven growth and many data products. Data science has given us a framework, which aims to create a conglomerate of skillsets, tools, and technologies. Drew Conway, the famous American data scientist who is known for his Venn diagram definition of data science as shown in Figure 1-2, has very rightly placed machine learning in the intersection of Hacking Skills and Math & Statistics Knowledge.

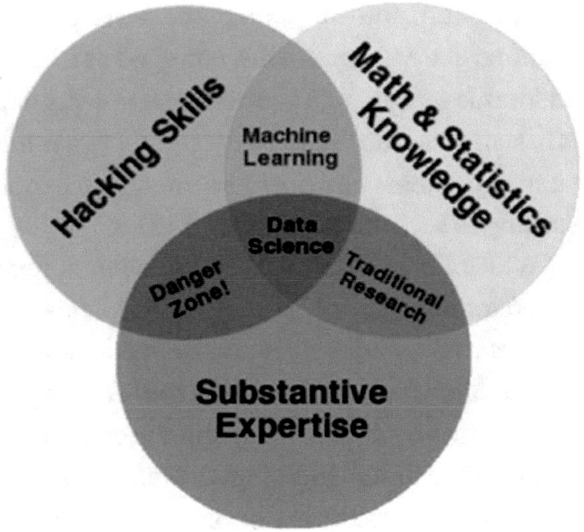

Figure 1-2. *Venn diagram definition of data science*

We strongly believe the fundamentals of these different fields of study are all derived from statistics and machine learning but different flavors, for reasons justifiable in its own context, were given to it, which helped the subject be molded into various systems and areas of research. This book will help trim down the number of different terminologies being used to describe the same set of algorithms and tools. It will present a simple-to-understand and coherent approach, the algorithms in machine learning and its practical use with R. Wherever it's appropriate, we will emphasize the need to go outside the scope of this book and guide our readers with the relevant materials. By doing so, we are re-emphasizing the need for mastering traditional approaches in machine learning and, at the same time, staying abreast with the latest development in tools and technologies in this space.

Our design of topics in this book are strongly influenced by data science framework but instead of wandering through the vast pool of tools and techniques you would find in the world of data science, we have kept our focus strictly on teaching practical ways of applying machine learning algorithms with R.

The rest of this chapter is organized to help readers understand the elements of probability and statistics and programming skills in R. Both of these will form the foundations for understanding and putting machine learning into practical use. The chapter ends with a discussion of technologies that apply ML to a real-world problem. Also, a generic machine learning process flow will be presented showing how to connect the dots, starting from a given problem statement to deploying ML models to working with real-world systems.

1.2 Probability and Statistics

Common sense and gut instincts play a key role for policymakers, leaders, and entrepreneurs in building nations and large enterprises. The question is, how do we change some intractable qualitative decision making into objectively understood quantitative decision making? That's where probability and statistics come in. Much of statistics is focused on analyzing existing data and drawing suitable conclusions using probability models. Though it's very common to use probabilities in many statistical modeling, we feel it's important to identify the different questions probability and statistics help us answer. An example from the book, *Learning Statistics with R: A Tutorial for Psychology Students and Other Beginners* by Daniel Navarro [8], University of Adelaide, helps us understand it much better. Consider these two pairs of questions:

1. What are the chances of a fair coin coming up heads 10 times in a row?
2. If my friend flips a coin 10 times and gets 10 heads. Is she playing a trick on me?

and

1. How likely it is that five cards drawn from a perfectly shuffled deck will all be hearts?
2. If five cards off the top of the deck are all hearts, how likely is it that the deck was shuffled?

In case of the coin toss, the first question could be answered if we know the coin is fair, there's a 50% chance that any individual coin flip will come up heads, in probability notation, P(heads) = 0.5. So, our probability is `P(heads 10 times in a row) =.0009765625` (since all the 10 coin tosses are independent of each other, we can simply compute (0.5)10 to arrive at this value). The probability value .0009765625 quantifies the chances of a fair coin coming up heads 10 times in a row.

On the other side, such a small probability would mean the occurrence of the event (heads 10 times in a row) is very rare, which helps to *infer* that my friend is playing some trick on me when she got all heads. Think about this—does tossing a coin 10 times give you strong evidence for doubting your friend? Maybe no; you may ask her to repeat the process several times. The more the data we generate, the better will be the inference. The second set of questions has the same thought process but is applied to a different problem. We encourage you to perform the calculations yourself to answer the question.

So, fundamentally, probability could be used as a tool in statistics to help us answer many such real-world questions using a model. We will explore some basics of both these worlds, and it will become evident that both converge at a point where it's hard to observe many differences between the two.

1.2.1 Counting and Probability Definition

Imagine we are conducting an experiment with coin flips, in which we will flip three coins eight times each. Each combination of heads and tails constitutes a unique outcome. For example, HHH is a unique outcome. The possible outcomes are the following: (HHH, HHT, HTH, HTT, THH, THT, TTH, and TTT). Figure 1-3 shows a basic illustration of this experiment, with three coins, a total of eight possible outcomes (HHH, HHT, HTH, HTT, THH, THT, TTH, and TTT) are present. This set is called the *sample space*.

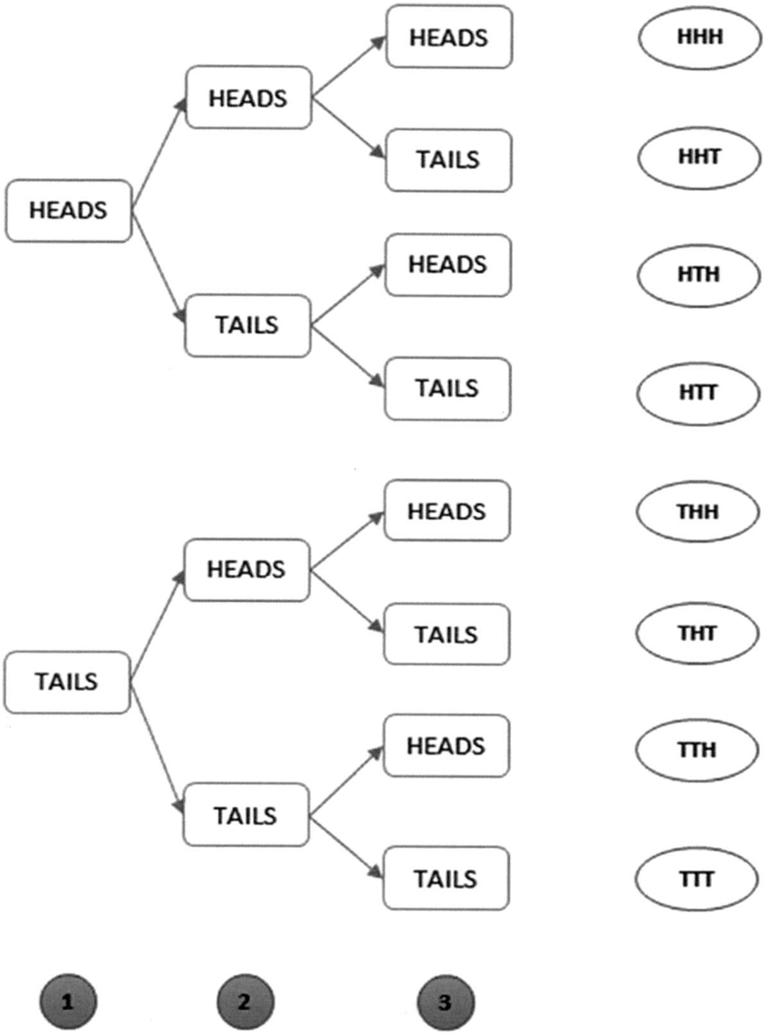

Figure 1-3. *Sample space of three-coin tossing experiment*

It's easy to count the total number of possible outcomes in such a simple example with three coins, but as the size and complexity of the problem increase, manually counting is not an option. A more formal approach is to use combinations and permutations. If the order is of significance, we call it a *permutation*; otherwise, generally the term *combination* is used. For instance, if we say it doesn't matter which coin gets heads or tails out of the three coins, we are only interested in number of heads, which is like saying there is no significance to the order, then our total number of possible combination will be {HHH, HHT, HTT, TTT}. This means HHT and HTH are the same, since there are two heads on these outcomes. A more formal way to obtain the number of possible outcome is shown in Table 1-1. It's easy to see that, for the value n = 2 (heads and tails) and k = 3 (three coins), we get eight possible permutations and four combinations.

Table 1-1. *Permutation and Combinations*

	Permutation	Combination
With Replacement	n^k	$\binom{n+k-1}{k}$
Without Replacement	$\frac{n!}{(n-k)!}$	$\binom{n}{k}$

Relating back to the example first illustrated, suppose we are interested in event E, which constitutes two of the three coins flipped appearing as heads. Order in this instance does not matter, so it is a combination and there is replacement. As such, the following probability is yielded:

$$P(\text{Two heads}) = \frac{\text{number of outcomes favourable to E}}{\text{total number of outcomes}} = \frac{4}{8} = 0.5$$

This way of calculating the probability using the counts or frequency of occurrence is also known as the *frequentist probability*. There is another class called the *Bayesian probability* or conditional probability, which we will explore later in the chapter.

1.2.2 Events and Relationships

In the previous section, we saw an example of an event. Let's go a step further and set a formal notion around various events and their relationship with each other.

1.2.2.1 Independent Events

A and B are independent if occurrence of A gives no additional information about whether B occurred. Imagine that Facebook enhances their Nearby Friends feature and tells you the probability of your friend visiting the same cineplex for a movie in the weekends where you frequent. In the absence of such a feature in Facebook, the information that you are a very frequent visitor to this cineplex doesn't really increase or decrease the probability of you meeting your friend at the cineplex. This is because the events—A, you visiting the cineplex for a movie and B, your friend visiting the cineplex for a movie—are independent.

On the other hand, if such a feature exists, we can't deny you would try your best to increase or decrease your probability of meeting your friend depending on if he or she is close to you or not. And this is only possible because the two events are now linked by a feature in Facebook.

Let's take another example of a dependent. When the sun is out in Pleasantville it never rains; however, if the sun is not out, it will definitely rain. Farmer John cannot harvest crops in the rain. Therefore, any individual harvest is dependent on it not raining.

In the commonly used set theory notations, A and B (both have a non-zero probability) are independent *iff* (read as if and only if) one of the following equivalent statements holds:

1. The probability of events A and B occurring at the same time is equal to the product of probability of event A and probability of event B

$$P(A \cap B) = P(A)P(B)$$

where, $\cap$ represent intersection of the two events and probability of A given B.

2. The probability of event A given B has already occurred is equal to the probability of A

$$P(A|B) = P(A)$$

3. Similarly, the probability of event B given A has already occurred is equal to the probability of B

$$P(B|A) = P(B)$$

For the event A = Tossing two heads, and event B = Tossing head on first coin, so $P(A \cap B) = 3/8 = 0.375$ whereas $P(A)P(B) = 4 / 8 * 4 / 8 = 0.25$ which is not equal to $P(A \cap B)$. Similarly, the other two conditions can also be validated.

1.2.2.2 Conditional Independence

In the Facebook Nearby Friends example, we were able to ascertain that the probability of you and your friend both visiting the cineplex at the same time has to do something with your location and intentions. Though intentions are very hard to quantify, it's not the case with location. So, if we define the event C to be, being in a location near to cineplex, then it's not difficult to calculate the probability. But even when you both are nearby, it's not necessary that you and your friend would visit the cineplex. More formally, this is where we define conditionally, A and B are independent given C if $P(A \cap B| C) = P(A | C)P(B| C)$.

Note here that independence does not imply conditional independence, and conditional independence does not imply independence. It's in a way saying, A and B together are independent of another event, C.

1.2.2.3 Bayes Theorem

On the contrary, if A and B are not independent but rather information about A reveals some detail about B or vice versa, we would be interested in calculating $P(A | B)$, read as probability of A given B. This has a profound application in modeling many real-world problems. The widely used form of such conditional probability is called the *Bayes Theorem* (or *Bayes Rule*). Formally, for events A and B, the Bayes Theorem is represented as:

$$P(A|B) = \frac{P(B|A)P(A)}{P(B)}$$

where, $P(B) \neq 0$, P(A) is then called a prior probability and $P(A | B)$ is called posterior probability, which is the measure we get after an additional information B is known. Let's look at the Table 1-2, a two-way contingency table for our Facebook Nearby example, to explain this better.

Table 1-2. *Facebook Nearby Example of Two-Way Contingency Table*

	Nearby (within 1 miles)	Far	Total
Visit Cineplex	10	2	**12**
Didn't Visit Cineplex	2	11	**13**
Total	**12**	**13**	**25**

So, if we would like to know P(Visiting Cineplex | Nearby), in other words, the probability of your friend visiting the cineplex given he or she is nearby (within one mile) the cineplex. A word of caution, we are saying the probability of your friend visiting the cineplex, not the probability of you meeting the friend. The latter would be a little more complex to model, which we skip here to keep our focus intact on the Bayes Theorem. Now, assuming we know the historical data (let's say, the previous month) about your friend as shown in the Table 1-2, we know:

$$P(\text{Visit Cineplex}|\text{Nearby}) = \left(\frac{10}{12}\right) = 0.83$$

This means in the previous month, your friend was 10 times within one mile (nearby) of the cineplex and visited it. Also, there have been two instances when he was nearby but didn't visit the cineplex. Alternatively, we could have calculated the probability as:

$$P(\text{Visit Cineplex} \mid \text{Nearby}) = \frac{P(\text{Nearby} \mid \text{Visit Cineplex}) * P(\text{Visit Cineplex})}{P(\text{Nearby})}$$

$$= \frac{\left(\frac{10}{12}\right) * \left(\frac{12}{25}\right)}{\left(\frac{12}{25}\right)} = \left(\frac{10}{12}\right) = 0.83$$

This example is based on the two-way contingency table and provides a good intuition around conditional probability. We will deep dive into the machine learning algorithm called *Naive Bayes* as applied to a real-world problem, which is based on the Bayes Theorem, later in Chapter 6.

1.2.3 Randomness, Probability, and Distributions

David S. Moore et. al.'s book, *Introduction to the Practice of Statistics [9]*, is an easy-to-comprehend book with simple mathematics, but conceptually rich ideas from statistics. It very aptly points out, "random" in statistics is not a synonym for "haphazard" but a description of a kind of order that emerges in the long run. They further explain that we often deal with unpredictable events in our life on a daily basis that we generally term as random, like the example of Facebook's Nearby Friends, but we rarely see enough repetition of the same random phenomenon to observe the long-term regularity that probability describes.

In this excerpt from the book, they capture the essence of randomness, probability, and distributions very concisely.

> "We call a phenomenon random if individual outcomes are uncertain but there is nonetheless a regular distribution of outcomes in a large number of repetitions. The probability of any outcome of a random phenomenon is the proportion of times the outcome would occur in a very long series of repetitions."

This leads us to define a random variable that stores such random phenomenon numerically. In any experiment involving random events, a random variable, say X, based on the outcomes of the events will be assigned a numerical value. And the probability distribution of X helps in finding the probability for a value being assigned to X.

For example, if we define X = {number of head in three coin tosses}, then X can take values 0, 1, 2, and 3. Here we call X a discrete random variable. However, if we define X = {all values between 0 and 2}, there can be infinitely many possible values, so X is called a continuous random variable.

```
par(mfrow=c(1,2))

X_Values <-c(0,1,2,3)
X_Props <-c(1/8,3/8,3/8,1/8)
barplot(X_Props, names.arg=X_Values, ylim=c(0,1), xlab =" Discrete RV X
Values", ylab ="Probabilities")

x   <-seq(0,2,length=1000)
y   <-dnorm(x,mean=1, sd=0.5)
plot(x,y, type="l", lwd=1, ylim=c(0,1),xlab ="Continuous RV X Values",
ylab ="Probabilities")
```

This code will plot the distribution of X, a typical probability distribution function, and will look like Figure 1-4. The second plot showing continuous distribution is a normal distribution with mean = 1 and standard deviation = 0.5. It's also called the *probability density function*. Don't worry if you are not familiar with these statistical terms; we will explore these in more detail later in the book. For now, it is enough to understand the random variable and what we mean by its distribution.

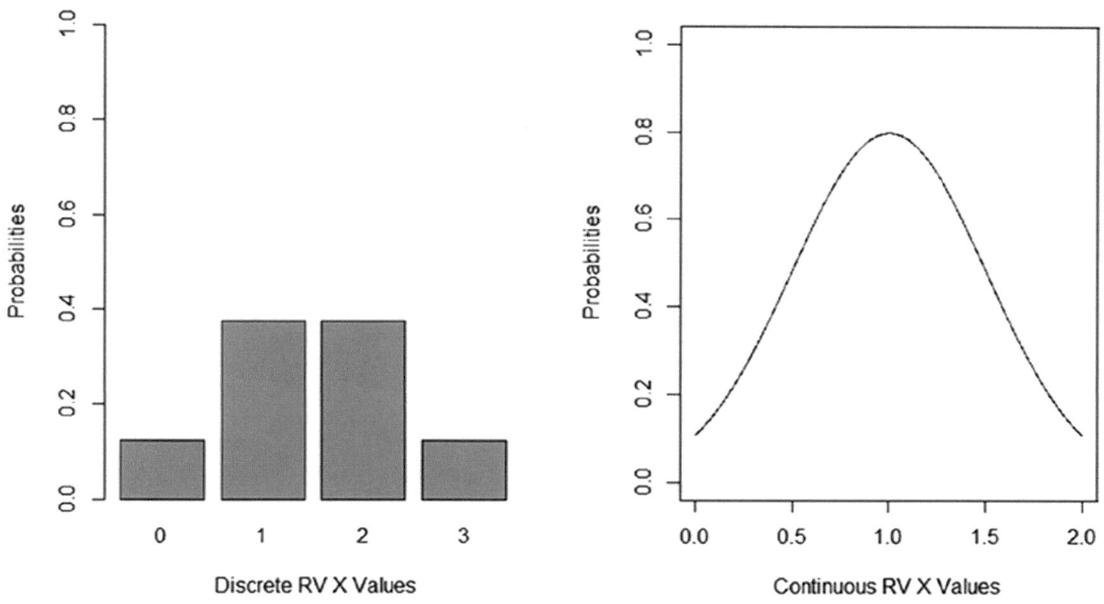

Figure 1-4. *Probability distribution with a discrete and continuous random variable*

1.2.4 Confidence Interval and Hypothesis Testing

Suppose you were running a socioeconomic survey for your state among a chosen sample from the entire population (assuming it's chosen totally at random). As the data starts to pour in, you feel excited and, at the same time, a little confused on how you should analyze the data. There could be many insights that can come from data and it's possible that every insight may not be completely valid, as the survey is only based on a small randomly chosen sample.

Law of Large Numbers (more detailed discussion on this topic in Chapter 3) in statistics tells us that the sample mean must approach the population mean as the sample size increases. In other words, we are saying it's not required that you survey each and every individual in your state but rather choose a sample large enough to be a close representative of the entire population. Even though measuring uncertainty gives us power to make better decisions, in order to make our insights statistically significant, we need to create a hypothesis and perform certain tests.

1.2.4.1 Confidence Interval

Let's start by understanding the confidence interval. Suppose that a 10-yearly census survey questionnaire contains information on income levels. And say, in the year 2005, we find that for the sample size of 1000, repeatedly chosen from the population, the sample mean $\overline{x}$ follows the normal distribution with population mean μ and standard error $\sigma / \sqrt{n}$. If we know the standard deviation, σ, to be $1500, then

$$\sigma_{\overline{x}} = \frac{1500}{\sqrt{1000}} = 47.4.$$

Now, in order to define confidence interval, which generally takes a form like this

```
estimate ± margin of error
```

A 95% confidence interval (CI) is twice the standard error (also called margin of error) plus or minus the mean. In our example, suppose the $\overline{x} = 990$ dollars and standard deviation as computed is $47.4, then we would have a confidence interval (895.2,1084.8), i.e., 990 ± 2 * 47.4. If we repeatedly choose many samples, each would have a different confidence interval but statistics tells us that 95% of the time, CI will contain the true population mean μ. There are other stringent CIs like 99.7% but 95% is a golden standard for all practical purposes. Figure 1-5 shows 25 samples and the CIs. The normal distribution of the population helps to visualize the number of CIs where the estimate μ wasn't contained in the CI; in this figure, there is only one such CI.

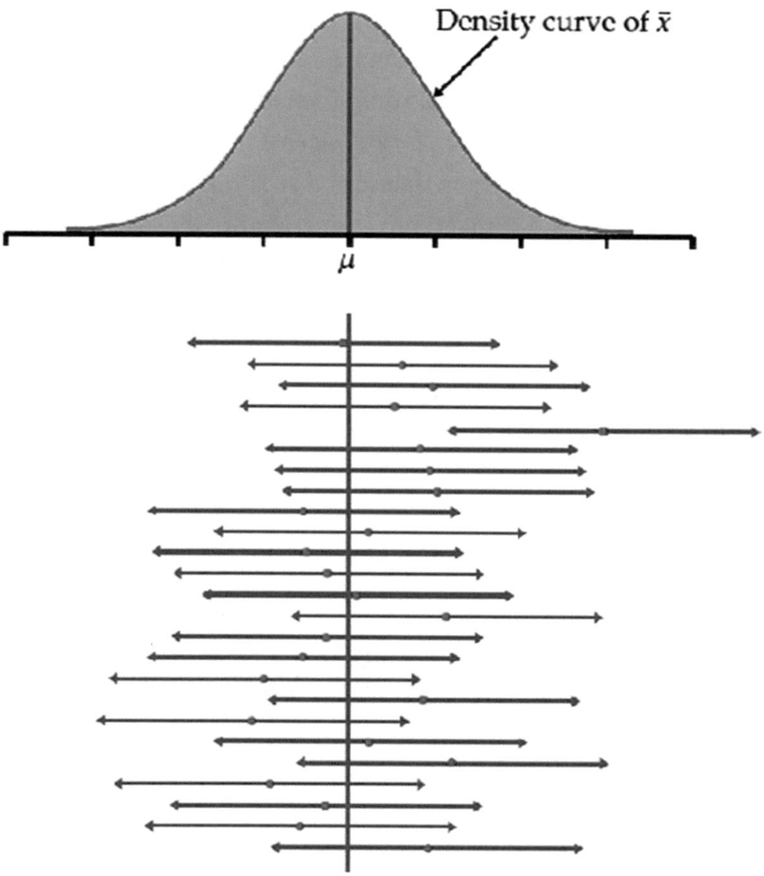

Figure 1-5. *Confidence interval*

1.2.4.2 Hypothesis Testing

Hypothesis testing is sometimes also known as a *test of significance*. Although CI is a strong representative of the population estimate, we need a more robust and formal procedure for testing and comparing an assumption about population parameters of the observed data. The application of hypothesis is wide spread, starting from assessing what's the reliability of a sample used in a survey for an opinion poll to finding out the efficacy of a new drug over an existing drug for curing a disease. In general, hypothesis tests are tools for checking the validity of a statement around certain statistics relating to an experiment design. If you recall, the high-level architecture of IBM's DeepQA has an important step called *hypothesis generation* in coming out with the most relevant answer for a given question.

The hypothesis testing consists of two statements that are framed on the population parameter, one of which we want to reject. As we saw while discussing CI, the sampling distribution of the sample mean $\bar{x}$ follows a normal distribution $N(\mu, \sigma / \sqrt{n})$. One of most important concepts is the *Central Limit Theorem* (a more detailed discussion on this topic is in Chapter 3), which tells us that for large samples, the sampling distribution is approximately normal. Since normal distribution is one of the most explored distributions with all of its properties well known, this approximation is vital for every hypothesis test we would like to perform.

Before we perform the hypothesis test, we need to construct a confidence level of 90%, 95%, or 99%, depending on the design of the study or experiment. For doing this, we need a number z *, also referred to as the critical value, so that normal distribution has a defined probability of 0.90, 0.95, or 0.99 within +-z* standard deviation of its mean. Figure 1-6 shows the value of z* for different confidence interval. Note that in our example in the Section 1.2.4.1, we approximated z* = 1.960 for 95% confidence interval to 2.

z*	1.645	1.960	2.576
Confidence Level	90%	95%	99%

Figure 1-6. *The z* score and confidence level*

In general, we could choose any value of z* to pick the appropriate confidence level. With this explanation, let's take our income example from the census data for the year 2015. We need to find out how the income has changed over the last 10 years, i.e., from 2005 to 2015. In the year 2015, we find the estimate of our mean value for income as $2300. The question to ask here would be, since both the values $900 (in the year 2005) and $2300 are estimates of the true population mean (in other words, we have taken a representative sample but not the entire population to calculate this mean) but not the actual mean, do these observed means from the sample provide the evidence to conclude that income has increased? We might be interested in calculating some probability to answer this question. Let's see how we can formulate this in a hypothesis testing framework. A hypothesis test starts with designing two statements like so:

> H_o : There is no difference in the mean income or true mean income
>
> H_a : The true mean incomes are not the same

Abstracting the details at this point, the consequence of the two statements would simply lead toward accepting H_o or rejecting it. In general, the null hypothesis is always a statement of "no difference" and the alternative statement challenges this null. A more numerically concise way of writing these two statements would be:

$$H_o : \text{Sample Mean } \overline{x} = 0$$
$$H_a : \text{Sample Mean } \overline{x} \neq 0$$

In case we reject H_o, we have two choices to make, whether we want to test $\overline{x} > 0$, $\overline{x} < 0$ or simply $\overline{x} \neq 0$, without bothering much about direction, which is called *two-side* test. If you are clear about the direction, a *one-side test* is preferred.

Now, in order to perform the significance test, we would understand the standardized test statistics z, which is defined as follows:

$$z = \frac{\text{estimate} - \text{hypothesized value}}{\text{standard deviation of the estimate}}$$

Alternatively:

$$z = \frac{\overline{x} - \mu_0}{\sigma / \sqrt{n}}$$

Substituting the value 1400 for the estimate of the difference of income between the year 2005 and 2015, and 1500 for standard deviation of the estimate (this SD is computed with the mean of all the samples drawn from the population), we obtain

$$z = \frac{1400 - 0}{1500} = 0.93$$

The difference in income between 2005 and 2015 based on our sample is \$1400, which corresponds to 0.93 standard deviations away from zero (z = 0.93). Because we are using a two-sided test for this problem, the evidence against null hypothesis, H_o, is measured by the probability that we observe a value of Z as extreme or more extreme than 0.93. More formally, this probability is

$$P(Z \leq -0.93 \text{ or } Z \geq 0.93)$$

where Z has the standard normal distribution N(0, 1). This probability is called *p-value*. We will use this value quite often in regression models.

From standard z-score table, the standard normal probabilities, we find:

$$P(Z \geq 0.93) = 1 - 0.8238 = 0.1762)$$

Also, the probability for being extreme in the negative direction is the same:

$$P(Z \leq -0.93) = 0.1762$$

Then, the p-value becomes:

$$P = 2P(Z \geq 0.93) = 2^{*}(0.1762) = 0.3524$$

Since the probability is large enough, we have no other choice but to stick with our null hypothesis. In other words, we don't have enough evidence to reject the null hypothesis. It could also be stated as, there is 35% chance of observing a difference as extreme as the $1400 in our sample if the true population difference is zero. A note here, though; there could be numerous other ways to state our result, all of it means the same thing.

Finally, in many practical situations, it's not enough to say that the probability is large or small, but instead it's compared to a significance or confidence level. So, if we are given a 95% confidence interval (in other words, the interval that includes the true value of μ with 0.95 probability), values of μ that are not included in this interval would be incompatible with the data. Now, using this threshold $\alpha = 0.05$ (95% confidence), we observe the P-value is greater than 0.05 (or 5%), which means we still do not have enough evidence to reject H_0. Hence, we conclude that there is no difference in the mean income between the year 2005 and 2015.

There are many other ways to perform hypothesis testing, which we leave for the interested readers to refer to detailed text on the subject. Our major focus in the coming chapters is to do hypothesis testing using R for various applications in sampling and regression.

We introduce the field of probability and statistics, both of which form the foundation of data exploration and our broader goal of understanding the predictive modeling using machine learning.

1.3 Getting Started with R

R is *GNU S*, a freely available language and environment for statistical computing and graphics that provides a wide variety of statistical and graphical techniques: linear and nonlinear modeling, statistical tests, time series analysis, classification, clustering, and lot more than what you could imagine.

Although covering the complete topics of R is beyond the scope of this book, we will keep our focus intact by looking at the end goal of this book. The getting started material here is just to provide the familiarity to readers who don't have any previous exposure to programming or scripting languages. We strongly advise that the readers follow R's official website for instructions on installing and some standard textbook for more technical discussion on topics.

1.3.1 Basic Building Blocks

This section provides a quick overview of the building blocks of R, which uniquely makes R the most sought out programming language among statisticians, analysts, and scientists. R is an easy-to-learn and an excellent tool for developing prototype models very quickly.

1.3.1.1 Calculations

As you would expect, R provides all the arithmetic operations you would find in a scientific calculator and much more. All kind of comparisons like >, >=, <, and <=, and functions such as acos, asin, atan, ceiling, floor, min, max, cumsum, mean, and median are readily available for all possible computations.

1.3.1.2 Statistics with R

R is one such language that's very friendly to academicians and people with less programming background. The ease of computing statistical properties of data has also given it a widespread popularity among data analysts and statisticians. Functions are provided for computing quantile, rank, sorting data, and matrix manipulation like crossprod, eigen, and svd. There are also some really easy-to-use functions for building linear models quite quickly. A detailed discussion on such models will follow in later chapters.

1.3.1.3 Packages

The strength of R lies with its community of contributors from various domains. The developers bind everything in one single piece called a package, in R. A simple package can contain few functions for implementing an algorithm or it can be as big as the base package itself, which comes with the R installers. We will use many packages throughout the book as we cover new topics.

1.3.2 Data Structures in R

Fundamentally, there are only five types of data structures in R, and they are most often used. Almost all other data structures are built on these five. Hadley Wickham, in his book *Advanced R [10]*, provides an easy-to-comprehend segregation of these five data structures, as shown in Table 1-3.

Table 1-3. *Data Structures in R*

Dimension	Type	
	Homogeneous	Heterogeneous
1d	*Vector*	*List*
2d	*Matrix*	*Data Frame*
nd	*Array*	*N/A*

Some other data structures derived from these five and most commonly used are listed here:

- *Factors*: This one is derived from a vector
- *Data tables*: This one is derived from a data frame

The homogeneous type allows for only a single data type to be stored in vector, matrix, or array, whereas the Heterogeneous type allows for mixed types as well.

1.3.2.1 Vectors

Vectors are the simplest form of data structure in R and yet are very useful. Each vector stores all elements of same type. This could be thought as a one-dimensional array, similar to those found in programming languages like C/C++

```
car_name <-c("Honda","BMW","Ferrari")
car_color =c("Black","Blue","Red")
car_cc =c(2000,3400,4000)
```

1.3.2.2 Lists

Lists internally in R are collections of generic vectors. For instance, a list of automobiles with name, color, and cc could be defined as a list named cars, with a collection of vectors named name, color, and cc inside it.

```
cars <-list(name =c("Honda","BMW","Ferrari"),
color =c("Black","Blue","Red"),
cc =c(2000,3400,4000))
cars
 $name
[1] "Honda"     "BMW"       "Ferrari"

$color
[1] "Black"    "Blue"    "Red"

$cc
[1] 2000 3400  4000
```

1.3.2.3 Matrixes

Matrixes are the data structures that store multi-dimensional arrays with many rows and columns. For all practical purposes, its data structure helps store data in a format where every row represents a certain collection of columns. The columns hold the information that defines the observation (row).

```
mdat <-matrix(c(1,2,3, 11,12,13), nrow =2, ncol =3, byrow =TRUE,
dimnames =list(c("row1", "row2"),
c("C.1", "C.2", "C.3")))
mdat

      C.1 C.2 C.3
 row1   1   2   3
 row2  11  12  13
```

1.3.2.4 Data Frames

Data frames extend matrixes with the added capability of holding heterogeneous types of data. In a data frame, you can store character, numeric, and factor variables in different columns of the same data frame. In almost every data analysis task, with rows and columns of data, a data frame comes as a natural choice for storing the data. The following example shows how numeric and factor columns are stored in the same data frame.

```
L3 <-LETTERS[1:3]
fac <-sample(L3, 10, replace =TRUE)
df <-data.frame(x =1, y =1:10, fac = fac)
```

```
class(df$x)
 [1]  "numeric"
class(df$y)
 [1]  "integer"
class(df$fac)
 [1]  "factor"
```

1.3.3 Subsetting

R has one of the most advanced, powerful, and fast subsetting operators compared to any other programming language. It's powerful to an extent that, except for few cases, which we will discuss in the next section, there is no looping construct like `for` or `while` required, even though R explicitly provides one if needed. Though its very powerful, syntactically it could sometime turn out to be an nightmare or gross error could pop up if careful attention is not paid in placing the required number of *parentheses*, *brackets,* and *commas*. The operators `[`, `[[`, and `$` are used for subsetting, depending on which data structure is holding the data. It's also possible to combine subsetting with assignment to perform some really complicated function with very few lines of code.

1.3.3.1 Vectors

For vectors, the subsetting could be done by referring to the respective index of the elements stored in a vector. For example, `car_name[c(1,2)]` will return elements stored in index 1 and 2 and `car_name[-2]` returns all the elements except for second. It's also possible to use binary operators to instruct the vector to retrieve or not retrieve an element.

```
car_name <-c("Honda","BMW","Ferrari")

#Select 1st and 2nd index from the vector
car_name[c(1,2)]
 [1] "Honda" "BMW"
#Select all except 2nd index
car_name[-2]
 [1] "Honda"    "Ferrari"

#Select 2nd index
car_name[c(FALSE,TRUE,FALSE)]
 [1] "BMW"
```

1.3.3.2 Lists

Subsetting in lists is similar to subsetting in a vector; however, since a list is a collection of many vectors, you must use double square brackets to retrieve an element from the list. For example, `cars[2]` retrieves the entire second vector of the list and `cars[[c(2,1)]]` retrieves the first element of the second vector.

```
cars <-list(name =c("Honda","BMW","Ferrari"),
color =c("Black","Blue","Red"),
cc =c(2000,3400,4000))

#Select the second list with cars
cars[2]
 $color
 [1] "Black" "Blue" "Red"
#select the first element of second list in cars
cars[[c(2,1)]]
 [1] "Black"
```

1.3.3.3 Matrixes

Matrixes have a similar subsetting as vectors. However, instead of specifying one index to retrieve the data, we need two index here—one that signifies the row and the other for the column. For example, `mdat[1:2,]` retrieves all the columns of the first two rows, whereas `mdat[1:2,"C.1"]` retrieves the first two rows and the `C.1` column.

```
mdat <-matrix(c(1,2,3, 11,12,13), nrow =2, ncol =3, byrow =TRUE,
dimnames =list(c("row1", "row2"),
c("C.1", "C.2", "C.3")))

#Select first two rows and all columns
mdat[1:2,]
      C.1 C.2 C.3
 row1   1   2   3
 row2  11  12  13

#Select first columns and all rows
mdat[,1:2]
      C.1 C.2
 row1   1   2
 row2  11  12

#Select first two rows and first column
mdat[1:2,"C.1"]
 row1 row2
    1   11

#Select first row and first two columns
mdat[1,1:2]
 C.1 C.2
   1   2
```

1.3.3.4 Data Frames

Data frames work similarly to matrixes, but they have far more advanced subsetting operations. For example, it's possible to provide conditional statements like `df$fac == "A"`, which will retrieve only rows where the column `fac` has a value `A`. The operator `$` is used to refer to a column.

```
L3 <-LETTERS[1:3]
fac <-sample(L3, 10, replace =TRUE)
df <-data.frame(x =1, y =1:10, fac = fac)

#Select all the rows where fac column has a value "A"
df[df$fac=="A",]
    x  y fac
 2  1  2   A
 5  1  5   A
 6  1  6   A
 7  1  7   A
 8  1  8   A
 10 1 10   A

#Select first two rows and all columns
df[c(1,2),]
   x y fac
 1 1 1   B
 2 1 2   A

#Select first column as a vector
df$x
  [1] 1 1 1 1 1 1 1 1 1 1
```

1.3.4 Functions and the Apply Family

As the standard definition goes, functions are the fundamental building blocks of any programming language and R is no different. Every single library in R has a rich set of functions used to achieve a particular task without writing the same piece of code repeatedly. Rather, all that is required is a function call. The following simple example is a function that returns the nth root of a number with two arguments, num and `nroot`, and contains a function body for calculating the nth root of a real positive number.

```
nthroot <-function(num, nroot) {
return (num ^(1/nroot))
                  }
nthroot(8,3)
 [1] 2
```

This example is a user-defined function, but there are so many such functions across the vast collection of packages contributed by R community worldwide. We will next discuss a very useful function family from the base package of R, which has found its application in numerous scenarios.

The following description and examples are borrowed from *The New S Language* by Becker, R. A. et al. [11]

- `lapply` returns a list of the same length as of input X, each element of which is the result of applying a function to the corresponding element of X.
- `sapply` is a user-friendly version and wrapper of `lapply` by default returning a vector, matrix or, if you use `simplify = "array"`, an array if appropriate. Applying `simplify2array()`. `sapply(x, f, simplify = FALSE, USE.NAMES = FALSE)` is the same as `lapply(x, f)`.
- `vapply` is similar to `sapply`, but has a prespecified type of return value, so it can be safer (and sometimes faster) to use.
- `tapply` applies a function to each cell of a ragged array, that is, to each (non-empty) group of values given by a unique combination of the levels of certain factors.

```
#Generate some data into a variable x

x <-list(a =1:10, beta =exp(-3:3), logic =c(TRUE,FALSE,FALSE,TRUE))

#Compute the list mean for each list element using lapply
lapply(x, mean)
 $a
 [1] 5.5

 $beta
 [1] 4.535125

 $logic
 [1] 0.5
```

```
#Compute the quantile(0%, 25%, 50%, 75% and 100%) for the three elements of x
sapply(x, quantile)
             a        beta logic
 0%       1.00  0.04978707   0.0
 25%      3.25  0.25160736   0.0
 50%      5.50  1.00000000   0.5
 75%      7.75  5.05366896   1.0
 100%    10.00 20.08553692   1.0

#Generate some list of elements using sapply on sequence of integers
i39 <-sapply(3:9, seq) # list of vectors

#Compute the five number summary statistic using sapply and vapply with the
function fivenum

sapply(i39, fivenum)
       [,1] [,2] [,3] [,4] [,5] [,6] [,7]
 [1,]   1.0  1.0    1  1.0  1.0  1.0    1
 [2,]   1.5  1.5    2  2.0  2.5  2.5    3
 [3,]   2.0  2.5    3  3.5  4.0  4.5    5
 [4,]   2.5  3.5    4  5.0  5.5  6.5    7
 [5,]   3.0  4.0    5  6.0  7.0  8.0    9
vapply(i39, fivenum,c(Min. =0, "1st Qu." =0, Median =0, "3rd Qu." =0,
Max. =0))
         [,1] [,2] [,3] [,4] [,5] [,6] [,7]
 Min.     1.0  1.0    1  1.0  1.0  1.0    1
 1st Qu.  1.5  1.5    2  2.0  2.5  2.5    3
 Median   2.0  2.5    3  3.5  4.0  4.5    5
 3rd Qu.  2.5  3.5    4  5.0  5.5  6.5    7
 Max.     3.0  4.0    5  6.0  7.0  8.0    9
#Generate some 5 random number from binomial distribution with repetitions
allowed
groups <-as.factor(rbinom(32, n =5, prob =0.4))

#Calculate the number of times each number repeats
```

```
tapply(groups, groups, length) #- is almost the same as
  7 11 12 13
  1  1  1  2
#The output is similar to the function table
table(groups)
 groups
  7 11 12 13
  1  1  1  2
```

As you can see, every operation in the list involves a certain logic, which needs a loop (for or while loop) like traversal on the data. However, by using the apply family of functions, we can reduce writing programming codes to a minimum and instead call a single-line function with the appropriate arguments. It's functions like these that make R the most preferred programming language for even less experienced programmers.

1.4 Machine Learning Process Flow

In the real world, every use case has a different modeling need, so it's hard to present a very generic process flow that explains how you should build a machine learning model or data product. However, it's possible to suggest best practices for a data science workflow. Figure 1-7 details our suggested workflow for the process of solving a data science problem.

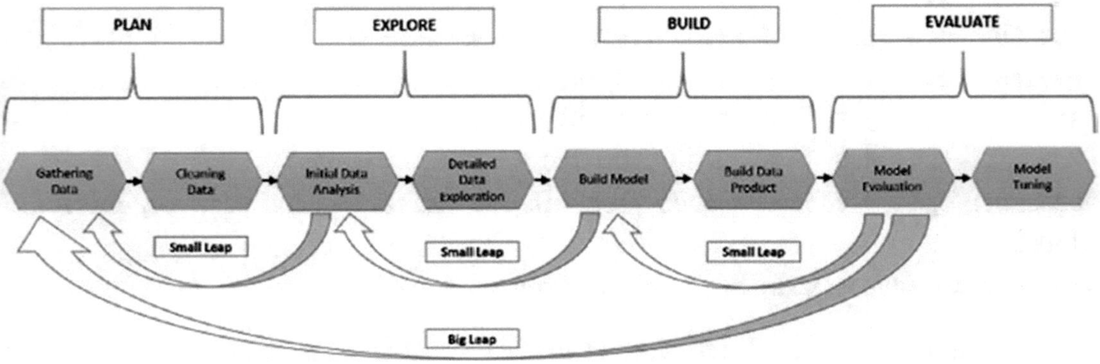

***Figure 1-7.** Machine leaning process flow*

The process flow has four main phases, which we will from here on refer to as *PEBE—Plan, Explore, Build,* and *Evaluate,* as shown in the Figure 1-7. Let's get into the details of each of these.

1.4.1 Plan

This phase forms the key component of the entire process flow. A lot of energy and effort needs to be spent on understanding the requirements, identifying every data source available at our disposal, and framing an approach for solving the problems being identified from the requirements. While gathering data is at the core of the entire process flow, considerable effort has to be spent in cleaning the data for maintaining the integrity and veracity of the final outputs of the analysis and model building. We will discuss many approaches for gathering various types of data and cleaning them up in Chapter 2.

1.4.2 Explore

Exploration sets the ground for analytic projects to take flight. A detailed analysis of possibilities, insights, scope, hidden patterns, challenges, and errors in the data are first discovered at this phase. A lot of statistical and visualization tools are employed to carry out this phase. In order to allow for greater flexibility for modification if required in later parts of the project, this phase is divided into two parts. The first is a quick initial analysis that's carried out to assess the data structure, including checking naming conventions, identifying duplicates, merging data, and further cleaning the data if required. Initial data analysis will help identify any additional data requirement, which is why you see a *small leap* of feedback loop built into the process flow.

In the second part, a more rigorous analysis is done by creating hypotheses, sampling data using various techniques, checking the statistical properties of the sample, and performing statistical tests to reject or accept the hypotheses. Chapters 2, 3, and 4 discuss these topics in detail.

1.4.3 Build

Most of the analytic projects either die out in the first or second phase; however, the one that reaches this phase has a great potential to be converted into a data product. This phase requires a careful study of whether a machine learning kind of model is required or a simple descriptive analysis done in the first two phases is more than sufficient. In the industry, unless you don't show a ROI on effort, time, and money required in building a ML model, the approval from the management is hard to come by. And since many ML algorithms are kind of a black box where the output is difficult to interpret, the business rejects them outright in the very beginning.

So, if you pass all these criteria and still decide to build the ML model, then comes the time to understand the technicalities of each algorithm and how it works on a particular set of data, which we will take up in Chapter 6. Once the model is built, it's always good to ask if the model satisfies your findings in the initial data analysis. If not, then it's advisable to take a *small leap* of feedback loop.

One reason you see *Build Data Product* in the process flow before the evaluation phase is to have a minimal viable output directed toward building a data product (not a full fledged product, but it could even be a small Excel sheet presenting all the analysis done until this point). We are essentially not suggesting that you always build a ML model, but it could even be a descriptive model that articulates the way you approached the problem and present the analysis. This approach helps with the evaluation phase, whether the model is good enough to be considered for building a more futuristic predictive model (or a data product) using ML or whether there still is a scope for refinement or whether this should be dropped completely.

1.4.4 Evaluate

This phase determines either the rise of another revolutionary disruption in the traditional scheme of things or the disappointment of starting from scratch once again. The *big leap* of feedback loop is sometimes unavoidable in many real-world projects because of the complexity it carries or the inability of data to answer certain questions. If you have diligently followed all the steps in the process flow, it's likely that you may just want to further spend some effort in tuning the model rather than taking the big leap to start all from the scratch.

It's highly unlikely that you can build a powerful ML model in just one iteration. We will explore in detail all the criteria for evaluating the model's goodness in Chapter 7 and further fine-tune the model in Chapter 8.

1.5 Other Technologies

While we place a lot of emphasis on the key role played by programming languages and technologies like R in simplifying many ML process flow tasks which otherwise are complex and time consuming, it would not be wise to ignore the other competing technologies in the same space. Python is another preferred programming language that has found quite a good traction in the industry for building production-ready ML process flows. There is an increased demand for algorithms and technologies with capabilities of scaling ML models or analytical tasks to a much larger dataset and executing them at real-time speed. The later part needs a much more detailed discussion on big data and related technologies, which is beyond the scope of this book.

Chapter 9, in a nutshell, will talk about such scalable approaches and other technologies that can help you build the same ML process flows with robustness and using industry standards. However, do remember that every approach/technology has its own pros and cons, so wisely deciding the right choice before the start of any analytic project is vital for successful completion.

1.6 Summary

In this chapter, you learned about the evolution of machine learning from statistics to contemporary data science. We also looked at the fundamental subjects like probability and statistics, which form the foundations of ML. You had an introduction to the R programming language, with some basic demonstrations in R. We concluded the chapter with the machine learning process flow the PEBE framework.

In the coming chapters, we will go into the details of data exploration for better understanding and take a deep dive into some real-world datasets.

CHAPTER 2

Data Preparation and Exploration

As we emphasized in our introductory chapter on applying machine learning (ML) algorithms with a simplified process flow, in this chapter, we go deeper into the first block of machine learning process flow—data exploration and preparation.

The subject of data exploration was very formally introduced by John W. Tukey almost four decades ago with his book entitled *Exploratory Data Analysis* (EDA). The methods discussed in the book were profound and there aren't many software programs that include all of it. Tukey put forth certain very effective ways for exploring data that could prove very vital in understanding the data before building the machine learning models. There are a wide variety of books, articles, and software codes that explain data exploration, but we will focus our attention on techniques that help us look at the data with more granularity and bring useful insights to aid us in model building. Tukey, in his book, *The Future of Data Analysis*, defined data analysis as:

> Procedures for analyzing data, techniques for interpreting the results of such procedures, ways of planning the gathering of data to make its analysis easier, more precise or more accurate, and all the machinery and results of (mathematical) statistics which apply to analyzing data.[1]

We will decode this entire definition in detail throughout this chapter but essentially, data exploration at large involves looking at the statistical properties of data and wherever possible, drawing some very appealing visualizations to reveal certain not so obvious patterns. In a broad sense, calculating statistical properties of data and visualization go hand-in-hand, but we have tried to give separate attention in order to bring out the best of both. Moreover, this chapter will go beyond data exploration and cover the various techniques available for preparing the data more suitable for the

K. Ramasubramanian and A. Singh, *Machine Learning Using R*, https://doi.org/10.1007/978-1-4842-4215-5_2

analysis and modeling, which includes imputation of missing data, removing outliers, and adding derived variables. This data preparation procedure is normally called initial data analysis (IDA).

This chapter also explores the process of data wrangling to prepare and transform the data. Once the data is structured, we could think about various descriptive statistics that explain the data more insightfully. In order to build the basic vocabulary for understanding the language of data, we discuss first the basic types of variables, data formats, and the degree of cleanliness. And then, the entire data wrangling process will be explained followed by descriptive statistics. The chapter ends with demonstrations using R. The examples help in seeing the theories taking a practical shape with real-world examples.

Broadly speaking, the chapter will focus on IDA and EDA. Even though we have a chapter dedicated to data visualization, which plays a pivotal role in understanding the data, EDA will give visualization its due emphasis in this chapter.

2.1 Planning the Gathering of Data

The data in the real world can be in numerous types and formats. It could be structured or unstructured, readable or obfuscated, and small or big; however, having a good plan for data gathering keeping in mind the end goal, will prove to be beneficial and will save a lot of time during data analysis and predictive modeling. Such a plan needs to include a lot of information around variable types, data formats, and source of data. We describe in this section many fundamentals to understanding the types, formats, and sources of that data.

A lot of data nowadays is readily available, but a true data-driven company will always have a strategic plan for making sure the data is gathered the way they want. Ideas from Business Intelligence (BI) can help in designing data schemas, cubes, and many insightful reports, but our focus is on laying a very generic framework, from understanding the nuances of data types to identifying the sources of data.

2.1.1 Variables Types

In general, we have two basic types of variables in any given data, categorical and continuous. Categorical variables include the qualitative attributes of the data such as gender or country name. Continuous variables are quantitative, for example, the salary of employees in a company.

2.1.1.1 Categorical Variables

Categorical variables can be classified into *nominal, binary,* and *ordinal.* We explain each type in a little more detail.

Nominal

These are variables with two or more categories without any regard for ordering. For example, in polling data from a survey, this could be the variable state or candidate names. The number of states and candidates are definite and it doesn't matter what order we choose to present our data. In other words, the order of state or candidate name has no significance in its relative importance in explaining the data.

Binary

A special case of nominal variables with exactly two categories such as gender, possible outcomes of a single coin toss, a survey questionnaire with a checkbox for telephone number as mobile or landline, or the outcome of election win or loss (assuming no tie).

Ordinal

Just like nominal variables, we can have two or more categories in ordinal variables with an added condition that the categories are ordered. For example, a customer rating for a movie in Netflix or a product in Amazon. The variable rating has a relative importance on a scale of 1 to 5, 1 being the lowest rating and 5 the highest for a movie or product by a particular customer.

2.1.1.2 Continuous Variables

Continuous variables are subdivided into *interval* and *ratio.*

Interval

The basic distinction is that they can be measured along a continuous range and they have a numerical value. For example, the temperature in degrees Celsius or Fahrenheit is an interval variable. Note here that the temperature at 0° C is not the absolute zero, which simply means 0° C has certain degree of temperature measure than just saying the value means none or no measure.

Ratio

In contrast, ratio variables include distance, mass, and height. Ratio reflects the fact that you can use the ratio of measurements. So, for example, a distance of 10 meters is twice the distance of 5 meters. A value 0 for a ratio variable means a none or no measure.

2.1.2 Data Formats

Increasing digital landscapes and diversity in software systems has led to the plethora of file formats available for encoding the information or data in a computer file. There are many data formats that are accepted as the gold standard for storing information and have widespread usage, independent of any software, but yet there are many other formats in use, generally because of the popularity of a given software package. Moreover, many data formats specific to scientific applications or devices are also available.

In this section, we discuss the commonly used data formats and show demonstrations using R for reading, parsing, and transforming the data. The basic data types in R as described in Chapter 1—like vectors, matrices, data frames, list, and factors—will be used throughout this chapter for all demonstrations.

2.1.2.1 Comma-Separated Values

CSV or TXT is one of the most widely used data exchange formats for storing tabular data containing many rows and columns. Depending on the data source, the rows and columns have a particular meaning associated with them. Typical information looks like the following example of employee data in a company. In R, the `read.csv` function is widely used to read such data. The `argumentssep` specifies the delimiting character and `header` takes `TRUE` or `FALSE`, depending on whether the dataset contains the column names or not.

```
read.csv("employees.csv", header =TRUE, sep =",")
   Code First.Name Last.Name Salary.US.Dollar.
 1 15421       John     Smith             10000
 2 15422      Peter      Wolf             20000
 3 15423       Mark   Simpson             30000
 4 15424      Peter    Buffet             40000
 5 15425     Martin    Luther             50000
```

2.1.2.2 XLS Files

Microsoft Excel file format (.xls or .xlsx) has been undisputedly the most popular data file format in the business world. The primary purpose being the same as CSV files, but Excel files offer many rich mathematical computations and elegant data presentation capabilities. Excel features calculation, graphing tools, pivot tables, and a macro programming language called Visual Basic for Applications. The programming feature of Excel has been utilized by many industries to automate their data analysis and manual calculations. This wide traction of Excel has resulted in many data analysis software programs that provide an interface to read the Excel data. There are many ways to read an Excel file in R, but the most convenient and easy way is to use the package `xlsx`.

```
library(xlsx)
read.xlsx("employees.xlsx",sheetName ="Sheet1")
    Code First.Name Last.Name Salary.US.Dollar.
 1 15421       John     Smith             10000
 2 15422      Peter      Wolf             20000
 3 15423       Mark   Simpson             30000
 4 15424      Peter    Buffet             40000
 5 15425     Martin    Luther             50000
```

2.1.2.3 Extensible Markup Language: XML

Markup languages have a very rich history of evolution by their first usage by William W. Tunnicliffe in 1967 for presentation at a conference. Later, Charles Goldfarb formalized the IBM Generalized Markup Language between the year 1969 and 1973. Goldfarb is more commonly regarded as the father of markup languages. Markup languages have seen many different forms, including TeX, HTML, XML, and XHTML and are constantly being improved to suit numerous applications. The basics for all these markup language is to provide a system for annotating a document with a specific syntactic structure.

Adhering to a markup language while creating documents ensures that the syntax is not violated and any human or software reader knows exactly how to parse the data in a given document. This feature of markup languages has found a wide range of use, starting from designing configuration files for setting up software in a machine to employing them in communications protocols.

Our focus here is the Extensible Markup Language widely known as XML. There are two basics constructs in any markup language, the first is markup and the second is the content. Generally, strings that create a markup either start with the symbol < and end with a >, or they start with the character & and end with a ;. Strings other than these characters are generally the content. There are three important markup types—tag, element, and attribute.

Tags

A tag is a markup construct that begins with < and ends with >. It has three types.

– Start tags: `<employee_id>`

– End tags: `</employee_id>`

– Empty tags: `</>`

Elements

Elements are the components that either begin with a start tag and end with an end tag, both are matched while parsing, or contain only an empty element tag. Examples of elements:

- `<employee_id>John </employee_id>`
- `<employee_name type="permanent"/>`

Attributes

Within a start tag or empty element tag, an attribute is a markup construct consisting of a name/value pair. In the following example, the element `designation` has two attributes, `emp_id` and `emp_name`.

- `<designation emp_id="15421" emp_name="John"> Assistant Manager </designation>`
- `<designation emp_id="15422" emp_name="Peter"> Manager </designation>`

Consider the following example XML file storing the information on athletes in a marathon.

```
<marathon>
<athletes>
<name>Mike</name>
<age>25</age>

<awards>
Two time world champion. Currently, worlds No. 3
</awards>
<titles>6</titles>
</athletes>
<athletes>
<name>Usain</name>
<age>29</age>
<awards>
Five time world champion. Currently, worlds No. 1
</awards>
<titles>17</titles>
</athletes>
</marathon>
```

Using the package XML and plyr in R, you can convert this file into a data.frame as follows:

```
library(XML)
library(plyr)

xml:data <-xmlToList("marathon.xml")

#Excluding "description" from print
ldply(xml:data, function(x) { data.frame(x[!names(x)=="description"]) } )
       .id  name age
 1 athletes  Mike  25
 2 athletes Usain  29
                                                        awards titles
 1  \n      Two time world champion. Currently, worlds No. 3\n      6
 2  \n     Five time world champion. Currently, worlds No. 1\n     17
```

2.1.2.4 Hypertext Markup Language: HTML

Hypertext Markup Language, commonly known as HTML, is used to create web pages. A HTML page, when combined with Cascading Style Sheets (CSS), can produce beautiful static web pages. The web page can further be made dynamic and interactive by embedding a script written in language such as JavaScript. Today's modern websites are a combination of HTML, CSS, JavaScript, and many more advanced technologies like Flash players. Depending on the purpose, a website could be made rich with all these elements. Even when the modern websites are getting more sophisticated, the core HTML design of web pages still stands against the test of times with newer features and advanced functionality. Although HTML is now filled with rich style and elegance, the content still remains very central.

The ever-exploding number of websites has made it difficult for someone to find relevant content on a particular subject of interest and that's where companies like Google saw a need to crawl, scrape, and rank web pages for relevant content. This process generates a lot of data, which Google uses to help users with their search queries. These kind of process exploits the fact that HTML pages have a distinctive structure for storing content and reference links to external web pages.

There are five key elements in a HTML file that are scanned by the majority of web crawlers and scrappers:

Headers

A simple header might look like

```
<head>
<title>Machine Learning with R </title>
</head>
```

Headings

There are six heading tags, h1 to h6, with decreasing font sizes. They look like

```
<h1>Header </h1>
<h2>Headings </h2>
<h3>Tables </h3>
<h4>Anchors </h4>
<h5>Links </h5>
<h6>Links </h6>
```

Paragraphs

A paragraph could contain more than a few words or sentences in a single block.

```
<p>Paragraph 1</p>
<p>Paragraph 2</p>
```

Tables

A tabular data of rows and columns could be embedded into HTML tables with the following tags

```
<table>
<tbody>
<thead>
<tr>Define a row </tr>
</thead>
</tbody>
</table>
<table> Tag declares the main table structure.
<tbody> Tag specifies the body of the table.
<thead> Tag defines the table header.
<tr> Tag defines each row of data in the table
```

Anchors

Designers can use anchors to anchor an URL to some text on a web page. When users view the web page in a browser, they can click the text to activate the link and visit the page. Here's an example

```
<a href="https://www.apress.com/"> Welcome to Machine Learning
using R!'</a>
```

With all these elements, a sample HTML file will look like the following snippet.

```
<!DOCTYPE html>
<html>
<body>
<h1>Machine Learning usingR</h1>
<p>Hope you having fun time reading this book !!</p>
```

```
<h1>Chapter 2</h1>
<h2>Data Exploration and Preparation</h2>
<a  href="https://www.apress.com/">Apress Website Link</a>
</body>
</html>
```

Python is one of most powerful scripting languages for building web scraping tools. Although R also provides many packages to do the same job, it's not very robust. Like Google, you can try to build a web-scrapping tool, which extracts all the links from a HTML web page like the one shown previously. The following code snippet in R shows how to extract an URL from an HTML file.

```
library(XML)
url <- "html_example.html"
doc <-htmlParse(url)
xpathSApply(doc, "//a/@href")
                          href
 "https://www.apress.com/"
```

2.1.2.5 JSON

JSON is a widely used data interchange format in many application programming interfaces like Facebook Graph API, Google Maps, and Twitter API. It is used especially to transmit data between a server and web application, as an alternative to XML.

It might also be used to contain profile information that can be easily shared across your system components using the simple JSON format.

```
{
"data":[
      {
"id": "A1_B1",

"from":{
"name": "Jerry", "id": "G1"
         },
"message": "Hey! Hope you like the book so far",
"actions":[
              {
```

```
"name": "Comment",
"link": "http://www.facebook.com/A1/posts/B1"
            },
            {
"name": "Like",
"link": "http://www.facebook.com/A1/posts/B1"
            }
         ],
"type": "status",
"created_time": "2016-08-02T00:24:41+0000",
"updated_time": "2016-08-02T00:24:41+0000"
      },
      {
"id": "A2_B2",
"from":{
"name": "Tom", "id": "G2"
         },
"message": "Yes. Easy to understand book",
"actions":[
            {
"name": "Comment",
"link": "http://www.facebook.com/A2/posts/B2"
            },
            {
"name": "Like",
"link": "http://www.facebook.com/A2/posts/B2"
            }
         ],
"type": "status",
"created_time": "2016-08-03T21:27:44+0000",
"updated_time": "2016-08-03T21:27:44+0000"
      }
   ]
}
```

Using the library rjson, you can read such JSON files into R and convert the data into a data.frame. The following R code displays the first three columns of the data.frame.

```
library(rjson)
url <- "json_fb.json"
document <-fromJSON(file=url, method='C')

as.data.frame(document)[,1:3]
   data.id data.from.name data.from.id
 1   A1_B1      Jerry                 G1
```

2.1.3 Types of Data Sources

Depending on the source of data, the format could vary. At times, identifying the type and format of data is not very straight forward, but broadly classifying, we might gather data that has a clear structure. Some might be semi-structured and other might look like total junk. Data gathering at large is not just an engineering effort but a great skill.

2.1.3.1 Structured Data

Structured data is everywhere and it's always easier to understand, represent, store, query, and process. So, if you dream of an ideal world, all data will have rows and columns stored in a tabular manner. The widespread development around the various business applications, database technology, business intelligent system, and spreadsheet tools has given rise to enormous amounts of clean and good looking data. Every row and column is well defined within a connected schematic tables in a database. The data coming from CSV and Excel files generally has this structure built into it. We will show many examples of such data throughout the book to explain the relevant concepts.

2.1.3.2 Semi-Structured Data

Although structured data gives us plenty of scope to experiment and ease of use, it's not always possible to represent information in rows and column. The kind of data generated from Twitter and Facebook has significantly moved away from the traditional Relational Database Management System (RDBMS) paradigms, where everything has a predefined schema, to a world of NoSQL (Chapter 9 covers some of the NoSQL systems), where data is semi-structured. Both Twitter and Facebook rely heavily on JSON or BSON (Binary JSON). Databases like MongoDB and Cassandra store this kind of NoSQL data. The JSON and XML formats are some examples of semi-structured data.

2.1.3.3 Unstructured Data

The biggest challenge in data engineering has been dealing with unstructured data like images, videos, web logs, and click stream. The challenge is pretty much in handling the volume and velocity of this data-generation process on top of not finding any patterns.

Despite having many sophisticated software systems for handling such data, there are no defined processes for using this data in modeling or insight generation. Unlike semi-structured data, where we have many APIs and tools to process the data into a required format, here, huge effort is spent in processing this data to a structured form. Big data technologies like Hadoop and Spark are often deployed for such purposes. There has been significant work on unstructured textual data generated from human interactions. For instance, Twitter Sentiment Analysis on tweets (covered in Chapter 6).

2.2 Initial Data Analysis (IDA)

Collection of data is the first mammoth task in any data science project, and it forms the first building block of machine learning process flow presented in Chapter 1. Once the data is ready, then comes what we call the primary investigation or more formally, *Initial Data Analysis* (IDA). IDA makes sure our data is clean, correct, and complete for further exploratory analysis. The process of IDA involves preparing the data with the right naming conventions and data types for the variables, checking for missing and outlier values, and merging data from multiple sources to develop one coherent data source for further EDA. IDA is commonly referred to as *data wrangling*.

It's widely believed that data wrangling consumes a significant amount of time (approximately 50-80% of the effort) and it's something that can't be overlooked. More than a painful activity, data wrangling is a crucial step in generating understanding and insights from data. It's not mere a process of cleaning and transforming the data but it helps to enrich and validate the data before something serious is done with it.

There are many thought processes around data wrangling; we will explain them broadly with demonstrations in R.

2.2.1 Discerning a First Look

The process of wrangling starts with a judicious and very shrewd look at your data from the start. This first look builds the intuition and understanding of patterns and trends. There are many useful functions in R that help you get a first grasp of your data in a quick and clear way.

2.2.1.1 Function str()

The `str()` function in R comes in very handy when you first look at the data. Referring back to the employee data we used earlier, the `str()` output will look something like what's shown in the following R code snippet. The output shows four useful tidbits about the data.

- The number of rows and columns in the data
- Variable name or column header in the data
- Data type of each variable
- Sample values for each variable

Depending on how many variables are contained in the data, spending a few minutes or an hour on this output will provide significant understanding of the entire dataset.

```
emp <-read.csv("employees.csv", header =TRUE, sep =",")
str(emp)
 'data.frame':    5 obs. of 4 variables:
  $ Code               : int 15421 15422 15423 15424 15425
  $ First.Name         : Factor w/ 4 levels "John","Mark",..: 1 4 2 4 3
  $ Last.Name          : Factor w/ 5 levels "Buffet","Luther",..: 4 5 3 1 2
  $ Salary.US.Dollar.: int 10000 20000 30000 40000 50000
```

2.2.1.2 Naming Convention: make.names()

In order to be consistent with the variable names throughout the course of the analysis and preparation phase, it's important that the variable names in the dataset follow the standard R naming conventions. The step is critical for two important reasons:

- When merging multiple datasets, it's convenient if the common columns on which the merge happens have the same variable name.
- It's also a good practice with any programming language to have clean names (no spaces or special characters) for the variables.

R has this function called `make.names()`. To demonstrate it, let's make our variable names dirty and then will use `make.names` to clean them up. Note that `read.csv` functions have a default behavior of cleaning the variable names before they loads the data into `data.frame`. But when we are doing many operations on data inside our program, it's possible that the variable names will fall out of convention.

```
#Manually overriding the naming convention
names(emp) <-c('Code','First Name','Last Name', 'Salary(US Dollar)')

# Look at the variable name
emp
   Code First Name Last Name Salary(US Dollar)
 1 15421       John     Smith             10000
 2 15422      Peter      Wolf             20000
 3 15423       Mark   Simpson             30000
 4 15424      Peter    Buffet             40000
 5 15425     Martin    Luther             50000

# Now let's clean it up using make.names
names(emp) <-make.names(names(emp))

# Look at the variable name after cleaning
emp
   Code First.Name Last.Name Salary.US.Dollar.
 1 15421       John     Smith             10000
 2 15422      Peter      Wolf             20000
 3 15423       Mark   Simpson             30000
 4 15424      Peter    Buffet             40000
 5 15425     Martin    Luther             50000
```

You could also write your custom column names instead of using the `make.names()` function

2.2.1.3 Table(): Pattern or Trend

Another reason it's important to look at your data closely up-front is to look for some kind of anomaly or pattern in the data. Suppose we wanted to see if there were any duplicates in the employee data, or if we wanted to find a common names among employees and reward them for a fun HR activity. These tasks are possible using the `table()` function. Its basic role is to show the frequency distribution in a one- or two-way tabular format.

```
#Find duplicates
table(emp$Code)

 15421 15422 15423 15424 15425
     1     1     1     1     1
#Find common names
table(emp$First.Name)

   John   Mark Martin Peter
      1      1      1     2
```

This clearly shows no duplicates and the name `Peter` appearing twice. These kind of patterns might be very useful to judge if the data has any bias for some variables, which will tie back to the final story we would want to write from the analysis.

2.2.2 Organizing Multiple Sources of Data into One

Often the data of our problem statements doesn't come from one place. A plethora of resources and abundance of information in the world always keep us thinking, is there data missing from whatever collection is available so far? We call it a tradeoff between the abundance of data and our requirements. Not all data is useful and not all our requirements will be met. So, when you believe there is no more data collection possible, the thought process goes around, how do you now combine all that you have into one single source of data? This process could be iterative in the sense that something needs to be added or deleted based on relevance.

2.2.2.1 Merge and dplyr Joins

The most useful operation while preparing the data is the ability to join or merge two different datasets into a single entity. This idea is easy to relate to the various joins of SQL queries. A standard text on SQL queries will explain the different forms of joins elaborately, but we will focus on the function available in R. Let's discuss the two functions in R, which help to join two datasets.

We will use another extended dataset of our employee example where we have the department and educational qualification and merge it with the already existing dataset of employees. Let's see the four very common type of joins using `merge` and `dplyr`. Though the output is same, there are many differences between `merge` and `dplyr` implementations. `dplyr` is somewhat regarded as more efficient than `merge`. The `merge()` function merges two data frames by common columns or row names, or does other versions of database `join` operations, whereas `dplyr` provides a flexible grammar of data manipulation focused on tools for working with data frames (hence the `d` in the name).

2.2.2.1.1 Using merge

Inner Join: Returns rows where a matching value for the variable `code` is found in both the `emp` and `emp-equal` data frames.

```
merge(emp, emp_qual, by ="Code")
   Code First.Name Last.Name Salary.US.Dollar.    Qual
 1 15421       John     Smith             10000 Masters
 2 15422      Peter      Wolf             20000     PhD
 3 15423       Mark   Simpson             30000     PhD
```

Left Join: Returns all rows from the first data frame even if a matching value for the variable `Code` is not found in the second.

```
merge(emp, emp_qual, by ="Code", all.x =TRUE)
   Code First.Name Last.Name Salary.US.Dollar.     Qual
 1 15421       John     Smith             10000  Masters
 2 15422      Peter      Wolf             20000      PhD
 3 15423       Mark   Simpson             30000      PhD
 4 15424      Peter    Buffet             40000     <NA>
 5 15425     Martin    Luther             50000     <NA>
```

Right Join: Returns all rows from second data frame even if a matching value for the variable `Code` is not found in the first.

```
merge(emp, emp_qual, by ="Code", all.y =TRUE)
   Code First.Name Last.Name Salary.US.Dollar.    Qual
1 15421       John     Smith             10000 Masters
2 15422      Peter      Wolf             20000     PhD
3 15423       Mark   Simpson             30000     PhD
4 15426       <NA>      <NA>                NA     PhD
5 15429       <NA>      <NA>                NA     Phd
```

Full Join: Returns all rows from the first and second data frame whether or not a matching value for the variable Code is found.

```
merge(emp, emp_qual, by ="Code", all =TRUE)
   Code First.Name Last.Name Salary.US.Dollar.    Qual
1 15421       John     Smith             10000 Masters
2 15422      Peter      Wolf             20000     PhD
3 15423       Mark   Simpson             30000     PhD
4 15424      Peter    Buffet             40000    <NA>
5 15425     Martin    Luther             50000    <NA>
6 15426       <NA>      <NA>                NA     PhD
7 15429       <NA>      <NA>                NA     Phd
```

Note in these outputs that if a match is not found, the corresponding values are filled with NA, which is nothing but a missing value. We will discuss later in IDA how to deal with such missing values.

2.2.2.1.2 dplyr

Inner Join: Returns rows where a matching value for the variable Code is found in both the emp and emp-equal data frames.

```
library(dplyr)

inner_join(emp, emp_qual, by ="Code")
   Code First.Name Last.Name Salary.US.Dollar.    Qual
1 15421       John     Smith             10000 Masters
2 15422      Peter      Wolf             20000     PhD
3 15423       Mark   Simpson             30000     PhD
```

Left Join: Returns all rows from the first data frame even if a matching value for the variable Code is not found in the second.

```
left_join(emp, emp_qual, by ="Code")
   Code First.Name Last.Name Salary.US.Dollar.    Qual
 1 15421       John     Smith             10000 Masters
 2 15422      Peter      Wolf             20000     PhD
 3 15423       Mark   Simpson             30000     PhD
 4 15424      Peter    Buffet             40000    <NA>
 5 15425     Martin    Luther             50000    <NA>
```

Right Join: Returns all rows from second data frame even if a matching value for the variable Code is not found in the first.

```
Right_join(emp, emp_qual, by ="Code")
   Code First.Name Last.Name Salary.US.Dollar.    Qual
 1 15421       John     Smith             10000 Masters
 2 15422      Peter      Wolf             20000     PhD
 3 15423       Mark   Simpson             30000     PhD
 4 15426       <NA>      <NA>                NA     PhD
 5 15429       <NA>      <NA>                NA     Phd
```

Full Join: Returns all rows from the first and second data frame whether or not a matching value for the variable Code is found.

```
Full_join(emp, emp_qual, by ="Code",)
   Code First.Name Last.Name Salary.US.Dollar.    Qual
 1 15421       John     Smith             10000 Masters
 2 15422      Peter      Wolf             20000     PhD
 3 15423       Mark   Simpson             30000     PhD
 4 15424      Peter    Buffet             40000    <NA>
 5 15425     Martin    Luther             50000    <NA>
 6 15426       <NA>      <NA>                NA     PhD
 7 15429       <NA>      <NA>                NA     Phd
```

Note that the output of the `merge` and `dplyr` functions is exactly the same for the respective joins. `dplyr` is syntactically more meaningful but instead of one `merge()` function, we now have four different functions. You can also see that `merge` and `dplyr` are similar to the `implicit` and `explicit` join statements in SQL query, respectively.

2.2.3 Cleaning the Data

The critical part of data wrangling is removing inconsistencies from the data, like missing values, and following a standard format in abbreviations. The process is a way to bring out the best quality of information from the data.

2.2.3.1 Correcting Factor Variables

Since R is a case-sensitive language, every categorical variable with a definite set of values like the variable `Qual` in our employee dataset with PhD and Masters as two values needs to be checked for any inconsistencies. In R, such variables are called *factors,* with PhD and Masters as its two levels. So, a value like PhD and Phd are treated differently, even though they mean the same thing. A manual inspection using the `table()` function will reveal such patterns. A way to correct this would be:

```
employees_qual <-read.csv("employees_qual.csv")

#Inconsistent
employees_qual
    Code    Qual
 1 15421 Masters
 2 15422     PhD
 3 15423     PhD
 4 15426     PhD
 5 15429     Phd

employees_qual$Qual =as.character(employees_qual$Qual)
employees_qual$Qual <-ifelse(employees_qual$Qual %in%c("Phd","phd","PHd"),
"PhD", employees_qual$Qual)
```

A quicker way to standardize the values would be to uppercase each string. However, with strings where you would like to keep the case-sensitivity intact, you could follow the previous example.

```
#Corrected
employees_qual
    Code    Qual
 1 15421 Masters
 2 15422     PhD
```

```
3 15423       PhD
4 15426       PhD
5 15429       PhD
```

2.2.3.2 Dealing with NAs

NAs (abbreviation for "Not Available") are missing values and will always lead to wrong interpretation, exceptions in function output, and cause models to fail if we live with them until the end. The best way to handle NAs is either to remove/ignore if we are sitting in a big pool of data However, if we only have a small dataset, we could think about feature imputation, which is the process of filling the missing values.

The technique of imputation has attracted many researchers to devise novel ideas but nothing can beat the simplicity that comes from the complete understanding of the data. Let's look at an example from the merge we did previously, in particular the output from the right join. It's not possible to impute `First` and `Last Name`, as it might not be relevant for any aggregate analysis we might want to do on our data. Rather, the variable that's important for us is `Salary`, where we don't want to see NA. So, here is how we input a value in the `Salary` variable.

```
emp <-read.csv("employees.csv")
employees_qual <-read.csv("employees_qual.csv")

#Correcting the inconsistency
employees_qual$Qual =as.character(employees_qual$Qual)
employees_qual$Qual <-ifelse(employees_qual$Qual %in%c("Phd","phd","PHd"),
"PhD", employees_qual$Qual)

#Store the output from right_join in the variables impute_salary
impute_salary <-right_join(emp, employees_qual, by ="Code")

#Calculate the average salary for each Qualification
ave_age <-ave(impute_salary$Salary.US.Dollar., impute_salary$Qual,
FUN = function(x) mean(x, na.rm =TRUE))

#Fill the NAs with the average values
impute_salary$Salary.US.Dollar. <-ifelse(is.na(impute_salary$Salary.
US.Dollar.), ave_age, impute_salary$Salary.US.Dollar.)
```

```
impute_salary
   Code First.Name Last.Name Salary.US.Dollar.    Qual
1 15421       John     Smith             10000 Masters
2 15422      Peter      Wolf             20000     PhD
3 15423       Mark   Simpson             30000     PhD
4 15426       <NA>      <NA>             25000     PhD
5 15429       <NA>      <NA>             25000     PhD
```

Here, the idea is that a particular qualification is eligible for paychecks of a similar value, but there certainly is some level of assumption we have taken, that the industry isn't biased on paychecks based on which institution the employee obtained the degree. However, if there is a significant bias, then a measure like average might not be a right method; instead something like median could be used. We will discuss these kinds of bias in greater detail in the descriptive analysis section.

2.2.3.3 Dealing with Dates and Times

In many machine learning models, date and time variables play a pivotal role. Date and time variables reveal a lot about temporal behavior such as sales data from supermarkets or online stores. We can likely find information such as the most frequented time at a supermarket daily or weekly. Moreover, we can do the same thing with different variables. Often, dealing with date variables is a painful task, primarily because of many available date formats, time zones, and daylight savings in few countries. These challenges makes any arithmetic calculation like difference between days and comparing two date values even more difficult.

The `lubridate` package is one of the most useful packages in R, and it helps in dealing with these challenges. The paper, "Dates and Times Made Easy with Lubridate," published in the *Journal of Statistical Software* by Grolemund, describes the capabilities the `lubridate` package offers. To borrow from the paper, `lubridate` helps users:

- Identify and parse date-time data
- Extract and modify components of a date-time, such as years, months, days, hours, minutes, and seconds
- Perform accurate calculations with date-times and timespans
- Handle time zones and daylight savings time

The paper gives an elaborate description with many examples, so we will take up here only two uncommon date transformations like dealing with time zone and daylight savings.

2.2.3.3.1 Time Zone

If we wanted to convert the date and time labeled in Indian Standard Time (IST) (the local time standard of the system where the code was run) to Universal Coordinated time zone (UTC), we use the following code:

```
library("lubridate")
date <-as.POSIXct("2016-03-13 09:51:48")
date
 [1] "2016-03-13 09:51:48 IST"
with_tz(date, "UTC")
 [1] "2016-03-13 04:21:48 UTC"
```

2.2.3.3.2 Daylight Savings Time

As the standard says, "daylight saving time (DST) is the practice of resetting the clocks with the onset of summer months by advancing one hour so that evening daylight stays an hour longer, while foregoing normal sunrise times."

For example, in the United States, the one-hour shift occurs at 02:00 local time, so in the spring, the clock is reset to advance by an hour from the last moment of 01:59 standard time to 03:00 DST. That day has 23 hours. Whereas in autumn, the clock is reset to go backward from the last moment of 01:59 DST to 01:00 standard time, repeating that hour, so that day has 25 hours. A digital clock will skip 02:00, exactly at the shift to summer time, and instead advance from 01:59:59.9 to 03:00:00.0.

```
dst_time <-ymd_hms("2010-03-14 01:59:59")
dst_time <-force_tz(dst_time, "America/Chicago")
dst_time
 [1] "2010-03-14 01:59:59 CST"
```

One second later, Chicago clock times read:

```
dst_time +dseconds(1)
 [1] "2010-03-14 03:00:00 CDT"
```

The `force_tz()` function forces a change of time zone based on the parameter we pass.

2.2.4 Supplementing with More Information

The best models are not built with raw data available at the beginning, but come from the intelligence shown in deriving a new variable from an existing one. For instance, a date variable from sales data of a supermarket could help in building variables like weekend (1/0), weekday (1/0), and bank holiday (1/0), or combing multiple variables like income and population could lead to Per Capita Income. Such creativity on derived variables usually comes with lots of experience and domain expertise. However, there could be some common approaches on standard variables such as date, which will be discussed in detail here.

2.2.4.1 Derived Variables

Deriving new variables requires lots of creativity. Sometimes it demands a purpose and situation where a derived variable helps to explain certain behaviors. For example, while looking at the sales trend of any online store, we see a sudden surge in volume on a particular day, so on further investigation we found the reason to be a heavy discounting for end-of-season sales. So, we include a new binary variable `EOS_Sales` assuming a value `1` if we had end of season sales or `0` otherwise. Doing so, we may aid the model in understanding why a sudden surge is seen in the sales.

2.2.4.2 n-Day Averages

Another useful technique for deriving such variables, especially in time series data from the stock market, is to derive variables like `last_7_days`, `last_2_weeks`, and `last_1_month` as average stock prices. Such variables work to reduce the variability in data like stock prices, which can sometime seem like noise and can hamper the performance of the model to a great extent.

2.2.5 Reshaping

In many modeling exercises, it's common practice to reshape the data into a more meaningful and usable format. Here, we show one example dataset from the World Bank on *World Development Indicators (WDI)*. The data has a wide set of variables explaining the various attributes for developments starting from the year 1950 until 2015. It's a very rich data and large dataset.

Here's a small sample of development indicators and its values for the country Zimbabwe for the years 1995 and 1998:

```
library(data.table)
WDI_Data <-fread("WDI_Data.csv", header =TRUE, skip =333555, select
=c(3,40,43))
setnames(WDI_Data, c("Dev_Indicators", "1995","1998"))
WDI_Data <-WDI_Data[c(1,3),]
```

Development indicators (DI):

```
WDI_Data[,"Dev_Indicators", with =FALSE]
                                          Dev_Indicators
 1: Women's share of population ages 15+ living with HIV (%)
 2:  Youth literacy rate, population 15-24 years, female (%)
```

DI value for the years 1995 and 1998:

```
WDI_Data[,2:3, with =FALSE]
        1995     1998
 1: 56.02648 56.33425
 2: NA             NA
```

This data has in each row a development indicator and columns representing its value from the year starting 1995 to 1998. Now, using the package `tidyr`, we will reshape this data to have the columns `1995` and `1998`, into one column called `Year`. This transformation will come pretty handy when we see the data visualization in Chapter 4.

```
library(tidyr)
gather(WDI_Data,Year,Value, 2:3)
                                          Dev_Indicators Year    Value
 1: Women's share of population ages 15+ living with HIV (%) 1995  56.02648
 2:  Youth literacy rate, population 15-24 years, female (%) 1995        NA
 3: Women's share of population ages 15+ living with HIV (%) 1998  56.33425
 4:  Youth literacy rate, population 15-24 years, female (%) 1998        NA
```

There are many such ways of reshaping our data, which we will describe as we look at the many case studies throughout the book.

2.3 Exploratory Data Analysis

Exploratory Data Analysis (EDA) provides a framework to choose the appropriate descriptive methods in various data analysis needs. Tukey, in his book *Exploratory Data Analysis* (EDA), emphasized the need to focus more on suggesting hypotheses using data rather than getting involved in many repetitive statistical hypothesis testing. Hypothesis testing in statistics is a tool for making certain confirmatory assertions drawn from data or more formally, statistically proving the significance of an insight. More on this later in the next section. EDA provides both visual and quantitative techniques for data exploration.

Tukey's EDA gave birth to two path-breaking developments in statistical theory: robust statistics and non-parametric statistics. Both of these ideas had a big role in redefining the way people perceived statistics. It's no more a complicated bunch of theorems and axioms but rather a powerful tool for exploring data. So, with our data in the most desirable format after cleaning up, we are ready to deep dive into the analysis.

Table 2-1 shows a simple example that we can use to understand statistics. Consider a marathon of approximately 26 miles and the finishing times (in hours) of 50 marathon runners. There are runners ranging from world-class elite marathoners to first-timers who walk all the way.

Table 2-1. *A Snippet of Data from the marathon.csv File*

ID	Type	Finishing Time
1	Professional	2.2
2	First-Timer	7.5
3	Frequents	4.3
4	Professional	2.3
5	Frequents	5.1
6	First-Timer	8.3

This dataset will be used throughout the section to explain the various exploratory analysis.

2.3.1 Summary Statistics

In statistics, what we call "summary statistics" for any numerical variables in the dataset are the genesis for data exploration. These are minimum, first quartile, median, mean, third quartile, and maximum. Summary statistics can be helpful for seeing how much the data varies from the mean, what is the average value of a variable, what are the range of values, and the implications these statistics might have in modeling and preprocessing. It's easy to calculate all these in R using the `summary` function.

```
marathon <-read.csv("marathon.csv")
summary(marathon)
       Id                    Type      Finish_Time
 Min.   : 1.00   First-Timer :17   Min.   :1.700
 1st Qu.:13.25   Frequents   :19   1st Qu.:2.650
 Median :25.50   Professional:14   Median :4.300
 Mean   :25.50                     Mean   :4.651
 3rd Qu.:37.75                     3rd Qu.:6.455
 Max.   :50.00                     Max.   :9.000
quantile(marathon$Finish_Time, 0.25)
  25%
 2.65
```

For categorical variables, the `summary` function simply gives the count of each category as seen with the variable Type. In case of the numerical variables, apart from minimum and maximum, which are quite straight forward to understand, we have mean, median, first quartile, and third quartile.

2.3.1.1 Quantile

If we divide our population of data into four equal groups, based on the distribution of values of a particular numerical variable, each of the three values creating the four divides are called first, second, and third quartile. In other words, the more general term is *quantile*; q-Quantiles are values that partition a finite set of values into q subsets of equal sizes.

For instance, dividing in four equal groups would mean a 3-quantile. In terms of usage, *percentile* is a more widely used terminology, which is a measure used in statistics indicating the value under which a given percentage of observations in a group of observations fall. If we divide something in 100 equal groups, we have 99-Quantiles, which leads us to define the first quartile as the 25th percentile and the third quartile as the 75th percentile. In simpler terms, the 25th percentile or first quartile is a value below which 25 percent of the observations are found. Similarly, 75th percentile or third quartile is a value below which 75 percent of the observations are found.

First quartile:

```
quantile(marathon$Finish_Time, 0.25)
   25%
 2.65
```

Second quartile or median:

```
quantile(marathon$Finish_Time, 0.5)
 50%
 4.3
```

```
median(marathon$Finish_Time)
 [1] 4.3
```

Third quartile:

```
quantile(marathon$Finish_Time, 0.75)
   75%
 6.455
```

The *interquartile range* is the difference between the 75th percentile and 25th percentile and would be the range that contains 50% of the data of any particular variable in the dataset. Interquartile range is a robust measure of statistical dispersion. We will discuss this further in a later part of the section.

```
quantile(marathon$Finish_Time, 0.75, names =FALSE)
-quantile(marathon$Finish_Time, 0.25, names =FALSE)
 [1] 3.805
```

2.3.1.2 Mean

Though *median* is a robust measure of the central tendency of any distribution of data, *mean* is a more traditional statistic for explaining the statistical property of the data distribution. The median is more robust because a single large observation can throw the mean off. We formally define this statistic in the next section.

```
mean(marathon$Finish_Time)
 [1] 4.6514
```

As you would expect, the summaries (mean and median are often counted as a measure of centrality) listed by the summary function's output are in the increasing order of their values. The reason for this is obvious from the way they are defined. And if these statistical definitions were difficult for you to contemplate, don't worry; we will turn to visualization for explanation. Though we have a dedicated chapter on it, here we discuss some very basic plots that are inseparable from theories around any exploratory analysis.

2.3.1.3 Frequency Plot

Frequency plot helps in understanding the distribution of values in a discrete or continuous variable. As seen in the plot in Figure 2-1, we how many first-timers, frequents, and professional runners participated in the marathon.

```
plot(marathon$Type, xlab ="Marathoners Type", ylab ="Number of
Marathoners")
```

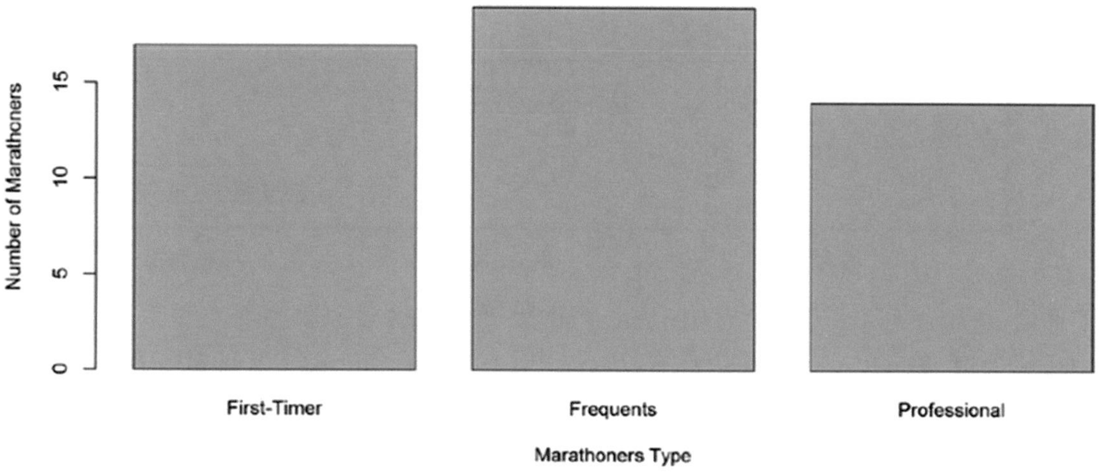

Figure 2-1. *Number of athletes in each type*

2.3.1.4 Boxplot

A *boxplot* is a form of visualization for summary statistics. Though looking at numbers is always useful, an equivalent representation in a visually appealing plot could serve as an excellent tool for better understanding, insight generation, and ease of explaining the data.

In the summary, we saw the values for each variable but were not able to look how the finish time varies for each type of runner. In other words, how type and finish time are related. Figure 2-2 clearly helps to illustrate this relationship. As expected, the boxplot clearly shows that professionals have a much better finish time than frequents and first-timers.

```
boxplot(Finish_Time ~Type,data=marathon, main="Marathon Data", xlab="Type of
Marathoner", ylab="Finish Time")
```

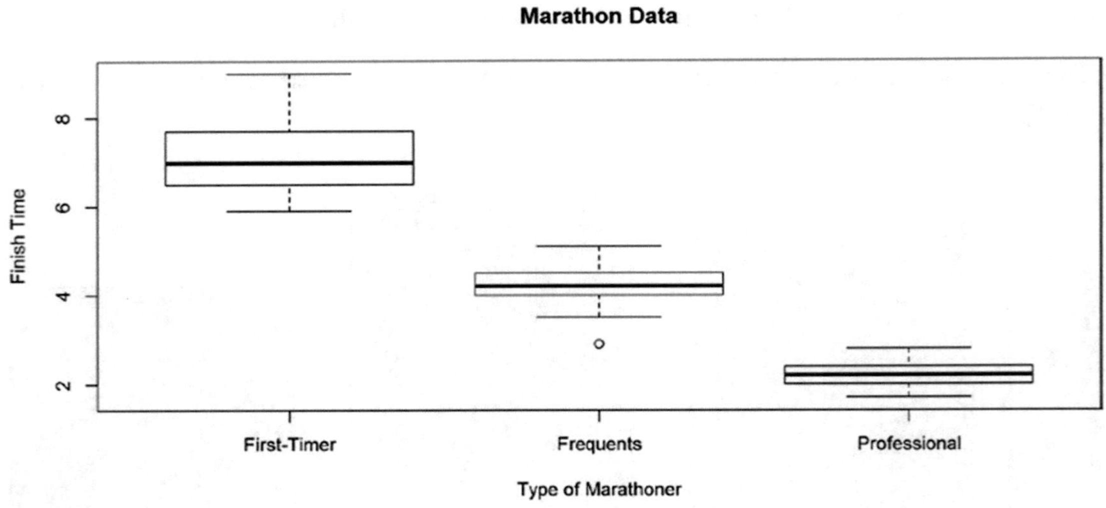

Figure 2-2. *Boxplot showing variation of finish times for each type of runner*

In Figure 2-2, the X-axis shows the three categories of people who participated in the marathon. The Y-axis shows the finish time of each category of people. In each of the box, the upper side, lower side, and the thick line represent the first quartile, third quartile, and the median of the finish times, respectively. The upper and the lower lines extending from the box indicate the max and min values of the finish time, respectively.

2.3.2 Moment

Apart from the summary statistics, we have other statistics like variance, standard deviation, skewness, kurtosis, covariance, and correlation. These statistics naturally lead us to look for some distribution in the data.

More formally, we are interested in the quantitative measure called the *moment*. Our data point represents a probability density function that describes the relative likelihood of a random variable to take on a given value. The random variables are the attributes of our dataset. In the marathon example, we have the `Finish_Time` variable describing the finishing time of each marathoner. So, for the probability density function, we are interested in the first five moments.

- The zeroth moment is the total probability (i.e., one)
- The first moment is the mean
- The second central moment is the variance; it's a positive square root of the standard deviation
- The third moment is the skewness
- The fourth moment (with normalization and shift) is the kurtosis

Let's look at the second, third, and fourth moments in detail.

2.3.2.1 Variance

Variance is a measure of the spread for the given set of numbers. The smaller the variance, the closer the numbers are to the mean and the larger the variance, the farther away the numbers are from the mean. Variance is an important measure for understanding the distribution of the data, more formally it's called *probability distribution*. In the next chapter, where various sampling techniques are discussed, we examine how a sample variance is considered to be an estimate of the full population variance, which forms the basis for a good sampling method. Depending on whether our variable is discrete or continuous, we can define the variance.

Mathematically, for a set of n equally likely numbers for a discrete random variable, variance can be represented as follows:

$$\sigma^2 = \frac{1}{n}\sum_{i=1}^{n}(x_i - \mu)^2$$

And more generally, if every number in our distribution occurs with a probability p_i, variance is given by:

$$\sigma^2 = \frac{1}{n}\sum_{i=1}^{n} p_i^* (x_i - \mu)^2$$

As seen in the formula, for every data point, we are measuring how far the number is from the mean, which translates into a measure of spread. Equivalently, if we take the square root of variance, the resulting measure is called the *standard deviation,* generally written as a *sigma*. The standard deviation has the same unit of measurement as of the variable, which makes it convenient to compare with the mean. Together, both mean and standard deviation can be used to describe any distribution of data. Let's take a look at the variance of the variable Finish_Time from our marathon data.

```
mean(marathon$Finish_Time)
 [1] 4.6514
var(marathon$Finish_Time)
 [1] 4.342155
sd(marathon$Finish_Time)
 [1] 2.083784
```

Looking at the values of mean and standard deviation, we could say, on average, that the marathoners have a finish time of 4.65 +/- 2.08 hours. Further, it's easy to notice from the following code snippet that each type of runner has their own speed of running and hence a different finish time.

```
tapply(marathon$Finish_Time,marathon$Type, mean)
  First-Timer    Frequents Professional
     7.154118     4.213158     2.207143
tapply(marathon$Finish_Time,marathon$Type, sd)
  First-Timer     Frequents Professional
    0.8742358     0.5545774    0.3075068
```

2.3.2.2 Skewness

As variance is a measure of spread, *skewness* measures asymmetry about the mean of the probability distribution of a random variable. In general, as the standard definition says, we could observe two types of skewness:

- *Negative skew:* The left tail is longer; the mass of the distribution is concentrated on the right. The distribution is said to be left- skewed, left-tailed, or skewed to the left.
- *Positive skew:* The right tail is longer; the mass of the distribution is concentrated on the left. The distribution is said to be right-skewed, right-tailed, or skewed to the right.

Mathematicians discuss skewness in terms of the second and third moments around the mean. A more easily interpretable formula could be written using standard deviation.

$$g_1 = \frac{\sum_{i=1}^{N}(x_i - \mu)^3 / N}{\sigma^3}$$

This formula for skewness is referred to as the *Fisher-Pearson coefficient of skewness.* Many software programs actually compute the adjusted Fisher-Pearson coefficient of skewness, which could be thought of as a normalization to avoid too high or too low values of skewness:

$$G_1 = \frac{\sqrt{(N(N-1))}}{N-1} \frac{\sum_{i=1}^{N}(x_i - \mu)^3 / N}{\sigma^3}$$

Let's use the histogram of beta distribution to demonstrate skewness (see Figure 2-3).

```
library("moments")
par(mfrow=c(1,3), mar=c(5.1,4.1,4.1,1))

# Negative skew
hist(rbeta(10000,2,6), main ="Negative Skew" )
skewness(rbeta(10000,2,6))
 [1] 0.7166848

# Positive skew
hist(rbeta(10000,6,2), main ="Positive Skew")
skewness(rbeta(10000,6,2))
 [1] -0.6375038
```

```
# Symmetrical

hist(rbeta(10000,6,6), main ="Symmetrical")

skewness(rbeta(10000,6,6))
 [1] -0.03952911
```

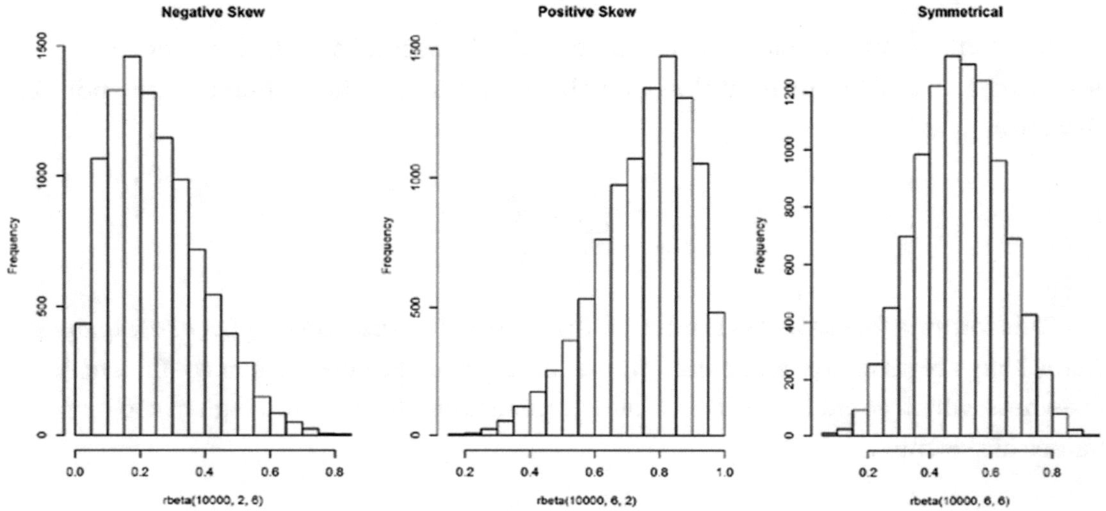

Figure 2-3. *Distribution showing symmetrical versus negative and positive skewness*

For our marathon data, the skewness is close to 0, indicating a symmetrical distribution. See Figure 2-4.

```
hist(marathon$Finish_Time, main ="Marathon Finish Time")

skewness(marathon$Finish_Time)
 [1] 0.3169402
```

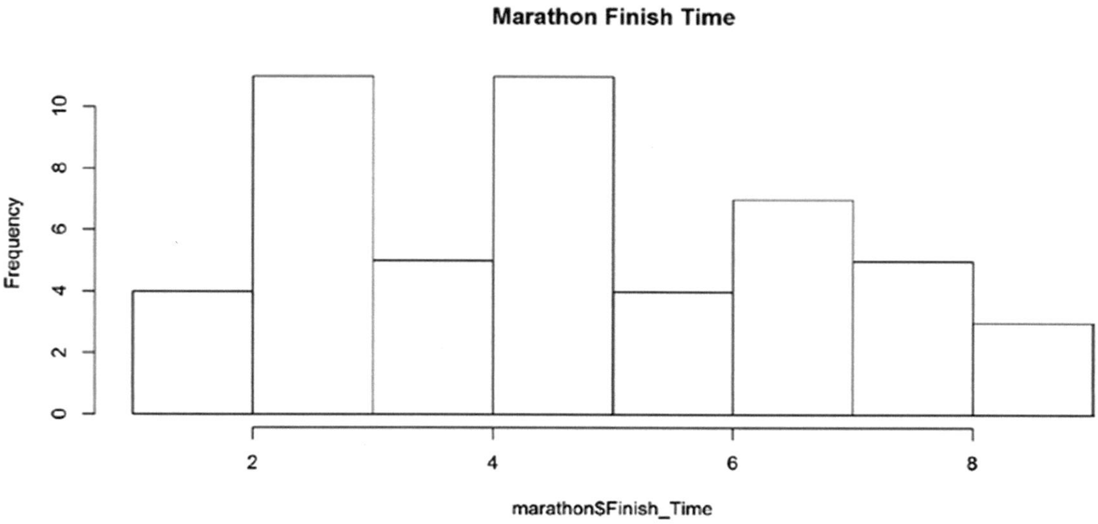

Figure 2-4. *Distribution of finish time of athletes in marathon data*

2.3.2.3 Kurtosis

Kurtosis is a measure of *peakedness* and *tailedness* of the probability distribution of a random variable. Similar to skewness, kurtosis is also used to describe the shape of the probability distribution function. In other words, kurtosis explains the variability due to a few data points having extreme differences from the mean, rather than lots of data points having smaller differences from the mean. Higher values indicate a higher and sharper peak and lower values indicate a lower and less distinct peak. Mathematically, kurtosis is discussed in terms of the fourth moment around the mean. It's easy to find that the kurtosis for a standard normal distribution is 3, a distribution known for its symmetry, and since kurtosis like skewness measures any asymmetry in data, many people use the following definition of kurtosis:

$$\text{kurtosis} = \frac{\sum_{i=1}^{N}(x_i - \mu)^4 / N}{\sigma^4} - 3$$

Generally, there are three types of kurtosis:

- *Mesokurtic*: Distributions with a kurtosis value close to 3, which means in the previous formula, the term before 3 becomes 0, a standard normal distribution with mean 0 and standard deviation 1.

- *Platykurtic*: Distributions with a kurtosis value < 3. Comparatively, a lower peak and shorter tails than normal distribution.
- *Leptokurtic*: Distributions with a kurtosis value > 3. Comparatively, a higher peak and longer tails than normal distribution.

While the kurtosis statistic is often used by many to numerically describe a sample, it is said that "there seems to be no universal agreement about the meaning and interpretation of kurtosis". Tukey suggests that, like variance and skewness, kurtosis should be viewed as a "vague concept" that can be formalized in a variety of ways. See Figure 2-5.

```
#leptokurtic
set.seed(2)
random_numbers <-rnorm(20000,0,0.5)
plot(density(random_numbers), col ="blue", main ="Kurtosis Plots", lwd=2.5,
asp =4)
kurtosis(random_numbers)
 [1] 3.026302
#platykurtic
set.seed(900)
random_numbers <-rnorm(20000,0,0.6)
lines(density(random_numbers), col ="red", lwd=2.5)
kurtosis(random_numbers)
 [1] 2.951033
#mesokurtic
set.seed(3000)
random_numbers <-rnorm(20000,0,1)
lines(density(random_numbers), col ="green", lwd=2.5)
kurtosis(random_numbers)
 [1] 3.008717
legend(1,0.7, c("leptokurtic", "platykurtic","mesokurtic" ),
lty=c(1,1),
lwd=c(2.5,2.5),col=c("blue","red","green"))
```

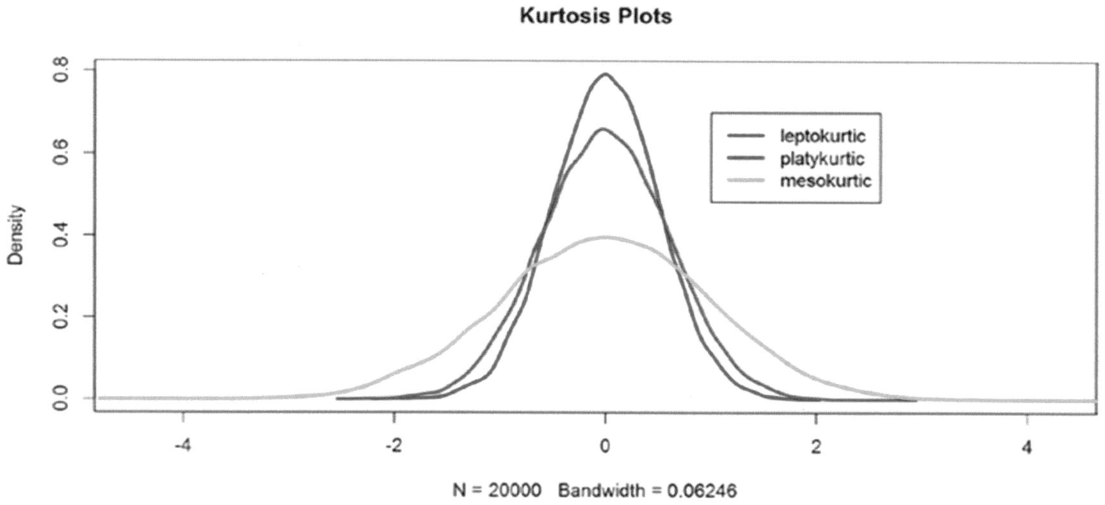

***Figure 2-5.** Showing kurtosis plots with simulated data*

Comparing these kurtosis plots to the marathon finish time, it's platykurtic with a very low peak and short tail (see Figure 2-6).

```
plot(density(as.numeric(marathon$Finish_Time)), col ="blue", main
="KurtosisPlots", lwd=2.5, asp =4)

kurtosis(marathon$Finish_Time)
 [1] 1.927956
```

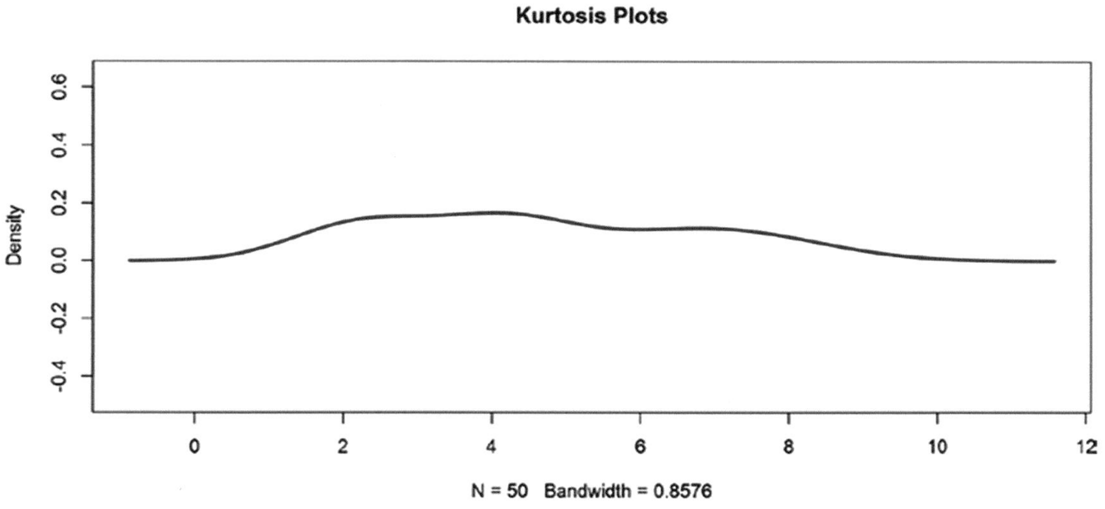

***Figure 2-6.** Showing kurtosis plot of finish time in marathon data*

2.4 Case Study: Credit Card Fraud

In order to apply the concepts explained so far in this chapter, this section presents simulated data on credit card fraud. The data is approximately 200MB, which is big enough to explain most of the ideas discussed. Reference to this dataset will be made quite often throughout the book. So, if you have any thoughts of skipping this section, we strongly advise you not to do so.

2.4.1 Data Import

We will use the package `data.table`. It offers fast aggregation of large data (e.g., 100GB in RAM), fast ordered joins, fast add/modify/delete of columns by group using no copies at all, list columns, and a fast file reader (`fread`). Moreover, it has a natural and flexible syntax, for faster development. Let's start by looking at how this credit card fraud data looks.

```
library(data.table)
data <-fread("ccFraud.csv",header=T, verbose =FALSE, showProgress =FALSE)
str(data)
 Classes 'data.table' and 'data.frame':   10000000 obs. of 9 variables:
  $ custID      : int 1 2 3 4 5 6 7 8 9 10 ...
  $ gender      : int 1 2 2 1 1 2 1 1 2 1 ...
  $ state       : int 35 2 2 15 46 44 3 10 32 23 ...
  $ cardholder  : int 1 1 1 1 1 2 1 1 1 1 ...
  $ balance     : int 3000 0 0 0 0 5546 2000 6016 2428 0 ...
  $ numTrans    : int 4 9 27 12 11 21 41 20 4 18 ...
  $ numIntlTrans: int 14 0 9 0 16 0 0 3 10 56 ...
  $ creditLine  : int 2 18 16 5 7 13 1 6 22 5 ...
  $ fraudRisk   : int 0 0 0 0 0 0 0 0 0 0 ...
  - attr(*, ".internal.selfref")=<externalptr>
```

The `str` displays variables in the dataset with few sample values. The following are the nine variables:

- *custID*: A unique identifier for each customer
- *gender*: Gender of the customer

- *state*: State in the United States where the customer lives
- *cardholder*: Number of credit cards the customer holds
- *balance*: Balance on the credit card
- *numTrans*: Number of transactions to date
- *numIntlTrans*: Number of international transactions to date
- *creditLine*: The financial services corporation, such as Visa, MasterCard, and American Express
- *fraudRisk*: Binary variable: 1 means customer being frauded, 0 means otherwise

2.4.2 Data Transformation

Further, it's clear that variables like `gender`, `state`, and `creditLine` are mapped to numeric identifiers. In order to understand the data better, we need to remap these numbers back to their original meanings. We can do this using the `merge` function in R. The file `US State Code Mapping.csv` contains the mapping for every U.S. state and the numbers in state variables in the datasets. Similarly, `Gender Map.csv` and `credit line map.csv` contain the mapping for the variables `gender` and `creditLine`, respectively.

Mapping U.S. states:

```
library(data.table)
US_state <-fread("US_State_Code_Mapping.csv",header=T, showProgress =FALSE)
data<-merge(data, US_state, by ='state')
```

Mapping gender:

```
library(data.table)
Gender_map<-fread("Gender Map.csv",header=T)
data<-merge(data, Gender_map, by ='gender')
```

Mapping credit line:

```
library(data.table)
Credit_line<-fread("credit line map.csv",header=T)
data<-merge(data, Credit_line, by ='creditLine')
```

Setting variable names and displaying new data:

```
setnames(data,"custID","CustomerID")
setnames(data,"code","Gender")
setnames(data,"numTrans","DomesTransc")
setnames(data,"numIntlTrans","IntTransc")
setnames(data,"fraudRisk","FraudFlag")
setnames(data,"cardholder","NumOfCards")
setnames(data,"balance","OutsBal") setnames(data,"StateName","State")
```

```
str(data)
 Classes 'data.table' and 'data.frame':   10000000 obs. of 11 variables:
  $ creditLine : int  1 1 1 1 1 1 1 1 1 1 ...
  $ CustomerID : int  4446 59161 136032 223734 240467 248899 262655 324670
390138 482698 ...
  $ NumOfCards : int  1 1 1 1 1 1 1 1 1 1 ...
  $ OutsBal    : int  2000 0 2000 2000 2000 0 0 689 2000 0 ...
  $ DomesTransc: int  31 25 78 11 40 47 15 17 48 25 ...
  $ IntTransc  : int  9 0 3 0 0 0 0 9 0 35 ...
  $ FraudFlag  : int  0 0 0 0 0 0 0 0 0 0 ...
  $ State      : chr  "Alabama" "Alabama" "Alabama" "Alabama" ...
  $ Gender     : chr  "Male" "Male" "Male" "Male" ...
  $ CardType   : chr  "American Express" "American Express" "American
Express" "American Express" ...
  $ CardName   : chr  "SimplyCash® Business Card from American Express"
"SimplyCash® Business Card from American Express" "SimplyCash® Business Card
from American Express" "SimplyCash® Business Card from American Express" ...
  -attr(*, ".internal.selfref")=<externalptr>
  -attr(*, "sorted")= chr "creditLine"
```

2.4.3 Data Exploration

Since the data wasn't too dirty, we managed to skip most of the data-wrangling approaches steps described earlier in the chapter. However, in real-world problems, the data transformation task is not so easy; it requires painstaking effort and data engineering. We will use such approaches in later case studies in the book. In this case, our data is ready to be explored in more detail. Let's start the exploration.

```
summary(data[,c("NumOfCards","OutsBal","DomesTransc",
"IntTransc"),with =FALSE])
   NumOfCards        OutsBal        DomesTransc        IntTransc
 Min.   :1.00   Min.   :    0   Min.   :  0.00   Min.   : 0.000
 1st Qu.:1.00   1st Qu.:    0   1st Qu.: 10.00   1st Qu.: 0.000
 Median :1.00   Median : 3706   Median : 19.00   Median : 0.000
 Mean   :1.03   Mean   : 4110   Mean   : 28.94   Mean   : 4.047
 3rd Qu.:1.00   3rd Qu.: 6000   3rd Qu.: 39.00   3rd Qu.: 4.000
 Max.   :2.00   Max.   :41485   Max.   :100.00   Max.   :60.000
```

So, if we want to understand the behavior of the number of transactions between men and women, it looks like there is no difference. Men and women shop equally, as shown in Figure 2-7.

```
boxplot(I(DomesTransc +IntTransc ) ~Gender, data = data)
title("Number of Domestic Transaction")
```

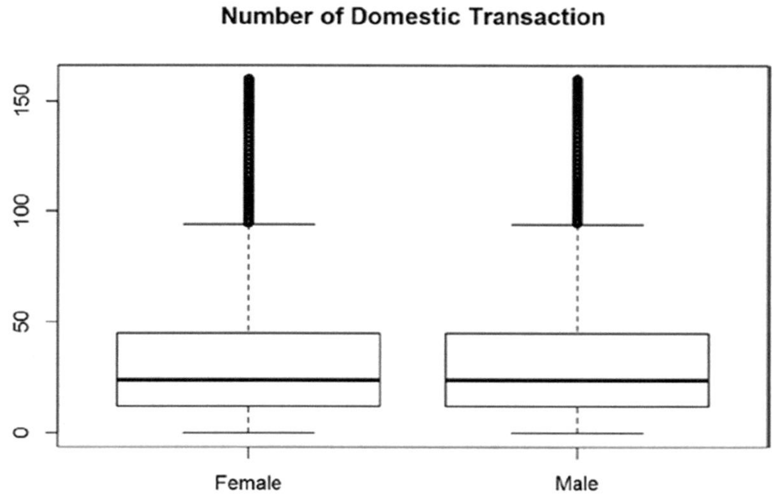

***Figure 2-7.** The number of domestic transactions sorted by male and female*

```
tapply(I(data$DomesTransc +data$IntTransc),data$Gender, median)
 Female   Male
     24     24
```

```
tapply(I(data$DomesTransc +data$IntTransc),data$Gender, mean)
   Female      Male
 32.97612  32.98624
```

Now let's look at the frequencies of the categorical variables.

Distribution of frauds across the card type are shown here. This type of frequency table tell us which categorical variable is prominent for the fraud cases.

```
table(data$CardType,data$FraudFlag)

                          0       1
American Express    2325707  149141
Discover             598246   44285
MasterCard          3843172  199532
Visa                2636861  203056
```

You can see from the frequency table that highest frauds have happened to Visa cards, followed by MasterCard and American Express. The lowest frauds are reported from Discover. The number of frauds defines the event rate for modeling purposes. Event rate is the proportion of events (i.e., fraud) versus the number of records for each category.

Similarly, you can see frequency plots for fraud and gender and fraud and state.

```
table(data$Gender,data$FraudFlag)

               0       1
   Female 3550933  270836
   Male   5853053  325178
```

Frauds are reported more from males; the event rate of fraud in the male category is 325178/(325178+5853053) = 5.2%. Similarly, the event rate in the female category is 270836/(270836+3550933) = 7.1%. Hence, while males have more frauds, the event rate is higher for female customers. In both cases, the event rate is low, so we need to look for sampling so that we get a high event rate in the modeling dataset.

2.5 Summary

In this chapter, we discussed various data preparation methods, like handling missing values, merging two datasets, computing derived variables, and dealing with date and time variables. Often in real-world datasets, the data needs a lot of cleaning to make it usable for deriving insights or building models. Exploratory data analysis provides a way to understand the various statistical properties of data, like mean, variance, standard deviation, skewness, and kurtosis, which helps in spotting abnormalities and in generating useful insights.

In upcoming chapters, we explain how to enrich this data to be able to model it and quantify these relationships for a predictive model. The next chapter will help you understand how you can reduce your dataset and at the same time enhance its properties to be able to apply machine learning algorithms.

While it's always good to say that more data implies a better model, there might be occasions where the luxury of sufficient amount of data is not there or computational power is limited to only allow a certain size of dataset. In such situations, statistics could help sample a precise and informative subset of data without compromising much on the quality of the model. Chapter 3 focuses on many such sampling techniques that will help in achieving this objective.

CHAPTER 3

Sampling and Resampling Techniques

In Chapter 2, we introduced the concept of data import and exploration techniques. Now you are equipped with the skills to load data from different sources and how to store them in an appropriate format. In this chapter we will discuss important data sampling methodologies and their importance in machine learning algorithms. Sampling is an important block in our machine learning process flow and it serves the dual purpose of cost savings in data collection and reduction in computational cost without compromising the power of the machine learning model.

> *"An approximate answer to the right problem is worth a good deal more than an exact answer to an approximate problem."*
>
> —John Tukey

John Tukey statement fits well into the spirit of sampling. As the technological advancement brought large data storage capabilities, the incremental cost of applying machine learning techniques is huge. Sampling helps us balance between the cost of processing high volumes of data with marginal improvement in the results. Contrary to the general belief that sampling is useful only for reducing a high volume of data to a manageable volume, sampling is also important to improve statistics garnered from small samples. In general, machine learning deals with huge volumes of data, but concepts like bootstrap sampling can help you get insight from small sample situations as well.

The learning objectives of this chapter are as follows:

- Introduction to sampling
- Sampling terminology

K. Ramasubramanian and A. Singh, *Machine Learning Using R*, https://doi.org/10.1007/978-1-4842-4215-5_3

- Non-probability sampling and probability sampling
- Business implication of sampling
- Statistical theory on sample statistics
- Introduction to resampling
- Monte Carlo method: Acceptance-Rejection sampling
- Computational time saving illustration

Different sampling techniques will be illustrated using the credit card fraud data introduced in Chapter 2.

3.1 Introduction to Sampling

Sampling is a process that selects units from a population of interest, in such a way that the sample can be generalized for the population with statistical confidence. For instance, if an online retailer wanted to know the average ticket size of an online purchase over the last 12 months, we might not want to average the ticket size over the population (which may run into millions of data points for big retailers), but we can pick up a representative sample of purchases over last 12 months and estimate the average for the sample. The sample average then can be generalized for the population with some statistical confidence. The statistical confidence will vary based on the sampling technique used and the size.

In general, sampling techniques are applied to two scenarios, for creating a manageable dataset for modeling and for summarizing population statistics. The following two broad categorizations can be presented as objectives of sampling:

- Model sampling
- Survey sampling

Figure 3-1 shows the difference between the two business objectives. The sample survey design and evaluation are out of scope of this book, so will keep our focus on model sampling alone.

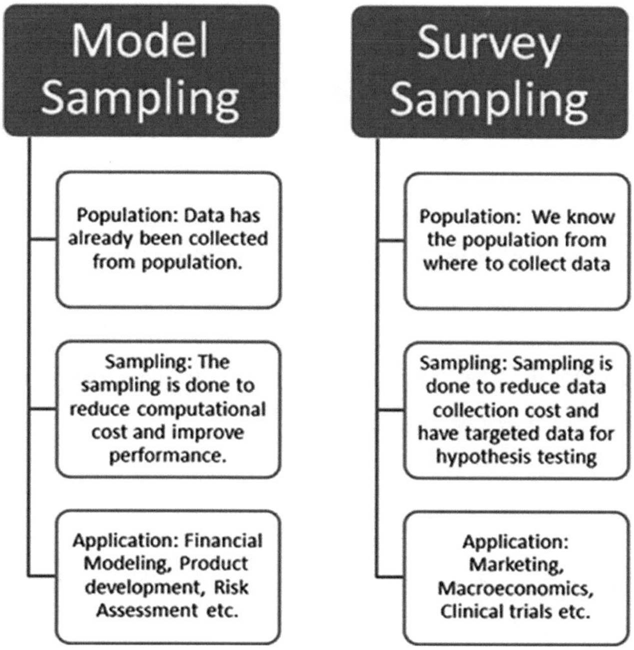

Figure 3-1. *Objectives of sampling*

This classification is also helpful in identifying the end objectives of sampling. This helps in choosing the right methodology for sampling and the right exploratory technique. In the context of the machine learning model building flow, our focus will be around model sampling. The assumption is that the data has already been collected and our end objective is to garner insight from that data, rather than develop a systematic survey to collect it.

3.2 Sampling Terminology

Before we get into details of sampling, let's define some basic terminology of sampling that we will be using throughout the book. The statistics and probability concepts discussed in Chapter 1 will come in handy in understanding the sampling terminology. This section lists the definition and mathematical formulation in sampling.

3.2.1 Sample

A *sample* is a set of units or individuals selected from a parent population to provide some useful information about the population. This information can be in the general shape of distribution, basic statistics, properties of population distribution parameters, or information of some higher moments. Additionally, the sample can be used to estimate test statistics for hypothesis testing. A representative sample can be used to estimate properties of population or to model population parameters.

For instance, the National Sample Survey Organization (NNSO) collects sample data on unemployment by reaching out to limited households, and then this sample is used to provide data for national unemployment.

3.2.2 Sampling Distribution

The distribution of the means of a particular size of samples is called the *sampling distribution* of means; similarly the distribution of the corresponding sample variances is called the sampling distribution of the variances. These distributions are the fundamental requirements for performing any kind of hypothesis testing.

3.2.3 Population Mean and Variance

Population mean is the arithmetic average of the population data. All the data points contribute toward the population mean with equal weight. Similarly, population variance is the variance calculated using all the data points in the data.

Population mean: $\mu = \frac{\sum_{i=1}^{n} x_i}{n}$

Population Variance: $\sigma^2 = \frac{1}{n}\sum_{i=1}^{n}(x_i - \mu)^2$

3.2.4 Sample Mean and Variance

Any subset you draw from the population is a sample. The mean and variance obtained from that sample are called *sample statistics*. The concept of degrees of freedom is used when a sample is used to estimate distribution parameters; hence, you will see for sample variance that the denominator is different than the population variance.

Sample mean: $\bar{x} = \frac{1}{n}\sum_{i=1}^{n} x_i$

Sample variance: $s^2 = \frac{1}{n-1}\sum_{i=1}^{n}(x_i - \bar{x})^2$

3.2.5 Pooled Mean and Variance

For k sample of size n_1, n_2, n_3, ..., n_k taken from the same population, the estimated population mean and variance are defined as follows.

Estimated population mean:

$$\bar{x}_p = \frac{\sum_{i=1}^{k}\bar{x}_i}{\sum_{i=1}^{k}(n_i)} = \frac{(n_1)\bar{x}_1 + (n_2)\bar{x}_2 + \cdots + (n_k)\bar{x}_k}{n_1 + n_2 + \cdots + n_k}$$

Estimated population variance:

$$s_p^2 = \frac{\sum_{i=1}^{k}(n_i - 1)s_i^2}{\sum_{i=1}^{k}(n_i - 1)} = \frac{(n_1 - 1)s_1^2 + (n_2 - 1)s_2^2 + \cdots + (n_k - 1)s_k^2}{n_1 + n_2 + \cdots + n_k - k}$$

In real-life situations, we usually can have multiple samples drawn from the same population at different points in space/location and time. For example, assume we have to estimate average income of bookshop owner in a city. We will get samples of bookshop owners' income from different parts of city at different points in time. At a later point of time, we can combine the individual mean and variance from different samples to get an estimate for population using pooled mean and variance.

3.2.6 Sample Point

A possible outcome in a sampling experiment is called a *sample point*. In many types of sampling, all the data points in the population are not sample points.

Sample points are important when the sampling design becomes complex. The researcher may want to leave some observations out of sampling, alternatively the sampling process by design itself can give less probability of selection to the undesired data point. For example, suppose you have gender data with three possible values—Male, Female, and Unknown. You may want to discard all Unknowns as an error, this is keeping the observation out of sampling. Otherwise, if the data is large and the Unknowns are a very small proportion then the probability to sample them is negligible. In both cases, Unknown is not a sample point.

3.2.7 Sampling Error

The difference between the true value of a population statistic and the sample statistic is the *sampling error*. This error is attributed to the fact that the estimate has been obtained from the sample.

For example, suppose you know by census data that monthly average income of residents in Boston is \$3,000 (the population mean). So, we can say that true mean of income is \$3,000. Let's say that a market research firm performed a small survey of residents in Boston. We find that the sample average income from this small survey is \$3,500. The sampling error is then \$3,500 - \$3,000, which equals \$500. Our sample estimates are over-estimating the average income, which also points to the fact that the sample is not a true representation of the population.

3.2.8 Sampling Fraction

The *sampling fraction* is the ratio of sample size to population size, $f = \frac{n}{N}$.

For example, if your total population size is 500,000 and you want to draw a sample of 2,000 from the population, the sampling fraction would be f = 2,000/50,000 = 0.04. In other words, 4% of population is sampled.

3.2.9 Sampling Bias

Sampling bias occurs when the sample units from the population are not characteristic of (i.e., do not reflect) the population. Sampling bias causes a sample to be unrepresentative of the population.

Connecting back to the example from sampling error, we found out that the sample average income is way higher than the census average income (true average). This means our sampling design has been biased toward higher income residents of Boston. In that case, our sample is not a true representation of Boston residents.

3.2.10 Sampling Without Replacement (SWOR)

Sampling without replacement requires two conditions to be satisfied:

- Each unit/sample point has a finite non-zero probability of selection
- Once a unit is selected, it is removed from the population

In other words, all the units have some finite probability of being sampled strictly only once.

For instance, if we have a bag of 10 balls marked with numbers 1 to 10, then each ball has selection probability of 1/10 in a random sample done without replacement. Suppose we have to choose three balls from the bag, then after each selection the probability of selection increases as number of balls left in bag decreases. So, for the first ball the probability of getting selected is 1/10, for the second it's 1/9, and for the third it's 1/8.

3.2.11 Sampling with Replacement (SWR)

Sampling with replacement differs from SWOR by the fact that a unit can be sampled more than once in the same sample. Sampling with replacement requires two conditions to be satisfied:

- Each unit/sample point has a finite non-zero probability of selection
- A unit can be selected multiple times, as the sampling population is always the same

In sampling with replacement, the unit can be sampled more than once and each time has the same probability of getting sampled. This type of sampling virtually expands the size of population to infinity as you can create as many samples of any size from this method. Connecting back to our previous example in SWOR, if we have to choose three balls with SWR, each ball will have the exact same finite probability of 1/10 for sampling.

The important thing to note here is sampling with replacement technically makes the population size infinite. Be careful while choosing SWR, as in most cases each observation is unique and counting it multiple times creates bias in your data. Essentially it will mean you are allowing a repetition of observation. For example, 100 people having the same name, income, age, and gender in the sample will create bias in the dataset.

3.3 Credit Card Fraud: Population Statistics

The credit card fraud dataset is a good example of how to build a sampling plan for machine learning algorithms. The dataset is huge, with 10 million rows and multiple features. This section will show you how the key sampling measure of population can be calculated and interpreted for this dataset. The following statistical measures will be shown:

- Population mean
- Population variance
- Pooled mean and variance

To explain these measures, we chose the outstanding balance feature as the quantity of interest.

3.4 Data Description

Here's a quick recap from Chapter 2 to describe the following variables in the credit card fraud data:

- `custID`: A unique identifier for each customer
- `gender`: Gender of the customer
- `state`: State in the United States where the customer lives

- cardholder: Number of credit cards the customer holds
- balance: Balance on the credit card
- numTrans: Number of transactions to date
- numIntlTrans: Number of international transactions to date
- creditLine: The financial services corporation, such as Visa, MasterCard, or American Express
- fraudRisk: Binary variable: 1 means customer is being frauded, 0 means otherwise

The structure of the data.frame after reading from the CSV file could be explored using str(data).

```
str(data)
 Classes 'data.table' and 'data.frame':   10000000 obs. of 14 variables:
  $ creditLine : int  1 1 1 1 1 1 1 1 1 1 ...
  $ gender     : int  1 1 1 1 1 1 1 1 1 1 ...
  $ state      : int 1 1 1 1 1 1 1 1 1 1 ...
  $ CustomerID : int 4446 59161 136032 223734 240467 248899 262655 324670
                 390138 482698 ...
  $ NumOfCards : int 1 1 1 1 1 1 1 1 1 1 ...
  $ OutsBal    : int 2000 0 2000 2000 2000 0 0 689 2000 0 ...
  $ DomesTransc: int 31 25 78 11 40 47 15 17 48 25 ...
  $ IntTransc  : int 9 0 3 0 0 0 0 9 0 35 ...
  $ FraudFlag  : int 0 0 0 0 0 0 0 0 0 0 ...
  $ State      : chr "Alabama" "Alabama" "Alabama" "Alabama" ...
  $ PostalCode : chr "AL" "AL" "AL" "AL" ...
  $ Gender     : chr "Male" "Male" "Male" "Male" ...
  $ CardType   : chr "American Express" "American Express" "American
                 Express" "American Express" ...
  $ CardName   : chr "SimplyCash® Business Card from American Express"
                "SimplyCash® Business Card from American Express"
                "SimplyCash® Business Card
                 from American Express" "SimplyCash® Business Card from
                 American Express" ...
 - attr(*, ".internal.selfref")=<externalptr>
 - attr(*, "sorted")= chr "creditLine"
```

As stated earlier, we chose outstanding balance as the variable/feature of interest. In the `str()` output for data descriptive, we can see the outstanding balance is stored in a variable named `OutsBal`, which is of type `integer`. Being a continuous variable, mean and variance can be defined for this variable.

3.5 Population Mean

Mean is a more traditional statistic for measuring the central tendency of any distribution of data. The mean outstanding balance of our customers in the credit card fraud dataset turns out to be $4,109.92. This is our first understanding about the population. Population mean tells us that on average, the customers have an outstanding balance of $4,109.92 on their cards.

```
Population_Mean_P <-mean(data$OutsBal)
```

The average outstanding balance on cards is $4,109.92.

3.6 Population Variance

Variance is a measure of spread for the given set of numbers. The smaller the variance, the closer the numbers are to the mean and the larger the variance, the farther away the numbers are from the mean. For the outstanding balance, the variance is 15974788 and standard deviation is 3996.8. The variance by itself is not comparable across different populations or samples. Variance is required to be seen along with the mean of the distribution. Standard deviation is another measure and it equals the square root of the variance.

```
Population_Variance_P <-var(data$OutsBal)
```

The variance in the average outstanding balance is 15974788.
Standard deviation of outstanding balance is $3996.847.

3.7 Pooled Mean and Variance

Pooled mean and variance estimate population mean and variance respectively when multiple samples are drawn independently of each other. To illustrate the pooled mean and variance compared to true population mean and variance, we will first create five random samples of size 10K, 20K, 40K, 80K, and 100K and calculate their mean and variance.

Using these samples, we will estimate the population mean and variance by using pooled mean and variance formula. Pooled values are useful because estimates from a single sample might produce a large sampling error, whereas if we draw many samples from the same population, the sampling error is reduced. The estimate in a collective manner will be closer to the true population statistics.

In the following R snippet, we are creating five random samples using the sample() function. sample() is an built-in function that's been used multiple times in the book. Another thing to note is that the sample() function works with some random seed value, so if you want to create the sample with same observations as ours, use the set.seed(937) function in R. This will make sure that each time you run the code, you get the same random sample.

```
set.seed(937)
i<-1
n<-rbind(10000,20000,40000,80000,100000)
Sampling_Fraction<-n/nrow(data)
sample_mean<-numeric()
sample_variance<-numeric()
for(i in 1:5)
{
    sample_100K <-data[sample(nrow(data),size=n[i], replace =FALSE, prob
    =NULL),]
    sample_mean[i]<-round(mean(sample_100K$OutsBal),2)
    sample_variance[i] <-round(var(sample_100K$OutsBal),2)
}
```

```
Sample_statistics <-cbind (1:5,c('10K','20K','40K','80K','100K'),sample_
mean,sample_variance,round(sqrt(sample_variance),2),Sampling_Fraction)
```

```
knitr::kable(Sample_statistics, col.names =c("S.No.", "Size","Sample_
Mean","Sample_Variance","Sample SD","Sample_Fraction"))
```

In Table 3-1, basic properties of the five samples are presented. The highest sample fraction is for the biggest sample size. A good thing to notice is that, as the sample size increases, the sample variance gets smaller.

***Table 3-1.** Sample Statistics*

S.No.	Size	Sample_Mean	Sample_Variance	Sample SD	Sample_Fraction
1	10K	4092.48	15921586.32	3990.19	0.001
2	20K	4144.26	16005696.09	4000.71	0.002
3	40K	4092.28	15765897.18	3970.63	0.004
4	80K	4127.18	15897698.44	3987.19	0.008
5	100K	4095.28	15841598.06	3980.15	0.01

Now let's use the pooled mean and variance formula to calculate the population mean from the five samples we drew from the population and then compare them with population mean and variance.

```
i<-1
Population_mean_Num<-0
Population_mean_Den<-0
for(i in 1:5)
{
  Population_mean_Num =Population_mean_Num +sample_mean[i]*n[i]
  Population_mean_Den =Population_mean_Den +n[i]
}

Population_Mean_S<-Population_mean_Num/Population_mean_Den


cat("The pooled mean ( estimate of population mean) is",Population_Mean_S)
 The pooled mean ( estimate of population mean) is 4108.814
```

The pooled mean is $4,108.814. Now we apply this same process to calculate the pooled variance from the samples. Additionally, we will show the standard deviation as an extra column to make dispersion comparable to the mean measure.

```
i<-1
Population_variance_Num<-0
Population_variance_Den<-0
for(i in 1:5)
{
  Population_variance_Num =Population_variance_Num +(sample_
  variance[i])*(n[i] -1)
  Population_variance_Den =Population_variance_Den +n[i] -1
}

Population_Variance_S<-Population_variance_Num/Population_variance_Den

Population_SD_S<-sqrt(Population_Variance_S)

cat("The pooled variance (estimate of population variance) is", Population_
Variance_S)
 The pooled variance (estimate of population variance) is 15863765
cat("The pooled standard deviation (estimate of population standard
deviation) is", sqrt(Population_Variance_S))
 The pooled standard deviation (estimate of population standard deviation)
 is 3982.934
```

The pooled standard deviation is $3,982.934. Now we have both pooled statistics and population statistics. Here, we create a comparison between the two and see how well the pooled statistics estimated the population statistics:

```
SamplingError_percent_mean<-round((Population_Mean_P -sample_mean)/
Population_Mean_P,3)
SamplingError_percent_variance<-round((Population_Variance_P -sample_
variance)/Population_Variance_P,3)

Com_Table_1<-cbind(1:5,c('10K','20K','40K','80K','100K'),Sampling_
Fraction,SamplingError_percent_mean,SamplingError_percent_variance)

knitr::kable(Com_Table_1, col.names =c("S.No.","Size","Sampling_
Frac","Sampling_Error_Mean(%)","Sampling_Error_Variance(%)"))
```

Table 3-2 shows the comparison of the population mean and the variance against each individual sample. The bigger the sample, the closer the mean estimate to the true population estimate.

Table 3-2. *Sample Versus Population Statistics*

S.No.	Size	Sampling_Frac	Sampling_Error_Mean(%)	Sampling_Error_Variance(%)
1	10K	1000	0.004	0.003
2	20K	500	-0.008	-0.002
3	40K	250	0.004	0.013
4	80K	125	-0.004	0.005
5	100K	100	0.004	0.008

Create the same view for pooled statistics against the population statistics. The difference is expressed as a percentage of differences among pooled/sample to the true population statistics (see Tables 3-3 and 3-4).

```
SamplingError_percent_mean<-(Population_Mean_P -Population_Mean_S)/
Population_Mean_P
SamplingError_percent_variance<-(Population_Variance_P -Population_
Variance_S)/Population_Variance_P

Com_Table_2 <-cbind(Population_Mean_P,Population_Mean_S,SamplingError_
percent_mean)
Com_Table_3 <-cbind(Population_Variance_P,Population_
Variance_S,SamplingError_percent_variance)

knitr::kable(Com_Table_2)

knitr::kable(Com_Table_3)
```

Table 3-3. *Population Mean and Sample Mean Difference*

Population_Mean_P	Population_Mean_S	SamplingError_percent_mean
4109.92	4108.814	0.000269

Table 3-4. *Population Variance and Sample Variance*

Population_Variance_P	Population_Variance_S	SamplingError_percent_variance
15974788	15863765	0.0069499

Pooled mean is close to the true mean of the population. This shows that given multiple samples, the pooled statistics are more likely to capture true statistics values. You have now seen how a sample so small in size when compared to population gives you estimates so close to the population estimate.

Does this example give you a tool of dealing with big data by using small samples from them? By now you might have started thinking about the cost-benefit analysis of using sampling. This is very relevant to machine learning algorithms churning millions of data points. More data points does not necessarily mean all of them contain meaningful patterns/trends/information. Sampling will try to save you from the weeds and help you focus on meaningful datasets for machine learning.

3.8 Business Implications of Sampling

Sampling is applied at multiple stages of model development and decision making. Sampling methods and interpretation are driven by business constraints and statistical methods chosen for inference testing. There is a delicate balance set by data scientists between the business implications and how statistical results stay valid and relevant. Most of the time, the problem is given by business and data scientists have to work in a targeted manner to solve the problem.

For instance, suppose the business wants to know why customers are not returning to their website. This problem will dictate the terms of sampling. To know why customers are not coming back, do you really need a representative sample of the whole population of your customers? Or you will just take a sample of customers who didn't return? Or rather you would like to only study a sample of customers who return and negate the results? Why not create a custom mixed bag of all returning and not returning customers? As you can observe, lots of these questions, along with practical limitations on time, cost, computational capacity, will be deciding factors on how to go about gathering data for this problem.

3.8.1 Shortcomings of Sampling

- Sampling bias can cause wrong inference
- Representative sampling is always not possible due to size, type, and requirements
- It is not exact science but an approximation within certain confidence limits
- In a sample survey, we have issues of manual errors, inadequate response, and absence of informants

3.9 Probability and Non-Probability Sampling

The sampling methodology largely depends on what we want to do with the sample. Whether we want to generate a hypothesis about population parameters or want to test a hypothesis. We classify sampling method into two major buckets—probability sampling and non-probability sampling. The comparison in Figure 3-2 provides the high-level differences between them.

Probability (Random) Sampling	Non-Probability (Non-Random) Sampling
Can be generalized to population defined by sampling frame	Cannot be generalized beyond the sample
Can apply statistical methods, Hypothesis testing, confidence bounds	Exploratory research, helps in generating Hypothesis, Analytical inference
Can estimate population statistics/parameters from sample	Population statistics/parameters are not of interest
Reduces Bias by varying sample design	Biased, Sample adequacy can't be known
Random selection from population	No defined population; Cheaper, easier and convenient to carry out

Figure 3-2. *Probability versus non-probability sampling*

In *probability sampling*, the sampling methods draws each unit with some finite probability. The sampling frame that maps the population unit to sample unit is created based on the probability distribution of the random variable utilized for sampling. These types of methods are commonly used for model sampling, and have high reliability to draw population inference. They eliminate bias in parameter estimation and can be generalized to the population. Contrary to non-probability sampling, we need to know the population beforehand to sample from. This makes this method costly and sometimes difficult to implement.

Non-probability sampling is sampling based on subjective judgment of experts and business requirements. This is a popular method where the business needs don't need to align with statistical requirements or it is difficult to create a probability sampling frame. The non-probability sampling method does not assign probability to population units and hence it becomes highly unreliable to draw inferences from the sample. Non-probability sampling have bias toward the selected classes as the sample is not representative of population. Non-probability methods are more popular with exploratory research for new traits of population that can be tested later with more statistical rigor. In contrast to probability techniques, it is not possible to estimate population parameters with accuracy using non-probability techniques.

3.9.1 Types of Non-Probability Sampling

In this section, we briefly touch upon the three major types of non-probability sampling methods. As these techniques are more suited to survey samples, we will not discuss them in detail.

3.9.1.1 Convenience Sampling

In convenience sampling, the expert will choose the data that is easily available. This technique is the cheapest and consumes less time. For our case, suppose that the data from New York is accessible but for other states, the data is not readily accessible. So we choose data from one state to study whole United States. The sample would not be a representative sample of population and will be biased. The insights also cannot generalized to the entire population. However, the sample might allow us to create some hypotheses that can later be tested using random samples from all the states.

3.9.1.2 Purposive Sampling

When the sampling is driven by the subjective judgment of the expert, it's called purposive sampling. In this method the expert will sample those units that help him establish the hypothesis he is trying to test. For our case, if the researcher is only interested in looking at American Express cards, he will simply choose some units from the pool of records from that card type. Further, there are many types of purposive sampling methods, e.g., maximum variance sampling, extreme case sampling, homogeneous sampling, etc., but these are not discussed in this book, as they lack representativeness of population, which is required for unbiased machine learning methods.

3.9.1.3 Quota Sampling

As the name goes, quota sampling is based on a prefixed quota for each type of cases, usually the quota decided by an expert. Fixing a quota grid for sampling ensures equal or proportionate representation of subjects being sampled. This technique is popular in marketing campaign design, A/B testing, and new feature testing.

In this chapter we cover sampling methods with examples drawn from our credit card fraud data. We encourage you to explore more non-probability sampling in context of the business problem at your disposal. There are times when experience can beat statistics, so non-probability sampling is equally important in many use cases.

3.10 Statistical Theory on Sampling Distributions

Sampling techniques draw their validity from well-established theorems and time-tested methods from statistics. For studying sampling distribution, we need to understand two important theorems from statistics:

- Law of Large Numbers
- Central Limit Theorem

This section explains these two theorems with some simulations.

3.10.1 Law of Large Numbers: LLN

In general, as the sample size increases in a test, we expect the results to be more accurate, having smaller deviations in the expected outcomes. The Law of Large Numbers formalizes this with help of the probability theory. The first notable reference to this concept was given by Italian mathematician Gerolamo Cardano in the 16th Century, when he observed and stated that empirical statistics get closer to their true value as the number of trials increases.

In later years, a lot of work was done to get different form of the Law of Large Numbers. The example we are going to discuss for a coin toss was first proved by Bernoulli and later he provided proof of his observations. Aleksander Khinchin provided the most popular statement for the Law of Large Numbers, also called the Weak Law of Large Numbers. The Weak Law of Large Numbers is alternatively called the Law of Averages.

3.10.1.1 Weak Law of Large Numbers

In probability space, the sample average converges to an expected value as the sample size trends to infinity. In other words, as the number of trials or sample size grows, the probability of getting close to the true average increases. The weak law is also called Khinchin's Law to recognize his contribution.

The Weak Law of Large Numbers states that the sample averages converge in probability toward the expected value $X_n \xrightarrow{p} \mu \ when\ n \rightarrow \infty$.

Alternatively, for any positive number $\in$

$$\lim_{n\to\infty} \text{pr}\left(\left|\overline{X}_n - \mu\right| > \varepsilon\right) = 0.$$

3.10.1.2 Strong Law of Large Numbers

It is important to understand the subtle difference between the Weak and Strong Laws of Large Numbers. The Strong Law of Large Numbers states that the sample average will converge to true average by probability 1, while the Weak Law only states that they will converge. Hence, the Strong Law is more powerful to state while estimating population mean by sample means.

The Strong Law of Large Numbers states that the sample average converges almost surely to the expected value $\overline{X}_n \xrightarrow{\text{a.s.}} \mu$ *when* $n \to \infty$.

Equivalent to

$$\operatorname{pr}\left(\lim_{n\to\infty} \overline{X}_n - \mu\right) = 1$$

Note There are multiple representations and proofs for the Law of Large Numbers. You are encouraged to refer to any graduate level text of probability to learn more.

Without getting into the statistical details of this theorem, we will set up an example to understand. Consider a coin toss example whereby a coin toss outcome follows a binomial distribution.

Suppose you have a biased coin and you have to determine what the probability is of getting "heads" in any toss of the coin. According to LLN, if you perform the coin toss experiment multiple times, you will be able to find the actual probability of getting heads.

Note that for a unbiased coin, you can use the classical probability theory and get the probability, `P(head)= Total no. of favorable outcomes/Total number of outcomes = 1/2`. But for a biased coin, you have unequal probability associated with each event and hence cannot use the classical approach. We will set up a coin toss experiment to determine the probability of getting heads in a coin toss.

3.10.1.3 Steps in Simulation with R Code

Step 1: Assume some value of binomial distribution parameter, `p=0.60(say)`, which we will be estimating using the Law of Large Numbers.

```
# Set parameters for a binomial distribution Binomial(n, p)
# n -> no. of toss
# p -> probability of getting a head
library(data.table)
n <-100
p <-0.6
```

In the previous code snippet, we set the true mean for our experiment. Which is to say we know that our population is coming from a binomial distribution with p=0.6. The experiment will now help us estimate this value as the number of experiments increases.

Step 2: Sample a point from a binomial distribution (p).

```
#Create a data frame with 100 values selected samples from Binomial(1,p)
set.seed(917);
dt <-data.table(binomial =rbinom(n, 1, p) ,count_of_heads =0, mean =0)

# Setting the first observation in the data frame

ifelse(dt$binomial[1] ==1, dt[1, 2:3] <-1, 0)
 [1] 1
```

We are using a built-in function rbinom() to sample binomial distributed random variable with parameter, p=0.6. This probability value is chosen such that the coin is biased. If the coin is not biased, then we know the probability of heads is 0.5.

Step 3: Calculate the probability of heads as the number of heads/total no. of coin tosses.

```
# Let's run an experiment large number of times (till n) and see how the
average of heads -> probability of heads converge to a value

for (i in 2 :n)
  {
    dt$count_of_heads[i] <-ifelse(dt$binomial[i] ==1, dt$count_of_
    heads[i]<- dt$count_of_heads[i -1]+1, dt$count_of_heads[i -1])
    dt$mean[i] <-dt$count_of_heads[i] /i
}
```

At each step, we determine if the outcome is heads or tails. Then, we count the number of heads and divide by the number of trials to get an estimated proportion of heads. When you run the same experiment a large number of times, LLN states that you will converge to the probability (expectation or mean) of getting heads in an experiment. For example, at trial 30, we will be counting how many heads so far and divide by 30 to get the average number of heads.

Step 4: Plot and see how the average over the sample is converging to p=0.60.

```
# Plot the average no. of heads -> probability of heads at each experiment
stage plot(dt$mean, type='l', main ="Simulation of average no. of heads",
xlab="Size of Sample", ylab="Sample mean of no. of Heads")
abline(h = p, col="red")
```

Figure 3-3 shows that as the number of experiments increases, the probability is converging to the true probability of heads (0.6). You are encouraged to run the experiment a large number of times to see the exact convergence. This theorem helps us estimate unknown probabilities by method of experiments and create the distribution for inference testing.

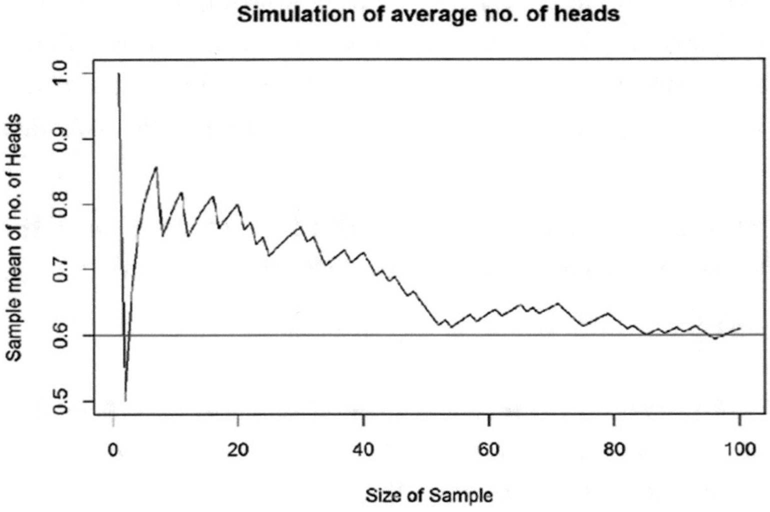

Figure 3-3. *Simulation of the coin toss experiment*

3.10.2 Central Limit Theorem

The Central Limit Theoremc is another very important theorem in probability theory and it allows hypothesis testing using the the sampling distribution. In other words, the Central Limit Theorem states that sample averages of large number of iterations of independent random variables, each with well-defined means and variances, are approximately normally distributed.

The first written explanation of this concept was provided by de Moivre in his work back in the early 18th Century when he used normal distribution to approximate the number of heads from the tossing experiment of a fair coin. Pierre-Simon Laplace published *Théorie analytique des probability* in 1812, where he expanded the idea of de Moivre by approximating binomial distribution with normal distribution. The precise proof of CLT was provided by Aleksandr Lyapunov in 1901 when he defined it in general terms and proved precisely how it worked mathematically. In probability, this is one the most popular theorems along with the Law of Large Numbers.

In context of this book, we will mathematically state by far the most popular version of the Central Limit Theorem (Lindeberg-Levy CLT).

For a sequence of i.i.d random variables {X1, X2, ...} with a well defined expectation and variance (E[Xi] = μ and Var[Xi] = σ2<∞), as n trends to infinity $\sqrt{n}$ $(S_n - \mu)$ converge in distribution to a normal N(0, sigma^2)

$$\sqrt{n}\left(\left(\frac{1}{n}\sum_{i=1}^{n}X_i\right)-\mu\right)\xrightarrow{d}=N\left(0,\sigma^2\right)$$

There are other versions of this theorem, such as Lyapunov CLT, Lindeberg CLT, Martingale difference CLT, and many more. It is important to understand how the Law of Large Numbers and the Central Limit Theorem tie together in our sampling context. The Law of Large Numbers states that the sample mean converges to the population mean as the sample size grows, but it does not talk about distribution of sample means. The Central Limit Theorem provides us with the insight into the distribution around the mean and states that it converges to a normal distribution for large number of trials. Knowing the distribution then allows us to do inferential testing, as we are able to create confidence bounds for a normal distribution.

We will again set up a simple example to explain the theorem. As a simple example, we will start sampling from an exponential distribution and will show the distribution of the sample mean.

3.10.2.1 Steps in Simulation with R Code

Step 1: Set a number of samples (say r=5000) to draw from a mixed population.

```
#Number of samples
r<-5000
#Size of each sample
n<-10000
```

In the previous code, r represented the number of samples to draw, and n represented the number of units in each sample. As per CLT, the larger the number of samples, the better the convergence to a normal distribution.

Step 2: Start sampling by drawing a sample of sizes n (say n=10000 each). Draw samples from normal, uniform, Cauchy, gamma, and other distributions to test the theorem for different distributions. Here, we take an exponential distribution with parameter ($\lambda = 0.6$)

```
#Produce a matrix of observations with n columns and r rows. Each row is
one sample
lambda<-0.6
Exponential_Samples =matrix(rexp(n*r,lambda),r)
```

Now, the Exponential_Samples data frame contains the series of i.i.d samples drawn from exponential distribution with the parameter, $\lambda = 0.6$

Step 3: Calculate the sum, means, and variance of all the samples for each sample.

```
all.sample.sums <-apply(Exponential_Samples,1,sum)
all.sample.means <-apply(Exponential_Samples,1,mean)
all.sample.vars <-apply(Exponential_Samples,1,var)
```

The previous step calculated the sum, mean, and variance of all the i.i.d samples. Now in the next step, we will observe the distribution of the sums, means, and variances. As per CLT, we will observe that the mean is following a normal distribution.

Step 4: Plot the combined sum, means, and variances.

```
par(mfrow=c(2,2))
hist(Exponential_Samples[1,],col="gray",main="Distribution of One Sample")
hist(all.sample.sums,col="gray",main="Sampling Distribution of
      the Sum")
hist(all.sample.means,col="gray",main="Sampling Distribution of the Mean")
hist(all.sample.vars,col="gray",main="Sampling Distribution of
      the Variance")
```

Figure 3-4 shows the plots of an exponential sample and sum, mean, and standard deviation of the all r samples.

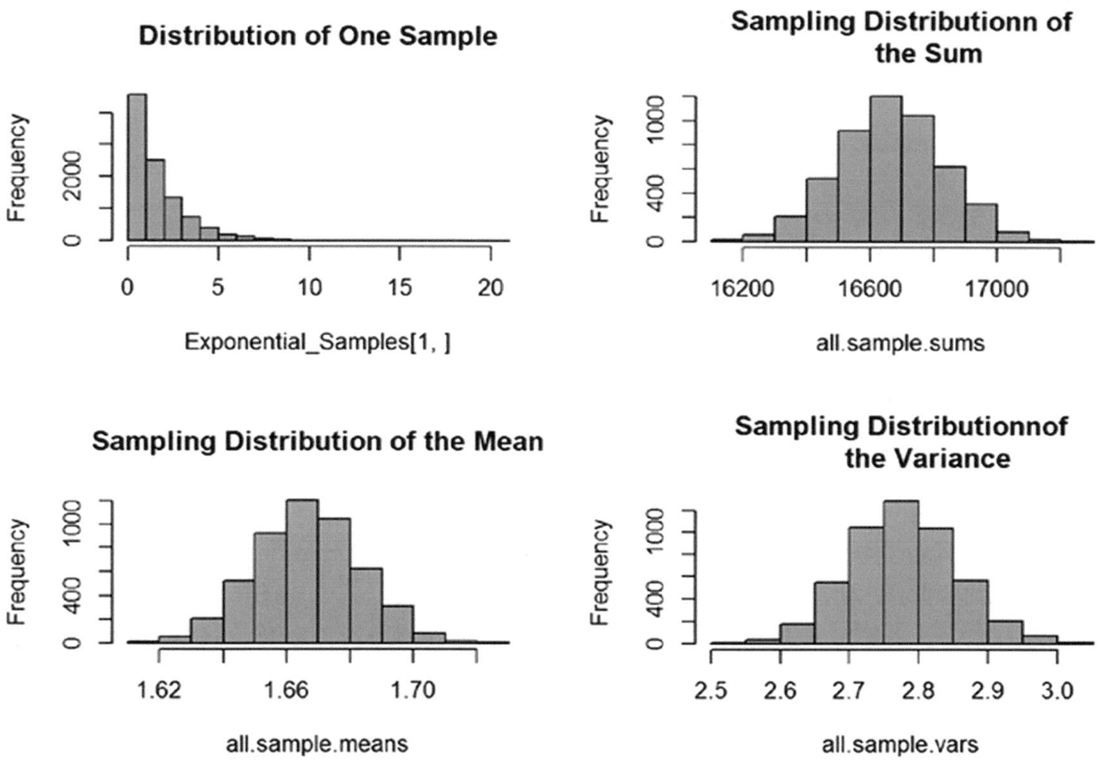

Figure 3-4. *Sampling distribution plots*

Figure 3-4 shows the distribution of statistics of the samples, i.e., the sum, mean, and variance. The first plot shows the histogram of the first sample from the exponential distribution. You can see the distribution of units in the sample is exponential. The visual inspection shows that the statistics estimated from the i.i.d samples are following a distribution close to a normal distribution.

Step 5: Repeat this experiment with other distributions and see that the results are consistent with the CLT for all the distributions.

There are some other standard distributions that can be used to validate the results of the Central Limit Theorem. Our example just discussed the exponential distribution; you are encouraged to use the following distribution to validate the Central Limit Theorem.

```
Normal_Samples =matrix(rnorm(n*r,param1,param2),r),

Uniform_Samples =matrix(runif(n*r,param1,param2),r),
```

```
Poisson_Samples =matrix(rpois(n*r,param1),r),

Cauchy_Samples =matrix(rcauchy(n*r,param1,param2),r),

Bionomial_Samples =matrix(rbinom(n*r,param1,param2),r),

Gamma_Samples =matrix(rgamma(n*r,param1,param2),r),

ChiSqr_Samples =matrix(rchisq(n*r,param1),r),

StudentT_Samples =matrix(rt(n*r,param1),r))
```

It is a good practice to not rely on visual inspection and perform formal tests to infer any properties of distribution. Histogram and a formal test of normality is a good way to establish both visually and by parametric testing that the distribution of means is actually normally distributed (as claimed by CLT).

Next, we perform a Shapiro-Wilk test to check for normality of distribution of means. Other normality tests are discussed briefly in Chapter 6. One of the most popular non-parametric normality tests is the KS one sample test, which is discussed in Chapter 7.

```
#Do a formal test of normality on the distribution of sample means

  Mean_of_sample_means <-mean (all.sample.means)
  Variance_of_sample_means <-var(all.sample.means)

# testing normality by Shapiro wilk test
shapiro.test(all.sample.means)

  Shapiro-Wilk normality test

data: all.sample.means
W = 0.99979, p-value = 0.9263
```

You can see that the p-value is significant (>0.05) from the Shapiro-Wilk test, which means that we can't reject the null hypothesis that the distribution is normally distributed. The distribution is indeed normally distributed with a mean = 1.66 and variance = 0.00027.

Visual inspection can be done by plotting histograms. Additionally, for clarity, let's superimpose the normal density function on the histogram to confirm if the distribution is normally distributed (see Figure 3-5).

```
x <-all.sample.means
h<-hist(x, breaks=20, col="red", xlab="Sample Means",
main="Histogram with Normal Curve")
xfit<-seq(min(x),max(x),length=40)
yfit<-dnorm(xfit,mean=Mean_of_sample_means,sd=sqrt(Variance_of_sample_
means)) yfit <-yfit*diff(h$mids[1:2])*length(x)
lines(xfit, yfit, col="blue", lwd=2)
```

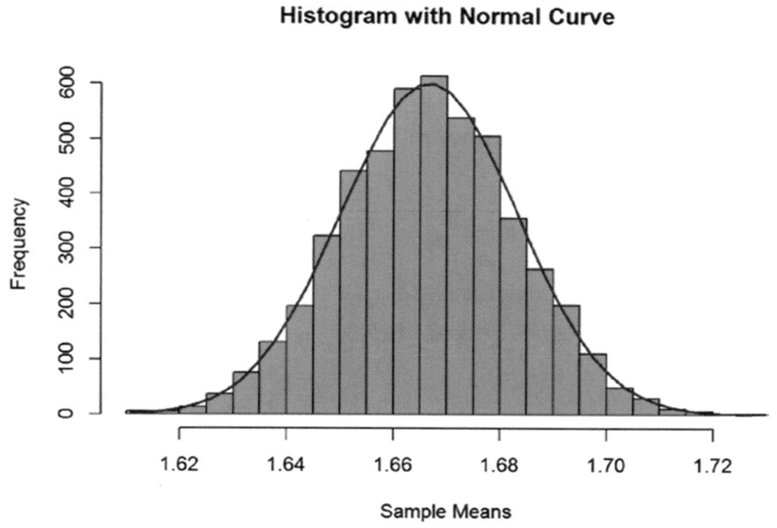

Figure 3-5. *Distribution of sample means with normal density lines*

The most important points to remember about the Law of Large Numbers and CLT are:

- As the sample size grows large, you can expect a better estimate of the population/model parameters. This being said, a large sample size will provide you with unbiased and more accurate estimates for hypothesis testing.
- The Central Limit Theorem helps you get a distribution and hence allows you to get a confidence interval around parameters and apply inference testing. The important thing is that CLT doesn't assume any distribution of population from which samples are drawn, which frees you from distribution assumptions.

3.11 Probability Sampling Techniques

In this section, we introduce some of the popular probability sampling techniques and show how to perform them using R. All the sampling techniques are explained using our credit card fraud data. As a first step of explaining the individual techniques, we create the population statistics and distribution and then compare the same sample properties with the population properties to ascertain the sampling outputs.

3.11.1 Population Statistics

We will look at some basic features of data. These features will be called as population statistics/parameters. We will then show different sampling methods and compare the result with population statistics.

1. Population data dimensions

str() shows us the column names, type, and a few values in the column. You can see that the dataset is a mix of integers and characters.

```
str(data)
 Classes 'data.table' and 'data.frame':   10000000 obs. of 14 variables:
  $ creditLine : int  1 1 1 1 1 1 1 1 1 1 ...
  $ gender     : int  1 1 1 1 1 1 1 1 1 1 ...
  $ state      : int  1 1 1 1 1 1 1 1 1 1 ...
  $ CustomerID : int 4446 59161 136032 223734 240467 248899 262655 324670
                 390138 482698 ...
  $ NumOfCards : int 1 1 1 1 1 1 1 1 1 1 ...
  $ OutsBal    : int 2000 0 2000 2000 2000 0 0 689 2000 0 ...
  $ DomesTransc: int 31 25 78 11 40 47 15 17 48 25 ...
  $ IntTransc  : int 9 0 3 0 0 0 0 9 0 35 ...
  $ FraudFlag  : int 0 0 0 0 0 0 0 0 0 0 ...
  $ State      : chr "Alabama" "Alabama" "Alabama" "Alabama" ...
  $ PostalCode : chr "AL" "AL" "AL" "AL" ...
  $ Gender     : chr "Male" "Male" "Male" "Male" ...
  $ CardType   : chr "American Express" "American Express" "American
                 Express" "American Express" ...
  $ CardName   : chr "SimplyCash® Business Card from American Express"
```

```
"SimplyCash® Business Card from American Express" "SimplyCash® Business Card
from American Express" "SimplyCash® Business Card from American Express" ...
  - attr(*, ".internal.selfref")=<externalptr>
  - attr(*, "sorted")= chr "creditLine"
```

2. Population mean for measures

   a. *Outstanding balance*: On average, each card carries an outstanding amount of $4,109.92.

```
mean_outstanding_balance <- mean(data$OutsBal)
mean_outstanding_balance
```

```
[1] 4109.92
```

   b. *Number of international transactions*: Average number of international transactions is 4.04.

```
mean_international_trans <- mean(data$IntTransc)
mean_international_trans
```

```
[1] 4.04719
```

   c. *Number of domestic transactions:* Average number of domestic transactions is very high compared to international transactions; the number is 28.9 ~ 29 transactions.

```
mean_domestic_trans <- mean(data$DomesTransc)
mean_domestic_trans
```

```
[1] 28.93519
```

3. Population variance for measures

   a. *Outstanding balance:*

```
Var_outstanding_balance <- var(data$OutsBal)
Var_outstanding_balance
```

```
[1] 15974788
```

   b. *Number of international transactions*:

```
Var_international_trans <- var(data$IntTransc)
Var_international_trans
```

```
[1] 74.01109
```

c. *Number of domestic transactions:*

```
Var_domestic_trans <- var(data$DomesTransc)
Var_domestic_trans
```

```
[1] 705.1033
```

4. Histogram

a. *Outstanding balance* (see Figure 3-6):

```
hist(data$OutsBal, breaks=20, col="red",
xlab="Outstanding Balance",
main="Distribution of Outstanding Balance")
```

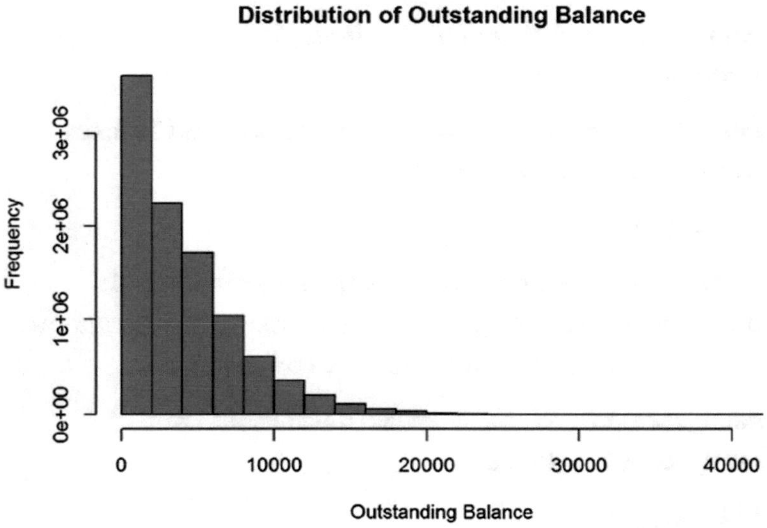

Figure 3-6. *Histogram of outstanding balance*

b. *Number of international transactions* (see Figure 3-7):

```
hist(data$IntTransc, breaks=20, col="blue",
xlab="Number of International
Transactions",
main="Distribution of International Transactions")
```

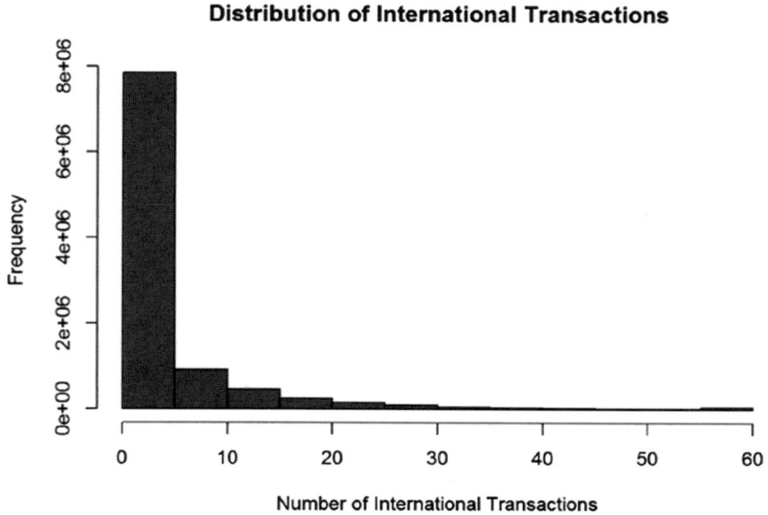

Figure 3-7. *Histogram of number of international transactions*

c. *Number of domestic transactions* (see Figure 3-8):

```
hist(data$DomesTransc, breaks=20, col="green",
xlab="Number of Domestic
Transactions",
main="Distribution of Domestic Transactions")
```

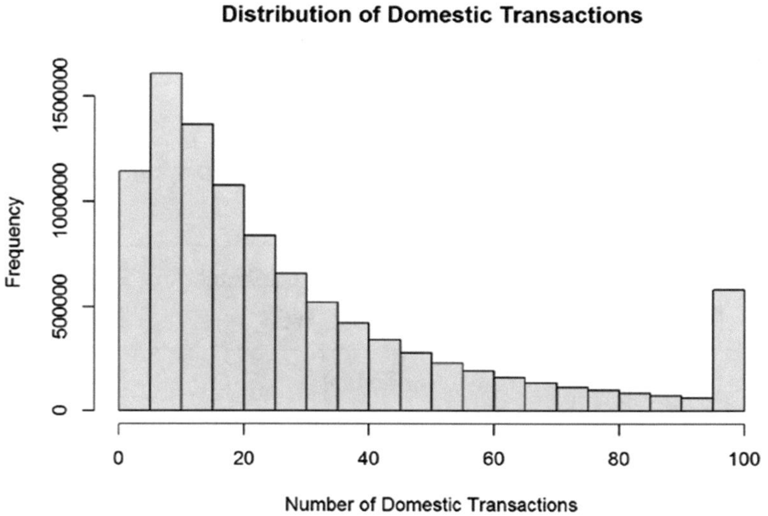

Figure 3-8. *Histogram of number of domestic transactions*

Figure 3-8 shows the mean, variance, and distribution of a few important variables from our credit card fraud dataset. These population statistics will be compared to sample statistics to see which sampling techniques provide a representative sample.

3.11.2 Simple Random Sampling

Simple random sampling is a process of selecting a sample from the population where each unit of population is selected at random. Each unit has the same individual probability of being chosen at any stage during the sampling process, and the subset of k individuals has the same probability of being chosen for the sample as any other subset of k individuals.

Simple random is a basic type of sampling, hence it can be a component of more complex sampling methodologies. In coming topics, you will see simple random sampling form an important component of other probability sampling methods, like stratified sampling and cluster sampling.

Simple random sampling is typically without replacement, i.e., by the design of sampling process, we make sure that no unit can be selected more than once. However, simple random sampling can be done with replacement, but in that case the sampling units will not be independent. If you draw a small size sample from a large population, sampling without replacement and sampling with replacement will give approximately the same results, as the probability of each unit to be chosen is very small. Table 3-5 compares the statistics from simple random sampling with and without replacement. The values are comparable, as the population size is very big (~10 million). We will see this fact in our example.

Table 3-5. *Comparison Table with Population Sampling with and Without Replacement*

CardType	OutstandingBalance_ Population	OutstandingBalance_ Random_WOR	OutstandingBalance_ Random_WR
American Express	3820.896	3835.064	3796.138
Discover	4962.420	4942.690	4889.926
MasterCard	3818.300	3822.632	3780.691
Visa	4584.042	4611.649	4553.196

Advantages:

- It is free from classification error
- Not much advanced knowledge is required of the population
- Easy interpretation of sample data

Disadvantages:

- Complete sampling frame (population) is required to get representative sample
- Data retrieval and storage increases cost and time
- Simple random sample carries the bias and errors present in the population, and additional interventions are required to get rid of those

Function: Summarise

Summarise is a function in the dplyr library. This function helps aggregate the data by dimensions. This works similar to a pivot table in Excel.

- group_by: This argument takes the categorical variable by which you want to aggregate the measures.
- mean(OutsBal): This argument gives the aggregating function and the field name on which aggregation is to be done.

```
#Population Data :Distribution of Outstanding Balance across Card Type

library (dplyr)

summarise (group_by (data,CardType),Population_OutstandingBalance=mean
(OutsBal))
Source: local data table [4 x 2]

          CardType Population_OutstandingBalance
 1 American Express                     3820.896
 2       MasterCard                     3818.300
 3             Visa                     4584.042
 4         Discover                     4962.420
```

The call of the summarise function by CardType shows the average outstanding balance by card type. Discover cards have the highest average outstanding balance.

Next, we draw a random sample of 100,000 records by using a built-in function `sample()` from the `base` library. This function creates a sampling frame by randomly selecting indexes of data. Once we get the sampling frame, we extract the corresponding records from the population data.

Function: Sample

Note some important arguments of the `sample()` function:

- `nrow(data)`: This tells the size of data. Here it is 10,000,000 and hence it will create an index of 1 to 10,000,000 and then randomly select index for sampling.
- `size`: Allows users to provide how many data points to sample from the population. In our case, we have set `n` to 100,000.
- `replace`: This argument allows users to state if the sampling should be done without replacement (`FALSE`) or with replacement (`TRUE`).
- `prob`: This is vector of probabilities for obtaining the sampling frame. We have set this to `NULL`, so that they all have the same weight/probability.

```
set.seed(937)
# Simple Random Sampling Without Replacement
library("base")

sample_SOR_100K <-data[sample(nrow(data),size=100000, replace =FALSE,
prob
=NULL),]
```

Now, let's again see how the average balance looks for the simple, random sample. As you can see the order of average balances has been maintained. Note that the average is very close to the population average as calculated in the previous step for population.

```
#Sample Data : Distribution of Outstanding Balance across Card Type

library(dplyr)

summarise(group_by(sample_SOR_100K,CardType),Sample_Outstanding
Balance=mean (OutsBal))
Source: local data table [4 x 2]
```

```
          CardType Sample_OutstandingBalance
1       MasterCard                  3822.632
2 American Express                  3835.064
3             Visa                  4611.649
4         Discover                  4942.690
```

Function: KS.test()

This is one of the non-parametric tests for comparing the empirical distribution functions of data. This function helps determine if the data points are coming from the same distribution or not. It can be done as one sample test, i.e., the data Empirical Distribution Function (EDF) compared to some preset PDF of distribution (normal, cauchy, etc.), two sample test, i.e., when we want to see if the distribution of two samples is the same or not.

As one of the important features of sampling is to make sure the distribution of data does not change after sampling (except when it is done intentionally), we will use two sample tests to see if the sample is a true representation of the population by checking if the population and sample are drawn from the same distribution.

The important arguments are the two data series and hypothesis to test, two tail, one tail. We are choosing the more conservative two tail test for this example. Two tail test means that we want to make sure the equality is used in the null hypothesis.

```
#Testing if the sampled data comes from population or not. This makes sure that sampling does not change the original distribution
ks.test(data$OutsBal,sample_SOR_100K$OutsBal,alternative="two.sided")
  Two-sample Kolmogorov-Smirnov test

 data: data$OutsBal and sample_SOR_100K$OutsBal
 D = 0.003042, p-value = 0.3188
 alternative hypothesis: two-sided
```

The KS test results clearly states that the sample and population have the same distribution. Hence, we can say that the sampling has not changed the distribution. By the nature of sampling, the simple random sampling without replacement retains the distribution of data.

For visual inspection, Figure 3-9 shows the histograms for the population and the sample. As you can see, the distribution is the same for both.

```
par(mfrow =c(1,2))
hist(data$OutsBal, breaks=20, col="red", xlab="Outstanding Balance",
main="Histogram for Population Data")

hist(sample_SOR_100K$OutsBal, breaks=20, col="green", xlab="Outstanding
Balance",
main="Histogram for Sample Data (without replacement)")
```

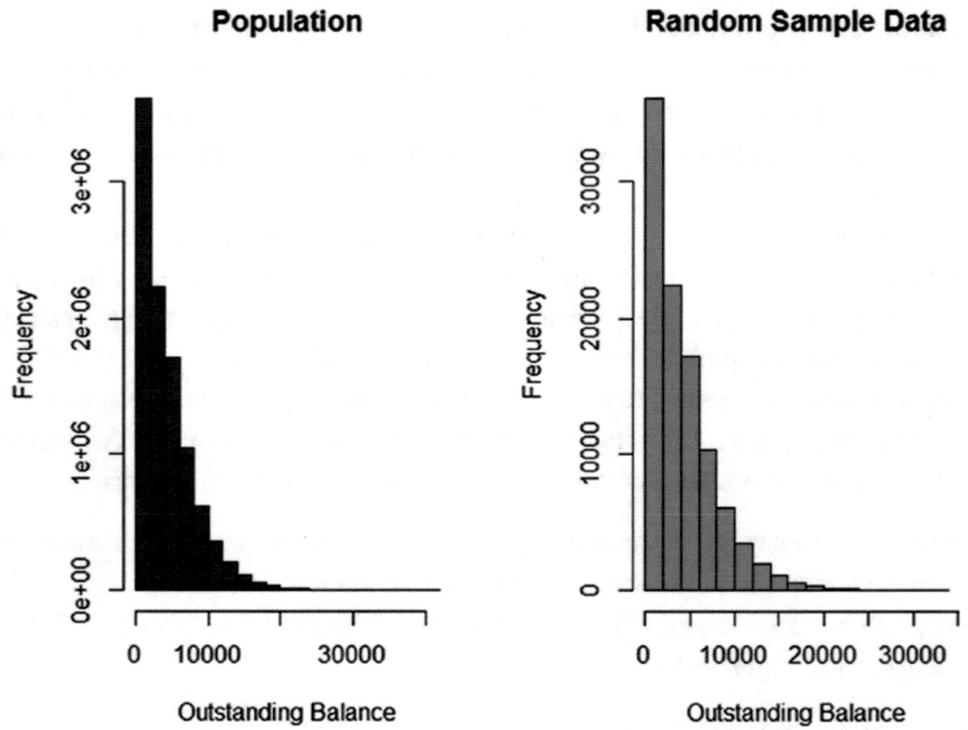

Figure 3-9. *Population versus sample (without replacement) distribution*

Now we will do a formal test on the mean of the outstanding balance from the population and our random sample. Theoretically, we will expect the t-test on means of two to be TRUE and hence we can say that the mean of the sample and population are the same with 95% confidence.

```
# Let's also do t.test for the mean of population and sample.

t.test(data$OutsBal,sample_SOR_100K$OutsBal)
```

```
 Welch Two Sample t-test

data:  data$OutsBal and sample_SOR_100K$OutsBal
t = -0.85292, df = 102020, p-value = 0.3937
alternative hypothesis: true difference in means is not equal to 0
95 percent confidence interval:
 -35.67498 14.04050
sample estimates:
mean of x mean of y
 4109.920 4120.737
```

These results show that the means of population and sample are the same as the p-value of `t.test` is insignificant. We cannot reject the null hypothesis that the means are equal.

Here we will show you similar testing performed for simple random sample with replacement. As you will see, we don't see any significant change in the results as compared to simple random sample, as the population size is very big and replacement essentially doesn't alter the sampling probability of a record in any material way.

```
set.seed(937)
# Simple Random Sampling With Replacement
library("base")

sample_SR_100K <-data[sample(nrow(data),size=100000, replace =TRUE, prob
=NULL),]
```

In this code, for simple random sampling with replacement, we set `replace` to `TRUE` in the sample function call.

The following code shows how we performed the KS test on the distribution of the population and the sample drawn with replacement. The test shows that the distributions are the same and the p-value is insignificant, which fails to reject the null of equal distribution.

```
ks.test(data$OutsBal,sample_SR_100K$OutsBal,alternative="two.sided")
 Warning in ks.test(data$OutsBal, sample_SR_100K$OutsBal, alternative =
 "two.sided"): p-value will be approximate in the presence of ties

  Two-sample Kolmogorov-Smirnov test

 data: data$OutsBal and sample_SR_100K$OutsBal
 D = 0.0037522, p-value = 0.1231
 alternative hypothesis: two-sided
```

We create the histogram of population and sample with replacement. The plots look the same, coupled with a formal KS test, and we can see that both samples with replacement and populations have the same distribution (see Figure 3-10). Be cautious about this when the population size is small.

```
par(mfrow =c(1,2))
hist(data$OutsBal, breaks=20, col="red", xlab="Outstanding Balance",
main="Population ")

hist(sample_SR_100K$OutsBal, breaks=20, col="green", xlab="Outstanding
Balance", main=" Random Sample Data ( WR)")
```

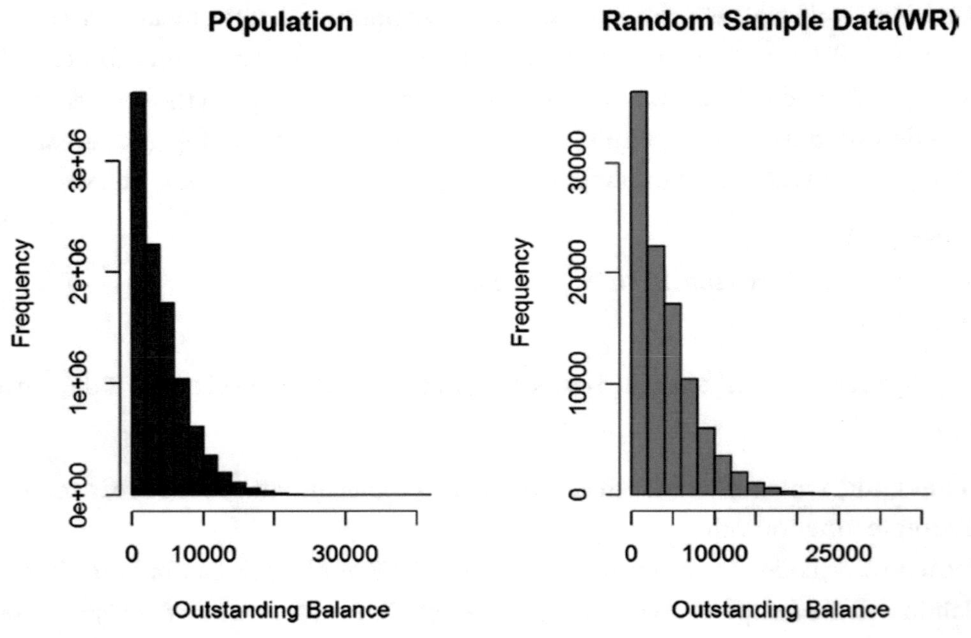

***Figure 3-10.** Population versus sample (with replacement) distribution*

The distribution is similar for population and random sample drawn with replacement. We summarize the simple random sampling by comparing the summary results from population, simple random sample without replacement, and simple random sample with replacement.

```
population_summary <-summarise(group_by(data,CardType),OutstandingBalan
ce_Population=mean(OutsBal))
random_WOR_summary<-summarise(group_by(sample_SOR_100K,CardType),Outstanding
Balance_Random_WOR=mean(OutsBal))
random_WR_summary<-summarise(group_by(sample_SR_100K,CardType),OutstandingBa
lance_Random_WR=mean(OutsBal))
compare_population_WOR<-merge(population_summary,random_WOR_summary,
by="CardType")
compare_population_WR <-merge(population_summary,random_WR_summary,
by="CardType")

summary_compare<-cbind(compare_population_WOR,compare_population_
WR[,OutstandingBalance_Random_WR]) colnames(summary_compare)
[which(names(summary_compare) == "V2")] <- "OutstandingBalance_Random_WR"

knitr::kable(summary_compare)
```

Table 3-5 shows that both with and without replacement, simple random sampling gave similar values of mean across card types, which were very close to the true mean of the population.

Key points:

- Simple random sampling gives representative samples from the population.
- Sampling with and without replacement can give different results with different samples sizes, so extra care should be taken to choosing the method when the population size is small.
- The appropriate sample size for each problem differs based on the confidence we want with our testing, business purposes, cost benefit analysis, and other reasons. You will get a good understanding of what is happening in each sampling techniques and can choose the best one that suits the problem at hand.

3.11.3 Systematic Random Sampling

Systematic sampling is a statistical method in which the units are selected with a systematically ordered sampling frame. The most popular form of systematic sampling is based on a circular sampling frame, where we transverse the population from start to end and then again continue from start in a circular manner. In this approach the probability of each unit to be selected is the same and hence this approach is sometimes called the equal-probability method. But you can create other systematic frames according to your need to perform systematic sampling.

In this section, we discuss the most popular circular approach to systematic random sampling. In this method, sampling starts by selecting a unit from the population at random and then every kth element is selected. When the list ends, the sampling starts from the beginning. Here, the k is known as the skip factor, and it's calculated as follows

$$k = \frac{N}{n}$$

where N is population size and n is sample size.

This approach to systematic sampling makes this functionally similar to simple random sampling, but it is not the same because not every possible sample of a certain size has an equal probability of being chosen (e.g., the seed value will make sure that the adjacent elements are never selected in the sampling frame). However, this method is efficient if variance within the systematic sample is more than the population variance.

Advantages:

- Easy to implement
- Can be more efficient

Disadvantages:

- Can be applied when the population is logically homogeneous
- There can be a hidden pattern in the sampling frame, causing unwanted bias

Let's create an example of systematic sampling from our credit card fraud data.

Step 1: Identify a subset of the population that can be assumed to be homogeneous. A possible option is to subset the population by state. In this example, we use Rhode Island, the smallest state in the United States, to assume homogeneity.

Note Creating homogeneous sets from the population by some attribute is discussed in Chapter 6.

For illustration purposes, let's create a homogeneous set by subsetting the population with the following business logic. Subset the data and pull the records whose international transactions equal 0 and domestic transactions are less than or equal to 3.

Assuming the previous subset forms a set of homogeneous population, the assumption in subsetting is also partially true as the customers who do not use card domestically are likely not to use them internationally at all.

```
Data_Subset <-subset(data, IntTransc==0&DomesTransc<=3)
summarise(group_by(Data_Subset,CardType),OutstandingBalance=mean(OutsBal))
 Source: local data table [4 x 2]

          CardType OutstandingBalance
 1 American Express           3827.894
 2       MasterCard           3806.849
 3             Visa           4578.604
 4         Discover           4924.235
```

Assuming the subset has homogeneous sets of cardholders by card type, we can go ahead with systematic sampling. If the set is not homogeneous, then it's highly likely that systematic sampling will give a biased sample and hence not provide a true representation of the population. Further, we know that the data is stored in R data frame by an internal index (which will be the same as our customer ID), so we can rely on internally ordered index for systematic sampling.

Step 2: Set a sample size to sample from the population.

```
#Size of population ( here the size of card holders from Data Subset)
Population_Size_N<-length(Data_Subset$OutsBal)

# Set a the size of sample to pull (should be less than N), n. We will
assume n=5000

Sample_Size_n<-5000
```

Step 3: Calculate the skip factor using this formula:

$$k = \frac{N}{n}$$

The skip factor will give the jump factor while creating the systematic sampling frame. Essentially, with a seed (or starting index) of c, items will be selected after skipping k items in order.

```
#Calculate the skip factor

k =ceiling(Population_Size_N/Sample_Size_n)

#ceiling(x) rounds to the nearest integer that's larger than x.
#This means ceiling (2.3) = 3

cat("The skip factor for systematic sampling is ",k)
 The skip factor for systematic sampling is 62
```

Step 4: Set a random seed value of index and then create a sequence vector with seed and skip (sample frame). This will take a seed value of index, say `i`, then create a sampling frame as i,i+k,i+2k ...and so on until it has a total of `n` (sample size) indexes in the sampling frame.

```
r =sample(1:k, 1)
systematic_sample_index =seq(r, r +k*(Sample_Size_n-1), k)
```

Step 5: Sample the records from the population by sample frame. Once we have our sampling frame ready, it is nothing but a list of indices, so we pull those data records corresponding to the sampling frame.

```
systematic_sample_5K<-Data_Subset[systematic_sample_index,]
```

Let's now compare the systematic sample with a simple random sample of the same size of 5000. As from the previous discussion, we know that the simple random sampling is a true representation of the population, so we can use that as a proxy for population properties.

```
set.seed(937)
# Simple Random Sampling Without Replacement
library("base")

sample_Random_5K <-Data_Subset[sample(nrow(Data_Subset),size=5000, replace
=FALSE, prob =NULL),]
```

Here is the result of summary comparison by card type for outstanding balances. The comparison is important to show what differences in mean will appear if we would have chosen a simple random sample instead of a systematic sample.

```
sys_summary <-summarise(group_by(systematic_sample_5K,CardType),OutstandingB
alance_Sys=mean(OutsBal))
random_summary<-summarise(group_by(sample_Random_5K,CardType),OutstandingBal
ance_Random=mean(OutsBal))

summary_mean_compare<-merge(sys_summary,random_summary, by="CardType")

print(summary_mean_compare)
 Source: local data table [4 x 3]

          CardType OutstandingBalance_Sys OutstandingBalance_Random
 1 American Express               3745.873                  3733.818
 2         Discover               5258.751                  4698.375
 3       MasterCard               3766.037                  3842.121
 4             Visa               4552.099                  4645.664
```

Again, we will emphasize on testing the sample EDF with population EDF to make sure that the sampling has not distorted the distribution of data. This steps will be repeated for all the sampling techniques, as this ensures that the sampling is stable for modeling purposes.

```
ks.test(Data_Subset$OutsBal,systematic_sample_5K$OutsBal,alternative="two.
sided")
 Warning in ks.test(Data_Subset$OutsBal, systematic_sample_5K$OutsBal,
 alternative = "two.sided"): p-value will be approximate in the presence of
 ties
```

```
    Two-sample Kolmogorov-Smirnov test

data: Data_Subset$OutsBal and systematic_sample_5K$OutsBal
D = 0.010816, p-value = 0.6176
alternative hypothesis: two-sided
```

The KS test results show that the distribution is the same and hence the sample is a representation of the population by distribution. Figure 3-11 shows the histograms to show how the distribution is for a homogeneous data subset and a systematic sample. We can see that the distribution has not changed drastically.

```
par(mfrow =c(1,2))
hist(Data_Subset$OutsBal, breaks=50, col="red", xlab="Outstanding Balance",
main="Homogenous Subset Data")

hist(systematic_sample_5K$OutsBal, breaks=50, col="green",
xlab="Outstanding
mBalance", ain="Systematic Sample ")
```

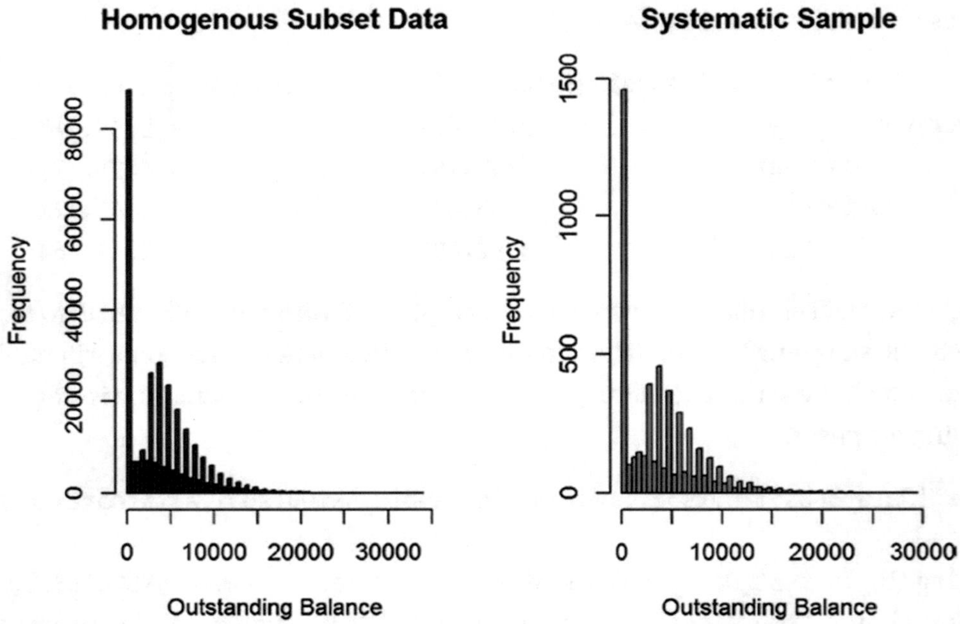

Figure 3-11. *Homogeneous population and systematic sample distribution*

Key points:

- Systematic sampling is equivalent to simple random sampling if done on a homogeneous set of data points. Also, a large population size suppresses the bias associated with systematic sampling for smaller sampling fractions.
- Business and computational capacity are important criteria to choose a sampling technique when the population size is large. In our example, the systematic sampling gives a representative sample with a lower computational cost. (There is no call to the random number generator, and hence no need to transverse the complete list of records.)

3.11.4 Stratified Random Sampling

When the population has sub-populations that vary, it is important for the sampling technique to consider the variations at the subpopulation (stratum) level and sample them independently at the stratum level. Stratification is the process of identifying homogeneous groups by featuring that group by some intrinsic property. For instance, customers living in the same city can be thought of as belonging to that city stratum. The strata should be mutually exclusive and collectively exhaustive, i.e., all units of the population should be assigned to some strata and one unit can only belong to one strata.

Once we form the stratum then a simple random sampling or systematic sampling is performed at the stratum level independently. This improves the representativeness of sample and generally reduces the sampling error. Dividing the population in stratum also helps you calculate the weighted average of the population, which has less variability than the total population combined.

There are two generally accepted methods of identifying stratified sample size:

- *Proportional allocation:* Samples equal proportions of the data from each stratum. In this case, the same sampling fraction is applied for all the stratum in the population. For instance, your population has four types of credit cards and you assume that each credit card type forms a homogeneous group of customers. Assume the number of each type of customers in each stratum is N1+N2+N3+N4=total, then in proportional allocation you will get a sample having the same proportion from each stratus (n1/N1=n2/N2=n3/N3=n4/N4=sampling fraction).

- *Optimal allocation:* Samples proportions of data proportionate to the standard deviation of the distribution of stratum variable. This results in large samples from the strata with the highest variability, which means the sample variance is reduced.

Another important feature of stratified sampling is that it makes sure that at least one unit is sampled from each strata, even if the probability of it getting selected is zero. It is recommended to limit the number of strata and make sure enough units are present in each stratum to do sampling.

Advantages:

- Greater precision than simple random sampling of the same sample size
- Due to higher precision, it is possible to work with small samples and hence reduce cost
- Avoid unrepresentative samples, as this method samples at least one unit from each stratum

Disadvantages:

- Not always possible to partition the population in disjointed groups
- Overhead of identifying homogeneous stratum before sampling, adding to administrative cost
- Thin stratum can limit the representative sample size

To construct an example of stratified sampling with credit card fraud data, we first have to check the stratums and then go ahead with sampling from stratum. For our example, we will create a stratum based on the `CardType` and `State` variables.

Here, we explain step by step how to go about performing stratified sampling.

Step 1: Check the stratum variables and their frequency in the population.

Let's assume that `CardType` and `State` are stratum variables. In other words, we believe the type of card and the state can be used as a criteria to stratify the customers in logical buckets. Here are the frequencies by our stratum variables. We expect stratified sampling to maintain the same proportion of records in the stratified sample.

```
#Frequency table for CardType in Population
table(data$CardType)

 American Express          Discover        MasterCard              Visa
          2474848            642531           4042704           2839917
#Frequency table for State in Population
table(data$State)

          Alabama American Samoa          Arizona         Arkansas       California
            20137         162574           101740           202776          1216069
         Colorado    Connecticut         Delaware          Florida          Georgia
           171774         121802            20603            30333           608630
             Guam         Hawaii            Idaho         Illinois          Indiana
           303984          50438           111775            60992           404720
             Iowa         Kansas         Kentucky        Louisiana            Maine
           203143          91127           142170           151715           201918
         Maryland  Massachusetts         Michigan        Minnesota      Mississippi
           202444          40819           304553           182201           203045
         Missouri        Montana         Nebraska           Nevada    New Hampshire
           101829          30131            60617           303833            20215
       New Jersey     New Mexico         New York   North Carolina     North Dakota
            40563         284428            81332            91326           608575
             Ohio       Oklahoma           Oregon     Pennsylvania     Rhode Island
           364531         122191           121846           405892            30233
   South Carolina   South Dakota        Tennessee            Texas             Utah
           152253          20449           203827           812638            91375
          Vermont       Virginia       Washington    West Virginia        Wisconsin
           252812          20017           202972           182557            61385
          Wyoming
            20691
```

The cross table breaks the whole population by the stratum variables, CardType and State. Each stratum represents a set of customers having similar behaviors as they come from the same stratum. The following output is trimmed for easy readability.

```
#Cross table frequency for population data
table(data$State,data$CardType)

                   American Express Discover MasterCard   Visa
  Alabama                      4983     1353       8072   5729
  American Samoa              40144    10602      65740  46088
  Arizona                     25010     6471      41111  29148
  Arkansas                    50158    12977      82042  57599
  California                 301183    78154     491187 345545
  Colorado                    42333    11194      69312  48935
  Connecticut                 30262     7942      49258  34340
  Delaware                     4990     1322       8427   5864
```

Step 2: Random sample without replacement from each stratum, consider sampling 10% of the size of the stratum.

We are choosing the most popular way of stratified sampling, proportional sampling. We will be sampling 10% of the records from each stratum.

Function: `stratified()`

The `stratified` function samples from a `data.frame` or a `data.table` in which one or more columns can be used as a "stratification" or "grouping" variable. The result is a new `data.table` with the specified number of samples from each group. The standard function syntax is shown here:

```
stratified(indt, group, size, select = NULL, replace = FALSE, keep.rownames
= FALSE, bothSets = FALSE, ...)
```

- `group`: This argument allows users to define the stratum variables. Here we have chosen `CardType` and `State` as the stratum variables. So in total, we will have four (card types) X 52 (states) stratum to sample from.
- `size`: In general, size can be passed as a number (equal numbers from each strata) or as a sampling fraction. We will use the sampling fraction of 0.1. For other options type `?stratified` in the console.
- `replace`: This allows you to choose sampling with or without replacement. We have set it as `FALSE`, which means sampling without replacement.

We will be using this function to perform stratified random sampling.

We can also do the stratified sampling using our standard `sample()` function as well with following steps:

1. Create subsets of the data by stratum variables.
2. Calculate the sample size for sampling fraction of 0.1, for each stratum.
3. Do a simple random sampling from each stratum for the sample size as calculated.

The previous results and the `stratified()` results will be the same. But the `stratified()` function will be faster to execute. You are encouraged to implement this algorithm and try the other functions.

```
set.seed(937)
#We want to make sure that our sampling retain the same proportion of the
cardtype in the sample
#Do choose a random sample without replacement from each stratum consisting
of 10% of total size of stratum
library(splitstackshape)
stratified_sample_10_percent<-stratified(data, group=c("CardType","State"),
size=0.1,replace=FALSE)
```

Step 3: Check if the proportions of data points in the sample are the same as the population.

Here is the output of stratified sample by `CardType, State`, and by cross tabulation. The values show that the sampling has been done across the stratum with the same proportion. For example, number of records Alabama and American Express is 4980, in stratified sample the number of Alabama and American Express cardholders is 1/10 of the population, i.e., 498. For all other stratum, the proportion is the same.

```
#Frequency table for CardType in sample
table(stratified_sample_10_percent$CardType)

 American Express          Discover        MasterCard              Visa
           247483             64250            404268            283988
#Frequency table for State in sample
table(stratified_sample_10_percent$State)
```

```
        Alabama American Samoa          Arizona        Arkansas       California
           2013           16257           10174           20278           121606
       Colorado     Connecticut        Delaware         Florida          Georgia
          17177           12180            2060            3032            60862
           Guam          Hawaii           Idaho        Illinois          Indiana
          30399            5044           11177            6099            40471
           Iowa          Kansas        Kentucky       Louisiana            Maine
          20315            9113           14218           15172            20191
       Maryland   Massachusetts        Michigan       Minnesota      Mississippi
          20245            4081           30455           18220            20305
       Missouri         Montana        Nebraska          Nevada    New Hampshire
          10183            3013            6061           30383             2022
     New Jersey      New Mexico        New York North Carolina     North Dakota
           4056           28442            8133            9132            60856
           Ohio        Oklahoma          Oregon    Pennsylvania     Rhode Island
          36453           12219           12184           40589             3023
 South Carolina    South Dakota       Tennessee           Texas             Utah
          15225            2046           20382           81264             9137
        Vermont        Virginia      Washington   West Virginia        Wisconsin
          25281            2002           20297           18255             6138
        Wyoming
           2069
#Cross table frequency for sample data
table(stratified_sample_10_percent$State,stratified_sample_10_
percent$CardType)
                  American Express Discover MasterCard  Visa
  Alabama                      498      135        807   573
  American Samoa              4014     1060       6574  4609
  Arizona                     2501      647       4111  2915
  Arkansas                    5016     1298       8204  5760
  California                 30118     7815      49119 34554
  Colorado                    4233     1119       6931  4894
  Connecticut                 3026      794       4926  3434
  Delaware                     499      132       843    586
```

You can see that the proportion has remained the same. Here, we compare the properties of sample and population. The `summarise()` function shows the average of outstanding balance by strata. You can perform a pairwise `t.test` to see that the sampling has not altered the means of outstanding balance belonging to each strata. You are encouraged to do testing on the means by `t.test()`, as shown in this simple random sampling section.

```
# Average outstanding balance by stratum variables
summary_population<-summarise(group_by(data,CardType,State),OutstandingBalan
ce_Stratum=mean(OutsBal))

#We can see below that we want to make sure that our sampling retains the
same proportion of the cardtype in the sample
summary_sample<-summarise(group_by(stratified_sample_10_percent,CardType,Sta
te),OutstandingBalance_Sample=mean(OutsBal))

#Mean Comparison by stratum
summary_mean_compare<-merge(summary_population,summary_sample,
by=c("CardType","State"))
```

Again, we will do a KS test to compare the distribution of the stratified sample. We can see that the KS test shows that both have the same distribution.

```
ks.test(data$OutsBal,stratified_sample_10_percent$OutsBal,alternative="two.
sided")
  Two-sample Kolmogorov-Smirnov test

 data:  data$OutsBal and stratified_sample_10_percent$OutsBal
 D = 0.00073844, p-value = 0.7045
 alternative hypothesis: two-sided
```

Figure 3-12 shows the histograms to show how the distribution of outstanding balance looks for the sample and population. The visual comparison clearly shows that the sample is representative of the population.

```
par(mfrow =c(1,2))
hist(data$OutsBal, breaks=50, col="red", xlab="Outstanding Balance",
main="Population ")
```

```
hist(stratified_sample_10_percent$OutsBal, breaks=50, col="green",
xlab="Outstanding Balance",
main="Stratified Sample")
```

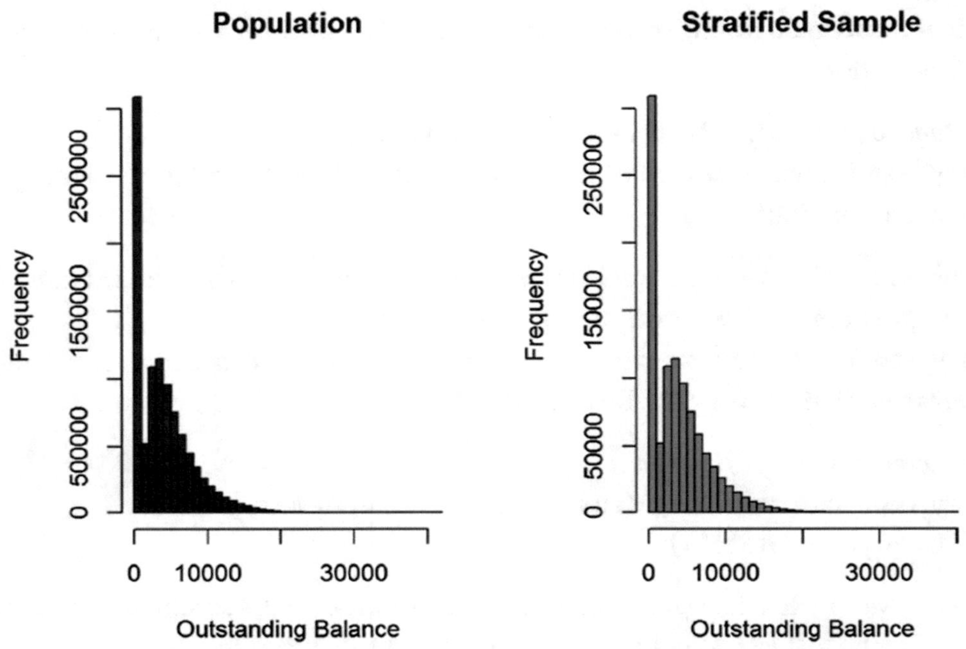

Figure 3-12. *Population and stratified sample distribution*

The distribution plot in Figure 3-12 reemphasizes the test results, both population and stratifies random sample have the same distribution. The stratified random sample is representative of the population.

Key points:

- Stratified sampling should be used when you want to make sure the proportion of data points remains the same in the sample. This not only ensures representativeness but also ensures that all the stratum gets a representation in the sample.
- Stratified sampling can also help you systematically design the proportion of records from each stratum, so you can design a stratified sampling plan to change the representation as per business need. For instance, you are modeling a binomial response function, and the even rate or the proportion of 1 is very small in the dataset.

Then you can do a stratified random sampling from stratum (0 or 1 response) and try to sample so that the proportion of 1 increases to facilitate modeling.

3.11.5 Cluster Sampling

Many times, populations contain heterogeneous groups that are statistically evident in the population. In those cases, it is important to first identify the heterogeneous groups and then plan the sampling strategy. This technique is popular among marketing and campaign designers, as they deal with characteristics of heterogeneous groups within a population.

Cluster sampling can be done in two ways:

- *Single-stage sampling*: All of the elements within selected clusters are included in the sample. For example, you want to study a particular population feature that's dominant in a cluster, so you might want to first identify the cluster and its element and just take all the units of that cluster.
- *Two-stage sampling*: A subset of elements within selected clusters is randomly selected for inclusion in the sample. This method is similar to stratified sampling but differs in the sense that here the clusters are parent units while in former case it was strata. Strata variables may themselves be divided into multiple clusters on the measure scale.

For a fixed sample size, the cluster sampling gives better results when most of the variation in the population is within the groups, not between them. It is not always straightforward to choose sampling methods. Many times the cost per sample point is less for cluster sampling than for other sampling methods. In these kinds of cost constraints, cluster sampling might be a good choice.

It is important to point out the difference between strata and cluster. Although both are overlapping subsets of the population, they are different in many respects.

- While all strata are represented in the sample; in clustering only a subset of clusters are in the sample.
- Stratified sampling gives best result when units within strata are internally homogeneous. However, with cluster sampling, the best results occur when elements within clusters are internally heterogeneous.

Advantages:

- Cheaper than other methods for data collection, as the cluster of interest requires less cost to collect and store and requires less administrative cost.
- Clustering takes a large population into account in terms of cluster chunks. Since these groups/clusters are so large, deploying any other technique would be very difficult. Clustering is feasible only when we are dealing with large populations with statistically significant clusters present in them.
- Reduction in variability of estimates is observed with other methods of sampling, but this may not be an ideal situation every time.

Disadvantages:

- *Sampling error:* This is high due to the design of the sampling process. The ratio between the number of subjects in the cluster study and the number of subjects in an equally reliable, randomly sampled unclustered study is called *design effect,* which causes the high sampling error.
- *Sampling bias:* The chosen sample in cluster sampling will be taken as representative of the entire population and if that cluster has a biased opinion then the entire population is inferred to have the same opinion. This may not be the actual case.

Before we show you cluster sampling, let's artificially create clusters in our data by subsetting the data by international transaction. We will subset the data with a conditional statement on international transaction. Here you can see we are artificially creating five clusters.

```
# Before i explain cluster sampling, lets try to subset the data such that
we have clear samples to explain the importance of cluster sampling
#Subset the data into 5 subgroups
Data_Subset_Clusters_1 <-subset(data, IntTransc >2&IntTransc <5)
Data_Subset_Clusters_2 <-subset(data, IntTransc >10&IntTransc <13)
Data_Subset_Clusters_3 <-subset(data, IntTransc >18&IntTransc <21)
Data_Subset_Clusters_4 <-subset(data, IntTransc >26&IntTransc <29)
Data_Subset_Clusters_5 <-subset(data, IntTransc >34)
```

```
Data_Subset_Clusters<-rbind(Data_Subset_Clusters_1,Data_Subset_
Clusters_2,Data_
Subset_Clusters_3,Data_Subset_Clusters_4,Data_Subset_Clusters_5)

str(Data_Subset_Clusters)
 Classes 'data.table' and 'data.frame':   1291631 obs. of 14 variables:
  $ creditLine : int  1 1 1 1 1 1 1 1 1 1 ...
  $ gender     : int  1 1 1 1 1 1 1 1 1 1 ...
  $ state      : int  1 1 1 1 1 1 1 1 1 1 ...
  $ CustomerID : int 136032 726293 1916600 2180307 3186929 3349887 3726743
                 5121051 7595816 8058527 ...
  $ NumOfCards : int 1 1 1 1 1 1 1 1 2 1 ...
  $ OutsBal    : int 2000 2000 2000 2000 2000 2000 0 0 2000 2000 ...
  $ DomesTransc: int 78 5 5 44 43 51 57 23 5 15 ...
  $ IntTransc  : int  3 4 3 3 4 4 3 3 4 3 ...
  $ FraudFlag  : int 0 0 0 0 0 0 0 0 0 0 ...
  $ State      : chr "Alabama" "Alabama" "Alabama" "Alabama" ...
  $ PostalCode : chr "AL" "AL" "AL" "AL" ...
  $ Gender     : chr "Male" "Male" "Male" "Male" ...
  $ CardType   : chr "American Express" "American Express" "American
                 Express" "American Express" ...
  $ CardName   : chr "SimplyCash® Business Card from American Express"
"SimplyCash® Business Card from American Express" "SimplyCash® Business Card
from American Express" "SimplyCash® Business Card from American Express"
...
  - attr(*, ".internal.selfref")=<externalptr>
```

We explicitly created clusters based on the International transactions. The clusters are created to show clustering sampling.

One-stage cluster sampling will mean randomly choosing clusters out of five clusters for analysis. While two-stage sampling will mean randomly choosing a few clusters and then doing stratified random sampling from them. In Figure 3-13, we first create clusters using k-means (discussed in detail in Chapter 6) and then apply stratified sampling, assuming the cluster is the stratum variable.

The k-means function creates clusters based on the centroid-based k-means clustering method. Since we have explicitly created five clusters, we will call k-means to form five clusters based on the international transaction values. We already know that the function will give us exactly five clusters as we created in the previous step. This has been done only for illustration purposes. In real situations, you have to find out the clusters present in the population data.

```
# Now we will treat the Data_Subset_Clusters as our population
library(stats)

kmeans_clusters <-kmeans(Data_Subset_Clusters$IntTransc, 5, nstart =25)

cat("The cluster center are ",kmeans_clusters$centers)
 The cluster center are 59.11837 22.02696 38.53069 47.98671 5.288112
```

Next, we take a random sample of records just to plot them neatly, as plotting with a large number of records will not be clear (see Figure 3-13).

```
set.seed(937)
# For plotting lets use only 100000 records randomly chosen from total
data.
library(splitstackshape)
PlotSample<-Data_Subset_Clusters[sample(nrow(Data_Subset_
Clusters),size=100000, replace =TRUE, prob =NULL),]

plot(PlotSample$IntTransc, col = kmeans_clusters$cluster)
points(kmeans_clusters$centers, col =1:5, pch =8)
```

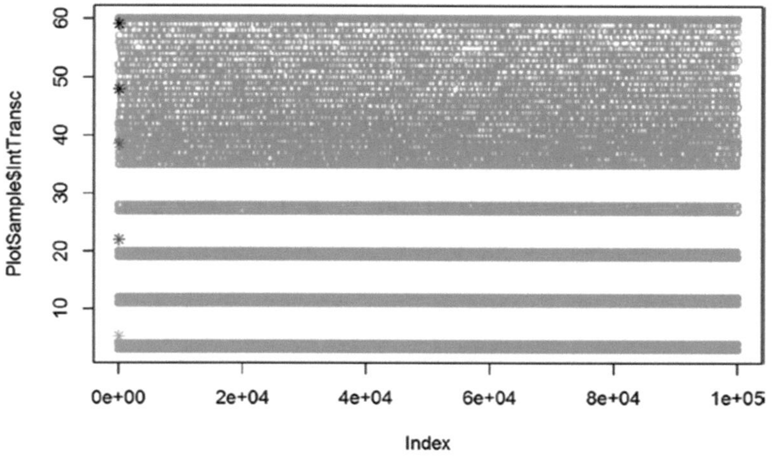

***Figure 3-13.** Input data segmented by the set of five classes by number of international transactions*

```
cluster_sample_combined<-cbind(Data_Subset_Clusters,kmeans_
clusters$cluster)

setnames(cluster_sample_combined,"V2","ClusterIdentifier")
```

Now, we show you the number of records summarized by each cluster. Take note of these numbers, as we will show you the two-stage cluster sampling. The sample will have the same proportion across the clusters.

```
print("Summary of no. of records per clusters")
 [1] "Summary of no. of records per clusters"
table(cluster_sample_combined$ClusterIdentifier)

      1      2      3      4      5
  67871 128219  75877  44771 974893
```

Here, we are assuming the cluster identifier as the stratum variable and using the `stratified()` function to draw a sample having 10% of the stratum population, respectively.

```
set.seed(937)
library(splitstackshape)
cluster_sample_10_percent<-stratified(cluster_sample_combined,group=c("Clust
erIdentifier"),size=0.1,replace=FALSE)
```

This step has created the two-stage cluster sample, i.e., randomly selected 10% of the records from each cluster. Let's plot the clusters with the cluster centers (see Figure 3-14).

```
print("Plotting the clusters for random sample from clusters")
 [1] "Plotting the clusters for random sample from clusters"
plot(cluster_sample_10_percent$IntTransc, col = kmeans_clusters$cluster)
points(kmeans_clusters$centers, col =1:5, pch =8)
```

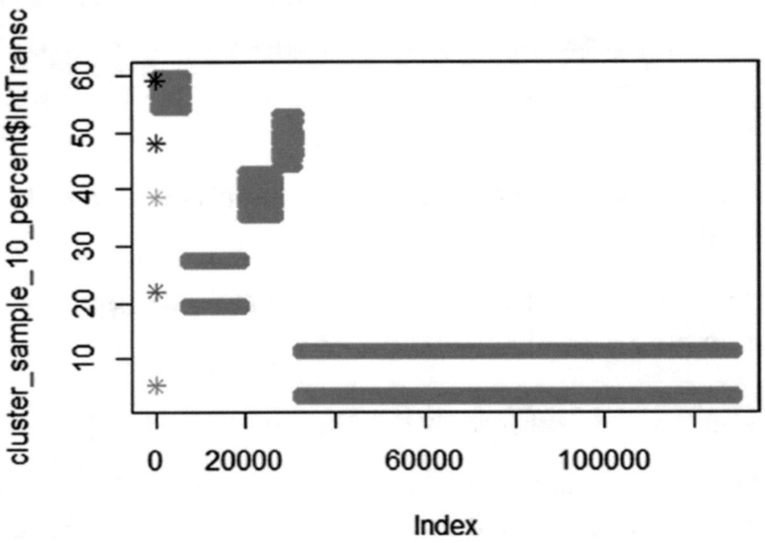

Figure 3-14. *Clusters formed by K-means (star sign represents the centroid of the cluster)*

Next is the frequency distribution of the cluster sample. Go back and see the same proportions as on population used for clustering. The stratified sampling at stage two of clustering sampling has ensured that the proportions of data points remain the same, i.e., 10% of the stratum size.

```
print("Summary of no. of records per clusters")
 [1] "Summary of no. of records per clusters"
table(cluster_sample_10_percent$ClusterIdentifier)

     1     2     3     4     5
  6787 12822  7588  4477 97489
```

Let's now show how cluster sampling has impacted the distribution of outstanding balance compared with the population and cluster samples.

```
population_summary <-summarise(group_by(data,CardType),OutstandingBalan
ce_Population=mean(OutsBal))
 Warning in gmean(OutsBal): Group 1 summed to more than type 'integer'
 can hold so the result has been coerced to 'numeric' automatically, for
 convenience.
cluster_summary<-summarise(group_by(cluster_sample_10_percent,CardType),Outs
tandingBalance_Cluster=mean(OutsBal))

summary_mean_compare<-merge(population_summary,cluster_summary,
by="CardType")

print(summary_mean_compare)
 Source: local data table [4 x 3]

          CardType OutstandingBalance_Population
 1 American Express                      3820.896
 2         Discover                      4962.420
 3       MasterCard                      3818.300
 4             Visa                      4584.042
Variables not shown: OutstandingBalance_Cluster (dbl)
```

This summary shows how the mean of the outstanding balance impacted by cluster sampling based on the international transactions. For visual inspection, we will create histograms in Figure 3-15. You will see that the distribution is impacted marginally. This could be because the clusters we created assume international transactions buckets were homogeneous and hence did not have a great impact on the outstanding balance. To be sure, you are encouraged to do a `t.test()` to see if the means are significantly the same or not.

```
par(mfrow =c(1,2))
hist(data$OutsBal, breaks=50, col="red", xlab="Outstanding Balance",
main="Histogram for Population Data")

hist(cluster_sample_10_percent$OutsBal, breaks=50, col="green",
xlab="Outstanding Balance",
main="Histogram for Cluster Sample Data ")
```

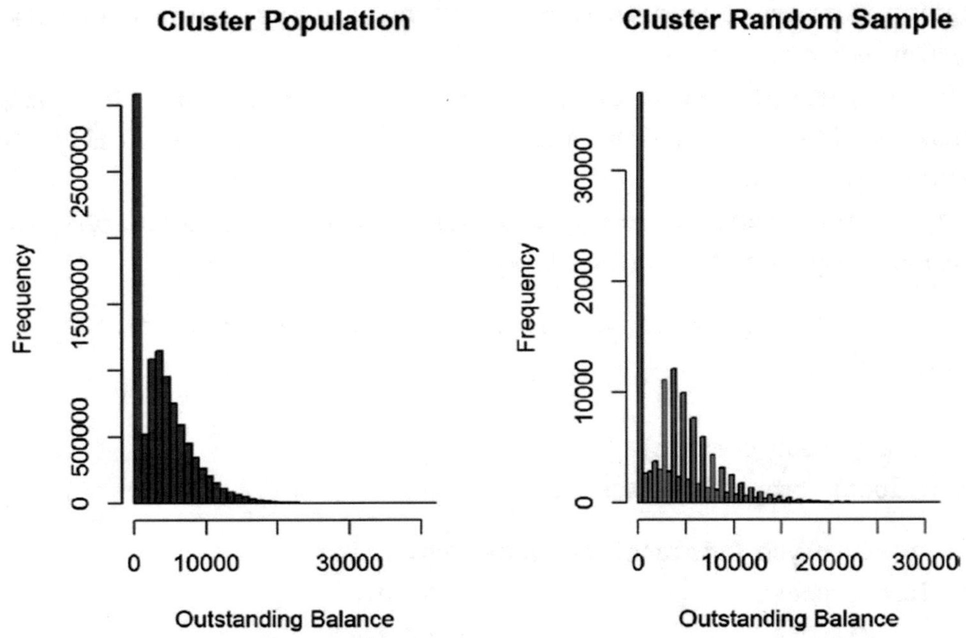

Figure 3-15. *Cluster population and cluster random sample distribution*

In other words, clustering sampling is the same as the stratified sampling; the only difference is that the stratum variable exists in data and is an intrinsic property of data, while in clustering first we identify clusters and then do random sampling from those clusters.

Key points:

- Cluster sampling should be done only when there is strong evidence of clusters in population and you have strong business reason to justify the clusters and their impact on the modeling outcome.
- Cluster sampling should not be confused with stratified sampling. In stratified sampling, the stratum are formed on the attributes in the dataset while clusters are created based on similarity of subject in population by some relation, e.g., distance from centroid, the same multivariate features, etc. Pay close attention while implementing clustering sampling and clusters need to exist and should make a business case of homogeneity.

3.11.6 Bootstrap Sampling

In statistics, bootstrapping is any sampling method, test, or measure that relies on a sampling random sampling with replacement. Theoretically, you can create infinite size population to sample in bootstrapping. It is an advanced topic in statistics and widely used in cases where you have to calculate sampling measure of statistics—e.g., mean, variance, bias, etc.—from a sample estimate of the same.

Bootstrapping allows estimation of the sampling distribution of almost any statistic using random sampling methods. Jackknife predates the modern bootstrapping technique. A Jackknife estimator of a parameter is found by repeatedly leaving out an observation and calculating the estimate. Once all the observation points are exhausted the average of the estimates is taken as the estimator. For a sample size of N, a Jackknife estimate can also be found by aggregating the estimates of each N-1 estimate in the sample. It is important to understand the Jackknife approach, as it provides the basic idea behind the bootstrapping method of a sample metric estimation.

The Jackknife estimate of a parameter can be found by estimating the parameter for each subsample and omitting the ith observation to estimate the previously unknown value of a parameter (say $\overline{x_i}$).

$$\overline{x}_i = \frac{1}{n-1}\sum_{j \neq i}^{n} x_j$$

The Jackknife technique can used to estimate variance of an estimator.

$$\text{Var}_{(\text{jackknife})} = \frac{n-1}{n}\sum_{i=1}^{n}\left(\overline{x}_i - \overline{x}_{(.)}\right)^2$$

where $\overline{x}_i$ is the parameter estimate based on leaving out the ith observation, and $\overline{x}_{(.)}$ is the estimator based on all of the subsamples.

In 1977, B. Efron of Stanford University published his noted paper, "Bootstrap Methods: Another Look at the Jackknife". This paper provides the first detailed account of bootstrapping for a variety of sample metric estimation problems. Statistically, the paper tried to address the following problem: Given a random sample, X= (x_1,x_2,...X_n) from an unknown probability distribution F, estimate the sampling distribution of some prespecified random variable R(X,F) on the basis of the observed data x. We leave it to you to explore the statistical detail of the method.

When you don't know the distribution of the population (or you don't even have a population), bootstrapping comes in handy to create hypothesis testing for the sampling estimates. The bootstrapping technique will sample data from the empirical distribution obtained from the sample. In the case where a set of observations can be assumed to be from an independent and identically distributed population, this can be implemented by constructing a number of resamples with replacement of the observed dataset (and of equal size to the observed dataset). This comes in very handy when we have a small dataset and we are unsure about the distribution of the estimator to perform hypothesis testing.

Advantages:

- Simple to implement; it provides an easy way to calculate standard errors and confidence intervals for complex unknown sampling distributions.
- With increasing computing power, the bootstrap results get better.
- One popular application of bootstrapping is to check for stability of estimates.

Disadvantages:

- Bootstrapping is asymptotically consistent, but does not provide finite sample consistency.
- This is an advanced technique, so you need to be fully aware of the assumptions and properties of estimates derived from the bootstrap methods.

In our R example, we will show how bootstrapping can be used to estimate a population parameter to create a confidence interval around that estimate. This helps in checking the stability of the parameter estimate and perform a hypothesis test. We will be creating the example on a business relevant linear regression methodology.

Note Bootstrapping techniques are more relevant to estimation problems when you have a very small sample size and it is difficult to find the distribution of the actual population.

First, we fit a linear regression model on population data (without intercept). The model will be fit with response variable as an outstanding variable and predictor being number of domestic transactions. Business intuition says that the outstanding balance should be positively correlated with the number of domestic transactions. A positive correlation between dependent and independent variables implies the sign of the linear regression coefficient should be positive.

The coefficient that we get is the true value of the estimate coming from the population. This is the population parameter estimate, as it is calculating the full population.

```
set.seed(937)
library(boot)
# Now we need the function we would like to estimate

#First fit a linear model and know the true estimates, from population data
summary(lm(OutsBal ~0 +DomesTransc, data = data))

Call:
lm(formula = OutsBal ~ 0 + DomesTransc, data = data)

Residuals:
   Min     1Q Median     3Q    Max
 -7713  -1080   1449   4430  39091

Coefficients:
            Estimate Std. Error t value Pr(>|t|)
DomesTransc 77.13469    0.03919    1968   <2e-16 ***
---
Signif. codes:  0 '***' 0.001 '**' 0.01 '*' 0.05 '.' 0.1 ' ' 1

Residual standard error: 4867 on 9999999 degrees of freedom
Multiple R-squared: 0.2792, Adjusted R-squared: 0.2792
F-statistic: 3.874e+06 on 1 and 9999999 DF, p-value: < 2.2e-16
```

You can see the summary of the linear regression model fit on the population data. Now we will take a small sample of population (sampling fraction =10000/10,000,000=1/1000). Hence, our challenge is to estimate the coefficient of domestic transactions from a very small dataset.

In this context, sampling can be seen as a process to create a larger set of samples from a small set of values to get an estimate of the true distribution of the estimate.

```
set.seed(937)
#Assume that we are only having 10000 data points and have to do the
hypothesis test around significance of coefficient domestic transactions. As
the dataset is small we will use the bootstarting to create the distribution
of coefficient and then create a confidence interval to test the
hypothesis.

sample_10000 <-data[sample(nrow(data),size=10000, replace =FALSE, prob
=NULL),]
```

Now we have a small sample to work with. Let's define a function named `Coeff`, which will return the coefficient of the domestic transaction variable.

It has a three arguments:

- `data`: This will be the small dataset that you want to bootstrap. In our case, this is the sample dataset of 10,000 records.
- `b`: A random frame of indexes to choose each time the function is called. This will make sure each time a dataset is selected from a model that it's randomly chosen from the input data.
- `formula`: This is an optional field. But this will be the functional form of the model which will be estimated by the linear regression.

Here we have just incorporated the formula in the `return` statement.

```
# Function to return Coefficient of DomesTransc
Coeff =function(data,b,formula){
# b is the random indexes for the bootstrap sample
    d =data[b,]
return(lm(OutsBal ~0 +DomesTransc, data = d)$coefficients[1])
# that's for the beta coefficient
}
```

Now we can start bootstrap, so we will be using the `boot()` function from the boot library. It is very powerful function for both parametric and non-parametric boot strapping. We consider this an advanced topic and will not be covering details of this function. Interested readers are advised to read the function documents from CRAN.

The inputs we are using for our example are:

- `data`: This is the small sample data we created in the previous step.
- `statistics`: This is a function that will return the estimated value of the interested parameter. Here, our function `Coeff` will return the value of coefficient of the domestic transactions.
- `R`: This the number of bootstrap samples you want to create. A general rule of thumb is the more bootstrap samples you have, the narrower the confidence band.

Note For this example, we are considering a smaller number of samples to be sure the confidence band is broad and with what confidence we can see the original estimate from the population.

Here we call the function with `R=50`.

```
set.seed(937)
# R is how many bootstrap samples
bootbet =boot(data=sample_10000, statistic=Coeff, R=50)
```

```
names(bootbet)
  [1] "t0"        "t"         "R"         "data"      "seed"
  [6] "statistic" "sim"       "call"      "stype"     "strata"
 [11] "weights"
```

Now plot the histograms and qq plots for the estimated values of the coefficient (see Figure 3-16).

```
plot(bootbet)
```

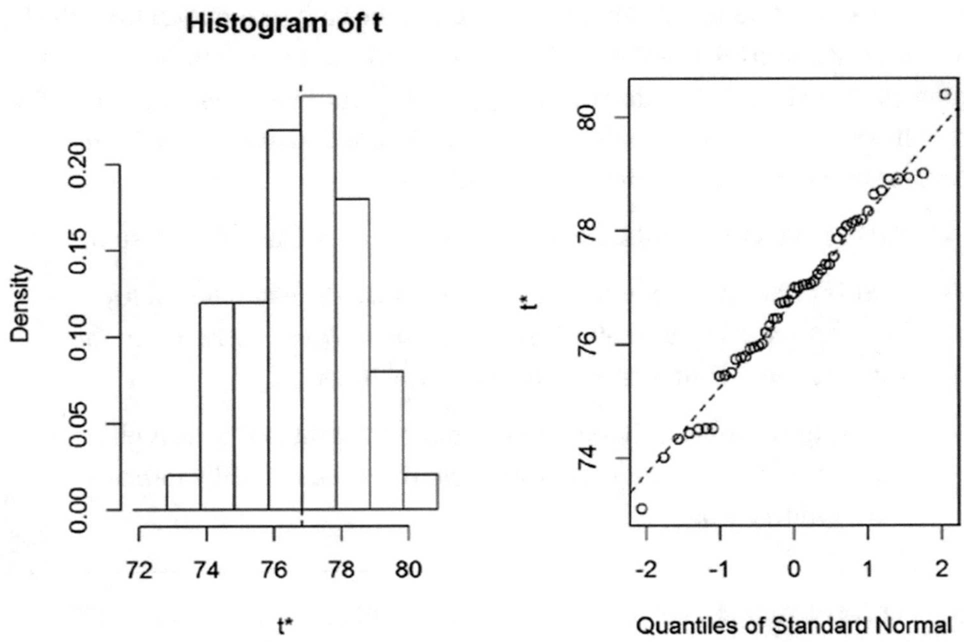

***Figure 3-16.** Histogram and QQ plot of estimated coefficient*

Now, we plot the histogram of parameter estimates. We can see in Figure 3-17 that the bootstrap sample uncovered the distribution of the parameter. We can form a confidence interval around this and do hypothesis testing.

```
hist(bootbet$t, breaks =5)
```

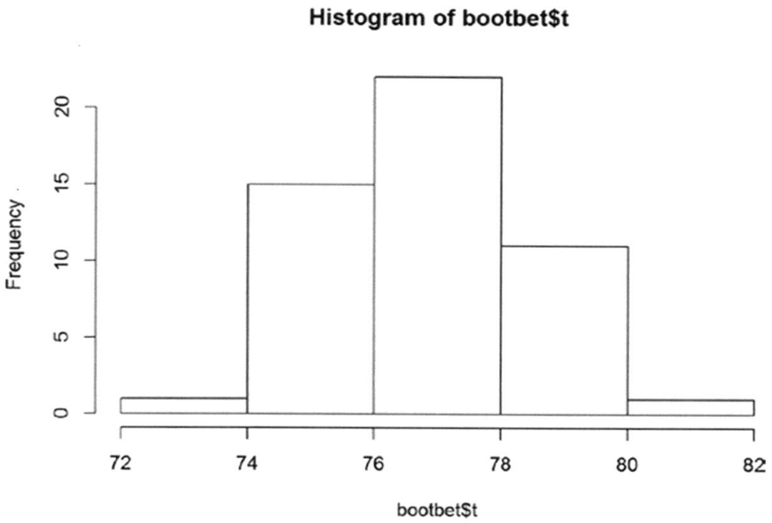

***Figure 3-17.** Histogram of parameter estimate from bootstrap*

Here we calculate the mean and variance of the estimated values from bootstrapping. Considering the distribution of coefficient is normally distributed, you can create a confidence band around the mean for the true value.

```
mean(bootbet$t)
 [1] 76.77636
var(bootbet$t)
          [,1]
 [1,] 2.308969
```

Additionally, to show how the distribution looks superimposed on a normal distribution from the previous parameters, do this:

```
x <-bootbet$t
h<-hist(x, breaks=5, col="red", xlab="Boot Strap Estimates",
main="Histogram with Normal Curve")
xfit<-seq(min(x),max(x),length=40)
yfit<-dnorm(xfit,mean=mean(bootbet$t),sd=sqrt(var(bootbet$t)))
yfit <-yfit*diff(h$mids[1:2])*length(x)
lines(xfit, yfit, col="blue", lwd=2)
```

In Figure 3-18, you can see that we have been able to find the distribution of the coefficient and hence can do hypothesis testing on it. This also provided us with a close estimate of the true coefficient. If you look closely, this idea is very close to what Jackknife originally proposed. With more computing power, we have just expanded the scope of that method from the mean and standard deviation to any parameter estimation.

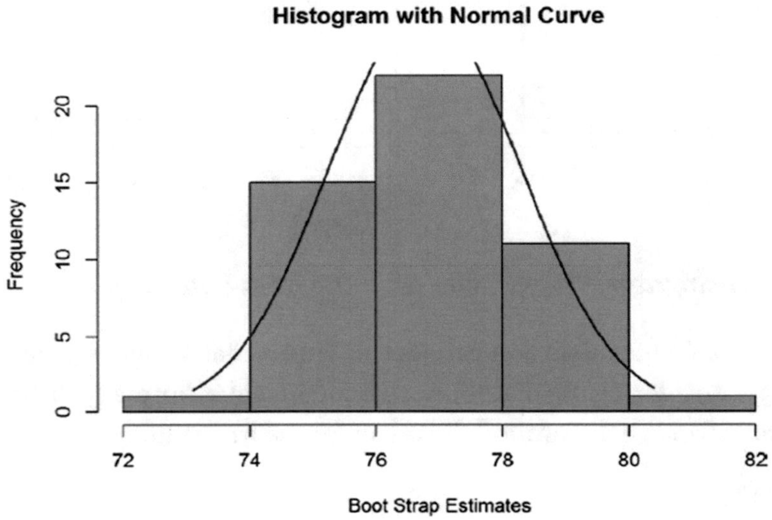

Figure 3-18. *Histogram with normal density function*

The following code does a `t.test()` on the bootstrap values on coefficients with the true estimate of the coefficient from the population data. This will tell us how close we got to the estimate from a smaller sample and with what confidence we would be able to accept or reject the bootstrapped coefficient.

```
t.test(bootbet$t, mu=77.13)

  One Sample t-test

 data: bootbet$t
 t = -1.6456, df = 49, p-value = 0.1062
 alternative hypothesis: true mean is not equal to 77.13
 95 percent confidence interval:
```

```
 76.34452 77.20821
sample estimates:
mean of x
 76.77636
```

Key points:

- Bootstrapping is a powerful technique that comes in handy when we have little knowledge of the distribution of parameter and only a small dataset is available.
- This technique is advanced in nature and involves a lot of assumptions, so proper statistical knowledge is required to use bootstrapping techniques.

3.12 Monte Carlo Method: Acceptance-Rejection Method

In modern times, Monte Carlo methods have become a separate field of study in statistics. Monte Carlo methods leverage the computationally heavy random sampling techniques to estimate the underlying parameters. This technique is important in stochastic equations where an exact solution is not possible. The Monte Carlo techniques are very popular in the financial world, specifically in financial instrument valuation and forecasting.

In statistics, acceptance-rejection methods are very basic techniques to sample observations from a distribution. In this method, random sampling is done from a distribution and, based on preset conditions, the observation is accepted or rejected. Hence, it lies in the broad bucket of a Monte Carlo method.

In this method, we first estimate the empirical distribution of the dataset (r empirical density function: EDF) by looking at cumulative probability distribution. After we get the EDF, we set the parameters for another known distribution. The known distribution will be covering the EDF.

Now we start sampling from the known distribution and accept the observations if it lies within the EDF; otherwise, we reject it. In other words, rejection sampling can be performed by following these steps:

1. Sample a point from the proposed distribution (say x).
2. Draw a vertical line at this sample point x up to the curve of proposed distribution (see Figure 3-19).
3. Sample uniformly along this line from 0 to max (PDF), where PDF stands for probability density function. If a sample's value is greater than the maximum value, reject it; otherwise accept it.

This method helps us draw a sample of any distribution from the known distribution. These methods are very popular in stochastic calculus for financial product valuation and other stochastic processes.

To illustrate this method, we will draw a sample from a beta distribution with parameters of (3,10). The beta distribution looks like Figure 3-19.

```
curve(dbeta(x, 3,10),0,1)
```

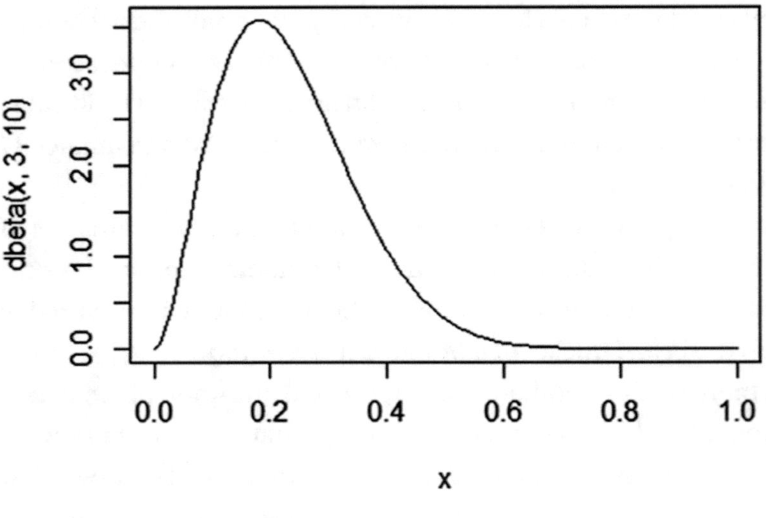

Figure 3-19. *Beta distribution plot*

We first create a sample of 5000 with random values between 0 and 1. Now we calculate the beta density corresponding to the 5000 random values sample.

```
set.seed(937)
sampled <-data.frame(proposal =runif(5000,0,1))

sampled$targetDensity <-dbeta(sampled$proposal, 3,10)
```

Now, we calculate the maximum probability density for our proposed distribution (beta PDF). Once we have maximum density and sample density for 5000 cases, we start our sampling by rejection as follows. Create a random number between 0 and 1:

```
Reject the value as coming from beta distribution if the value is more than
the sample density we calculated for pre-known beta distribution maxDens
=max(sampled$targetDensity, na.rm = T)
sampled$accepted =ifelse(runif(5000,0,1) <sampled$targetDensity /maxDens,
TRUE, FALSE)
```

Figure 3-20 shows plot of EDF of beta (3,10) and the histogram of the sample dataset. We can see we have been able to create the desired sample by accepting values from a random numbers that lie below the red line, i.e., PDF of beta distribution.

```
hist(sampled$proposal[sampled$accepted], freq = F, col ="grey", breaks
=100)
curve(dbeta(x, 3,10),0,1, add =T, col ="red")
```

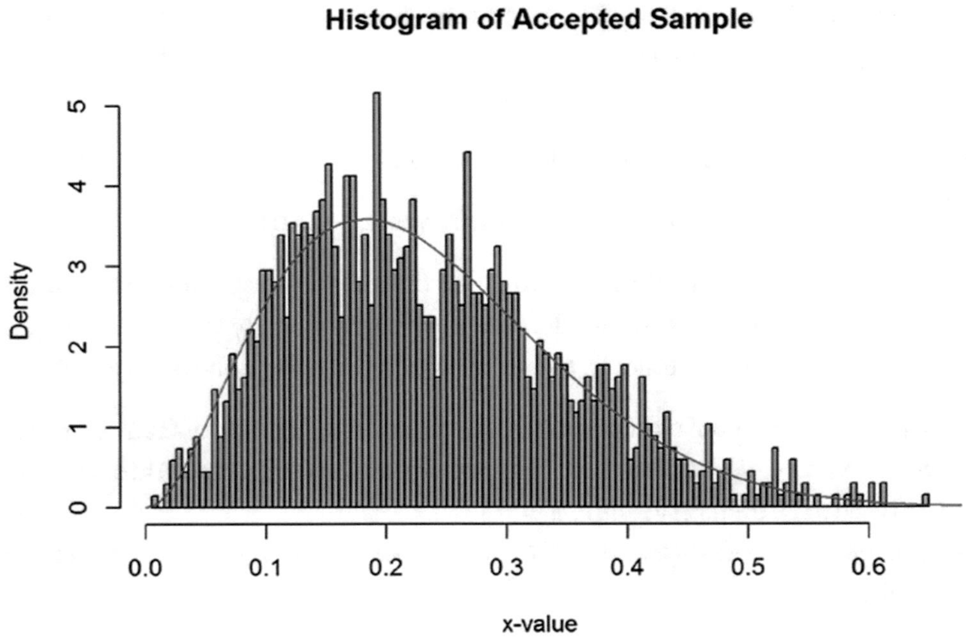

Figure 3-20. *Sampling by rejection*

3.13 Summary

In this chapter we covered different sampling techniques and showed how these sampling techniques reduce the volume of data to process and the same time retain properties of the data. The best sampling method to apply to any population is simple random sampling without replacement.

We also discussed bootstrap sampling, which is an important concept as you can estimate distribution of any parameter using this method. At the end, we showed an illustration of sampling by rejection, which allows us to create any distribution from known distributions. This technique is based on the Monte Carlo simulation and is very popular in financial services.

This chapter plays an important role in reducing the volume of data to apply in our machine learning algorithms, thereby keeping the population variance intact.

In the next chapter, we look at the properties of data with visualization. If we use the appropriate sampling, the same visualization and trends will appear from populations as they do from the sample.

CHAPTER 4

Data Visualization in R

Data visualization is the process of creating and studying the visual representation of data to bring some meaningful insights.

Data visualization specifically deals with visualizing the information in a given data. This can include multiple types of charts, graphs, colors, and line plots. Data visualization is an effective way to present data because it shifts the balance between perception and cognition to take fuller advantage of the brain's abilities. The ways we encode the information is very important to make direct pathways into the brain cognition. The core tools used to encode information in a visualization are color, size, shape, numbers.

The first step for data science is to understand the data; only then do we start thinking about model and algorithm. There are many benefits to embrace data visualization as an integral part of data science process. Some of the direct benefits of the data visualization are:

- Identifying red spots in data, starting diagnostics
- Tracking and identifying relations among different attributes
- Seeing the trends and fallouts to understand the reasons
- Summarizing complicated long spreadsheets and databases into visual art
- Having an easy-to-use and very impactful way to store and present information and others

The market has many paid visualization software suites and on-demand cloud applications that can create meaningful visuals by the click of a button. However, we will explore the power of open source packages and tools for creating visualization in R.

Any kind of data visualization fundamentally depends on four key elements of data presentation, namely *Comparison, Relationship, Distribution,* and *Composition.*

K. Ramasubramanian and A. Singh, *Machine Learning Using R*, https://doi.org/10.1007/978-1-4842-4215-5_4

Comparison is used to see the differences between multiple items at a given point in time or to see the relative change in a variable over a time period. A *relationship* element helps in finding correlations between two or more variables with an increase or decrease in values. Scatter and bubble chart are some examples in this category. *Distribution* charts like column and line histograms show the spread of data. For instance, data with skewness toward left or right could be easily spotted. *Composition* refers to a stacked chart with multiple components like a pie chart or stacked column/area chart. In our PEBE ML process flow, visualization plays a key role in the exploration phase.

Visualization serves as an aid in story telling by harnessing the power of data. There are plenty of examples to show patterns emerging from simple plots, which otherwise is difficult to find even after using sophisticated statistics. Throughout this chapter, we will explore the four elements of data presentation with suitable examples and highlight the importance of the role that visualization plays in better understanding the data to its finest of detail.

4.1 Introduction to the ggplot2 Package

R developers have created a good collection in the visualization tool library. Being open source, these packages get updated very rapidly with new features. Another remarkable development in R tools for visualization is that the developers have been able to create functions that can replicate some of the high computational 3D plots and model outputs.

`ggplot2` is a data visualization package created by Hadley Wickham in 2005. It's an implementation of Leland Wilkinson's Grammar of Graphics—a general scheme for data visualization that breaks up graphs into semantic components such as scales and layers. It is also important to state here that the other powerful plotting function that we have used multiple time is `plot()`.

There are some other packages that we use in this chapter and you can explore more of them. Some of them are `googleVis()`, `ggmap()`, `ggrepel()`, `waterfall()`, and `rCharts()`. These are all highly recommended.

4.2 World Development Indicators

Good data visualization tells a story with numbers.

In this chapter we will be discussing chart types with some examples. Half of the chapter discusses economic indicators to build visualizations. The specific plots and graphs will be discussed with World Bank's development indicator data. The World Bank collects data to monitor economic indicators across the world. For details of the data and economic principles, visit `http://www.worldbank.org/`.

The following section is a quick introduction of core indicators. A suitable visualization used for understanding its meaning and impact will be presented in the following sections. There has been lot of good research using many of the World Bank's data by social scientists in various sectors. We have cherry picked a few really impactful parts of that research and brought the real essence of the data into view. As we move from one example to the other, there will be emphasis given to the right type of visualization and extracting meaning out of the data without looking at the hundreds of rows and columns of a CSV or Excel file. Many of these visualizations are also provided on the World Bank website; however, here in this book, you will learn how to use the `ggplot` package available in R to produce different graphs, charts, and plots. Instead of following a traditional approach of learning the grammar of graphics and then discussing a lot of theory on visualization, in this book, we have chosen a theme (World Bank's development indicators) and will take you through a journey by means of storytelling.

4.3 Line Chart

A *line chart* is a basic visualization chart type in which information is displayed in a series of data points called *markers* connected by line segments. Line charts are used for showing trends in multiple categories of a variable. For instance, Figure 4-1 shows the growth of the Gross Domestic Product (GDP) over the years for the top 10 countries based on their most recent reported GDP figures. It helps in visualizing the trend in GDP growth for all these countries in a single plot.

```
library(reshape)
library(ggplot2)

GDP <-read.csv("Dataset/Total GDP 2015 Top 10.csv")
names(GDP) <-c("Country", "2010","2011","2012","2013","2014","2015")
```

The following code uses a very important function that will be repeated in later sections as well, called melt().

The melt function takes data in wide formats and stacks a set of columns into a single column of data. You can think of it as melting the current dimensions and getting simpler dimensions. Melt() is available in the reshape2() package. In the following code, you will, after reshaping the dataset, reduce it to three columns. The columns are stacked versions of the same information along multiple columns. The melt() function can only melt the categorical attributes; the numeric ones are aggregated.

```
GDP_Long_Format <-melt(GDP, id="Country")
names(GDP_Long_Format) <-c("Country", "Year","GDP_USD_Trillion")
```

The following code stacks various layers of the visualization on ggplot() function's output (see Figure 4-1). You are encouraged to refer to the ggplot documentation for more options.

```
ggplot(GDP_Long_Format, aes(x=Year, y=GDP_USD_Trillion, group=Country)) +
geom_line(aes(colour=Country)) +
geom_point(aes(colour=Country),size =5) +
theme(legend.title=element_text(family="Times",size=20),
legend.text=element_text(family="Times",face ="italic",size=15),
plot.title=element_text(family="Times", face="bold", size=20),
axis.title.x=element_text(family="Times", face="bold", size=12),
axis.title.y=element_text(family="Times", face="bold", size=12)) +
xlab("Year") +
ylab("GDP (in trillion USD)") +
ggtitle("Gross Domestic Product - Top 10 Countries")
```

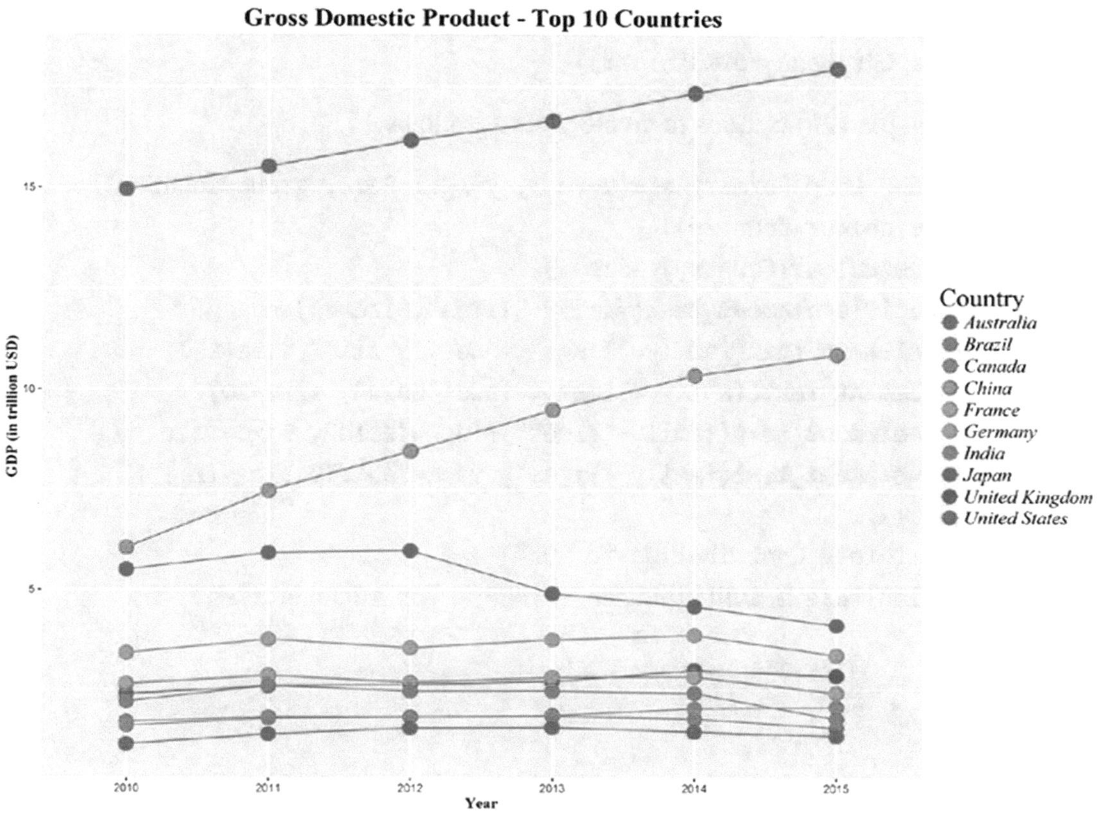

***Figure 4-1.** A line chart showing the top 10 countries based on their GDP*

Clearly, among the top 10, the United States is leading the race, followed by China and Japan. So, without looking at the data, we are seeing rich information being shown in this visualization. Now, the obvious next question that comes to your mind is, what makes any country's GDP go up or down? Let's try to understand for these countries, how much percentage of their GDP is contributed by agriculture (see Figure 4-2), the service sector (see Figure 4-3), and industry (see Figure 4-4).

```
# Agriculture

Agri_GDP <-read.csv("Dataset/Agriculture - Top 10 Country.csv")
```

Again, we melt the data into smaller numbers of columns to allow plotting.

```
Agri_GDP_Long_Format <-melt(Agri_GDP, id ="Country")
names(Agri_GDP_Long_Format) <-c("Country", "Year", "Agri_Perc")
```

```
Agri_GDP_Long_Format$Year <-substr(Agri_GDP_Long_Format$Year,
2,length(Agri_GDP_Long_Format$Year))
```

Apply the ggplot2() options to create plots as follows:

```
ggplot(Agri_GDP_Long_Format, aes(x=Year, y=Agri_Perc, group=Country)) +
geom_line(aes(colour=Country)) +
geom_point(aes(colour=Country),size =5) +
theme(legend.title=element_text(family="Times",size=20),
legend.text=element_text(family="Times",face ="italic",size=15),
plot.title=element_text(family="Times", face="bold", size=20),
axis.title.x=element_text(family="Times", face="bold", size=12),
axis.title.y=element_text(family="Times", face="bold", size=12)) +
xlab("Year") +
ylab("Agriculture % Contribution to GDP") +
ggtitle("Agriculture % Contribution to GDP - Top 10 Countries")
```

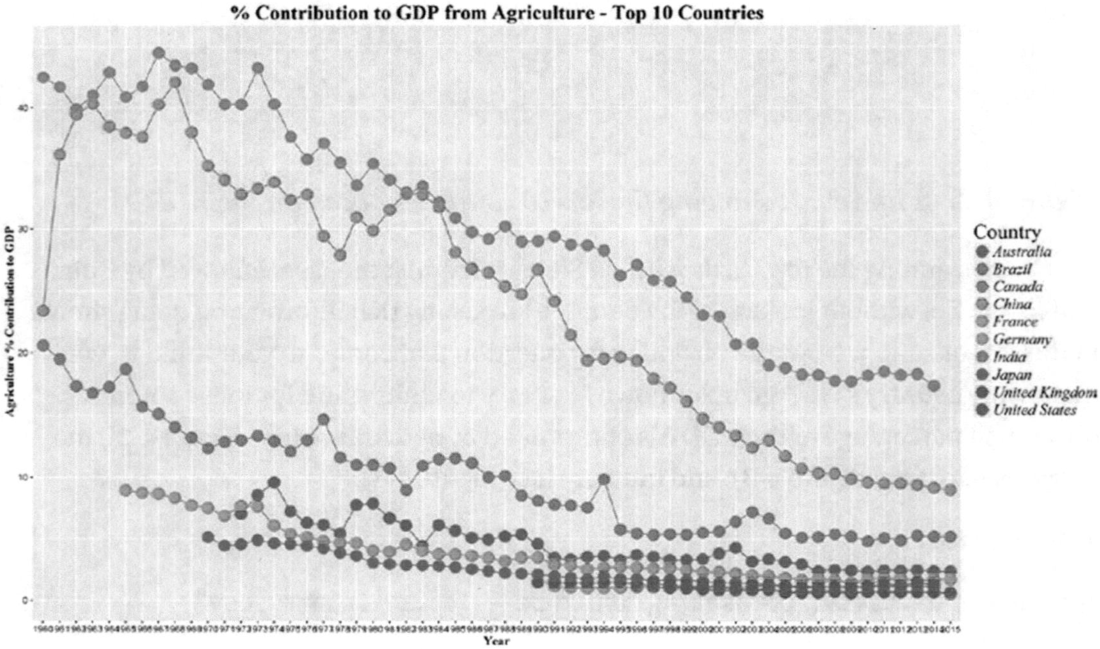

Figure 4-2. *A line chart showing the top 10 countries based on percent contribution to GDP from agriculture*

While countries like India and Brazil, which didn't get the top three spots when we looked at the GDP, tops the list in agriculture (along with China, which comes in the top three here as well). This shows the dependence on agriculture in these countries economies.

```
# Service

Service_GDP <-read.csv("Services - Top 10 Country.csv")

Service_GDP_Long_Format <-melt(Service_GDP, id ="Country")
names(Service_GDP_Long_Format) <-c("Country", "Year", "Service_Perc")

Service_GDP_Long_Format$Year <-substr(Service_GDP_Long_Format$Year,
2,length(Service_GDP_Long_Format$Year))

ggplot(Service_GDP_Long_Format, aes(x=Year, y=Service_Perc, group=Country)) +
geom_line(aes(colour=Country)) +
geom_point(aes(colour=Country),size =5) +
theme(legend.title=element_text(family="Times",size=20),
legend.text=element_text(family="Times",face ="italic",size=15),
plot.title=element_text(family="Times", face="bold", size=20),
axis.title.x=element_text(family="Times", face="bold", size=12),
axis.title.y=element_text(family="Times", face="bold", size=12)) +
xlab("Year") +
ylab("Service sector % Contribution to GDP") +
ggtitle("Service sector % Contribution to GDP - Top 10 Countries")
```

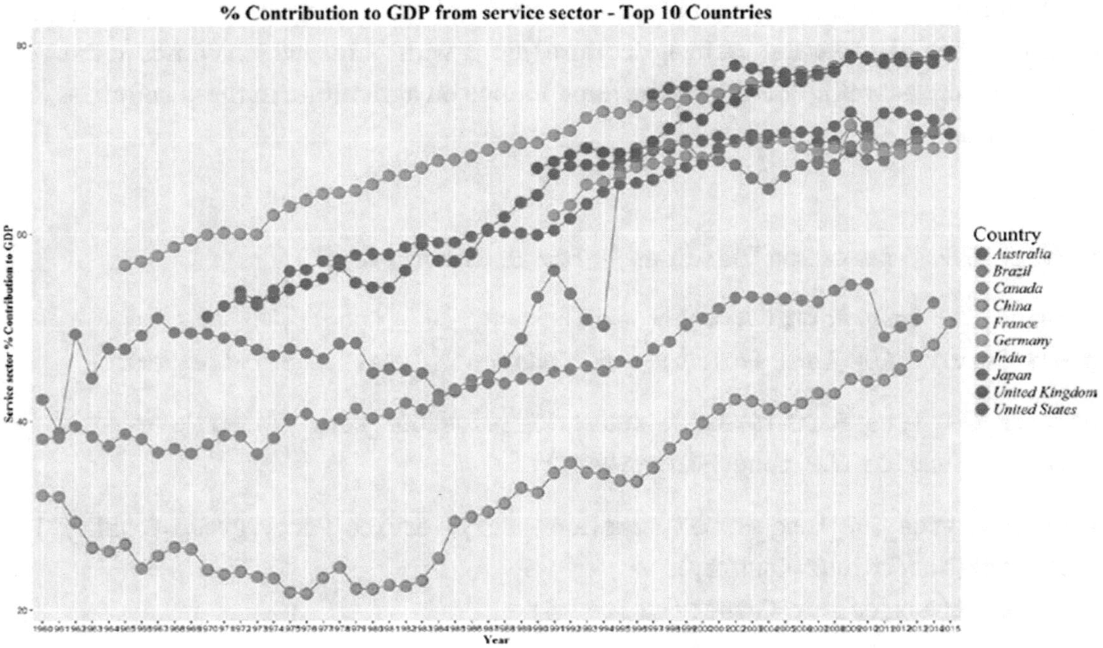

Figure 4-3. *A line chart showing the top 10 countries based on percent contribution to GDP from the service sector*

Now, contrary to agriculture, looking at the service sector, you will understand the reason behind the large GDP of the United States, China, and the United Kingdom. These countries have typically built their strong economies with service sectors. So, when you hear about Silicon Valley in the United States and London being the world's largest financial center, it's actually their economies' biggest growth drivers.

```
# Industry

Industry_GDP <-read.csv("Industry - Top 10 Country.csv")

Industry_GDP_Long_Format <-melt(Industry_GDP, id ="Country")
names(Industry_GDP_Long_Format) <-c("Country", "Year", "Industry_Perc")
Industry_GDP_Long_Format$Year <-substr(Industry_GDP_Long_Format$Year,
2,length(Industry_GDP_Long_Format$Year))

ggplot(Industry_GDP_Long_Format, aes(x=Year, y=Industry_Perc,
group=Country)) +
geom_line(aes(colour=Country)) +
```

```
geom_point(aes(colour=Country),size =5) +
theme(legend.title=element_text(family="Times",size=20),
legend.text=element_text(family="Times",face ="italic",size=15),
plot.title=element_text(family="Times", face="bold", size=20),
axis.title.x=element_text(family="Times", face="bold", size=12),
axis.title.y=element_text(family="Times", face="bold", size=12)) +
xlab("Year") +
ylab("Industry % Contribution to GDP") +
ggtitle("Industry % Contribution to GDP - Top 10 Countries")
```

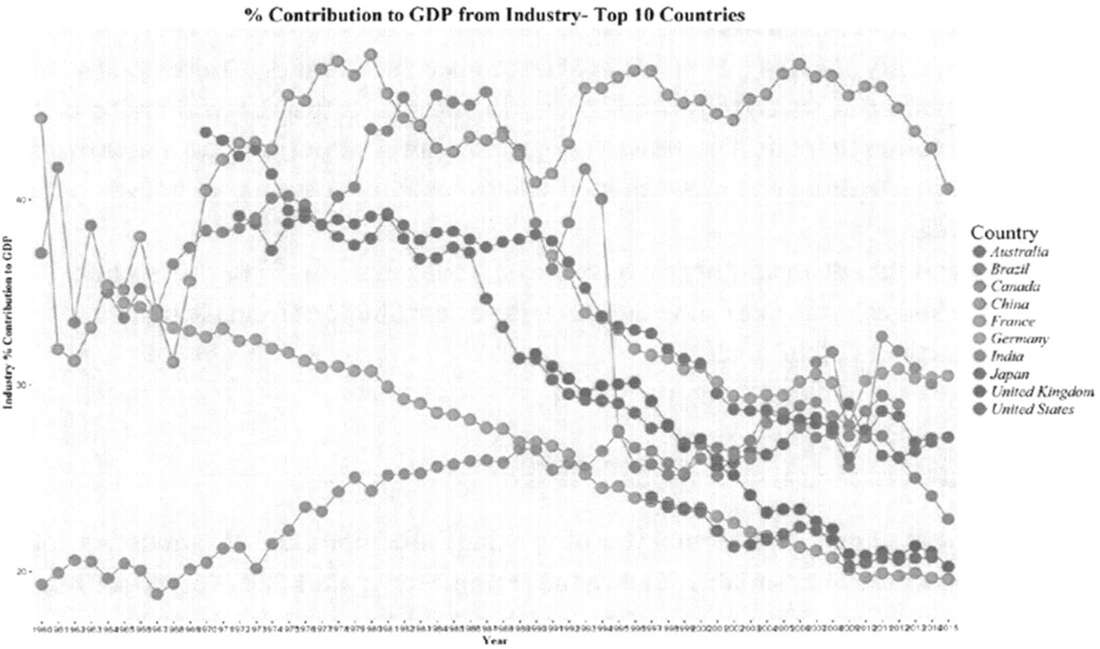

Figure 4-4. *A line chart showing the top 10 countries based on percent contribution to GDP from industry*

After looking at agriculture and service sector, industry is the third biggest component in the GDP pie. And this particular component is by far led by China and their manufacturing industry. This is why you see many big brands like Apple embedding a label in their products that says, "Designed by Apple in California. Assembled in China". It's not just mobile phones or companies like Apple, China is a manufacturing hub for many product segments like apparel and accessories, automobile parts, motorcycle parts, furniture, and the list goes on.

So, the overall trend shows while the industry and the service sector keep increasing in their contributions to GDP, agriculture has seen a steady decrease over the years. Is this a signal of growth or a compromise of our food sources in the name of more lucrative sectors? Perhaps we will leave that question for the economic experts to answer. However, we definitely see how this visualization can show us insights that would have been difficult otherwise to interpret from the raw data.

In concluding remarks, among these big economies, many countries are witnessing a drastic drop in their industry output, like China, France, Australia, and Japan. India is the only country among these 10, where there has been a steady increase of industrial output over the years, which is a sign of development. Having said that, it still remains to see how agriculture and the service sector are balanced for the unprecedented growth in Industry. Even in this situation of unbalanced economies of developed and developing countries, what really helps to keep the balance is that the world is lot more free when it comes to trade. If you have strong agricultural output, you are free to export your production to other countries where it's deficient and the same goes with the other sectors as well.

Before we embark on another story through visualization, the following section shows a stacked column chart showing percentage contributions from each of the sectors to the world's total GDP.

4.4 Stacked Column Charts

Stacked column charts are an elegant way of showing the composition of various categories that make up a particular variable. Here in the example in Figure 4-5, it's easy to see how much percentage contribution each of these sectors has in the world's total GDP.

```
library(plyr)

World_Comp_GDP <-read.csv("World GDP and Sector.csv")

World_Comp_GDP_Long_Format <-melt(World_Comp_GDP, id ="Sector")
names(World_Comp_GDP_Long_Format) <-c("Sector", "Year", "USD")

World_Comp_GDP_Long_Format$Year <-substr(World_Comp_GDP_Long_Format$Year,
2,length(World_Comp_GDP_Long_Format$Year))
```

```
# calculate midpoints of bars

World_Comp_GDP_Long_Format_Label <-ddply(World_Comp_GDP_Long_Format, .(Year),
   transform, pos =cumsum(USD) -(0.5 *USD))

ggplot(World_Comp_GDP_Long_Format_Label, aes(x = Year, y = USD, fill =
Sector)) +
geom_bar(stat ="identity") +
geom_text(aes(label = USD, y = pos), size =3) +
theme(legend.title=element_text(family="Times",size=20),
legend.text=element_text(family="Times",face ="italic",size=15),
plot.title=element_text(family="Times", face="bold", size=20),
axis.title.x=element_text(family="Times", face="bold", size=12),
axis.title.y=element_text(family="Times", face="bold", size=12)) +
xlab("Year") +
ylab("% of GDP") +
ggtitle("Contribution of various sector in the World GDP")
```

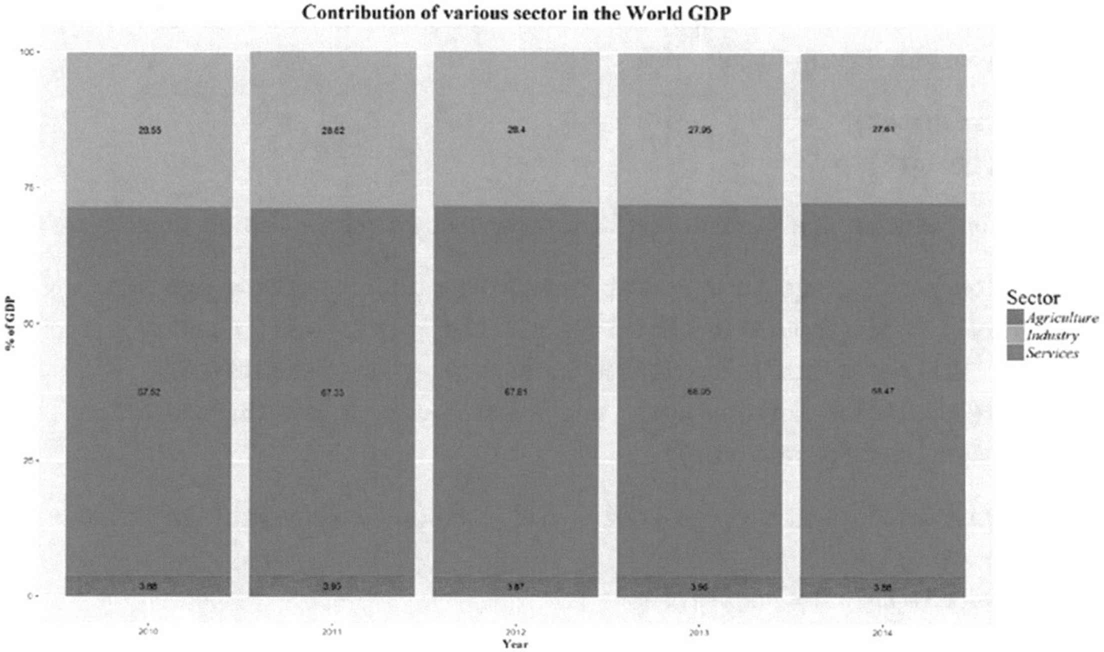

***Figure 4-5.** A stacked column chart showing the contribution of various sectors to the world's GDP*

It's clear from the stacked column chart in Figure 4-5 that the service sector has a major contribution all the years, followed by industry, and then agriculture. As the size of each block does not change meaning, the GDP has grown with similar ratios among these sectors.

Next, let's see the age dependency ratio measure in the stacked chart.

The age dependency ratio is a good measure to show how this line plots and the stacked column chart can help investigate the measure. As defined by the World Bank, the *age dependency ratio* is the ratio of dependents—people younger than 15 or older than 64—to the working-age population—those aged between 15-64.

If the age dependency ratio is very high for a country, the government's expenditure goes up on health, social security, and education, which are mostly spent on people younger than 14 or older than 64 (the numerator) because the number of people supporting these expenditures (people aged between 15-64) is less (the denominator). This also means individuals in the workforce have to take more of the burden to support their dependents than what is recommended. And at times, this leads to social issues like child labor (people aged less than 14 years ending up in the adult workforce). So, many developing economies where age dependency is high have to deal with these issues. The stacked line chart in Figure 4-6 shows how the working age ratio has been decreasing over the years for the top 10 countries.

```
library(reshape2)
library(ggplot2)

Population_Working_Age <-read.csv("Age dependency ratio - Top 10 Country.csv")

Population_Working_Age_Long_Format <-melt(Population_Working_Age, id
="Country") names(Population_Working_Age_Long_Format) <-c("Country",
"Year", "Wrk_Age_Ratio") Population_Working_Age_Long_Format$Year
<-substr(Population_Working_Age_ Long_Format$Year, 2,length(Population_
Working_Age_Long_Format$Year))

ggplot(Population_Working_Age_Long_Format, aes(x=Year, y=Wrk_Age_Ratio,
group=Country)) +
geom_line(aes(colour=Country)) +
geom_point(aes(colour=Country),size =5) +
theme(legend.title=element_text(family="Times",size=20),
```

```
legend.text=element_text(family="Times",face ="italic",size=15),
plot.title=element_text(family="Times", face="bold", size=20),
axis.title.x=element_text(family="Times", face="bold", size=12),
axis.title.y=element_text(family="Times", face="bold", size=12)) +
xlab("Year") +
ylab("Working age Ratio") +
ggtitle("Working age Ratio - Top 10 Countries")
```

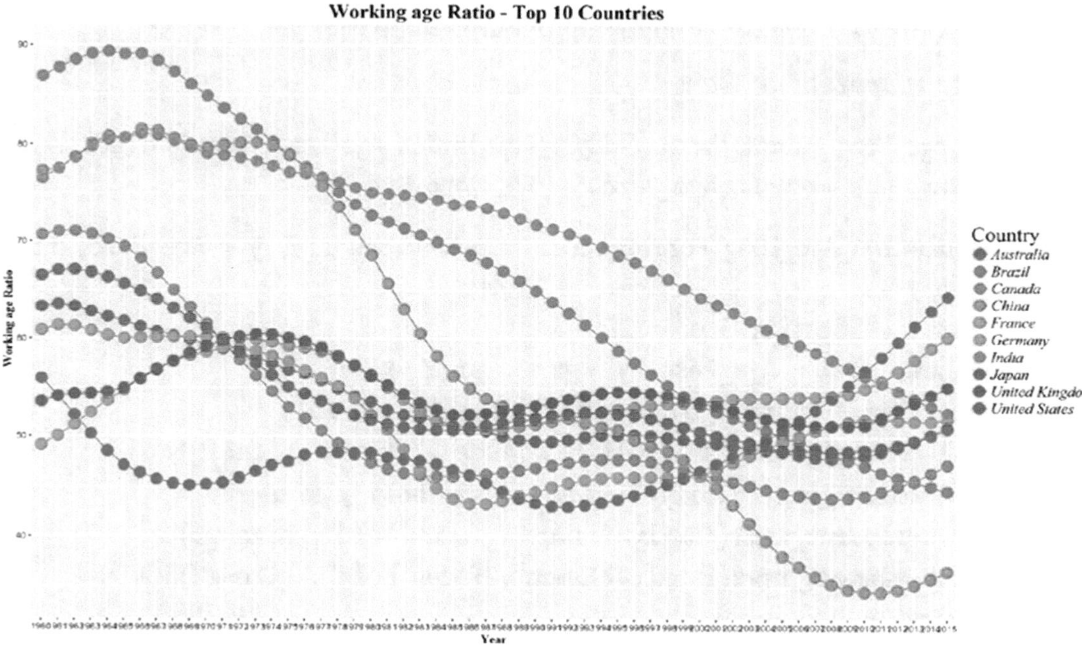

***Figure 4-6.** A stacked line chart showing the top 10 countries based on their working age ratio*

If you look at the line charts in Figures 4-6 and 4-7, you will notice, in recent years, countries like Japan and France have the largest ageing population, hence a higher age dependency ratio, whereas, countries like India and China have a strong and large population of young people and thus show a steady decrease in this ratio over the years. For instance, in the year 2015, India and China reported 65.6% and 73.22% of their population aged between 15 and 64, respectively (34.41% and 26.78% with people aged below 14 and above 65, respectively). The same percentage for Japan and France is 60.8 and 62.4, respectively (33.19% and 37.57%, with people aged below 14 and above 65, respectively).

```
library(reshape2)
library(ggplot2)
library(plyr)

Population_Age <-read.csv("Population Ages - All Age - Top 10 Country.csv")

Population_Age_Long_Format <-melt(Population_Age, id ="Country")
names(Population_Age_Long_Format) <-c("Country", "Age_Group", "Age_Perc")
Population_Age_Long_Format$Age_Group <-substr(Population_Age_Long_
Format$Age_Group, 2,length(Population_Age_Long_Format$Age_Group))

# calculate midpoints of bars

Population_Age_Long_Format_Label <-ddply(Population_Age_Long_Format, .(Country),
   transform, pos =cumsum(Age_Perc) -(0.5 *Age_Perc))

ggplot(Population_Age_Long_Format_Label, aes(x = Country, y = Age_Perc, fill
= Age_Group)) +
geom_bar(stat ="identity") +
geom_text(aes(label = Age_Perc, y = pos), size =3) +
theme(legend.title=element_text(family="Times",size=20),
legend.text=element_text(family="Times",face ="italic",size=15),
plot.title=element_text(family="Times", face="bold", size=20),
axis.title.x=element_text(family="Times", face="bold", size=12),
axis.title.y=element_text(family="Times", face="bold", size=12)) +
xlab("Country") +
ylab("% of Total Population") +
ggtitle("Age Group - % of Total Population - Top 10 Country")
```

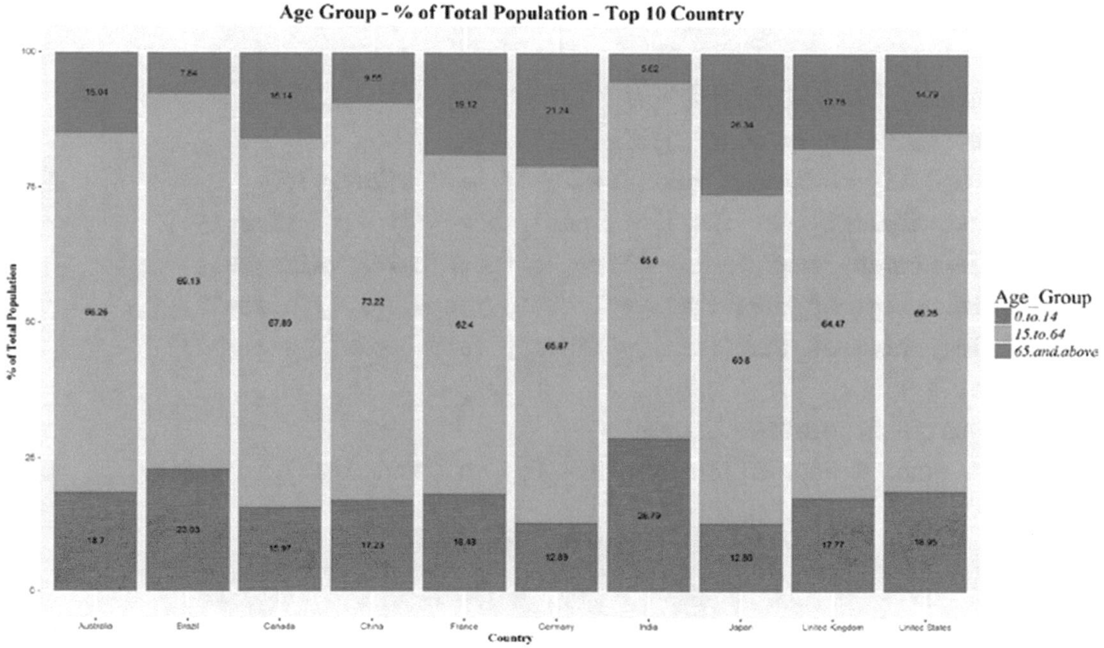

Figure 4-7. *A stacked bar chart showing the constituents of different age groups as a percentage of the total population*

In a way, if you look at it, many economic factors—like income parity, inflation, imports and exports, GDP, and many more—have a direct or indirect effect on population growth and ageing. With population growth slowing down, as shown in Figure 4-8, for most of countries, there is a need for good public polices and awareness campaigns from the government in order to balance the ageing and younger population over the coming years.

```
library(reshape2)
library(ggplot2)

Population_Growth <-read.csv("Population growth (annual %) - Top 10
Country.csv")

Population_Growth_Long_Format <-melt(Population_Growth, id ="Country")
names(Population_Growth_Long_Format) <-c("Country", "Year", "Annual_Pop_Growth")
Population_Growth_Long_Format$Year <-substr(Population_Growth_Long_
Format$Year, 2,length(Population_Growth_Long_Format$Year))
```

```
ggplot(Population_Growth_Long_Format, aes(x=Year, y=Annual_Pop_Growth,
group=Country)) +
geom_line(aes(colour=Country)) +
geom_point(aes(colour=Country),size =5) +
theme(legend.title=element_text(family="Times",size=20),
legend.text=element_text(family="Times",face ="italic",size=15),
plot.title=element_text(family="Times", face="bold", size=20),
axis.title.x=element_text(family="Times", face="bold", size=12),
axis.title.y=element_text(family="Times", face="bold", size=12)) +
xlab("Year") +
ylab("Annual % Population Growth") +
ggtitle("Annual % Population Growth - Top 10 Countries")
```

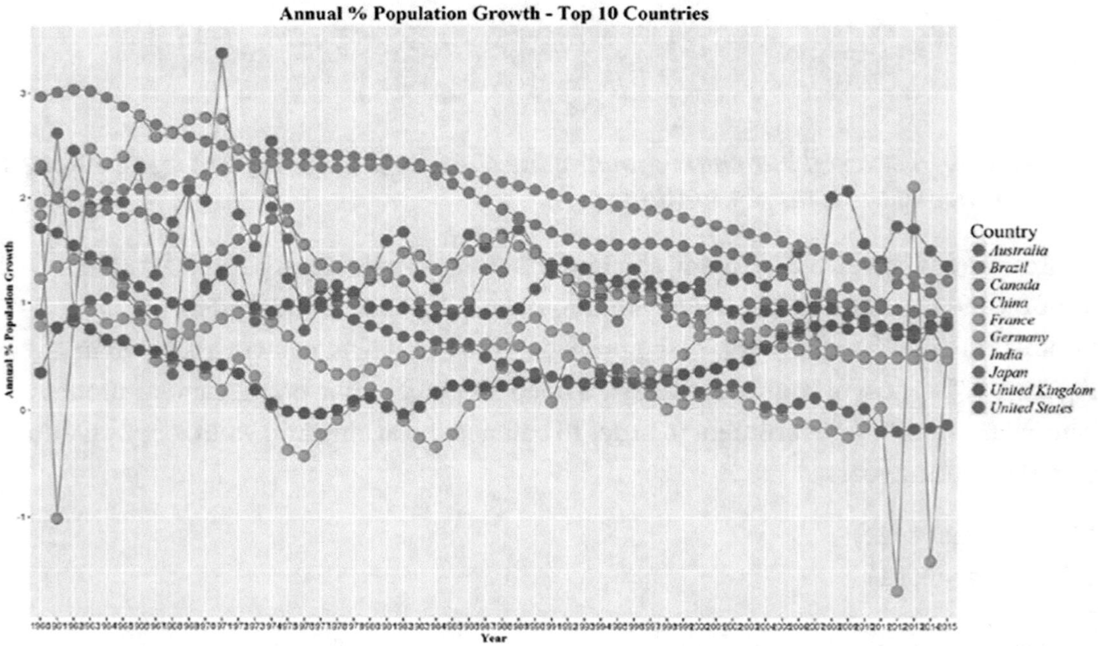

***Figure 4-8.** A line chart showing the top 10 countries and their annual percentage of population growth*

These plots are very interesting to peruse. The population growth for a few countries is very erratic while for others, it's stable and decreasing. For instance, see the population growth of India, which has been steadily decreasing, while for the United States it stabilized and then increased.

4.5 Scatterplots

A *scatterplot* is a graph that helps identify if there is a relationship between two variables. Scatterplots use Cartesian coordinates to show two variables on an x- and y-axis. Higher dimensional scatterplots are also possible but they are difficult to visualize, hence two-dimensional scattercharts are very popular. If we add dimensions of color or shape or size, so we can present more than two variables on a two-dimensional scatterplot as well. In this case, we will look at a population growth indicator from the World Bank's development indicators.

Any economy's strength is its people, and it is most important to measure if the citizens are doing well in terms of their financials, health, education, and all the basic necessities. A robust and strong economy is only built if it's designed and planned to keep the citizens at the center of everything. So, while GDP as an indicator signifies the growth of the country, there are many indicators that measure how well people are growing with the GDP. So, before we look at such indicators, let's try to explore the basic characteristics of the data using some of the widely used visualization tools, like scatterplots, boxplots, and histograms. Let's see if there are some patterns emerging from the population growth data and the GDP of the top 10 countries.

```
library(reshape2)
library(ggplot2)

GDP_Pop <-read.csv("GDP and Population 2015.csv")

ggplot(GDP_Pop, aes(x=Population_Billion, y=GDP_Trilion_USD))+
geom_point(aes(color=Country),size =5) +
theme(legend.title=element_text(family="Times",size=20),
legend.text=element_text(family="Times",face ="italic",size=15),
plot.title=element_text(family="Times", face="bold", size=20),
axis.title.x=element_text(family="Times", face="bold", size=12),
axis.title.y=element_text(family="Times", face="bold", size=12)) +
xlab("Population ( in Billion)") +
ylab("GDP (in Trillion US $)") +
ggtitle("Population Vs GDP - Top 10 Countries")
```

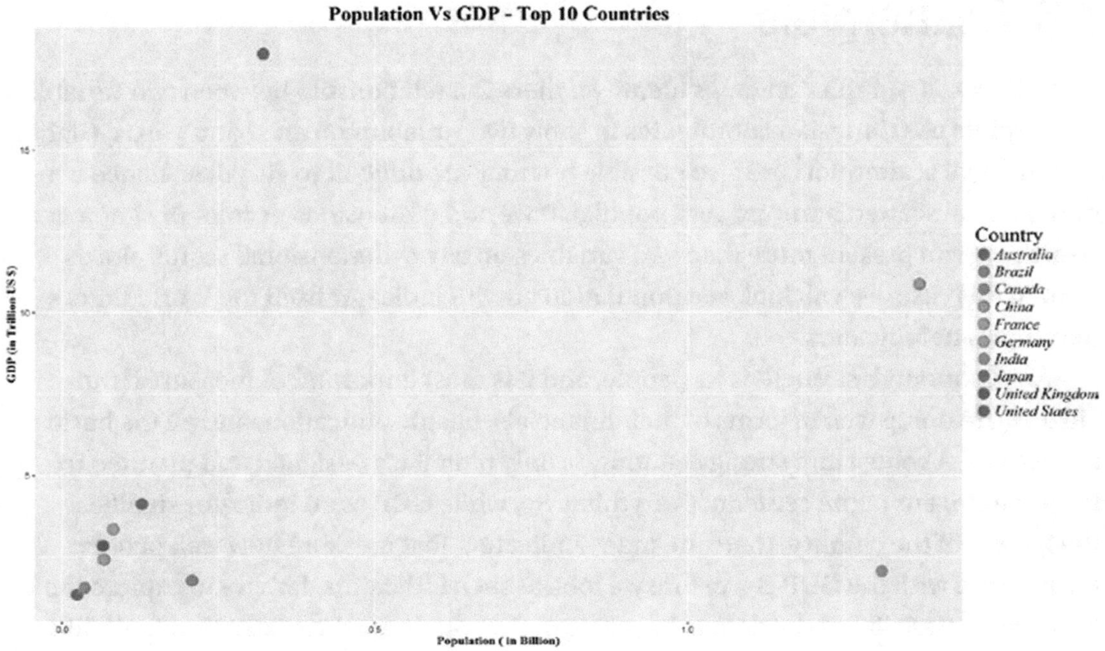

***Figure 4-9.** A scatterplot showing the relationship between population and GDP for the top 10 countries*

The scatterplot in Figure 4-9 shows that for countries like United States (US) since 2009, the population has been relatively low compared to other countries in the top 10; however, the United States, being the worlds' largest economy, has a very large GDP, taking the point high in the y-axis of the scatterplot. Similarly, if you look at China, with the worlds' largest population of 1.37 billion and 10.8 trillion of US dollars of GDP, it's represented by a point on the extreme right of the x-axis.

4.6 Boxplots

Boxplots are a compact way of representing the five-number summary described in Chapter 1, namely median, first and third quartiles (25th and 75th percentile) and min and max. The upper side of the vertical rectangular box represents the third quartile and the lower, the first quartile. The difference between the two points is known as the *interquartile range,* which consists of 50% of the data. A line dividing the rectangle represents the median. It also contains a line extending on both sides (known as whiskers) of the rectangle, which indicate the variability outside the first and third quartile. And finally the points plotted, which are shown as extensions of the lines, are called *outliers*. Numerically, these points have a value more than twice the standard deviation of the variable.

```
# GDP

GDP_all <-read.csv("Dataset/WDi/GDP All Year.csv")
GDP_all_Long_Format <-melt(GDP_all, id ="Country")
names(GDP_all_Long_Format) <-c("Country", "Year", "GDP_USD_Trillion")
GDP_all_Long_Format$Year <-substr(GDP_all_Long_Format$Year, 2,length(GDP_
all_Long_Format$Year))

ggplot(GDP_all_Long_Format, aes(factor(Country), GDP_USD_Trillion)) +
geom_boxplot(aes(fill =factor(Country)))+
theme(legend.title=element_text(family="Times",size=20),
legend.text=element_text(family="Times",face ="italic",size=15),
plot.title=element_text(family="Times", face="bold", size=20),
axis.title.x=element_text(family="Times", face="bold", size=12),
axis.title.y=element_text(family="Times", face="bold", size=12)) +
xlab("Country") +
ylab("GDP (in Trillion US $)") +
ggtitle("GDP (in Trillion US $): Boxplot - Top 10 Countries")
```

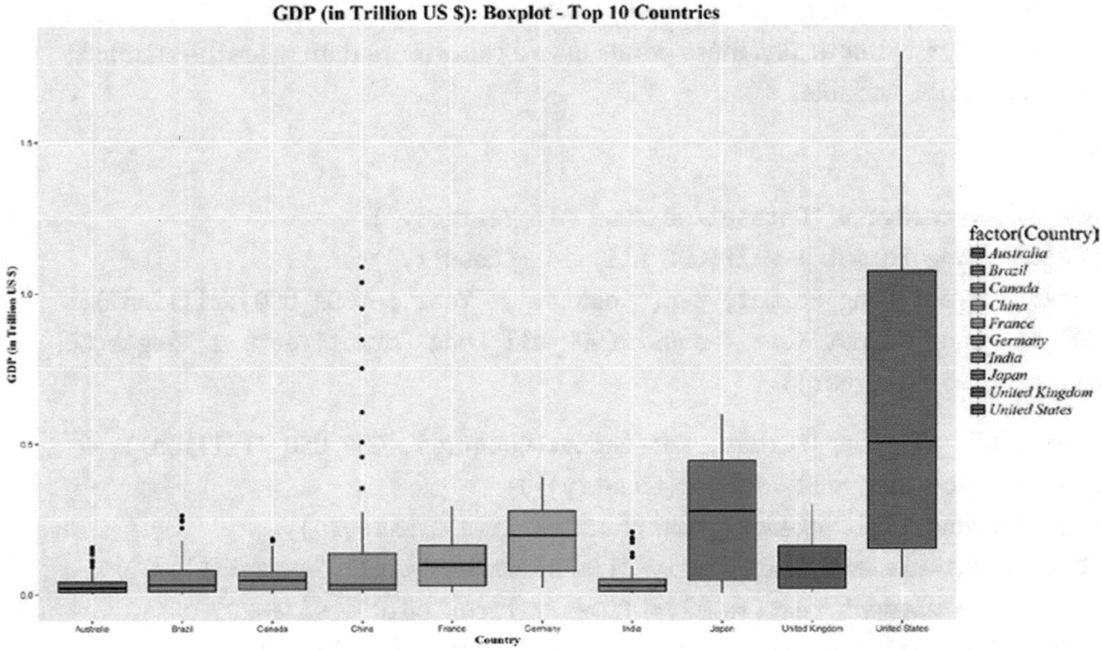

Figure 4-10. *A boxplot showing the GDP (in trillion US$) for the top 10 countries*

A boxplot is a wonderful representation of the degree of dispersion (spread), skewness, and outliers in a single plot. Using `ggplot`, it's possible to stack the different categories of the variables together side-by-side to see a comparison. For instance, looking at Figure 4-10, you see a boxplot of GDP by country. This contains the GDP data from 1962 to 2015. You see that the United States has shown the highest level of growth (degree of dispersion) with no outliers, indicating a sustained growth with no extreme highs or lows, whereas in China shows a high number of outliers, which roughly indicates the country has seen many unpredicted growths between 1962 and 2015. This interpretation is prone to error as we haven't looked at the reasons for these outliers in the data. An economist might intuitively generate some insights by just glancing at this plot; however, a naive analyst might end up producing some erroneous conclusions if they didn't give attention to the details. So, always hold onto the excitement of seeing a beautiful visualization and carefully analyze the other statistical properties of the data before making conclusions.

```
# Population

Population_all <-read.csv("Population All Year.csv")
Population_all_Long_Format <-melt(Population_all, id ="Country")
names(Population_all_Long_Format) <-c("Country", "Year", "Pop_Billion")
Population_all_Long_Format$Year <-substr(Population_all_Long_Format$Year,
2,length(Population_all_Long_Format$Year))

ggplot(Population_all_Long_Format, aes(factor(Country), Pop_Billion)) +
geom_boxplot(aes(fill =factor(Country))) +
theme(legend.title=element_text(family="Times",size=20),
legend.text=element_text(family="Times",face ="italic",size=15),
plot.title=element_text(family="Times", face="bold", size=20),
axis.title.x=element_text(family="Times", face="bold", size=12),
axis.title.y=element_text(family="Times", face="bold", size=12)) +
xlab("Country") +
ylab("Population (in Billion)") +
ggtitle("Population (in Billion): Boxplot - Top 10 Countries")
```

The boxplot for population of these 10 countries (in Figure 4-11) shows a similar trend but with no outliers. India and China are clearly emerging as the largest countries in terms of population.

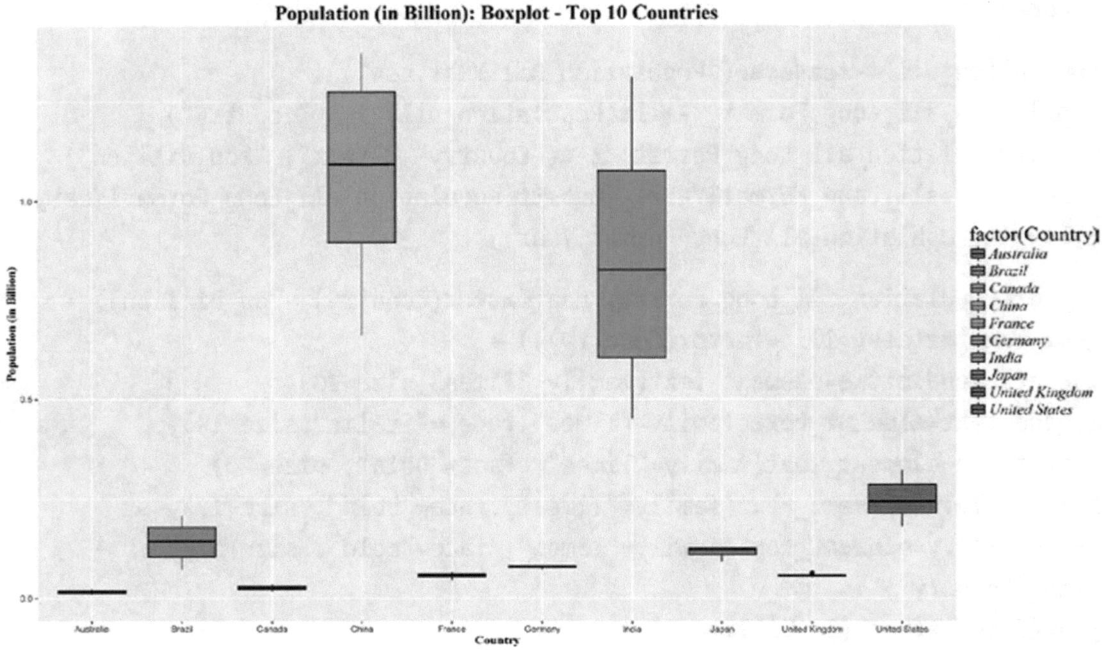

Figure 4-11. *A boxplot showing the population (in billions) for the top 10 countries*

4.7 Histograms and Density Plots

A *histogram* is one of the most basic and easy to understand graphical representations of numerical data. It consists of rectangular boxes. The width of each rectangle has a certain range and the height signifies the number of data points within that range. Constructing a histogram begins with dividing the entire range of values into non-overlapping and equal sized smaller bins (the rectangles). Histograms show an estimate of the probability distribution of a continuous variable.

Now imagine if you increase the number of bins to a large number in the histogram. What happens as a result is that you get a smooth surface and the rectangles appear to diminish into an area with some density. Alternatively, you could also use a density plot. Here we will show a histogram and then a density plot separately.

```
# Population

Population_all <-read.csv("Population All Year.csv")
Population_all_Long_Format <-melt(Population_all, id ="Country")
names(Population_all_Long_Format) <-c("Country", "Year", "Pop_Billion")
Population_all_Long_Format$Year <-substr(Population_all_Long_Format$Year,
2,length(Population_all_Long_Format$Year))

#Developed Country

Population_Developed <-Population_all_Long_Format[!(Population_all_Long_
Format$Country %in%c('India','China','Australia','Brazil','Canada','France',
'United States')),]

ggplot(Population_Developed, aes(Pop_Billion, fill = Country)) +
geom_histogram(alpha =0.5, aes(y = ..density..),col="black") +
theme(legend.title=element_text(family="Times",size=20),
legend.text=element_text(family="Times",face ="italic",size=15),
plot.title=element_text(family="Times", face="bold", size=20),
axis.title.x=element_text(family="Times", face="bold", size=12),
axis.title.y=element_text(family="Times", face="bold", size=12)) +
xlab("Population (in Billion)") +
ylab("Frequency") +
ggtitle("Population (in Billion): Histogram")
```

Figures 4-12 shows the distribution of population for three countries—Germany, Japan, and the United Kingdom.

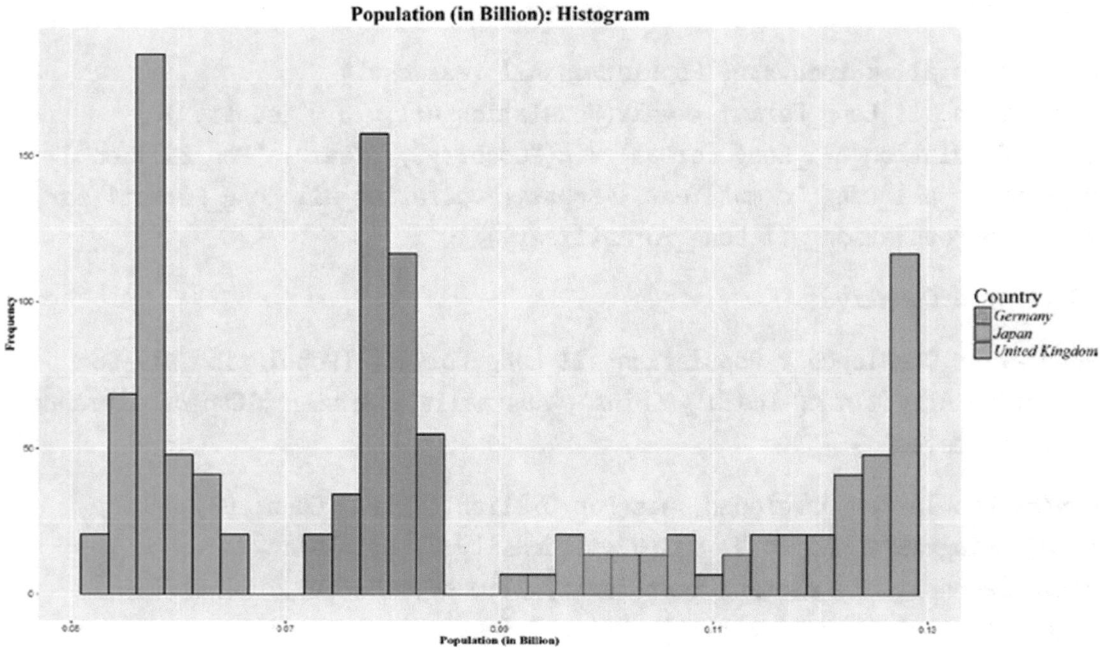

Figure 4-12. *A histogram showing GDP and population for three developed countries*

This distribution can be shown in density scales as well; Figures 4-13 through 4-15 are plots showing density scales.

```
ggplot(Population_Developed, aes(Pop_Billion, fill = Country)) +
geom_density(alpha =0.2, col="black") +
theme(legend.title=element_text(family="Times",size=20),
legend.text=element_text(family="Times",face ="italic",size=15),
plot.title=element_text(family="Times", face="bold", size=20),
axis.title.x=element_text(family="Times", face="bold", size=12),
axis.title.y=element_text(family="Times", face="bold", size=12)) +
xlab("Population (in Billion)") +
ylab("Frequency") +
ggtitle("Population (in Billion): Density")

#Developing Country
```

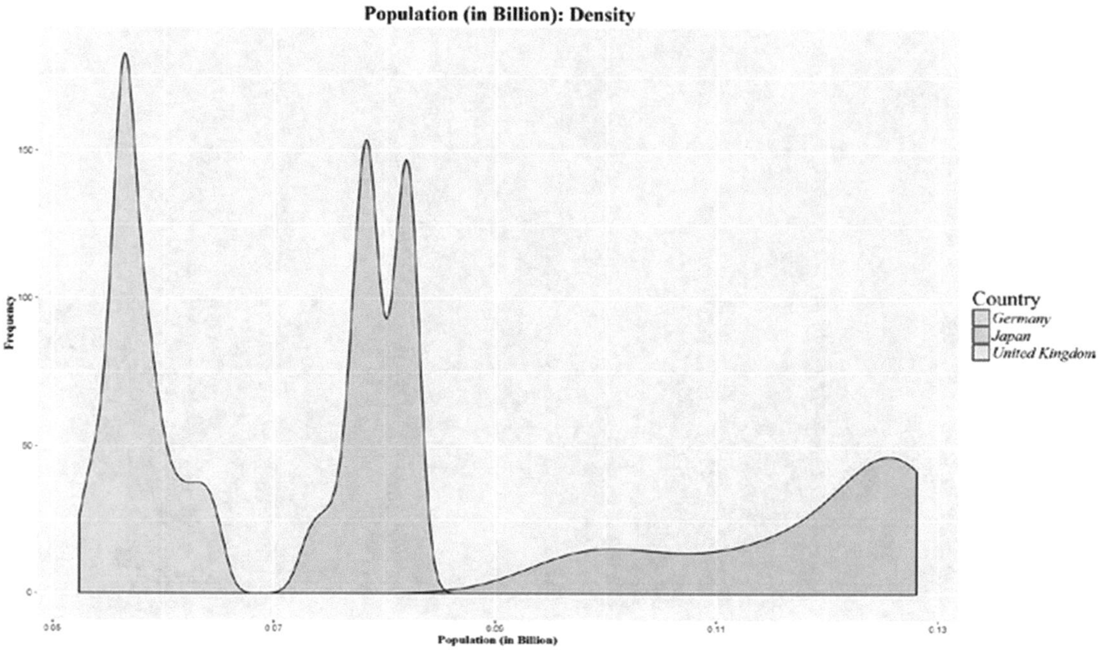

Figure 4-13. *A density plot showing GDP and population for three developed countries*

```
Population_Developing <-Population_all_Long_Format[Population_all_Long_
Format$Country %in%c('India','China'),]

#Histogram

ggplot(Population_Developing, aes(Pop_Billion, fill = Country)) +
geom_histogram(alpha =0.5, aes(y = ..density..),col="black") +
theme(legend.title=element_text(family="Times",size=20),
legend.text=element_text(family="Times",face ="italic",size=15),
plot.title=element_text(family="Times", face="bold", size=20),
axis.title.x=element_text(family="Times", face="bold", size=12),
axis.title.y=element_text(family="Times", face="bold", size=12)) +
xlab("Population (in Billion)") +
ylab("Frequency") +
ggtitle("Population (in Billion): Histogram")
```

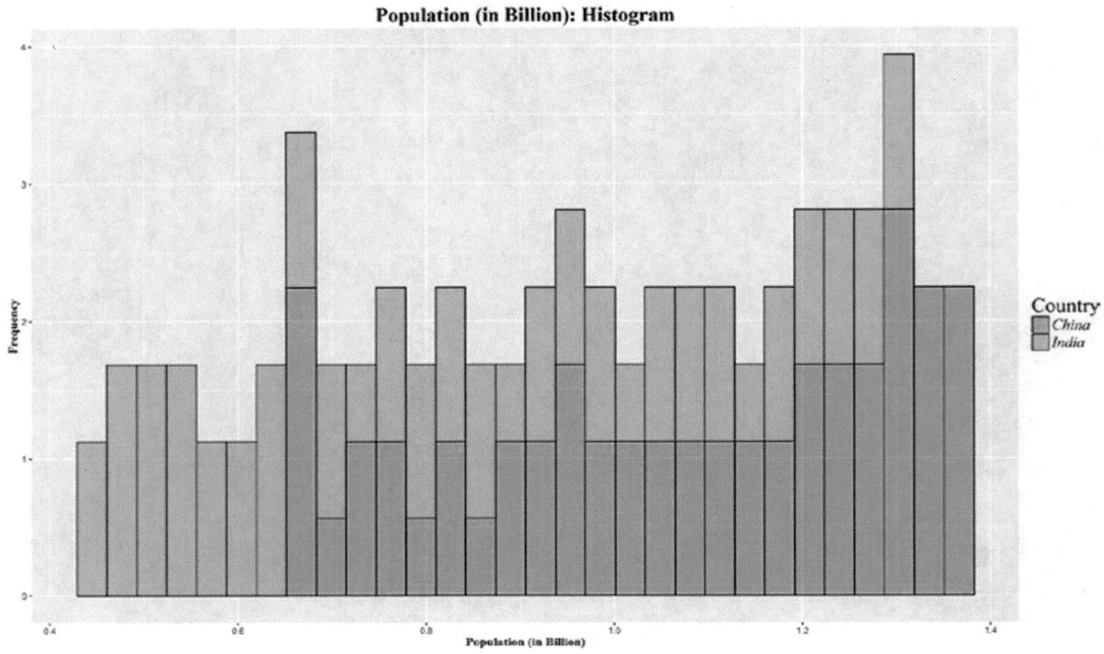

***Figure 4-14.** A histogram showing GDP and population for two developing countries*

```
#Density

ggplot(Population_Developing, aes(Pop_Billion, fill = Country)) +
geom_density(alpha =0.2, col="black") +
theme(legend.title=element_text(family="Times",size=20),
legend.text=element_text(family="Times",face ="italic",size=15),
plot.title=element_text(family="Times", face="bold", size=20),
axis.title.x=element_text(family="Times", face="bold", size=12),
axis.title.y=element_text(family="Times", face="bold", size=12)) +
xlab("Population (in Billion)") +
ylab("Frequency") +
ggtitle("Population (in Billion): Density Plot")
```

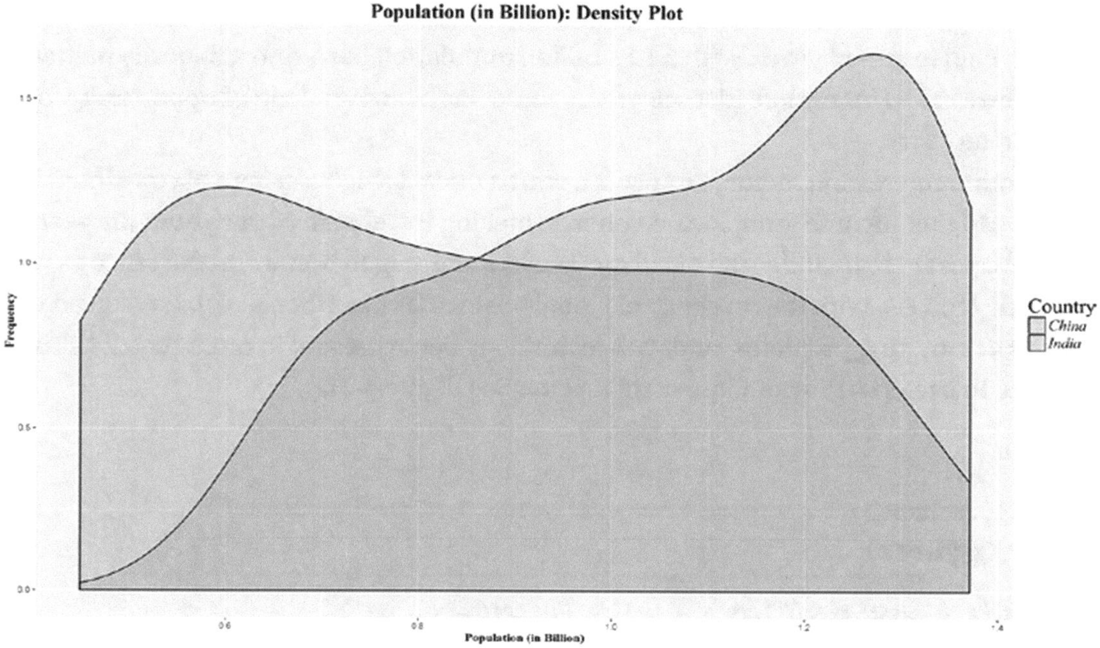

Figure 4-15. *A density plot showing GDP and population for two developing countries*

Looking at the histograms and density plots in Figures 4-12 through 4-15, you can see over the years, how the population data for these developed and developing nations is distributed. Now, since we have explored the data in detail, let's get a little more specific about the indicators based on population but split by different cohorts, like country and age.

4.8 Pie Charts

In India, the lowest consumption group spends almost close to 53% of their money on food and beverages as compared to the higher consumption group with by far the lowest among other groups at 12%. On the other hand, their spending on housing stands at 39%. This has one clear indication—the lowest consumption group with less disposable income spends a lot on basic survival needs like food, whereas the higher income group is looking for nice places to buy homes. The middle income group has something very similar to the higher group, but they have a larger pie allocated for food as well, which stands at 21%.

So, in India, businesses around real estates and food industry have flourished to an all time high in recent years. With a 1.31 billion population base, and a majority of them in the lowest, low, or middle income group, India has become a land of opportunity for the food industry.

Another interesting sector is transport, which finds its highest share of contribution from the higher income group, which often is making travel plans throughout the year. The transport here includes the usual mode of commuting to home and the office as well as holiday travels. With the presence of global businesses like Uber, which has solved the world's commuting problems, and with technology being present in more than 28 cities of India, this tells us the potential of this sector. See Figure 4-16.

```
# India

library(reshape2)
library(ggplot2)

GCD_India <-read.csv("India - USD - Percentage.csv")

GCD_India_Long_Format <-melt(GCD_India, id ="Sector")
names(GCD_India_Long_Format) <-c("Sector", "Income_Group","Perc_Cont")

ggplot(data=GCD_India_Long_Format, aes(x=factor(1), fill =factor(Sector))) +
geom_bar(aes(weight = Perc_Cont), width=1) +
coord_polar(theta="y", start =0) +
facet_grid(facets=. ~Income_Group) +
scale_fill_brewer(palette="Set3") +
xlab(“) +
ylab(“) +
labs(fill='Sector') +
ggtitle("India - Percentage share of each sector by Consumption Segment")
```

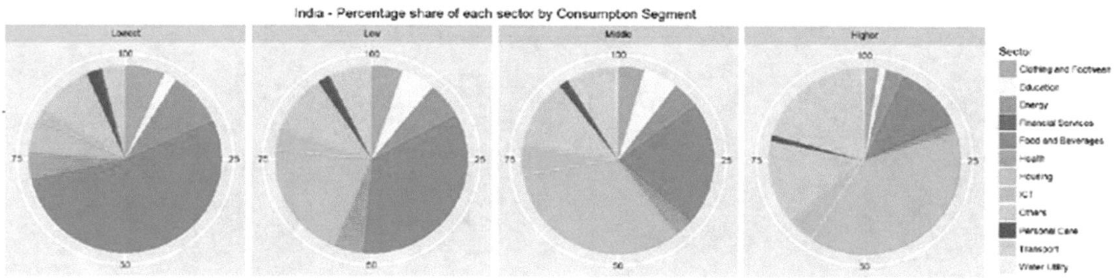

Figure 4-16. *A pie chart showing the percentage share of each sector by consumption segment in India*

In contrast to India, if you look at China, the need for food and housing is more evenly distributed among different income groups, whereas what emerges very distinctively in China is the spending on information and communication technologies (ICT) by the higher income group, which stands at 14% of the total spend (see Figure 4-17). This puts China more into the league of developed nations, where such high adaptability and spend on ICT could be seen.

```
# China

library(reshape2)
library(ggplot2)

GCD_China <-read.csv("China - USD - Percentage.csv")

GCD_China_Long_Format <-melt(GCD_China, id ="Sector")
names(GCD_China_Long_Format) <-c("Sector", "Income_Group","Perc_Cont")

ggplot(data=GCD_China_Long_Format, aes(x=factor(1), fill =factor(Sector))) +
geom_bar(aes(weight = Perc_Cont), width=1) +
coord_polar(theta="y", start =0) +
facet_grid(facets=. ~Income_Group) +
scale_fill_brewer(palette="Set3") +
xlab(“) +
ylab(“) +
labs(fill='Sector') +
ggtitle("China - Percentage share of each sector by Consumption Segment")
```

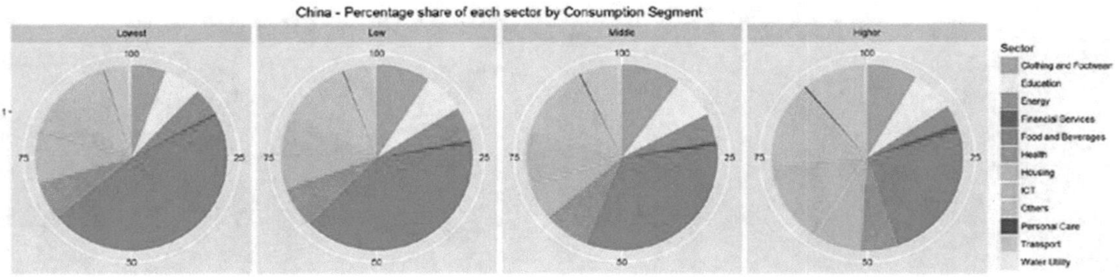

***Figure 4-17.** A pie chart showing the percentage share of each sector by consumption segment in China*

The pie chart in Figure 4-17 is very intuitive. Look at the lowest segment, the pie chart on extreme left. Almost half of the consumption is for food and beverages, as for the poor, the first priority is food. As you move to the higher segment, the priories shift and things like education and ICT (computing devices) go up substantially.

4.9 Correlation Plots

The best way to show how much one indicator relates to another is by computing the correlation. Though we won't go into the details of the mathematics behind correlation, those of you who thought that correlations are only seen through an nxn matrix are in for a surprise. Here comes the visual representation of it using the `corrplot` library in R. Correlation as a statistical measure is discussed in Chapter 6.

`Corrplot()` is a R package that can be used for graphical display of a correlation matrix. It also contains some algorithms to do matrix reordering. In addition, `corrplot` is good at details, including choosing color, text labels, color labels, and layout.

In this last section of the chapter, we want to tie together a few development indicators discussed in the previous sections—like GDP and population—with some indicators that contribute to their growth. The World Bank data used from 1961 to 2014 at an overall world level. For instance, fertility rate (births per women) highly correlates to population growth rate. See Figure 4-18.

```
library(corrplot)
library(reshape2)
library(ggplot2)
```

```
correlation_world <-read.csv("Correlation Data.csv")

corrplot(cor(correlation_world[,2:6],method ="pearson"),diag =FALSE,
title ="Correlation Plot", method ="ellipse",
tl.cex =0.7, tl.col ="black", cl.ratio =0.2
        )
```

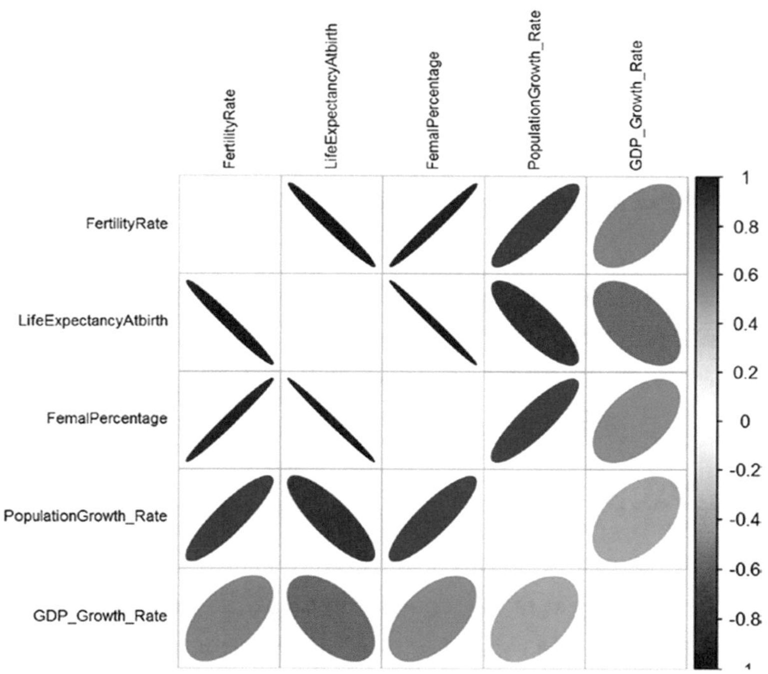

***Figure 4-18.** A plot showing correlation between various world development indicators*

There are many methods with the `corrplot` function (the method used in the `cor` function defines which correlation measure to use; here we use a Pearson correlation) with which you can experiment to see different shapes in this plot. We prefer the "ellipse," for two reasons. The ellipse can give us size and directional elements to capture more information. The combination of color, size, and position encapsulates a numeric value into a visual representation. For example, a correlation between fertility rate and population growth has a value greater than 0 (reflected in the shades of blue), and the direction of the ellipse represents a positive or negative correlation. The size represents the value; a thin ellipse would mean either a low or negative correlation and vice versa.

This way of leveraging the color, shape, and position gives us more dimensions to present a visualization in 2D, which otherwise would have been difficult to visualize. Some of the insights we get from this plot without even looking at the correlation matrix are as follows:

- As the fertility rates go down, we can see an increased life expectancy.
- With increase in the life expectancy, people start to live longer and there is greater burden on the economy to meet their healthcare needs. As a result, we see its negative correlation with GDP growth rate. Although it would be a gross mistake to say it's only the increase in life expectancy causing the GDP growth rate to go down, it is fair to point out the negative correlation that exists between the two variables.
- An increase in females also shows a positive (although not too high) correlation with GDP growth rate. This might mean that female contribution in household income growth and hence the spending increase has some effect on the country's GDP.

4.10 Heatmaps

Carrying on with the indicators and their correlations in the last section, heatmaps are visualizations of data where values are represented as different shades of colors. The darker the shade, the higher the value. For example, heatmaps can help us visualize how different regions of the world are responding to the development indicators.

The heatmap in Figure 4-19 shows six development indicators and how its scaled values (between 0 to 1) compare in different regions. Some insights we could derive from this heatmap are:

- The East Asia and Pacific region has the world's highest population (mostly contributed by China), followed by South Asia (contribution from India).
- North America, with its very low population, has the highest GDP per capita value (GDP/Population). It also has the lowest fertility rate and highest life expectancy, which comes from the fact that both of these indicators are highly correlated. Sub-Saharan Africa has the lowest GDP and GDP per capita.

- Interestingly, life expectancy throughout the world now looks healthy in terms of its scaled value. This perhaps is because of the improved healthcare services and reduced fertility rates. So, it seems most of the countries in the world are able to use contraceptives and enjoy the economic benefits of a smaller family.

```
library(corrplot)
library(reshape2)
library(ggplot2)

library("scales")
#Heatmaps

bc <-read.csv("Region Wise Data.csv")

bc_long_form <-melt(bc, id =c("Region","Indicator"))
names(bc_long_form) <-c("Region","Indicator","Year", "Inc_Value")
bc_long_form$Year <-substr(bc_long_form$Year, 2,length(bc_long_form$Year))

bc_long_form_rs <-ddply(bc_long_form, .(Indicator), transform ,rescale
=rescale(Inc_Value))

ggplot(bc_long_form_rs, aes(Indicator,  Region)) +geom_tile(aes(fill
= rescale),colour ="white") +scale_fill_gradient(low ="white",high
="steelblue") +
theme_grey(base_size =11) +scale_x_discrete(expand =c(0, 0)) +
scale_y_discrete(expand =c(0, 0)) +
theme(
axis.text.x =element_text(size =15 *0.8, angle =330, hjust =0, colour
="black",face="bold"),
axis.text.y =element_text(size =15 *0.8, colour ="black",face="bold"))+
ggtitle("Heatmap - Region Vs World Development Indicators") +
theme(text=element_text(size=12),
title=element_text(size=14,face="bold"))
```

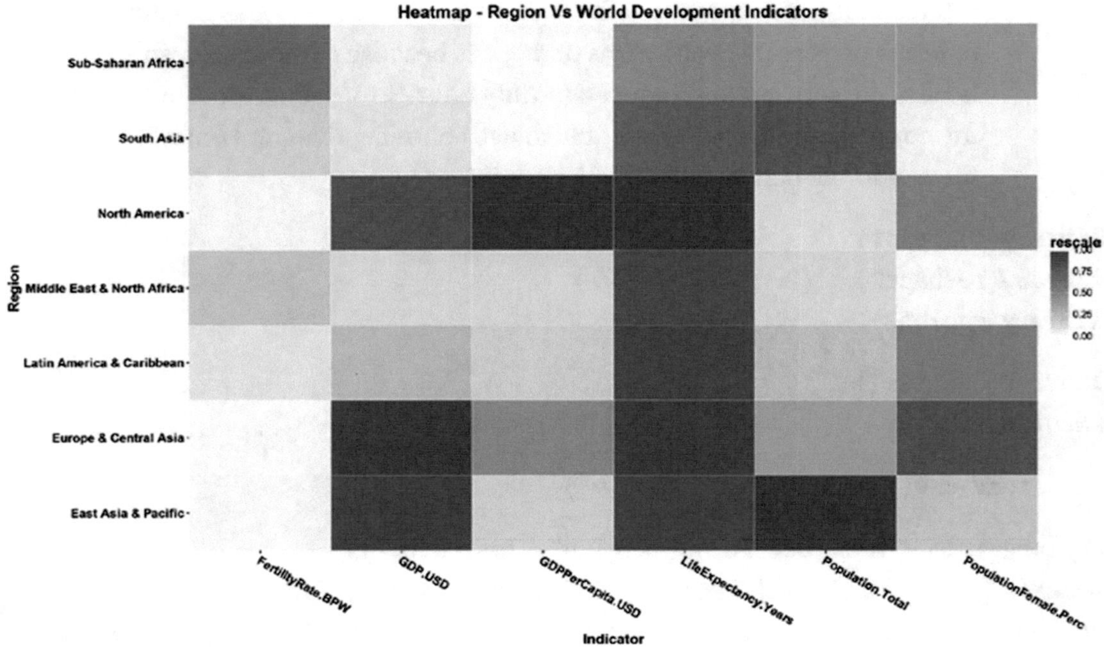

Figure 4-19. *A heatmap between regions and their various world development indicators*

4.11 Bubble Charts

In order to appreciate bubble charts, you need to first watch the TED talk by Hans Rosling, called "The best stats you've ever seen". He is a Swedish medical doctor, academic, statistician, and public speaker. Hans co-founded Gapminder Foundations, a non-profit organization promoting the use of data to explore development issues. They came out with software named Trendalyzer, which was later acquired by Google and rebranded as googleViz or otherwise known as Google Motion Charts. Google didn't commercialize this product, but rather made it available free publicly.

In this section, we use a dataset made available by Gapminder, which has the data around continent, country, life expectancy, and GDP per capita from 1995 to 2007. Though it looks good in 2D and in static charts, it's a visual delight to see these bubbles move in a motion chart (see Figure 4-20).

```
library(corrplot)
library(reshape2)
library(ggplot2)
library("scales")

#Bubble chart

bc <-read.delim("BubbleChart_GapMInderData.txt")
bc_clean <-droplevels(subset(bc, continent != "Oceania"))
str(bc_clean)
 'data.frame':     1680 obs. of 6 variables:
  $ country  : Factor w/ 140 levels "Afghanistan",..: 1 1 1 1 1 1 1 1 1 1
...
  $ year     : int 1952 1957 1962 1967 1972 1977 1982 1987 1992 1997 ...
  $ pop      : num 8425333 9240934 10267083 11537966 13079460 ...
  $ continent: Factor w/ 4 levels "Africa","Americas",..: 3 3 3 3 3 3 3 3 3
3 ...
  $ lifeExp  : num 28.8 30.3 32 34 36.1 ...
  $ gdpPercap: num 779 821 853 836 740 ...
bc_clean_subset <-subset(bc_clean, year ==2007)
bc_clean_subset$year =as.factor(bc_clean_subset$year)

ggplot(bc_clean_subset, aes(x = gdpPercap, y = lifeExp)) +scale_x_log10() +
geom_point(aes(size =sqrt(pop/pi)), pch =21, show.legend =FALSE) +
scale_size_continuous(range=c(1,40)) +
facet_wrap(~continent) +
aes(fill  =  continent)  +
scale_fill_manual(values =c("#FAB25B", "#276419", "#529624", "#C6E79C")) +
xlab("GDP Per Capita(in US $)")+
ylab("Life Expectancy(in years)")+
ggtitle("Bubble Chart - GDP Per Capita Vs Life Expectancy") +
theme(text=element_text(size=12),
title=element_text(size=14,face="bold"))
```

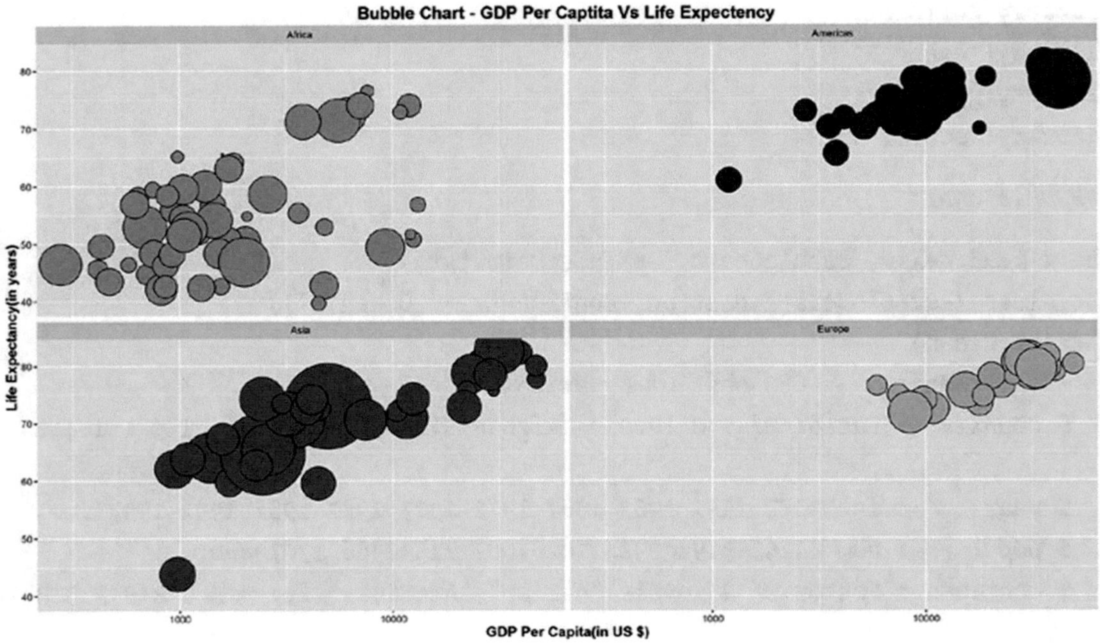

Figure 4-20. *A bubble chart showing GDP per capita vs life expectancy*

The book, *Lattice: Multivariate Data Visualization with R available via SpringerLink,* by Deepayan Sarkar, Springer (2008), has a comprehensive analysis on bubble charts. If you want a deeper understanding of this visualization, refer to this book.

The bubble chart in Figure 4-20 shows the plot between life expectancy and GDP per capita for the year 2007. The size of the bubble indicates the population of countries in that continent. The bigger the bubble, the larger the population. You can see that Asia contains multiple large bubbles because of the India and China presence, whereas Europe consists of mostly less populated countries and a high GDP per capita and life expectancy. America has some densely populated areas at the same time as a high value for both the indicators.

```
library(corrplot)
library(reshape2)
library(ggplot2)
library("scales")

bc <-read.csv("Bubble Chart.csv")
```

```
ggplot(bc, aes(x = GDPPerCapita, y = LifeExpectancy)) +scale_x_log10() +
geom_point(aes(size =sqrt(Population/pi)), pch =21, show.legend =FALSE) +
scale_size_continuous(range=c(1,40)) +
facet_wrap(~Country) +
aes(fill  =  Country)  +
xlab("GDP Per Capita(in US $)")+
ylab("Life Expectancy(in years)")+
ggtitle("Bubble Chart - GDP Per Capita Vs Life Expectancy - Four
Countries")
+
theme(text=element_text(size=12),
title=element_text(size=14,face="bold"))
```

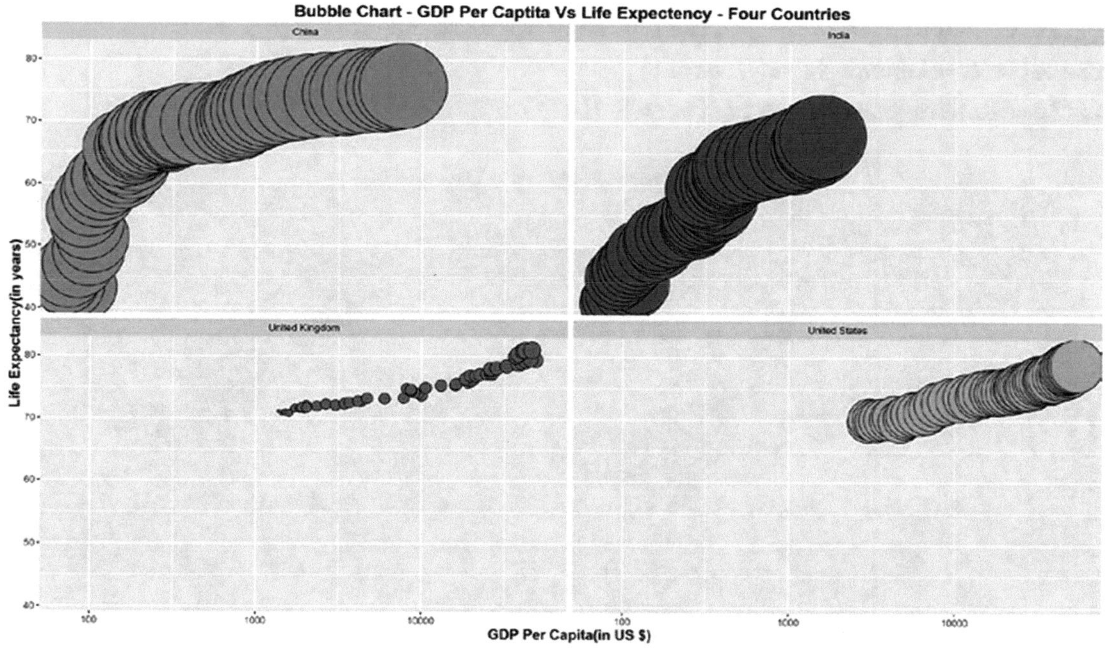

***Figure 4-21.** A bubble chart showing GDP per capita vs life expectancy for four countries*

The bubble chart in Figure 4-21 is for the two most developed and two fastest developing countries. Note that the developing nations, China and India, are quickly catching up in GDP and life expectancy to the developed nations over the years, despite their large populations.

```
library(corrplot)
library(reshape2)
library(ggplot2)
library("scales")

bc <-read.csv("Bubble Chart.csv")

ggplot(bc, aes(y = FertilityRate, x = LifeExpectancy)) +scale_x_log10() +
geom_point(aes(size =sqrt(Population/pi)), pch =21, show.legend =FALSE) +
scale_size_continuous(range=c(1,40)) +
facet_wrap(~Country) +
aes(fill = Country) +
ylab("Fertility rate, total (births per woman)")+
xlab("Life Expectancy(in years)")+
ggtitle("Bubble Chart - Fertility rate Vs Life Expectancy") +
theme(text=element_text(size=12),
title=element_text(size=14,face="bold"))
```

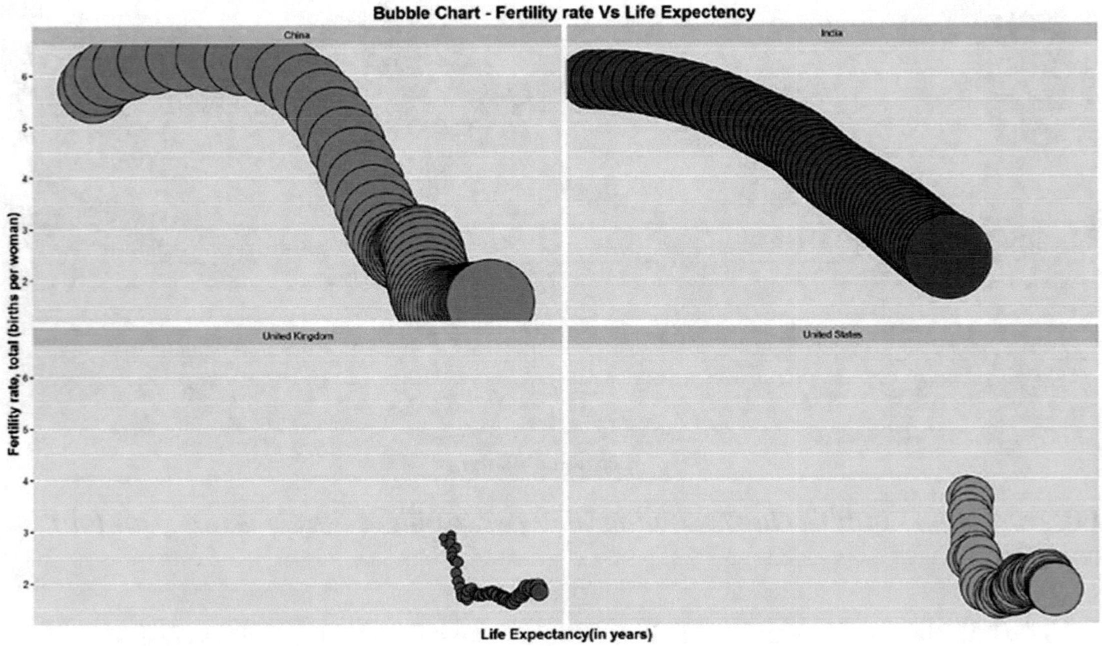

***Figure 4-22.** A bubble chart showing fertility rate vs life expectancy*

It's evident from the chart in Figure 4-22 that, with decreasing fertility rates, the life expectancy is getting longer for all these four nations. India steadily reduced the gap between itself and China in terms of life expectancy. There were 14 years between them to begin with and it fell to 6 or 7 years.

4.12 Waterfall Charts

A *waterfall chart* helps visualize the cumulative effect of sequential changes (addition and deletion) in the values. Just like a waterfall, it shows the flow of values in and out of the main values. Waterfall charts are also known as *flying bricks charts* or *Mario charts* due to the apparent suspension of columns (bricks) in midair. They are very popular in accounting and stock management visualizations, as the quantities keep on changing in a sequential manner. We will be using the `waterfall` package to create an example on hypothetical data of border control.

`Waterfall()` is an R package that provides support for creating waterfall charts in R using both traditional base and lattice graphics. The package details can be found at `https://cran.r-project.org/web/packages/waterfall/waterfall.pdf`.

The data we have is of border control, where each month the footfall of people is counted. More people going out than coming in means the net migration is negative, and when more people come in than out, the migration is positive. If we record this exchange over the border for 12 months, we can see the net migration. The waterfall chart will show us how it changed over these months (see Figure 4-23).

```
#Read the Footfall Data
footfall <-read.csv("Dataset/Waterfall Shop Footfall Data.csv",header = T)

#Display the data for easy read
footfall
#Convert the Months into factors to retain the order in chart
footfall$Month <-factor(footfall$Month)
footfall$Time_Period <-factor(footfall$Time_Period)

#Load waterfall library
library(waterfall)
library(lattice)
```

```
#Plot using waterfall
waterfallplot(footfall$Net,names.arg=footfall$Month, xlab ="Time
Period(Month)",ylab="Footfall",col = footfall$Type,main="Footfall by Month")
```

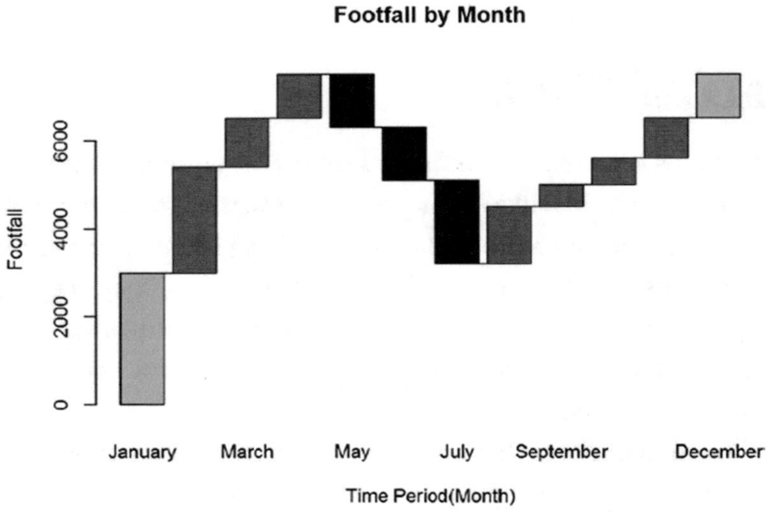

***Figure 4-23.** Waterfall plot of footfall at the border*

The green blocks are starting or ending blocks, corresponding to January and December, respectively. The red blocks are people coming in while the black blocks are people going out. When you follow this over a year, you can see that positive migration happened most of the year, except in three months where more people went out (the black blocks).

The following plot is alternative view of the same waterfall charts (see Figure 4-24).

```
waterfallchart(Net~Time_Period, data=footfall,col = footfall$Type,xlab
="Time Period(Month)",ylab="Footfall",main="Footfall by Month")
```

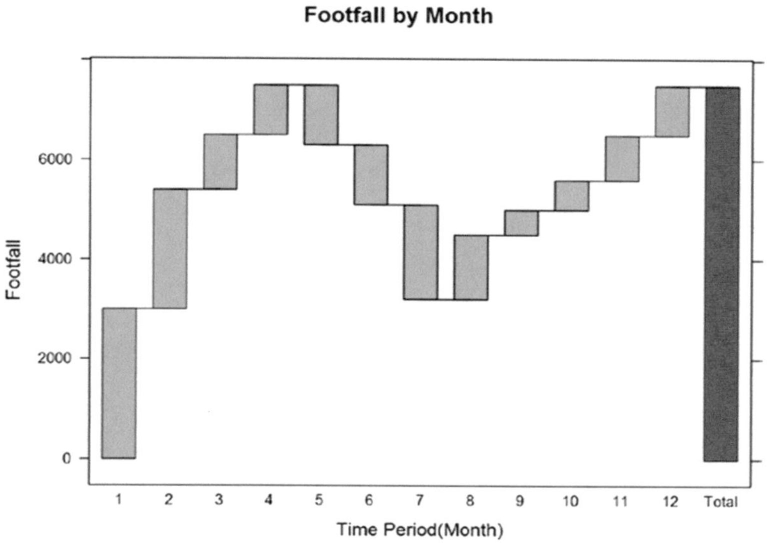

Figure 4-24. *Waterfall chart with net effect*

The plot in Figure 4-24 is similar to the previous one, with the only difference of the total column at the end. The total column presents the final net value in our counter of footfall after the year ended.

The same plot can be created to show the percentage of footfall contribution by month. This will show how the ending footfall count each month is proportional to the total end footfall. The sum of such percentage should be 100 and is divided into 12 months.

```
waterfallchart(Month~Footfall_End_Percent, data=footfall)
```

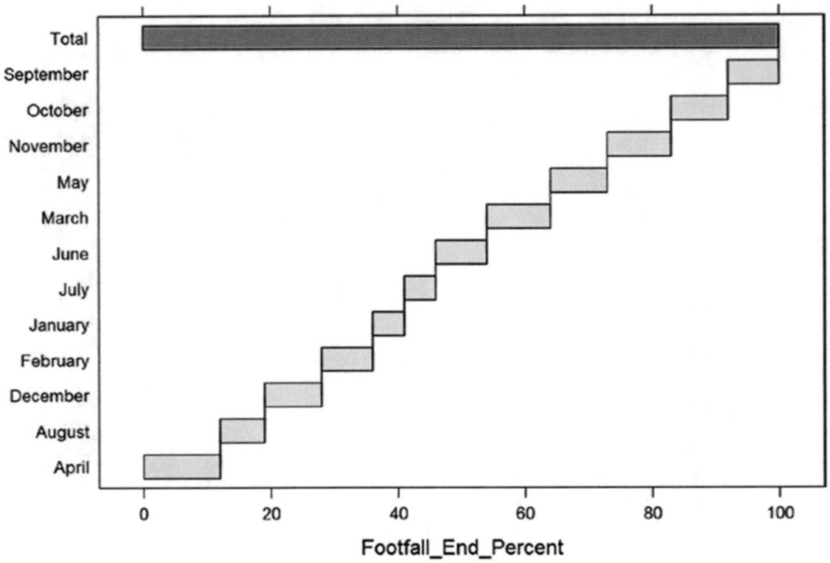

Figure 4-25. *Footfall end count as percentage of total end count*

Note that the end count fluctuated during the month of April, followed by March and November. The interpretation will vary based on what you are more interested in from the plots in Figures 4-24 and 4-25.

4.13 Dendogram

Dendograms are visual representations specifically useful in clustering analysis. They are tree diagrams frequently used to illustrate the formation of clusters as is done in hierarchical clusters. Chapter 6 explains how hierarchical clustering works. Dendograms are popular in computational biology where similarities among species can be presented using histograms to classify them.

Dendograms are native to the basic `plot()` command. There are some other packages as well for more detailed dendograms like `ggdendro()` and `dendextend()`.

The y-axis in dendograms measures the closeness (or similarity) of an individual data point of clusters.

The x-axis lists the elements in the dataset (and hence they look messy on the leaf nodes).

The dendogram helps in choosing the right numbers of clusters by showing how the tree grows with distance matrix (or height) on the y-axis. Cut the tree where you feel substantially separated clusters can be seen on dendogram. A cut means a like y=c, where c is 1, 2, or 3..n and c is the number of clusters.

Here, we create an example with iris data, and in the end show how good the clusters fit to the actual data.

```
library(ggplot2)
data(iris)
# prepare hierarchical cluster on iris data
hc <-hclust(dist(iris[,1:2]))

# using dendogram objects
hcd <-as.dendrogram(hc)

#Zoom Into it at level 1
plot(cut(hcd, h =1)$upper, main ="Upper tree of cut at h=1")
```

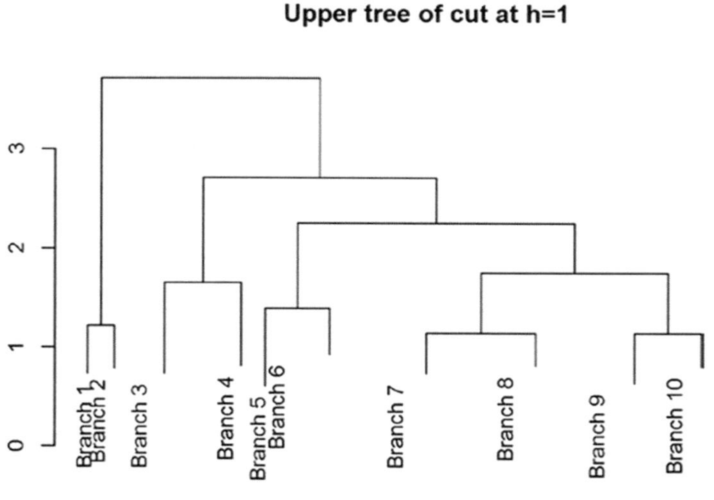

Figure 4-26. *Dendogram with distance/height up to h=1*

Looking at the dendogram in Figure 4-26, the best cut seems like it will be somewhere between 2 and 3, as the clusters have to be complete. We will go ahead with three clusters and see how they fit into our prior knowledge of clusters.

```
#lets show how cluster looks looks like if we have cut the tree at y=3
clusterCut <-cutree(hc, 3)

iris$clusterCut <-as.factor(clusterCut)

ggplot(iris, aes(Petal.Length, Petal.Width, color = iris$Species)) +
geom_point(alpha =0.4, size =3.5) +geom_point(col = clusterCut) +
scale_color_manual(values =c('black', 'red', 'green'))
```

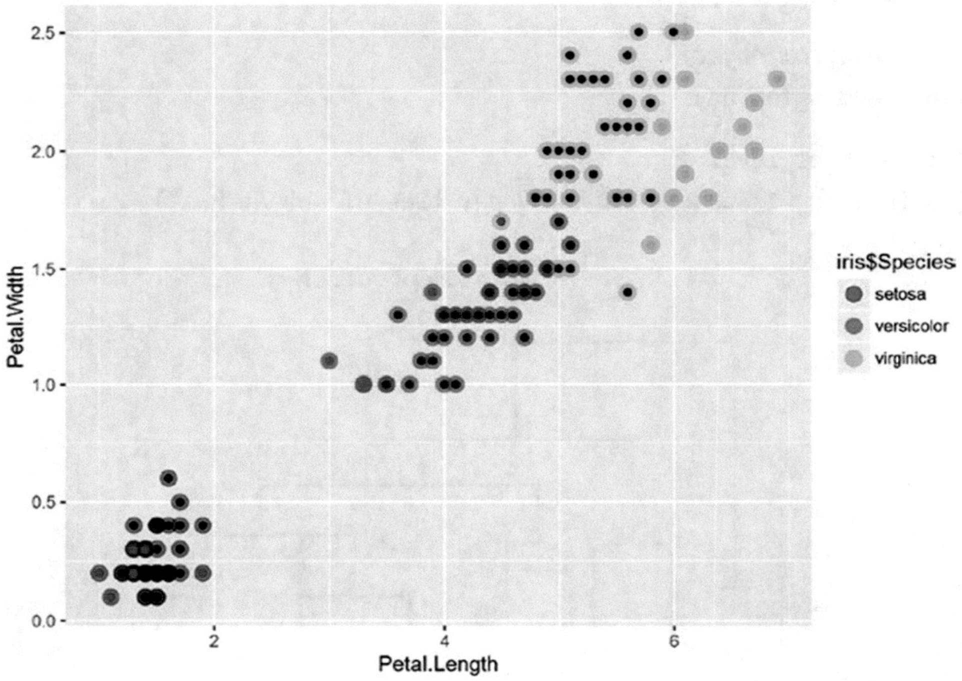

***Figure 4-27.** Clusters by actual classification of species in iris data*

We can see in the plots in Figure 4-27 that most of the clusters we predicted and the already existing classification of species match. This also means the variables we use for clustering petal width and petal length are important features for the type of species they belong to.

4.14 Wordclouds

Wordclouds are word plots with frequency weighted to the size of the words. The more frequently a word appears, the bigger the word. You can look at text data and quickly identify the most prominent themes discussed. The earliest example of weighted lists of English keywords were the "subconscious files" in Douglas Coupland's *Microserfs* (1995). After that, this has become a prominent way of quickly perceiving the most frequent terms and for locating a word alphabetically to determine its relative importance.

In R, we have the `wordcloud()` package, which is used in this section to create a wordcloud. The details of this package are available at `https://cran.r-project.org/web/packages/wordcloud/wordcloud.pdf`.

In this section, we show a good example of how wordclouds can be useful. We have just copied multiple job descriptions from the Internet for a data science position. Now the wordcloud on this document will tell us which words occur most frequency in the job descriptions and hence give us an idea about what the hot skills in the market are and the demand of other qualities (see Figure 4-28).

```
#Load the text file

job_desc <-readLines("Dataset/wordcloud.txt")

library(tm)
library(SnowballC)
library(wordcloud)
 Loading required package: RColorBrewer
jeopCorpus <-Corpus(VectorSource(job_desc))

jeopCorpus <-tm_map(jeopCorpus, PlainTextDocument)
#jeopCorpus <- tm_map(jeopCorpus, content_transformer(tolower))
#Remove punctuation marks
jeopCorpus <-tm_map(jeopCorpus, removePunctuation)
#remove English stopwords and some more custom words
jeopCorpus <-tm_map(jeopCorpus, removeWords,(c("Data","data","Experi","work"
,"develop","use","will","can","you","busi", stopwords('english'))))
#Create the document matrix
jeopCorpus <-tm_map(jeopCorpus, stemDocument)
```

```
#Creating the color pellet for the word images

pal <-brewer.pal(9,"YlGnBu")
pal <-pal[-(1:4)]
set.seed(146)
#creating the wordcloud
wordcloud(words = jeopCorpus, scale=c(3,0.5), max.words=100, random.
order=FALSE,
rot.per=0.10, use.r.layout=FALSE, colors=pal)
```

Figure 4-28. *Wordcloud of job descriptions*

The wordcloud shows that the key trends in data science positions are experienced people, analyst positions, Hadoop, statistics, Python, and others. This way, without even going through all the data, we have been able to extract the prominent requirements for a data science position.

4.15 Sankey Plots

Sankey plots are also called river plots. They are used to show how the different elements of data are connected, with the density of connecting lines presenting the strength of connection. They help show the flow of connected items from one factor to another.

It is highly recommended that users explore a powerful visualization package for making lot of beautiful charts in R: `Rcharts()`. The source of this package, with lots of examples, can be found at `https://github.com/ramnathv/rCharts`.

In the following example, we will use another powerful visualization tool, called `googleVis()`. `GoogleVis` is an R interface to the Google Charts API, allowing users to create interactive charts based on data frames. Charts are displayed locally via the R HTTP help server. A modern browser with an Internet connection is required and for some charts a Flash player. The data remains local and is not uploaded to Google. (Source: `https://cran.r-project.org/web/packages/googleVis/googleVis.pdf`.)

In our example, we will show how the `HousePrice` flows among different attributes; we have chosen three layers of plot with Type of House, Estate type, and Type of Sale.

```
#Load the data from sankey.csv
sankey_data <-read.csv("Dataset/sankey2.csv",header=T)

library(googleVis)
plot(
gvisSankey(sankey_data, from="Start",
to="End", weight="Weight",
options=list(
height=250,
sankey="{link:{color:{fill:'lightblue'}}}"
            ))
)
```

Note The visualization is loaded on a web browser, so you don't need a working Internet connection to load this example.

```
starting httpd help server ...
 done
```

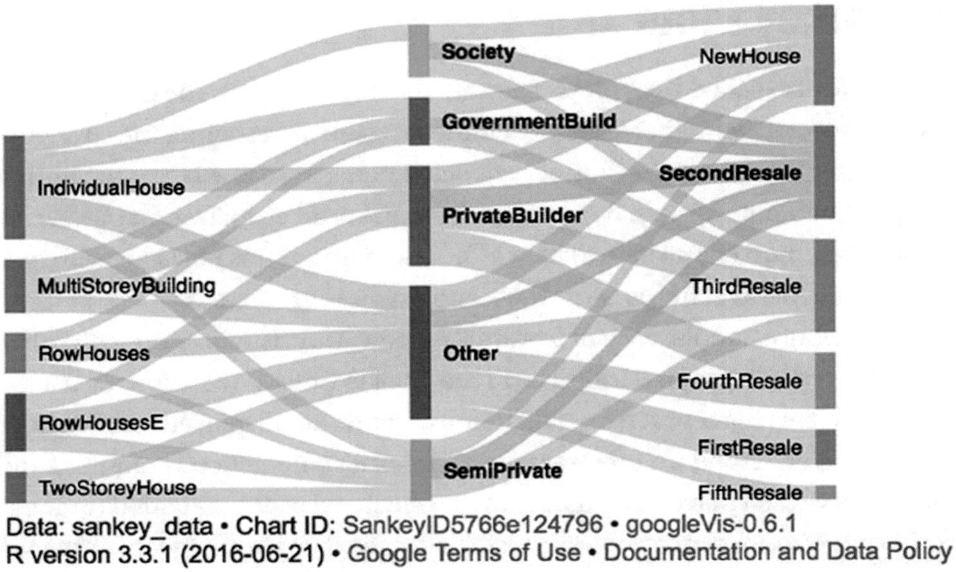

Figure 4-29. *The Sankey chart for house sale data*

The Sankey chart shown in Figure 4-29 provides us with some important information, like the most popular house type is the individual house. They then are available in all the types of states. Further, the societies only have individual houses and they have gone through new house sale, second resale, and third resale only. You can use these plots to explain a lot of other insights as well.

4.16 Time Series Graphs

We have already shown time series plots in earlier sections in this chapter. Essentially, when the data is time indexed, like GDP data, we take time on the x-axis and plot the data to see how it has been changing over time. We can use time series plots to evaluate patterns and behavior in data over time.

R has powerful libraries to plot multiple types of time series plots. A good read for you can be found at `https://cran.r-project.org/web/packages/timeSeries/vignettes/timeSeriesPlot.pdf`.

For our example, we will try to show two time plots to understand some stark behavior:

- GDP of eight countries overlaid on a single plot to show how the GDP growth varied for these countries over the last 25 years.
- Tracing the GDP growth of three countries during the recession of 2008.

The first example plots GDP growth over 25 years for eight countries/areas (the Arab world, UAE (United Arab Emirates), Australia, Bangladesh, Spain, United Kingdom, India, and the United States).

```
library(reshape2)
library(ggplot2)
library(ggrepel)

time_series <-read.csv("Dataset/timeseries.csv",header=TRUE);

mdf <-melt(time_series,id.vars="Year");

mdf$Date <-as.Date(mdf$Year,format="%d/%m/%Y");

names(mdf)=c("Year","Country","GDP_Growth","Date");

ggplot(data=mdf,aes(x=Date,y=GDP_Growth)) +geom_line(aes(color=Country),
size=1.5)
```

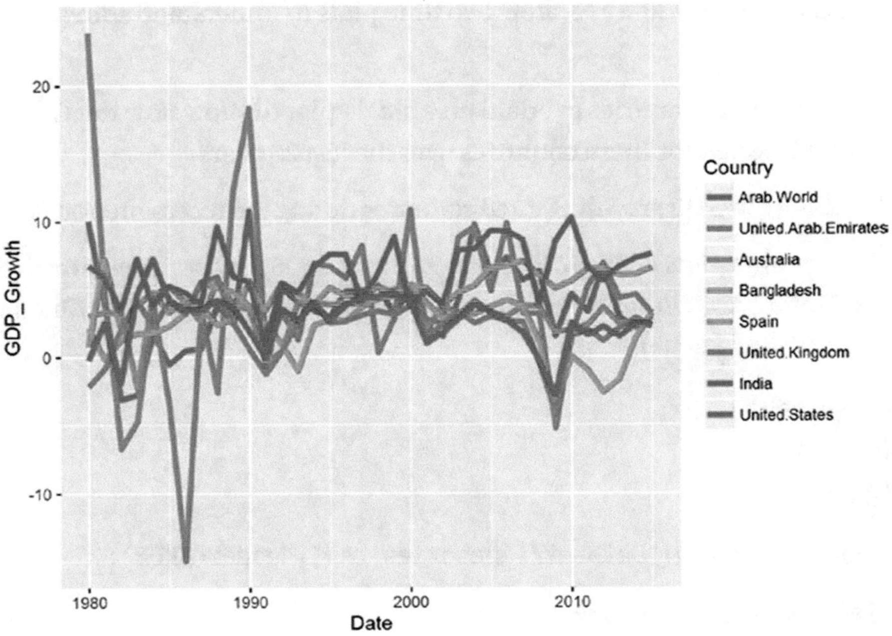

Figure 4-30. *GDP growth for eight countries*

The plot in Figure 4-30 shows that the most volatile economy among the eight countries is UAE. They showed phenomenal growth after the 1990s. You can also see during 2007-2009 that all the economies showed lower GDP growth, due to a worldwide recession.

In the following plots, we will see how the recessions impacted three major economies and to what extent (the United States, the UK, and India).

```
#Now lets just see the growth rates for India, US and UK during recession
years (2006,2007,2008,2009,2010)

mdf_2 <-mdf[mdf$Country %in%c("India","United.States","United.Kingdom")
&(mdf$Date >as.Date("2005-01-01") &mdf$Date <as.Date("2011-01-01")),]

mdf_2$GDP_Growth <-round(mdf_2$GDP_Growth,2)

tp <-ggplot(data=mdf_2,aes(x=Date,y=GDP_Growth)) +geom_line(aes(color=
Country),size=1.5)
tp +geom_text_repel(aes(label=GDP_Growth))
```

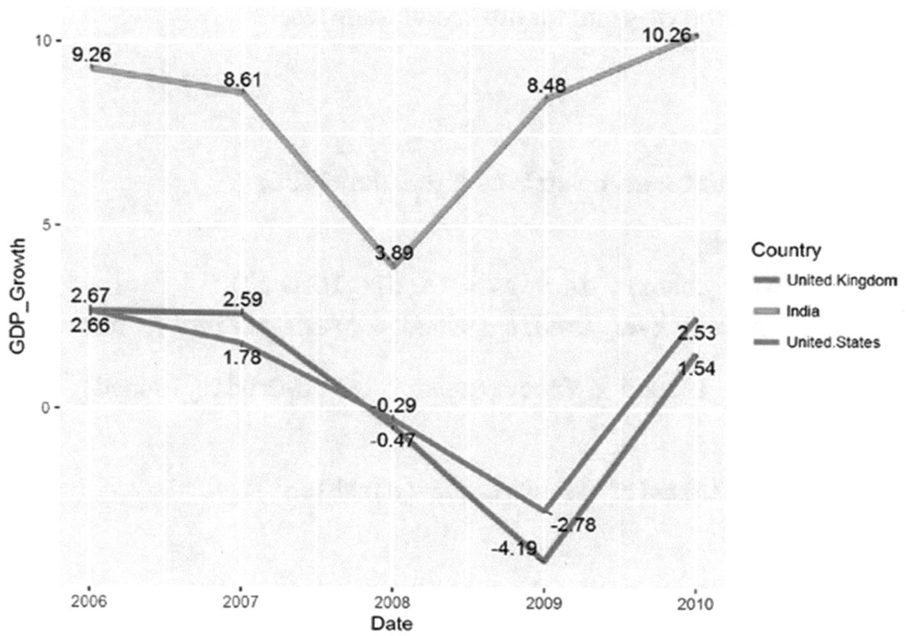

Figure 4-31. *GDP growth during the recession*

You can see in Figure 4-31, that in 2008, that the United States and the UK showed negative growth, while India's growth slowed but was not negative. The United States and the UK were in a deep recession in 2009 as well, while India started picking up. After 2009, all the economies were on the recovery path.

4.17 Cohort Diagrams

Cohort diagrams are two-dimensional diagrams used to present events that occur to a set of observations (individuals) belonging to different cohorts. They are very popular in credit analysis, marketing analysis, and other demographic studies. Cohort diagrams are also sometimes called *Lexis diagrams*.

A cohort is a group of people that's assumed to behave differently than others based on demographics. In our credit example, we assume the cohorts as the year in which credit was issued. This means each year applicants will be treated as a cohort and then we track how many of them still remain unpaid in the following years. In cohort plots, time is usually represented on the horizontal axis, while the value of interest is represented on the vertical axis.

Let's create the cohort diagram for our credit example.

```
library(ggplot2)
require(plyr)

cohort <-read.csv("Dataset/cohort.csv",header=TRUE)

#we need to melt data
cohort.chart <-melt(cohort, id.vars ="Credit_Issued")
colnames(cohort.chart) <-c('Credit_Issued', 'Year_Active', 'Active_Num')

cohort.chart$Credit_Issued <-factor(cohort.chart$Credit_Issued)

#define palette
blues <-colorRampPalette(c('lightblue', 'darkblue'))

#plot data
p <-ggplot(cohort.chart, aes(x=Year_Active, y=Active_Num,
group=Credit_Issued))
p +geom_area(aes(fill = Credit_Issued)) +
scale_fill_manual(values =blues(nrow(cohort))) +
ggtitle('Active Credit Cards Volume')
```

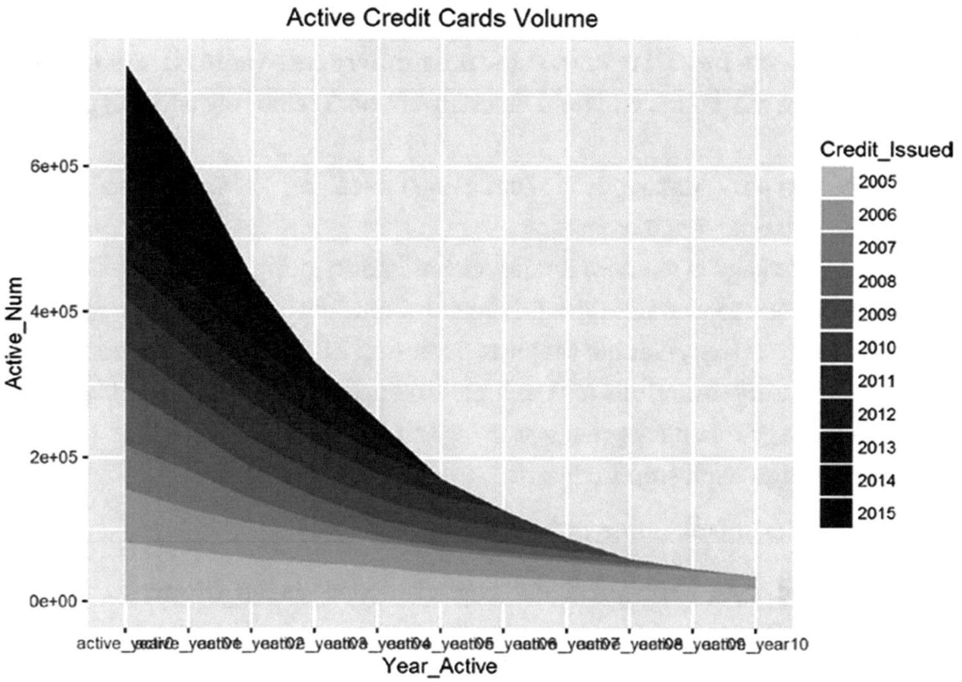

Figure 4-32. *The cohort plot for credit card active by year of issue*

The plot in Figure 4-32 shows how each cohort volume changes with the number of active years. You can see how the active number of cards decreases over the years. The decline rate can be estimated by the slope of each cohort and can be tested against others to see if some particular cohort behaved differently.

4.18 Spatial Maps

Spatial maps have become very popular in recent days. They are powerful presentations of data that's tagged with locations on a map. If the information is geotagged, we can create powerful visual presentations of the data. You can see lots of applications of them—weather reporting, demographics, crime monitoring, trails monitoring, and some very interesting crowd behavior tracking using Twitter data, Flikr data, and other geotagged personal data.

We recommend a good read, available at `https://journal.r-project.org/archive/2013-1/kahle-wickham.pdf`.

To show an example, we have selected the crime records data from the National Crime Records Bureau, India. We show how the robbery cases across the states can be shown on an Indian map. This will help us compare data relatively without getting into the data itself.

Data source: `https://data.gov.in/catalog/cases-reported-and-value-property-stolen-place-occurrence`.

The `Ggmap()` package is used for spatial visualization along with `ggplot2`. It is a collection of functions to visualize spatial data and models on top of static maps from various online sources (e.g., Google Maps and Stamen Maps). It includes tools common to those tasks, including functions for geolocation and routing. (Source: `https://cran.r-project.org/web/packages/ggmap/ggmap.pdf`.)

Let's walk through each step in detail:

1. Load the crime data into `crime_data`:

```
crime_data <-read.csv("Dataset/Case_reported_and_value_of_property_taken_
away.csv",header=T)

#install.packages("ggmap")
library(ggmap)
```

2. Pull an example map to check if the `ggplot()` function is working or not:

```
#Example map to test if ggmap is able to pull graphs or not
qmap(location ="New Delhi, India")
Map from URL : http://maps.googleapis.com/maps/api/staticmap?center=New
+Delhi,+India&zoom=10&size=640x640&scale=2&maptype=terrain&language=en-
EN&sensor=false
Information from URL : http://maps.googleapis.com/maps/api/geocode/
json?address=New%20Delhi,%20India&sensor=false
```

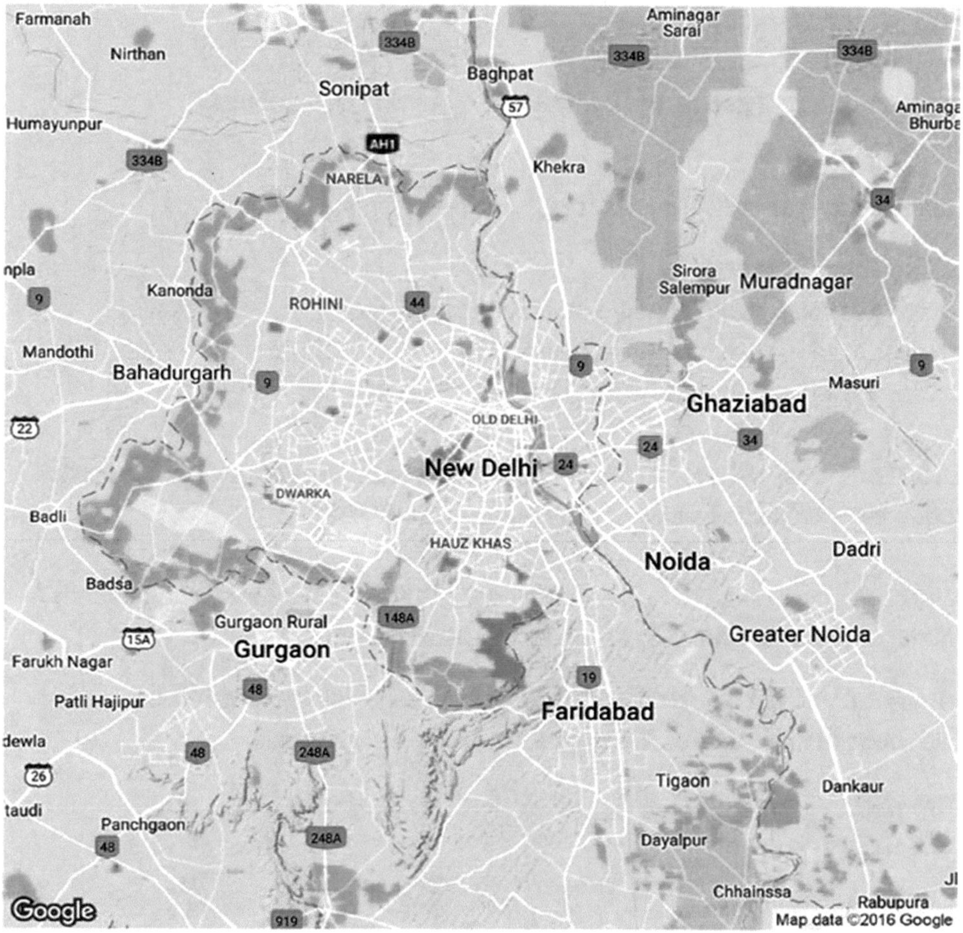

Figure 4-33. *An example map pulled using ggplot()—New Delhi India*

The plot in Figure 4-33 confirms that the ggmap() can pull the maps by passing the location into the function.

3. Get the geolocation of all the states of India present in the crime data:

```
crime_data$geo_location <-as.character(crime_data$geo_location)
crime_data$robbery =as.numeric(crime_data$robbery)

#lets just see the stats fpr 2010
mydata <-crime_data[crime_data$year == '2010',]
```

```
#Summarize the data by state
library(dplyr)
mydata <-summarise(group_by(mydata, geo_location),robbery_
count=sum(robbery))

#get Geop code for all the cities

for (i in 1:nrow(mydata)) {
  latlon =geocode(mydata$geo_location[i])
  mydata$lon[i] =as.numeric(latlon[1])
  mydata$lat[i] =as.numeric(latlon[2])
}
 Information from URL : http://maps.googleapis.com/maps/api/geocode/
json?address=A&N%20Islands,%20India&sensor=false
.....
 Information from URL : http://maps.googleapis.com/maps/api/geocode/
json?address=West%20Bengal,%20India&sensor=false
```

4. Here you can see that each state has been geotagged with the central coordinates in longitude and latitude duplets.

```
head(mydata)
 # A tibble: 6 × 4
               geo_location robbery_count      lon      lat
                      <chr><dbl><dbl><dbl>
 1        A&N Islands, India            14 10.89779 48.37054
 2    Andhra Pradesh, India          1120 79.73999 15.91290
 3 Arunachal Pradesh, India           138 94.72775 28.21800
 4              Assam, India          1330 92.93757 26.20060
 5              Bihar, India          3106 85.31312 25.09607
 6         Chandigarh, India           134 76.77942 30.73331
#write the data with geocode for future reference
mydata <-mydata[-8,]
row.names(mydata) <-NULL

write.csv(mydata,"Dataset/Crime Data for 2010 from NCRB with geocodes.
csv",row.names =FALSE)
```

5. Create a data frame, with an aggregated number of robberies in the state, its longitude, and its latitude.

```
Robbery_By_State =data.frame(mydata$robbery_count, mydata$lon, mydata$lat)

colnames(Robbery_By_State) <-c('robbery','lon','lat')
```

6. Find the center of India on the map and then pull the map of India to store in IndiaMap.

```
india_center =as.numeric(geocode("India"))
 Information from URL : http://maps.googleapis.com/maps/api/geocode/
json?add
ress=India&sensor=false
IndiaMap <-ggmap(get_googlemap(center=india_center, scale=2, zoom=5,maptype
='terrain'));
 Map from URL : http://maps.googleapis.com/maps/api/
staticmap?center=20.5936
84,78.96288&zoom=5&size=640x640&scale=2&maptype=terrain&sensor=false
```

7. Plot the India map overlaid by orange circles showing the robbery count for each state. The bigger the circle, the higher the robbery rate:

```
circle_scale_amt <-0.005

IndiaMap +geom_point(data=Robbery_By_State,aes(x=lon,y=lat), col="orange",
alpha=0.4, size=Robbery_By_State$robbery*circle_scale_amt) +scale_size_
continuous(range=range(mv_num_collisions$robbery))
```

Looking at the spatial visualizations, it's easy to see the distribution of robbery cases in India. We can quickly do the comparative analysis also by state. In the plots in Figure 4-34, Maharashtra, then UP, and then Bihar top the list of robberies registered in 2010.

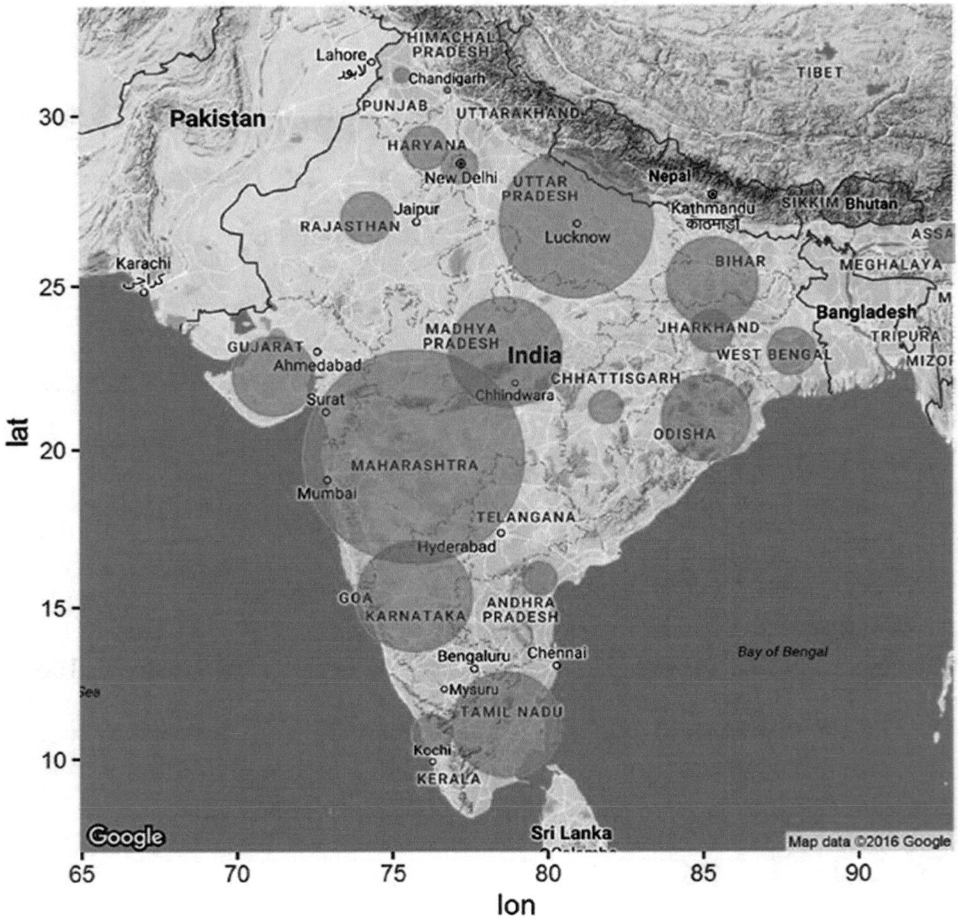

Figure 4-34. *India map with robbery counts in 2010*

4.19 Summary

Data visualization is an art and science at the same time. What information to show comes from scientific reasoning while how to show it comes from the cognitive capabilities of brain. It is proved that the brain processes images faster than numbers, so it becomes very important for a professional to compress the information in meaningful visuals rather than long data feeds.

In this chapter, we discussed many types of visualization plots and charts that can be used to build a story around what the data is telling us. We started with World Bank data and showed how to track the changes in key indicators using line charts and columns charts. We also saw how histograms and density plots save us from generalization our inferences by looking at overall levels, as histograms show the distribution within. Pie charts are a good way to show the contribution of individual components. Boxplots were used to show the extreme values in our dataset. Overall, the correlation plot, heatmaps, and finally bubble charts have many commonalities in terms of the rich information they show in a relatively small real estate of a chart. While similarities exist, you need to carefully choose the right graphs and plots to represent your data.

Waterfall charts were used to show how a sequential flow of information can be captured in more intuitive ways. Similar to waterfall charts are the Sankey plots, drawn for different purposes. Sankey plots show properties of connection among different components in a flow visualization. Dendograms have specific uses in clustering and analysis of similarities among subjects. Time series plots are very important for time-indexed data; using time series plots enables you to see how in recession years the GDP growth went negative among three countries.

Another popular chart is the cohort chart. These charts are very popular in analyzing groups of people over time for some key characteristic changes. We used a credit card example where different cohorts were shown on different time periods from issuance of credit. The last and one of most powerful charts are spatial maps. They are presentations of information on maps. Any data that's geotagged can be presented using spatial maps. Overall, R has scalable libraries to create powerful visualizations.

It's of foremost importance that you understand the audience of your presentation before choosing an appropriate visualization technique. As stated, data visualization has a vast scope and we will continuously use many such plots, charts, and graphs throughout the book.

In the next chapter, we will explore another aspect of data exploration, which is feature engineering. If we have hundreds and thousands of variables or features, how do we decide which particular feature is useful in building a ML model? Such questions will be answered to set the stage to start building our ML model in Chapter 6.

CHAPTER 5

Feature Engineering

In machine learning, feature engineering is a blanket term covering both statistical and business judgment aspects of modeling real-world problems. Feature engineering is a term coined to give due importance to the domain knowledge required to select sets of features for machine learning algorithms. It is one of the reasons that most of the machine learning professionals call it an informal process.

In order to quantify meaningful relationships between the response variable and predictor variables, we need to know the individual properties of the features and how they interact with each other. Descriptive statistics and distribution of features provide us with insight into what they are and how they behave in our dataset.

The learning objectives of this chapter are as follows:

- Introduction to feature engineering
- Feature ranking
- Variable subset selection
- Dimensionality reduction

The chapter includes some hands-on examples to apply the general statistical method to these concepts within the feature engineering space. The latter part of the chapter will discuss some examples to show how business-critical thinking helps feature selection.

The illustrations in this chapter are based on loan default data. The data contain the loss on a given loan. The loss on each loan is graded between 1 and 100. For the cases where the full loan was recovered, the value of loan loss is set to 0, which means there was no default on that loan. A loss of 60 means that only 40% of the loan was recovered. The data is set up to create a default prediction model.

The data feature names are annonymized to bring focus on the statistical quantification of relationship among features. There are some key terms associated with the loan default in financial services industry, Probability of Default (PD), Exposure at

K. Ramasubramanian and A. Singh, *Machine Learning Using R*, https://doi.org/10.1007/978-1-4842-4215-5_5

Default (EAD), and Loss Given Default (LGD). While the focus of this chapter is to show how statistical methods work, you are encouraged to draw parallel analogies to your business problems, in which case a good reference point could be loan default.

5.1 Introduction to Feature Engineering

With technological advances, it's now possible to collect a lot of data at just a fraction of the cost. In many cases, to improve modeling output, we are merging lots of data from third-party sources, external open sources into internal data. This creates huge sets of features for machine learning algorithms. All the features in our consideration set might not be important from a machine learning perspective and even if they are, all of them might not be needed to attain a level of confidence in model predictions.

The other aspect is time and complexity; the machine learning algorithms are resource intensive and time increases exponentially for each feature added to the model. A data scientist has to bring in a balance between this complexity and benefit in the final model accuracy.

To completely understand the feature engineering concepts, we have to focus on two separate but supporting processes:

- Feature selection (or variable selection)
- Business/domain knowledge

The former is statistics-intensive and provides empirical evidence as to why a certain feature or set of features is important for the machine learning algorithm. This is based on quantifiable and comparable metrics created either independent of the response variable or otherwise. The latter is more to put the business logic to make sure the features make sense and provide the right insights the business is looking for.

For instance, suppose the unemployment rate is used for identifying loan defaults in a region. For the set of data, it might be possible that unemployment rate might not be significant at the 95% confidence level, but is significant at the 90% confidence level. If a business believes that unemployment rate is an important variable, then we might want to create an exception in the variable selection where the unemployment rate is captured with relaxed statistical constraints.

The main benefits that come out of a robust and structured variable selection are:

- Improved predictive performance of the model
- Faster and less complex machine learning process
- Better understanding of underlying data relationships
- Explainable and implementable machine learning models/solutions

The first three benefits are intuitive and can be relayed back to our prior discussion. Let's invest some time to give due importance to the fourth point here. Business insights are generally driven from simple and explainable models. The more complicated a machine is, the more difficult it is to explain. Try to think about features as business action points. If the machine being built has features that cannot be explained in clear terms back to the business, the business loses the value as the model output is not actionable. That means the whole purpose of machine learning is lost.

Any model that you develop has to be deployed in the live environment for use by the end users. For a live environment, each added feature in the model means an added data feed into the live system, which in turn may mean accessing a whole new database. This creates a lot of IT system changes and dependencies within the system. The implementation and maintenance costs then have to be weighted upon the inalienability of the model and the essence of keeping so many variables. If the same underlying behavior can be explained with fewer features, implementation should be done with fewer features. Agility to compute and provide quick results often outweighs a better model with more features.

The feature selection methods are broadly divided into three groups—filter, wrapper, and embedded. In the next few sections, we explain these three methods with examples in Section 5.4

5.2 Understanding the Data

The data used in this chapter is credit risk data from a public competition. Credit risk modeling is one of the most involved modeling problems in the banking industry. The process of building a credit risk model is not only complicated in terms of data but also requires in-depth knowledge of business and market dynamics.

> *A credit risk is the risk of default on a debt that may arise from a borrower failing to make required payments.*

A little more background on key terms from credit risk modeling will be helpful for you to relate these data problems to other similar domain problems. We briefly introduce a few key concepts in credit risk modeling.

- *Willingness to pay and ability to pay*: The credit risk model tries to quantify these two aspects of any borrower. Ability to pay can be quantified by studying the financial conditions of the borrower (variable like income, wealth, etc.), while the tough part is measuring willingness to pay, where we use a variable which captures behavioral properties (variables like default history, fraudulent activities, etc.).
- *Probability of default (PD)*: PD is a measure that indicates how likely the borrower is going to default in the next period. The higher the value, the higher the chances of default. It is a measure having value between 0 and 1 (boundary inclusive). Banks want to lend money to borrowers having a low PD.
- *Loss given default (LGD)*: LGD is a measure of how much the lender is likely to lose if the borrower defaults in the next period. Generally, lenders have some kind of collateral with them to limit downside risk of default. In simplistic terms, this measure is the amount lent minus the value of the collateral. This is usually measured as a percentage. Borrowers having high LGDs are a risk.
- *Exposure at default (EAD)*: EAD is the amount that the bank/lender is exposed at the current point in time. This is the amount that the lender is likely to lose if the borrower defaults right now. This is one of the closely watched metrics in any bank credit risk division.

These terms will help you think through how we can influence the information from the same data with a tweaked way to do feature engineering. All these metrics can be predicted from the same loan default data, but the way we go about selecting features will differ.

5.2.1 Data Summary

Data summary of the input data will provide vital information about the data. For this chapter, we need to understand some of the features of the data before we apply different techniques. To show how to apply statistical methods, select the feature set for modeling. The important features that we will be looking are as follows:

- Properties of dependent variable
- Feature availability: continuous or categorical
- Setting up data assumptions

5.2.2 Properties of Dependent Variable

In our dataset, *loss* is the variable used as the dependent variable in the figures in this chapter. The modeling is to be done for credit loss. Loan is a type of credit and we will use credit loss and loan loss interchangeably. The `loss` variable has values between 0 and 100. We will see the `loss` variable's distribution in this chapter.

The following code loads the data and shows the dimension of the dataset created. Dimension means the number of records multiplied by the number of features.

```
Input the data and store in data table

library(data.table)

data <-fread ("Dataset/Loan Default Prediction.csv",header=T, verbose
=FALSE, showProgress =TRUE)

Read 105471 rows and 771 (of 771) columns from 0.476 GB file in 00:01:02
dim(data)
 [1] 105471    771
```

There are 105,471 records with 771 attributes. Out of 771, there is one dependent series and one primary key. We have 769 features to create a feature set for this credit loss model.

We know that the dependent variable is loss on a scale of 0 to 100. For analysis purposes, we will analyze the dependent variable as continuous and discrete. As a continuous variable, we will look at descriptive statistics and, as a discrete variable, we will look at the distribution.

```
#Summary of the data
summary(data$loss)
     Min.  1st Qu.  Median    Mean  3rd Qu.     Max.
   0.0000   0.0000  0.0000  0.7996   0.0000 100.0000
```

The highest loss that is recorded is 100, which is equivalent to saying that all the outstanding credit on the loan was lost. The mean is close to 0 and the first and third quartiles are 0. Certainly the loss cannot be dealt with as a continuous variable, as most of the values are concentrated toward 0. In other words, the number of cases with default is low.

```
hist(data$loss,
main="Histogram for Loss Distribution ",
xlab="Loss",
border="blue",
col="red",
las=0,
breaks=100,
prob =TRUE)
```

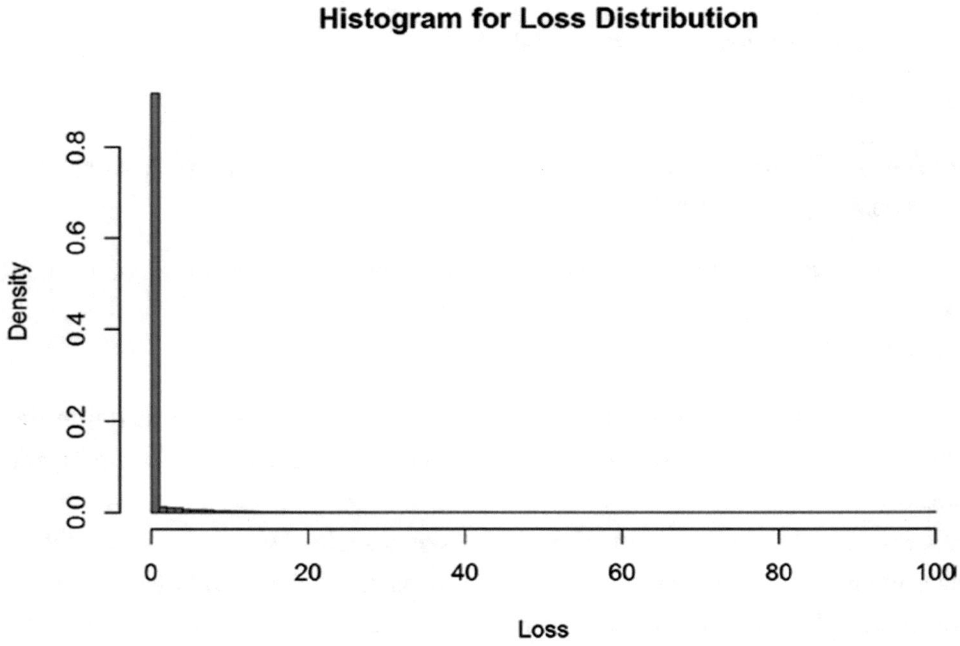

Figure 5-1. *Distribution of loss (including no default)*

The distribution of loss in Figure 5-1 shows that loss is equal to zero for most of the distribution. We can see that using loss as a continuous variable is not possible in this setting. So we will convert our dependent variable into a dichotomous variable, with 0 representing a non-default and 1 a default. The problem is to reduce to the default prediction, and we now know what kind of machine learning algorithm we intend to use down the line. This prior information will help us choose the appropriate feature selection methods and metrics to use in feature selection.

Let's now see for the cases where there is default (i.e., loss not equal to zero), how the loss is distributed (recall the LGD measure).

```
#Sub-set the data into NON Loss and Loss ( e.g., loss > 0)

subset_loss <-subset(data,loss !=0)

#Distribution of cases where there is some loss registered

hist(subset_loss$loss,
main="Histogram for Loss Distribution ( Only Default cases) ",
xlab="Loss",
border="blue",
col="red",
las=0,
breaks=100,
prob =TRUE)
```

Below distribution plot exclude non-default cases, in other words for only use cases where Loss >0.

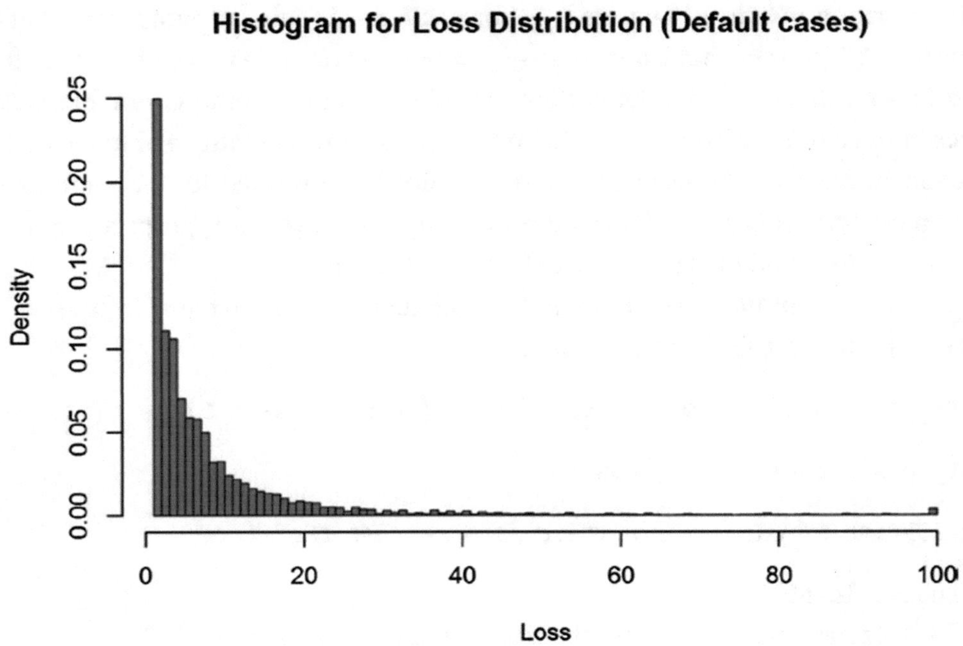

Figure 5-2. *Distribution of loss (excluding no default)*

In more than 90% of the cases, we have a loss below 25%, hence the Loss Given Default (LGD) is low (see Figure 5-2). The company can recover a high amount of what's due. For further discussion around feature selection, we will create a dichotomous variable called `default`, which will be 0 if the loss is equal to 0 and 1 otherwise.

```
default = 0 , there is no default and hence no lossdefault = 1, there is a
default
#Create the default variable

data[,default :=ifelse(data$loss ==0, 0,1)]

#Distribution of defaults
table(data$default)

     0     1
 95688  9783
#Event rate is defined as ratio of default cases in total population
```

```
print(table(data$default)*100/nrow(data))

        0         1
90.724465  9.275535
```

So we have converted our dependent variable into a dichotomous variable and our features selection problem will be geared toward finding the best set of features to model this default behavior for our data. The distribution table states that we have 9.3% of the cases of default in our dataset. This is sometimes called an *event rate* in the model development data.

5.2.3 Features Availability: Continuous or Categorical

The data has 769 features to create a model for the credit loss. We have to identify how many of these features are continuous and categorical. This will allow us to design the feature selection process appropriately, as many metrics are not directly comparable for ordering, e.g., correlation of the continuous variable is different than the correlation measure for categorical variables.

Tip If you don't have any prior knowledge of a feature's valid values, you can treat variables with more than 30 levels as continuous and ones with fewer than 30 levels as categorical variables.

The following code snippet does three things to identify the type of treatment a variable needs to be given, i.e., continuous or categorical:

- Removes the id, loss, and default indicators from this analysis, as these variables are identifier or dependent variable.
- Finds the unique values in each feature; if the number of unique values is less than or equal to 30, assigns that feature to categorical set.
- If the number of unique values is greater than 30, assigns it to be continuous.

This idea is working for us; however, you have be cautious about variables like ZIP code (it is a nominal variable), states (number of states can be more than 30 and they are characters), and other features having character values.

```
continuous <-character()
categorical <-character()
#Write a loop to go over all features and find unique values
p<-1
q<-1
for (i in names(data))
{
  unique_levels =length(unique(data[,get(i)]))

  if(i %in%c("id","loss","default"))
  {
    next;
  }

  else
  {
    if (unique_levels <=30 |is.character(data[,get(i)]))
    {
#     cat("The feature ", i, " is a categorical variable")
      categorical[p] <-i
      p=p+1
# Making the
     data[[i]] <-factor(data[[i]])
    }
    else
    {
#    cat("The feature ", i, " is a continuous variable")
     continuous[q] <-i
     q=q+1

    }
  }
}
```

```
# subtract 1 as one is dependent variable = default
cat("\nTotal number of continuous variables in feature set ",
length(continuous) -1)

 Total number of continuous variables in feature set 717
# subtract 2 as one is loss and one is id
cat("\nTotal number of categorical variable in feature set ",
length(categorical) -2)

   Total number of categorical variable in feature set 49
```

These iterations have divided the data into categorical and continuous variables with each having 49 and 717 features in them, respectively. We will ignore the domain-specific meaning of these features, as our focus is on statistical aspects of feature selection.

5.2.4 Setting Up Data Assumptions

To explain the different aspects of feature selection, we will be using some assumptions:

- We do not have any prior knowledge of feature importance or domain-specific restrictions.
- The machine/model we want to create will predict the dichotomous variable `default`.
- The order of steps is just for illustration; multiple variations do exist.

5.3 Feature Ranking

Feature ranking is one of the most popular methods of identifying the explanatory power of a feature against the set purpose of the model. In our case the purpose is to predict a 0 or 1. The explanatory power has to be captured in a predefined metric, so we can put the features in an ordinal manner.

In our problem setup, we can use the following steps to get feature rankings:

- For each feature fit, use a logistic model (a more elaborate treatment of this topic is covered in Chapter 6) with the dependent variable being `default`.
- Calculate the Gini coefficient. Here, the Gini coefficient is the metric we defined to measure the explanatory power of the feature.
- Rank order features using the Gini coefficient, where a higher Gini coefficient means greater explanatory power of the feature.

`MLmetrics` is a collection of evaluation metrics—including loss, score, and utility functions—that measure regression, classification, and ranking performance. This is a useful package for calculating classifiers' performance metrics. We will be using the function `Gini()` in this package to get the Gini coefficient.

The following code snippet implements the following steps:

- For each feature in data, fits a logistic regression using the `logit` link function.
- Calculates the Gini coefficient on all the data (you can also train on training data and calculate Gini on the testing data).
- Orders all the features by the Gini coefficient (higher to lower).

```
library(MLmetrics)
performance_metric_gini <-data.frame(feature =character(), Gini_value
=numeric())

#Write a loop to go over all features and find unique values
for (feature in names(data))
{
  if(feature %in%c("id","loss","default"))
  {
   next;
  }
```

```
  else
  {
tryCatch({glm_model <-glm(default ~get(feature),data=data,family=binomial(l
ink="logit"));

      predicted_values <-predict.glm(glm_model,newdata=data,type="response");

      Gini_value <-Gini(predicted_values,data$default);

      performance_metric_gini <-rbind(performance_metric_
gini,cbind(feature,Gini_value));},error=function(e){})
  }
}

performance_metric_gini$Gini_value <-as.numeric(as.character(performance_
metric_gini$Gini_value))
#Rank the features by value of Gini coefficient

Ranked_Features <-performance_metric_gini[order(-performance_metric_
gini$Gini_value),]

print("Top 5 Features by Gini Coefficients\n")
 [1] "Top 5 Features by Gini Coefficients\n"
head(Ranked_Features)
     feature Gini_value
 710    f766  0.2689079
 389    f404  0.2688113
 584    f629  0.2521622
 585    f630  0.2506394
 269    f281  0.2503371
 310    f322  0.2447725
```

Tip When you are running loops over large datasets, it is possible that the loop might stop due to some errors. To escape that, consider using the `trycatch()` function in R.

The ranking methods tells us that the top six features by their individual predicted power are f766, f404, f629, f630, f281, and f322. The top feature in the Gini coefficient is 0.268 (or 26.8%). Now using the set of top five features, let's create a logistical model and see the same performance metric.

The following code uses the top six features to fit a logistical model on our data. After fitting the model, it then prints out the Gini coefficient of the model.

```
#Create a logistic model with top 6 features (f766,f404,f629,f630,f281 and f322)

glm_model <-glm(default ~f766 +f404 +f629 +f630 +f281
+f322,data=data,family =binomial(link="logit"));

predicted_values <-predict.glm(glm_model,newdata=data,type="response");

Gini_value <-Gini(predicted_values,data$default);

summary(glm_model)

Call:
glm(formula = default ~ f766 + f404 + f629 + f630 + f281 + f322,
    family = binomial(link = "logit"), data = data)

Deviance Residuals:
    Min       1Q    Median       3Q      Max
-0.7056  -0.4932   -0.4065  -0.3242  3.3407

Coefficients:
             Estimate Std. Error z value Pr(>|z|)
(Intercept) -3.071639   2.160885  -1.421    0.155
f766        -1.609598   2.150991  -0.748    0.454
f404         0.351095   2.147072   0.164    0.870
f629        -0.505835   0.077767  -6.505 7.79e-11 ***
f630        -0.090988   0.057619  -1.579    0.114
f281        -0.004073   0.008245  -0.494    0.621
f322         0.262128   0.055992   4.682 2.85e-06 ***
---
```

```
Signif. codes:  0 '***' 0.001 '**' 0.01 '*' 0.05 '.' 0.1 ' ' 1

(Dispersion parameter for binomial family taken to be 1)

    Null deviance: 65044 on 105147 degrees of freedom
Residual deviance: 62855 on 105141 degrees of freedom
  (323 observations deleted due to missingness)
AIC: 62869

 Number of Fisher Scoring iterations: 6
Gini_value
 [1] 0.2824955
```

The model result shows that four features (f766, f404, f630, and f281) are not significant. The standard errors are very high for these features. This gives us an indication that the features themselves are highly correlated and hence are not adding value by being in the model. As you can see, the Gini coefficient has not improved, even after adding more variables. The reason for the top features being insignificant could be that all of them are highly correlated. To investigate this multicollinearity issue, we will create the correlation matrix for the six features.

```
#Create the correlation matrix for 6 features (f766,f404,f629,f630,f281 and f322)

top_6_feature <-data.frame(data$f766,data$f404,data$f629,data$f630,data$f28
1,data$f322)

cor(top_6_feature, use="complete")
           data.f766  data.f404  data.f629  data.f630  data.f281
 data.f766  1.0000000  0.9996710  0.6830923  0.6420238  0.8067094
 data.f404  0.9996710  1.0000000  0.6827368  0.6416069  0.8065005
 data.f629  0.6830923  0.6827368  1.0000000  0.9114775  0.6515478
 data.f630  0.6420238  0.6416069  0.9114775  1.0000000  0.6102867
 data.f281  0.8067094  0.8065005  0.6515478  0.6102867  1.0000000
 data.f322 -0.7675846 -0.7675819 -0.5536863 -0.5127184 -0.7280321
```

```
           data.f322
data.f766 -0.7675846
data.f404 -0.7675819
data.f629 -0.5536863
data.f630 -0.5127184
data.f281 -0.7280321
data.f322  1.0000000
```

It's clear from the correlation structure that the features f766, f404, f630, and f281 are highly correlated and hence the model results shows them to be insignificant. This exercise shows that while feature ranking helps in measuring and quantifying the individual power of variables, it might not be directly used as a method of variable selection for model development.

Guyon and Elisseeff provide the following criticism for this variable ranking method:

> *[The] variable ranking method leads to the selection of a redundant subset. The same performance could possibly be achieved with a smaller subset of complementary variables.*

You can verify this fact by looking at the correlation matrix and the significant variables in the model. The two significant variables are complementary and provide the similar Gini coefficient.

5.4 Variable Subset Selection

Variable subset selection is the process of selecting a subset of features (or variables) to use in the machine learning model. In previous section, we tried to create a subset of variables using the individual ranking of variables but observed the limitations of feature ranking as a variable selection method. Now we formally introduce the process of variable subset selection. We will be discussing one method from each broad category and will show an example using the credit loss data. You are encouraged to compare the results and assess what method suits your machine learning problem best.

Isabelle Guyon and Andre Elisseeff provided comprehensive introduction to various methods of variable (or feature) selection. They call the criteria for different methods measuring "usefulness" or "relevance" of features to qualify them to be part of the variable subset. The three broad methods—filter, wrapper, and embedded—are illustrated with our credit loss data.

5.4.1 Filter Method

The filter method uses the intrinsic properties of variables, ignoring the machine learning method itself. This method is useful for classification problems where each variable adds incremental classification power.

Criterion: Measure feature/feature subset "relevance"

Search: Order features by individual feature ranking or nested subset of features

Assessment: Using statistical tests

Statistical Approaches

1. Information gain
2. Chi-square test
3. Fisher score
4. Correlation coefficient
5. Variance threshold

Results

1. Relatively more robust against overfitting
2. Might not select the most "useful" set of features

For this method we will be showing the variance threshold approach, which is based on the basic concept that the variables that have high variability also have higher information in them. Variance threshold is a simple baseline approach. In this method, we remove all the variables having variance less than a threshold. This method automatically removes the variables having zero variance.

Note The features in our dataset are not standardized and hence we cannot do direct comparison of variances. We will be using the coefficient of variation (CV) to choose the top five features for model building. Also, the following exercise is shown only for continuous features; for categorical variables, use a chi.square test.

Coefficient of Variance (CoV), also known as relative standard deviation, provides a standardized measure of dispersion of a variable. It is defined as the ratio of standard deviation to the mean of the variable:

$$c_v = \frac{\sigma}{\mu}$$

Here, we calculate the mean and variance of each continuous variable, then we take a ratio of them to calculate the Coefficient of Variance (CoV). The features are then ordered by decreasing coefficient of variance.

```
#Calculate the variance of each individual variable and standardize the
variance by dividing with mean()

coefficient_of_variance <-data.frame(feature =character(), cov =numeric())

#Write a loop to go over all features and calculate variance
for (feature in names(data))
{
  if(feature %in%c("id","loss","default"))
  {
   next;
  }
  else if(feature %in%continuous)
  {
tryCatch(
      {cov <-abs(sd(data[[feature]], na.rm =TRUE)/mean(data[[feature]],na.
rm =TRUE));
      if(cov !=Inf){
      coefficient_of_variance <-rbind(coefficient_of_variance,cbind(feature,
cov));} else {next;}},error=function(e){})

  }
  else
  {
    next;
  }
}
```

```
coefficient_of_variance$cov <-as.numeric(as.character(coefficient_of_
variance$cov))

#Order the list by highest to lowest coefficient of variation

Ranked_Features_cov <-coefficient_of_variance[order(-coefficient_of_
variance$cov),]

print("Top 5 Features by Coefficient of Variance\n")
 [1] "Top 5 Features by Coefficient of Variance\n"
head(Ranked_Features_cov)
     feature       cov
 295    f338 164.46714
 378    f422 140.48973
 667    f724  87.22657
 584    f636  78.06823
 715    f775  70.24765
 666    f723  46.31984
```

The coefficient of variance provided the top six features by order of their CoV values. The features that show up in the top six (f338, f422, f724, f636, f775, and f723) are then used to fit a binomial logistic model. We calculate the Gini coefficient of the model to assess if these variables improve the Gini over individual features, as discussed earlier.

```
#Create a logistic model with top 6 features (f338,f422,f724,f636,f775 and f723)

glm_model <-glm(default ~f338 +f422 +f724 +f636 +f775
+f723,data=data,family
=binomial(link="logit"));

predicted_values <-predict.glm(glm_model,newdata=data,type="response");

Gini_value <-Gini(predicted_values,data$default);

summary(glm_model)

 Call:
 glm(formula = default ~ f338 + f422 + f724 + f636 + f775 + f723,
     family = binomial(link = "logit"), data = data)
```

```
Deviance Residuals:
    Min       1Q   Median       3Q      Max
-1.0958  -0.4839  -0.4477  -0.4254   2.6363

Coefficients:
              Estimate Std. Error  z value Pr(>|z|)
(Intercept) -2.206e+00  1.123e-02 -196.426  < 2e-16 ***
f338        -1.236e-25  2.591e-25   -0.477    0.633
f422         1.535e-01  1.373e-02   11.183  < 2e-16 ***
f724         1.392e+01  9.763e+00    1.426    0.154
f636        -1.198e-06  2.198e-06   -0.545    0.586
f775         6.412e-02  1.234e-02    5.197 2.03e-07 ***
f723        -5.181e+00  4.623e+00   -1.121    0.262
---
Signif. codes:  0 '***' 0.001 '**' 0.01 '*' 0.05 '.' 0.1 ' ' 1

(Dispersion parameter for binomial family taken to be 1)

    Null deviance: 59064 on 90687 degrees of freedom
Residual deviance: 58898 on 90681 degrees of freedom
  (14783 observations deleted due to missingness)
AIC: 58912

 Number of Fisher Scoring iterations: 6
cat("The Gini Coefficient for the fitted model is ",Gini_value);
 The Gini Coefficient for the fitted model is   0.1445109
```

This method does not show any improvement on the number of significant variables among the top six, i.e., only two features are significant—f422 and f775. Also, the model's overall performance is worse, i.e., the Gini coefficient is 0.144 (14.4% only). For completeness of analysis purposes, let's create the correlation matrix for these six features. We want to see if the variables are correlated and hence are insignificant.

```
#Create the correlation matrix for 6 features (f338,f422,f724,f636,f775 and f723)

top_6_feature <-data.frame(as.double(data$f338),as.double(data$f422),as.
double(data$f724),as.double(data$f636),as.double(data$f775),as.
double(data$f723))
```

```
cor(top_6_feature, use="complete")
                       as.double.data.f338. as.double.data.f422.
 as.double.data.f338.          1.000000e+00          0.009542857
 as.double.data.f422.          9.542857e-03          1.000000000
 as.double.data.f724.          4.335480e-02          0.006249059
 as.double.data.f636.         -6.708839e-05          0.011116608
 as.double.data.f775.          5.537591e-03          0.050666549
 as.double.data.f723.          5.048078e-02          0.005556227
                       as.double.data.f724. as.double.data.f636.
 as.double.data.f338.          0.0433548003        -6.708839e-05
 as.double.data.f422.          0.0062490589         1.111661e-02
 as.double.data.f724.          1.0000000000        -1.227539e-04
 as.double.data.f636.         -0.0001227539         1.000000e+00
 as.double.data.f775.          0.0121451180        -7.070228e-03
 as.double.data.f723.          0.9738147134        -2.157437e-04
                       as.double.data.f775. as.double.data.f723.
 as.double.data.f338.           0.005537591         0.0504807821
 as.double.data.f422.           0.050666549         0.0055562270
 as.double.data.f724.           0.012145118         0.9738147134
 as.double.data.f636.          -0.007070228        -0.0002157437
 as.double.data.f775.           1.000000000         0.0190753853
 as.double.data.f723.           0.019075385         1.0000000000
```

You can clearly see that the correlation structure is not dominating the feature set, but the individual feature relevance is driving their selection into the modeling subset. This is expected as well as we selected the variables based on CoV, which is independent of any other variable.

5.4.2 Wrapper Methods

Wrapper methods use a search algorithm to search the space of possible feature subsets and evaluate each subset by running a model on the subset. Wrappers can be computationally expensive and have the risk of overfitting to the model.

***Criterion*:** Measure feature subset "usefulness"

***Search*:** Search the space of all feature subsets and select the set with the highest score

***Assessment*:** Cross-validation

Statistical Approaches

1. Recursive feature elimination
2. Sequential feature selection algorithms
    1. Sequential Forward Selection
    2. Sequential Backward Selection
    3. Plus-l Minus-r Selection
    4. Bidirectional Search
    5. Sequential Floating Selection
3. Genetic algorithm

Results

1. Give the most useful features for model building
2. Can cause overfitting

We will be discussing sequential methods for illustration purposes. The most popular sequential methods are forward and backward selection. A similar variation of both combined is called a *stepwise* method.

Steps in a forward variable selection algorithm are as follows:

1. Choose a model with only one variable, which gives the maximum value in your evaluation function.
2. Add the next variable that improves the evaluation function by a maximum value.
3. Keep repeating Step 2 until there is no more improvement by adding a new variable.

As you can see, this method is computationally intensive and iterative. It's important to start with a set of variables carefully chosen for the problem. Using all the features available might not be cost effective. Filter methods can help shorten your list of variables to a manageable set for wrapper methods.

To set up the illustrative example, let’s take a subset of 10 features from the total set of features. Let's have the top five continuous variables from our filter method output and randomly choose five from the categorical variables.

```
#Pull 5 variables we had from highest coefficient of variation (from filter method)(f338,f422,f724,f636 and f775)

predictor_set <-c("f338","f422","f724","f636","f775")

#Randomly Pull 5 variables from categorical variable set ( Reader can apply filter method to categorical variable and can choose these 5 variables systematically as well)
set.seed(101);
ind <-sample(1:length(categorical), 5, replace=FALSE)
p<-1
for (i in ind)
{
  predictor_set [5+p] <-categorical[i]
  p=p+1
}

#Print the set of 10 variables we will be working with

print(predictor_set)
  [1] "f338" "f422" "f724" "f636" "f775" "f222" "f33" "f309" "f303" "f113"
#Replaced f33 by f93 as f33 does not have levels

predictor_set[7] <- "f93"

#Print final list of variables

print(predictor_set)
  [1] "f338" "f422" "f724" "f636" "f775" "f222" "f93" "f309" "f303" "f113"
```

We are preparing to predict the probability of someone defaulting in the next one-year time period. Our objective is to select the model based on the following characteristics:

- A fewer number of predictors is preferable
- Penalize a model having a lot of predictors
- Penalize a model for a bad fit

To measure these effects, we will be using the Akaike Information Criterion (AIC) measure as the evaluation metric. AIC is founded on the information theory; it measures the quality of a model relative to other models. While comparing it to other models, it deals with the tradeoff between the goodness of the fit of the model and the complexity of the model. Complexity of the model is represented by the number of variables in the model, where more variables mean greater complexity.

In statistics, AIC is defined as:

$$AIC = 2k - 2\ln(L) = 2k + Deviance$$

where k is the number of parameters (or features).

Note AIC is a relative measure; hence, it does not tell you anything about the quality of the model in the absolute sense.

To illustrate the feature selection by forward selection, we need to first develop two models, one with all features and one with no features:

- *Full model*: A model with all the variables included in it. This model provides an upper limit on the complexity of the model.
- *Null model*: A model with no variables in it, just an intercept term. This model provides a lower limit on the complexity of the model.

Once we have these two models, we can start the feature selection based on the AIC measure. These models are important for AIC to use as a measure of model fit, as AIC will be measured relative to these extreme cases in the model. Let's first create a full model with all the predictors and see its summary (the output is truncated):

```
# Create a small modeling dataset with only predictors and dependent variable
library(data.table)
data_model <-data[,.(id,f338,f422,f724,f636,f775,f222,f93,f309,f303,f113,de
fault),]
#make sure to remove the missing cases to resolve errors regarding null values

data_model<-na.omit(data_model)
```

```
#Full model uses all the 10 variables
full_model <-glm(default ~f338 +f422 +f724 +f636 +f775 +f222 +f93 +f309
+f303 +f113,data=data_model,family=binomial(link="logit"))

#Summary of the full model
summary(full_model)

 Call:
 glm(formula = default ~ f338 + f422 + f724 + f636 + f775 + f222 +
     f93 + f309 + f303 + f113, family = binomial(link = "logit"),
     data = data_model)

Deviance Residuals:
    Min        1Q    Median        3Q       Max
-0.9844  -0.4803   -0.4380   -0.4001    2.7606

Coefficients:
              Estimate Std. Error z value Pr(>|z|)
(Intercept) -2.423e+00  3.146e-02 -77.023  < 2e-16 ***
f338        -1.379e-25  2.876e-25  -0.480 0.631429
f422         1.369e-01  1.387e-02   9.876  < 2e-16 ***
f724         3.197e+00  1.485e+00   2.152 0.031405 *
f636        -9.976e-07  1.851e-06  -0.539 0.589891
f775         5.965e-02  1.287e-02   4.636 3.55e-06 ***
......Output truncated
---
 Signif. codes:  0 '***' 0.001 '**' 0.01 '*' 0.05 '.' 0.1 ' ' 1

 (Dispersion parameter for binomial family taken to be 1)

     Null deviance: 58874 on 90287 degrees of freedom
 Residual deviance: 58189 on 90214 degrees of freedom
 AIC: 58337

Number of Fisher Scoring iterations: 12
```

This output shows the summary of the full model build using all 10 variables. Now, let's similarly create the null model:

```
#Null model uses no variables
null_model <-glm(default ~1 ,data=data_model,family=binomial(link="logit"))

#Summary of the full model
summary(null_model)
```

```
 Call:
 glm(formula = default ~ 1, family = binomial(link = "logit"),
     data = data_model)

Deviance Residuals:
    Min       1Q    Median       3Q      Max
-0.4601  -0.4601  -0.4601  -0.4601   2.1439

Coefficients:
            Estimate Std. Error z value Pr(>|z|)
(Intercept) -2.19241    0.01107    -198   <2e-16 ***
---
Signif. codes:  0 '***' 0.001 '**' 0.01 '*' 0.05 '.' 0.1 ' ' 1

(Dispersion parameter for binomial family taken to be 1)

    Null deviance: 58874 on 90287 degrees of freedom
Residual deviance: 58874 on 90287 degrees of freedom
AIC: 58876

Number of Fisher Scoring iterations: 4
```

At this stage, we have seen the extreme model performance, having all the variables in the model and a model without any variables (basically the historical average of the dependent variable). With these extreme models, we will perform forward selection with the null model and start adding variables to it.

Forward selection will be done in iterations over the variable subset. Observe that the base model for the first iteration is the null model with AIC of 58876. Below that is the list of variables to choose from to add to the model.

```
#summary of forward selection method
forwards <-step(null_model,scope=list(lower=formula(null_
model),upper=formula(full_model)), direction="forward")
 Start:  AIC=58876.26
 default ~ 1

        Df Deviance    AIC
 + f222  7    58522  58538
 + f422  1    58743  58747
 + f113  7    58769  58785
 + f303 24    58780  58830
 + f775  1    58841  58845
 + f93   7    58837  58853
 + f309 23    58806  58854
 + f724  1    58870  58874
 <none>       58874  58876
 + f636  1    58873  58877
 + f338  1    58874  58878
```

Iteration 1: The model added f222 in the model.

```
 Step:  AIC=58538.39
 default ~ f222

        Df Deviance    AIC
 + f422  1    58405  58423
 + f113  7    58461  58491
 + f303 24    58434  58498
 + f775  1    58495  58513
 + f93   7    58486  58516
 + f309 23    58462  58524
 + f724  1    58518  58536
 <none>       58522  58538
 + f636  1    58522  58540
 + f338  1    58522  58540
```

Iteration 2: The model added f422 in the model.

```
Step:  AIC=58422.87
default ~ f222 + f422

       Df Deviance   AIC
+ f113  7    58346 58378
+ f303 24    58323 58389
+ f93   7    58370 58402
+ f775  1    58383 58403
+ f309 23    58353 58417
+ f724  1    58401 58421
<none>       58405 58423
+ f636  1    58404 58424
+ f338  1    58404 58424
```

Iteration 3: The model added f113 in the model.

```
Step:  AIC=58377.8
default ~ f222 + f422 + f113

       Df Deviance   AIC
+ f303 24    58265 58345
+ f775  1    58325 58359
+ f309 23    58295 58373
+ f724  1    58342 58376
<none>       58346 58378
+ f636  1    58345 58379
+ f338  1    58345 58379
+ f93   7    58338 58384
```

Iteration 4: The model added f303 in the model.

```
Step:  AIC=58345.04
default ~ f222 + f422 + f113 + f303

       Df Deviance   AIC
+ f775  1    58245 58327
+ f724  1    58261 58343
<none>       58265 58345
+ f636  1    58264 58346
```

```
+ f338  1    58265  58347
+ f309 23    58225  58351
+ f93   7    58257  58351
```

Iteration 5: The model added f775 in the model.

```
Step:  AIC=58326.96
default ~ f222 + f422 + f113 + f303 + f775

       Df Deviance   AIC
+ f724  1    58241  58325
<none>       58245  58327
+ f636  1    58244  58328
+ f338  1    58244  58328
+ f309 23    58202  58330
+ f93   7    58237  58333
```

Iteration 6: The model added f724 in the model.

```
Step:  AIC=58325.08
default ~ f222 + f422 + f113 + f303 + f775 + f724

       Df Deviance   AIC
<none>       58241  58325
+ f636  1    58240  58326
+ f338  1    58240  58326
+ f309 23    58199  58329
+ f93   7    58233  58331
```

In last iteration, i.e., iteration six, you can see that our model has reached the minimal set of variables. The next suggestion is `<none>`, which means we are better off not adding any variables to the model. Now let's see how our final forward selection model looks:

```
#Summary of final model with forward selection process
formula(forwards)
 default ~ f222 + f422 + f113 + f303 + f775 + f724
```

The forward selection method says that the best model with AIC criteria can be created with these six features: f222, f422, f113, f303, f775, and f724. Other features selection methods, like backward selection, stepwise selection, etc. can be done in a similar manner. In the next section, we introduce embedded methods that are computationally better than wrapper methods.

5.4.3 Embedded Methods

Embedded methods are similar to wrapper methods because they also optimize the objective function, usually a model of performance evaluation functions. The difference with the wrapper method is that an intrinsic model building metric is used during the learning of the model. Essentially, this is a search problem but a guided search, and hence is computationally less expensive.

Criterion: Measure feature subset "usefulness"

Search: Search the space of all feature subsets guided by the learning process

Assessment: Cross-validation

Statistical Approaches

1. L1 (LASSO) regularization
2. Decision tree
3. Forward selection with Gram-Schimdth orthogonalization
4. Gradient descent methods

Results

1. Similar to wrapper but with guided search
2. Less computationally expensive
3. Less prone to overfitting

For this method, we will be showing a regularization technique. In machine learning space, *regularization* is the process of introducing additional information to prevent overfitting while searching through the variable subset space. In this section, we will show an illustration of L1 regularization for variable selection.

L1 regularization for variable selection is also called LASSO (Least Absolute Shrinkage and Selection Operator). This method was introduced by Robert Tibshirani in his famous 1996 paper titled "Regression Shrinkage and Selection via the Lasso," published in the *Journal of the Royal Statistical Society*.

In L1 or LASSO regression, we add a penalty term against the complexity to reduce the degree of overfitting or the variance of the model by adding bias. So the objective function to minimize looks like this:

$$\text{regularization cost} = \text{cost} + \text{regularization penalty}$$

In LASSO regularization, the general form is given for the objective function:

$$\frac{1}{N}\sum_{i=1}^{N} f(x_i, y_i, \alpha, \beta)$$

The LASSO regularized version of the estimator will be the solution to:

$$\min_{\alpha,\beta} \frac{1}{N}\sum_{i=1}^{N} f(x_i, y_i, \alpha, \beta) \ \textit{subject to} \ \|\beta\|_1 \le t$$

where only β is penalized, while α is free to take any allowed value. Adding the regularization cost makes our objective function minimize the regularization cost.

The objective function for the penalized logistic regression uses the negative binomial log-likelihood, and is as follows:

$$\min_{(\beta_0,\beta)\in\mathbb{R}^{p+1}} -\left[\frac{1}{N}\sum_{i=1}^{N} y_i \cdot \left(\beta_0 + x_i^T\beta\right) - \log\left(1 + e^{\left(\beta_0 + x_i^T\beta\right)}\right)\right] + \lambda\left[(1-\alpha)\|\beta\|_2^2 / 2 + \alpha\|\beta\|_1\right].$$

Logistic regression is often plagued with degeneracy when p>Np>N and exhibits wild behavior even when N is close to p; the elastic-net penalty alleviates these issues and regularizes and selects variables as well.

We will run this example on a set of 10 continuous variables in the dataset.

```
#Create data frame with dependent and independent variables (Remove NA)

data_model <-na.omit(data)

y <-as.matrix(data_model$default)

x <-as.matrix(subset(data_model, select=continuous[250:260]))

library("glmnet")
We will be using package glmnet() to show the
#Fit a model with dependent variable of binomial family
fit =glmnet(x,y, family="binomial")
```

```
#Summary of fit model
summary(fit)
            Length Class     Mode
a0           44    -none-    numeric
beta        440    dgCMatrix S4
df           44    -none-    numeric
dim           2    -none-    numeric
lambda       44    -none-    numeric
dev.ratio    44    -none-    numeric
nulldev       1    -none-    numeric
npasses       1    -none-    numeric
jerr          1    -none-    numeric
offset        1    -none-    logical
classnames    2    -none-    character
call          4    -none-    call
nobs          1    -none-    numeric
```

Figure 5-3 shows the plot between the fraction of deviance explained by each of these 10 variables.

```
#Plot the output of glmnet fit model
plot (fit, xvar="dev", label=TRUE)
```

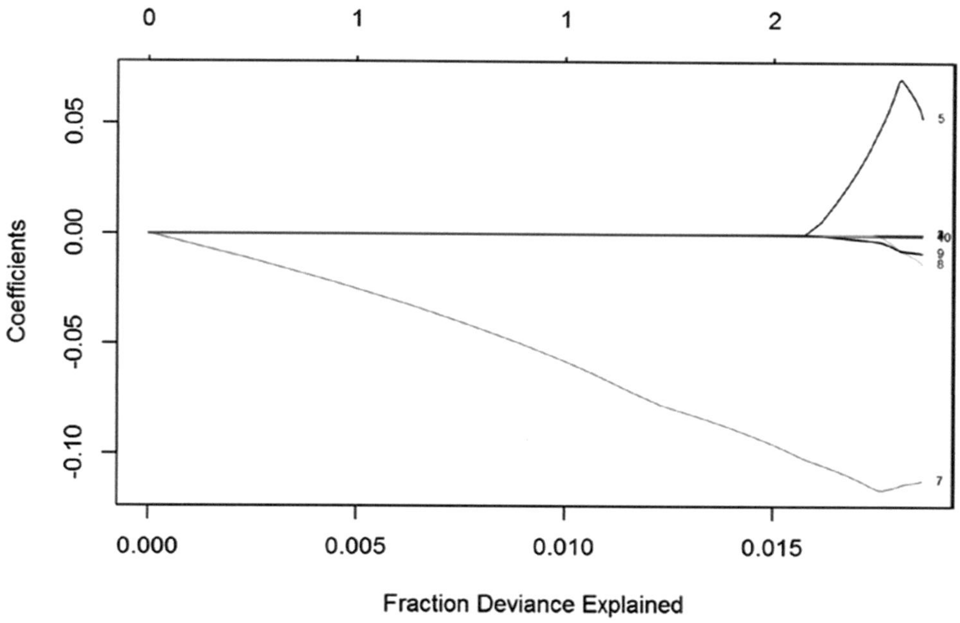

Figure 5-3. *Coefficient and fraction of deviance explained by each feature/variable*

In the plot with 10 variables shown in Figure 5-3, you can see the coefficient of all the variables except that #7 and #5 are 0. As the next step, we will cross-validate our fit. For logistic regression, we will use `cv.glmnet`, which has similar arguments and usage in Gaussian. For instance, let's use a misclassification error as the criteria for 10-fold cross-validation.

```
#Fit a cross-validated binomial model
fit_logistic =cv.glmnet(x,y, family="binomial", type.measure ="class")

#Summary of fitted Cross-Validated Linear Model

summary(fit_logistic)
Length Class  Mode
lambda     43     -none- numeric
cvm        43     -none- numeric
cvsd       43     -none- numeric
cvup       43     -none- numeric
cvlo       43     -none- numeric
nzero      43     -none- numeric
```

```
name          1     -none- character
glmnet.fit 13      lognet list
lambda.min  1      -none- numeric
lambda.1se  1      -none- numeric
```

The plot in Figure 5-4 is explaining how the misclassification rate changes over our set of features brought into the model. The plot shows that the model is pretty bad, as the variables we provided perform badly on the data.

```
#Plot the results
plot (fit_logistic)
```

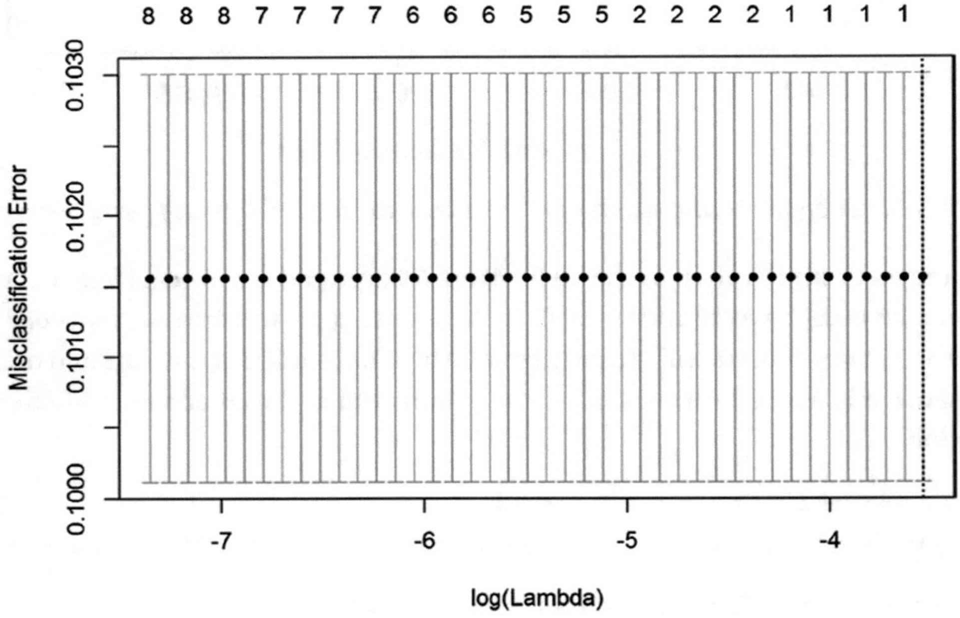

***Figure 5-4.** Misclassification error and log of penalization factor (lambda)*

For a good model, Figure 5-4 will show an upward trend in the red dots. This is when you know what variability you are measuring in your dataset.

We can now pull the regularization factor from the glmnet() fit model. We pulled out the variable coefficient and variable names action.

```
#Print the minimum lambda - regularization factor
print(fit_logistic$lambda.min)
```

```
 [1] 0.003140939
print(fit_logistic$lambda.1se)
 [1] 0.03214848
#Against the lambda minimum value we can get the coefficients
param <-coef(fit_logistic, s="lambda.min")

param <-as.data.frame(as.matrix(param))

param$feature<-rownames(param)

#The list of variables suggested by the embedded method

param_embeded <-param[param$`1`>0,]

print(param_embeded)
                  1 feature
 f279 8.990477e-03    f279
 f298 2.275977e-02    f298
 f322 1.856906e-01    f322
 f377 1.654554e-04    f377
 f452 1.326603e-04    f452
 f453 1.137532e-05    f453
 f471 1.548517e+00    f471
 f489 1.741923e-02    f489
```

The final features suggested by the LASSO method are f279, f298, f322, f377, f452, f453, f471, and f489. Feature selection is a very statistically intense topic. You are encouraged to read more about the methods and make sure their chosen methodology fits the business problem you are trying to solve. In most of the real scenarios, data scientists have to design a mixture of techniques to get the desired set of variables for machine learning.

5.5 Principal Component Analysis

In recent years, there has been explosion in the amount as well as the type of data available at the data scientist's disposal. The traditional machine learning algorithms partly break down because of the volume of data and mostly because of the number of variables associated with each observation. The *dimension* of the data is the number of variables we have for each observation in our data.

In machine learning problems, the addition of each feature into the dataset exponentially increases the requirement of data points to train the model. The learning algorithm needs an enormous amount of data to search the right model in the higher dimensional space. With a fixed number of training samples, the predictive power reduces as the dimensionality increases, and this is known as the *Hughes* phenomenon (named after Gordon F. Hughes).

Dimensionality reduction is a process of features extraction rather than a feature selection process. Feature extraction is the process of transforming the data in the high-dimensional space to a space with fewer dimensions. The data transformation may be linear, as in Principal Component Analysis (PCA), but many nonlinear dimensionality reduction techniques also exist. For multidimensional data, tensor representation can be used in dimensionality reduction through multilinear subspace learning. For example, by use of PCA, you can reduce a set of variables into a smaller set of variables (principal components) to model with, e.g., rather than using all 100 features in raw form, you can use the top 10 PCA factors to build the model with similar performance to the actual full model.

PCA is based on the covariance matrix; it is a second order method. A covariance matrix is a matrix whose element in the i, j position is the covariance between the ith and jth elements of a random vector.

For illustration of PCA, we will work with 10 randomly chosen continuous variables from our data and create the principal components and check their significance in explaining the data.

Here are the steps for principal component analysis:

1. Load the data as a data frame.
2. Normalize/scale the data.
3. Apply the `prcomp()` function to get the principal components.

This performs a principal components analysis on the given data matrix and returns the results as an object of class `prcomp`.

```
#Take a subset of 10 features
pca_data <-data[,.(f381,f408,f495,f529,f549,f539,f579,f634,f706,f743)]

pca_data <-na.omit(pca_data)
```

```
head(pca_data)
       f381 f408   f495        f529  f549 f539   f579   f634    f706
 1: 1598409    5 238.58 1921993.90 501.0  552 462.61  0.261  4.1296
 2:  659959    6   5.98  224932.72 110.0   76  93.77 11.219  4.1224
 3: 2036578   13  33.61  192046.42 112.0  137 108.60 16.775  9.2215
 4:  536256    4 258.23  232373.41 161.0  116 127.84  1.120  3.2036
 5: 2264524   26   1.16   52265.58  21.0   29  20.80 17.739 21.0674
 6: 5527421   22  38.91  612209.01 375.9  347 317.27 11.522 17.8663
         f743
 1:    -21.82
 2:    -72.44
 3:    -79.48
 4:     18.15
 5: -10559.05
 6:   8674.08

#Normalize the data before applying PCA
 analysis mean=0, and sd=1
scaled_pca_data <-scale(pca_data)

head(scaled_pca_data)
           f381       f408       f495       f529       f549       f539
 [1,] -0.5692025 -0.6724669  1.7551841  0.4825810  0.9085923  0.9507127
 [2,] -0.6549414 -0.6186983 -0.9505976 -0.4712597 -0.5448800 -0.6449880
 [3,] -0.5291705 -0.2423176 -0.6291842 -0.4897436 -0.5374454 -0.4404970
 [4,] -0.6662432 -0.7262356  1.9837680 -0.4670777 -0.3552967 -0.5108955
 [5,] -0.5083448  0.4566750 -1.0066675 -0.5683081 -0.8757215 -0.8025467
 [6,] -0.2102394  0.2416004 -0.5675306 -0.2535894  0.4435555  0.2634886
           f579        f634       f706       f743
 [1,]  1.0324757 -0.30383519 -0.5885608 -0.1716417
 [2,] -0.5546476  0.06876713 -0.5890247 -0.1751343
 [3,] -0.4908339  0.25768651 -0.2604470 -0.1756200
 [4,] -0.4080440 -0.27462681 -0.6482307 -0.1688839
 [5,] -0.8686385  0.29046517  0.5028836 -0.8986722
 [6,]  0.4070758  0.07906997  0.2966099  0.4283437
```

Do the decomposition on the scaled series:

```
pca_results <-prcomp(scaled_pca_data)

print(pca_results)
 Standard deviations:
  [1] 1.96507747 1.63138621 0.98482612 0.96399979 0.92767640 0.61171578
  [7] 0.55618915 0.13051700 0.12485945 0.03347933

 Rotation:
                PC1          PC2         PC3         PC4          PC5
 f381  0.05378102  0.467799305  0.12132602 -0.42802089  0.126159741
 f408  0.15295858  0.564941709 -0.01768741 -0.07653169  0.024978144
 f495 -0.20675453 -0.006500783 -0.16011133 -0.40648723 -0.872112347
 f529 -0.43704261  0.071515698  0.03229563  0.02515962  0.023404863
 f549 -0.48355364  0.131867970  0.03001595  0.07933850  0.098468782
 f539 -0.49110704  0.119977024  0.03264945  0.06070189  0.084331260
 f579 -0.48599970  0.130907456  0.03066637  0.07796726  0.098436970
 f634  0.08047589  0.148642810  0.80498132  0.42520275 -0.369686177
 f706  0.13666005  0.563301330 -0.06671534 -0.04782415  0.003828164
 f743  0.05999412  0.261771729 -0.55039555  0.66778245 -0.243211544
                PC6         PC7          PC8         PC9          PC10
 f381 -0.73377400 -0.14656999  0.020865868  0.06391263  2.449224e-03
 f408  0.33818854  0.09731467  0.100148531 -0.71887123  1.864559e-03
 f495  0.05113531 -0.05328517  0.010515158 -0.01387541  2.371417e-03
 f529 -0.16222155  0.87477550  0.099118491  0.01647113  3.417335e-03
 f549  0.10180105 -0.29558279  0.504078886  0.07149433 -6.123361e-01
 f539  0.02135767 -0.16116039 -0.811700032 -0.13982619 -1.664926e-01
 f579  0.09037093 -0.27164477  0.222859021  0.03262620  7.728324e-01
 f634 -0.07273691 -0.01754913 -0.002658235  0.01905427 -2.230924e-05
 f706  0.42035273  0.10600450 -0.130052945  0.67259788 -5.277646e-03
 f743 -0.34249087 -0.04793683  0.007771732 -0.01404485  3.873828e-04
```

Here is the summary of 10 principal components we get after applying the `prcomp()` function.

```
summary(pca_results)
 Importance of components:
                          PC1    PC2     PC3     PC4     PC5     PC6
Standard deviation     1.9651 1.6314 0.98483 0.96400 0.92768 0.61172
Proportion of Variance 0.3861 0.2661 0.09699 0.09293 0.08606 0.03742
Cumulative Proportion  0.3861 0.6523 0.74928 0.84221 0.92827 0.96569
                           PC7    PC8     PC9    PC10
Standard deviation     0.55619 0.1305 0.12486 0.03348
Proportion of Variance 0.03093 0.0017 0.00156 0.00011
Cumulative Proportion  0.99663 0.9983 0.99989 1.00000
```

The plot in Figure 5-5 shows the variance explained by each principal component. You can see that the first five principal components will be able to present ~90% of the information stored in 10 variables.

```
plot(pca_results)
```

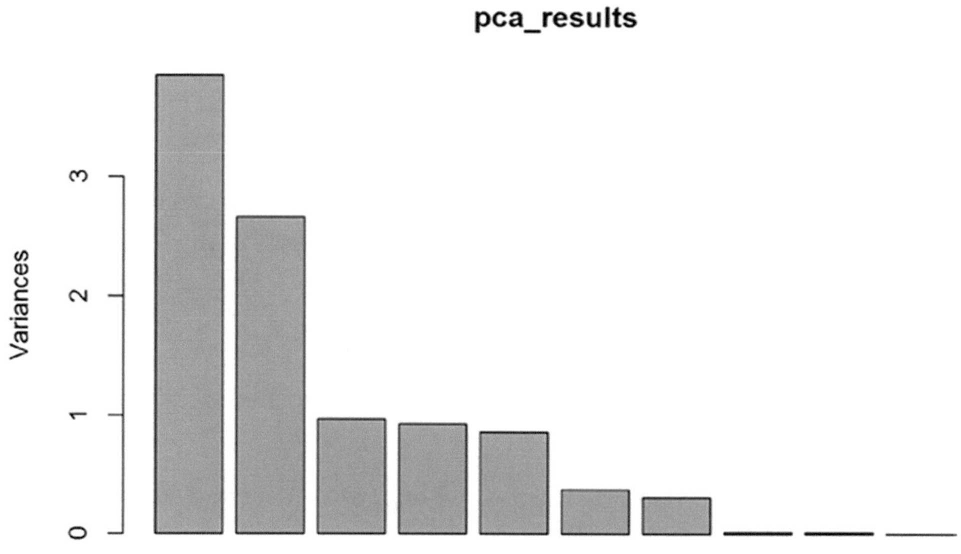

***Figure 5-5.** Variance explained by principal components*

The plot in Figure 5-6 is a relationship between principal component 1 and principal component 2. As we know, the decomposition is orthogonal, and we can see the orthogonality in the plot by looking at the 90 degrees between PC1 and PC2.

```
#Create the biplot with principal components
biplot(pca_results, col =c("red", "blue"))
```

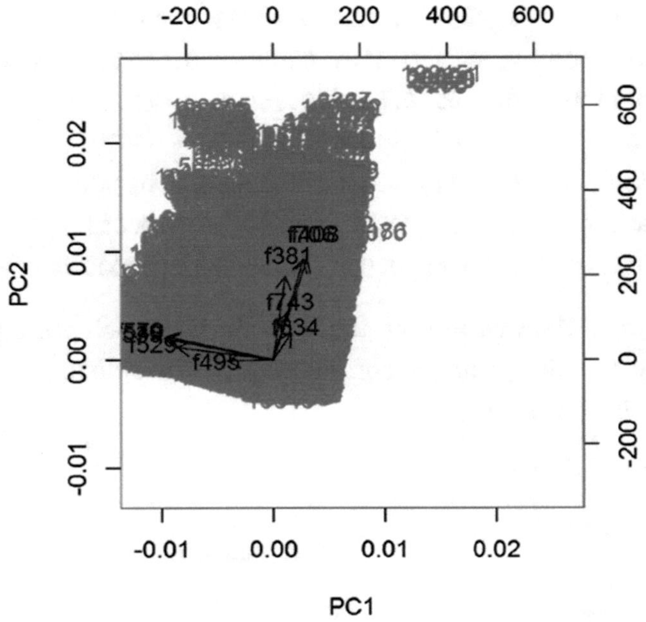

***Figure 5-6.** Orthogonality of principal components 1 and 2*

So instead of using 10 variables for machine learning, you can use these top five principal components to train the model and still preserve 90% of the information.

Advantages of principal component analysis include:

- Reduces the time and storage space required.
- Removes multicollinearity and improves the performance of the machine learning model.
- Makes it easier to visualize the data when reduced to very low dimensions such as 2D or 3D.

We further recommend the research paper, "An Introduction to Variable and Feature Selection," by Isabelle Guyon et al. for a comprehensive checklist involving the decision-making process of feature engineering.

5.6 Summary

Feature engineering is an integral part of machine learning model development. The volume of data can be reduced by applying sampling techniques. Feature selection helps reduce the width of the data by selecting the most powerful features. We developed understanding of three core methods of variable selection—filter, wrapper, and embedded. Toward the end of this chapter, we showed examples of the Principal Component Analysis and learned how PCA can reduce dimensionality without losing the taste and value.

The next chapter is the core of this book, Chapter 6. The chapter shows you how to bring your business problems to your IT system and then try to solve them using machine learning.

CHAPTER 6

Machine Learning Theory and Practice

The world is quickly adapting the use of machine learning (ML). Whether its driverless cars, the intelligent personal assistant, or machines playing the games like Go and Jeopardy against humans, ML is pervasive. The availability and ease of collecting data coupled with high computing power has made this field even more conducive to researchers and businesses to explore data-driven solutions for some of the most challenging problems. This has led to a revolution and outbreak in the number of new startups and tools leveraging ML to solve problems in sectors such as healthcare, IT, HR, automobiles, manufacturing, and the list is ever expanding.

The abstraction layer between the complicated machine learning algorithms and its implementation has reached an all-time high with the efforts from ML researchers, ML engineers, and developers. Today, you don't have to understand the statistics behind the ML algorithms to be able to apply them to a real-world dataset, rather just knowing how to use a tool is sufficient (which has its pros and cons), which need you to explore and clean the data and put it into an appropriate format. Many large enterprises have come out with certain APIs that provide analytics-as-a-service with capabilities to build predictive models using ML. This does not stop here—companies like Google, Facebook, and IBM have already taken the lead to make some of their systems completely open source, which means the way Android revolutionized the mobile industry, these ML systems are going to do the same for the next generation of fully automated machines.

So now it remains to see from where the next path-breaking, billion-dollar, disruptive idea is going to come. Though all these might sound like a distant dream, it's fast approaching. The past two decades gave us Google, Twitter, WhatsApp, Facebook, and so many others in the technology fields. All these billion-dollar enterprises have data and use it to make possibilities that we didn't know about a few years back. Computer vision to online location maps has changed the way we work in this century. Who would have

K. Ramasubramanian and A. Singh, *Machine Learning Using R*, https://doi.org/10.1007/978-1-4842-4215-5_6

thought that sitting in one place, you could find the best route from one place to another, or a drone could perform a search and help rescue operation? These possibilities did not exist a few decades ago but now they are a reality. All these are driven by data and what we have been able to learn from that data. The future belongs to enterprises and individuals who embrace the power of data.

In this chapter, we are going to deep dive into the fascinating and exciting world of machine learning, where we have tried to maintain a fine balance between theory and tool-centric practical aspects of the subject. As this chapter is the crux of this entire book, we take up some real industry data to illustrate the algorithm and, at the same time, make you understand how the concepts you learned in previous chapters are connected to this chapter. This means, you will now start to see how the ML process flow, PEBE, which we proposed in Chapter 1, is going to play a key role. Chapters 2 to 5 were the foundation and prerequisite for effectively and efficiently running an ML algorithm. We learned about properties of data, data types, hidden patterns through visualization, sampling, and creating best sets of features to apply an ML algorithm. The chapters after this one are more about how to measure the performance of models, improve them, and what technology can help you take ML to an actual scalable environment.

In this chapter, we briefly touch on the mathematical background of each algorithm and then show you how to run that R and interpret results. The following are the three ways this chapter empowers you to quickly get started with ML and learn with a right blend of theory and practice:

- *The statistical background:* We introduce the core formulation/statistical concept behind the ML concept/algorithm. Since the statistical concepts make the discussion intense and fairly complicated for beginners and intermediate readers, we have designed a much lighter version of these concepts and expect the interested readers to refer a more detailed literature for the same (we have provided sufficient references wherever possible).

- *Demo in R:* Set up the R environment and write R script to work with the datasets provided for a real-world problem. This approach of quickly getting started with R programming after the theoretical foundation on the problem and ML algorithm has been adopted keeping in mind industry professionals who are looking for a quick prototyping and researchers who wants to get started with practical implementations of ML algorithm. Industry professionals might tend to identify the problem statement in their domain of work and apply a brute force approach to try all possible ML algorithms, whereas researchers tend to master the foundational elements and then proceed to the implementation side of things. This chapter is suitable for both.

- *Real-world use case:* The dataset we have chosen to explain. The ML algorithms are from real scenarios curated for the purpose of explaining the concepts. This means our examples are built on real data, making sure we emulate a real-world scenario, where the model results are not always good. Sometime you get good results, sometimes very poor. A few algorithms work best, some don't work on the same data. This approach will help you see all algorithms of the same type with the same denominator to compare and make judicious decisions based on the actual problem at hand. We have discouraged the use of examples that explain the concepts in an ideal situation, and create a falsehood about performance, e.g., rather than choosing a linear regression-based example with R-square (a performance metric) of 90%, we presented a real-world case, where it could be even as poor as 30%, and discuss further how to improve it. This builds a strong case on how to approach an ML model-building process in the real world. However, wherever required, we have taken up a few standard datasets as well from a few popular repositories for easy explanation of certain concepts.

We have very broadly divided the ML algorithms into different categories in Section 6.2 and discuss some selective algorithms from each group in this and coming chapters. Some of these modules are touched on in previous chapters as well, where we felt it was more relevant. Normally, other books on the subject would have dedicated the entire book to such groups; however, based on our PEBE framework for machine learning process flow, we have consolidated all the ML algorithms into one chapter, providing you a much needed comprehensive guide for ML.

6.1 Machine Learning Types

In the machine learning literature, there are multiple ways in which we group the algorithms to study them in a collective manner. The following are two types of grouping:

- *Learning type based grouping*: This is to do with what type of response variable (or labels) we have in the training data. The broad types of learning are supervised, unsupervised, semi-supervised, and reinforcement learning.
- *Problem type based grouping*: This grouping is driven by "what" the model is trying to achieve. Each group has a similar set of algorithmic approach and principles. We show this grouping and a few popular techniques within them.

There are numerous ways in which ML algorithms are applied to a particular problem. As a result, for the same problem, there could be many different ML models possible. Chapters 7 and 8 discuss a few ways to choose the best among them and combine a few to create a new ensemble. So, coming out with the best ML model is an art that requires a lot of patience and trial and error. Figure 6-1 shows different types of learning with sample use cases.

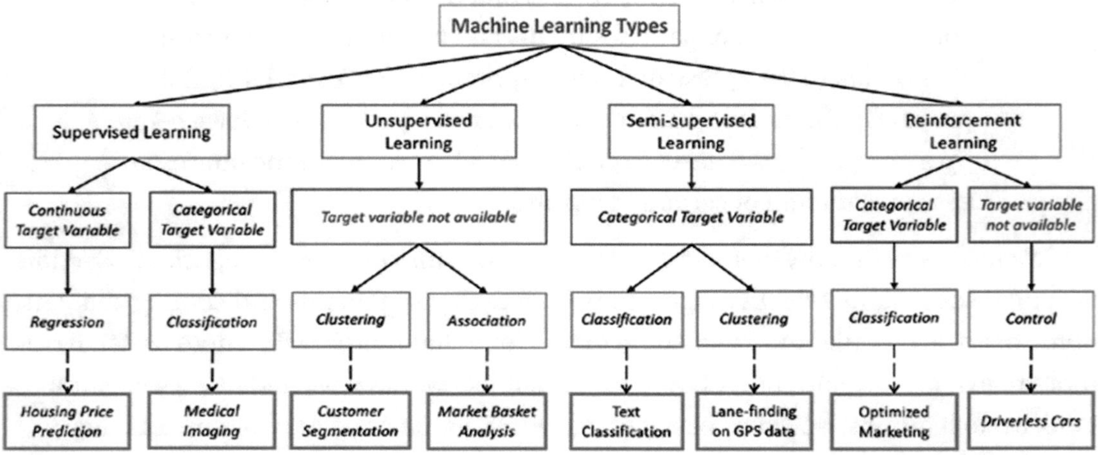

Figure 6-1. *Machine learning types*

6.1.1 Supervised Learning

Supervised learning applies in dataset with a response variable (also called label). The response variable could be either continuous or categorical. The algorithm learns the response variable against the provided set of predictor variables. For example, if the dataset belongs to a set of patients, each instance will have a response variable identifying whether a patient has cancer or not (categorical). Or in a dataset of house prices in a given state or country, the response variable could be the price of the house.

Keep in mind that defining the problem (defining a problem will be more clear when we discuss the real-world use cases later in the chapter) clearly is important for us to start in the right direction. Further, the problem is a classification task if the response variable is categorical, and a regression task, if it's continuous. Though this rule is largely true in all cases, there are certain problems that are a mix of both classification and regression. In the banking sector, one important model is to predict if a customer will default on their loan or not. Supervised learning with examples from the customer's past will learn the pattern of customers who have defaulted versus non-defaulters. We discuss this example while explaining *logistic regression*, which is a type of supervised learning algorithm.

6.1.2 Unsupervised Learning

In case of datasets with no response variable, there is no help for learning from the predictor variables, in other words, the learning has to be unsupervised. The learning happens based on some measure of similarity or distance between each row in the dataset. The most commonly used technique in unsupervised learning is *clustering*. Other methods like Association Rule Mining (ARM) are based on the frequency of an event like a purchase in a market basket, server crashes in log mining, and so on. Some applications of unsupervised learning are customer segmentation in marketing, social network analysis, image segmentation, climatology, and many more. In this book, we explain the value (or worth) of a house using variables like store area, lawn area, and so on. The data will be used with algorithms like k-means and hierarchical clusterings.

6.1.3 Semi-Supervised Learning

In the previous two types, either there are no labels for all the observation in the dataset or labels are present for all the observations. Semi-supervised learning deals with dataset with partially filled response variables. In many practical situations, the cost to label is quite high, since it requires skilled human experts to do that. So, in the absence of labels in the majority of the observations but present in a few, semi-supervised algorithms are the best candidates for the model building. These methods exploit the idea that even though the group memberships of the unlabeled data are unknown, this data carries important information about the group parameters. The most extensive literature on this topic is provided in the book, *Semi-Supervised Learning*. MIT Press, Cambridge, MA, by Chapelle, O. et al.[1]

6.1.4 Reinforcement Learning

Both supervised and unsupervised learning algorithms need clean and accurate data to produce the best results. Also, the data needs to be comprehensive in order to work on the unseen instances. For example, if the problem of predicting cancer based on patients' medical history didn't have data for a particular type of cancer, the algorithm will produce many false alarms when deployed in real time. Reinforcement learning is an ideal choice in cases, where only an initial state of the data is available as an input and there is no single possible response but rather many outcomes are possible. The world of robotics and innovation in driverless cars is all coming from this class of ML algorithm. The reinforcement learning algorithm continuously learns from the environment in an iterative fashion. In the process, the it learns from its experiences of the environment until it explores the full range of possible states. Some applications of the RL algorithm are computer played board games (Chess, Go), robotic hands, and self-driving cars.

A detailed discussion of semi-supervised and RL algorithms is beyond the scope of this book; however, we will reference them wherever necessary.

6.2 Groups of Machine Learning Algorithms

The ML algorithms could be grouped based on the similarity of approach and algorithm output. This will help you create use cases within the same group for a more diverse set of problems. Another benefit of organizing algorithms in this manner is ease of working with R libraries, which are designed to contain all relevant/similar functions in a single library. This helps the users explore all options/diagnostics for a problem using a single library. The list is ever-expanding with new use cases emerging from academia and

[1]Chapelle O, Schölkopf B, Zien A (eds.) (2006). Semi-Supervised Learning. MIT Press, Cambridge, MA.

industries. We mention which of these algorithms are covered in this book and let you explore more from other sources.

- *Regression-based methods:* Regression-based methods are the most popular and widely used in academia and research. They are easy to explain and easy to put into a live production environment. In this class of methods, the relationship between dependent variable and set of independent variables is estimated by the probabilistic method or by error function minimization. We cover linear regression, polynomial regression, and logistic regression in this chapter. See Figure 6-2.

	Algorithms
Regression Analysis	Ordinary Least Squares Regression (OLSR)
	Linear Regression
	Logistic Regression
	Stepwise Regression
	Polynomial Regression
	Locally Estimated Scatterplot Smoothing (LOESS)

Figure 6-2. *Regression algorithms*

- *Distance-based algorithms:* Distance-based or event-based algorithms are used for learning representations of data and creating a metric to identify whether an object belongs to the class of interest or not. They are sometimes called memory-based learning, as they learn from set of instances/events captured in the data. We use K-Nearest Neighbor and Learning Vector Quantization in creating ensembles in Chapter 8. See Figure 6-3.

	Algorithms
Distance-based Algorithms	k-Nearest Neighbor (kNN)
	Learning Vector Quantization (LVQ)
	Self-Organizing Map (SOM)

Figure 6-3. *Distance-based algorithms*

- *Regularization methods:* Regularization methods are essentially an extension of regression methods. Regularization algorithms introduce a penalization term to the loss function (as discussed in Chapter 5) for balancing between the complexity of the model and improvement in results. They are very powerful and useful techniques when dealing with data with a high number of features and large data volume. We introduced L1 regularization in Chapter 5 as an embedded method of variable subset selection. See Figure 6-4.

	Algorithms
Regularization Algorithms	Ridge Regression
	Least Absolute Shrinkage and Selection Operator (LASSO)
	Elastic Net
	Least-Angle Regression (LARS)

Figure 6-4. *Regularization algorithms*

- *Tree-based algorithms:* These algorithms are based on sequential conditional rules applied on the actual data. The rules are generally applied serially and a classification decision is made when all the conditions are met. These methods are very popular in decision-making engines and classification problems. They are fast and distributed algorithms. We discuss algorithms like CART, Iterative Dichotomizer, CHAID, and C5.0 in this chapter and use them to train our ensemble model in Chapter 8. See Figure 6-5.

	Algorithms
Decision Tree Algorithms	Classification and Regression Tree (CART)
	Iterative Dichotomiser 3 (ID3)
	C4.5 and C5.0 (different versions of a powerful approach)
	Chi-squared Automatic Interaction Detection (CHAID)
	Random Forest
	Conditional Decision Trees

Figure 6-5. *Decision tree algorithms*

- *Bayesian algorithms:* These algorithms might not be called learning algorithms, as they work the Bayes Theorem prior and post distributions. The machine essentially does not learn from an iterative process but uses inference from distributions of variable. These methods are very popular and easy to explain, used mostly in classification and inference testing. We cover the Naïve Bayes model in this chapter and introduce basic ideas from probability to explain them. See Figure 6-6.

	Algorithms
Bayesian Algorithms	Naive Bayes
	Gaussian Naive Bayes
	Multinomial Naive Bayes
	Bayesian Belief Network (BBN)
	Bayesian Network (BN)

***Figure 6-6.** Bayesian algorithms*

- *Clustering algorithms:* These algorithms generally work on simple principle of maximization of intracluster similarities and minimization of intercluster similarities. The measure of similarity determines how the clusters need to be formed. These are very useful in marketing and demographic studies. Mostly these are unsupervised algorithms, which group the data for maximum commonality. We discuss k-means, expectation-minimization, and hierarchical clustering. We also discuss distributed clustering. See Figure 6-7.

	Algorithms
Clustering Algorithms	k-Means
	k-Medians
	Partitioning Around Medoids (PAM)
	Hierarchical Clustering

***Figure 6-7.** Clustering algorithms*

- *Association rule mining:* In these algorithms, the relationship among the variables is observed and used to quantify the relationship for predictive and exploratory objectives. These methods have been proved to be very useful to build and mine relationships among large multi-dimensional datasets. Popular recommendation systems are based on some variation of association rule mining algorithms. We discuss Apriori and Eclet algorithms in this chapter. See Figure 6-8.

	Algorithms
Association Rule Mining Algorithms	Apriori algorithm
	Eclat algorithm
	FP-growth algorithm
	Context Based Rule Mining

Figure 6-8. *Association rule mining*

- *Artificial Neural Networks (ANN):* Inspired by the biological neural networks, these are powerful enough to learn non-linear relationships and recognize higher order relationships among variables. They can implement both supervised and unsupervised learning process. There is a stark difference between the complexity of traditional neural networks and deep learning neural networks (discussed later in this chapter). We discuss perceptron and back-propagation in this chapter. See Figure 6-9.

	Algorithms
Artificial Neural Network Algorithms	Perceptron
	Back-Propagation
	Hopfield Network
	Radial Basis Function Network (RBFN)

Figure 6-9. *Artificial neural networks*

- *Deep learning:* These algorithms work on complex neural structures that can abstract higher level of information from a huge dataset. They are computationally heavy and hard to train. In simple terms, you can think of them as very large, multiple hidden layer neural nets. We have a dedicated an entire Chapter 11 on deep learning. See Figure 6-10.

	Algorithms
Deep Learning Algorithms	Deep Boltzmann Machine (DBM)
	Deep Belief Networks (DBN)
	Convolutional Neural Network (CNN)
	Stacked Auto-Encoders

Figure 6-10. *Deep learning algorithms*

- *Ensemble learning:* This is a set of algorithms that is built by combining results from multiple machine learning algorithms. These methods have become very popular due to their ability to provide superior results and the possibility of breaking them into independent models to train on a distributed network. We discuss bagging, boosting, stacking, and blending ensembles in Chapter 8. See Figure 6-11.

	Algorithms
Ensemble Algorithms	Boosting
	Bagging
	AdaBoost
	Stacked Generalization (blending)
	Gradient Boosting Machines (GBM)

Figure 6-11. *Ensemble learning*

- *Text mining:* It is also known as text analytics and is a subfield of Natural Language Processing, which in turn is a subfield of machine learning. It provides certain algorithms and approaches to deal with unstructured textual data, commonly obtained from call center logs, customer reviews, and so on. The algorithms in this group can deal with highly unstructured text data to bring insights and/or create features for applying machine learning algorithms. We discuss text summarization, sentimental analysis, word cloud, and topic identification. See Figure 6-12.

	Algorithms
Text Mining	Automatic summarization
	Named entity recognition (NER)
	Optical character recognition (OCR)
	Part-of-speech tagging
	Sentiment analysis
	Speech recognition
	Topic Modeling

Figure 6-12. *Text mining algorithms*

The list of algorithms discussed has multiple implementations in R, Python, and other statistics packages. All the methods don't have readily available R packages for implementation. Some algorithms are not fully supported in the R environment and have to be used by calling APIs, e.g., text mining and deep neural nets. The research community is working toward bringing all the latest algorithms into R either via a package or APIs.

Torsten Hothorn maintains an exhaustive list of packages available in R for implementing machine learning algorithms. (Reference: CRAN Task View: Machine Learning & Statistical Learning at `https://cran.r-project.org/web/views/MachineLearning.html`.)

We recommend you keep an eye on this list and keep following up with the latest package releases. In the next section, we present a brief taxonomy of all the real-world datasets that are going to be used in this chapter and in the coming chapters for demos using R.

6.3 Real-World Datasets

Throughout this chapter, we are going to use many real-world datasets and build use cases to demonstrate the various ML algorithms. In this section, a brief taxonomy of datasets associated with each use case is presented before we start with the demos using R.

6.3.1 House Sale Prices

The selling price of a house depends on many variables; this dataset presents a combination of factors to predict the selling price. Table 6-1 presents the metadata of this House Sale Price dataset.

Table 6-1. *House Sale Price Dataset*

House Sale Prices			
Variable	Description	Code/Values	Variable Name
1	Unique Identifier of House Property	1 to 1201	HOUSE_ID
2	Selling price of the house	Positive Integer	HousePrice
3	Storage space area in sq.ft	Positive Integer	StoreArea
4	Area of the House Basement	Positive Integer	BasementArea
5	Area of the Lawn in sq.ft	Positive Integer	LawnArea
6	Width of street connected the House in feet	Positive Integer	StreetHouseFront
7	Location of the Property	Location Names	Location
8	The type of connectivity to house	Types of Road	ConnectivityType
9	The type of building construction	Type of building construction	BuidlingType
10	The year house was built	Date (Year)	ConstructionYear
11	The type of estate/society	SemiPrivate, Government, etc	EstateType
12	The year in which house sale took place	Date (Year)	SellingYear
13	Rating of house based on quality and location	1- Worst ... 10-Best	Rating
14	Indicator for fresh sale or resale	NewHouse, FirstResale, etc	SaleType

6.3.2 Purchase Preference

This data contains transaction history for customers who have bought a particular product. For each `customer_ID`, multiple data points are simulated to capture the purchase behavior. The data is originally set for solving multi-class models with four possible products from the insurance industry. The features are generic enough so that they could be adapted for another industry like automobile or retail, where you could have data about the car purchases, consumer goods, and so on. See Table 6-2.

Table 6-2. *Purchase Preferences*

Purchase Preference			
Variable	Description	Code/Values	Variable Name
1	Unique Identifier of Customer	1 to 1201	CUSTOMER_ID
2	Choice of Product Purchased	1, 2,3 and 4	ProductChoice
3	Customer member reward points	1-13	MembershipPoints
4	The mode of payment by the customer	Cash, CreditCard ,etc	ModeOfPayment
5	Customer resident city	City Name	ResidentCity
6	Numberof months since the first purchase made by the customer	Positive Integer	PurchaseTenure
7	Channel of purchase	Online/Offline	Channel
8	Income of customer	1- Lowest ... 9 - Highest	IncomeClass
9	Buying propensity rating of the customer	VeryHigh, High, Medium, Low, Unknown	CustomerPropensity
10	Age of customer as on last purchase	Positive Integer	CustomerAge
11	Martial Status of customer	1- Married, 0- Single	MartialStatus
12	Months since the last purchase	Positive Integer	LastPurchaseDuration

6.3.3 Twitter Feeds and Article

We collected some Twitter feeds to generate results for applying text mining algorithms. The feeds are taken from National News Channel Twitter accounts as of September 30, 2016. The handles used are `@TimesNow` and `@CNN`. One article available on the Internet has been used for summarization. The original article can be found at `http://www.yourarticlelibrary.com/essay/essay-on-india-after-independence/41354/`.

6.3.4 Breast Cancer

We will be using the Breast Cancer Wisconsin (Diagnostic) dataset from the UCI machine learning repository. The features in the dataset are computed from a digitized image of a fine needle aspirate (FNA) of a breast mass. Each variable, except for the first and last, was converted into 11 primitive numerical attributes with values ranging from 0 to 10. They describe characteristics of the cell nuclei present in the image. Table 6-3 lists the features available.

Table 6-3. *Breast Cancer Wisconsin*

Breast Cancer Wisconsin			
Variable	Description	Code/Values	Variable Name
1	Sample code number	1-699	Id (V1)
2	Clump Thickness	1-10	Cl.thickness (V2)
3	Uniformity of Cell Size	1-10	Cell.size (V3)
4	Uniformity of Cell Shape	1-10	Cell.shape (V4)
5	Marginal Adhesion	1-10	Marg.adhesion (V5)
6	Single Epithelial Cell Size	1-10	Epith.c.size (V6)
7	Bare Nuclei	1-10	Bare.nuclei (V7)
8	Bland Chromatin	1-10	Bl.cromatin (V8)
9	Normal Nucleoli	1-10	Normal.nucleoli (V9)
10	Mitoses	1-10	Mitoses (V10)
11	Class	2 - Benign 4 - Malignant)	Class (V11)

6.3.5 Market Basket

We will use a real-world data from a small supermarket. Each row of this data contains a customer transaction with a list of products (from now on, we will use the term *items*) they purchased. Since the items were too many in a typical supermarket, we have aggregated them to the category level. For example, "baking needs" covers a number of different products like dough, baking soda, butter, and so on. For illustration, let's take a small subset of the data consisting of five transactions and nine items, as shown in Table 6-4.

Table 6-4. *Market Basket Data*

Market Basket Data	
Transaction	Items
T1	bread and cake,baking needs,biscuits,canned fruit
T2	bread and cake,baking needs,Jams spreads,canned vegetables
T3	bread and cake, frozen foods
T4	frozen foods, laundry needs, deodorants soap
T5	Jams spreads,laundry needs

6.3.6 Amazon Food Reviews

The Amazon Fine Food Reviews dataset consists of 568,454 food reviews that Amazon users left up to October 2012. A subset of this data is being used for text mining approaches in this chapter to show text summarization, categorization, and part-of-speech extraction. Table 6-5 contains the metadata of Amazon Fine Food Reviews dataset.

Table 6-5. *Amazon Food Reviews*

Amazon Fine Food Reviews			
Variable	Description	Code/Values	Variable Name
1	Id of the reviewer	1 - 35173	Id
2	Unique identifier for the product	Alphanumeric	ProductId
3	Unique identifier for the user	Alphanumeric	UserId
4	ProfileName	Alphanumeric	ProfileName
5	Number of users who found the review helpful	Positive Integer	HelpfulnessNumerator
6	Number of users who indicated whether they found the review helpful	Positive Integer	HelpfulnessDenominator
7	Rating between 1 and 5	1 - 5	Score
8	Timestamp for the review	Date timestamp	Time
9	Brief summary of the review	Character	Summary
10	Text of the review	Character	Text

The rest of the chapter will discuss every machine learning algorithm based on the grouping discussed earlier and consistently explain every algorithm by discussing statistical background, demonstration in R, and using a real-world use case.

6.4 Regression Analysis

In previous chapters, we were trying to set the stage for modeling techniques to work for our desired objective. This chapter touches on some of the out-of-box techniques in statistical learning and machine learning space. At this stage you might want to focus on the algorithmic approaches and not worry much about how statistical assumptions play a role in machine learning algorithms. For completeness, we discuss in Chapter 8 how statistical learning differs from machine learning.

The section of regression analysis will focus on building a thought process around how the modeling techniques establish and quantify a relation among response variables and predictors. We will start by identifying how strong and what type of relationship they share and try to see if the relationship can be modeled with an assumption around a distribution or not like normal distribution. We will also address some of the important diagnostic features of popular techniques and explain what significance they have in model selection.

The focus of these techniques is to find relationships that are statistically significant and do not bear any distributional assumptions. The techniques do not establish causation (best understood with the notion which says "a strong association is not a proof of causation"), but give the data scientist indication of how the data series is related given some assumptions around parameters. Causation establishment lies with the prudence and business understanding of the process.

The concept of causation is important to keep in mind, as most of the time our thought process deviates from how relationships quantified by a model have to be interpreted. For example, a statistical model will be able to quantify relationships between completely irrelevant measures, say electricity generation and beer consumption. The linear model will be able to quantify a relationship among them. But does beer consumption relate to electricity generation? Or does more electricity generation mean more beer consumption? Unless you try very hard, it's difficult to prove. Hence, a clear understanding of the process in discussion and domain knowledge is important. You have to challenge the assumptions to get the real value out of the data. This curse of causation needs to be kept in mind while we discuss correlation and other concepts in regression.

Any regression analysis involves three key sets of variables:

- Dependent or response variables (Y): Input series
- Independent or predictor variables (X): Input series
- Model parameters: Unknown parameters to be estimated by the regression model

For more than one independent variable and single dependent variable, these quantities can be thought of as a matrix.

The regression relationship can be shown as a function that maps from set of independent variable space to dependent variable space. This relationship is the foundation of prediction/forecasting:

$$Y \approx f(\mathrm{X},\beta)$$

This notation looks more like a mathematical modeling, and the Statistical Modeling scholars use a little different notation for the same relationship:

$$E(Y|X) = f(X,\beta)$$

In statistical modeling, regression analysis estimates the conditional expectation of dependent variable for known values of independent variables, which is nothing but the average value of dependent for given values of independent variables. Other important concept to understand before we expand the idea of regression is around parametric and non-parametric methods. The discussion in this section will be based on parametric methods, while there exist other sets of techniques that are non-parametric.

- ***Parametric methods*** assume that the sample data is drawn from a known probability distribution based on a fixed set of parameters. For instance, linear regression assumes normal distribution, whereas logistic assumes binomial distribution, etc. This assumption allows the methods to be applied to small datasets as well.
- ***Non-parametric methods*** do not assume any probability distribution in prior, rather they construct empirical distributions from the underlying data. These methods require a high volume of data to model estimation. There exists a separate branch on non-parametric regressions, which is out of scope of this book, e.g., kernel regression, Nonparametric Multiplicative Regression (NPMR), etc. A good resource to read more on this topic is "Artificial Intelligence: A Modern Approach" by Stuart Russell and Peter Norvig.[2]

Further, using a parametric method allows you to easily create confidence intervals around the estimated parameters; we will use this in our model diagnostic measures. In this book we will be working with two types of input data—continuous input with

[2]Stuart Russell and Peter Norvig. 2009. Artificial Intelligence: A Modern Approach (3rd ed.). Prentice Hall Press, Upper Saddle River, NJ, USA.

normality assumption and logistic regression with binomial assumption. Also, a small primer on generalized framework will be provided for further reading.

6.5 Correlation Analysis

> *The object of statistical science is to discover methods of condensing information concerning large groups of allied facts into brief and compendious expressions suitable for discussion.*
>
> —Sir Francis Galton (1822-1911)

Correlation can be seen as a broader term used to represent the statistical relationship between two variables. Correlation, in principle, provides a single measure of relationship among the variables. There are multiple ways in which a relationship can be quantified, due to this same reason we have so many types of correlation coefficients in statistics.

For measuring linear relationships, Pearson correlation is the best measure. Pearson correlation, also called the Pearson *Product-Moment Correlation Coefficient,* is sensitive to linear relationships. It also exists for non-linear relationships but doesn't provide any useful information in those cases.

Let's assume two random variables, X and Y with their means as μ_X and μ_Y and standard deviations as σ_X and σ_Y. The population correlation coefficient is defined as

$$\rho X,Y = \frac{\mathrm{E}\left[(X-\mu_X)(Y-\mu_Y)\right]}{\sigma_X\sigma_Y}$$

We can infer from this, two important features of this measure:

- It ranges from -1 (negative correlated) and +1 (positively correlated), which can be derived from Cauchy-Schwarz inequality.
- This is defined only when the standard deviation is finite and non-zero.

Similarly, for a sample from the population, the measure is defined as follows:

$$r_{xy} = \frac{\sum_{i=1}^{n}(x_i-\bar{x})(y_i-\bar{y})}{ns_xs_y} = \frac{\sum_{i=1}^{n}(x_i-\bar{x})(y_i-\bar{y})}{\sqrt{\sum_{i=1}^{n}(x_i-\bar{x})^2\sum_{i=1}^{n}(y_i-\bar{y})^2}},$$

Let's create some scatter plots with our house price data and see what kind of relationship we can quantify using the Pearson correlation.

Dependent variable: HousePrice

Independent variable: StoreArea

```
Data_HousePrice <-read.csv("Dataset/House Sale Price Dataset.
csv",header=TRUE);

#Create a vectors with Y-Dependent, X-Independent
y <-Data_HousePrice$HousePrice;
x<-Data_HousePrice$StoreArea;

#Scatter Plot
plot(x,y, main="Scatterplot HousePrice vs StoreArea",
xlab="StoreArea(sqft)", ylab="HousePrice($)", pch=19,cex=0.3,col="red")

#Add a fit line to show the relationship direction
abline(lm(y~x)) # regression line (y~x)
lines(lowess(x,y), col="green") # lowess line (x,y)
```

The plot in Figure 6-13 shows the scatter plot between HousePrice and StoreArea. The curved line is a locally smoothed fitted line. It can be seen that there is a linear relationship among the variables.

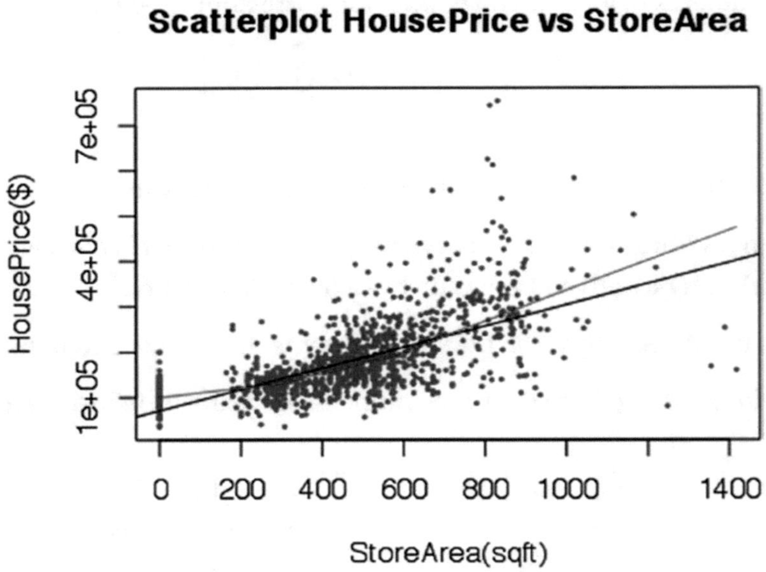

Figure 6-13. *Scatter plot between HousePrice and StoreArea*

```
#Report the correlation coefficient of this relation
cat("The correlation among HousePrice and StoreArea is  ",cor(x,y));
 The correlation among HousePrice and StoreArea is   0.6212766
```

From these plots, we can make the following observations:

- The relationship is in a positive direction, so on average the house price increases with the size of the store. This is an intuitive relationship, hence we can draw causality. The bigger the store space, the better the house, which means it's more costly.
- The correlation is 0.62. This is a moderately strong relationship on a linear scale.
- The curved line is a LOWESS (Locally Weighted Scatterplot Smoothing) plot, which shows that it is not very different from the linear regression line. Hence, the linear relationship is worth exploring for a model.
- If you see closely, there is a vertical line at `StoreArea` = 0. This vertical line is saying that the prices vary for the house where there is no store area. We need to look at other factors that are driving the house prices.

We have discussed in detail how to find the set of variables that fit the data best. So in coming sections we will not focus on how we got to that model, but show more about how to run and interpret them in R.

6.5.1 Linear Regression

Linear regression is a process of fitting a linear predictor function to estimate unknown parameters from the underlying data. In general, the model predicts the conditional mean of Y given X, which is assumed to be an affine function of X.

Affine function: as linear regression estimated model does have an intercept term and hence it is not just a linear function of X but an affine function.

Essentially, the linear regression model will help you with:

- Prediction or forecasting
- Quantifying the relationship among variables

While the former has to do with if there are some unknown Xs then what is the expected value for Y, the later deals with on the historical data of how these variables were related in quantifiable terms (e.g., parameters and p-values).

Mathematically, the simple linear relationship looks like this:

For a set of n duplets $(xi,yi), i=1,\ldots,n$, the relationship function is described as:

$$y_i = \alpha + \beta x_i + \varepsilon_i.,$$

and the objective of linear regression is to estimate this line:

$$y = \alpha + \beta x$$

where y is the predicted response (or fitted value) · is the intercept, i.e., average response value if the independent variable is zero, and β is the parameter for x, i.e., change in y by per unit change in x.

There are many ways to fit this line with the given dataset. This differs with the type of loss function we want to minimize, e.g., ordinary least square, least absolute deviation, ridge etc. Let's look at the most popular method of Ordinary Least Square (OLS).

In OLS, the algorithm minimizes the squares error. The minimization problem can be defined as follows:

$$\text{Find } \min_{\alpha,\beta} Q(\alpha,\beta), \qquad \text{for} Q(\alpha,\beta) = \sum_{i=1}^{n} \varepsilon_i^2 = \sum_{i=1}^{n} (y_i - \alpha - \beta x_i)^2$$

Being a parametric method, we can have a closed form solution for this optimization. The closed form solution for estimating coefficients (or parameters) is by using the following equations:

$$\bar{\beta} = \frac{\sum x_i y_i - \frac{1}{n}\sum x_i \sum y_i}{\sum x_i^2 - \frac{1}{n}\left(\sum x_i\right)^2} = \frac{\text{Cov}[x,y]}{\sigma_x^2}, \qquad \bar{\alpha} = \bar{y} - \bar{\beta}\bar{x}.$$

Where, $\sigma^2{}_x$ is the variance of x. The derivation of this solution can be found at `https://onlinecourses.science.psu.edu/stat414/node/278`.

OLS has special properties for a linear regression model under certain assumptions on the residual. Carl Friedrich Gauss and Andrey Markov jointly developed Gauss-Markov Theorem that states that if the following conditions are satisfied:

- Expectation (mean) of residuals is zero (normality of residuals)
- Residuals are un-correlated and (no auto-correlation)
- Residuals have equal variance (homoscedasticity)

then Ordinary Lease Square estimation gives Best Linear Unbiased Estimator of coefficients (or parameter estimates). We now explain the key terms that comprise the best estimator, i.e., bias, consistent, and efficient.

6.5.2 Simple Linear Regression

Now we can move on to estimating the linear models using the OLS technique. The `lm()` package in R provides us with the capability to run OLS for linear regressions. The `lm()` function can be used to carry out regression, single stratum analysis of variance, and analysis of covariance. It is part of the base `stats()` package in R.

Now, we will create a simple linear regression and understand how to interpret the `lm()` output for this simple case. Here we are fitting linear regression model with OLS technique on the following.

Dependent variable: `HousePrice`

Independent variable: `StoreArea`

Further our correlation analysis showed that these two variables have a positive linear relation and hence we will expect a positive sign to the parameter estimates of `StoreArea`. Let's run and interpret the results.

```
# fit the model
fitted_Model <-lm(y~x)
# Display the summary of the model
summary(fitted_Model)
```

```
Call:
lm(formula = y ~ x)
```

```
Residuals:
    Min      1Q  Median      3Q     Max
-280115  -33717   -4689   24611  490698

Coefficients:
             Estimate Std. Error t value Pr(>|t|)
(Intercept) 70677.227   4261.027   16.59   <2e-16 ***
x             232.723      8.147   28.57   <2e-16 ***
---
Signif. codes:  0 '***' 0.001 '**' 0.01 '*' 0.05 '.' 0.1 ' ' 1

Residual standard error: 63490 on 1298 degrees of freedom
Multiple R-squared:  0.386,  Adjusted R-squared:  0.3855
F-statistic:   816 on 1 and 1298 DF,  p-value: < 2.2e-16
```

The estimated equation for our example is

$$y = 70677.227 + (232.723)x$$

where y is `HousePrice` and x is `StoreArea`. This implies for a unit increase in x (`StoreArea`), the y (`HousePrice`) will be increased by $232.72. Intercept, being constant, tells us the `HousePrice` when there is no `StoreArea`, and can be thought of as a registration fee.

Let's discuss the `lm()` summary output to understand the model better. The same explanation can be extended to multiple linear regression in the next section.

- *Call*: Output the model equation that was fitted in the `lm()` function.
- *Residuals*: This gives interquartile range of residuals and Min, Max, and Median on residuals. A negative median means that at least half of the residuals are negative, i.e., the predicted values are more than the actual values in more than 50% of the prediction.
- *Coefficients*: This is a table giving model parameter estimates (or coefficient), standard error, t-value, and p-value of the student t-test.
- *Diagnostics*: Residual standard error, and multiple and adjusted R-square and F-statistics for variance testing.

It is important to expand the coefficient's component of the `lm()` summary output. This output provides vital information about the model predictors and their coefficients:

- *Estimate:* The fitted value for that parameter. This value directly uses the model equation to do prediction and to understand the relationship with the dependent variable. For example, in our model, the predictor variable x (store area) has a coefficient of 232.7.
- *Standard Error (std. Error):* The standard deviation of the distribution of the parameter estimate. In other words, the estimate is the mean value of coefficients and the standard deviation of that is the standard error. The standard error can be calculated as:

$$S_{\bar{x}} = \frac{s}{\sqrt{n}}$$

Where s is the sample standard deviation and n is the size of the sample.

The lower the standard error with respect to the estimate, the better the model estimate.

- *t-value and p-value:* Student t-test is a hypothesis test that checks if the test statistics follow a t-distribution. Statistically the p-value reported against each parameter is the p-value of one sample t-test.

We test that the value of parameter is statistically different from zero. If we fail to reject the null hypothesis then we can say the respective parameter is not significant in our model.

- The t-statistics for one sample t-test is as follows:

$$t = \frac{\bar{x} - \mu_0}{s / \sqrt{n}}$$

where $\bar{x}$ is the sample mean, s is the sample standard deviation of the sample, and n is the sample size. For our linear model, the t-value of x is 28.57 and the p-value is ~0. This means the estimate of x is not 0 and hence it is significant in the model.

Once we understand how the model looks and what the significance of each predictor is, we move on to see how the model fits the actual value. This is done by plotting actual values against the predicted values:

```
res <-stack(data.frame(Observed = y, Predicted =fitted(fitted_Model)))
res <-cbind(res, x =rep(x, 2))

#Plot using lattice xyplot(function)
library("lattice")
xyplot(values ~x, data = res, group = ind, auto.key =TRUE)
```

The plot in Figure 6-14 shows the fitted values with the actual values. You can see that the plot shows the linear relationship predicted by our model, stacked with the scatter plot of the original.

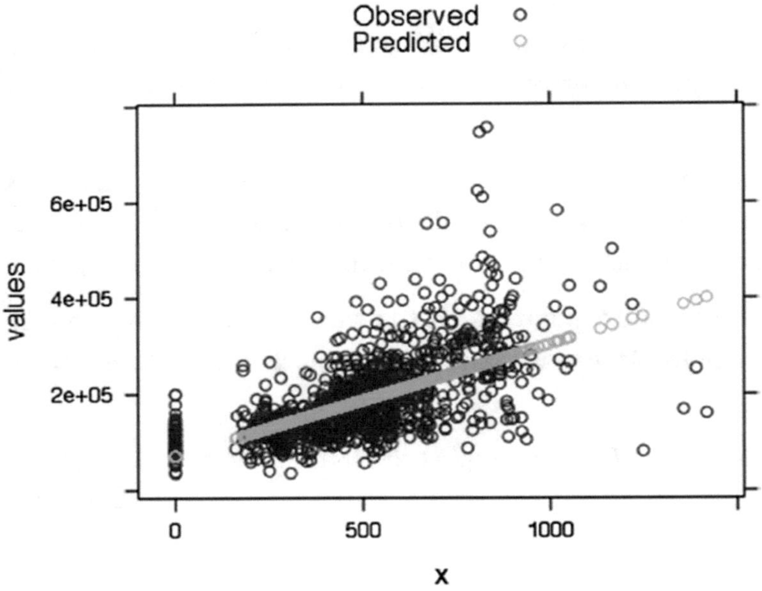

***Figure 6-14.** Scatter plot of actual versus predicted*

Now, this was a model with only one explanatory variable (`StoreArea`), but there are other variables available that show significant relationships with `HousePrices`. The regression framework allow us to add multiple explanatory variables or independent variables to the regression analysis. We introduce multiple linear regression in the next section.

6.5.3 Multiple Linear Regression

The ideas of simple linear regression can be extended to multiple independent variables. The linear relationship in multiple linear regression then becomes

$$y_i = \beta_1 x_{i1} + \cdots + \beta_p x_{ip} + \varepsilon_i = x_i^T \beta + \varepsilon_i, \qquad i = 1, \ldots, n,$$

For multiple regression, the matrix representation is very popular as it makes the concepts of matrix computation explanation easy.

$$\mathrm{y} = \mathrm{X}\beta + \varepsilon,$$

In our previous example we just used one variable to explain the dependent variable, StoreArea. In multiple linear regression we will use StoreArea, StreetHouseFront, BasementArea, LawnArea, Rating, and SaleType as independent variables to estimate a linear relationship with HousePrice.

The least square estimation function remains the same except there will be new variables as predictors. To run the analysis on multiple variables, we introduce one more data cleaning step, missing value identification. We either want to input the missing value or leave it out of our analysis. We choose leaving it out by using the na.omit() function R. The following code first finds the missing cases and then removes them.

```
# Use lm to create a multiple linear regression
Data_lm_Model <-Data_HousePrice[,c("HOUSE_ID","HousePrice","StoreArea","Str
eetHouseFront","BasementArea","LawnArea","Rating","SaleType")];

# below function we display number of missing values in each of the
variables in data
sapply(Data_lm_Model, function(x) sum(is.na(x)))
        HOUSE_ID       HousePrice        StoreArea StreetHouseFront
               0                0                0              231
    BasementArea         LawnArea           Rating         SaleType
               0                0                0                0
#We have preferred removing the 231 cases which correspond to missing
values in StreetHouseFront. Na.omit function will remove the missing cases.
Data_lm_Model <-na.omit(Data_lm_Model)
rownames(Data_lm_Model) <-NULL
#categorical variables has to be set as factors
```

```
Data_lm_Model$Rating <-factor(Data_lm_Model$Rating)
Data_lm_Model$SaleType <-factor(Data_lm_Model$SaleType)
```

Now we have cleaned up the data from the missing values and can run the `lm()` function to fit our multiple linear regression model.

```
fitted_Model_multiple <-lm(HousePrice ~StoreArea +StreetHouseFront
+BasementArea +LawnArea +Rating   +SaleType,data=Data_lm_Model)
summary(fitted_Model_multiple)
```

```
Call:
lm(formula = HousePrice ~ StoreArea + StreetHouseFront + BasementArea +
    LawnArea + Rating + SaleType, data = Data_lm_Model)

Residuals:
    Min      1Q  Median      3Q     Max
-485976  -19682   -2244   15690  321737

Coefficients:
                       Estimate Std. Error t value Pr(>|t|)
(Intercept)           2.507e+04  4.827e+04   0.519  0.60352
StoreArea             5.462e+01  7.550e+00   7.234 9.06e-13 ***
StreetHouseFront      1.353e+02  6.042e+01   2.240  0.02529 *
BasementArea          2.145e+01  3.004e+00   7.140 1.74e-12 ***
LawnArea              1.026e+00  1.721e-01   5.963 3.39e-09 ***
Rating2              -8.385e+02  4.816e+04  -0.017  0.98611
Rating3               2.495e+04  4.302e+04   0.580  0.56198
Rating4               3.948e+04  4.197e+04   0.940  0.34718
Rating5               5.576e+04  4.183e+04   1.333  0.18286
Rating6               7.911e+04  4.186e+04   1.890  0.05905 .
Rating7               1.187e+05  4.193e+04   2.830  0.00474 **
Rating8               1.750e+05  4.214e+04   4.153 3.54e-05 ***
Rating9               2.482e+05  4.261e+04   5.825 7.61e-09 ***
Rating10              2.930e+05  4.369e+04   6.708 3.23e-11 ***
SaleTypeFirstResale   2.146e+04  2.470e+04   0.869  0.38512
SaleTypeFourthResale  6.725e+03  2.791e+04   0.241  0.80964
SaleTypeNewHouse      2.329e+03  2.424e+04   0.096  0.92347
```

```
SaleTypeSecondResale -5.524e+03  2.465e+04  -0.224  0.82273
SaleTypeThirdResale  -1.479e+04  2.613e+04  -0.566  0.57160
---
Signif. codes:  0 '***' 0.001 '**' 0.01 '*' 0.05 '.' 0.1 ' ' 1

Residual standard error: 41660 on 1050 degrees of freedom
Multiple R-squared:  0.7644, Adjusted R-squared:  0.7604
F-statistic: 189.3 on 18 and 1050 DF,  p-value: < 2.2e-16
```

The estimated model has six independent variables, with four continuous variables (`StoreArea`, `StreetHouseFront`, `BasementArea`, and `LawnArea`) and two categorical variables (`Rating` and `SaleType`). From the results of the `lm()` function, we can see that `StoreArea`, `StreetHouseFront`, `BasementArea`, and `LawnArea` are significant at 95% confidence level, i.e., statistically different from zero. While all levels of `SaleType` are insignificant, hence statistically they are equal to zero. The higher ratings are significant but not the lower ones. The model should drop the `SaleType` and be re-estimated to keep only significant variables.

Now we will see how the actual versus predicted values look for this model by plotting them after ordering the series by house prices.

```
#Get the fitted values and create a data frame of actual and predicted get
predicted values

actual_predicted <-as.data.frame(cbind(as.numeric(Data_lm_Model$HOUSE_
ID),as.numeric(Data_lm_Model$HousePrice),as.numeric(fitted(fitted_Model_
multiple))))

names(actual_predicted) <-c("HOUSE_ID","Actual","Predicted")

#Ordered the house by increasing Actual house price
actual_predicted <-actual_predicted[order(actual_predicted$Actual),]

#Find the absolute residual and then take mean of that
library(ggplot2)
```

```
#Plot Actual vs Predicted values for Test Cases
ggplot(actual_predicted,aes(x =1:nrow(Data_lm_Model),color=Series)) +
geom_line(data = actual_predicted, aes(x =1:nrow(Data_lm_Model),
y = Actual, color ="Actual")) +
geom_line(data = actual_predicted, aes(x =1:nrow(Data_lm_Model),
y = Predicted, color ="Predicted"))  +xlab('House Number') +ylab('House
Sale Price')
```

The plot in Figure 6-15 shows the actual and predicted values on a value ordered `HousePrice`.

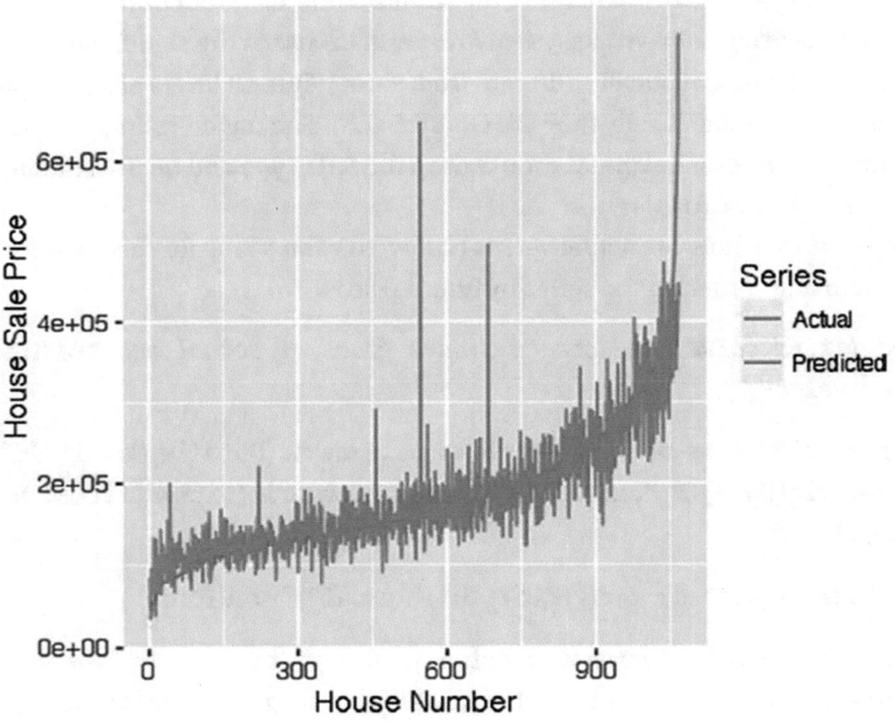

***Figure 6-15.** The actual versus predicted plot*

We have arranged the house prices in increasing order to see less cluttered actual versus predicted plot. The plot shows that our model closely follows the actual prices. There are a few cases of outlier/high values on actual which the model is not able to predict, and that is fine as our model is not influenced by outliers.

6.5.4 Model Diagnostics: Linear Regression

Model diagnostics is an important step in the model-selection process. There is a difference between model performance evaluation, discussed in Chapter 7, and the model selection process. In model evaluation, we check how the model performs on unseen data (testing data), but in model diagnostic/selection, we see how the model fitting itself looks on our data. This includes checking the p-value significance of the parameter estimates, normality, auto-correlation, homoscedasticity, influential/outlier points, and multicollinearity. There are other test as well to see how well the model follows the statistical assumptions, strict exogeneity, anova tables, and others but we will focus on only a few in the following sections.

6.5.4.1 Influential Point Analysis

In linear regression, extreme values can create issues in the estimation process. A few high leverage values introduce bias in the estimators and create other aberrations in the residuals. So it is important to identify influential points in data. If the influential points seem too extreme, we have to discard them from our analysis as *outliers*.

A specific statistical measure that we will show, among others, is Cook's distance. This method is used to find an estimate of the influence data point when doing an OLS estimation.

Cook's distance is defined as follows:

$$D_i = \frac{e_i^2}{s^2 p}\left[\frac{h_i}{(1-h_i)^2}\right],$$

where $s^2 \equiv (n-p)^{-1} \mathrm{e}^{\top}\mathrm{e}$ is the mean squared error of the regression model and $h_i \equiv \mathbf{x}_\mathrm{i}^\mathrm{T}\left(\mathbf{X}^\mathrm{T}\mathbf{X}\right)^{-1}\mathbf{x}_\mathrm{i}$ and $\mathrm{e} = \mathrm{y} - \check{\mathrm{y}} = (\mathrm{I} - \mathrm{H})y$ is denoted by e_i

In simple terms, Cook's distance measures the effect of deleting a given observation. In this way, if removal of some observation causes significant changes, that means those points are influencing the regression model. These points are assigned a large value to Cook's distance and are considered for further investigation.

The cutoff value for this statistics can be taken as $D_i > 4/n$, where n is the number of observations. If you adjust for the number of parameters in the model, then the cutoff can be taken as $D_i > 4/(n-k-1)$, where k is the number of variables in the model.

```
library(car);
 Influential Observations
# Cook's D plot
# identify D values > 4/(n-k-1)
cutoff <-4/((nrow(Data_lm_Model)-length(fitted_Model_
multiple$coefficients)-2))
plot(fitted_Model_multiple, which=4, cook.levels=cutoff)
```

The plot in Figure 6-16 shows the Cook's distance for each observation in our dataset.

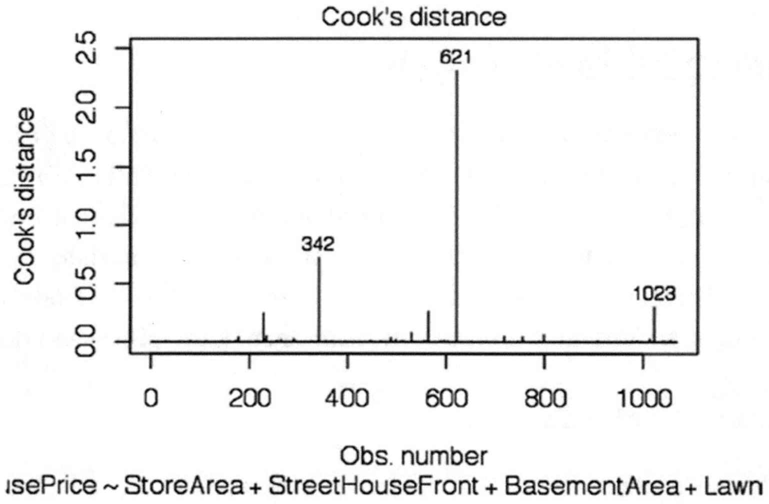

Figure 6-16. *Cook's distance for each observation*

You can see the observation numbers with a high Cook's distance are highlighted in the plot in Figure 6-16. These observations require further investigation.

```
# Influence Plot
influencePlot(fitted_Model_multiple,    id.method="identify",
main="Influence Plot", sub="Circle size is proportional to Cook's
Distance",id.location =FALSE)
```

The plot in Figure 6-17 shows a different view of Cook's distance. The circle size is proportional to the Cook's distance.

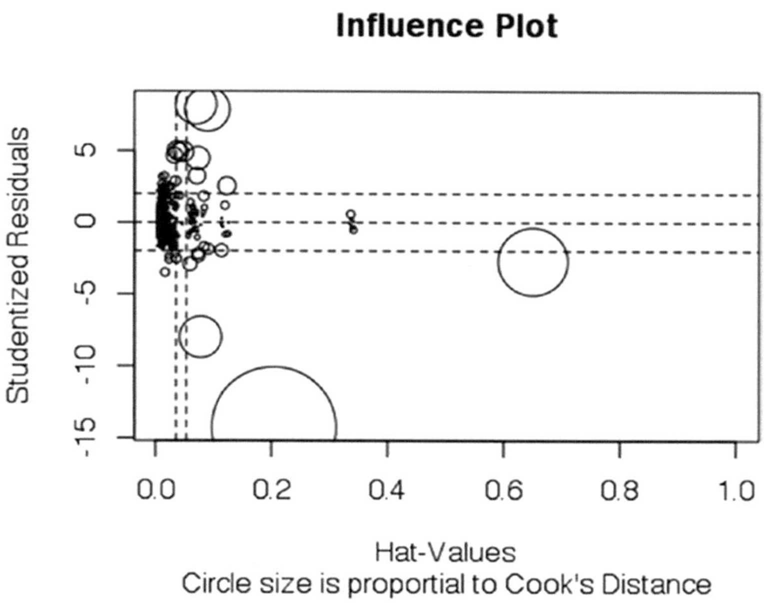

Figure 6-17. *Influence plot*

Also, the outlier test results are shown here:

```
#Outlier Plot
outlier.test(fitted_Model_multiple)
        rstudent unadjusted p-value Bonferonni p
 621  -14.285067          1.9651e-42   2.0987e-39
 229    8.259067          4.3857e-16   4.6839e-13
 564   -7.985171          3.6674e-15   3.9168e-12
 1023   7.902970          6.8545e-15   7.3206e-12
 718    5.040489          5.4665e-07   5.8382e-04
 799    4.925227          9.7837e-07   1.0449e-03
 235    4.916172          1.0236e-06   1.0932e-03
 487    4.673321          3.3491e-06   3.5768e-03
 530    4.479709          8.2943e-06   8.8583e-03
```

The observation numbers—342,621 and 102—as shown in Figure 6-17 (corresponding to HOUSE_ID 412, 759, and 1242) are the three main influence points. Let's pull out these records to see what values they have.

```
#Pull the records with highest leverage
Debug <-Data_lm_Model[c(342,621,1023),]

print(" The observed values for three high leverage points");
 [1] " The observed values for three high leverage points"
Debug
      HOUSE_ID HousePrice StoreArea StreetHouseFront BasementArea LawnArea
 342       412     375000       513              150         1236   215245
 621       759     160000      1418              313         5644    63887
 1023     1242     745000       813              160         2096    15623
      Rating      SaleType
 342       7      NewHouse
 621      10   FirstResale
 1023     10  SecondResale

print("Model fitted values for these high leverage points");
 [1] "Model fitted values for these high leverage points"

fitted_Model_multiple$fitted.values[c(342,621,1023)]
      342       621      1023
 441743.2 645975.9 439634.3

print("Summary of Observed values");
 [1] "Summary of Observed values"

summary(Debug)
     HOUSE_ID         HousePrice        StoreArea       StreetHouseFront
  Min.   : 412.0   Min.   :160000   Min.   : 513.0   Min.   :150.0
  1st Qu.: 585.5   1st Qu.:267500   1st Qu.: 663.0   1st Qu.:155.0
  Median : 759.0   Median :375000   Median : 813.0   Median :160.0
  Mean   : 804.3   Mean   :426667   Mean   : 914.7   Mean   :207.7
  3rd Qu.:1000.5   3rd Qu.:560000   3rd Qu.:1115.5   3rd Qu.:236.5
  Max.   :1242.0   Max.   :745000   Max.   :1418.0   Max.   :313.0

   BasementArea      LawnArea           Rating           SaleType
  Min.   :1236   Min.   : 15623   10      :2   FifthResale :0
  1st Qu.:1666   1st Qu.: 39755   7       :1   FirstResale :1
  Median :2096   Median : 63887   1       :0   FourthResale:0
```

```
 Mean   :2992   Mean   : 98252   2       :0   NewHouse    :1
 3rd Qu.:3870   3rd Qu.:139566   3       :0   SecondResale:1
 Max.   :5644   Max.   :215245   4       :0   ThirdResale :0
                                 (Other):0
```

Note that the house price for these three leverage points are far away from the mean or high density terms. The house price for two observations corresponds to the highest and lowest in the dataset. Also another interesting thing is the third observation corresponding to median house price is having a very high lawn area, certainly an influence point. Based on this analysis, we can either go back to check if these are data errors or choose to ignore them in our analysis.

6.5.4.2 Normality of Residuals

Residuals are core to the diagnostic of regression models. Normality of residual is an important condition for the model to be a valid linear regression model. In simple words, normality implies that the errors/residuals are random noise and our model has captured all the signals in data.

The linear regression model gives us the conditional expectation of function Y for given values of X. However, the fitted equation has some residual to it. We need the expectation of residual to be normally distributed with a mean of 0 or reducible to 0. A normal residual means that the model inference (confidence interval, model predictors' significance) is valid.

Distribution of studentized residuals (could be thought of as a normalized value) is a good way to see if the normality assumption is holding or not. But we may still want to formally test the residuals by normality tests like KS tests, Shapiro-Wilk tests, Anderson Darling tests, etc.

Here, we show the plot of studentized residual for a normal distribution, which should follow a bell curve.

```
library(stats)
library(IDPmisc)
 Loading required package: grid
library(MASS)
sresid <-studres(fitted_Model_multiple)
#Remove irregular values (NAN/Inf/NAs)
sresid <-NaRV.omit(sresid)
```

```
hist(sresid, freq=FALSE,
main="Distribution of Studentized Residuals",breaks=25)

xfit<-seq(min(sresid),max(sresid),length=40)
yfit<-dnorm(xfit)
lines(xfit, yfit)
```

The plot in Figure 6-18 is created using the studentized residuals. In the previous code, the residuals are studentized using the `studres()` function in R.

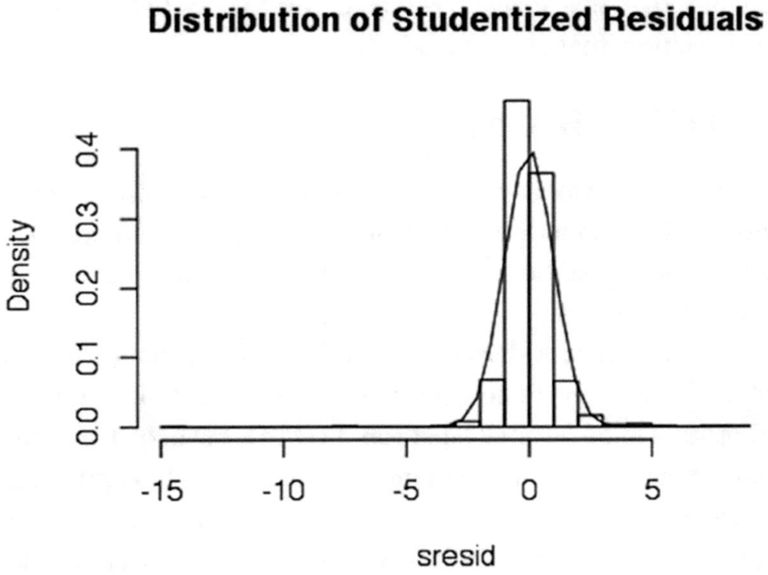

***Figure 6-18.** Distribution of studentized residuals*

The residual plot is close to a normal plot as the distribution forms a bell curve. However, we still want to do formal testing of the normality. We will show result of all three normality test but formally will introduce the test statistics for the most popular test of normality—one sample Kolmogorov-Smirnov Test or KS test. For rest of the tests, we encourage you to go through the R vignettes for the functions used here. It points to the most appropriate reference on the topic.

Formally, let's introduce the KS test here. The Kolmogorov–Smirnov statistic for a given cumulative distribution function F(x) is

$$D_n = \sup_x \left| F_n(x) - F(x) \right|$$

where *sup x* is the maximum of the set of distances.

The KS statistics give back the largest difference between the empirical distribution of residual and normal distribution. If the largest (`supremum`) is more than a critical value then we say the distribution is not normal (using the p-value of the test statistic). Here we have three tests for conformity of results:

```
# test on normality
#K-S one sample test
ks.test(fitted_Model_multiple$residuals,pnorm,alternative="two.sided")

  One-sample Kolmogorov-Smirnov test

 data:  fitted_Model_multiple$residuals
 D = 0.54443, p-value < 2.2e-16
 alternative hypothesis: two-sided
#Shapiro Wilk Test
shapiro.test(fitted_Model_multiple$residuals)

  Shapiro-Wilk normality test

 data:  fitted_Model_multiple$residuals
 W = 0.80444, p-value < 2.2e-16
#Anderson Darling Test
library(nortest)
ad.test(fitted_Model_multiple$residuals)

  Anderson-Darling normality test

 data:  fitted_Model_multiple$residuals
 A = 29.325, p-value < 2.2e-16
```

None of these three test thinks that the residuals are distributed normally. The p-values are less than 0.05, and hence we can reject the null hypothesis that the distribution is normal. This means we have to go back into our model and see what might be driving the non-normal behavior, dropping some variable or adding some variable, influential points, and other issues.

6.5.4.3 Multicollinearity

Multicollinearity is basically a problem of too much information in a pair of independent variables. This is a phenomenon when two or more variables are highly correlated, and hence causes inflated standard errors in the model fit. For testing this phenomenon, we can use the correlation matrix and see if they have a relationship with decent accuracy. If yes, the addition of one variable is enough for supplying the information required to explain the dependent variable.

For this section, we will use the variance inflation factor to determine the degree of multidisciplinary in the independent variables. Another popular method is the Colin index (Condition Index) number to detect multicollinearity.

The variance inflation factor (VIF) for multicollinearity is defined as follows:

$$\text{tolerance} = 1 - R_j^2, \qquad \text{VIF} = \frac{1}{\text{tolerance}}$$

where R_j^2 is the coefficient of determination of a regression of explanator j on all the other explanators.

Generally, cutoffs for detecting the presence of multicollinearity based on the metrics are:

- Tolerance less than 0.20
- VIF of 5 and greater indicating a multicollinearity problem

The simple solution to this problem is to drop the variable from these thresholds from the model building process.

```
library(car)
# calculate the vif factor
# Evaluate Collinearity
print(" Variance inflation factors are ");
 [1] " Variance inflation factors are "
vif(fitted_Model_multiple);
# variance inflation factors
                     GVIF Df GVIF^(1/(2*Df))
 StoreArea        1.767064  1        1.329309
 StreetHouseFront 1.359812  1        1.166110
 BasementArea     1.245537  1        1.116036
```

```
 LawnArea         1.254520  1         1.120054
 Rating           1.931826  9         1.037259
 SaleType         1.259122  5         1.023309
print("Tolerance factors are ");
 [1] "Tolerance factors are "
1/vif(fitted_Model_multiple)
                      GVIF        Df GVIF^(1/(2*Df))
 StoreArea        0.5659106 1.0000000       0.7522703
 StreetHouseFront 0.7353955 1.0000000       0.8575521
 BasementArea     0.8028664 1.0000000       0.8960281
 LawnArea         0.7971175 1.0000000       0.8928143
 Rating           0.5176450 0.1111111       0.9640796
 SaleType         0.7942043 0.2000000       0.9772220
```

Now we have the VIF values and tolerance value in the previous tables. We will simply apply the cutoffs for VIF and tolerance as discussed.

```
# Apply the cut-off to Vif
print("Apply the cut-off of 4 for vif")
 [1] "Apply the cut-off of 4 for vif"
vif(fitted_Model_multiple) >4
                  GVIF    Df GVIF^(1/(2*Df))
 StoreArea        FALSE FALSE           FALSE
 StreetHouseFront FALSE FALSE           FALSE
 BasementArea     FALSE FALSE           FALSE
 LawnArea         FALSE FALSE           FALSE
 Rating           FALSE  TRUE           FALSE
 SaleType         FALSE  TRUE           FALSE
# Apply the cut-off to Tolerance
print("Apply the cut-off of 0.2 for vif")
 [1] "Apply the cut-off of 0.2 for vif"
(1/vif(fitted_Model_multiple)) <0.2
                  GVIF    Df GVIF^(1/(2*Df))
 StoreArea        FALSE FALSE           FALSE
 StreetHouseFront FALSE FALSE           FALSE
 BasementArea     FALSE FALSE           FALSE
```

```
LawnArea            FALSE FALSE              FALSE
Rating              FALSE  TRUE              FALSE
SaleType            FALSE FALSE              FALSE
```

You can observe that the GVIF column is false for the cutoffs we set for multicollinearity. Hence, we can safely say that our model is not having a multicollinearity problem. And hence the standard errors are not inflated, so we can do hypothesis testing.

6.5.4.4 Residual Auto-Correlation

Correlation is defined among two different variables, while auto-correlation, also known as serial correlation, is the correlation of a variable with itself at different points in time or in a series. This type of relationship is very important and quite frequently used in time series modeling. Auto-correlation makes more sense when we have an inherent order in the observations, e.g., index by time, key, etc. If the residual shows that it has a definite relationship with prior residuals, i.e. auto-correlated, the noise is not purely by chance, which means we still have some more information that we can extract and put in the model.

To test for auto-correlation we will use the most popular method, the Durbin Watson test.

Given the process has defined the mean and variance, the auto-correlation statistics of Durbin Watson test can be defined as follows:

$$R(s,t) = \frac{\mathrm{E}\left[(X_t - \mu_t)(X_s - \mu_s)\right]}{\sigma_t \sigma_s}$$

This can be rewritten for our residual auto-correlation as d-Durbin Watson test statistics:

$$d = \frac{\sum_{t=2}^{T}(e_t - e_{t-1})^2}{\sum_{t=1}^{T} e_t^2}$$

where, `et` is the residual associated with the observation at time t.

To interpret the statistics, you can follow the rules outlined in Figure 6-19.

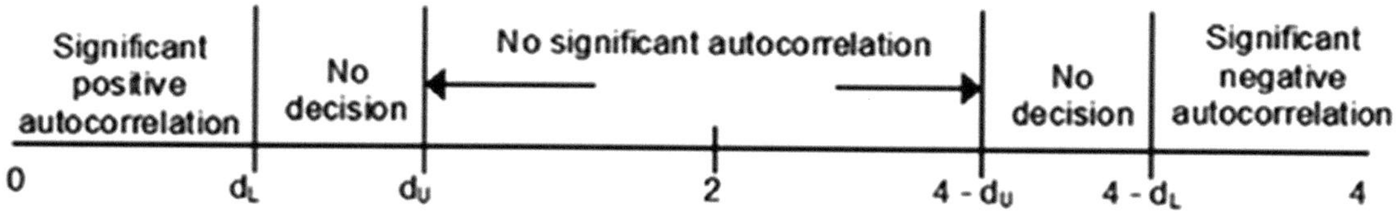

***Figure 6-19.** Durbin Watson statistics bounds*

Positive auto-correlations mean a positive error for one observation increases the chances of a positive error for another observation. While negative auto-correlation is the opposite. Both positive and negative auto-correlation are not desired in linear regression models. In Figure 6-20, it is clear that if the d-statistics value is close to 2, we can infer there if no auto-correlation in residual terms.

Another way to detect auto-correlation is by plotting the ACF plots and searching for spikes.

```
# Test for Autocorrelated Errors
durbinWatsonTest(fitted_Model_multiple)
  lag Autocorrelation D-W Statistic p-value
    1     -0.03814535      2.076011   0.192
  Alternative hypothesis: rho != 0
#ACF Plots
plot(acf(fitted_Model_multiple$residuals))
```

The plot in Figure 6-20 is called an Auto-Correlation Function (ACF) plot against different lags. This plot is popular in time series analysis as the data is time index, so we are using this plot here as a proxy for an auto-correlation explanation.

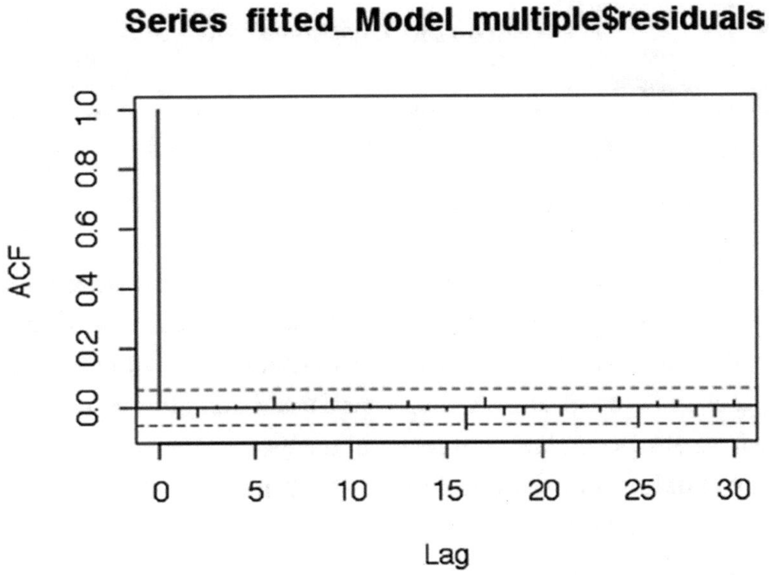

Figure 6-20. *Auto-correlation function (ACF) plot*

The Durbin Watson statistics show no auto-correlation among residuals, with d equal to 2.07. Also the ACF plots does not show spikes. Hence, we can say the residuals are free from auto-correlation.

6.5.4.5 Homoscedasticity

Homoscedasticity means all the random variables in the sequence or vector have finite and constant variance. This is also called homogeneity of variance. In the linear regression framework, homoscedastic errors/residuals will mean that the variance of errors is independent of the values of *x*. This means the probability distribution of *y* has the same standard deviation regardless of *x*.

There are multiple statistical tests for checking the homoscedasticity assumption, e.g., the Breush-Pagan test, the arch test, Bartlett's test, and so on. In this section our focus is on the Bartlett's test, developed in 1989 by Snedecor and Cochran.

To perform a Bartlett's test, first we create subgroups within our population data. For illustration we have created three groups of population data with 400, 400, and 269 observations in each group.

```
We can create three groups in data to see if the variance varies across
these three groups
gp<-numeric()
```

```
for( i in 1:1069)
{
  if(i<=400){
    gp[i] <-1;
  }else if(i<=800){
    gp[i] <-2;
  }else{
    gp[i] <-3;
  }
}
```

Now we define the hypothesis we will be testing in a Bartlett's test:

Ho: All three population variances are the same.

Ha: At least two are different.

Here, we perform a Bartlett's test with the function `Bartlett.test()`:

```
Data_lm_Model$gp <-factor(gp)
bartlett.test(fitted_Model_multiple$fitted.values,Data_lm_Model$gp)

  Bartlett test of homogeneity of variances

 data:  fitted_Model_multiple$fitted.values and Data_lm_Model$gp
 Bartlett's K-squared = 1.3052, df = 2, p-value = 0.5207
```

The Bartlett's test has a p-value of greater than 0.05, which means we fail to reject the null hypothesis. The subgroups have the same variance, and hence variance is homoscedastic.

Here, we show some more test for checking variances. This is done for reference purposes so that you can replicate other tests if required.

1. Breush-Pagan Test

   ```
   # non-constant error variance test - breush pagan test
   ncvTest(fitted_Model_multiple)
    Non-constant Variance Score Test
    Variance formula: ~ fitted.values
    Chisquare = 2322.866    Df = 1     p = 0
   ```

   These results are for a popular test for heteroscedasticity called the Breush-Pagan test. The p-value is 0, hence you can reject the null that the variance in heteroscedastic.

2. ARCH Test

```
#also show ARCH test - More relevant for a time series model
library(FinTS)
ArchTest(fitted_Model_multiple$residuals)

  ARCH LM-test; Null hypothesis: no ARCH effects

 data:  fitted_Model_multiple$residuals
 Chi-squared = 4.2168, df = 12, p-value = 0.9792
```

The test result for Bartlett's test and the Arch test clearly shows that the residuals are homoscedastic. The plot in Figure 6-21 is a residual versus fitted values plot. It is a scatter plot of residuals on the x-axis and fitted values (estimated responses) on the y-axis. The plot is used to detect non-linearity, unequal error variances, and outliers.

```
# plot residuals vs. fitted values
plot(fitted_Model_multiple$residuals,fitted_Model_multiple$fitted.
values)
```

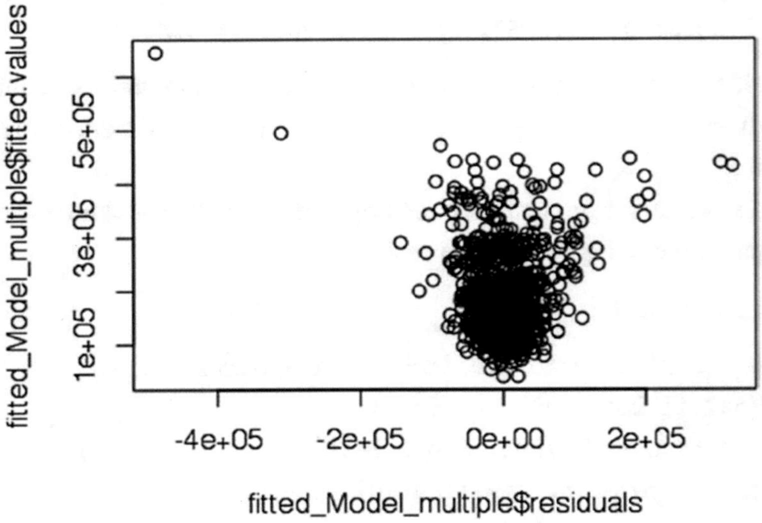

Figure 6-21. *Residuals versus fitted plot*

A plot of fitted values and residuals also does not show any behavior of increase or decrease. This means the residuals are homoscedastic as they don't vary with values of x.

In this section on model diagnostics, we explored the important test and process to identify problems with regression. Influential points can bring bias into the model estimates and reduce the performance of a model. We can explore a few options to reduce the problem by capping the values, creating bins and/or may be just remove them for analysis. Normality of residuals is important as we will expect a good model to capture all signals in the data and reduce the residual to just a white noise. Auto-correlation is a feature of indexed data, in this case if the residuals are not independent of each other and have auto-correlation then the model performance will be reduced. Homoscedasticity is another important diagnostic that tells us if the variance of dependent variable is independent of predictor/independent variable. All these diagnostics need to be done after fitting a regression model to make sure the model is reliable and statistically valid to be used in real settings.

Now we have tested major tests for linear regression and can now move onto polynomial regression. So far we have assumed that the relationship between dependent and independent variable was linear, but this may not be the case in real life. Linear relations show the same proportional change behavior at all levels. For example, the `HousePrice` increase when the store size changes from 10 sq. ft. to 20 sq. ft. is not the same as change of the same 10 sq. ft. from 2000 sq. ft. to 2010 sq. ft. But linear regression ignores this fact and assumes the same change at all levels.

The next section will extend the idea of linear regression to relationships with higher degree polynomials.

6.5.5 Polynomial Regression

The linear regression framework can be extended to polynomial relationship between variables. In polynomial regression, the relationship between independent variable x and dependent variable y is modeled as nth degree polynomial.

The polynomial regression model can be presented as follows:

$$y_i = a_0 + a_1 x_i + a_2 x_i^2 + \cdots + a_m x_i^m + \varepsilon_i \left(i = 1,2,\ldots,n \right)$$

There are multiple examples where the data does not follow linear dependent but higher degrees of relationship. In general, real life relations are not linear in true terms. Linear regression assume that the dependent variable can move only one direction with the same marginal change per unit independent variable.

For instance, HousePrice has a positive correlation with StoreArea. This means that if the StoreArea increases, the HousePrice will increase. So if StoreArea keeps on increasing the HousePrice prices will increase with the same rate (coefficient). But do you believe that a HousePrice can go to 1 million if the StoreArea is too big? No, StoreArea has a utility that keeps on decreasing as it increases and finally you will not see the same increase in HousePrice.

Economics provide a lot of good examples of such quadratic behavior, e.g., price elasticity, diminishing returns, etc. Also in normal planning we make use of quadratic and other high-level polynomial relationship like discount generation, pricing products, etc. We will show an example of how polynomial regression can help model some polynomial relationship.

Dependent variable: Price of a commodity

Independent variable: Quantity sold

The general principle is if the price is too cheap, people will not buy the commodity thinking it's not of good quality, but if the price is too high, people will not buy due to cost consideration. Let's try to quantify this relationship using linear and quadratic regression.

```
#Dependent variable : Price of a commodity

y <-as.numeric(c("3.3","2.8","2.9","2.3","2.6","2.1","2.5","2.9","2.4",
"3.0","3.1","2.8","3.3","3.5","3"));

#Independent variable : Quantity Sold

x<-as.numeric(c("50","55","49","68","73","71","80","84","79","92","91","90",
"110","103","99"));

#Plot Linear relationship
linear_reg <-lm(y~x)

summary(linear_reg)
```

```
 Call:
 lm(formula = y ~ x)
```

```
Residuals:
     Min       1Q   Median       3Q      Max
-0.66844 -0.25994  0.03346  0.20895  0.69004

Coefficients:
            Estimate Std. Error t value Pr(>|t|)
(Intercept) 2.232652   0.445995   5.006  0.00024 ***
x           0.007546   0.005463   1.381  0.19046
---
Signif. codes:  0 '***' 0.001 '**' 0.01 '*' 0.05 '.' 0.1 ' ' 1

Residual standard error: 0.3836 on 13 degrees of freedom
Multiple R-squared:  0.128,  Adjusted R-squared:  0.06091
F-statistic: 1.908 on 1 and 13 DF,  p-value: 0.1905
```

The model summary shows that the multiple R-square is merely 12% and the variable x is insignificant in the model. Also the coefficient of x is insignificant as the p-value is 0.19. Figure 6-22 shows the actual versus predicted scatter plot to see whether the values are getting fitted well or not.

```
res <-stack(data.frame(Observed =as.numeric(y), Predicted =fitted(linear_
reg)))
res <-cbind(res, x =rep(x, 2))

#Plot using lattice xyplot(function)
library("lattice")
xyplot(values ~x, data = res, group = ind, auto.key =TRUE)
```

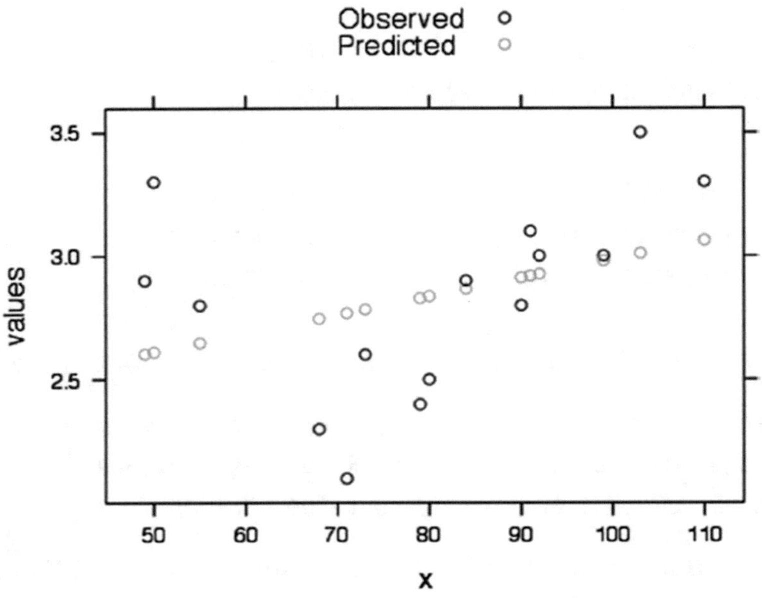

Figure 6-22. *Actual versus predicted plot linear model*

The plot provides additional proof that the linear relation is not evident from the plot. The values are not a right fit in the linear line predicted by the model.

Now, we move onto fitting a quadratic curve onto our data, to see if that helps us capture the curvilinear behavior of quantity by price.

```
#Plot Quadratic relationship
linear_reg <-lm(y~x +I(x^2) )

summary(linear_reg)

 Call:
 lm(formula = y ~ x + I(x^2))

 Residuals:
      Min       1Q   Median       3Q      Max
 -0.43380 -0.13005  0.00493  0.20701  0.33776

 Coefficients:
               Estimate Std. Error t value Pr(>|t|)
 (Intercept)  6.8737010  1.1648621   5.901 7.24e-05 ***
 x           -0.1189525  0.0309061  -3.849  0.00232 **
```

```
I(x^2)        0.0008145  0.0001976   4.122  0.00142 **
---
Signif. codes:  0 '***' 0.001 '**' 0.01 '*' 0.05 '.' 0.1 ' ' 1

Residual standard error: 0.2569 on 12 degrees of freedom
Multiple R-squared:  0.6391, Adjusted R-squared:  0.5789
F-statistic: 10.62 on 2 and 12 DF,  p-value: 0.002211
```

The model summary shows that the multiple R-square has improved to 63% after we introduce a quadratic term for *x,* and both variable *x* and *x*-square are statistically significant in the model. Let's plot the scatter plot and see if the values fit the data well. See Figure 6-23.

```
res <-stack(data.frame(Observed =as.numeric(y), Predicted =
fitted(linear_reg)))
res <-cbind(res, x =rep(x, 2))

#Plot using lattice xyplot(function)
library("lattice")
xyplot(values ~x, data = res, group = ind, auto.key =TRUE)
```

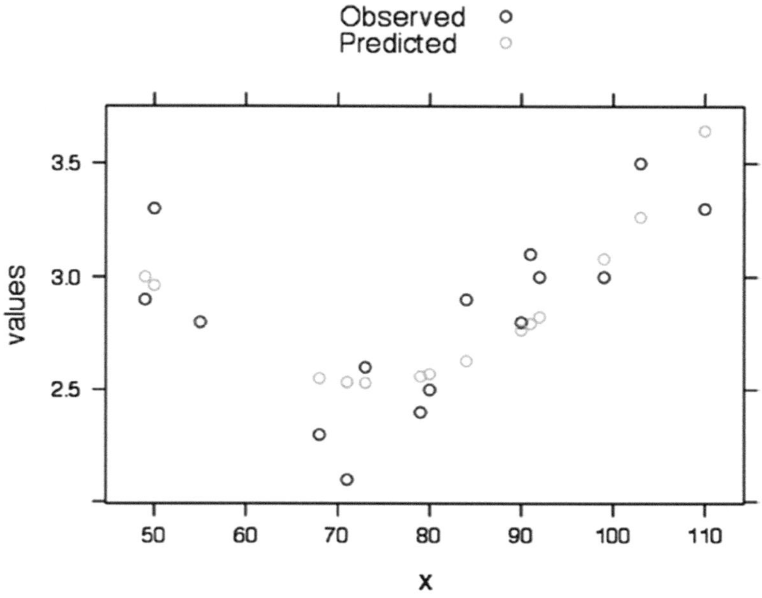

Figure 6-23. *Actual versus predicted plot quadratic polynomial model*

The model shows improvement in R-square and quadratic term is significant in model. The plot also shows a better fit in quadratic case than the linear case. The idea can be extended to higher degree polynomials, but that will cause overfitting. Also, many processes are normally not well represented by very high degree polynomial. If you are planning to use a polynomial of degree more than four, be very careful during the interpretation.

6.5.6 Logistic Regression

In linear regression we have seen that the dependent variable is a continuous variable having real values. Also, we have determined that the error requires to be normal for the regression equation to be valid. Now let's assume what will happen if the dependent variable is a having only two possible values (0 and 1), in other words binomially distributed. Then the error terms can not be normally distributed as:

$$ei = Binomial(Yi) - Gausssian(\beta 0 + \beta 1xi)$$

Hence, we need to move onto different framework to accommodate the cases where the dependent variable is not Gaussian but from an exponential family of distributions. After logistic regression we will touch on exponential distributions and show how they can be reduced to a linear form by a link function. The logistic regression models a relationship between predictor variables and a categorical response/dependent variable. For instance, the credit risk problem we were looking at in Chapter 5. The predictor variables were used to model the binomial outcome of default/No Default.

Logistic regression can be of three types based on the type of categorical (response) variable:

- ***Binomial logistic regression:*** Only two possible values for response variable(0/1). Typically we estimate the probability of it being 1 and based on some cutoff we predict the state of response variable.

  Binomial distribution probability mass function is given by

$$f(k;n;p) = \Pr(X = k) = \binom{n}{k} p^k (1-p)^{n-k}$$

  where k is number of successes, n is total number of trials, and p is the unit probability of success.

- ***Multinomial logistic regression*:** There are three or more values/levels for the categorical response variable. Typically, we calculate probability for each level and then, based on some classification (e.g., maximum probability), we assign the state of response variable.

The multinomial distribution probability mass function is given by

$$f(x_1,\ldots,x_k;n,p_1,\ldots,p_k) = \Pr(X_1 = x_1 \quad and \quad \ldots \quad and \quad X_k = x_k)$$

$$= \begin{cases} \dfrac{n!}{x_1!\cdots x_k!} p_1^{x_1} \cdots p_k^{x_k}, & \text{when } \sum_{i=1}^{k} x_i = n \\ 0 & \text{otherwise,} \end{cases}$$

$$for \quad non-negative \quad \text{int}egers \quad x_1,\ldots,x_k$$

where *xi* is set of predictor variables, *pk* is probability of each class (proportion), and *n* is number of trials (sample size).

- ***Ordered logistic regression*:** The response variable is a categorical variable with some built-in order in them. This method is the same as multinomial, with a key difference of having an inherent order in them. For example, a rating variable between 1 and 5.

Let's look at two important terms we will use in explaining the logistic regression.

6.5.7 Logit Transformation

For logistic regression, we use a transformation function, also called the link function, which creates a linear function from binomial distribution in independent variable. The link function used for binomial distribution is called the `logit` function (see Figure 6-24).

The `logit` function $\sigma(t)$ is defined as follows:

$$\sigma(t) = \frac{e^t}{e^t + 1} = \frac{1}{1 + e^{-t}}$$

The `logit` function curve looks like this:

```
curve((1/(1+exp(-x))),-10,10,col ="violet")
```

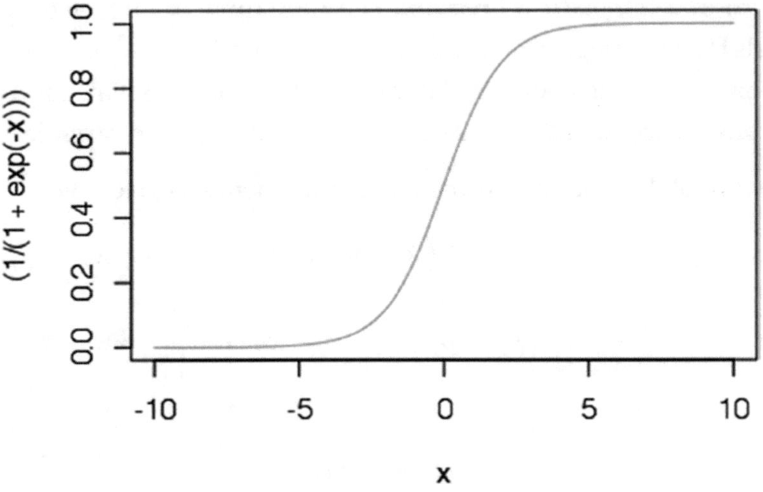

Figure 6-24. *Logit function*

You can observe that the `logit` function is capped from top by 1 and from bottom by 0. Extremely high values of x have very little effect on function value, the same for very small values. This way we can see the bounds are between 0 and 1 probability scale to fit a model.

In logistic regression, we use maximum likelihood estimation (MLE), while for multinomial we use iterative method to optimize on the `logLoss` function.

The `logit` function then convert the relationship into `logit` of odds ratio as a linear combination of independent variables. The inverse of the logistic function g, the `logit` (log odds), maps the relationship into a linear one:

$$g(F(x)) = \ln\left(\frac{F(x)}{1 - F(x)}\right) = \beta_0 + \beta_1 x$$

In this section we discuss logistic regression with binomial categorical variables, and in later part we touch at a high level how to extend this method into a multinomial class.

6.5.8 Odds Ratio

In Chapter 1, we discussed probability measure, which signifies the chance of having that event. The value of probability is always between 0 and 1, where 0 means definitely no occurrence of event and 1 being that event definitely happened.

We define probability odds, or simply odds, as the ratio of chance of the event happening and nothing happening

```
Odds in favor of event A = P(A)/1-P(A)
Odds against event A = (1-P(A))/P(A) = 1/Odds in favor
```

So now, an odds of 2 for event A will mean that event A is 2 times more likely of happening than not happening. The ratio can be generalized to any number of classes, where the interpretation changes to likelihood of an event happening against all possible events.

Odds ratio is a way to represent the relationship between presence/absence of an event “A” with the presence or absence of event “B”. For a binary case, we can create an example as shown:

$$Oddsratio = (OddsofA) / (OddsofB)$$

For example, let’s assume there are two types of event outcome, A and B. The probability of event A happening is 0.4 (P(A)) and event B is 0.6(P(B)). Then odds in favor of A are 0.66 (P(A)/1-P(A)), similarly, odds for B are 1.5 (P(B)/1-P(B)). This means the chances of event B happening is 1.5 times that of not happening.

Now the odds ratio is defined as a ratio of these odds, odds B by Odds A = 1.5/0.66 = 2.27 ~ 2. This is saying that the chances of B happening are twice that of event A happening. We can observe that this quantity is a relative measure, and hence we use concept of base levels in logistic regressions. The odds ratio from the model is relative to base level/class.

Now, we can introduce the relationship between `logit` and odds ratios. The logistic regression essentially models the following equation, which is a `logit` transform on the odds of the event and then coverts our problem to its linear form, as shown:

$$\operatorname{logit}\left(\mathrm{E}\left[Y_i \middle| x_{1,i},\ldots,x_{m,i}\right]\right) = \operatorname{logit}(p_i) = \ln\left(\frac{p_i}{1-p_i}\right) = \beta_0 + \beta_1 x_{1,i} + \cdots + \beta_m x_{m,i}$$

Hence in logistic regression, the odds ratio is the exponentiated coefficient of variables, signifying the relative chance of the event from reference class/event. Here, you can see how the odds ratio translates to exponentiated coefficients of logistic regression.

$$\mathrm{OR} = \frac{\mathrm{odds}(x+1)}{\mathrm{odds}(x)} = \frac{\dfrac{F(x+1)}{1-F(x+1)}}{\dfrac{F(x)}{1-F(x)}} = \frac{e^{\beta_0+\beta_1(x+1)}}{e^{\beta_0+\beta_1 x}} = e^{\beta_1}$$

6.5.8.1 Binomial Logistic Model

Let's use our purchase prediction data to build a logistic regression model and see its diagnostics. We will be subsetting the data to only have ProductChoice 1 and 3 as 1 and 0 respectively, in our analysis.

```
#Load the data and prepare a dataset for logistic regression
Data_Purchase_Prediction <-read.csv("~/Dropbox/Book Writing - Drafts/
Chapter Drafts/Final Artwork and Code/Chapter 6/Dataset/Purchase Prediction
Dataset.csv",header=TRUE);

Data_Purchase_Prediction$choice <-ifelse(Data_Purchase_
Prediction$ProductChoice ==1,1,
ifelse(Data_Purchase_Prediction$ProductChoice ==3,0,999));

Data_Logistic <-Data_Purchase_Prediction[Data_Purchase_Prediction$choice
%in%c("0","1"),c("CUSTOMER_ID","choice","MembershipPoints","IncomeClass","C
ustomerPropensity","LastPurchaseDuration")]

table(Data_Logistic$choice,useNA="always")

      0      1   <NA>
 143893 106603      0
Data_Logistic$MembershipPoints <-factor(Data_Logistic$MembershipPoints)
Data_Logistic$IncomeClass <-factor(Data_Logistic$IncomeClass)
Data_Logistic$CustomerPropensity <-factor(Data_Logistic$CustomerPropensity)
Data_Logistic$LastPurchaseDuration <-as.numeric(Data_
Logistic$LastPurchaseDuration)
```

Before we start the model, let's see the distribution of categorical variables over dependent categorical variables.

```
table(Data_Logistic$MembershipPoints,Data_Logistic$choice)

        0     1
 1  15516 13649
 2  19486 15424
 3  20919 15661
 4  20198 14944
 5  18868 13728
 6  16710 11883
 7  13635  9381
 8   9632  6432
 9   5566  3512
 10  2427  1446
 11   754   441
 12   165    95
 13    17     7
```

This distribution says that as the MemberShipPoints increase, both choice 0 and 1 decrease.

```
table(Data_Logistic$IncomeClass,Data_Logistic$choice)

       0     1
 1   145   156
 2   203   209
 3  3996  3535
 4 23894 18952
 5 47025 36781
 6 38905 27804
 7 21784 14715
 8  6922  3958
 9  1019   493
```

This distribution says that most of the customers are in income classes 4, 5, and 6. The choice distribution is equitable in both 0 and 1 across the income class bands.

```
table(Data_Logistic$CustomerPropensity,Data_Logistic$choice)

               0     1
   High     26604 10047
   Low      20291 19962
   Medium   27659 17185
   Unknown  36633 52926
   VeryHigh 32706  6483
```

The distribution is interesting as it tells that customers with very high propensity are very unlikely to buy the product represented by class 1. The distributions are good way to get a first-hand idea of your data. This exploratory task also helps in feature selections for models.

Now, we have all the relevant libraries and function loaded, we will show step by step how to develop the logistic regression and choose one of the models for evaluation in the next chapter. We will be developing models on full data, and the next chapter discusses performance evaluation metrics in detail.

```
library(dplyr)
#Get the average purchase rate by Rating and plot that

summarise(group_by(Data_Logistic,IncomeClass),Average_Rate=mean(choice))
print("Summary of Average Purchase Rate by IncomeClass")
 [1] "Summary of Average Purchase Rate by IncomeClass"
summary_Rating
 # A tibble: 9 × 2
   IncomeClass Average_Rate
        <fctr><dbl>
 1           1    0.5182724
 2           2    0.5072816
 3           3    0.4693932
 4           4    0.4423283
 5           5    0.4388827
 6           6    0.4167953
 7           7    0.4031617
 8           8    0.3637868
 9           9    0.3260582
```

```
plot(summary_Rating$IncomeClass,summary_Rating$Average_Rate,type="b",
xlab="Income Class", ylab="Average Purchase Rate observed", main="Purchase
Rate and Income Class")
```

Now we want to see how average purchase rate of product 1 varies over the income class. We plot the average purchase rate (proportion of 1) by each income class, as shown in Figure 6-25.

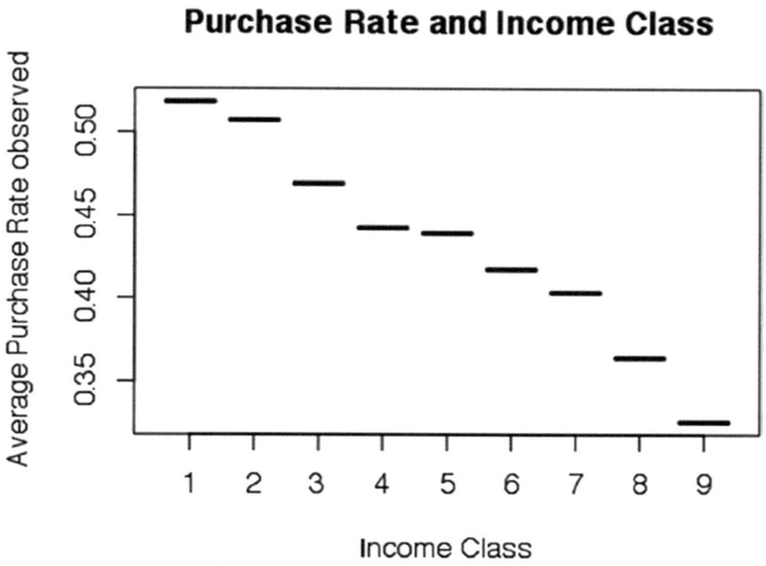

Figure 6-25. *Purchase rate and income class*

The plot in Figure 6-25 shows that, as the income class increases, the propensity to buy the product 1 goes down. Similar plots can be created for other variables to see how the expected behavior of model probabilities should be after fitting a model.

Now we will clean up the data from NAs (missing values 0) and fit a binary logistic regression using the function `glm()`. GLM stands for generalized linear regression, which can handle exponential family of distributions. The function requires users to mention the family of distribution the dependent variable belong to and the link function you want to use. We have used the binomial family with `logit` as a link function.

```
#Remove the Missing values - NAs

Data_Logistic <-na.omit(Data_Logistic)
rownames(Data_Logistic) <-NULL
```

```
#Divide the data into Train and Test
set.seed(917);
index <-sample(1:nrow(Data_Logistic),round(0.7*nrow(Data_Logistic)))
train <-Data_Logistic[index,]
test <-Data_Logistic[-index,]
```

```
Fitting a logistic model
Model_logistic <-glm( choice ~MembershipPoints +IncomeClass
+CustomerPropensity +LastPurchaseDuration, data = train, family
=binomial(link ='logit'));
```

```
summary(Model_logistic)
```

```
 Call:
 glm(formula = choice ~ MembershipPoints + IncomeClass + Customer
 Propensity +
     LastPurchaseDuration, family = binomial(link = "logit"),
     data = train)

 Deviance Residuals:
    Min      1Q  Median      3Q     Max
 -1.631  -1.017  -0.614   1.069   2.223

 Coefficients:
                            Estimate Std. Error z value Pr(>|z|)
 (Intercept)                0.066989   0.145543   0.460 0.645323
 MembershipPoints2         -0.123408   0.020577  -5.997 2.01e-09 ***
 MembershipPoints3         -0.185540   0.020359  -9.113  < 2e-16 ***
 MembershipPoints4         -0.204938   0.020542  -9.977  < 2e-16 ***
 MembershipPoints5         -0.237311   0.020942 -11.332  < 2e-16 ***
 MembershipPoints6         -0.258884   0.021597 -11.987  < 2e-16 ***
 MembershipPoints7         -0.291123   0.022894 -12.716  < 2e-16 ***
 MembershipPoints8         -0.326029   0.025526 -12.773  < 2e-16 ***
 MembershipPoints9         -0.387113   0.031572 -12.261  < 2e-16 ***
 MembershipPoints10        -0.439228   0.044839  -9.796  < 2e-16 ***
 MembershipPoints11        -0.357339   0.078493  -4.553 5.30e-06 ***
 MembershipPoints12        -0.447326   0.164172  -2.725 0.006435 **
 MembershipPoints13        -1.349163   0.583320  -2.313 0.020728 *
```

```
IncomeClass2                 -0.412020   0.190461  -2.163 0.030520 *
IncomeClass3                 -0.342854   0.146938  -2.333 0.019631 *
IncomeClass4                 -0.389236   0.144433  -2.695 0.007040 **
IncomeClass5                 -0.373493   0.144169  -2.591 0.009579 **
IncomeClass6                 -0.442134   0.144244  -3.065 0.002175 **
IncomeClass7                 -0.455158   0.144548  -3.149 0.001639 **
IncomeClass8                 -0.509290   0.146126  -3.485 0.000492 ***
IncomeClass9                 -0.569825   0.160174  -3.558 0.000374 ***
CustomerPropensityLow         0.877850   0.018709  46.921  < 2e-16 ***
CustomerPropensityMedium      0.427725   0.018491  23.131  < 2e-16 ***
CustomerPropensityUnknown     1.208693   0.016616  72.744  < 2e-16 ***
CustomerPropensityVeryHigh -0.601513   0.021652 -27.781  < 2e-16 ***
LastPurchaseDuration         -0.063463   0.001211 -52.393  < 2e-16 ***
---
Signif. codes:  0 '***' 0.001 '**' 0.01 '*' 0.05 '.' 0.1 ' ' 1

(Dispersion parameter for binomial family taken to be 1)

    Null deviance: 235658  on 172985  degrees of freedom
Residual deviance: 213864  on 172960  degrees of freedom
AIC: 213916

Number of Fisher Scoring iterations: 4
```

The p-value of all the variables and levels is significant. This implies we have fit a model with variables having significant relationship with dependent variable. Now let's work out to get classification matrix for this model. This is done by method of balancing specificity and sensitivity. Details of these metrics are given in Chapter 6, and we give a brief explanation here and make use of that to create a good cutoff for classification from probabilities into classes.

```
#install and load package
library(pROC)
#apply roc function
cut_off <-roc(response=train$choice, predictor=Model_logistic$fitted.
values)
```

```
#Find threshold that minimizes error
e <-cbind(cut_off$thresholds,cut_off$sensitivities+cut_off$specificities)
best_t <-subset(e,e[,2]==max(e[,2]))[,1]

#Plot ROC Curve
plot(1-cut_off$specificities,cut_off$sensitivities,type="l",
ylab="Sensitivity",xlab="1-Specificity",col="green",lwd=2,
main ="ROC Curve for Train")
abline(a=0,b=1)

abline(v = best_t) #add optimal t to ROC curve
```

The plot in Figure 6-26 is between specificity and sensitivity. The plot is also called an ROC plot. The best cutoff is the value on the curve that maximizes sensitivity and minimizes specificity.

```
cat(" The best value of cut-off for classifier is ", best_t)
 The best value of cut-off for classifier is 0.4202652
```

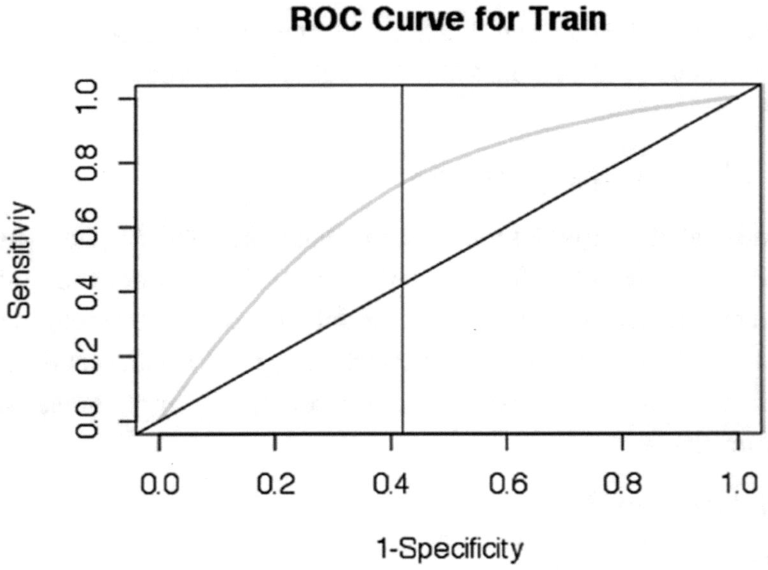

Figure 6-26. *ROC curve for train data*

Looking at the plot, we can see our choice of cutoff will provide best classification on the train data. We need to test this assumption on the test data and record the classification rate by using this cutoff of 0.42.

```
# Predict the probabilities for test and apply the cut-off
predict_prob <-predict(Model_logistic, newdata=test, type="response")

#Apply the cutoff to get the class
class_pred <-ifelse(predict_prob >0.41,1,0)
#Classification table
table(test$choice,class_pred)
    class_pred
         0     1
   0 24605 18034
   1  8364 23134
#Classification rate
sum(diag(table(test$choice,class_pred))/nrow(test))
 [1] 0.6439295
```

The model shows 64% good classification on the test data. This shows the model can capture the signals in the data well to distinguish between 0 and 1.

The logistic model diagnostic is different from linear regression models. In the following sections, we explore some common diagnostic metrics for logistic regression.

6.5.9 Model Diagnostics: Logistic Regression

Once we have fit the model, we have a two-step analysis to do on the logistic output:

1. If we are interested in final assignment of class, we focus on classifier and compare the exact classes assigned by using classifier on the predicted probabilities.

2. If we are interested in the probabilities, we look at the cases where the chances of the event are high are getting high probabilities.

Other than this, we want to look at the coefficients, R-square equivalents, and other tests to verify that our model has been fit with statistical validity. Another important thing to keep in mind while looking coefficients is that the logistic regression coefficients represent the change in the `logit` for each unit change in the predictor, which is not the same as linear regression.

We will show how to perform three diagnostic tests—the Wald test, the likelihood ratio test, and the deviance/pseudo R-square—and three measure of separation bivariate plots, gains/lift chart, and concordance ratio.

6.5.9.1 Wald Test

The Wald test is analogous to the t-test in linear regression. This is used to assess the contribution of individual predictors in a given model.

In logistic regression, the Wald statistic is

$$W_j = \frac{\beta_j^2}{SE_{\beta_j}^2}$$

Add β is coefficient and SE is standard error of coefficient β.

The Wald statistic is the ratio of the square of the regression coefficient to the square of the standard error of the coefficient, and it follows a chi-square distribution.
A significant Wald statistic implies that the predictor/independent variable is significant in the model.

Let's perform a Wald test on `MembershipPoints` and see if that is significant in the model or not.

```
#Wald test
library(survey)
regTermTest(Model_logistic,"MembershipPoints", method ="Wald")
 Wald test for MembershipPoints
  in glm(formula = choice ~ MembershipPoints + IncomeClass +
  CustomerPropensity +
     LastPurchaseDuration, family = binomial(link = "logit"),
     data = train)
 F =  31.64653  on  12  and  172960  df: p= < 2.22e-16
```

The p-value is less than 0.05, so at 95% confidence we can reject the null hypothesis that the coefficient's value is zero. Hence, the `MembershipPoints` is a statistically significant variable of the model.

6.5.9.2 Deviance

Deviance is calculated by comparing a null model and a saturated model. A null model is a model without any predictor in it, just the intercept term and a saturated model is the fitted model with some predictors in it. In logistic regression, deviance is used in lieu of the sums of squares calculations. The test statistic (often denoted by D) is twice the log of the likelihoods ratio, i.e., it is twice the difference in the log likelihoods:

Deviance

$$D = -2\ln \frac{\text{likelihood of the fitted model}}{\text{likelihood of the saturated model}}$$

The deviance statistic (D) follows a chi-square distribution. Smaller values indicate a better fit as the fitted model deviates less from the saturated model.

Here is the analysis of the deviance table.

```
#Anova table of significance
anova(Model_logistic, test="Chisq")
 Analysis of Deviance Table

 Model: binomial, link: logit

 Response: choice

 Terms added sequentially (first to last)

                       Df Deviance Resid. Df Resid. Dev  Pr(>Chi)
 NULL                                 172985     235658
 MembershipPoints      12    330.6    172973     235328 < 2.2e-16 ***
 IncomeClass            8    339.1    172965     234989 < 2.2e-16 ***
 CustomerPropensity     4  18297.4    172961     216691 < 2.2e-16 ***
 LastPurchaseDuration  1   2826.9    172960     213864 < 2.2e-16 ***
 ---
 Signif. codes:  0 '***' 0.001 '**' 0.01 '*' 0.05 '.' 0.1 ' ' 1
```

The chi-square test on all the variables is significant as the p-value is less than 0.05. All the predictors' contributions to the model are significant.

6.5.9.3 Pseudo R-Square

In linear regression, we have R-square measure (discussed in detail in Chapter 7), which measures the proportion of variance independently explained by the model. A similar measure in logistics regression is called pseudo R-square. The most popular of such measure used the likelihood ratio, which is presented as:

$$R_{\mathrm{L}}^2 = \frac{D_{\text{null}} - D_{\text{fitted}}}{D_{\text{null}}}.$$

It's the ratio of the difference in the deviance of null and the fitted model by the null model. The higher the value of this measure, the better the explaining power of the model. There are other similar measures not discussed in this chapter, like Cox and Snell R-square, Nagelkerke R-square, McFadden R-square, and Tjur R-square. Here we compute the pseudo R-square for our model.

```
# R square equivalent for logistic regression
library(pscl)
pR2(Model_logistic)
          llh        llhNull             G2       McFadden           r2ML
-1.069321e+05 -1.178291e+05  2.179399e+04  9.248135e-02  1.183737e-01
         r2CU
 1.591199e-01
```

The last three outputs from this function are McFadden's pseudo R-square, Maximum likelihood pseudo R-square (Cox & Snell) and Cragg and Uhler's or Nagelkerke's pseudo R-square. The R-square values are very low, signifying that the model might not be performing better than a null model.

6.5.9.4 Bivariate Plots

The most important diagnostic of logistic regression is to see how the actual probabilities and predicted probabilities behave by each level of single independent variables. These plots are called *bivariate* as there are two variables—actual and predicted—plotted against single independent variable levels. The plot have three important inputs:

- *Actual Probability:* The prior proportion of target level in each category of independent variable.

- *Predicted Probability:* The probability given by the model.
- *Frequency:* The frequency of a categorical variable (number of observations).

The plot essentially tells us how the model is behaving for different levels in our categorical variables. You can extend this idea to continuous variables as well by binning the continuous variable.

Another good thing about these plots is that you can determine for which cohort in your dataset the model performs better and where it need investigation. This cohort level diagnostic is not possible by looking at aggregated plots.

```
#The function code is provided separately in the appendix
source("actual_pred_plot.R")
MODEL_PREDICTION <-predict(Model_logistic, Data_Logistic, type
='response');
Data_Logistic$MODEL_PREDICTION <-MODEL_PREDICTION
#Print the plots MembershipPoints
actual_pred_plot  (var.by=as.character("MembershipPoints"),
var.response='choice',
data=Data_Logistic,
var.predict.current='MODEL_PREDICTION',
var.predict.reference=NULL,
var.split=NULL,
var.by.buckets=NULL,
sort.factor=FALSE,
errorbars=FALSE,
subset.to=FALSE,
barline.ratio=1,
title="Actual vs. Predicted Purchase Rates",
make.plot=TRUE
                  )
```

The plot in Figure 6-27 shows actual versus predicted against the frequency plot of `MembershipPoints`.

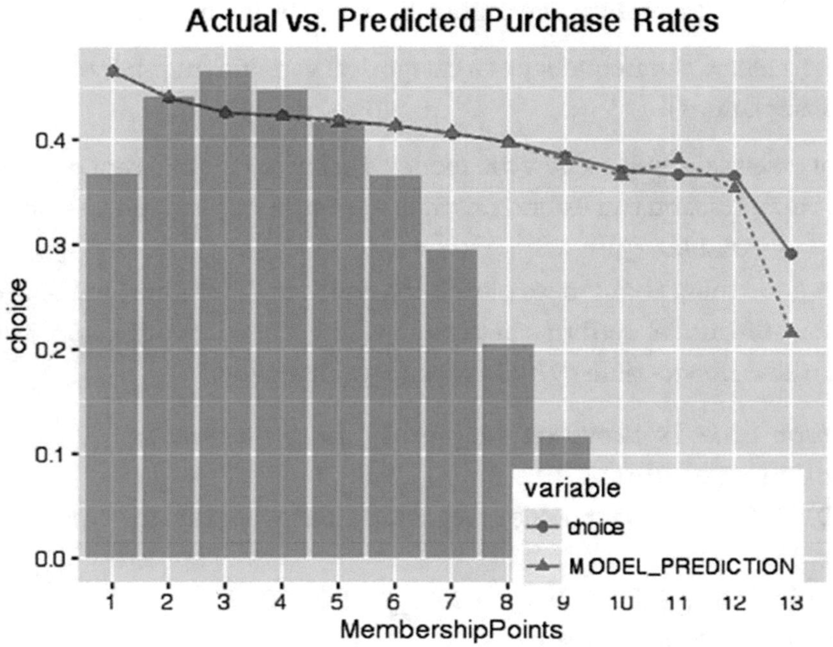

Figure 6-27. *Actual versus predicted plot against MembershipPoints*

For `MembershipPoints`, the actual and predicted probabilities follow each other. This means the model predicts the probabilities close to actual. Also, you can see in both cases customer having higher `MembershipPoints` are less likely to have product choice = 1, that is the same as seen in the actual and predicted.

```
#Print the plots IncomeClass
actual_pred_plot  (var.by=as.character("IncomeClass"),
var.response='choice',
data=Data_Logistic,
var.predict.current='MODEL_PREDICTION',
var.predict.reference=NULL,
var.split=NULL,
var.by.buckets=NULL,
sort.factor=FALSE,
errorbars=FALSE,
subset.to=FALSE,
barline.ratio=1,
```

```
title="Actual vs. Predicted Purchase Rates",
make.plot=TRUE
                    )
```

The plot in Figure 6-28 shows actual versus predicted against the frequency plot of `IncomeClass`.

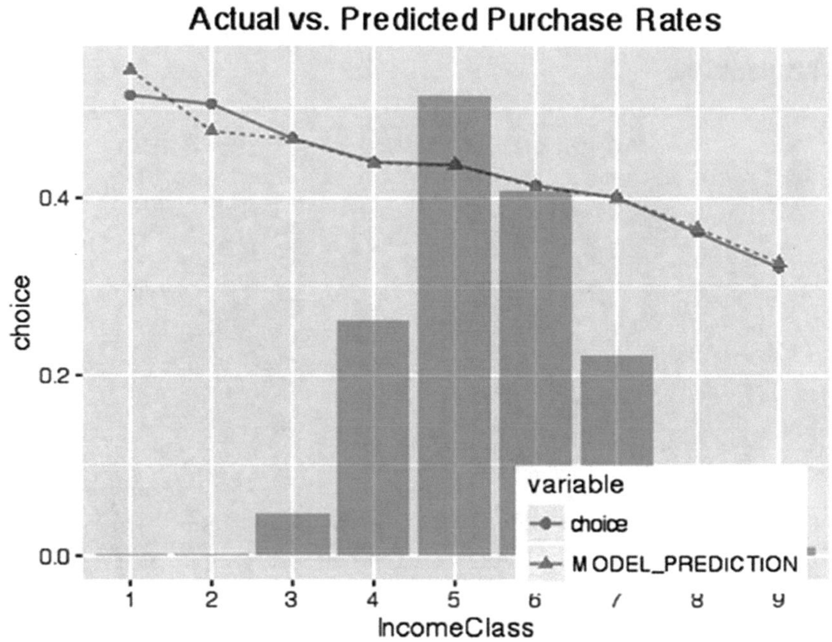

Figure 6-28. *Actual versus predicted plot against IncomeClass*

Again, the model behavior for `IncomeClass` is as expected. The model is able to predict the probabilities across different income classes as an actual observed rate.

```
#Print the plots CustomerPropensity
actual_pred_plot  (var.by=as.character("CustomerPropensity"),
var.response='choice',
data=Data_Logistic,
var.predict.current='MODEL_PREDICTION',
var.predict.reference=NULL,
var.split=NULL,
var.by.buckets=NULL,
sort.factor=FALSE,
```

```
errorbars=FALSE,
subset.to=FALSE,
barline.ratio=1,
title="Actual vs. Predicted Purchase Rates",
make.plot=TRUE
                    )
```

The plot in Figure 6-29 shows the actual versus predicted against the frequency plot of `CustomerPropensity`.

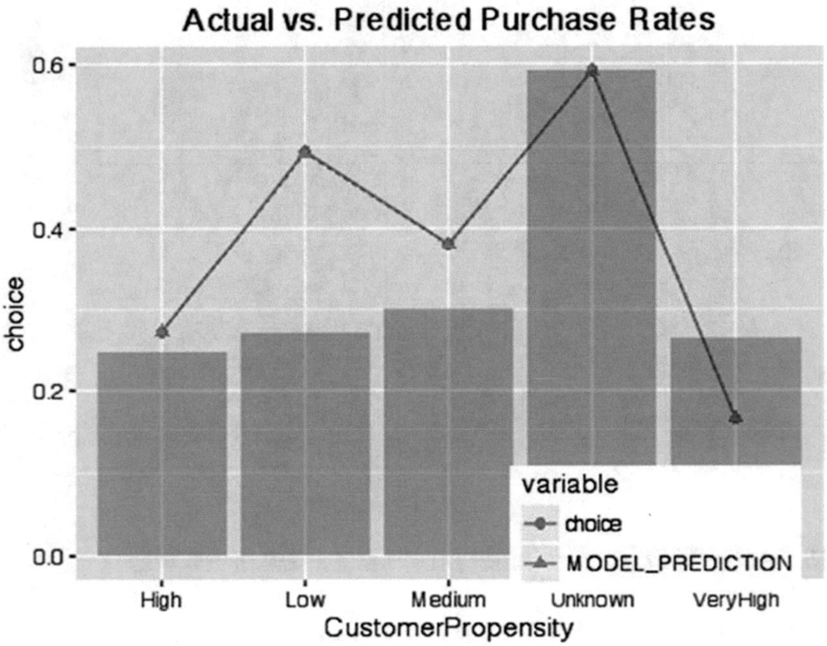

***Figure 6-29.** Actual versus predicted plot against CustomerPropensity*

The model shows good agreement with observed probabilities for `CustomerPropensity` as well. Similar plots can be plotted for continuous variable in our model after binning them appropriately. At least on categorical variables, the model performs well.

The model shows a good prediction against actual values across different categorical variable levels. It's a good model at the probability scale!

6.5.9.5 Cumulative Gains and Lift Charts

Cumulative gains and lift charts are visual ways to measure the effectiveness of predictive models. They consist of a baseline and the lift curve due to the predictive model. The more there is separation between baseline and predicted (lift) curve, the better the model.

In a Gains curve:

X-axis: % of customers

Y-axis: Percentage of positive predictions

Baseline: Random line (x% of customers giving x% of positive predictions)

Gains: The percentage of positive responses for the % of customers

In a Lift curve:

X-axis: % of customers

Y-axis: Actual lift (the ratio between the result predicted by our model and the result using no model)

```
library(gains)
library(ROCR)
library(calibrate)
MODEL_PREDICTION <-predict(Model_logistic, Data_Logistic, type
='response');

Data_Logistic$MODEL_PREDICTION <-MODEL_PREDICTION;
lift =with(Data_Logistic, gains(actual = Data_Logistic$choice, predicted =
Data_Logistic$MODEL_PREDICTION , optimal =TRUE));
pred =prediction(MODEL_PREDICTION,as.numeric(Data_Logistic$choice));

# Function to create performance objects. All kinds of predictor
evaluations are performed using this function.
gains =performance(pred, 'tpr', 'rpp');
# tpr: True positive rate
# rpp: Rate of positive predictions
auc =performance(pred, 'auc');
auc =unlist(slot(auc, 'y.values')); # The same as: auc@y.values[[1]]
auct =paste(c('AUC = '), round(auc, 2), sep ='')
```

```
#par(mfrow=c(1,2), mar=c(6,5,4,2));

plot(gains, col='red', lwd=2, xaxs='i', yaxs='i', main =paste('Gains
Chart ', sep =''),ylab='% of Positive Response', xlab='% of customers/
population');
axis(side =1, pos =0, at =seq(0, 1, by =0.10));
axis(side =2, pos =0, at =seq(0, 1, by =0.10));

lines(x=c(0,1), y=c(0,1), type='l', col='black', lwd=2,
ylab='% of Positive Response', xlab='% of customers/population');

legend(0.6, 0.4, auct, cex =1.1, box.col ='white')

gains =lift$cume.pct.of.total
deciles =length(gains);

for (j in 1:deciles)
{
  x =0.1;
  y =as.numeric(as.character(gains[[j]]));
lines(x =c(x*j, x*j),
y =c(0, y),
type ='l', col ='blue', lwd =1);
lines(x =c(0, 0.1*j),
y =c(y, y),
type ='l', col ='blue', lwd =1);
# Annotating the chart by adding the True Positive Rate exact numbers at
the specified deciles.
textxy(0, y, paste(round(y,2)*100, '%',sep=''), cex=0.9);
}
```

The chart in Figure 6-30 is the Gains chart for our model. This is plotted with the percentage of positive responses on the y-axis and the population percentage on the x-axis.

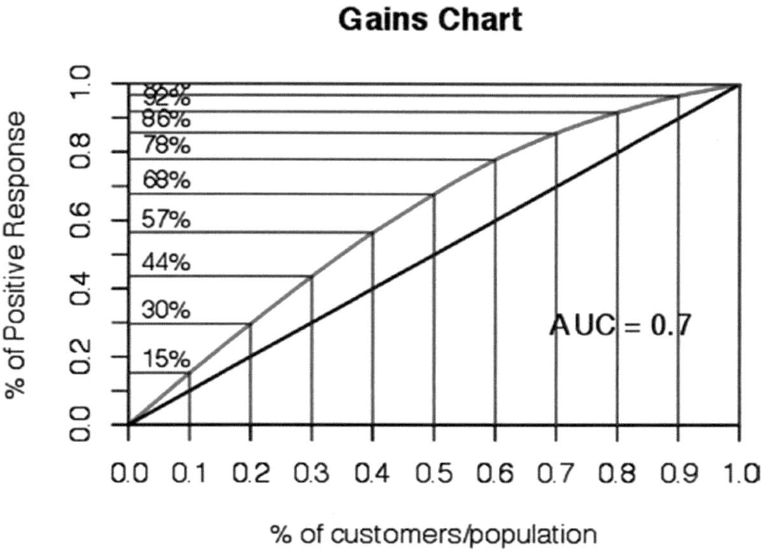

Figure 6-30. *Gains charts with AUC*

```
plot(lift,
xlab ='% of customers/population',
ylab ='Actual Lift',
main =paste('Lift Chart \n', sep =' '),
xaxt ='n');
axis(side =1, at =seq(0, 100, by =10), las =1, hadj =0.4);
```

The chart in Figure 6-31 is the Lift chart for our model. This is plotted with actual lift on the y-axis and population percentage on the x-axis.

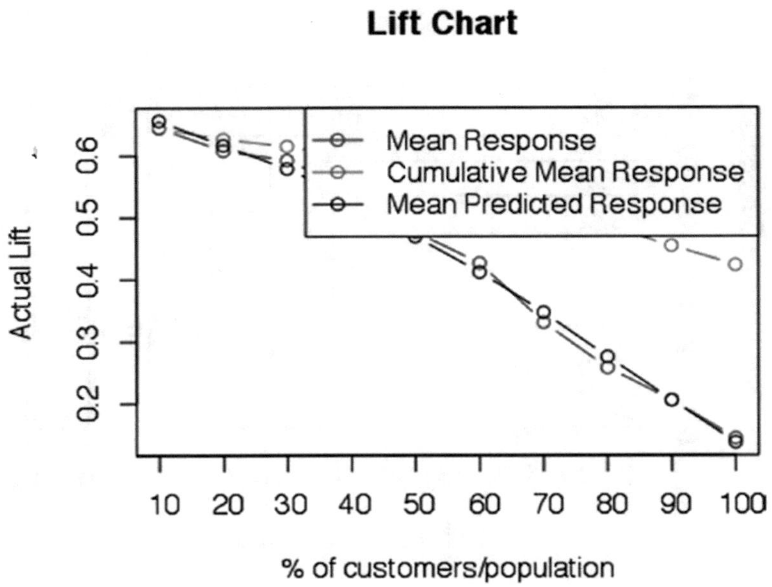

Figure 6-31. Lift chart

The Gains shows a good separation between model line and baseline. This shows that the model has good separation power. Also the AUC value of 0.7 means that the model will be able to roughly separate 70% of cases.

The Lift curve shows a lift of close to 70% for the first 10% of the population. This value needs to be the same as what we observed in the Gains chart, only the presentation has changed.

6.5.9.6 Concordance and Discordant Ratios

In any classification model based on raw probabilities, we need a classification methodology to separate these probability cases. In binary logistic, this is most of the time done by choosing a cutoff value and then creating an inequality to classify objects into 0 or 1.

To make sure such a cutoff exists and has good separation power, we have to see if the actual objects with state 1 in data are having higher probability than the actual state 0. For example, a pair of (Yi,Yj) be (0,1), then the predicted values (Pi,Pj) should have Pj>Pi, then we can choose a number between Pj and Pi, which will correctly classify a 1 as 1 and 0 as 0. Based on this understanding, we can divide all the possible pairs in data into three types:

- *Concordant pairs:* For (0,1) or (1,0) corresponding probabilities with 1 are greater than probabilities with 0
- *Discordant pairs:* For (0,1) or (1,0) corresponding probabilities with 0 are greater than probabilities with 1
- **Tied:** (0,0) and (1,0) pairs

The concordance ratio is then defined as the ratio of the number of concordant pairs by the total number of pairs. If our model produces a high concordance ratio then it will be able to classify the objects in classes more accurately.

```
#The function code is provided separately in R-code for Chapter 6
source("concordance.R")

#Call the concordance function to get these ratios
concordance(Model_logistic)
 $Concordance
 [1] 0.7002884

 $Discordance
 [1] 0.2991384

 $Tied
 [1] 0.0005731122

 $Pairs
 [1] 7302228665
```

The concordance is 69.9%, signifying that the model probabilities have good separation on ~70% cases. This is a good model to create a classifier for 0 and 1.

In this section of model diagnostics for logistic regression we discussed the diagnostics in broadly two bucket, model fit statistics and model classification power. The model fit statistics discussed Wald test, which is significance test for the parameter estimates, Deviance is similar measure to residual in linear regression and pseudo R-square, which is equivalent to R-square of liner regression. The other set of diagnostics were to identify if the model can be used to create a powerful classifier. The tests included were bivariate plots (plots of actual probability by predicted probabilities), cumulative gains and lift charts to show how well our model differentiates between two classes, and the concordance ratio, which tells us if we can have a good cutoff value for our classifier. These diagnostics provide us vital properties of the model and help the modeler to either improve or re-estimate the models.

In the next section, we move onto multi-class classification problems. Multi-class problems are one of the hardest problems to solve, as more number of classes bring ambiguity. It is difficult to create a good classifier in many cases. We discuss multiple ways you can do multi-class classification using machine learning. Multinomial logistic regression is one the popular ways to do multi-class classification.

6.5.10 Multinomial Logistic Regression

Multinomial logistic regression is used when we have more than one category for classification. The dependent variable in that case follows a multinomial distribution. In the background we create a logistic model for each class and then combine those into one single equation by making the probability constraint of the sum of all probabilities be 1. The equation setup for the multinomial logistic is shown here:

$$\Pr(Y_i = 1) = \frac{e^{\beta_1 \cdot X_i}}{1 + \sum_{k=1}^{K-1} e^{\beta_k \cdot X_i}}$$

$$\Pr(Y_i = 2) = \frac{e^{\beta_2 \cdot X_i}}{1 + \sum_{k=1}^{K-1} e^{\beta_k \cdot X_i}}$$

$$\cdots \qquad \cdots$$

$$\Pr(Y_i = K-1) = \frac{e^{\beta_{K-1} \cdot X_i}}{1 + \sum_{k=1}^{K-1} e^{\beta_k \cdot X_i}}$$

The estimation process has additional constraints on individual `logit` transformation, the sum of probabilities from all `logit` functions needs to be 1. As the estimation has to take care of this constraint, the estimation method is an iterative one. The best coefficients for the model are found by iterative optimization of the `logLoss` function.

For our purchase prediction problem, first we will fit a logistic model on our data. The `multinom()` function from the `nnet` package will be used to estimate the logistic equation for our multi-class problem (`ProductChoice` has four possible options). Once we get the probabilities for each class, we will create a classifier to assign classes to individual cases.

There will be two methods illustrated for the classifier:

- *Pick the highest probability:* Pick the class having the highest probability among all the possible classes. However, this technique suffers form class imbalance problem. Class imbalance occurs when prior distribution of high proportion class drive the predicted probability and hence the low proportion classes never got assigned the class using predicted probabilities maximum value.
- *Ratio of probabilities:* We can take a ratio of predicted probabilities by prior distribution and then choose a class based on the the highest ratio. Highest ratio will signify that the model picked the highest signal as the probabilities got normalized by prior proportion.

Let's fit a model and apply the two classifiers.

```
#Remove the data having NA. NA is ignored in modeling algorithms
Data_Purchase<-na.omit(Data_Purchase_Prediction)

rownames(Data_Purchase)<-NULL


#Random Sample for easy computation
Data_Purchase_Model <-Data_Purchase[sample(nrow(Data_Purchase),10000),]

print("The Distribution of product is as below")
 [1] "The Distribution of product is as below"
table(Data_Purchase_Model$ProductChoice)

    1    2    3    4
 2192 3883 2860 1065
#fit a multinomial logistic model
library(nnet)
mnl_model <-multinom (ProductChoice ~MembershipPoints +IncomeClass
+CustomerPropensity +LastPurchaseDuration +CustomerAge +MartialStatus, data
= Data_Purchase)
 # weights:  44 (30 variable)
 initial  value 672765.880864
```

```
 iter  10 value 615285.850873
 iter  20 value 607471.781374
 iter  30 value 607231.472034
 final  value 604217.503433
 converged
#Display the summary of model statistics
mnl_model
 Call:
 multinom(formula = ProductChoice ~ MembershipPoints + IncomeClass +
     CustomerPropensity + LastPurchaseDuration + CustomerAge +
     MartialStatus, data = Data_Purchase)

 Coefficients:
   (Intercept) MembershipPoints IncomeClass CustomerPropensityLow
 2  0.77137077      -0.02940732  0.00127305            -0.3960318
 3  0.01775506       0.03340207  0.03540194            -0.8573716
 4 -1.15109893      -0.12366367  0.09016678            -0.6427954
   CustomerPropensityMedium CustomerPropensityUnknown
 2               -0.2745419                -0.5715016
 3               -0.4038433                -1.1824810
 4               -0.4035627                -0.9769569
   CustomerPropensityVeryHigh LastPurchaseDuration CustomerAge
 2                  0.2553831           0.04117902 0.001638976
 3                  0.5645137           0.05539173 0.005042405
 4                  0.5897717           0.07047770 0.009664668
   MartialStatus
 2  -0.033879645
 3  -0.007461956
 4   0.122011042

 Residual Deviance: 1208435
 AIC: 1208495
```

The model result shows that it converged after 30 iterations. Now let's see a sample set of probabilities assigned by the model and then apply the first classifier that has picked the highest probability.

Here, we apply the highest probability classifier and see how it classifies the cases.

```
#Predict the probabilities
predicted_test <-as.data.frame(predict(mnl_model, newdata = Data_Purchase,
type="probs"))

head(predicted_test)
           1         2         3          4
 1 0.21331014 0.3811085 0.3361570 0.06942438
 2 0.05060546 0.2818905 0.4157159 0.25178812
 3 0.21017415 0.4503171 0.2437507 0.09575798
 4 0.24667443 0.4545797 0.2085789 0.09016690
 5 0.09921814 0.3085913 0.4660605 0.12613007
 6 0.11730147 0.3624635 0.4184053 0.10182971
#Do the prediction based in highest probability
test_result <-apply(predicted_test,1,which.max)

result <-as.data.frame(cbind(Data_Purchase$ProductChoice,test_result))
colnames(result) <-c("Actual Class", "Predicted Class")

table(result$`Actual Class`,result$`Predicted Class`)

          1      2      3
  1     302  91952  12365
  2     248 150429  38028
  3     170  90944  51390
  4      27  32645  16798
```

The model shows good result for classifying classes 1, 2, and 3, but for class 4 the model does not classify even a single case. This is happening because the classifier (picking the highest probability) is very sensitive to absolute probabilities. This is called *class imbalance* and is discussed at the start of the section.

Let's apply the second method we discussed at the start of the section, probability ratios, to classify. We will select the class based on the ratio of predicted probability to the prior probability/proportion. This way we will be ensuring that the classifier assigns the class that is providing the highest jump in probabilities. In other words, the ratio will normalize the probabilities by prior odds, therefore reducing the bias due to prior distributions.

```
prior <-table(Data_Purchase_Model$ProductChoice)/nrow(Data_Purchase_Model)

prior_mat <-rep(prior,nrow(Data_Purchase_Model))

pred_ratio <-predicted_test/prior_mat
#Do the prediction based in highest ratio
test_result <-apply(pred_ratio,1,which.max)

result <-as.data.frame(cbind(Data_Purchase$ProductChoice,test_result))

colnames(result) <-c("Actual Class", "Predicted Class")

table(result$`Actual Class`,result$`Predicted Class`)

        1      2      3      4
1   21251  64410  18935     23
2   28087 112480  48078     60
3   13887  77090  51476     51
4    4620  27848  16958     44
```

Now you can see the class imbalance problem is reduced to some extent. You are encouraged to try other methods of sampling to reduce this problem further. Multinomial models are very popular in multi-class classification problems; other alternatives algorithms for multi-class classification tend to be more complex than multinomial. Multinomial logistic classifiers more commonly used in natural language processing and multi-class problems than Naive Bayer classifiers.

6.5.11 Generalized Linear Models

Generalized linear models extend the idea of ordinary linear regression to other distributions of response variables in an exponential family.

In the GLM framework, we assume that the dependent variable is generated from an exponential family distribution. Exponential families include normal, binomial, Poisson, and gamma distributions, among others. The expectation in that case is defined as:

$$\mathrm{E}(\mathrm{Y}) = \mu = g^{-1}(\mathrm{X}\beta)$$

where *E(Y)* is the expected value of *Y; X*β is the linear predictor, a linear combination of unknown parameters β; *g* is the link function.

The model parameters, β, are typically estimated with maximum likelihood, maximum quasi-likelihood, or Bayesian techniques.

The `glm` function is very generic function that can accommodate many types of distributions in a response variable:

glm(formula, family=familytype(link=linkfunction), data=)

- `binomial, (link = "logit")`

  Binomial distribution is very common in the real world. Any problem that has two possible outcomes can be thought of as a binomial distribution. A simple example could be whether it will rain today (=1) or not (=0).

- `gaussian, (link= "identity")`

  Gaussian distribution is a continuous distribution, i.e., a normal distribution. All the problems in linear regression are modeled assuming Gaussian distribution on the dependent variable.

- `Gamma, (link= "inverse")`

  An example could be, "N people are waiting at a take-away. How long will it take to serve them"? OR time to failure of a machine in the industry.

- `poisson, (link = "log")`

  This is a common distribution in queuing examples. One example could be "How many calls will the call center receive today?".

The following exponential family is also supported by the `glm()` function in R. However, these distributions are not observed normally in day-to-day activities.

```
inverse.gaussian, (link = "1/mu^2")
quasi, (link = "identity", variance = "constant")
quasibinomial, (link = "logit")
quasipoisson, (link = "log")
```

6.5.12 Conclusion

Regression is one of the very first learning algorithms with a heavy influence from statistics but an elegantly simple design. Over the years, the complexity and diversity in regression techniques has increased many folds as new applications started emerging. In this book we gave a heavy share of pages to regression in order to bring the best out of the widely used regression techniques. We discussed from the most fundamental simple regression to the advanced polynomial regression ,with a heavy emphasis on demonstration in R. Interested readers are advised to refer further to some advanced text of the topic if they want to go deeper into regression theory.

We have also presented a detailed discussion of model diagnostics for regression, which is the most overlooked topic when developing real-world models but could bring monumental damage to the industry where it's applied, especially if it's not done properly.

In the next section, we cover a technique from the distance-based algorithm called support vector machine, which could be a really good binary classification model on higher dimensional datasets.

6.6 Support Vector Machine SVM

In the R function `libsvm` documentation titled "Support Vector Machine," by David Meyer is a crisp brief of SVM describing the class separation, handling overlapping classes, dealing with non-linearity, and modeling of problem solution. The following are the excerpts from the documentation:

a. Class separation

   SVM looks for the optimal hyperplane separating the two classes. (In two dimensions, a hyperplane is a line and in a p-dimensional space, a hyperplane is a flat affine subspace of hyperplane dimension p – 1.) It finds the optimal hyperplane by maximizing the margin between the closest points of the two classes (see Figure 6-57). In two-dimensional space, as shown in Figure 6-32, the points lying on the margins are called support vectors and the line passing through the midpoint of the margins is the optimal hyperplane.

A simple two-dimensional hyperplane for a linearly separable data is represented by the following two equations:

$$\vec{w} \cdot \vec{x} + b = 1$$

and

$$\vec{w} \cdot \vec{x} + b = -1$$

subject to the following constraint so that each observation lies on the correct side of the margin

$$y_i \left(\vec{w} \cdot \vec{x_i} + b \right) \geq 1, \qquad \text{for all } 1 \leq i \leq n.$$

b. Overlapping classes

If the data points reside on the wrong side of the discriminant margin, it could be weighted down to reduce its influence (in this setting, the margin is called a soft margin).

The following function, called the Hinge loss function, can be introduced to handle this situation

$$\max\left(0, 1 - y_i \left(\vec{w} \cdot \vec{x_i} + b \right)\right).$$

which becomes 0 if $\vec{x_i}$ lies on the correct side of the margin and the function value is proportional to the distance from the margin.

c. Non-linearity

If a linear separator couldn't be found, observations are usually projected into a higher-dimensional space using a kernel function where the observations effectively become linearly separable.

One popular Gaussian family kernel is the radial basis function. A radial basis function (RBF) is a real-valued function whose value depends only on the distance from the origin. The function can be defined here:

$$K(x,y) = \exp\left(-\frac{\|x-y\|^2}{2s^2}\right)$$

where $\|x-y\|^2$ is known as squared Euclidean distance between the observation x and y. There are other linear, polynomial, and sigmoidal kernels that could be used based on the data.

A program that can perform all these tasks is called a *support vector machine*. See Figure 6-32.

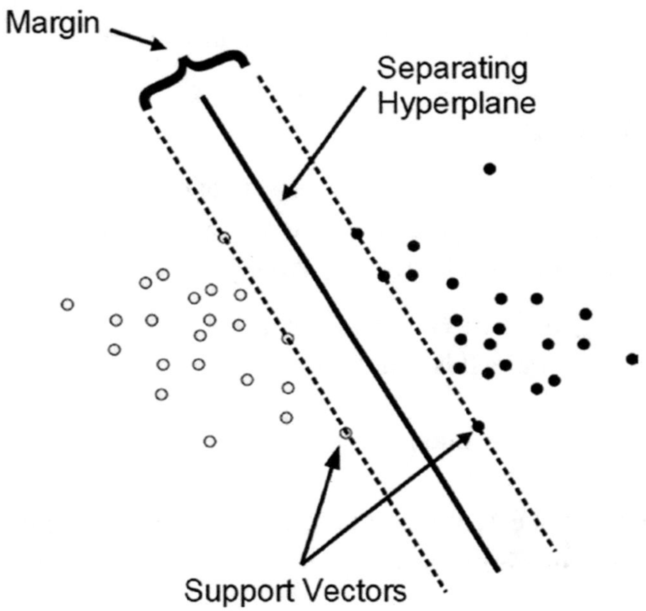

Figure 6-32. *Classification using support vector machine*

6.6.1 Linear SVM

The problem could be formulated as a quadratic optimization problem which can be solved by many known techniques. The following expressions could be converted to a quadratic function (the discussion of this topic is beyond the scope of this book).

6.6.1.1 Hard Margins

For the hard margins

Minimize $\|\vec{w}\|$, subject to $y_i\left(\vec{w}\cdot\vec{x_i}-b\right)\geq 1, \text{for } i=1,\ldots n$

6.6.1.2 Soft Margins

For the soft margins

$$\text{Minimize}\left[\frac{1}{n}\sum_{i=1}^{n}\max\left(0,1-y_i\left(\vec{w}\cdot\vec{x_i}+b\right)\right)\right]+\lambda\vec{w}^2,$$

where

Parameter • determines the tradeoff between increasing the margin and ensuring $\vec{x}_i$ lies on the correct side of the margin.

6.6.2 Binary SVM Classifier

Let's look at the classification of benign and malignant cells in our breast cancer dataset. We want to create a binary classifier to classify cells into benign and malignant.

a. Data summary

```
library(e1071)
library(rpart)

breast_cancer_data <-read.table("Dataset/breast-cancer-wisconsin.
data.txt",sep=",")
breast_cancer_data$V11 =as.factor(breast_cancer_data$V11)

summary(breast_cancer_data)
       V1                  V2               V3               V4
 Min.   :   61634  Min.   : 1.000  Min.   : 1.000  Min.   : 1.000
 1st Qu.: 870688   1st Qu.: 2.000  1st Qu.: 1.000  1st Qu.: 1.000
 Median :1171710   Median : 4.000  Median : 1.000  Median : 1.000
 Mean   :1071704   Mean   : 4.418  Mean   : 3.134  Mean   : 3.207
 3rd Qu.: 1238298  3rd Qu.: 6.000  3rd Qu.: 5.000  3rd Qu.: 5.000
 Max.   :13454352  Max.   :10.000  Max.   :10.000  Max.   :10.000
```

```
       V5                  V6                 V7            V8
 Min.   : 1.000    Min.   : 1.000    1       :402    Min.   : 1.000
 1st Qu.: 1.000    1st Qu.: 2.000    10      :132    1st Qu.: 2.000
 Median : 1.000    Median : 2.000    2       : 30    Median : 3.000
 Mean   : 2.807    Mean   : 3.216    5       : 30    Mean   : 3.438
 3rd Qu.: 4.000    3rd Qu.: 4.000    3       : 28    3rd Qu.: 5.000
 Max.   :10.000    Max.   :10.000    8       : 21    Max.   :10.000
                                     (Other): 56
       V9                V10          V11
 Min.   : 1.000    Min.   : 1.000    2:458
 1st Qu.: 1.000    1st Qu.: 1.000    4:241
 Median : 1.000    Median : 1.000
 Mean   : 2.867    Mean   : 1.589
 3rd Qu.: 4.000    3rd Qu.: 1.000
 Max.   :10.000    Max.   :10.000
```

b. Data preparation

```
split data into a train and test set
index <-1:nrow(breast_cancer_data)
test_data_index <-sample(index, trunc(length(index)/3))
test_data <-breast_cancer_data[test_data_index,]
train_data <-breast_cancer_data[-test_data_index,]
```

c. Model building

```
svm.model <-svm(V11 ~., data = train_data, cost =100, gamma =1)
```

d. Model evaluation

Normally, such a high level of accuracy is possible only if the feature being used and the data matches the real world very closely. Such a dataset in practical scenarios is difficult to build, however, in the world of medical diagnostics, the expectation is always very high in terms of accuracy, as error involves a significant risk to somebody's life.

Training set accuracy = 100%

```
library(gmodels)

svm_pred_train <-predict(svm.model, train_data[,-11])
CrossTable(train_data$V11, svm_pred_train,
prop.chisq =FALSE, prop.c =FALSE, prop.r =FALSE,
dnn =c('actual default', 'predicted default'))

   Cell Contents
|-------------------------|
|                       N |
|         N / Table Total |
|-------------------------|

Total Observations in Table:  466

               | predicted default
actual default |         2 |         4 | Row Total |
---------------|-----------|-----------|-----------|
             2 |       303 |         0 |       303 |
               |     0.650 |     0.000 |           |
---------------|-----------|-----------|-----------|
             4 |         0 |       163 |       163 |
               |     0.000 |     0.350 |           |
---------------|-----------|-----------|-----------|
  Column Total |       303 |       163 |       466 |
---------------|-----------|-----------|-----------|
```

Testing set accuracy = 95%

```
svm_pred_test <-predict(svm.model, test_data[,-11])
CrossTable(test_data$V11, svm_pred_test,
prop.chisq =FALSE, prop.c =FALSE, prop.r =FALSE,
dnn =c('actual default', 'predicted default'))

   Cell Contents
|-------------------------|
|                       N |
|         N / Table Total |
|-------------------------|
```

```
Total Observations in Table:  233

               | predicted default
actual default |          2 |          4 | Row Total |
---------------|------------|------------|-----------|
             2 |        142 |         13 |       155 |
               |      0.609 |      0.056 |           |
---------------|------------|------------|-----------|
             4 |          0 |         78 |        78 |
               |      0.000 |      0.335 |           |
---------------|------------|------------|-----------|
  Column Total |        142 |         91 |       233 |
---------------|------------|------------|-----------|
```

The binary SVM has done exceptionally well on the breast cancer dataset, which is the golden mark for the dataset as described in the UCI Machine Learning Repository. The classification matrix shows a correct classification of 95% (58.4% of malignant and 36.9% of benign cells correctly identified).

6.6.3 Multi-Class SVM

We introduced SVM as a binary classifier. However the idea of SVM can be extended to multi-class classification problems as well. Multi-class SVM can be used as a multi-class classifier by creating multiple binary classifiers. This method works similarly to the idea of multinomial logistic regression, where we build a logistic model for each pair of classes with base function.

Along the same lines, we can create a set of binary SVMs to do multi-class classification. The steps in implementing that will be as follows:

1. Create binary classifiers:
   - Between one class and the rest of the classes
   - Between every pair of classes (all possible pairs)
2. For any new cases, the SVM classifier adopts a winner-takes-all strategy, in which the class with highest output is assigned.

To implement this methodology, it is important that the output functions are calibrated to generate comparable scores, otherwise the classification will become biased.

There are other methods also for multi-class SVMs. One such is proposed by Crammer and Singer. They proposed a multi-class SVM method that casts the multi-class classification problem into a single optimization problem, rather than decomposing it into multiple binary classification problems.

We show quick example with our house worth data. The house net worth is divided into three classes—high, medium, and low. The multi-class SVM has to classify the houses into these categories. Here is the R implementation of the SVM multi-class classifier:

```
# Read the house Worth Data
Data_House_Worth <-read.csv("Dataset/House Worth Data.csv",header=TRUE);

library( 'e1071' )
#Fit a multiclass SVM
svm_multi_model <-svm( HouseNetWorth ~StoreArea +LawnArea, Data_House_Worth )

#Display the model
svm_multi_model

 Call:
 svm(formula = HouseNetWorth ~ StoreArea + LawnArea, data = Data_House_
 Worth)

 Parameters:
    SVM-Type:  C-classification
  SVM-Kernel:  radial
        cost:  1
       gamma:  0.5

 Number of Support Vectors:  120
#get the predicted value for all the set
res <-predict( svm_multi_model, newdata=Data_House_Worth )
```

```
#Classification Matrix
table(Data_House_Worth$HouseNetWorth,res)
         res
          High Low Medium
   High    122   1      7
   Low       6 122      7
   Medium    1   7     43
#Classification Rate

sum(diag(table(Data_House_Worth$HouseNetWorth,res)))/nrow(Data_House_Worth)
 [1] 0.9082278
```

Multi-class SVM gives us 90% good classification rate on house worth data. The prediction is good across all the classes.

6.6.4 Conclusion

Support vector machine, which initially was a non-probabilistic binary classifier with later variations to solve for multi-class problems as well, has proved to be one of the most successful algorithms in machine learning. A number of applications of SVM emerged over the years, and a few noteworthy ones are hypertext categorization, image classification, character recognition, and many more applications in biological sciences as well.

This section discussed a brief introduction to SVM with both binary and multi-class versions on breast cancer and house worth data. In the next section, we discuss the decision tree algorithm, which is another classification and as well as regression type model and a very popular approach in many fields of study.

6.7 Decision Trees

Unlike other ML algorithms based on statistical techniques, decision tree is a non-parametric model, having no underlying assumptions for the model. However, we should be careful in identifying the problems where a decision tree is appropriate and where not. Decision tree's ease of interpretation and understanding has found its use in many applications ranging from agriculture, where you could predict the chances of rain given the various environmental variables, to software development, where it's possible to estimate the development effort given the details about the modules. Over the years, tree-based approaches have evolved into a much broader scope in applicability as well as sophistication. They are available both in case of discrete and continuous response variables, which makes it a suitable solution in for both classification and regression problems.

More formally, a decision tree D consists of two types of nodes:

- A leaf node, which indicates the class/region defined by the response variable.
- A decision node, which specifies some test on a single attributes (predictor variable) with one branch and subtree for each possible outcome of the test.

A decision tree once constructed can be used to classify an observation by starting at the top decision node (called the root node) and moving down through the other decision nodes until a leaf is encountered using a recursive divide and conquer approach. Before we get into the details of how the algorithm works, let's get some familiarity with certain measures and their importance for the decision tree building process (see Figure 6-33).

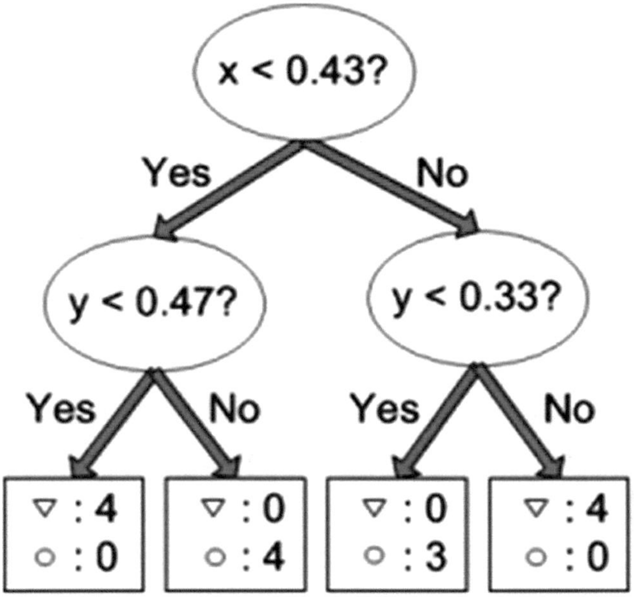

***Figure 6-33.** Decision tree with two attributes and a class*

6.7.1 Types of Decision Trees

Decision trees offer two types of implementations, one for regression and the other for classification problems. This means you could use decision tree for categorical as well as continuous response variables, which makes it a widely popular approach in the ML world. Next, we briefly describe how the two problems could be modeled using a decision tree.

6.7.1.1 Regression Trees

In problems where the response variable is continuous, regression trees are useful. They provide the same level of interpretability as linear regression and, on top of that, they are a very intuitive understanding of final output, which ties back to the domain of the problem. In the previous example in Figure 6-33, the regression tree is built to recursively split the two feature vector space into different regions based on various thresholds. Our objective in splitting the regions in every iteration is to minimize the Residual Sum of Squares (RSS) defined by the following equation:

$$\sum_{i:x_i \in R_1(j,s)} \left(yi - \hat{y}_{R1}\right)^2 + \sum_{i:x_i \in R_2(j,s)} \left(yi - \hat{y}_{R2}\right)^2,$$

Overall, the following are the two steps involved in regression tree building and prediction on new test data:

- Recursively split the feature vector space (X_1, X_2, ..., X_p) into distinct and non-overlapping regions
- For new observations falling into the same region, the prediction is equal to the mean of all the training observations in that region.

In a n-dimensional feature vector, Gini-index or Entropy, measures of classification power of node could be used to choose the right feature to split the space into different regions. Variance reduction (not covered in this book) is another popular approach that appropriately discretizes the range of continuous response variable in order to choose the right thresholds for splitting. See Figure 6-34.

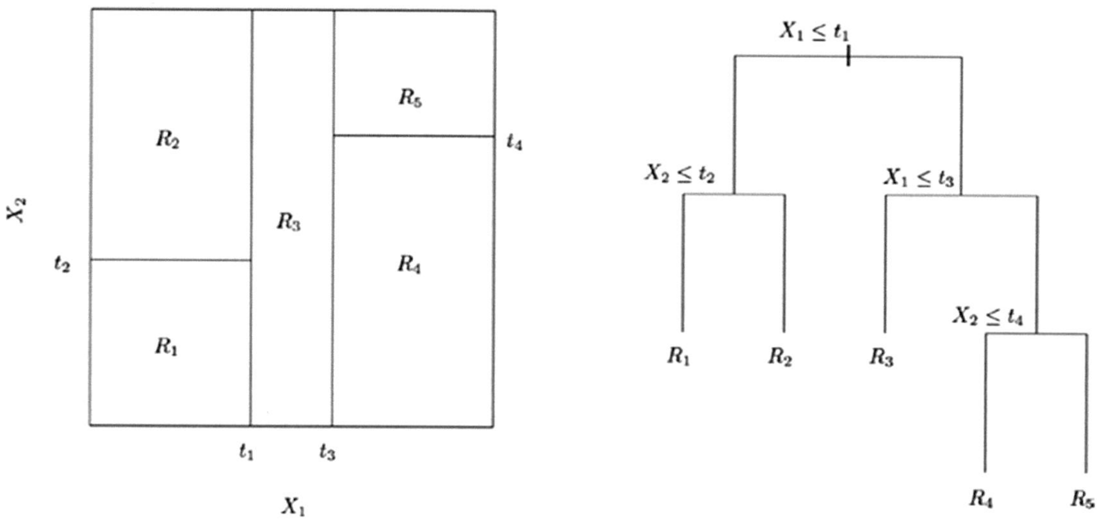

Figure 6-34. *Recursive binary split and its corresponding tree for two-dimensional feature space*

We will take up demonstration using a regression tree algorithm called Classification and Regression Tree (CART) later in this chapter, on the housing dataset described earlier in this chapter.

6.7.1.2 Classification Trees

Classification trees are more suitable for categorical or discrete response variables. The following are the key differences between classification trees and regression trees:

- We use classification error rate for making the splits in classification trees.
- Instead of taking the mean of the response variable in a particular region for prediction, here we use the most commonly occurring class of training observation as the prediction methodology.

Again, we could use Gini-Index or Entropy as a measure for selecting the best feature or attribute of splitting the observations into different classes.

In the coming sections, we discuss some popular classification decision tree algorithms like ID3 and C5.0.

6.7.2 Decision Measures

There are certain measures that are key to building a decision tree. In this section, we discuss a few measures associated with node purity (measure of randomness or heterogeneity). In the context of decision trees, a small value signifies that the node contains a majority of the observations from a single class. There are two widely used measures for node purity and another measure, called information gain, which uses either Gini-Index or Entropy to make decisions on node split.

6.7.2.1 Gini Index

A Gini-Index is calculated using

$$G = \sum_{k=1}^{K} \mathbf{p}_{mk} {}^{*} (1 - \mathbf{p}_{mk})$$

where, $\mathbf{p}_{mk}$ is the proportion of training observations in the mth region that are from the kth class.

For demonstration purposes, look at Figure 6-35. Suppose you have two classes where P1 proportion of all training observation belongs to class C_1 (triangle) and then P2 = 1-P1 belongs to C_2 (circle). The Gini-Index assumes a curve, as shown in Figure 6-35.

```
curve(x *(1-x) +(1 -x) *x, xlab ="P", ylab ="Gini-Index", lwd =5)
```

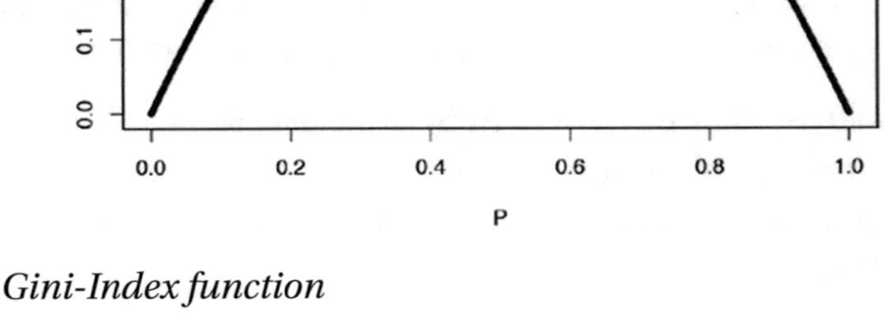

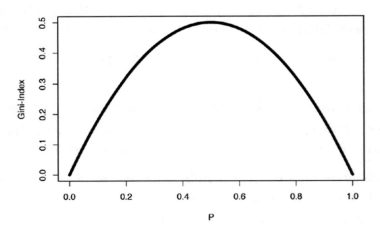

Figure 6-35. *Gini-Index function*

6.7.2.2 Entropy

Entropy is calculated using

$$E = -\sum_{k=1}^{K} \mathbf{p}_{mk} \log 2\left(1 - \mathbf{p}_{mk}\right)$$

The curve for entropy looks something like this:

```
curve(-x *log2(x) -(1 -x) *log2(1 -x), xlab ="x", ylab ="Entropy", lwd =5)
```

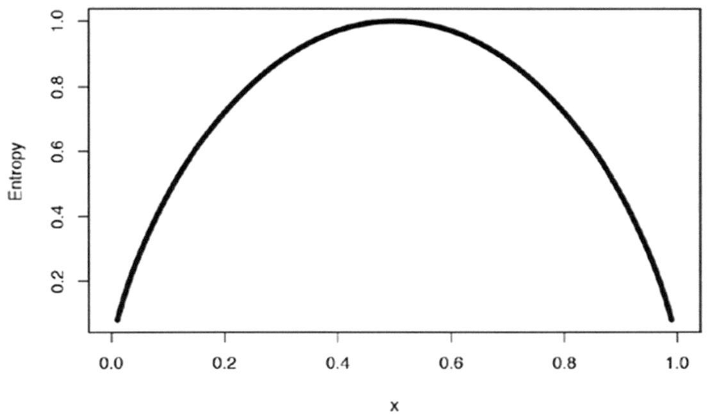

Figure 6-36. *The Entropy function*

Observe that both measures are very similar, however, there are some differences:

- Gini-Index is more suitable to continuous attributes and Entropy is better for discrete data.
- Gini-Index works well for minimizing misclassifications.
- Entropy is slightly slower than Gini-Index, as it involves logarithms (although this doesn't really matter much given today's fast computing machines).

6.7.2.3 Information Gain

Information gain is a measure that quantifies the change in the entropy before and after the split. It's an elegantly simple measure to decide the relevance of an attribute. In general, we could write information gain as:

$$\text{IG} = \left[\text{G}(\text{Parent}) - \text{Average}(\text{G}(\text{Children}))\right],$$

where G(Parent) is the Gini-Index (we could use Entropy as well) of parent node represented by an attribute before the split and G(Children) is the Gini-index of children nodes that will be generated after the split. For example, in Figure 6-33, all observations satisfying the parent node condition x<0.43 are its left child nodes and the remaining are its right.

6.7.3 Decision Tree Learning Methods

In this section, we discuss four widely used decision tree algorithms applied to our real-world datasets.

a. Data Summary

```
library(C50)
library(splitstackshape)
library(rattle)
library(rpart.plot)
library(data.table)

Data_Purchase <-fread("/Dataset/Purchase Prediction Dataset.
csv",header=T, verbose =FALSE, showProgress =FALSE)
str(Data_Purchase)
 Classes 'data.table' and 'data.frame':   500000 obs. of  12
 variables:
  $ CUSTOMER_ID         : chr  "000001" "000002" "000003" "000004" ...
  $ ProductChoice        : int  2 3 2 3 2 3 2 2 2 3 ...
  $ MembershipPoints     : int  6 2 4 2 6 6 5 9 5 3 ...
  $ ModeOfPayment        : chr  "MoneyWallet" "CreditCard"
                           "MoneyWallet" "MoneyWallet" ...
```

```
 $ ResidentCity         : chr  "Madurai" "Kolkata" "Vijayawada"
                          "Meerut" ...
 $ PurchaseTenure       : int  4 4 10 6 3 3 13 1 9 8 ...
 $ Channel              : chr  "Online" "Online" "Online"
                          "Online" ...
 $ IncomeClass          : chr  "4" "7" "5" "4" ...
 $ CustomerPropensity   : chr  "Medium" "VeryHigh" "Unknown"
                          "Low" ...
 $ CustomerAge          : int  55 75 34 26 38 71 72 27 33 29 ...
 $ MartialStatus        : int  0 0 0 0 1 0 0 0 0 1 ...
 $ LastPurchaseDuration: int  4 15 15 6 6 10 5 4 15 6 ...
 - attr(*, ".internal.selfref")=<externalptr>
#Check the distribution of data before grouping
table(Data_Purchase$ProductChoice)

     1      2      3      4
106603 199286 143893  50218
```

b. Data Preparation

```
#Pulling out only the relevant data to this chapter
Data_Purchase <-Data_Purchase[,.(CUSTOMER_ID,ProductChoice,Members
hipPoints,IncomeClass,CustomerPropensity,LastPurchaseDuration)]

#Delete NA from subset
Data_Purchase <-na.omit(Data_Purchase)
Data_Purchase$CUSTOMER_ID <-as.character(Data_Purchase$CUSTOMER_ID)

#Stratified Sampling
Data_Purchase_Model<-stratified(Data_Purchase, group=c
("ProductChoice"),size=10000,replace=FALSE)

print("The Distribution of equal classes is as below")
 [1] "The Distribution of equal classes is as below"
table(Data_Purchase_Model$ProductChoice)
```

```
    1     2     3     4
10000 10000 10000 10000
Data_Purchase_Model$ProductChoice <-as.factor(Data_Purchase_
Model$ProductChoice)
Data_Purchase_Model$IncomeClass <-as.factor(Data_Purchase_
Model$IncomeClass)
Data_Purchase_Model$CustomerPropensity <-as.factor(Data_Purchase_
Model$CustomerPropensity)

#Build the decision tree on Train Data (Set_1) and then test data
(Set_2) will be used for performance testing

set.seed(917);
train <-Data_Purchase_Model[sample(nrow(Data_Purchase_
Model),size=nrow(Data_Purchase_Model)*(0.7), replace =TRUE, prob
=NULL),]
train <-as.data.frame(train)

test <-Data_Purchase_Model[!(Data_Purchase_Model$CUSTOMER_ID
%in%train$CUSTOMER_ID),]
```

6.7.3.1 Iterative Dichotomizer 3

J. Ross Quinlan, a computer science researcher in data mining and decision theory, invented the most popular decision tree algorithms, C4.5 and ID3. Here is a brief explanation of how the ID3 algorithm works:

1. Calculates entropy for each attribute using the training observations.
2. Splits the observations into subsets using the attribute with minimum entropy or maximum information gain.
3. The selected attribute becomes the decision node.
4. Repeats the process with the remaining attribute on the subset.

For demonstration purposes, we will use a R Package called RWeka, which is a wrapper built on the tool Weka, which is a collection of machine learning algorithms for data mining tasks written in Java, containing tools for data preprocessing, classification, regression, clustering, association rules, and visualization. The RWeka package contains the interface code, and the Weka jar is in a separate package called RWekajars. For more information on Weka, see http://www.cs.waikato.ac.nz/ml/weka/.

Before using the ID3 function from the RWeka package, follow these instructions.

1. Install the RWeka package.
2. Set the environment variable WEKA_HOME to a folder location on your drive (e.g., D:\home) where you have sufficient access rights.
3. In the R console, run these two commands:

```
WPM("refresh-cache")
#looks for a package providing id3

WPM("install-package", "simpleEducationalLearningSchemes")
#load the package
```

a. Model Building

```
library(RWeka)
WPM("refresh-cache")
WPM("install-package", "simpleEducationalLearningSchemes")

 make classifier
ID3 <-make_Weka_classifier("weka/classifiers/trees/Id3")

ID3Model <-ID3(ProductChoice ~CustomerPropensity +IncomeClass ,
data = train)

summary(ID3Model)

 === Summary ===

 Correctly Classified Instances        9423               33.6536 %
 Incorrectly Classified Instances     18577               66.3464 %
 Kappa statistic                          0.1148
 Mean absolute error                      0.3634
 Root mean squared error                  0.4263
 Relative absolute error                 96.9041 %
 Root relative squared error             98.4399 %
 Total Number of Instances            28000
```

```
=== Confusion Matrix ===

    a    b    c    d   <-- classified as
 4061  987  929 1078 |    a = 1
 3142 1054 1217 1603 |    b = 2
 2127  727 1761 2290 |    c = 3
 2206  859 1412 2547 |    d = 4
```

b. Model Evaluation

Training set accuracy is present as part of the ID3 model output (33% correctly classified instances), so we needn't present that here. Let's look at the testing set accuracy.

Testing set accuracy = 32%. As you can observe, the accuracy is not exceptionally good. Moreover, given there are four classes of data, the accuracy is prone to be even less. The fact that training and testing accuracy are almost equal tells us that there is no overfitting kind of scenario.

```
library(gmodels)
purchase_pred_test <-predict(ID3Model, test)
CrossTable(test$ProductChoice, purchase_pred_test,
prop.chisq =FALSE, prop.c =FALSE, prop.r =FALSE,
dnn =c('actual default', 'predicted default'))
```

```
   Cell Contents
|-------------------------|
|                       N |
|         N / Table Total |
|-------------------------|

Total Observations in Table:  20002

               | predicted default
actual default |        1 |           2 |           3 |           4 | Row Total |
---------------|----------|-------------|-------------|-------------|-----------|
             1 |     2849 |         758 |         625 |         766 |      4998 |
               |    0.142 |       0.038 |       0.031 |       0.038 |           |
---------------|----------|-------------|-------------|-------------|-----------|
             2 |     2291 |         681 |         872 |        1151 |      4995 |
               |    0.115 |       0.034 |       0.044 |       0.058 |           |
---------------|----------|-------------|-------------|-------------|-----------|
```

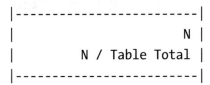

```
              3 |     1580 |       545 |      1151 |      1759 |      5035 |
                |    0.079 |     0.027 |     0.058 |     0.088 |           |
----------------|----------|-----------|-----------|-----------|-----------|
              4 |     1594 |       590 |      1066 |      1724 |      4974 |
                |    0.080 |     0.029 |     0.053 |     0.086 |           |
----------------|----------|-----------|-----------|-----------|-----------|
   Column Total |     8314 |      2574 |      3714 |      5400 |     20002 |
----------------|----------|-----------|-----------|-----------|-----------|
```

The accuracy isn't very impressive with the ID3 algorithm. One possible reason could be the multiple classes in our response variables. Generally, the ID3 is not known for performing exceptionally well on multi-class problems.

6.7.3.2 C5.0 Algorithm

In his book, *C4.5: Programs for Machine Learning*, J. Ross Quinlan[3] laid down a set of key requirements for using these algorithms for classification task, which are as follows:

- *Attribute-value description*: All information about one case should be expressible in terms of fixed collection of attributes (features) and it should not vary from one case to another.
- *Predefined classes*: As it happens in any supervised learning approach, the categories to which cases are to be assigned must be predefined.
- *Discrete classes*: The classes must be sharply delineated; a case either does or does not belong to a particular class and there must be far more cases than classes. So, clearly, problems with continuous response variable are not the right fit for this algorithm.
- *Sufficient data*: The amount of data required is affected by factors such as number of attributes and classes. As these increases, more data will be needed to construct a reliable model.
- *Logical classification models*: The description of the class should be logical expressions whose primitives are statements about the values of particular attributes. For example, `IF Outlook = "sunny" AND Windy = "false" THEN class = "Play"`.

Here we will use the C5.0 algorithm on our purchase prediction dataset, which is an extension of C4.5 for building the decision tree. C4.5 was a collective name given to a set of computer programs that constructs classification models. The following are some new features in C5.0 that are illustrated in Ross Quinlan's web page (`http://www.rulequest.com/see5-comparison.html`).

In the classic book, *Experiments in Induction*, Hunt et al.[4] describes many implementations of concept learning systems. Here is how Hunt's approach works.

Given a set of T training observations having C_1, C_2, ..., C_k classes, at a broad level, the following are the three possibilities involved in building the tree:

1. All the observations of T belongs to a single class C_i, the decision tree D for T is a leaf identifying class C_i.
2. T contains no class. C5.0 uses the most frequent class at the parent of this node.
3. T contains observations with a mixture of classes. A node condition (test) is chosen based on a single attribute (the attribute is chosen based on information gain), which generates a partitioned set of T_1, T_2, ..., T_n.

The split in third possibility is recursive in the algorithm, which is repeated until either all the observations are correctly classified or the algorithm runs out of attribute to split. Since this divide and conquer is a greedy approach that looks only at the immediate step to take a decision for split, its possible to end up in situation like overfitting. In order to avoid this, a technique called *pruning* is used, which reduces the overfit and generalizes better to unseen data. Fortunately, you don't have to worry about pruning since C5.0 algorithm, after building the decision tree, iterates back and replace the branches that do not increase the information gain.

Here, we will use our Purchase Preference dataset to build a C5.0 decision tree model on for product choice prediction based on the `ProductChoice` response variable.

a. Model Building

```
model_c50 <-C5.0(train[,c("CustomerPropensity",
"LastPurchaseDuration", "MembershipPoints")],
                  train[,"ProductChoice"],
control =C5.0Control(CF =0.001, minCases =2))
```

b. Model Summary

```
summary(model_c50)

 Call:
 C5.0.default(x = train[, c("CustomerPropensity",
  "LastPurchaseDuration", "MembershipPoints")], y =
train[, "ProductChoice"], control = C5.0Control(CF = 0.001,
minCases = 2))

 C5.0 [Release 2.07 GPL Edition]      Sun Oct 02 16:09:05 2016
 -------------------------------

 Class specified by attribute `outcome'

 Read 28000 cases (4 attributes) from undefined.data

 Decision tree:

 CustomerPropensity in {High,VeryHigh}:
 :...MembershipPoints <= 1: 4 (1264/681)
 :   MembershipPoints > 1:
 :   :...LastPurchaseDuration <= 6: 3 (3593/2266)
 :       LastPurchaseDuration > 6:
 :       :...CustomerPropensity = High: 3 (1665/1083)
 :           CustomerPropensity = VeryHigh: 4 (2140/1259)
 CustomerPropensity in {Low,Medium,Unknown}:
 :...MembershipPoints <= 1: 4 (3180/1792)
     MembershipPoints > 1:
     :...CustomerPropensity = Unknown: 1 (8004/4891)
         CustomerPropensity in {Low,Medium}:
         :...LastPurchaseDuration <= 2: 1 (2157/1417)
             LastPurchaseDuration > 2:
             :...LastPurchaseDuration > 13: 2 (1083/773)
                 LastPurchaseDuration <= 13:
                 :...CustomerPropensity = Medium: 3 (2489/1707)
                     CustomerPropensity = Low:
                     :...MembershipPoints <= 3: 2 (850/583)
                         MembershipPoints > 3: 1 (1575/1124)
```

```
Evaluation on training data (28000 cases):

     Decision Tree
   ----------------
   Size      Errors

     11 17576(62.8%)   <<

    (a)   (b)   (c)   (d)    <-classified as
   ----  ----  ----  ----
   4304   374  1345  1032    (a): class 1
   3374   577  1759  1306    (b): class 2
   2336   484  2691  1394    (c): class 3
   1722   498  1952  2852    (d): class 4

 Attribute usage:

 100.00% CustomerPropensity
 100.00% MembershipPoints
  55.54% LastPurchaseDuration

Time: 0.1 secs
```

plot(model_c50)

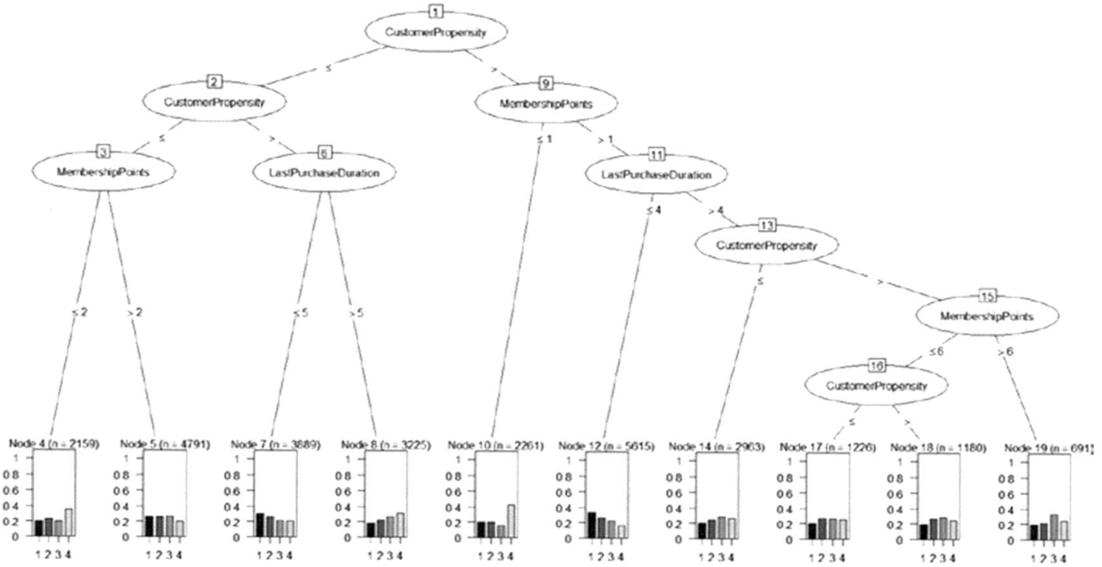

***Figure 6-37.** C5.0 decision tree on the purchase prediction dataset*

You can experiment with the parameters of C5.0 to see how the decision tree changes. As shown in Figure 6-37, if you traverse through any path, it forms one decision rule. For example, `Rule: CustomerPropensity in {High,VeryHigh}ANDMembershipPoints <= 1` is one path ending in a decision node, as shown in Figure 6-37.

c. Evaluation

Training set accuracy = 37%

```
library(gmodels)
purchase_pred_train <-predict(model_c50, train,type ="class")
CrossTable(train$ProductChoice, purchase_pred_train,
prop.chisq =FALSE, prop.c =FALSE, prop.r =FALSE,
dnn =c('actual default', 'predicted default'))

    Cell Contents
 |-------------------------|
 |                       N |
 |         N / Table Total |
 |-------------------------|
```

```
 Total Observations in Table:  28000

                 | predicted default
 actual default  |        1 |          2 |          3 |          4 |  Row Total |
 ----------------|----------|------------|------------|------------|------------|
               1 |     4304 |        374 |       1345 |       1032 |       7055 |
                 |    0.154 |      0.013 |      0.048 |      0.037 |            |
 ----------------|----------|------------|------------|------------|------------|
               2 |     3374 |        577 |       1759 |       1306 |       7016 |
                 |    0.120 |      0.021 |      0.063 |      0.047 |            |
 ----------------|----------|------------|------------|------------|------------|
               3 |     2336 |        484 |       2691 |       1394 |       6905 |
                 |    0.083 |      0.017 |      0.096 |      0.050 |            |
 ----------------|----------|------------|------------|------------|------------|
               4 |     1722 |        498 |       1952 |       2852 |       7024 |
                 |    0.061 |      0.018 |      0.070 |      0.102 |            |
 ----------------|----------|------------|------------|------------|------------|
    Column Total |    11736 |       1933 |       7747 |       6584 |      28000 |
 ----------------|----------|------------|------------|------------|------------|
```

Testing set accuracy = 36%

```
purchase_pred_test <-predict(model_c50, test)
CrossTable(test$ProductChoice, purchase_pred_test,
prop.chisq =FALSE, prop.c =FALSE, prop.r =FALSE,
dnn =c('actual default', 'predicted default'))
purchase_pred_test <-predict(model_c50, test)
CrossTable(test$ProductChoice, purchase_pred_test,
prop.chisq =FALSE, prop.c =FALSE, prop.r =FALSE,
dnn =c('actual default', 'predicted default'))
```

```
   Cell Contents
|-------------------------|
|                       N |
|         N / Table Total |
|-------------------------|
```

```
Total Observations in Table:  20002

               | predicted default
actual default |        1 |          2 |          3 |          4 | Row Total |
---------------|----------|------------|------------|------------|-----------|
             1 |     3081 |        279 |        895 |        743 |      4998 |
               |    0.154 |      0.014 |      0.045 |      0.037 |           |
---------------|----------|------------|------------|------------|-----------|
             2 |     2454 |        321 |       1317 |        903 |      4995 |
               |    0.123 |      0.016 |      0.066 |      0.045 |           |
---------------|----------|------------|------------|------------|-----------|
             3 |     1730 |        344 |       1843 |       1118 |      5035 |
               |    0.086 |      0.017 |      0.092 |      0.056 |           |
---------------|----------|------------|------------|------------|-----------|
             4 |     1176 |        349 |       1382 |       2067 |      4974 |
               |    0.059 |      0.017 |      0.069 |      0.103 |           |
---------------|----------|------------|------------|------------|-----------|
  Column Total |     8441 |       1293 |       5437 |       4831 |     20002 |
---------------|----------|------------|------------|------------|-----------|
```

As you can observe, the accuracy is not exceptionally good. Moreover, given there are four classes of data, the accuracy is prone to be even less. The fact that training and testing accuracy are almost equal tells us that there is no overfitting kind of scenario.

6.7.3.3 Classification and Regression Tree: CART

CART is a regression tree-based approach and, as explained in the Section 6.8.1.1, it uses the sum of squared deviation about the mean (residual sum of square) as the node impurity measure. Keep in mind that CART could also be used for classification problems, in which case (see Figure 6-38) Gini-Index is a more appropriate choice for impurity measure. Roughly, here is a short pseudo-code for the algorithm:

1. Start the algorithm at the root node.
2. For each attribute X, find the subset S that minimizes the residual sum of square (RSS) of the two children and chooses the split that gives the maximum information gain.

3. Check if a relative decrease in impurity is below a prescribed threshold.

4. If yes, splitting stops, otherwise repeat Step 2.

Let's see a demonstration of CART using the rpart function, which is available in the most commonly used package with rpart. It also provides methods to build decision trees like Random Forest, which we cover later in this chapter.

We will also use an additional parameter cp (complexity parameter) in the function call, which signifies that any split that does not decrease the overall lack of fit by a factor of cp would not be attempted by the model.

a. Building the Model

```
CARTModel <-rpart(ProductChoice ~IncomeClass +CustomerPropensity
+LastPurchaseDuration +MembershipPoints, data=train)

summary(CARTModel)
 Call:
 rpart(formula = ProductChoice ~ IncomeClass + CustomerPropensity +
     LastPurchaseDuration + MembershipPoints, data = train)
   n= 28000

           CP nsplit rel error    xerror        xstd
 1 0.09649081      0 1.0000000 1.0034376 0.003456583
 2 0.02582955      1 0.9035092 0.9035092 0.003739335
 3 0.02143710      2 0.8776796 0.8776796 0.003793749
 4 0.01000000      3 0.8562425 0.8562425 0.003833608

 Variable importance
   CustomerPropensity     MembershipPoints LastPurchaseDuration
                   53                   37                    8
          IncomeClass
                    2

 Node number 1: 28000 observations,    complexity param=0.09649081
   predicted class=1  expected loss=0.7480357  P(node) =1
     class counts:  7055  7016  6905  7024
    probabilities: 0.252 0.251 0.247 0.251
```

```
   left son=2 (14368 obs) right son=3 (13632 obs)
   Primary splits:
  CustomerPropensity   splits as  RLRLR,      improve=408.0354,
(0 missing)
  MembershipPoints     < 1.5 to the right,   improve=269.2781,
(0 missing)
  LastPurchaseDuration < 5.5 to the left,    improve=194.7965,
(0 missing)
  IncomeClass          splits as  LRLLLLRRRL, improve= 24.2665,
(0 missing)
  Surrogate splits:
  LastPurchaseDuration    < 5.5 to the left, agree=0.590, adj=0.159,
(0 split)
   IncomeClass         splits as  LLLLLLLRRR, agree=0.529, adj=0.032,
(0 split)
     MembershipPoints     < 9.5 to the left, agree=0.514, adj=0.002,
(0 split)

....

 Node number 7: 2066 observations
   predicted class=4  expected loss=0.5382381  P(node) =0.07378571
     class counts:   291   408   413   954
    probabilities: 0.141 0.197 0.200 0.462
library(rpart.plot)
library(rattle)

fancyRpartPlot(CARTModel)
```

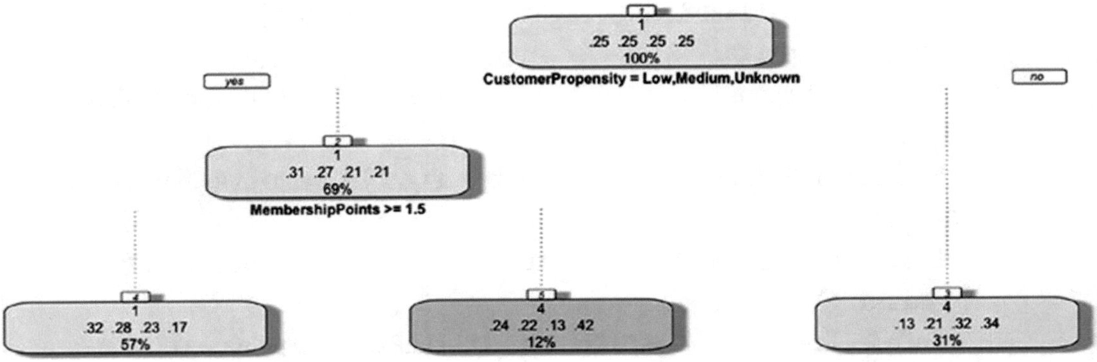

***Figure 6-38.** CART model*

b. Model Evaluation

```
Training set Accuracy = 27%
library(gmodels)

purchase_pred_train <-predict(CARTModel, train,type ="class")
CrossTable(train$ProductChoice, purchase_pred_train,
prop.chisq =FALSE, prop.c =FALSE, prop.r =FALSE,
dnn =c('actual default', 'predicted default'))

   Cell Contents
|-------------------------|
|                       N |
|         N / Table Total |
|-------------------------|

Total Observations in Table:  28000

               | predicted default
actual default |         1 |         3 |         4 | Row Total |
---------------|-----------|-----------|-----------|-----------|
             1 |      4253 |      1943 |       859 |      7055 |
               |     0.152 |     0.069 |     0.031 |           |
---------------|-----------|-----------|-----------|-----------|
             2 |      3452 |      2629 |       935 |      7016 |
               |     0.123 |     0.094 |     0.033 |           |
---------------|-----------|-----------|-----------|-----------|
```

```
              3 |      2384 |      3842 |       679 |      6905 |
                |     0.085 |     0.137 |     0.024 |           |
----------------|-----------|-----------|-----------|-----------|
              4 |      1901 |      3152 |      1971 |      7024 |
                |     0.068 |     0.113 |     0.070 |           |
----------------|-----------|-----------|-----------|-----------|
   Column Total |     11990 |     11566 |      4444 |     28000 |
----------------|-----------|-----------|-----------|-----------|
```

It looks like a poor model for this dataset. If you observe, the training model doesn't even predict any instance of class 3. We will skip the testing set evaluation. You are encouraged to try the housing dataset used in linear regression to appreciate the CART algorithm much better.

6.7.3.4 Chi-Square Automated Interaction Detection: CHAID

In this method, the R code being used for demonstration accepts only nominal or ordinal categorical predictors. For each predictor variable, the algorithm works by merging non-significant categories, wherein each final category of X will result in one child node, if the algorithm chooses X (based on adjusted p-value) to split the node.

The following algorithm is borrowed from the documentation of the CHAID package in R and the classic paper by G. V. Kass (1980), called "An Exploratory Technique for Investigating Large Quantities of Categorical Data."

1. If X has one category only, stop and set the adjusted p-value to be 1.
2. If X has two categories, go to Step 8.
3. Otherwise, find the allowable pair of categories of X (an allowable pair of categories for ordinal predictor is two adjacent categories, and for nominal predictor is any two categories) that is least significantly different (i.e., the most similar). The most similar pair is the pair whose test statistic gives the largest p-value with respect to the dependent variable Y. How to calculate p-value under various situations will be described in later sections.
4. For the pair having the largest p-value, check if its p-value is larger than a user-specified alpha-level `alpha2`. If it does, this pair is merged into a single compound category. Then a new set of categories of X is formed. If it does not, then go to Step 7.

5. (Optional) If the newly formed compound category consists of three or more original categories, then find the best binary split within the compound category where p-value is the smallest. Perform this binary split if its p-value is not larger than an alpha-level `alpha3`.

6. Go to Step 2.

7. (Optional) Any category having too few observations (as compared with a user-specified minimum segment size) is merged with the most similar other category, as measured by the largest of the p-values.

8. The adjusted p-value is computed for the merged categories by applying Bonferroni adjustments that are to be discussed later.

Splitting: The best split for each predictor is found in the merging step. The splitting step selects which predictor to be used to best split the node. Selection is accomplished by comparing the adjusted p-value associated with each predictor. The adjusted p-value is obtained in the merging step.

1. Select the predictor that has the smallest adjusted p-value (i.e., is most significant).

2. If this adjusted p-value is less than or equal to a user-specified alpha-level `alpha4`, split the node using this predictor. Otherwise, do not split and the node is considered a terminal node.

Stopping: The stopping step checks if the tree growing process should be stopped according to the following stopping rules.

1. If a node becomes pure; that is, all cases in a node have identical values of the dependent variable, the node will not be split.

2. If all cases in a node have identical values for each predictor, the node will not be split.

3. If the current tree depth reaches the user specified maximum tree depth limit value, the tree growing process will stop.

4. If the size of a node is less than the user-specified minimum node size value, the node will not be split.

5. If the split of a node results in a child node whose node size is less than the user-specified minimum child node size value, child nodes that have too few cases (as compared with this minimum) will merge with the most similar child node as measured by the largest of the p-values. However, if the resulting number of child nodes is 1, the node will not be split.
6. If the trees height is a positive value and equals the max height.

Let's now see a demonstration on our purchase prediction dataset.

Note For using the code in this section, use the following steps:

1. Download the `zip` or `.tar.gz` file according to your machine from `https://r-forge.r-project.org/R/?group_id=343`.
2. Extract the contents of the compressed file into a folder named `CHAID` and place it in the installation folder of R. The installation folder might look something like `C:\Program Files\R-3.2.2\library`.
3. That's it. You are ready to call the library (CHAID) inside your R script.

---

a. Building the Model

Since CHAID takes all categorical inputs, we are using the attributes `CustomerPropensity` and `IncomeClass` as predictor variables.

```
library("CHAID")
 Loading required package: partykit
 Loading required package: grid
ctrl <-chaid:control(minsplit =200, minprob =0.1)
CHAIDModel <-chaid(ProductChoice ~CustomerPropensity
+IncomeClass, data = train, control = ctrl)
print(CHAIDModel)
```

```
Model formula:
ProductChoice ~ CustomerPropensity + IncomeClass

Fitted party:
[1] root
|   [2] CustomerPropensity in High
|   |   [3] IncomeClass in , 1, 2, 3, 9: 2 (n = 169,
            err = 68.6%)
|   |   [4] IncomeClass in 4: 3 (n = 628, err = 65.0%)
|   |   [5] IncomeClass in 5: 4 (n = 1286, err = 70.2%)
|   |   [6] IncomeClass in 6: 3 (n = 1192, err = 67.0%)
|   |   [7] IncomeClass in 7: 3 (n = 662, err = 63.4%)
|   |   [8] IncomeClass in 8: 4 (n = 222, err = 59.9%)
|   [9] CustomerPropensity in Low: 2 (n = 4778, err = 72.0%)
|   [10] CustomerPropensity in Medium
|   |   [11] IncomeClass in , 1, 2, 3, 4, 5, 7: 3 (n = 3349,
             err = 73.5%)
|   |   [12] IncomeClass in 6, 8: 4 (n = 1585, err = 71.0%)
|   |   [13] IncomeClass in 9: 3 (n = 36, err = 44.4%)
|   [14] CustomerPropensity in Unknown
|   |   [15] IncomeClass in : 2 (n = 18, err = 0.0%)
|   |   [16] IncomeClass in 1: 4 (n = 15, err = 53.3%)
|   |   [17] IncomeClass in 2, 3, 4, 5, 6, 7, 8: 1 (n = 9524,
             err = 63.6%)
|   |   [18] IncomeClass in 9: 1 (n = 33, err = 39.4%)
|   [19] CustomerPropensity in VeryHigh
|   |   [20] IncomeClass in , 1, 3, 4, 5, 6, 9: 3 (n = 3484,
             err = 64.5%)
|   |   [21] IncomeClass in 2, 8: 4 (n = 268, err = 48.5%)
|   |   [22] IncomeClass in 7: 4 (n = 751, err = 58.2%)

Number of inner nodes:     5
Number of terminal nodes: 17
#plot(CHAIDModel)
```

b. Model Evaluation

The accuracy has no major improvement compared to C5.0 or ID3. However, it's interesting to see the accuracy is close to the C5.0 algorithm in spite of using only two attributes.

Training set accuracy: 32%

```
library(gmodels)
purchase_pred_train <-predict(CHAIDModel, train)
CrossTable(train$ProductChoice, purchase_pred_train,
prop.chisq =FALSE, prop.c =FALSE, prop.r =FALSE,
dnn =c('actual default', 'predicted default'))
```

```
   Cell Contents
|-------------------------|
|                       N |
|         N / Table Total |
|-------------------------|

Total Observations in Table:  28000

               | predicted default
actual default |        1 |          2 |          3 |          4 | Row Total |
---------------|----------|------------|------------|------------|-----------|
             1 |     3487 |       1367 |       1610 |        591 |      7055 |
               |    0.125 |      0.049 |      0.058 |      0.021 |           |
---------------|----------|------------|------------|------------|-----------|
             2 |     2617 |       1410 |       2047 |        942 |      7016 |
               |    0.093 |      0.050 |      0.073 |      0.034 |           |
---------------|----------|------------|------------|------------|-----------|
             3 |     1669 |       1031 |       3001 |       1204 |      6905 |
               |    0.060 |      0.037 |      0.107 |      0.043 |           |
---------------|----------|------------|------------|------------|-----------|
             4 |     1784 |       1157 |       2693 |       1390 |      7024 |
               |    0.064 |      0.041 |      0.096 |      0.050 |           |
---------------|----------|------------|------------|------------|-----------|
  Column Total |     9557 |       4965 |       9351 |       4127 |     28000 |
---------------|----------|------------|------------|------------|-----------|
```

Testing set accuracy: 32%

```
purchase_pred_test <-predict(CHAIDModel, test)
CrossTable(test$ProductChoice, purchase_pred_test,
prop.chisq =FALSE, prop.c =FALSE, prop.r =FALSE,
dnn =c('actual default', 'predicted default'))

   Cell Contents
|-------------------------|
|                       N |
|         N / Table Total |
|-------------------------|

Total Observations in Table:  20002

               | predicted default
actual default |        1 |         2 |         3 |         4 | Row Total |
---------------|----------|-----------|-----------|-----------|-----------|
             1 |     2493 |      1003 |      1048 |       454 |      4998 |
               |    0.125 |     0.050 |     0.052 |     0.023 |           |
---------------|----------|-----------|-----------|-----------|-----------|
             2 |     1929 |       901 |      1502 |       663 |      4995 |
               |    0.096 |     0.045 |     0.075 |     0.033 |           |
---------------|----------|-----------|-----------|-----------|-----------|
             3 |     1263 |       747 |      2034 |       991 |      5035 |
               |    0.063 |     0.037 |     0.102 |     0.050 |           |
---------------|----------|-----------|-----------|-----------|-----------|
             4 |     1318 |       776 |      2008 |       872 |      4974 |
               |    0.066 |     0.039 |     0.100 |     0.044 |           |
---------------|----------|-----------|-----------|-----------|-----------|
  Column Total |     7003 |      3427 |      6592 |      2980 |     20002 |
---------------|----------|-----------|-----------|-----------|-----------|
```

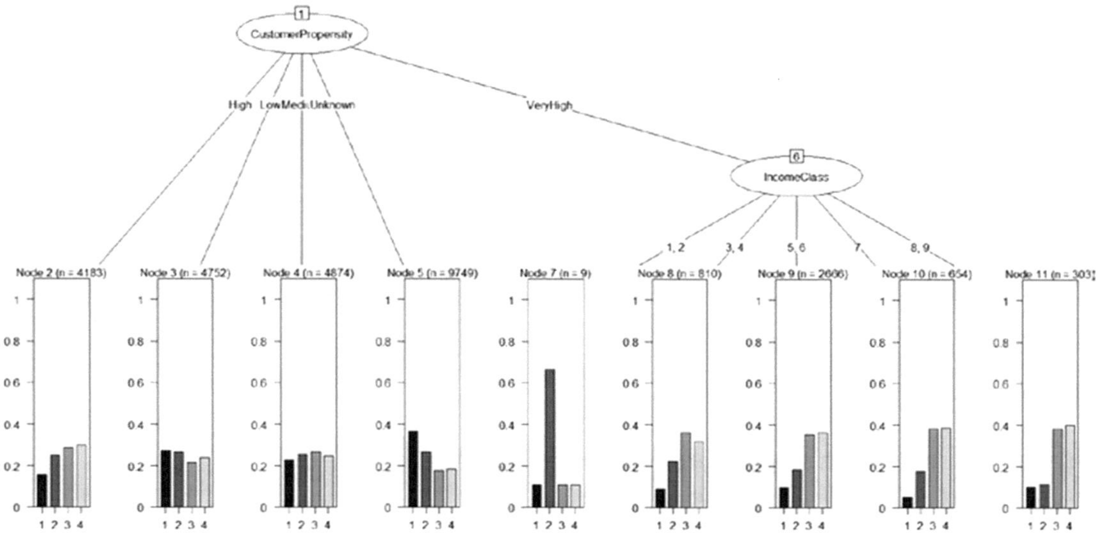

Figure 6-39. *CHAID decision tree*

The accuracy has no major improvement compared to C5.0 or ID3. However, it's interesting to see the accuracy is close to the C5.0 algorithm in spite of using only two attributes.

With 37% and 36% training and test set accuracy respectively, the C5.0 algorithm seems to have done the best among all the others. Although this accuracy might not be sufficient for using in any practical application, this example gives sufficient understanding of how the decision tree algorithms work. We encourage you to create a subset of the given dataset with only two classes and then see how each of these algorithms performs.

6.7.4 Ensemble Trees

Ensemble models in machine learning are a great way to improve your model accuracy by many folds. The best Kaggle competition-winning ML algorithms predominately use the ensemble approach. The idea is simple—instead of training one model on a set of observations, we use the power of multiple models (or multiple iteration of the same model on different subset of training data) combined together to train on the same set of observations. Chapter 8 takes a detailed approach on improving model performance using ensembles; however, we will keep our focus on ensemble models based on decision trees in this section.

6.7.4.1 Boosting

Boosting is an ensemble meta-algorithm in ML that helps reduce bias and variance and fits a sequence of weak learners on different weighted training observations (more on this in Chapter 8).

We will demonstrate this technique using C5.0 Ensemble model, which is an extension of what we discussed earlier in this chapter by adding a parameter trials = 10 in the C50 function call. This performs 10 boosting iterations in the model building process.

```
library(gmodels)

purchase_pred_train <-predict(ModelC50_boostcv10, train)
CrossTable(train$ProductChoice, purchase_pred_train,
prop.chisq =FALSE, prop.c =FALSE, prop.r =FALSE,
dnn =c('actual default', 'predicted default'))
```

```
   Cell Contents
|-------------------------|
|                       N |
|         N / Table Total |
|-------------------------|

Total Observations in Table:  28000

               | predicted default
actual default |        1 |          2 |          3 |          4 | Row Total |
---------------|----------|------------|------------|------------|-----------|
             1 |     3835 |        903 |       1117 |       1200 |      7055 |
               |    0.137 |      0.032 |      0.040 |      0.043 |           |
---------------|----------|------------|------------|------------|-----------|
             2 |     2622 |       1438 |       1409 |       1547 |      7016 |
               |    0.094 |      0.051 |      0.050 |      0.055 |           |
---------------|----------|------------|------------|------------|-----------|
             3 |     1819 |        812 |       2677 |       1597 |      6905 |
               |    0.065 |      0.029 |      0.096 |      0.057 |           |
---------------|----------|------------|------------|------------|-----------|
```

```
              4 |  1387 |     686 |    1577 |    3374 |    7024 |
                | 0.050 |   0.024 |   0.056 |   0.120 |         |
----------------|-------|---------|---------|---------|---------|
   Column Total |  9663 |    3839 |    6780 |    7718 |   28000 |
----------------|-------|---------|---------|---------|---------|
```

Testing set accuracy:

```
purchase_pred_test <-predict(ModelC50_boostcv10, test)
CrossTable(test$ProductChoice, purchase_pred_test,
prop.chisq =FALSE, prop.c =FALSE, prop.r =FALSE,
dnn =c('actual default', 'predicted default'))
```

```
   Cell Contents
|-------------------------|
|                       N |
|         N / Table Total |
|-------------------------|

Total Observations in Table:  20002

                | predicted default
 actual default |     1 |       2 |       3 |       4 | Row Total |
----------------|-------|---------|---------|---------|-----------|
              1 |  2556 |     769 |     770 |     903 |      4998 |
                | 0.128 |   0.038 |   0.038 |   0.045 |           |
----------------|-------|---------|---------|---------|-----------|
              2 |  2022 |     748 |    1108 |    1117 |      4995 |
                | 0.101 |   0.037 |   0.055 |   0.056 |           |
----------------|-------|---------|---------|---------|-----------|
              3 |  1406 |     701 |    1540 |    1388 |      5035 |
                | 0.070 |   0.035 |   0.077 |   0.069 |           |
----------------|-------|---------|---------|---------|-----------|
              4 |   970 |     548 |    1201 |    2255 |      4974 |
                | 0.048 |   0.027 |   0.060 |   0.113 |           |
----------------|-------|---------|---------|---------|-----------|
   Column Total |  6954 |    2766 |    4619 |    5663 |     20002 |
----------------|-------|---------|---------|---------|-----------|
```

Though the training set accuracy increases to 40%, the testing set accuracy has come down, indicating a slight overfitting in this model.

6.7.4.2 Bagging

This is another class of ML meta-algorithm, also known as *bootstrap aggregating*. It again helps in reducing the variance and overfitting on training observation. Explained next is the process of bagging:

1. Given a set of N training observations, generate m new training sets D_i each of size n where (n <<N) by uniform sampling with replacement. This sampling is called bootstrap sampling. (Refer to Chapter 3 for more details.)
2. Using these m training set, m models are fitted and the outputs are combined either by averaging the output (regression) or majority voting (for classification).

Certain version of algorithm could have even a sample set of smaller number of attributes than the original dataset like Random Forest. Let's use the Bagging CART and Random Forest algorithms here to demonstrate.

Note The following code might take a significant amount of time and RAM memory. If you want, you can reduce the size of the training set for quicker execution.

Bagging CART

```
control <-trainControl(method="repeatedcv", number=5, repeats=2)

# Bagged CART
set.seed(100)
CARTBagModel <-train(ProductChoice ~CustomerPropensity
+LastPurchaseDuration +MembershipPoints, data=train, method="treebag",
trControl=control)
 Loading required package: ipred
 Loading required package: plyr
 Warning: package 'plyr' was built under R version 3.2.5
 Loading required package: e1071
 Warning: package 'e1071' was built under R version 3.2.5
```

Training set accuracy = 42%

Testing set accuracy = 34%

Though the training set accuracy increases to 42%, the testing set accuracy has come down, indicating a slight overfitting in this model.

Training set accuracy:

```
library(gmodels)
purchase_pred_train <-predict(CARTBagModel, train)
CrossTable(train$ProductChoice, purchase_pred_train,
prop.chisq =FALSE, prop.c =FALSE, prop.r =FALSE,
dnn =c('actual default', 'predicted default'))
```

```
   Cell Contents
|-------------------------|
|                       N |
|         N / Table Total |
|-------------------------|

Total Observations in Table:  28000

               | predicted default
actual default |        1 |           2 |           3 |           4 | Row Total |
---------------|----------|-------------|-------------|-------------|-----------|
             1 |     3761 |        1208 |         885 |        1201 |      7055 |
               |    0.134 |       0.043 |       0.032 |       0.043 |           |
---------------|----------|-------------|-------------|-------------|-----------|
             2 |     2358 |        1970 |        1096 |        1592 |      7016 |
               |    0.084 |       0.070 |       0.039 |       0.057 |           |
---------------|----------|-------------|-------------|-------------|-----------|
             3 |     1685 |        1054 |        2547 |        1619 |      6905 |
               |    0.060 |       0.038 |       0.091 |       0.058 |           |
---------------|----------|-------------|-------------|-------------|-----------|
             4 |     1342 |         885 |        1291 |        3506 |      7024 |
               |    0.048 |       0.032 |       0.046 |       0.125 |           |
---------------|----------|-------------|-------------|-------------|-----------|
  Column Total |     9146 |        5117 |        5819 |        7918 |     28000 |
---------------|----------|-------------|-------------|-------------|-----------|
```

Testing set accuracy:

```
purchase_pred_test <-predict(CARTBagModel, test)
CrossTable(test$ProductChoice, purchase_pred_test,
prop.chisq =FALSE, prop.c =FALSE, prop.r =FALSE,
dnn =c('actual default', 'predicted default'))
```

```
   Cell Contents
|-------------------------|
|                       N |
|         N / Table Total |
|-------------------------|

Total Observations in Table:  20002

               | predicted default
actual default |        1 |        2 |        3 |        4 | Row Total |
---------------|----------|----------|----------|----------|-----------|
             1 |     2331 |     1071 |      657 |      939 |      4998 |
               |    0.117 |    0.054 |    0.033 |    0.047 |           |
---------------|----------|----------|----------|----------|-----------|
             2 |     1844 |     1012 |      928 |     1211 |      4995 |
               |    0.092 |    0.051 |    0.046 |    0.061 |           |
---------------|----------|----------|----------|----------|-----------|
             3 |     1348 |      875 |     1320 |     1492 |      5035 |
               |    0.067 |    0.044 |    0.066 |    0.075 |           |
---------------|----------|----------|----------|----------|-----------|
             4 |      979 |      759 |     1066 |     2170 |      4974 |
               |    0.049 |    0.038 |    0.053 |    0.108 |           |
---------------|----------|----------|----------|----------|-----------|
  Column Total |     6502 |     3717 |     3971 |     5812 |     20002 |
---------------|----------|----------|----------|----------|-----------|

Testing set Accuracy = 34%
```

Though the training set accuracy increases to 42%, the testing set accuracy has come down, indicating a slight overfitting in this model once again.

Random Forest

Random Forest is one of the most popular decision tree-based ensemble models. The accuracy of these models tends to be higher than most of the other decision trees. Here is a broad summary of how the Random Forest algorithm works:

1. Let N = Number of observations, n = number of decision trees (user input), and M = Number of variables in the dataset.
2. Choose a subset of m variables from M, where m << M, and build n decision trees using a random set of m variable.
3. Grow each tree as large as possible.
4. Use majority voting to decide the class of the observation.

A randomly chosen subset of N observations without replacement (normally 2/3) is used to build each decision tree. Now let's use our Purchase Preference dataset again for demonstration using R.

```
# Random Forest
set.seed(100)

rfModel <-train(ProductChoice ~CustomerPropensity +LastPurchaseDuration
+MembershipPoints, data=train, method="rf", trControl=control)
 Loading required package: randomForest
 randomForest 4.6-10
 Type rfNews() to see new features/changes/bug fixes.

 Attaching package: 'randomForest'
 The following object is masked from 'package:ggplot2':

     margin
```

Training set accuracy = 41%

Testing set Accuracy = 36%

This model seems to have the best training and testing accuracy so far in all our trials of other models. Observe that Random Forest has done slightly well in tackling the overfit problem compared to CART.

Training set accuracy:

```
library(gmodels)

purchase_pred_train <-predict(rfModel, train)
CrossTable(train$ProductChoice, purchase_pred_train,
prop.chisq =FALSE, prop.c =FALSE, prop.r =FALSE,
dnn =c('actual default', 'predicted default'))
```

```
   Cell Contents
|-------------------------|
|                       N |
|         N / Table Total |
|-------------------------|

Total Observations in Table:  28000

               | predicted default
actual default |        1 |          2 |          3 |          4 | Row Total |
---------------|----------|------------|------------|------------|-----------|
             1 |     4174 |        710 |       1162 |       1009 |      7055 |
               |    0.149 |      0.025 |      0.042 |      0.036 |           |
---------------|----------|------------|------------|------------|-----------|
             2 |     2900 |       1271 |       1507 |       1338 |      7016 |
               |    0.104 |      0.045 |      0.054 |      0.048 |           |
---------------|----------|------------|------------|------------|-----------|
             3 |     1970 |        701 |       2987 |       1247 |      6905 |
               |    0.070 |      0.025 |      0.107 |      0.045 |           |
---------------|----------|------------|------------|------------|-----------|
             4 |     1564 |        608 |       1835 |       3017 |      7024 |
               |    0.056 |      0.022 |      0.066 |      0.108 |           |
---------------|----------|------------|------------|------------|-----------|
  Column Total |    10608 |       3290 |       7491 |       6611 |     28000 |
---------------|----------|------------|------------|------------|-----------|
```

Testing set accuracy:

```
purchase_pred_test <-predict(rfModel, test)
CrossTable(test$ProductChoice, purchase_pred_test,
```

```
prop.chisq =FALSE, prop.c =FALSE, prop.r =FALSE,
dnn =c('actual default', 'predicted default'))

   Cell Contents
|-------------------------|
|                       N |
|         N / Table Total |
|-------------------------|

Total Observations in Table:  20002

               | predicted default
actual default |        1 |           2 |           3 |           4 | Row Total |
---------------|----------|-------------|-------------|-------------|-----------|
             1 |     2774 |         611 |         845 |         768 |      4998 |
               |    0.139 |       0.031 |       0.042 |       0.038 |           |
---------------|----------|-------------|-------------|-------------|-----------|
             2 |     2210 |         639 |        1194 |         952 |      4995 |
               |    0.110 |       0.032 |       0.060 |       0.048 |           |
---------------|----------|-------------|-------------|-------------|-----------|
             3 |     1531 |         602 |        1774 |        1128 |      5035 |
               |    0.077 |       0.030 |       0.089 |       0.056 |           |
---------------|----------|-------------|-------------|-------------|-----------|
             4 |     1100 |         462 |        1389 |        2023 |      4974 |
               |    0.055 |       0.023 |       0.069 |       0.101 |           |
---------------|----------|-------------|-------------|-------------|-----------|
  Column Total |     7615 |        2314 |        5202 |        4871 |     20002 |
---------------|----------|-------------|-------------|-------------|-----------|
```

There is another approach called *stacking*, which we cover in much greater detail in Chapter 8.

This model seems to have the best training and testing accuracy so far in all our trials of other models. Observe that Random Forest has done slightly well in tackling the overfit problem compared to CART.

In overall, under decision tree, the ensemble approach seems to do the best in predicting the product preferences.

6.7.5 Conclusion

These supervised learning algorithms have a wide-spread adaptability in industry and many research work. The underlying design of decision tree makes it easy to interpret and the model is very intuitive to connect with the real-world problem. The approaches like Boosting and Bagging have given rise to high accuracy models based on decision tree. In particular, Random Forest is now one of the most widely used models for many classification problems.

We presented a detailed discussion of decision tree where we started with the very first decision tree models like ID3 and then went on to present the contemporary Bagging CART and Random Forest algorithms as well.

In the next section, we discuss our first probabilistic model in this book. The Bayesian models are easy to implement and powerful enough to capture a lot of information from a given set of observations and its class labels.

6.8 The Naive Bayes Method

Naïve Bayes is a probabilistic model-based machine learning algorithm that was used in text categorization in its earlier use case. These methods fall in broad category of Bayesian algorithms in machine learning. Applications like document categorization and spam filters for emails were the first few areas where Naïve Bayes proved to be really effective as a classifier algorithm. The name of the algorithm is derived from the fact that it relies on one of the most powerful concepts in probability theory, the *Bayes theorem*, Bayes rule, or Bayes formula. In the coming sections, we will formally introduce the background necessary for understanding Naïve Bayes and demonstrate its application to our Purchase Prediction dataset.

6.8.1 Conditional Probability

Conditional probability plays a significant role in ascertaining the impact of one event on another. It could increase or decrease the probability of an event if it's known that another event has an influence on the event under study. Recall our Facebook nearby feature discussion in Chapter 1, where we computed this probability:

$$P(\text{Visit Cineplex} \mid \text{Nearby})$$

In other words, how does the information, "your friend is nearby the cineplex" affect the probability that you will visit the cineplex.

6.8.2 Bayes Theorem

The Bayes theorem (or Bayes rule or Bayes formula) defines the conditional probability between two events as

$$P(A|B) = \frac{P(B|A) \cdot P(A)}{P(B)}$$

where

P(A) is prior probability,

$P(A|B)$ is posterior probability and its read as the probability of the event A happening given the event B.

P(B) is marginal likelihood

$P(B|A)$ is likelihood

$P(B|A) \cdot P(A)$ could also be thought as joint probability, which denotes the probability of A intersection B; in other words, the probability of both event A and B happening together.

Rearranging the Bayes theorem, we could write it as

$$P(A|B) = \frac{P(B|A)}{P(B)} \cdot P(A)$$

where the term $P(B)$ signifies the impact event B has on the probability of A happening.

This will form the core of our Naïve Bayes algorithm. So, before we get there, let's understand briefly the three terms discussed in the Bayes theorem.

6.8.3 Prior Probability

Prior probability or *priors* signifies the certainty of an event occurring before some evidence is considered. Taking the same Facebook Nearby feature, what's the probability of your friend visiting the cineplex if you don't know anything about his current location?

6.8.4 Posterior Probability

The probability of the event A happening conditioned on another event gives us the posterior probability. So, in the Facebook Nearby feature, how his probability of visiting cineplex changes if we knew your friend is within one mile of the cineplex (defined as nearby). Such additional evidences are useful in increasing the certainty of a particular event. We will exploit this very fundamental in designing the Naïve Bayes algorithm.

6.8.5 Likelihood and Marginal Likelihood

If we slightly modify the Table 1-2 in Chapter 1, where you see a two-way contingency table (also called frequency table) for the Facebook Nearby example and transform it into a Likelihood table, as shown in Table 6-6, where each entry in the cells is now a conditional probability.

Table 6-6. *A Likelihood Table*

	Nearby	Far	**Total**
Visit Cineplex	10/12	2/12	**12**
Didn't Visit Cineplex	2/13	11/13	**13**
Total	**12/25**	**13/25**	**25**

Looking at the Table 6-6, it's now easy to compute the marginal likelihood P(Nearby) as 12/25 = 0.48. And the likelihood P (Nearby | Visit Cineplex) as 10/12 = 0.83. Marginal likelihood as you can observe, doesn't depend on the other event.

6.8.6 Naïve Bayes Methods

So, putting all these together, we get the final form of Naïve Bayes

$$\mathrm{P}(\text{Visit Cineplex} \mid \text{Nearby}) = \frac{\mathrm{P}(\text{Nearby} \mid \text{Visit Cineplex}) * \mathrm{P}(\text{Visit Cineplex})}{\mathrm{P}(\text{Nearby})}$$

Further generalizing this, let's suppose we have a dataset, represented by vector $x = (x_1,\ldots,x_n)$ with n features, independent of each other (This is a strong assumption in Naïve Bayes, and any dataset violating this property will perform poorly with Naïve Bayes), then a given observation could be classified with a probability $p(C_k|,x_1|,\ldots|,x_n)$ into any of the K classes C_k.

So, now using the Bayes theorem, we could write the conditional probability as

$$p(C_k|x) = \frac{p(C_k) \quad p(x|C_k)}{p(x)}$$

The numerator, $p(C_k) \quad p(x|C_k)$, which represents the joint probability could be expanded using the chain rule. However, we will leave that discussion to some advanced text on this topic.

At this point, we have discussed how the Bayes theorem server as a powerful way to model a real-world problem. Further, it's possible to show Naïve Bayes could be very effective if the likelihood tables are precomputed and a real-time implementation will just have to do a table lookup to do some quick computation. Naïve Bayes is elegantly simple yet powerful when assumptions are seriously considered while modeling the problem.

Now, let's apply this technique in our Purchase Preference dataset and see what we get.

a. Data Preparation

```
library(data.table)
library(splitstackshape)
library(e1071)
str(Data_Purchase)
 Classes 'data.table' and 'data.frame':   500000 obs. of  12
 variables:
  $ CUSTOMER_ID         : chr  "000001" "000002" "000003"
                          "000004" ...
  $ ProductChoice       : int  2 3 2 3 2 3 2 2 2 3 ...
  $ MembershipPoints    : int  6 2 4 2 6 6 5 9 5 3 ...
  $ ModeOfPayment       : chr  "MoneyWallet" "CreditCard"
                          "MoneyWallet" "MoneyWallet" ...
  $ ResidentCity        : chr  "Madurai" "Kolkata" "Vijayawada"
                          "Meerut" ...
  $ PurchaseTenure      : int  4 4 10 6 3 3 13 1 9 8 ...
```

```
 $ Channel              : chr  "Online" "Online" "Online"
                          "Online" ...
 $ IncomeClass          : chr  "4" "7" "5" "4" ...
 $ CustomerPropensity   : chr  "Medium" "VeryHigh" "Unknown"
                          "Low" ...
 $ CustomerAge          : int  55 75 34 26 38 71 72 27 33 29 ...
 $ MartialStatus        : int  0 0 0 0 1 0 0 0 0 1 ...
 $ LastPurchaseDuration: int  4 15 15 6 6 10 5 4 15 6 ...
 - attr(*, ".internal.selfref")=<externalptr>
#Check the distribution of data before grouping
table(Data_Purchase$ProductChoice)

      1      2      3      4
 106603 199286 143893  50218
#Pulling out only the relevant data to this chapter
Data_Purchase <-Data_Purchase[,.(CUSTOMER_ID,ProductChoice,Members
hipPoints,IncomeClass,CustomerPropensity,LastPurchaseDuration)]

#Delete NA from subset
Data_Purchase <-na.omit(Data_Purchase)
Data_Purchase$CUSTOMER_ID <-as.character(Data_Purchase$CUSTOMER_
ID)

#Stratified Sampling
Data_Purchase_Model<-stratified(Data_Purchase, group=c("ProductCho
ice"),size=10000,replace=FALSE)

print("The Distribution of equal classes is as below")
 [1] "The Distribution of equal classes is as below"
table(Data_Purchase_Model$ProductChoice)

     1     2     3     4
 10000 10000 10000 10000
Data_Purchase_Model$ProductChoice <-as.factor(Data_Purchase_
Model$ProductChoice)
Data_Purchase_Model$IncomeClass <-as.factor(Data_Purchase_
Model$IncomeClass)
```

```
Data_Purchase_Model$CustomerPropensity <-as.factor(Data_Purchase_
Model$CustomerPropensity)

set.seed(917);
train <-Data_Purchase_Model[sample(nrow(Data_Purchase_
Model),size=nrow(Data_Purchase_Model)*(0.7), replace =TRUE, prob
=NULL),]
train <-as.data.frame(train)

test <-as.data.frame(Data_Purchase_Model[!(Data_Purchase_
Model$CUSTOMER_ID %in%train$CUSTOMER_ID),])
```

b. Naïve Bayes Model

```
model_naiveBayes <-naiveBayes(train[,c(3,4,5)], train[,2])
model_naiveBayes

 Naive Bayes Classifier for Discrete Predictors

 Call:
 naiveBayes.default(x = train[, c(3, 4, 5)], y = train[, 2])

 A-priori probabilities:
 train[, 2]
         1         2         3         4
 0.2519643 0.2505714 0.2466071 0.2508571

 Conditional probabilities:
           MembershipPoints
 train[, 2]     [,1]     [,2]
          1 4.366832 2.385888
          2 4.212087 2.354063
          3 4.518320 2.391260
          4 3.659596 2.520176
```

```
              IncomeClass
train[, 2]                          1           2           3           4
         1 0.000000000 0.001417434 0.001842665 0.033451453 0.171651311
         2 0.002993158 0.001710376 0.002423033 0.032354618 0.173175599
         3 0.000000000 0.001158581 0.001737871 0.029543809 0.166980449
         4 0.000000000 0.001566059 0.001850797 0.019219818 0.151480638
              IncomeClass
train[, 2]           5           6           7           8           9
         1 0.337774628 0.265910702 0.142735648 0.040113395 0.005102764
         2 0.328962372 0.265250855 0.143529076 0.046465222 0.003135690
         3 0.325416365 0.275452571 0.148153512 0.046777697 0.004779146
         4 0.318479499 0.280466970 0.161161731 0.060791572 0.004982916

              CustomerPropensity
train[, 2]        High        Low     Medium    Unknown   VeryHigh
         1 0.09992913 0.17987243 0.16328845 0.49666903 0.06024096
         2 0.14438426 0.18258267 0.17901938 0.36944128 0.12457241
         3 0.18580739 0.13714699 0.19608979 0.25561188 0.22534395
         4 0.17283599 0.14635535 0.18180524 0.26153189 0.23747153
```

c. Model Evaluation

Training set accuracy: 41%

```
model_naiveBayes_pred <-predict(model_naiveBayes, train)
library(gmodels)

CrossTable(model_naiveBayes_pred, train[,2],
prop.chisq =FALSE, prop.t =FALSE,
dnn =c('predicted', 'actual'))
```

```
   Cell Contents
|-------------------------|
|                       N |
|           N / Row Total |
|           N / Col Total |
|-------------------------|

Total Observations in Table:  28000
```

```
             | actual
   predicted |         1 |           2 |           3 |           4 | Row Total |
-------------|-----------|-------------|-------------|-------------|-----------|
           1 |      4016 |        3077 |        2187 |        2098 |     11378 |
             |     0.353 |       0.270 |       0.192 |       0.184 |     0.406 |
             |     0.569 |       0.439 |       0.317 |       0.299 |           |
-------------|-----------|-------------|-------------|-------------|-----------|
           2 |       622 |         702 |         500 |         489 |      2313 |
             |     0.269 |       0.304 |       0.216 |       0.211 |     0.083 |
             |     0.088 |       0.100 |       0.072 |       0.070 |           |
-------------|-----------|-------------|-------------|-------------|-----------|
           3 |      1263 |        1635 |        2336 |        1890 |      7124 |
             |     0.177 |       0.230 |       0.328 |       0.265 |     0.254 |
             |     0.179 |       0.233 |       0.338 |       0.269 |           |
-------------|-----------|-------------|-------------|-------------|-----------|
           4 |      1154 |        1602 |        1882 |        2547 |      7185 |
             |     0.161 |       0.223 |       0.262 |       0.354 |     0.257 |
             |     0.164 |       0.228 |       0.273 |       0.363 |           |
-------------|-----------|-------------|-------------|-------------|-----------|
Column Total |      7055 |        7016 |        6905 |        7024 |     28000 |
             |     0.252 |       0.251 |       0.247 |       0.251 |           |
-------------|-----------|-------------|-------------|-------------|-----------|
```

Testing set accuracy: 34%

```
model_naiveBayes_pred <-predict(model_naiveBayes, test)
library(gmodels)

CrossTable(model_naiveBayes_pred, test[,2],
prop.chisq =FALSE, prop.t =FALSE,
dnn =c('predicted', 'actual'))
```

```
   Cell Contents
|-------------------------|
|                       N |
|           N / Row Total |
|           N / Col Total |
|-------------------------|

Total Observations in Table:  20002

             | actual
   predicted |         1 |           2 |           3 |           4 | Row Total |
-------------|-----------|-------------|-------------|-------------|-----------|
           1 |      2823 |        2155 |        1537 |        1493 |      8008 |
             |     0.353 |       0.269 |       0.192 |       0.186 |     0.400 |
             |     0.565 |       0.431 |       0.305 |       0.300 |           |
-------------|-----------|-------------|-------------|-------------|-----------|
           2 |       496 |         548 |         388 |         407 |      1839 |
             |     0.270 |       0.298 |       0.211 |       0.221 |     0.092 |
             |     0.099 |       0.110 |       0.077 |       0.082 |           |
-------------|-----------|-------------|-------------|-------------|-----------|
           3 |       885 |        1164 |        1746 |        1358 |      5153 |
             |     0.172 |       0.226 |       0.339 |       0.264 |     0.258 |
             |     0.177 |       0.233 |       0.347 |       0.273 |           |
-------------|-----------|-------------|-------------|-------------|-----------|
           4 |       794 |        1128 |        1364 |        1716 |      5002 |
             |     0.159 |       0.226 |       0.273 |       0.343 |     0.250 |
             |     0.159 |       0.226 |       0.271 |       0.345 |           |
-------------|-----------|-------------|-------------|-------------|-----------|
Column Total |      4998 |        4995 |        5035 |        4974 |     20002 |
             |     0.250 |       0.250 |       0.252 |       0.249 |           |
-------------|-----------|-------------|-------------|-------------|-----------|
```

There is a significant difference in the training and testing set accuracy, indicating a possibility of overfitting.

6.8.7 Conclusion

The techniques discussed in this section are based on probabilistic models, commonly known as Bayesian models. These models are easy to interpret and have been quite popular in applications like spam filtering and text classifications. Bayesian models offer the flexibility to add data incrementally to allow easy model updating as and when a new set of observation arrives. For this reason, probabilistic approaches like Bayesian have found their application in many real-world use cases. The model's adaptability to changing data is far easier than the other models.

In the next section, we take up the discussion of the unsupervised class of learning algorithms that are useful in many practical applications where availability of labeled data is less or not present at all. These algorithms are most famously regarded as pattern recognition algorithms and work based on certain similarity or distance-based methods.

6.9 Cluster Analysis

Clustering analysis involves grouping a set of objects into meaningful and useful clusters such that the objects within the cluster are homogeneous and the same objects are heterogeneous to objects of other clusters. The guiding principle of clustering analysis remains similar across different algorithms as minimizing intragroup variability and maximizing intergroup variability by some metric, e.g., distance connectivity, mean-variance, etc.

Clustering does not refer to specific algorithms but it's a process to create groups based on similarity measure. Clustering analysis use unsupervised learning algorithm to create clusters. Cluster analysis is sometimes presented as part of broader features analysis of data. Some researchers break the feature discovery exercise into cluster analysis of data:

- *Factor analysis*: Where we first reduce the dimensionality of data
- *Clustering*: Where we create clusters within data
- *Discriminant analysis*: Measure how well the data properties are captured

Clustering analysis will involve all or some of the three steps as standalone processes. This will give the insights into data distribution, which can be used to create better data decisions or the results can be used to feed into some further algorithm.

In machine learning, we are not always solving for some predefined target variable, exploratory data mining provide us a lot of information about the data itself. There are lots of applications of clustering in industry; here are some of them.

1. *Marketing*: The clustering algorithm can provide useful insights into how distinct groups exist in their customers. It can help answer questions like does this group share some common demographics? What features to look for while creating targeted marketing campaigns?

    - *Insurance*: Identify the features of group having highest average claim cost. Is the cluster made up of specific set of people? Is some specific feature driving this high claim cost?
    - *Seismology*: Earthquake epicenters show a cluster around continental faults. Clustering can help identify cluster of faults with a higher magnitude of probability than others.
    - *Government planning*: Clustering can help identify clusters of specific household for social schemes, and you can group households based on multiple attributes size, income, type, etc.
    - *Taxonomy*: It's very popular among biologists to use clustering to create taxonomy trees of groups and subgroups of similar species.

There are other methods as well to identify and creates similar groups like Q-analysis, multi-dimensional scaling, and latent class analysis. You are encouraged to read more about them in any marketing research methods textbook.

6.9.1 Introduction to Clustering

In this chapter we discuss and illustrate some of the common clustering algorithms. The definition of a cluster is loosely defined around the notion of what measure we use to find goodness of a cluster. The clustering algorithms largely depend on the the type of "clustering model" we assume for our underlying data.

Clustering model is a notion used to signify what kind of clusters we are trying to identify. Here are some common cluster models and the popular algorithms built on them.

- *Connectivity models*: Distance connectivity between observations is the measure, e.g., hierarchical clustering.
- *Centroid models*: Distance from mean value of each observation/cluster is the measure, e.g., k-means.
- *Distribution models*: Significance of statistical distribution of variables in the dataset is the measure, e.g., expectation-maximization algorithms.
- *Density models*: Density in data space is the measure, e.g., DBSCAN models.

Further clustering can be of two types:

- *Hard clustering*: Each object belongs to exactly one cluster
- *Soft clustering*: Each object has some likelihood of belonging to a different cluster

In the next section, we show R demonstrations of these algorithms to understand their output.

6.9.2 Clustering Algorithms

Clustering algorithms cannot differentiate between relevant and irrelevant variables. It is important for the researcher to carefully choose the variables based on which algorithm will start identifying patterns/groups in data. This is very important because the clusters formed can be very dependent on the variables included.

A good clustering algorithm can be evaluated based on two primary objectives:

- High intra-class similarity
- Low inter-class similarity

The other common notion among the clustering algorithm is the *measure of quality* of clustering. The similarity measure used and the implementation becomes important determinants of clustering quality measures. Another important factor in measuring quality of clustering in its ability to discover hidden patterns.

Let's first load the House Pricing dataset and see its data description. For posterior analysis (after building the model), we have appended the data with `HouseNetWorth`. This house net worth is a function of `StoreArea(sq.mt)` and `LawnArea(sq.mt)`.

From market research we will get data in raw format without any target variables. The clustering algorithm will show us if we can divide the data in the worth scales by different clustering algorithms.

```
# Read the house Worth Data
Data_House_Worth <-read.csv("Dataset/House Worth Data.csv",header=TRUE);

str(Data_House_Worth)
 'data.frame':    316 obs. of  5 variables:
  $ HousePrice    : int  138800 155000 152000 160000 226000 275000 215000
                    392000 325000 151000 ...
  $ StoreArea     : num  29.9 44 46.2 46.2 48.7 56.4 47.1 56.7 84 49.2 ...
  $ BasementArea : int  75 504 493 510 445 1148 380 945 1572 506 ...
  $ LawnArea      : num  11.22 9.69 10.19 6.82 10.92 ...
  $ HouseNetWorth: Factor w/ 3 levels "High","Low","Medium": 2 3 3 3 3 1 3
                    1 1 3 ...
#remove the extra column as well not be using this
Data_House_Worth$BasementArea <-NULL
```

A quick analysis of scatter plot in Figure 6-40 shows us that there is some relationship between the `LawnArea` and `StoreArea`. As this is a small dataset and well calibrated we can see and interpret the clusters (manual process if also clustering). However, we will assume that we didn't have this information prior and let the clustering algorithms tell us about these clusters.

```
library(ggplot2)
ggplot(Data_House_Worth, aes(StoreArea, LawnArea, color = HouseNetWorth))
+geom_point()
```

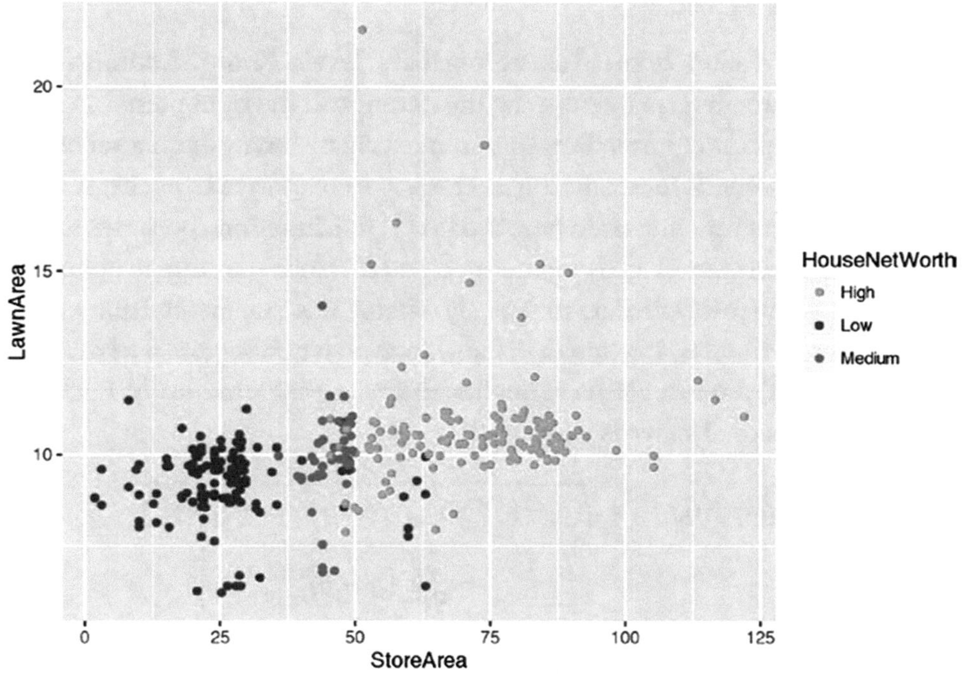

Figure 6-40. *Scatter plot between StoreArea and LawnArea for each HouseNetWorth group*

Let's use this data to illustrate different clustering algorithms.

6.9.2.1 Hierarchal Clustering

Hierarchical clustering is based on the connectivity model of clusters. The steps involved in the clustering process are:

1. Start with N clusters, N is number of elements (i.e., assign each element to its own cluster). In other words distances (similarities) between the clusters are equal to the distances (similarities) between the items they contain.

2. Now merge pairs of clusters with the closest to other (most similar clusters) (e.g., the first iteration will reduce the number of clusters to N - 1).

3. Again compute the distance (similarities) and merge with the closest one.

4. Repeat Steps 2 and 3 to exhaust the items until you get all data points in one cluster.

Now you will get a dendogram of clustering for all levels. Choose a cutoff at how many clusters you want to have by stopping the iteration at the right point.

In R, we use the `hclust()` function. Hierarchical cluster analysis on a set of dissimilarities and methods for analyzing it. This is part of the `stats` package.

Another important function used here is `dist()`; this function computes and returns the distance matrix computed by using the specified distance measure to compute the distances between the rows of a data matrix. By default, it is Euclidean distance.

In Cartesian coordinates, Euclidean distance between two vectors p = (p1, p2,..., pn) and q = (q1, q2,..., qn) are two points in Euclidean space. Mathematically, Euclidean distance in n-dimensional space is given by

$$d(p,q) = d(q,p) = \sqrt{(q_1 - p_1)^2 + (q_2 - p_2)^2 + \cdots + (q_n - p_n)^2}$$

$$= \sqrt{\sum_{i=1}^{n} (q_i - p_i)^2}.$$

Let's apply the `hclust` function and create our clusters.

```
# apply the hierarchal clustering algorithm
clusters <-hclust(dist(Data_House_Worth[,2:3]))

#Plot the dendogram
plot(clusters)
```

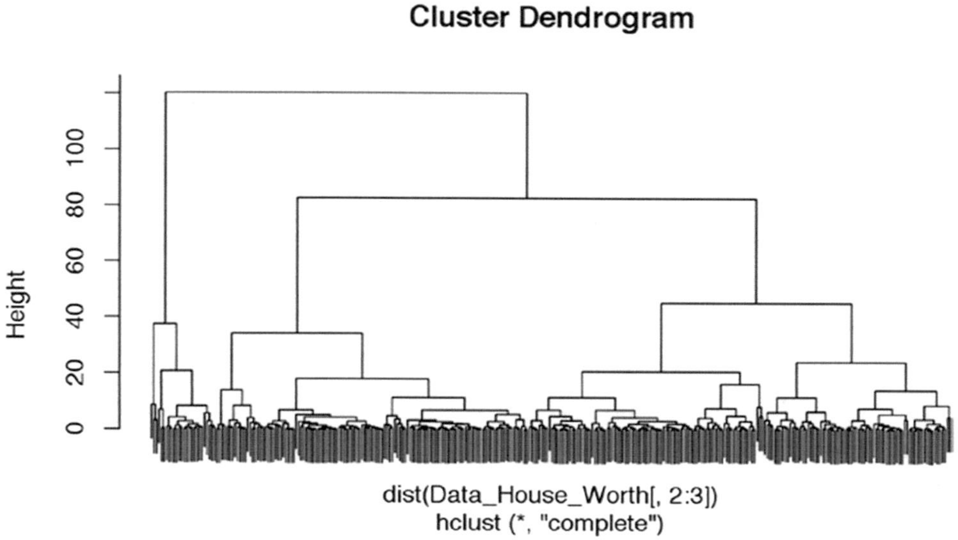

Figure 6-41. *Cluster dendogram*

Now we can see there are number of possible places where we can choose clusters. We will show cross-plot with two, three, and four clusters.

```
# Create different number of clusters
clusterCut_2 <-cutree(clusters, 2)
#table the clustering distribution with actual networth
table(clusterCut_2,Data_House_Worth$HouseNetWorth)

 clusterCut_2 High Low Medium
            1  104 135     51
            2   26   0      0
clusterCut_3 <-cutree(clusters, 3)
#table the clustering distribution with actual networth
table(clusterCut_3,Data_House_Worth$HouseNetWorth)

 clusterCut_3 High Low Medium
            1    0 122      1
            2  104  13     50
            3   26   0      0
clusterCut_4 <-cutree(clusters, 4)
#table the clustering distribution with actual networth
table(clusterCut_4,Data_House_Worth$HouseNetWorth)
```

```
clusterCut_4 High Low Medium
           1    0 122      1
           2   34   9     50
           3   70   4      0
           4   26   0      0
```

These three separate tables show how much the clusters able to capture the feature of net worth. Let's limit ourselves to three clusters as we know from additional knowledge that there are three groups of house by net worth. In statistical terms, the best number of clusters can be chosen by using elbow method and/or semi-partial R-square, validity index Pseudo F. More details can be learned from Timm, Neil H., *Applied Multivariate Analysis*, Springer, 2002.

```
ggplot(Data_House_Worth, aes(StoreArea, LawnArea, color = HouseNetWorth)) +
geom_point(alpha =0.4, size =3.5) +geom_point(col = clusterCut_3) +
scale_color_manual(values =c('black', 'red', 'green'))
```

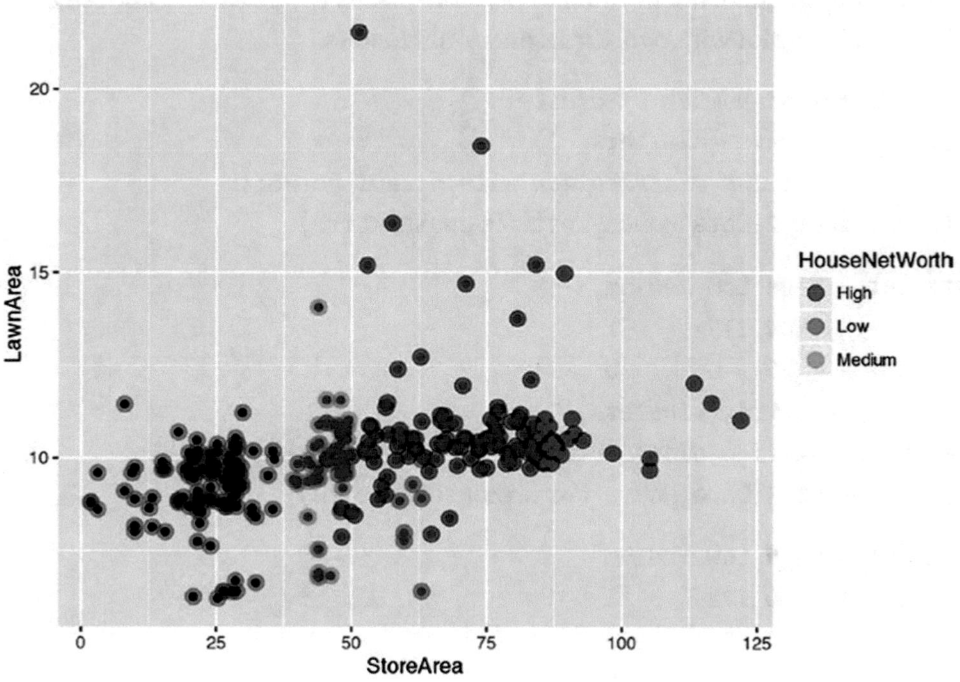

Figure 6-42. *Cluster plot with LawnArea and StoreArea*

You can see most of our "high", "medium" and "low" `NetHouseworth` points are overlapping with the three cluster created by `hclust`. In hindsight, if we didn't know the actual networth scales, we could have retrieved this information from this cluster analysis.

In the next section, we apply another clustering algorithm to the same data and see how the results look.

6.9.2.2 Centroid-Based Clustering

The following text borrowed from the original paper, "A K-Means Clustering Algorithm," by Hartigan et al. [6] gives the most crisp and precise description of the way k-means algorithm works, it says:

> *The aim of the K-means algorithm is to divide M points in N dimensions into K clusters so that the within-cluster sum of squares is minimized. It is not practical to require that the solution has minimal sum of squares against all partitions, except when M, N are small and K = 2. We seek instead "local" optima, solution such that no movement of a point from one cluster to another will reduce the within-cluster sum of squares.*

where, within cluster sum of squares (WCSS) is sum of distance of each observation in a cluster to its centroid. More technically, for a set of observations $(x_1, x_2, \ldots, x_n)$ and set of k clusters $C = \{C_1, C_2, \ldots, C_k\}$

$$WCSS = \sum_{i=1}^{k} \sum_{\mathbf{x} \in \mathbf{C}_i} \left\| \mathbf{x} - \mu_i \right\|^2$$

μ_i is the mean of points in C_i

Algorithm:

In the simplest form of the algorithm, it has two steps:

- *Assignment*: Assign each observation to the cluster that gives the minimum within cluster sum of squares (WCSS).
- *Update*: Update the centroid by taking the mean of all the observation in the cluster.

These two steps are iteratively executed until the assignments in any two consecutive iteration don't change, meaning either a point of local or global optima (not always guaranteed) is reached.

Note For interested readers, Hartigan et al., in their original paper, describes a seven-step procedure.

Let's use our HouseNetWorth data to show k-means clustering. Unlike the hierarchical cluster, to find the optimal value for k (number of cluster) here, we will use an Elbow curve. The curve shows the percentage of variance explained as a function of the number of clusters.

```
# Elbow Curve

wss <-(nrow(Data_House_Worth)-1)*sum(apply(Data_House_Worth[,2:3],2,var))
for (i in 2:15) {
  wss[i] <-sum(kmeans(Data_House_Worth[,2:3],centers=i)$withinss)
}
plot(1:15, wss, type="b", xlab="Number of Clusters",ylab="Within groups sum of squares")
```

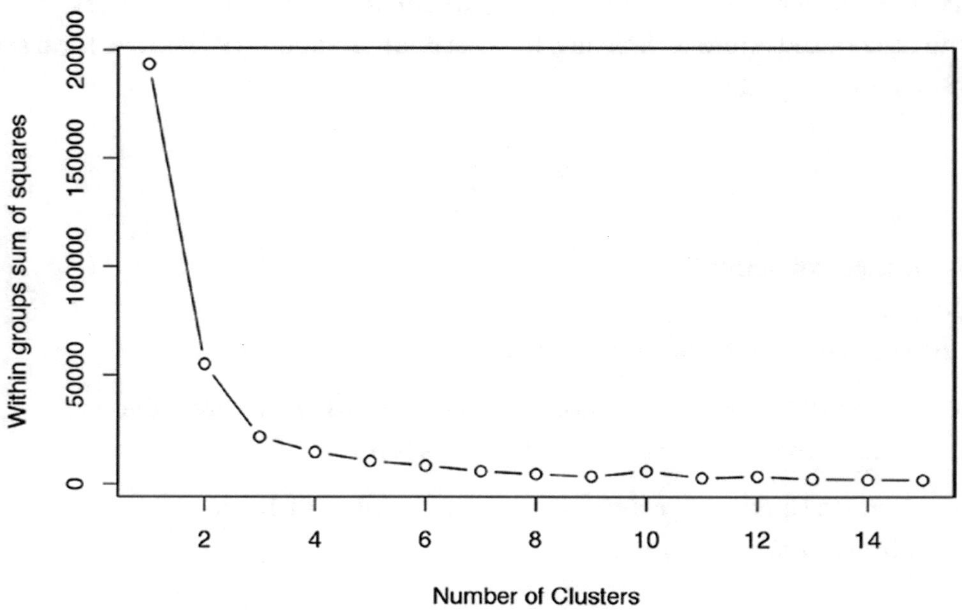

Figure 6-43. *Elbow curve for varying values of k (number of clusters) on the x-axis*

The elbow curve suggests that with three clusters, we were able to explain most of the variance in data. Beyond four clusters adding more clusters is not helping with explaining the groups (as the plot in Figure 6-43, shows, WCSS is saturating after three). Hence, we will once again choose k=3 clusters.

```
set.seed(917)
#Run k-means cluster of the dataset
Cluster_kmean <-kmeans(Data_House_Worth[,2:3], 3, nstart =20)

#Tabulate the cross distribution
table(Cluster_kmean$cluster,Data_House_Worth$HouseNetWorth)

     High Low Medium
  1    84   0      0
  2    46  13     50
  3     0 122      1
```

The table shows cluster 1 has only of "High" worth, while clusters 2 and 3 have all of it. While cluster 3 only represents the low worth except for one point. Here is the plot of clusters against the actual networth.

```
Cluster_kmean$cluster <-factor(Cluster_kmean$cluster)
ggplot(Data_House_Worth, aes(StoreArea, LawnArea, color = HouseNetWorth)) +
geom_point(alpha =0.4, size =3.5) +geom_point(col = Cluster_kmean$cluster) +
scale_color_manual(values =c('black', 'red', 'green'))
```

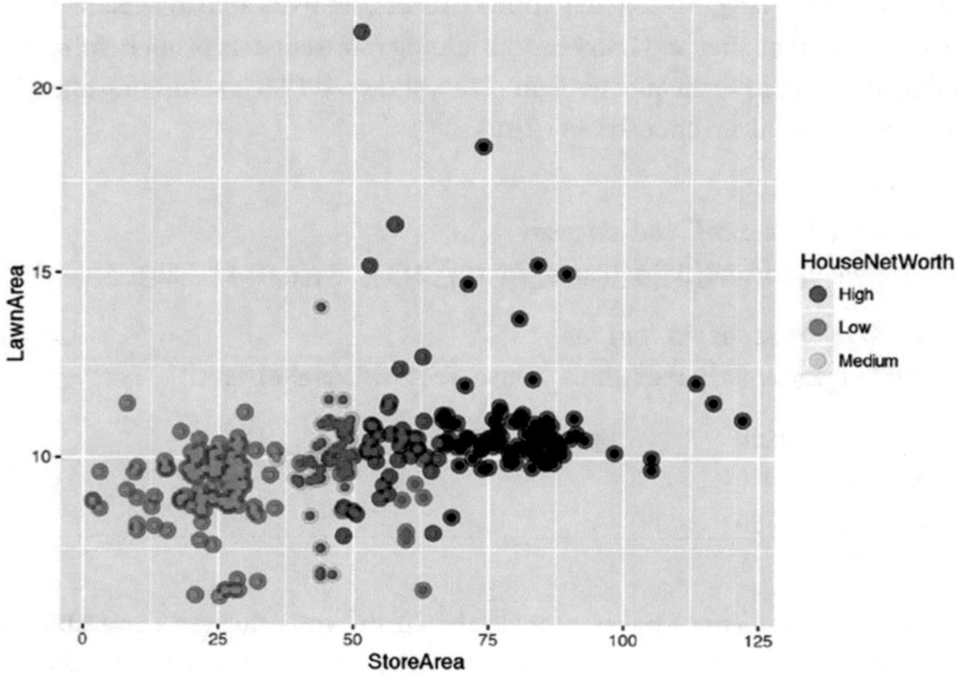

Figure 6-44. *Cluster plot using k-means*

In Figure 6-44, we can see in k-means have captured the clusters very well.

6.9.2.3 Distribution-Based Clustering

Distribution methods are iterative methods that optimize distributions of datasets in clusters. Gaussian distribution is nothing but normal distribution. This method works in three steps:

1. First randomly choose Gaussian parameters and fit it to a set of data points.
2. Iteratively optimize the distribution parameters to fit as many points it can.
3. Once it converges to a local minima, you can assign data points closer to that distribution of that cluster.

Although this algorithm create complex models, it does capture correlation and dependence among the attributes. The downside is that these methods usually suffer from an overfitting problem. Here, we show an example of an algorithm on our house worth data.

```
library(EMCluster, quietly =TRUE)

ret <-init.EM(Data_House_Worth[,2:3], nclass =3)
ret
 Method: em.EMRnd.EM
  n = 316, p = 2, nclass = 3, flag = 0, logL = -1871.0336.
 nc:
 [1]  48 100 168
 pi:
 [1] 0.2001 0.2508 0.5492
ret.new <-assign.class(Data_House_Worth[,2:3], ret, return.all =FALSE)

#This has assigned a class to each case
str(ret.new)
 List of 2
  $ nc   : int [1:3] 48 100 168
  $ class: num [1:316] 1 3 3 1 3 3 3 3 3 3 ...
# Plot results
plotem(ret,Data_House_Worth[,2:3])
```

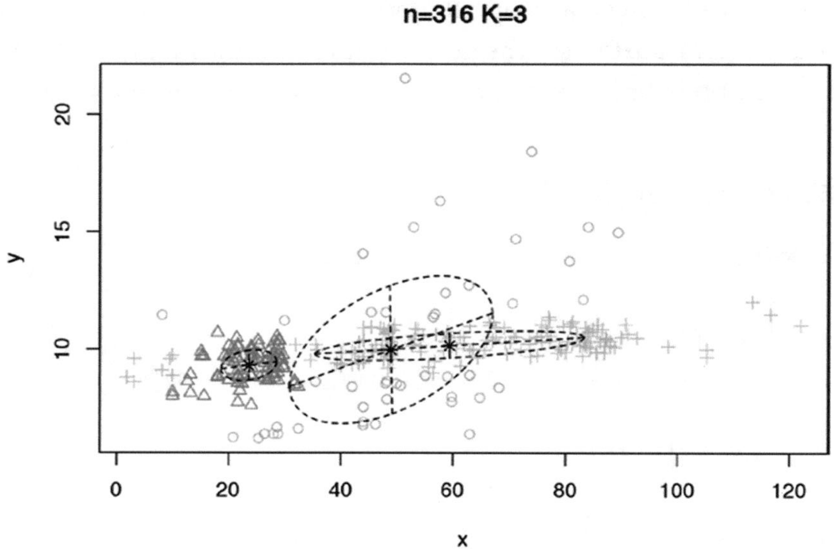

***Figure 6-45.** Clustering plot-based on the EM algorithm*

The low worth and high worth is captured well in the algorithm, while the medium ones are far more scattered, which is not well represented in the cluster. Now let's see how the scatter plot looks by clustering with this method.

```
ggplot(Data_House_Worth, aes(StoreArea, LawnArea, color = HouseNetWorth)) +
geom_point(alpha =0.4, size =3.5) +geom_point(col = ret.new$class) +
scale_color_manual(values =c('black', 'red', 'green'))
```

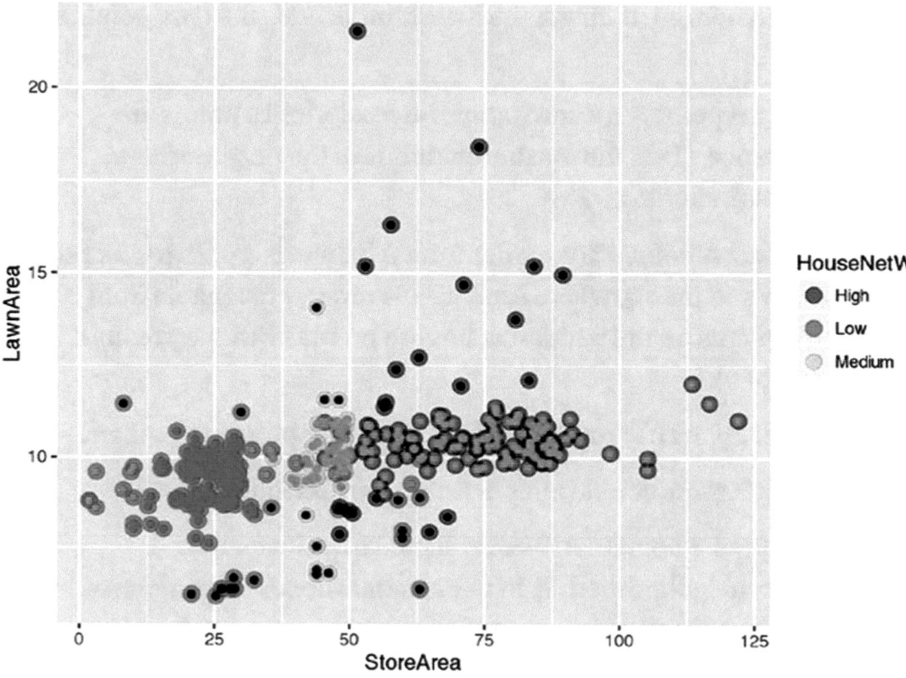

Figure 6-46. *Cluster plot for the EM algorithm*

Again, the plot is good for high and low classes, but isn't doing very well for the medium class. There are some cases scattered in high `LawnArea` values as well, but comparatively it's still captured better in the high cluster. If you observe, this method isn't as good as what we saw in the case of `hclust` or k-means, as there are many more overlaps of points between two clusters.

6.9.2.4 Density-Based Clustering

Density-based spatial clustering of applications with noise (DBSCAN) is a data clustering algorithm proposed by Martin Ester, Hans-Peter Kriegel, Jörg Sander, and Xiaowei Xu in 1996.

This algorithm works on a parametric approach. The two parameters involved in this algorithm are:

- `e`: The radius of our neighborhoods around a data point p.
- `minPts`: The minimum number of data points we want in a neighborhood to define a cluster.

Once these parameters are defined, the algorithm divides the data points into three points:

- *Core points*: A point *p* is a core point if at least `minPts` points are within distance · (· is the maximum radius of the neighborhood from *p*) of it (including *p*).
- *Border points*: A point *q* is a border from *p* if there is a path p1, ..., pn with p1 = p and pn = q, where each pi+1 is directly reachable from *pi* (all the points on the path must be core points, with the possible exception of *q*).
- *Outliers*: All points not reachable from any other point are outliers.

The steps in DBSCAN are simple after defining the previous steps:

1. Pick at random a point that is not assigned to a cluster and calculate its neighborhood. If, in the neighborhood, this point has `minPts` then make a cluster around that; otherwise, mark it as an outlier.
2. Once you find all the core points, start expanding that to include border points.
3. Repeat these steps until all the points are assigned either to a cluster or to an outlier.

```
library(dbscan)
 Warning: package 'dbscan' was built under R version 3.2.5
cluster_dbscan <-dbscan(Data_House_Worth[,2:3],eps=0.8,minPts =10)
cluster_dbscan
 DBSCAN clustering for 316 objects.
 Parameters: eps = 0.8, minPts = 10
 The clustering contains 5 cluster(s) and 226 noise points.

   0   1   2   3   4   5
 226  10  25  24  15  16

 Available fields: cluster, eps, minPts
#Display the hull plot
hullplot(Data_House_Worth[,2:3],cluster_dbscan$cluster)
```

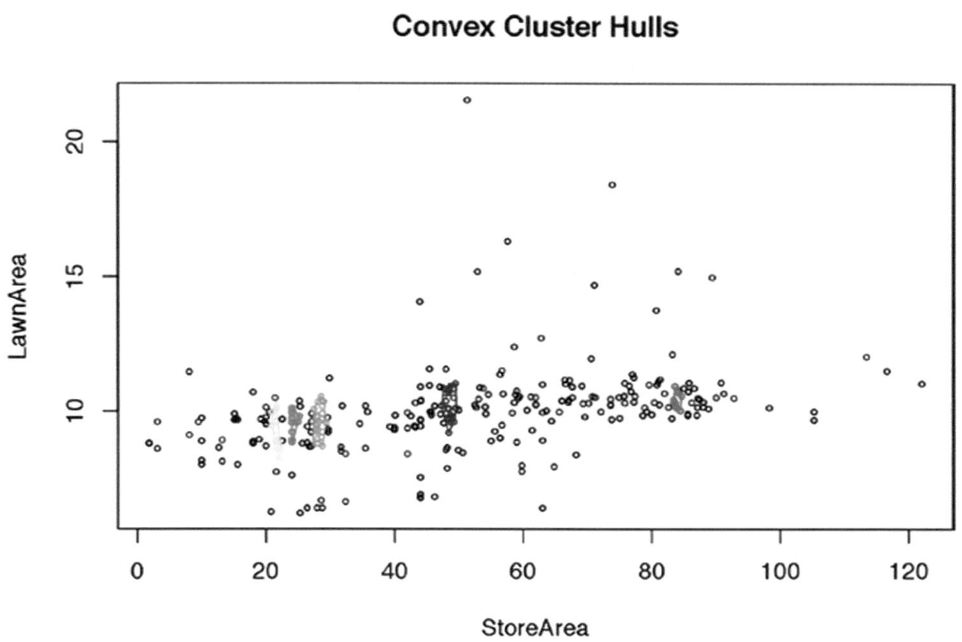

Figure 6-47. *Plot for convex cluster hulls for the EM algorithm*

The result shows that DBSCAN has found five clusters and assigned 226 cases as noise/outliers. The hull plot shows the separation is good, so we can play around with the parameters to get more generalized or specialized clusters.

6.9.3 Internal Evaluation

When a clustering result is evaluated based on the data that was clustered, it is called an internal evaluation. These methods usually assign the best score to the algorithm that produces clusters with high similarity within a cluster and low similarity between clusters.

6.9.3.1 Dunn Index

J Dunn proposed this index in 1974 through his published work titled, "Well Separated Clusters and Optimal Fuzzy Partitions," in the *Journal of Cybernetics*.[7]

The Dunn index aims to identify dense and well-separated clusters. It is defined as the ratio between the minimal intercluster distances to the maximal intracluster distance. For each cluster partition, the Dunn index can be calculated using the following formula.

$$D = \frac{\min\limits_{1 \le i < j \le n} d(i,j)}{\max\limits_{1 \le k \le n} d'(k)}$$

where *d(i,j)* represents the distance between clusters *i* and *j*, and *d'(k)* measures the intra-cluster distance of cluster *k*.

```
library(clValid)
#Showing for hierarchical cluster with clusters = 3
dunn(dist(Data_House_Worth[,2:3]), clusterCut_3)
 [1] 0.009965404
```

The Dunn index has a value between zero and infinity and should be maximized. The Dunn score with high value are more desirable; here the value is too low, suggesting it's not a good cluster.

6.9.3.2 Silhouette Coefficient

The silhouette coefficient contrasts the average distance to elements in the same cluster with the average distance to elements in other clusters. Objects with a high silhouette value are considered well clustered; objects with a low value may be outliers.

```
library(cluster)
#Showing for k-means cluster with clusters = 3
sk <-silhouette(clusterCut_3,dist(Data_House_Worth[,2:3]))

plot(sk)
```

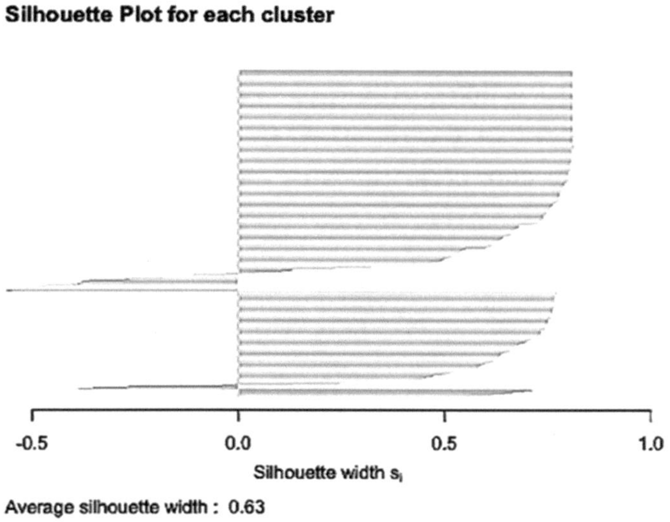

Figure 6-48. *Silhouette plot*

The silhouette plot in Figure 6-48 shows how the three clusters behave on a silhouette width.

6.9.4 External Evaluation

External evaluations are similar to evaluations done on test data. The data used for testing is not used for training the model. The test data is then evaluated and labels assigned by experts or some third-party benchmarks. Then clustering results on these already labeled items provide us the metric for how good the clusters grouped our data. As the metric depends on external inputs, it is called external evaluation.

The method is simple if we know what the actual clusters will look like. Then we can have these evaluations. In our case we already know the house worth indicator, hence we can calculate these evaluation metrics. In reality, our data is already labeled before clustering and hence we can do external evaluation on the same data as we used for clustering.

6.9.4.1 Rand Measure

The Rand index is similar to classification rate in multi-class classification problems. This measures how many items that are returned by the cluster and expert (labeled) are common and how many differ. If we assume expert labels (or external labels) to be correct, this measures the correct classification rate. It can be computed using the following formula [8]:

$$RI = \frac{TP + TN}{TP + FP + FN + TN}$$

where *TP* is the number of true positives, *TN* is the number of true negatives, *FP* is the number of false positives, and *FN* is the number of false negatives.

```
#Unsign result from EM Algo
library(EMCluster)
clust <-ret.new$class
orig <-ifelse(Data_House_Worth$HouseNetWorth == "High",2,
ifelse(Data_House_Worth$HouseNetWorth == "Low",1,2))
RRand(orig, clust)
    Rand adjRand  Eindex
  0.7653  0.5321  0.4099
```

The Rand index value is high, 0.76, indicating a good clustering fit by our EM method.

6.9.4.2 Jaccard Index

The Jaccard index is similar to the Rand index. The Jaccard index measures the overlap of external labels and labels generated by the cluster algorithms. The Jaccard index value varies between 0 and 1, 0 implying no overlap, while 1 means identical datasets. The Jaccard index is defined by the following formula:

$$J(A,B) = \frac{|A \cap B|}{|A \cup B|} = \frac{TP}{TP + FP + FN}$$

where *TP* is the number of true positives, *FP* is the number of false positives, and *FN* is the number of false negatives.

```
#Unsign result from EM Algo
#Unsign result from EM Algo
library(EMCluster)
clust <-ret.new$class
orig <-ifelse(Data_House_Worth$HouseNetWorth == "High",2,
ifelse(Data_House_Worth$HouseNetWorth == "Low",1,2))
Jaccard.Index(orig, clust)
 [1] 0.1024096
```

The index value is low, suggesting only 10% of the values are common. This implies the overlap on the original and cluster is low. Not a good cluster formation.

6.9.5 Conclusion

These supervised learning algorithms have a wide-spread adaptability in industry and research. The underlying design of decision tree makes it easy to interpret and the model is very intuitive to connect with the real-world problem. The approaches like boosting and bagging have given rise to high accuracy models based on decision trees. In particular, Random Forest is now one of the widely used models for many classification problems.

We presented a detailed discussion of decision tree where we started with the very first decision tree models like ID3 and went on to present the contemporary bagging CART and Random Forest algorithms as well.

In the next section, we see association rule mining, which works on transactional data and has found application in market basket analysis and led to many powerful recommendation algorithms.

6.10 Association Rule Mining

Association rule learning is a method for discovering interesting relations between variables in large databases. It is intended to identify strong rules discovered in databases using some measures of interestingness. Based on the concept of strong rules, Rakesh Agrawal et al. introduced association rules for discovering regularities between products in large-scale transaction data recorded by point-of-sale (POS) systems in supermarkets.

For example, the rule $\{\text{onions,potatoes}\} \Rightarrow \{\text{burger}\}$ found in the sales data of a supermarket would indicate that if a customer buys onions and potatoes together, they are likely to also buy hamburger meat. Library is another good example where rule mining plays an important role to keep books and stock up. The Hossain and Rashedur paper entitled "Library Material Acquisition Based on Association Rule Mining" is a good read to expand the idea of association rule mining that can be applied in real situations.

6.10.1 Introduction to Association Concepts

Transactional data is generally a rich source of information for a business. In the traditional scheme of things, businesses were looking at such data from the perspective of reporting and producing dashboards for the executives to understand the health of their business. In the pioneer research paper, "Mining Association Rules between Sets of Items in Large Databases," by Agrawal et al., they proposed an alternative to use this data:

- Boosting the sale of a product (item) in a store
- Impact of discontinuing a product
- Bundling multiple products together for promotions
- Better shelf planning in a physical supermarket
- Customer segmentation based on buying patterns

Consider the Market Basket data, where Item set, $I =$ {bread and cake, baking needs, biscuits, canned fruit, canned vegetables, frozen foods, laundry needs, deodorants soap, and jam spreads}

Database, $D = T_1, T_2, T_3, T_4, T_5$

And {bread and cake, baking needs, Jams spreads} is a subset of the item set I and $\{\text{bread and cake, baking needs}\} \Rightarrow \{\text{Jams spreads}\}$ is a typical rule.

The following sections describe some useful measures that can help us iterate through the algorithm.

6.10.1.1 Support

Support is the proportion of transactions in which an item set appears. We will denote it by *supp(X)*, where *X* is an item set. For example,
$\text{supp}(\{\text{bread and cake,baking needs}\}) = 2/5 = 0.4$ and
$\text{supp}(\{\text{bread and cake}\}) = 3/5 = 0.6$.

6.10.1.2 Confidence

While support helps in understanding the strength of an item set, confidence indicates the strength of a rule. For example, in the rule $\{\text{bread and cake, baking needs}\} \Rightarrow \{\text{Jams spreads}\}$, confidence is the conditional probability of finding the item set {Jams spreads} (RHS) in transactions under the condition that these transactions also contain the {bread and cake, baking needs } (LHS).

More technically, confidence is defined as

$$\text{conf}(X \Rightarrow Y) = \frac{\text{supp}(X \cup Y)}{\text{supp}(X)},$$

The rule $\{\text{bread and cake, baking needs}\} \Rightarrow \{\text{Jams spreads}\}$ has a confidence of $0.2/0.4 = 0.5$, which means 50% of the time when the customer buys {bread and cake, baking needs }, they buy {Jams spreads} as well.

6.10.1.3 Lift

If the LHS and RHS of a rule is independent of each other, i.e., the purchase of one doesn't depend on the other, then lift is a ratio between the observed support to the expected support. So, if lift = 1, LHS and RHS are independent of each other and it doesn't make any sense to have such a rule, whereas if the lift is > 1, it tells the degree to which the two occurrences are dependent on one another.

More technically

$$\text{lift}(X \Rightarrow Y) = \frac{\textbf{supp}(X \cup Y)}{\textbf{supp}(X) \times \textbf{supp}(Y)}$$

The rule $\{\text{bread and cake, baking needs}\} \Rightarrow \{\text{Jams spreads}\}$ has a lift of $\frac{0.2}{0.4 \times 0.4} = 1.25$, which means people who buy {bread and cake, baking needs } are nearly 1.25 times more likely to buy {Jams spreads} than the typical customer.

There are some other measures like conviction, leverage, and collective strength; however, these three are found to be widely used in all the literature and sufficient for the understanding of the Apriori algorithm.

Things might work well for small examples like these, however, in practicality, a typical database of transactions is very large. Agrawal et al. proposed a simple yet fast algorithm to work on large databases.

1. In the first step, all possible candidate item sets are generated.
2. Then the rules are formed using these candidate item sets.
3. The rule with the highest lift is generally the preferred choice.

Later, many variations of the Apriori algorithm have been devised but in its original form. Here are the steps involved in the Apriori algorithm for generating candidate item sets:

1. Determine the support of the one element item sets (aka singletons) and discard the infrequent items/item sets.
2. Form candidate item sets with two items (both items must be frequent), determine their support, and discard the infrequent item sets.
3. Form candidate item sets with three items (all contained pairs must be frequent), determine their support, and discard the infrequent item sets.
4. Continue by forming candidate item sets with four, five, and so on, items until no candidate item set is frequent.

6.10.2 Rule-Mining Algorithms

We will use the Market Basket data to demonstrate this algorithm in R

```
library(arules)
MarketBasket <-read.transactions("Dataset/MarketBasketProcessed.csv",
sep =",")
summary(MarketBasket)
 transactions as itemMatrix in sparse format with
  4601 rows (elements/itemsets/transactions) and
  100 columns (items) and a density of 0.1728711
```

```
most frequent items:
bread and cake          fruit      vegetables      milk cream   baking needs
          3330           2962            2961            2939           2795
       (Other)
         64551

element (itemset/transaction) length distribution:
sizes
  1   2   3   4   5   6   7   8   9  10  11  12  13  14  15  16  17  18
 30  15  14  36  44  75  72 111 144 177 227 227 290 277 286 302 239 247
 19  20  21  22  23  24  25  26  27  28  29  30  31  32  33  34  35  36
193 191 170 199 160 153 108 125  90  94  59  43  45  35  36  27  16  11
 37  38  39  40  41  42  43  47
 11   6   4   5   4   1   1   1

   Min. 1st Qu.  Median    Mean 3rd Qu.    Max.
   1.00   12.00   16.00   17.29   22.00   47.00

includes extended item information - examples:
              labels
1  canned vegetables
2      750ml red imp
3       750ml red nz
#Transactions - First two
inspect(MarketBasket[1:2])
  items
1 {baking needs,
   beef,
   biscuits,
   bread and cake,
   canned fruit,
   dairy foods,
   fruit,
   health food other,
   juice sat cord ms,
   lamb,
   puddings deserts,
```

```
    sauces gravy pkle,
    small goods,
    stationary,
    vegetables,
    wrapping}
 2 {750ml white nz,
    baby needs,
    baking needs,
    biscuits,
    bread and cake,
    canned vegetables,
    cheese,
    cleaners polishers,
    coffee,
    confectionary,
    dishcloths scour,
    frozen foods,
    fruit,
    juice sat cord ms,
    margarine,
    mens toiletries,
    milk cream,
    party snack foods,
    razor blades,
    sauces gravy pkle,
    small goods,
    tissues paper prd,
    vegetables,
    wrapping}
# Top 20 frequently bought product
itemFrequencyPlot(MarketBasket, topN =20)
```

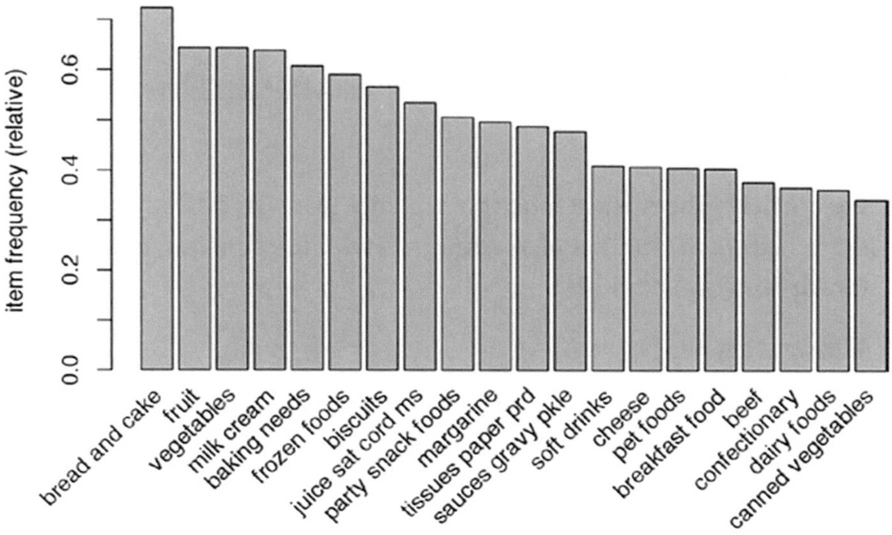

Figure 6-49. *Item frequency plot in the market basket data*

```
# Scarcity in the data - More white space means, more scarcity
image(sample(MarketBasket, 100))
```

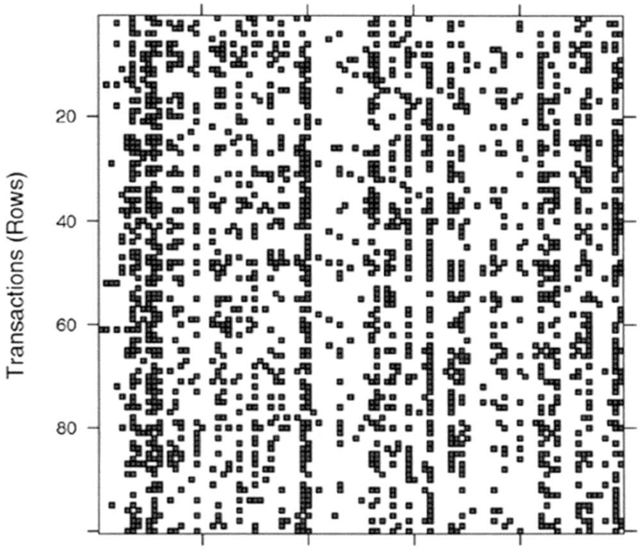

Figure 6-50. *Scarcity visualization in transactions of market basket data*

6.10.2.1 Apriori

The support and confidence could be modified to allow for flexibility in this model.

a. Model Building

We are using the Apriori function from the package `arules` to demonstrate the market basket analysis with the constant values for `support` and `confidence`:

```
library(arules)

MarketBasketRules<-apriori(MarketBasket, parameter =list(support
=0.2, confidence =0.8, minlen =2))
MarketBasketRules

 Parameter specification:
  confidence minval smax arem  aval originalSupport support minlen maxlen
         0.8    0.1    1 none FALSE            TRUE     0.2      2     10
  target   ext
   rules FALSE

 Algorithmic control:
  filter tree heap memopt load sort verbose
     0.1 TRUE TRUE  FALSE TRUE    2    TRUE

 writing ... [190 rule(s)] done [0.00s].
 creating S4 object  ... done [0.00s].
```

b. Model Summary

The top five rules and lift:

```
{beef,fruit} => {vegetables} - 1.291832
{biscuits,bread and cake,frozen foods,vegetables} => {fruit} -
1.288442
{biscuits,milk cream,vegetables} => {fruit} - 1.275601
{bread and cake,fruit,sauces gravy pkle} =>{vegetables} - 1.273765
{biscuits, bread and cake,vegetables} => {fruit} - 1.270252

summary(MarketBasketRules)
```

```
set of 190 rules

rule length distribution (lhs + rhs):sizes
 2  3  4  5
 4 93 84  9

   Min. 1st Qu.  Median    Mean 3rd Qu.    Max.
  2.000   3.000   3.000   3.516   4.000   5.000

summary of quality measures:
    support          confidence          lift
 Min.    :0.2002   Min.    :0.8003   Min.    :1.106
 1st Qu.:0.2082   1st Qu.:0.8164   1st Qu.:1.138
 Median :0.2260   Median :0.8299   Median :1.160
 Mean    :0.2394   Mean    :0.8327   Mean    :1.169
 3rd Qu.:0.2642   3rd Qu.:0.8479   3rd Qu.:1.187
 Max.    :0.3980   Max.    :0.8941   Max.    :1.292

mining info:
         data ntransactions support confidence
 MarketBasket          4601     0.2        0.8
```

Sorting grocery rules by lift:

```
inspect(sort(MarketBasketRules, by ="lift")[1:5])
   lhs                          rhs           support confidence     lift
 1 {beef,
    fruit}                  => {vegetables} 0.2143012  0.8313659 1.291832
 2 {biscuits,
    bread and cake,
    frozen foods,
    vegetables}             => {fruit}      0.2019126  0.8294643 1.288442
 3 {biscuits,
    milk cream,
    vegetables}             => {fruit}      0.2206042  0.8211974 1.275601
 4 {bread and cake,
    fruit,
    sauces gravy pkle} => {vegetables} 0.2184308  0.8197390 1.273765
```

```
 5 {biscuits,
    bread and cake,
    vegetables}         => {fruit}      0.2642904  0.8177539 1.270252
# store as  data frame
MarketBasketRules_df <-as(MarketBasketRules, "data.frame")
str(MarketBasketRules_df)
 'data.frame':    190 obs. of  4 variables:
  $ rules     : Factor w/ 190 levels "{baking needs,beef} => {bread and
                cake}",..: 189 106 163 174 60 116 115 118 16 120 ...
  $ support   : num  0.203 0.226 0.223 0.398 0.201 ...
  $ confidence: num  0.835 0.811 0.804 0.8 0.815 ...
  $ lift      : num  1.15 1.12 1.11 1.11 1.13 ...
```

6.10.2.2 Eclat

Eclat is another algorithm for association rule mining. This algorithm uses simple intersection operations for equivalence class clustering along with bottom-up lattice traversal. The following two references talk about the algorithm in detail:

- Mohammed J. Zaki, Srinivasan Parthasarathy, Mitsunori Ogihara, and Wei Li, 1997, "New Algorithms for Fast Discovery of Association Rules," Technical Report 651, Computer Science Department, University of Rochester, Rochester, NY 14627.
- Christian Borgelt (2003), "Efficient Implementations of Apriori and Eclat," Workshop of Frequent Item Set Mining Implementations (FIMI), Melbourne, FL, USA.

a. Model Building

```
library(arules)
With support = 0.2

MarketBasketRules_Eclat<-eclat(MarketBasket, parameter
=list(support =0.2, minlen =2))

 parameter specification:
  tidLists support minlen maxlen            target   ext
     FALSE     0.2      2     10 frequent itemsets FALSE
```

```
 algorithmic control:
  sparse sort verbose
       7   -2    TRUE

 writing  ... [531 set(s)] done [0.00s].
 Creating S4 object  ... done [0.00s].
With support = 0.1
MarketBasketRules_Eclat<-eclat(MarketBasket, parameter =list(supp
=0.1, maxlen =15))

 parameter specification:
  tidLists support minlen maxlen            target   ext
     FALSE     0.1      1     15 frequent itemsets FALSE

 algorithmic control:
  sparse sort verbose
       7   -2    TRUE

 writing  ... [7503 set(s)] done [0.00s].
 Creating S4 object  ... done [0.00s].
Observe the increase in the number of rules by decreasing the
support. Experiment with the support value to see how the rules
are changing.
```

b. Model Summary

The top five rules and support:

```
{bread and cake,milk cream} 0.5079331
{bread and cake,fruit} 0.5053249
{bread and cake,vegetables} 0.4994566
{fruit,vegetables} 0.4796783
{baking needs,bread and cake} 0.4762008

summary(MarketBasketRules_Eclat) # the model with support = 0.1
 set of 531 itemsets

 most frequent items:
 bread and cake     vegetables            fruit   baking needs   frozen foods
            196            137              136            130            122
```

```
        (Other)
           772

element (itemset/transaction) length distribution:sizes
  2   3   4   5
187 260  81   3

   Min. 1st Qu.  Median    Mean 3rd Qu.    Max.
  2.000   2.000   3.000   2.812   3.000   5.000

summary of quality measures:
    support
 Min.   :0.2002
 1st Qu.:0.2118
 Median :0.2378
 Mean   :0.2539
 3rd Qu.:0.2768
 Max.   :0.5079

includes transaction ID lists: FALSE

mining info:
         data ntransactions support
 MarketBasket          4601     0.2
```

Sorting grocery rules by support:

```
inspect(sort(MarketBasketRules_Eclat, by ="support")[1:5])
   items              support
 1 {bread and cake,
    milk cream}      0.5079331
 2 {bread and cake,
    fruit}           0.5053249
 3 {bread and cake,
    vegetables}      0.4994566
 4 {fruit,
    vegetables}      0.4796783
```

```
 5 {baking needs,
    bread and cake} 0.4762008
# store as  data frame
groceryrules_df <-as(groceryrules, "data.frame")
str(groceryrules_df)
 'data.frame':    531 obs. of  2 variables:
  $ items  : Factor w/ 531 levels "{baking needs,beef,bread and cake}",..:
             338 250 239 358 357 302 96 334 426 341 ...
  $ support: num  0.203 0.213 0.226 0.203 0.2 ...
```

The results are shown based on the support of the item sets rather than the lift. This is because Eclat only mines frequent item sets. There are no output of the lift measure, for which Apriori is a more suitable approach. Nevertheless, this output shows the top five item sets with highest support, which could be further used to generate rules.

6.10.3 Recommendation Algorithms

In the preceding section, we saw association rule mining, which could have been used to generate product recommendations for customer based on their purchase history. For n-products, each customer will be represented by n-dimensional 0-1 vector, where 1 means the customer has brought the corresponding product, 0 otherwise. Based on the rules with highest lift, we could recommend the product on the RHS of the rule to all the customers who bought products in the LHS.

This might work if the scarcity in the data isn't too high; however, there are more robust and efficient algorithms, collectively known as the *recommendation algorithm*. Originally, the use case of these algorithms got its popularity from Amazon's product and Netflix's movie recommendation system. A significant amount of research has been done in this area in the last couple of years. One of the most elegant implementations of a recommender algorithm can be found in the `recommenderlab` package in R, developed by Michael Hahsler. It has been well documented in the CRAN articles by the title, "recommenderlab: A Framework for Developing and Testing Recommendation Algorithms," (`https://cran.r-project.org/web/packages/recommenderlab/vignettes/recommenderlab.pdf`). This article not only elaborates on the usage of the package but also gives a good introduction of the various recommendation algorithms.

In this book, we discuss the collaborative filtering-based approach for food recommendations using the Amazon Fine Foods Review dataset. The data has one row for each user and their ratings between 1 to 5 (lowest to highest), as described earlier in the text mining section. Two of the most popular recommendation algorithms, user-based and item-based collaborative filtering, are presented in this book. We encourage you to refer to the recommenderlab article from CRAN for a more elaborate discussion.

6.10.3.1 User-Based Collaborative Filtering (UBCF)

The UBCF algorithm works on the assumption that users with similar preferences will rate similarly. For example, if a user A likes spaghetti noodles with a rating of 4 and if user B has similar taste as user A, he will rate the spaghetti close enough to 4. This approach might not work if you consider only two users; however if instead of two, we find three users closest to user A and consider their rating for spaghetti noodles in a collaborative manner (could be as simple as taking an average), we could produce a much accurate rating of user B to spaghetti noodles. For a given user-product (item) rating matrix, as shown in Figure 6-51, the algorithm works as follows:

1. We compute the similarity between two users using either cosine similarity or Pearson correlation, two of the most widely used approaches for comparing two vectors.

$$\text{sim}_{\text{Pearson}}\left(\vec{x},\vec{y}\right)=\frac{\sum_{i\in I}\left(\vec{x}_i\bar{\vec{x}}\right)\left(\vec{y}_i\bar{\vec{y}}\right)}{\left(|I|-1\right)\ \text{sd}\left(\vec{x}\right)\ \text{sd}\left(\vec{y}\right)}$$

   and

$$\text{sim}_{\text{Cosine}}\left(\vec{x},\vec{y}\right)=\frac{\vec{x}\cdot\vec{y}}{\|\vec{x}\|\cdot\|\vec{y}\|},$$

2. Based on the similarity measure, choose the k-nearest neighbor to the user to whom recommendation has to be given.
3. Take an average of the ratings of the k-nearest neighbors.
4. Recommend the top N products based on the rating vector.

Some additional notes about the previous algorithm:

- We could normalize the rating matrix to remove any user bias.
- In this approach we treat each user equally in terms of similarity; however, it's possible that some users in the neighborhood are more similar to U_a than others. In this case, we could assign certain weights to allow for some flexibility.

Note NA ratings are treated as 0.

	P1	P2	P3	P4	P5	P6	P7	P8	P9	Pearson Correlation	Nearest Neighbours
U1	3.0	2.0	1.0	5.0	NA	5.0	2.0	3.0	4.0	-0.51183	9
U2	3.0	1.0	NA	5.0	2.0	3.0	3.0	5.0	NA	-0.20919	7
U3	2.0	5.0	NA	1.0	5.0	NA	5.0	2.0	3.0	0.18997	4
U4	1.0	NA	5.0	NA	5.0	2.0	3.0	NA	3.0	0.49016	1
U5	5.0	5.0	2.0	NA	5.0	2.0	3.0	5.0	NA	0.29417	3
U6	NA	2.0	3.0	NA	NA	2.0	5.0	2.0	5.0	-0.16467	6
U7	5.0	3.0	NA	5.0	5.0	1.0	5.0	3.0	2.0	0.06012	5
U8	2.0	5.0	2.0	3.0	5.0	NA	NA	3.0	3.0	0.48511	2
U9	3.0	5.0	2.0	3.0	3.0	5.0	2.0	1.0	NA	-0.50175	8
Ua	2.0	NA	2.0	NA	5.0	NA	NA	3.0	3.0		
Ra	**2.7**	**3.3**	**3.0**	**1.0**	**5.0**	**1.3**	**2.0**	**2.7**	**2.0**		

Figure 6-51. *Illustration of UBCF*

As shown in Figure 6-51, for a new user, U_a, with a rating vector <2.0,NA,2.0,NA, 5.0,NA,NA,3.0,3.0>, we would like to find the missing ratings. Based on the Pearson correlation, for $k = 3$, the users, U_4, U_8, and U_5 are the nearest neighbors to U_a. Take an average of ratings by these users and you will get <2.7,3.3,3.0,1.0,5.0,1.3,2.0,2.7,2.0>. We might recommend product P5 and P2 to U_a based on these rating vectors.

6.10.3.2 Item-Based Collaborative Filtering (IBCF)

IBCF is similar to UBCF, but here items are compared with items based on the relationship between items inferred from the rating matrix. A similarity matrix is thus obtained using again either cosine or Pearson correlation.

Since IBCF removes any user bias and could be precomputed, it's generally considered more efficient but is known to produce slightly inferior results to UBCF.

Let's now use the Amazon Fine Food Review and apply the UBCF and IBCF algorithms from the recommender lab package in R.

a. Loading Data

```
library(data.table)

fine_food_data <-read.csv("Food_Reviews.csv",stringsAsFactors
=FALSE)
fine_food_data$Score <-as.factor(fine_food_data$Score)

str(fine_food_data[-10])
 'data.frame':    35173 obs. of  9 variables:
  $ Id                     : int  1 2 3 4 5 6 7 8 9 10 ...
  $ ProductId              : chr  "B001E4KFG0" "B00813GRG4"
                             "B000LQOCH0" "B000UA0QIQ" ...
  $ UserId                 : chr  "A3SGXH7AUHU8GW" "A1D87F6ZCVE5NK"
                             "ABXLMWJIXXAIN" "A395BORC6FGVXV" ...
  $ ProfileName            : chr  "delmartian" "dll pa" "Natalia
                             Corres \"Natalia Corres\"" "Karl" ...
  $ HelpfulnessNumerator   : int  1 0 1 3 0 0 0 0 1 0 ...
  $ HelpfulnessDenominator: int  1 0 1 3 0 0 0 0 1 0 ...
  $ Score                  : Factor w/ 5 levels "1","2","3","4",..:
                             5 1 4 2 5 4 5 5 5 5 ...
  $ Time                   : int  1303862400 1346976000 1219017600
                             1307923200 1350777600 1342051200
                             1340150400 1336003200 1322006400
                             1351209600 ...
  $ Summary                : chr  "Good Quality Dog Food" "Not as
                             Advertised" "\"Delight\" says it all"
                             "Cough Medicine" ...
```

b. Data Preparation

```
library(caTools)

# Randomly split data and use only 10% of the dataset
set.seed(90)
split =sample.split(fine_food_data$Score, SplitRatio =0.05)

fine_food_data =subset(fine_food_data, split ==TRUE)
select_col <-c("UserId","ProductId","Score")

fine_food_data_selected <-fine_food_data[,select_col]
rownames(fine_food_data_selected) <-NULL
fine_food_data_selected$Score =as.numeric(fine_food_data_
selected$Score)

#Remove Duplicates
fine_food_data_selected <-unique(fine_food_data_selected)
```

c. Creation Rating Matrix

We will use a function called `dcast` to create the rating matrix from the review ratings from the Amazon Fine Food Review dataset:

```
library(recommenderlab)
#RatingsMatrix

RatingMat <-dcast(fine_food_data_selected,UserId ~ProductId,
value.var ="Score")
User=RatingMat[,1]
Product=colnames(RatingMat)[2:ncol(RatingMat)]
RatingMat[,1] <-NULL
RatingMat <-as.matrix(RatingMat)
dimnames(RatingMat) =list(user = User , product = Product)

realM <-as(RatingMat, "realRatingMatrix")
```

d. Exploring the Rating Matrix

```
#distribution of ratings
hist(getRatings(realM), breaks=15, main ="Distribution of
Ratings", xlab ="Ratings", col ="grey")
```

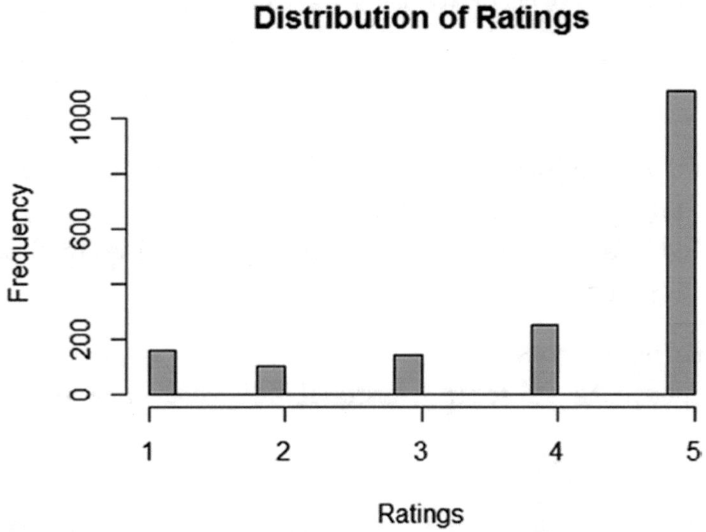

***Figure 6-52.** Distribution of ratings*

```
#Sparse Matrix Representation
head(as(realM, "data.frame"))
                  user        item rating
 467  A10012K7DF3SBQ B000SATIG4      3
 1381 A10080F3B083XV B004BKP68Q      5
 428  A1031BS8KG7I02 B000PDY3P0      5
 1396 A1074ZS6AOHJCU B004JQTAKW      1
 951   A107MO1RZUQ8V B001RVFDOO      5
 1520 A108GQ9A91JIP4 B005K4Q1VI      1
#The realRatingMatrix can be coerced back into a matrix which is
identical to the original matrix
identical(as(realM, "matrix"),RatingMat)
 [1] TRUE
#Scarcity in Rating Matrix
image(realM, main ="Raw Ratings")
```

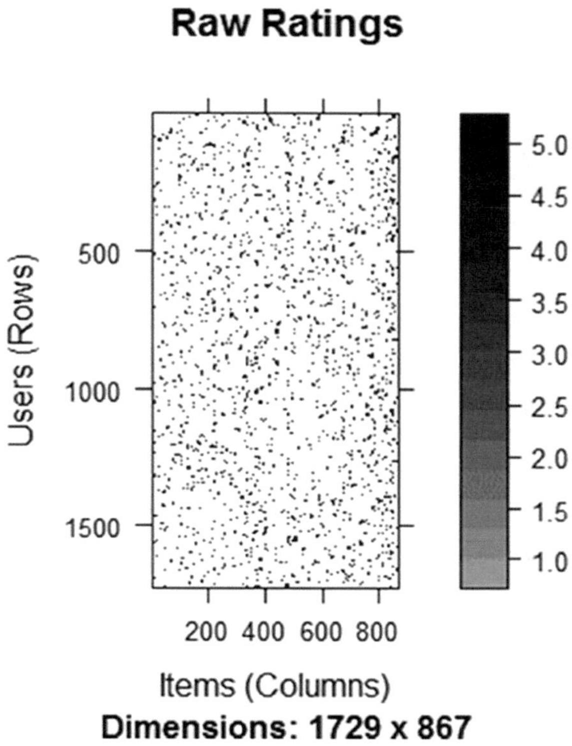

Figure 6-53. *Raw ratings by users*

e. UBCF Recommendation Model

```
#UBCF Model
r_UBCF <-Recommender(realM[1:1700], method ="UBCF")
r_UBCF
 Recommender of type 'UBCF' for 'realRatingMatrix'
 learned using 1700 users.
#List of objects in the model output
names(getModel(r_UBCF))
 [1] "description" "data"        "method"      "nn"
"sample"
 [6] "normalize"   "verbose"
#Recommend product for the rest of 29 left out observations
recom_UBCF <-predict(r_UBCF, realM[1700:1729], n=5)
recom_UBCF
```

```
 Recommendations as 'topNList' with n = 5 for 30 users.
#Display the recommendation
reco <-as(recom_UBCF, "list")
reco[lapply(reco,length)>0]
 $AY6MB5S44GMH4
 [1] "B000084EK5" "B000084EKL" "B000084ETV" "B00008DF91"
     "B00008JOLO"

 $AYOMAHLWRQHUG
 [1] "B000084EK5" "B000084EKL" "B000084ETV" "B00008DF91"
     "B00008JOLO"

 $AYX86RC7QV2UT
 [1] "B000084EK5" "B000084EKL" "B000084ETV" "B00008DF91"
     "B00008JOLO"

 $AZ4IFJ01WKBTB
 [1] "B000084EK5" "B000084EKL" "B000084ETV" "B00008DF91"
     "B00008JOLO"
```

Similarly, you can extract such recommendations for IBCF.

f. Evaluation

```
set.seed(2016)
scheme <-evaluationScheme(realM[1:1700], method="split", train = .9,
k=1, given=1, goodRating=3)

scheme
 Evaluation scheme with 1 items given
 Method: 'split' with 1 run(s).
 Training set proportion: 0.900
 Good ratings: >=3.000000
 Data set: 1700 x 867 rating matrix of class 'realRatingMatrix'
with 1729 ratings.
algorithms <-list(
"random items" =list(name="RANDOM", param=NULL),
"popular items" =list(name="POPULAR", param=NULL),
```

```
"user-based CF" =list(name="UBCF", param=list(nn=50)),
"item-based CF" =list(name="IBCF", param=list(k=50))
)

results <-evaluate(scheme, algorithms, type ="topNList",
n=c(1, 3, 5, 10, 15, 20))
 RANDOM run fold/sample [model time/prediction time]
   1  [0sec/0.91sec]
 POPULAR run fold/sample [model time/prediction time]
   1  [0.03sec/2.14sec]
 UBCF run fold/sample [model time/prediction time]
   1  [0sec/71.13sec]
 IBCF run fold/sample [model time/prediction time]
   1  [292.13sec/0.46sec]
plot(results, annotate=c(1,3), legend="bottomright")
```

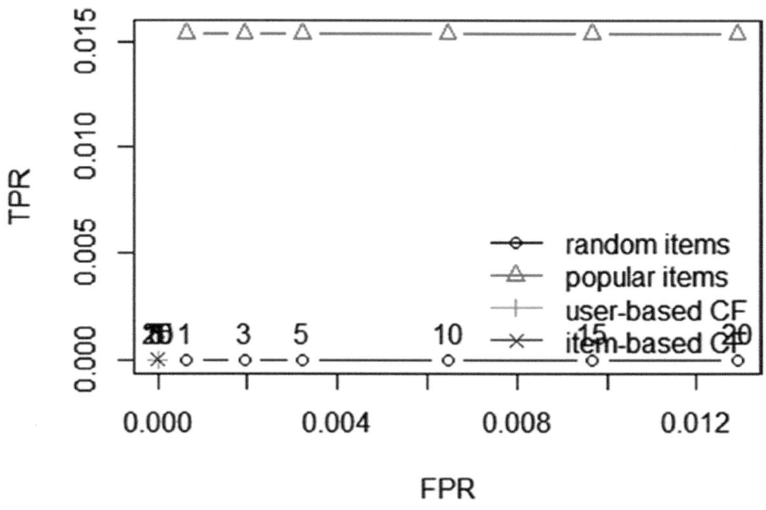

***Figure 6-54.** True positive ratio versus false positive ratio*

You can see that the ROC curve shows the poor accuracy of these recommendations on this data. It could be because of sparsity and high bias in ratings.

6.10.4 Conclusion

Association rule mining could also be thought of as a frequent version of the probabilistic model like Naïve Bayes. Although we don't call the terms directly as probabilities, they have the same roots. These algorithms are particularly well known for their ability to work with transaction data in a supermarket or e-commerce platforms where customers usually buy more than one product in a single transaction.

Finding some interesting patterns in such transactions could help reveal a whole new direction to the business or increase customer experience through product recommendation. In this section we started out with association rule mining algorithms like Apriori and went on to discuss the recommendation algorithms, which are closely related but take a different approach. Though much of the literature classifies the recommendation algorithm as a separate topic of its own, we have kept it under association rule mining, to show how the evolution happened.

In the next chapter, we discuss one of the widely used models in the world of artificial intelligence, which derives its root from the biological neural network structures in human beings.

6.11 Artificial Neural Networks

We start building this section on neural networks and then introduce deep learning toward the end, which is an extension of the neural network. In recent times, deep learning has been getting quite a lot of attention from the research community and industry for its high accuracies. Neural network-based algorithms have become very popular in recent years and take center stage in machine learning algorithms. From a statistical leaning point of view, they have become very popular in machine learning for two main reasons:

- We no longer need to make any assumptions about our data; any type of data works in neural networks (categorical and numerical).
- They are scalable techniques, can take in billions of data points, and can capture a very high level of abstraction.

It is important to mention here that neural networks are inspired from the way the human brain learns. The recent development in these fields have led to training of far dense neural networks, hence making possible to capture signals that other machine learning techniques can't.

6.11.1 Human Cognitive Learning

Artificial neural networks are inspired from biological neural networks. The human brain is one such large neural network, with neurons being the unit processing in this big network. To understand how signals are processed in brain, we need to understand the structure of a building block of brain neural network, *neurons*.

In Figure 6-55, you can see anatomy of a neuron. The structure of neuron and its function will help us build our artificial neural networks in computer systems.

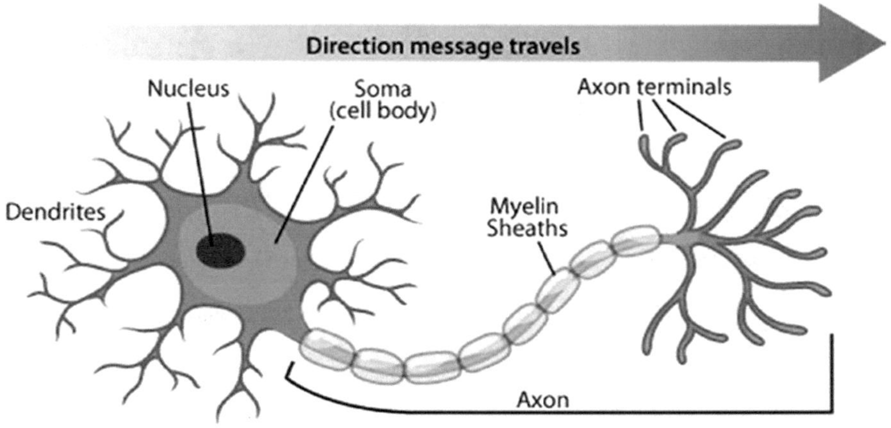

Figure 6-55. *Neuron anatomy*

A neuron is a smallest unit of neural network, and can be excited by electronic signals. It can process and transmit information through electrical and chemical signals. The excited state of neuron can be thought as the 1 state in a transistor and a 0 state if not excited. The neuron takes input from the dendrites and transmits the signals generated (processed) in the cell body through axons. Each axon then connects to other neurons in the network. The next neuron then again processes the information and passes it to another neuron.

Other important issues include the process by which the transfer of signals take place. The process takes place through synapses. There is a concept of chemical and electrical synapses, while electrical synapse works very fast and transfer continuous signals, chemical synapse works on an activation energy concept. The neuron will only transmit a signal if the strength of signal is more than a threshold. These important features allow neurons to differentiate between signal and noise.

A big network of such tiny neurons builds up in our nervous system, run by a dense neural network in our brain. Our brain learns and stores all the information in that densely packed neural network in our head. Scientists started investigating how our brain works and started experimenting with the learning process using an artificial equivalent of neurons.

Now when you have a structure of brain architecture, let's try to understand how we human learn something. I will take a simple example of golf and how a golfer learns what the best force is to hit a ball.

Learning steps:

1. You hit the ball with some force (seed value of force, F1).
2. The ball falls short of the hole, say by 3m (error is 3m).
3. You know the ball fell short, so in the next shot, you apply more force by delta (i.e., F2 = F1 + delta).
4. The ball again falls short by 50 cm (error is 50 cm).
5. Again you found that the ball fell short, so you increase the force by delta (i.e., F3 = F2 + delta).
6. Now you will observe the ball went went beyond on hole by 2m (error -2 m).
7. Now you know that too much force was applied, so you change the rate of force increase (learning rate), say `delta2`.
8. Again you hit the ball with a new force with `delta2` as improvement over the second shot (F4 = F2 + delta2).
9. Now the ball falls very close to hole, say 25 cm.
10. Now you know the previous `delta2` worked for you, so you try again with the same delta, and this time it goes into the hole.

This process is simply based on learning and updating yourself for better results. There might be many ways to learn how to correct and by what magnitude to improve. This biological idea of learning from a large number of events is successfully translated by researchers into artificial neural network learning, the most powerful tool the data scientist has.

Warren McCulloch and Walter Pitts (1943) paper entitled, "A Logical Calculus of Ideas Immanent in Nervous Activity"[12], laid the foundation of a computational framework for neural networks. After their path-breaking work, the further development of neural networks split into biological processes and machine learning (applied neural networks).

It will help to look back at the biological architecture and learning method while reading through the rest of neural networks.

6.11.2 Perceptron

A *perceptron* is basic unit of artificial neural network that takes multiple inputs and produces binary outputs. In machine learning terminology, it is a supervised learning algorithm that can classify an input into binary 0 or 1 class. In simpler terms, it is a classification algorithm than can do classification based on a linear predictor function combining weights (parameters) of the feature vector. See Figure 6-56.

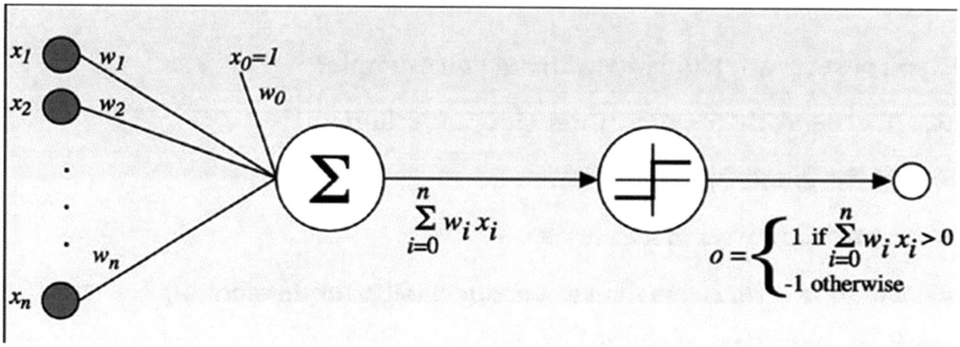

Figure 6-56. *Working of a perceptron (mathematically)*

In machine learning, the perceptron is defined as a binary classifier function that maps its input x (a real-valued vector) to an output value f(x) (a single binary value):

$$f(x) = \begin{cases} 1 & \text{if } w \cdot x + b > 0 \\ 0 & \text{otherwise} \end{cases}$$

where w is a vector of real-valued weights, $w \cdot x$ is the dot product $\sum_{i=0}^{m} w_i x_i$, where m is the number of inputs to the perceptron and b is the bias. Bias is independent of input values and helps fix the decision boundary.

The learning algorithm for a single perceptron can be stated as follows:

1. Initialize the weights to some feasible values.
2. For each data point in a training set, do Steps 3 and 4.
3. Calculate the output with previous step weights.

$$y_j(t) = f\left[w(t) \cdot x_j\right]$$
$$= f\left[w_0(t)x_{j,0} + w_1(t)x_{j,1} + w_2(t)x_{j,2} + \cdots + w_n(t)x_{j,n}\right]$$

   This is the output you will get with the current weights in the perceptron.

4. Update the weights:

$$w_i(t+1) = w_i(t) + \left(d_j - y_j(t)\right)x_{j,i}, \text{ for all features } 0 \le i \le n.$$

Did you observe any similarity with our golf example?

5. In general, there can be three stopping criteria:

- All the points in training set are exhausted
- A preset number of iterations
- Iteration error is less than a user-specified error threshold, γ

Iteration error is defined as follows:

$$\frac{1}{s}\sum_{j=1}^{s}\left|d_j - y_j(t)\right|$$

Now let's explain a simple example using a sample perceptron to make it clear how powerful a classifier it can be.

NAND gate is a Boolean operator that gives the value zero if and only if all the operands have a value of 1, and otherwise has a value of 1 (equivalent to NOT AND).

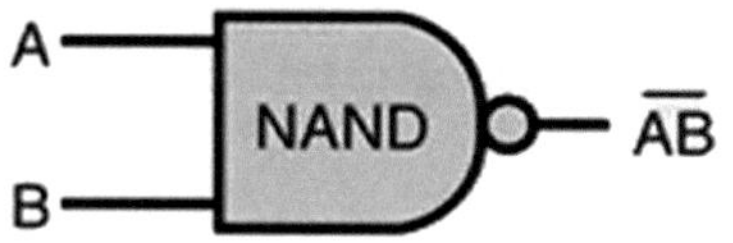

A	B	Out
0	0	1
0	1	1
1	0	1
1	1	0

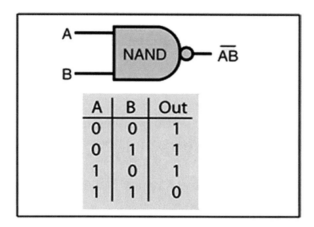

Figure 6-57. *NAND gate operator*

Now we will try to recreate this NAND gate with the perceptron in Figure 6-58 and see if it gives us the same output as the previous output, by applying the weights logic.

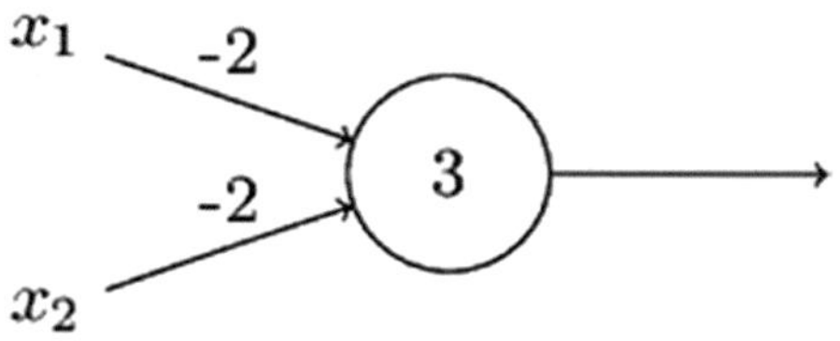

Figure 6-58. *NAND gate perceptron*

There are two inputs to the perceptron x1 and x2 with possible values of 0 and 1. Hence, there can be four types of input and we know the output as well for NAND, as per Figure 6-58.

The perceptron is a function of weights, and if the dot product of weights is greater than 1 then it gives output one. For our example, we chose the weights as w1=w2= -2 and bias = 3. Now let's compute the perceptron for inputs and see the output.

1. 00 (-2)0 + (-2)0 + 3 = 3 >0, output is 1
2. 01 (-2)0 + (-2)1 + 3 = 1 >0, output is 1
3. 10 (-2)1 + (-2)1 + 3 = 1 >0, output is 1
4. 11 (-2)1 + (-2)1 + 3 = -1 <0, output is 0

Our perceptron just implemented a NAND gate!

Now that the basic concepts of neural networks are set, we can jump to increasing the complexity and bring more power to these basic concepts.

6.11.3 Sigmoid Neuron

Neural networks have a special kind of neurons, called *sigmoid neurons*. They allow a continuous output, which a perceptron does not provide. The output of sigmoid neuron is on a continuous scale.

A sigmoid function is a mathematical function having an S-shaped curve (a sigmoid curve). The function is defined as follows:

$$S(t) = \frac{1}{1+e^{-t}}.$$

Other examples/variations of the sigmoid function are the ogee curve, gompertz curve, and logistic curve. Sigmoids are used as activation functions (recall chemical synapse) in neural networks. See Figure 6-59.

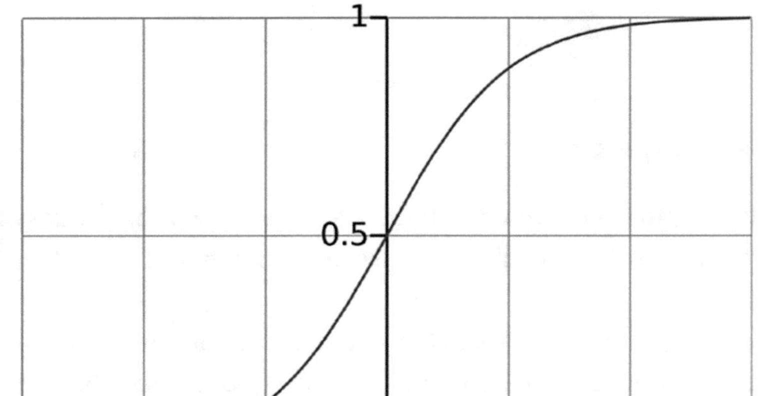

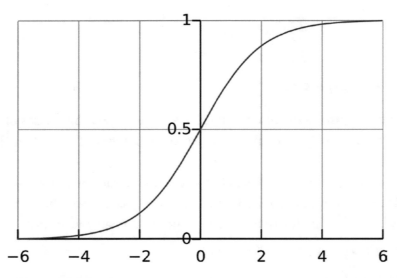

Figure 6-59. *Sigmoid function*

In neural networks, a sigmoid neuron has multiple inputs x1, x2,.. , xn. But the output is on a scale of 0 to 1. Similar to perceptron, the sigmoid neuron has weights for each input, i.e., w1,w2,... and an overall bias. To draw similarity with perceptron, observe for very large input (input dot product with weights plus bias) the sigmoid perceptron tends to 1, the same as perceptron but asymptotically. This holds true for highly negative value as well.

Now that we have covered the basic parts of the neural network, let's discuss the architecture of neural networks in the next section.

6.11.4 Neural Network Architecture

The simple perceptron cannot do a good job of classification beyond linear ones, so the example in Figure 6-60 will show what we mean by linear separability.

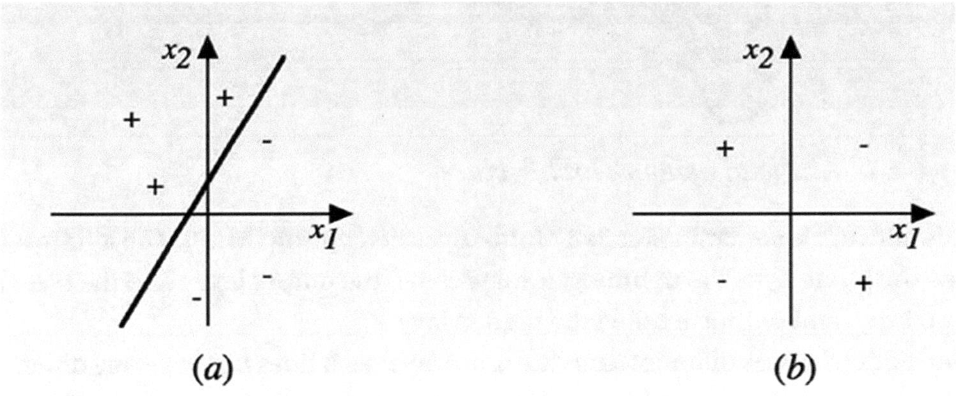

Figure 6-60. *Linear separability*

In Figure 6-60(a) on the left, you can draw a line (linear function of weights and bias) to separate + from -, but take a look at the image at right. In Figure 6-60(b), the + and - are not linearly separable. We need to expand our neural network architecture to include more perceptrons to do non-linear separation.

Similar to what happens in biological systems to learn complicated things, we take the idea of network of neurons as network of perceptrons for our artificial neural network. Figure 6-61 shows a simple expansion of perceptrons to a network of perceptrons.

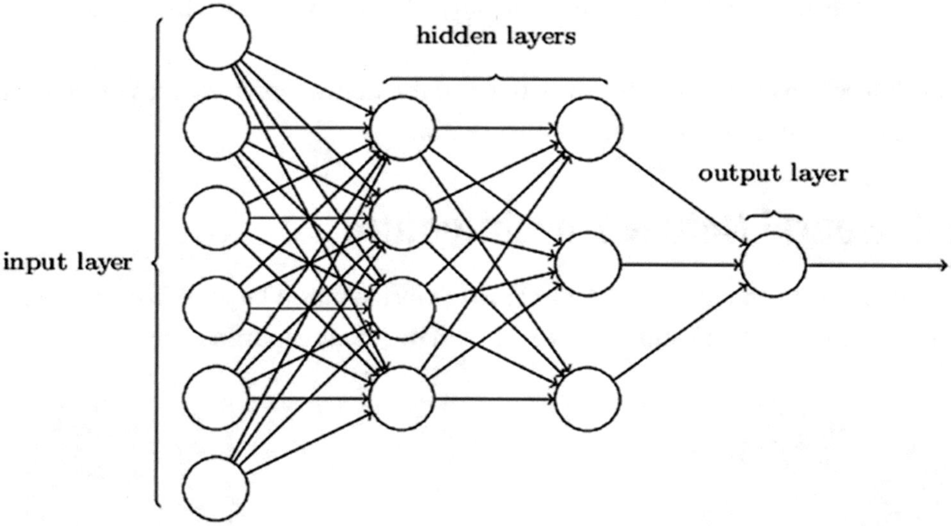

Figure 6-61. *Artificial network architecture*

This network is sometimes called Multi-Layer Perceptron (MLP). The leftmost layer is called the input layer, the rightmost layer is called the output layer, and the layer in between input and output is called the hidden layer.

The hidden layer is different from the input layer as it does not have any direct input. While the number of input and output layer design and number is determined by the inputs and outputs respectively, finding the hidden layer design and number is not straightforward. The researchers have developed many design heuristics for the hidden layers; these different heuristics help the network behave the way they want it to. In this section it's good to talk about two more features of neural nets:

- *Feedforward Neural Networks (FFNN):* As you can see from the simple architecture, if the input to each layer is in one direction we call that network a feed-forward neural network. This network makes sure that there are no loops within the neural network. There are many other types of neural networks, especially deep learning has expanded the list, but this is the most generic framework.
- *Specialization versus generalization:* This is a general concept that relates to the complexity of architecture (size and number of hidden layers). If you have too many hidden layers/complicated architecture, the neural network tend to be very specialized; in machine learning

terms, it overfits. This is called a specialized neural network. The other extreme is if you use a simple architecture that the model will be very generalized and would not fit the data properly. A data scientist has to keep this balance in mind while designing the neural net.

Artificial neural networks have three main components to set up the training exercise:

- *Architecture*: Number of layers, weights matrix, bias, connections, etc.
- *Rules*: Refer to the mechanism of how the neurons behave in response to signals from each other.
- *Learning rule:* The way in which the neural network's weights change with time.

In the next section, we touch on supervised and unsupervised learning, which will relate to the concepts we have been learning in the book for dependent variables and no dependent variable (like clustering).

6.11.5 Supervised versus Unsupervised Neural Nets

We present a quick recap of this subject with an illustration by Andrew NG in his Coursera course. We show a simple and intuitive example to differentiate between supervised and unsupervised learning (see Figure 6-62).

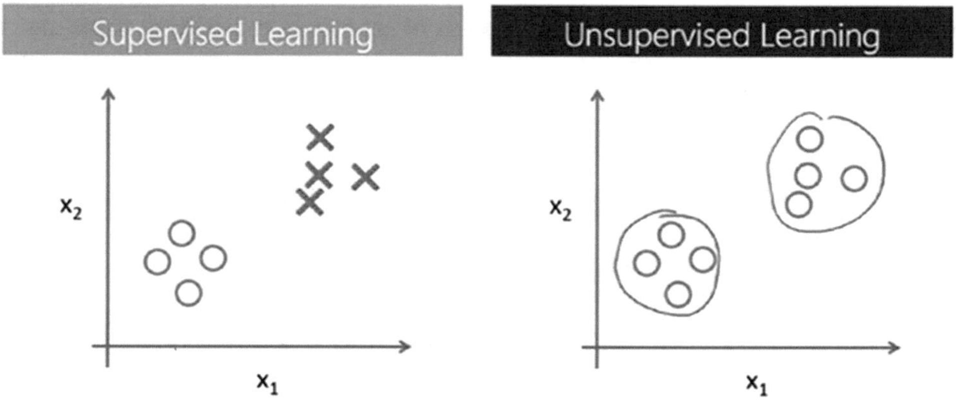

Figure 6-62. *Supervised versus unsupervised learning*

The image on the left has labeled the data as two different types, so the algorithm knows that the objects are different, while on the right we have the same objects but didn't tell the algorithm which is which.

So in very simple terms, supervised learning is when we provide the machine learning algorithm the output against each input. While learning is unsupervised when we don't supply the output and the algorithms themselves have to figure out the different set of outputs.

Examples:

- *Supervised learning*: `HousePrice` is given in our data against each input variable. Our learning algorithm will try to learn after multiple iterations how to determine the house price based on underlying features (e.g., linear regression).
- *Unsupervised learning*: We just provide the house feature data without a target variable. In that case, the algorithm will do categorization based on similar set of features (e.g., clustering).

In the next section, we introduce a supervised learning algorithm for neural networks and show an example of neural net in R. R is not one of the preferred platforms for neural network and deep leaning. We will limit ourselves to simple examples.

6.11.6 Neural Network Learning Algorithms

Learning algorithm determine how our machine learning process will choose a model for our underlying data. The general principle is to select the model that minimizes our cost function. A learning algorithm finds the best solution for problem by controlling the training of the neural networks. Most of the learning algorithms work on the principle of non-linear optimization and statistical estimation.

Next, we touch on the broader classed of learning algorithms for neural nets.

6.11.6.1 Evolutionary Methods

Evolutionary methods are derived from the evolutionary process in biology, and evolution can be in terms of reproduction, mutation, selection, and recombination. A fitness function is used to determine the performance of the model, and based on this function we select our final model.

The steps involved in this learning method are as follows:

1. Create a population of solutions (i.e., weights on all the inputs).
2. Apply the fitness function to see how this initial population performed with initial population.
3. Select the best solution set from Step 2, and then breed with other solutions (e.g., change weight on one variable with another solution).
4. Evaluate again on the fitness function and continue with Steps 3 and 4 until you get a solution.

Genetic algorithms are inspired by this evolutionary process.

6.11.6.2 Gene Expression Programming

Gene expression programming is also a type of evolutionary learning algorithm. The learning method is inspired by home gene expression happens in biological body. The gene expression learning program are implemented as complex tree structures adapting to change in sizes, shape, and composition.

Though this deemed to be an improvement over genetic algorithm, the general sentiment is that this has not been able to improve the learning results drastically. In computer programming, gene expression programming (GEP) is an evolutionary algorithm.

6.11.6.3 Simulated Annealing

Simulated annealing is a very different approach from the evolutionary approach. This method works on a probabilistic approach to approximate the global optimum for cost function. The method searches for a solution in large space with simulation.

The steps are involved in this method are:

1. Start the iteration with some random value/solution weights.
2. At each iteration, the algorithm gets probabilities to decide whether to stay in the same state or move to some neighbor state.

3. If moved to the next state, check the value of cost function. If it's lower than the previous, it was a successful move.
4. Repeat Steps 2 and 3 until either you get the desired results or you want to stop the iterations.

This method uses heavy computation power. However, it is a good improvement over the issue of model convergence to local optimum due to lack of a probabilistic jump.

6.11.6.4 Expectation Maximization

Expectation minimization is a statistical learning method that uses an iterative method to find maximum likelihood or maximum posterior estimate. The algorithm typically process in two steps:

1. Generating the Expectation function for log-likelihood using the current estimate for the parameters (take some random seed value for starting iterations).
2. Maximizing the Expectation function by tuning the parameters, and then using these parameters in the next iteration.

These two steps, when done iteratively, cause the algorithm to converge to the parameters, maximizing the log-likelihood of the function.

6.11.6.5 Non-Parametric Methods

Non-parametric efforts are exactly the opposite of the expectation-maximization method. In non-parametric, we don't make any assumptions on the underlying data distribution. This allows complex representation of the function as no constraints come from the distribution.

In neural networks, the model is represented by an unknown function of weighted sum of several sigmoids, each of which is a function of explanatory variables. The algorithm then does a non-linear least square optimization to get the final weights of the underlying objective function.

6.11.6.6 Particle Swarm Optimization

The particle swarm optimization algorithm is developed by observing how birds flock or a fish school finds the best shape to move at the least resistance and highest velocity. In this algorithm, we have notion of position and velocity for particles. Particles are a population of candidate solutions.

The algorithm tries to search the solution set in a large space, and each particle's movement is controlled by mathematical formula around velocity (how fast the flock can move?) and position (how the position of particle in the flock influences the velocity). Though it's a very powerful learning methodology, it does not guarantee a global optimal solution.

6.11.7 Feed-Forward Back-Propagation

Back-propagation learning is one of the most popular learning methodologies in neural networks. This is also called the "back-propagation of errors" method. In conjunction with some optimization methods like the gradient descent method, it can be used to train artificial neural networks.

This is a supervised learning method, as the name suggests a propagation of errors. Recall the golf example. Though this method can be used for unsupervised learning, it largely remains the best method to train a feed-forward neural network.

Another important point to consider here is generally this method works on the gradient descent principle, so the neuron function (activation function) should be differential. Otherwise the gradient descent cannot be calculated and the method fails. See Figure 6-63.

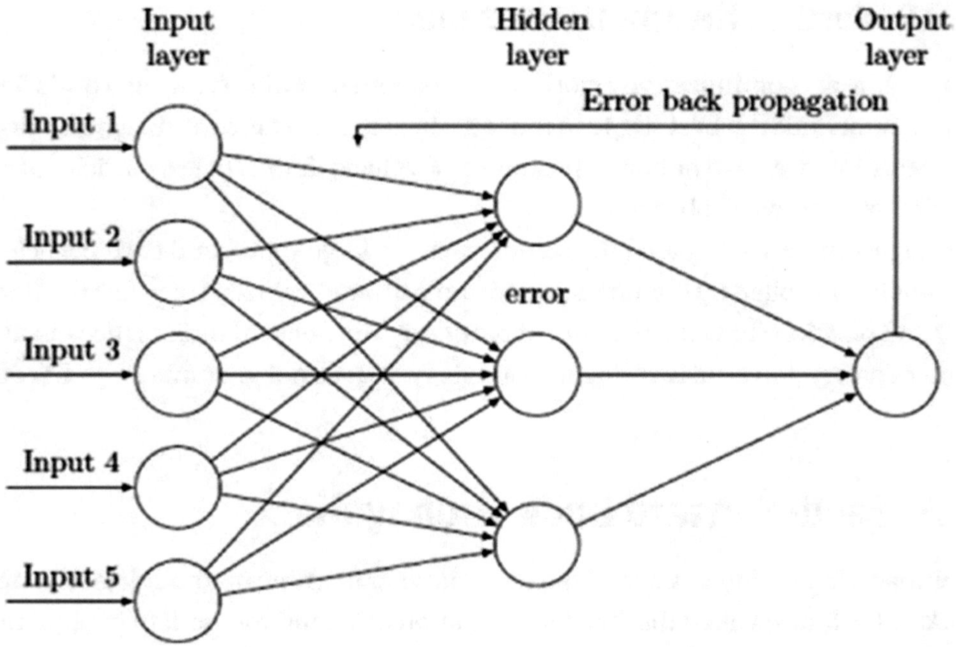

***Figure 6-63.** Workings of the back-propagation method*

The algorithm can be simply executed using the following steps. We will give a mathematical representation of error correction when the sigmoid function is used as the activation function:

1. Feed-forward the network with input and get the output.
2. Backward propagation of output, to calculate delta at each neuron (error).
3. Multiply the delta and input activation function to get the gradient of weight.
4. Update the weight by subtracting a ratio from the gradient of the weight.

This algorithm will be correcting for error in each iteration and coverage to a point where it has no more reducible error.

Mathematically, for each neuron *j*, its output o_j is defined as

$$o_j = \varphi(\text{net}_j) = \varphi\left(\sum_{k=1}^{n} w_{kj} o_k\right)$$

To update the weight w_{ij} using gradient descent, you must choose a learning rate, α. The change in weight, which is added to the old weight, is equal to the product of the learning rate and the gradient, multiplied by -1:

$$\Delta w_{ij} = -\alpha \frac{\partial E}{\partial w_{ij}} = \begin{cases} -\alpha o_i (o_j - t_j) o_j (1 - o_j) & \text{if } j \text{ is an output neuron,} \\ -\alpha o_i \left(\sum_{l \in L} \delta_l w_{jl}\right) o_j (1 - o_j) & \text{if } j \text{ is an inner neuron.} \end{cases}$$

The -1 is required in order to update in the direction of a minimum, not a maximum, of the error function.

6.11.7.1 Purchase Prediction: Neural Network-Based Classification

Let's run our purchase prediction data with the nnet package in R and see how neural networks perform compared to our logistic regression example discussed in the regression section.

```
#Load the data and prepare a dataset for logistic regression
Data_Purchase_Prediction <-read.csv("Dataset/Purchase Prediction Dataset.
csv",header=TRUE);

Data_Purchase_Prediction$choice <-ifelse(Data_Purchase_
Prediction$ProductChoice ==1,1,
ifelse(Data_Purchase_Prediction$ProductChoice ==3,0,999));
Data_Neural_Net <-Data_Purchase_Prediction[Data_Purchase_Prediction$choice
%in%c("0","1"),]

#Remove Missing Values
Data_Neural_Net <-na.omit(Data_Neural_Net)
rownames(Data_Neural_Net) <-NULL
```

Usually scaling the continuous variables in the intervals [0,1] or [-1,1] tends to give better results. Convert the categorical variables into binary variables.

```
#Transforming the continuous variables
cont <-Data_Neural_
Net[,c("PurchaseTenure","CustomerAge","MembershipPoints","IncomeClass")]

maxs <-apply(cont, 2, max)
mins <-apply(cont, 2, min)

scaled_cont <-as.data.frame(scale(cont, center = mins, scale = maxs -mins))

#The dependent variable
dep <-factor(Data_Neural_Net$choice)

Data_Neural_Net$ModeOfPayment <-factor(Data_Neural_Net$ModeOfPayment);

flags_ModeOfPayment =data.frame(Reduce(cbind,
lapply(levels(Data_Neural_Net$ModeOfPayment), function(x){(Data_Neural_
Net$ModeOfPayment ==x)*1})
))

names(flags_ModeOfPayment) =levels(Data_Neural_Net$ModeOfPayment)
Data_Neural_Net$CustomerPropensity <-factor(Data_Neural_
Net$CustomerPropensity);

flags_CustomerPropensity =data.frame(Reduce(cbind,
lapply(levels(Data_Neural_Net$CustomerPropensity), function(x){(Data_
Neural_Net$CustomerPropensity ==x)*1})
))
names(flags_CustomerPropensity) =levels(Data_Neural_Net$CustomerPropensity)

cate <-cbind(flags_ModeOfPayment,flags_CustomerPropensity)

#Combine all data into single modeling data
Dataset <-cbind(dep,scaled_cont,cate);

#Divide the data into train and test
set.seed(917);
index <-sample(1:nrow(Dataset),round(0.7*nrow(Dataset)))
```

```
train <-Dataset[index,]
test <-Dataset[-index,]
```

Now we will use the built-in back propagation algorithm from the nnet() package in R.

```
library(nnet)
i <-names(train)
form <-as.formula(paste("dep ~", paste(i[!i %in% "dep"], collapse =" + ")))
nn <-nnet.formula(form,size=10,data=train)
 # weights:  181
 initial  value 151866.965727
 iter  10 value 108709.305804
 iter  20 value 107666.702615
 iter  30 value 107382.819447
 iter  40 value 107267.937386
 iter  50 value 107203.589847
 iter  60 value 107138.952084
 iter  70 value 107084.361878
 iter  80 value 107037.998279
 iter  90 value 107003.328743
 iter 100 value 106970.152142
 final  value 106970.152142
 stopped after 100 iterations
predict_class <-predict(nn, newdata=test, type="class")

#Classification table
table(test$dep,predict_class)
    predict_class
         0     1
   0 28776 13863
   1 11964 19534
#Classification rate
sum(diag(table(test$dep,predict_class))/nrow(test))
 [1] 0.6516314
```

In the previous architecture, we used 10 neurons in one hidden layer. The accuracy comes out to be 65%, which is 1% more than what we saw in logistic regression. Neural net has improved prediction on 0 while deteriorated on 1. (Do you want to try an ensemble? We will discuss this in Chapter 8.)

Look at the neural net with 10 hidden neurons; it is able to improve prediction for 0s. If you extend this training to deep learning, even a minuscule signal can be captured. In deep learning, we will run the same example with multi-layer deep architecture. See Figures 6-64 through 6-66.

```
library(NeuralNetTools)
 Warning: replacing previous import by 'scales::alpha' when loading
 'NeuralNetTools'
# Plot the neural network
plotnet(nn)
```

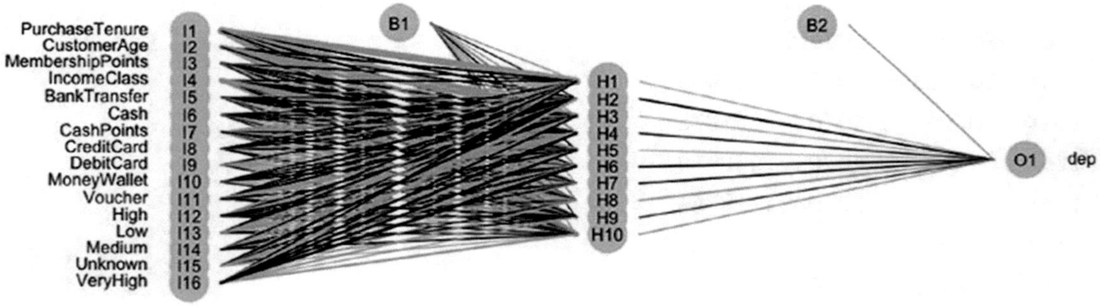

***Figure 6-64.** One hidden layer neural network*

```
#get the neural weights
neuralweights(nn)
 $struct
 [1] 16 10  1

 $wts
 $wts$`hidden 1 1`
  [1]  -1.7688041 -20.6924206   2.3683340   0.3254776   0.3755354
  [6]  -0.4381737  -0.9342264  -0.4396708   0.2488121  -0.8040053
 [11]  -0.2513980   1.1595037  -0.5800809   0.9427963  -0.5210107
 [16]  -0.5680854   0.9942396
```

```
$wts$`hidden 1 2`
 [1]  0.3785581  2.7997630  0.0419642 -1.8159788 -2.0329127  0.2695198
 [7]  0.3923006 -2.1276359  0.3242286  0.4522314  0.5254541  1.2197842
[13] -0.1996586  2.2651791  0.4066352  3.6192206 -5.2330743

$wts$`hidden 1 3`
 [1]  -1.4357242 -12.9881898 -12.3360008   1.1062240   3.6054822
 [6]   1.5317392   0.6969328  -6.2048082   0.9177840  -0.1734451
[11]   0.1648537   2.1053240   0.6816542  -2.9358718  -1.0474676
[16]  -0.4098642   1.5974077

$wts$`hidden 1 4`
 [1] -5.30486658  2.93556841 -9.97245085  0.30268208  6.59471280
 [6]  1.95089306  0.69071825  0.31481250 -0.06330620 -1.00934374
[11]  0.93998141 -9.14052075 -6.52385269 -1.32746226 -1.07514308
[16]  0.06271666  3.52729817

$wts$`hidden 1 5`
 [1]   2.24357572  -7.90629807  -2.19299184   0.78657421 -13.42029541
 [6]   1.35697587   0.76688140  -4.08706478   2.90349734  -0.59422438
[11]   2.21698054  -0.08467332   1.68745126  -0.43716182  -0.34025868
[16]  -2.29645501   2.73500554

$wts$`hidden 1 6`
 [1] -3.7195678  1.5885211  0.9809355 -0.8999143 -3.3623349 -1.6354780
 [7] -1.0924695  0.3577909 -0.4331445 -0.9332748 -0.6803754  1.4831636
[13]  0.1024139 -5.6953417  0.8179687 -3.9350386  4.9241476

$wts$`hidden 1 7`
 [1] -0.8225491 -4.8242434 -2.9266563  2.5035607  0.1378938 -0.3450762
 [7] -0.6713392  1.0763017 -0.2546451 -0.8533341 -0.5570266 -0.2484610
[13]  1.3856182 -1.1600616  1.2339496 -1.2949715 -0.7762755

$wts$`hidden 1 8`
 [1] -3.86805085  2.35232847 -2.48545877 -0.14794972  0.07481260
 [6]  0.70845847  0.38961887 -2.34134097 -2.32810205 -0.80392872
[11] -0.08502893 -1.81432815  0.05929793 -0.19809056 -0.27217330
[16]  0.47082670 -4.67137272
```

```
 $wts$`hidden 1 9`
  [1]   0.80066147   2.72835254  -6.01889627 -10.63057306   7.63526853
  [6]  -1.85188181  -0.59883189   0.86011432   2.28279639  -0.80140313
 [11]  -3.41439405   4.47209147   3.98812529   0.05217016   1.42120448
 [16]  -2.87977768  -1.80152670

 $wts$`hidden 1 10`
  [1]  -1.41326881 -16.86494495  -0.25563167   0.02405375  -5.82554392
  [6]   0.20502350   0.68081754  -4.30017547   0.24592770   0.94533019
 [11]   0.51276882  -0.10970560   1.52611041   1.41750276   2.40763017
 [16]  -1.56584208  -5.13504576

 $wts$`out 1`
  [1] -2.0906131 -0.8660608  2.5900163 -0.9717815  1.1467203 -0.8147543
  [7]  2.3220405  1.7924673 -3.5013152  0.2313364 -2.3259027
# Plot the importance
olden(nn)
```

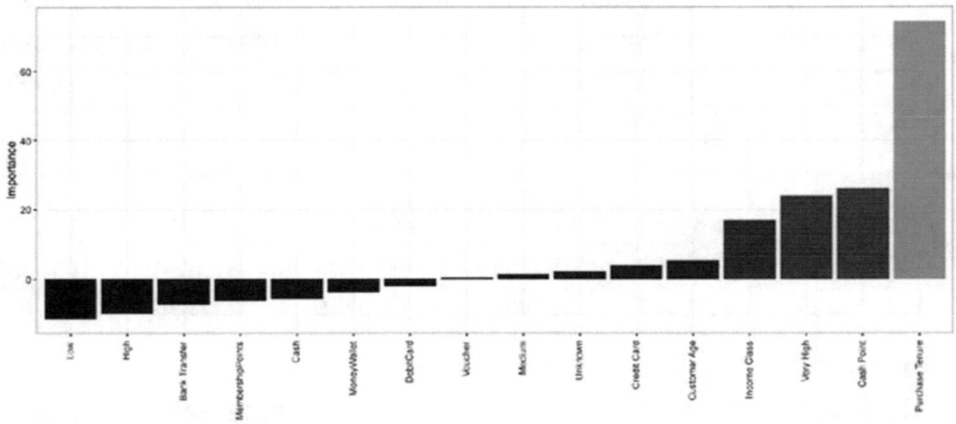

***Figure 6-65.** Attribute importance by olden method*

```
#variable importance by garson algorithm
garson(nn)
```

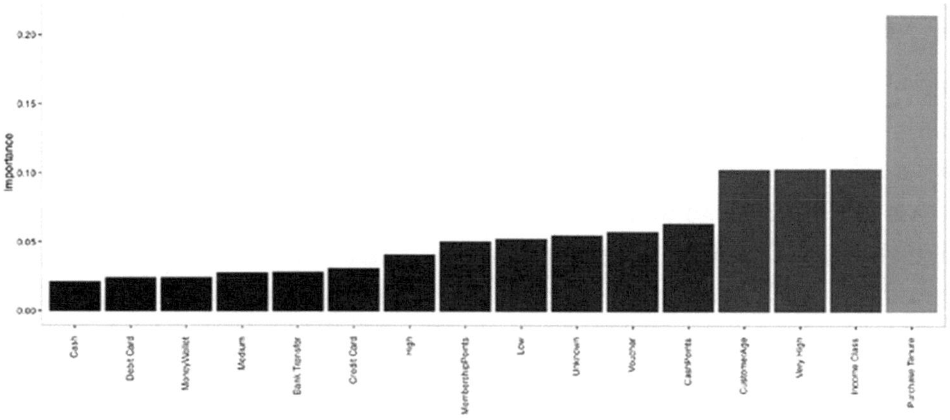

Figure 6-66. *Attribute importance by Garson method*

We showed how to create a neural network and test for its weight and prediction. R libraries have been expanding very fast in neural networks. It will be good for you to keep updated with the new tools being created by the research community. *Artificial Intelligence: A Modern Approach* by Stuart Russell and Peter Norvig is a great book to dig deeper into artificial neural networks.

6.11.8 Conclusion

Neural networks are very powerful tools that can learn from any dataset without any assumptions on input data. Further, the new research in their architecture and learning methods has given rise to deep neural networks. This has enabled the whole field of deep learning in various fields, specifically the fields having high volume and high abstraction in data. Deep neural nets are making possible computer vision, speech recognition, gene matching, and other complex problems.

In the next section, we delve into the world of unstructured data. You will see how some of the simple techniques could transform a completely unstructured textual data to a matrix of numerical observations, which then could be used with many other algorithms for classification, clustering, and so on.

6.12 Text-Mining Approaches

In recent years, text data has been increased manifold. Particularly, the digitally generated or digitally stored text data has increased a lot. A big part of big data world is that this text data is generated and stored in large volumes. Another important aspect of text data is that it can be generated by anybody and has implications on businesses.

For example, a bad product review can damage the market image of the product or a social media post about a social cause can create a campaign. In all these cases, text data plays a pivotal role of influencing behavior. In the 21st Century, it has become important for organizations to invest in text data and understand what insights it has on consumer behavior or product performance.

Brandwatch (`https://www.brandwatch.com/2016/05/44-twitter-stats-2016/`) published data around Twitter statics; let's look at some of that data.

- Twitter has 310 million active users (each user is a source of text data)
- 83% of the world's leaders are on Twitter (leaders tweets are text data that influences markets, people, policies, and so on)
- 500 million tweets are sent daily (isn't this big data?)
- 65.8% of U.S. companies with 100+ employees use Twitter for marketing (how can we use this data to manage and outshine in the marketing programs?)
- 80% of Twitter users have mentioned a brand in a tweet (doesn't this compel us to look at the treasure of information hidden in text data?)

These statistics tell us that text data is important to analyze in today's world. Being massive in nature, we need advanced machine learning methods and enhanced natural language processing to harness the power of text data. Some statistics suggest 80% of the information we store today is in text format, signifying the commercial value of text mining.

Formally, text analysis involves information retrieval, lexical analysis to study word frequency distributions, tagging/annotation, information extraction, data mining techniques including link and association analysis, visualization, pattern recognition, and predictive analytics. The end goal is to use unstructured data in text and convert that into data for analysis by using powerful techniques of Natural Language Processing and other mathematical methods (e.g., frequency plots, Singular Value Decomposition, etc.).

In this section, we introduce basics of text analytics using R. Toward the end of chapter, we show an example of how to use the Microsoft API to unlock powerful text-mining tools that are currently not available in R.

6.12.1 Introduction to Text Mining

The explosion in the amount of unstructured data has led to numerous use cases on text mining. The ability to process textual data very fast and convert it into a numeric feature matrix has opened up a plethora of machine learning algorithms to be used on such data. The field of Natural Language Processing (NLP), though a vast field, could be thought of as a subfield of ML. In an alternative view, the text mining approaches help in turning text into data for analysis, via the application of NLP and analytical methods.

In the following section, we go a little deeper into text mining concepts like text categorization, summarization, TF-IDF, Part of Speech (POS) tagging, and simple visualization using WordCloud.

We will use the Amazon Fine food reviews dataset for a couple of text mining approaches.

Let's start by looking at the data briefly and then choose a smaller subset for all the demonstrations.

a. Data Summary

```
library(data.table)

fine_food_data <-read.csv("Dataset/Food_Reviews.csv",
stringsAsFactors =FALSE)
fine_food_data$Score <-as.factor(fine_food_data$Score)

str(fine_food_data[-10])
 'data.frame':    35173 obs. of  9 variables:
  $ Id                     : int  1 2 3 4 5 6 7 8 9 10 ...
  $ ProductId              : chr  "B001E4KFG0" "B00813GRG4"
                             "B000LQOCH0" "B000UA0QIQ" ...
  $ UserId                 : chr  "A3SGXH7AUHU8GW" "A1D87F6ZCVE5NK"
                             "ABXLMWJIXXAIN" "A395BORC6FGVXV" ...
  $ ProfileName            : chr  "delmartian" "dll pa" "Natalia
                             Corres \"Natalia Corres\"" "Karl" ...
  $ HelpfulnessNumerator   : int  1 0 1 3 0 0 0 0 1 0 ...
```

```
 $ HelpfulnessDenominator: int  1 0 1 3 0 0 0 0 1 0 ...
 $ Score                 : Factor w/ 5 levels "1","2","3","4",..:
                           5 1 4 2 5 4 5 5 5 5 ...
 $ Time                  : int  1303862400 1346976000 1219017600
                           1307923200 1350777600 1342051200
                           1340150400 1336003200 1322006400
                           1351209600 ...
 $ Summary               : chr  "Good Quality Dog Food" "Not as
                           Advertised" "\"Delight\" says it all"
                           "Cough Medicine" ...
# Last column - Customer review in free text

head(fine_food_data[,10],2)
 [1] "I have bought several of the Vitality canned dog food
products and have found them all to be of good quality. The
product looks more like a stew than processed meat and it smells
better. My Labrador is finicky and she appreciates this product
better than  most."
 [2] "Product arrived labeled as Jumbo Salted Peanuts...the
peanuts were actually small sized unsalted. Not sure if this was
an error or if the vendor intended to represent the product as
\"Jumbo\"."
```

b. Data Preparation

```
library(caTools)

# Randomly split data and use only 10% of the dataset
set.seed(90)
split =sample.split(fine_food_data$Score, SplitRatio =0.10)

fine_food_data =subset(fine_food_data, split ==TRUE)
select_col <-c("Id","HelpfulnessNumerator","HelpfulnessDenominator",
"Score","Summary","Text")
fine_food_data_selected <-fine_food_data[,select_col]
```

6.12.2 Text Summarization

This applies the method of Gong & Liu (2001) for generic text summarization of text document D via latent semantic analysis:

1. Decompose the document D into individual sentences and use these sentences to form the candidate sentence set S and set k = 1.
2. Construct the terms by sentences matrix A for the document D.
3. Perform the SVD on A to obtain the singular value matrix, and the right singular vector matrix V^t. In the singular vector space, each sentence i is represented by the column vector.
4. Select the kth right singular vector from matrix V^t.
5. Select the sentence that has the largest index value with the kth right singular vector and include it in the summary.
6. If k reaches the predefined number, terminate the operation; otherwise, increment k by 1 and go back to Step 4.

(Cited directly from Gong & Liu, 2001, p. 21)[9]

Let's see how good the summarization works here in our Amazon fine food review dataset. In order to compare our results, we use the summary attribute in the dataset and do a qualitative assessment of the output.

a. Original Text

```
fine_food_data_selected[2,6]
```

[1] "McCann's Instant Oatmeal is great if you must have your oatmeal but can only scrape together two or three minutes to prepare it. There is no escaping the fact, however, that even the best instant oatmeal is nowhere near as good as even a store brand of oatmeal requiring stovetop preparation. Still, the McCann's is as good as it gets for instant oatmeal. It's even better than the organic, all-natural brands I have tried. All the varieties in the McCann's variety pack taste good. It can be prepared in the microwave or by adding boiling water so it is convenient in the extreme when time is an issue.

McCann's use of actual cane sugar instead of high fructose corn syrup helped me decide to buy this product. Real sugar tastes better and is not as harmful as the other stuff. One thing I do not like, though, is McCann's use of thickeners. Oats plus water plus heat should make a creamy, tasty oatmeal without the need for guar gum. But this is a convenience product. Maybe the guar gum is why, after sitting in the bowl a while, the instant McCann's becomes too thick and gluey."

b. Summary Generated by `genericSummary`

```
library(LSAfun)
genericSummary(fine_food_data_selected[2,6],k=1)
```

[1] "There is no escaping the fact, however, that even the best instant oatmeal is nowhere near as good as even a store brand of oatmeal requiring stovetop preparation."

c. Multiple Summaries Generated by `genericSummary`

```
library(LSAfun)
genericSummary(fine_food_data_selected[2,6],k=2)
```

[1] "There is no escaping the fact, however, that even the best instant oatmeal is nowhere near as good as even a store brand of oatmeal requiring stovetop preparation."

[2] "It can be prepared in the microwave or by adding boiling water so it is convenient in the extreme when time is an issue."

d. Summary from the Dataset

```
fine_food_data_selected[2,5]
```

[1] "Best of the Instant Oatmeals"

Observe the striking similarity of context of the text and the summary generated by the function. Text summarization has many wide ranging application. Google uses it to display the most relevant piece of information while returning the query results from a given web page, a lot of NLP approaches deal with text summary rather than processing the large chuck of textual data, Facebook could build use cases to automatically summarize the user post(ensuring the anonymity) to target the right ads and many more such applications.

6.12.3 TF-IDF

Term Frequency/Inverse Term frequency (TF_IDF) is the frequency of words, which is key in terms of transforming the bag of words into a numeric matrix, thus allowing for many ML algorithms to be applied to them.

a. *Term frequency* $tf_{i,j}$: Counts the number of occurrences $n_{i,j}$ of a term t_i in a document d_j. In the case of normalization, the term frequency $tf_{i,j}$ is divided by $\sum k n_{k,j}$.

b. *Inverse document frequency:* idf_i, for a term t_i is defined as

$$idf_i = \log_2 \frac{|D|}{|\{d|t_i \in d\}|}$$

where |D| denotes the total number of documents and $|\{d|t_i \in d\}|$ is the number of documents where the term t_i appears.

Intuitively, if you see, *I* has two properties:

- Certain terms that occur too frequently have little power in determining the reliance of a document. idf_i weighs down the too frequently occurring word.
- The terms that occur just a few times in a document have more relevance. idf_i weigh up the less frequently occurring word.

  For example, in a collection of document related to sport, the word "game" might be too frequent word, however any article with word "cricket" might show a high relevance to classify the article into a particular game.

c. *Term frequency/inverse document frequency (TF-IDF):* The product of $tf_{i,j} \cdot idf_i$

Let's create a tf-idf matrix from the bag-of-word approach in text mining. A tf-idf matrix is a numerical representation of a collection of documents (represented by rows) and words contained in it (represented by columns).

```
library(tm)
 Warning: package 'tm' was built under R version 3.2.3
 Loading required package: NLP
fine_food_data_corpus <-VCorpus(VectorSource(fine_food_data_selected$Text))

#Standardize the text - Pre-Processing

fine_food_data_text_dtm <-DocumentTermMatrix(fine_food_data_corpus, control
=list(
tolower =TRUE,
removeNumbers =TRUE,
stopwords =TRUE,
removePunctuation =TRUE,
stemming =TRUE
))

# save frequently-appearing terms( more than 500 times) to a character
vector
fine_food_data_text_freq <-findFreqTerms(fine_food_data_text_dtm, 500)

# create DTMs with only the frequent terms
fine_food_data_text_dtm <-fine_food_data_text_dtm[ , fine_food_data_text_
freq]

tm::inspect(fine_food_data_text_dtm[1:5,1:10])
 <<DocumentTermMatrix (documents: 5, terms: 10)>>
 Non-/sparse entries: 8/42
 Sparsity           : 84%
 Maximal term length: 6
 Weighting          : term frequency (tf)

     Terms
```

```
 Docs also bag buy can coffee dog eat find flavor food
    1    1   0   0   0      0   0   0    0      0    0
    2    0   0   1   2      0   0   0    0      0    0
    3    0   0   0   0      2   0   0    0      0    0
    4    0   0   0   0      0   0   1    1      0    0
    5    0   0   0   0      0   0   0    1      2    0
#Create a tf-idf matrix
fine_food_data_tfidf <-weightTfIdf(fine_food_data_text_dtm, normalize
=FALSE)

tm::inspect(fine_food_data_tfidf[1:5,1:10])
 <<DocumentTermMatrix (documents: 5, terms: 10)>>
 Non-/sparse entries: 8/42
 Sparsity           : 84%
 Maximal term length: 6
 Weighting          : term frequency - inverse document frequency (tf-idf)

     Terms
 Docs     also bag      buy      can   coffee dog      eat     find   flavor
    1 3.04583   0 0.000000 0.000000 0.00000   0 0.000000 0.000000 0.000000
    2 0.00000   0 2.635882 4.525741 0.00000   0 0.000000 0.000000 0.000000
    3 0.00000   0 0.000000 0.000000 5.82035   0 0.000000 0.000000 0.000000
    4 0.00000   0 0.000000 0.000000 0.00000   0 2.960361 2.992637 0.000000
    5 0.00000   0 0.000000 0.000000 0.00000   0 0.000000 2.992637 4.024711
     Terms
 Docs food
    1    0
    2    0
    3    0
    4    0
    5    0
```

6.12.4 Part-of-Speech (POS) Tagging

Parts of speech are useful features for finding named entities like people or organizations in a text and other information extraction tasks. This could help in classifying named entities in text into categories like people, company, locations, expression of time, and so on. This is found in many applications in molecular biology, bioinformatics, and medical communities.

We will use the Amazon food review dataset to extract POS tags using R. Figure 6-67 shows the mappings of the abbreviations of the PoS produced by the R script to the part of speech (POS) in the English language.

Number	Tag	Description
1	CC	Coordinating conjunction
2	CD	Cardinal number
3	DT	Determiner
4	EX	Existential *there*
5	FW	Foreign word
6	IN	Preposition or subordinating conjunction
7	JJ	Adjective
8	JJR	Adjective, comparative
9	JJS	Adjective, superlative
10	LS	List item marker
11	MD	Modal
12	NN	Noun, singular or mass
13	NNS	Noun, plural
14	NNP	Proper noun, singular
15	NNPS	Proper noun, plural
16	PDT	Predeterminer
17	POS	Possessive ending
18	PRP	Personal pronoun

Number	Tag	Description
19	PRPS	Possessive pronoun
20	RB	Adverb
21	RBR	Adverb, comparative
22	RBS	Adverb, superlative
23	RP	Particle
24	SYM	Symbol
25	TO	*to*
26	UH	Interjection
27	VB	Verb, base form
28	VBD	Verb, past tense
29	VBG	Verb, gerund or present participle
30	VBN	Verb, past participle
31	VBP	Verb, non-3rd person singular present
32	VBZ	Verb, 3rd person singular present
33	WDT	Wh-determiner
34	WP	Wh-pronoun
35	WPS	Possessive wh-pronoun
36	WRB	Wh-adverb

Figure 6-67. *Part-of-speech mapping*

a. Preprocessing

```
library("NLP")
library(tm)

fine_food_data_corpus <-Corpus(VectorSource(fine_food_data_
selected$Text[1:3]))
fine_food_data_cleaned <-tm_map(fine_food_data_corpus,
PlainTextDocument)

#tolwer
fine_food_data_cleaned <-tm_map(fine_food_data_cleaned, tolower)
fine_food_data_cleaned[[1]]
```

```
 [1] "twizzlers, strawberry my childhood favorite candy, made in
lancaster pennsylvania by y & s candies, inc. one of the oldest
confectionery firms in the united states, now a subsidiary of the
hershey company, the company was established in 1845 as young and
smylie, they also make apple licorice twists, green color and blue
raspberry licorice twists, i like them all<br /><br />i keep it in
a dry cool place because is not recommended it to put it in the
fridge. according to the guinness book of records, the longest
licorice twist ever made measured 1.200 feet (370 m) and weighted
100 pounds (45 kg) and was made by y & s candies, inc. this
record-breaking twist became a guinness world record on july 19,
1998. this product is kosher! thank you"
fine_food_data_cleaned <-tm_map(fine_food_data_cleaned,
removeWords, stopwords("english"))
fine_food_data_cleaned[[1]]
 [1] "twizzlers, strawberry  childhood favorite candy,
made  lancaster pennsylvania  y & s candies, inc. one   oldest
confectionery firms   united states, now  subsidiary   hershey
company,  company  established  1845  young  smylie,  also make
apple licorice twists, green color  blue raspberry licorice
twists,  like  <br /><br /> keep    dry cool place    recommended
put    fridge. according   guinness book  records,  longest
licorice twist ever made measured 1.200 feet (370 m)  weighted 100
pounds (45 kg)   made  y & s candies, inc.  record-breaking twist
became  guinness world record  july 19, 1998.  product  kosher!
thank "
fine_food_data_cleaned <-tm_map(fine_food_data_cleaned,
removePunctuation)
fine_food_data_cleaned[[1]]
 [1] "twizzlers strawberry  childhood favorite candy
made  lancaster pennsylvania  y  s candies inc one   oldest
confectionery firms   united states now  subsidiary   hershey
company  company  established  1845  young  smylie  also make
apple licorice twists green color  blue raspberry licorice
twists  like  br br  keep    dry cool place    recommended
```

```
put    fridge according   guinness book  records  longest licorice
twist ever made measured 1200 feet 370 m  weighted 100 pounds 45
kg   made  y  s candies inc  recordbreaking twist became  guinness
world record  july 19 1998  product  kosher thank "
fine_food_data_cleaned <-tm_map(fine_food_data_cleaned,
removeNumbers)
fine_food_data_cleaned[[1]]
 [1] "twizzlers strawberry  childhood favorite candy
made  lancaster pennsylvania  y  s candies inc one   oldest
confectionery firms   united states now  subsidiary   hershey
company  company  established    young  smylie  also make
apple licorice twists green color  blue raspberry licorice
twists  like  br br  keep    dry cool place    recommended
put    fridge according   guinness book  records  longest
licorice twist ever made measured  feet  m  weighted  pounds  kg
made  y  s candies inc  recordbreaking twist became  guinness
world record  july    product  kosher thank "
fine_food_data_cleaned <-tm_map(fine_food_data_cleaned,
stripWhitespace)
fine_food_data_cleaned[[1]]
 [1] "twizzlers strawberry childhood favorite candy made lancaster
pennsylvania y s candies inc one oldest confectionery firms united
states now subsidiary hershey company company established young
smylie also make apple licorice twists green color blue raspberry
licorice twists like br br keep dry cool place recommended put
fridge according guinness book records longest licorice twist
ever made measured feet m weighted pounds kg made y s candies inc
recordbreaking twist became guinness world record july product
kosher thank "
```

b. PoS Extraction

```
library(openNLP)
 Warning: package 'openNLP' was built under R version 3.2.3
library(NLP)
```

```
fine_food_data_string <-NLP::as.String(fine_food_data_
cleaned[[1]])

sent_token_annotator <-Maxent_Sent_Token_Annotator()
word_token_annotator <-Maxent_Word_Token_Annotator()
fine_food_data_string_an <-annotate(fine_food_data_string,
list(sent_token_annotator, word_token_annotator))

pos_tag_annotator <-Maxent_POS_Tag_Annotator()
fine_food_data_string_an2 <-annotate(fine_food_data_string, pos_
tag_annotator, fine_food_data_string_an)

 Variant with POS tag probabilities as (additional) features.
head(annotate(fine_food_data_string, Maxent_POS_Tag_
Annotator(probs =TRUE), fine_food_data_string_an2))
  id type     start end features
   1 sentence     1 524 constituents=<<integer,77>>
   2 word         1   9 POS=NNS, POS=NNS, POS_prob=0.7822268
   3 word        11  20 POS=VBP, POS=VBP, POS_prob=0.3488425
   4 word        22  30 POS=NN, POS=NN, POS_prob=0.8055908
   5 word        32  39 POS=JJ, POS=JJ, POS_prob=0.6114238
   6 word        41  45 POS=NN, POS=NN, POS_prob=0.9833723
 Determine the distribution of POS tags for word tokens.
fine_food_data_string_an2w <-subset(fine_food_data_string_an2,
type == "word")
tags <-sapply(fine_food_data_string_an2w$features, `[[`, "POS")
table(tags)
 tags
   ,  CC  CD  IN  JJ JJS  NN NNS  RB  VB VBD VBG VBN VBP VBZ
   1   2   1   1  10   2  28   9   5   1   6   2   4   2   3
plot(table(tags), type ="h", xlab="Part-Of_Speech",
ylab ="Frequency")
```

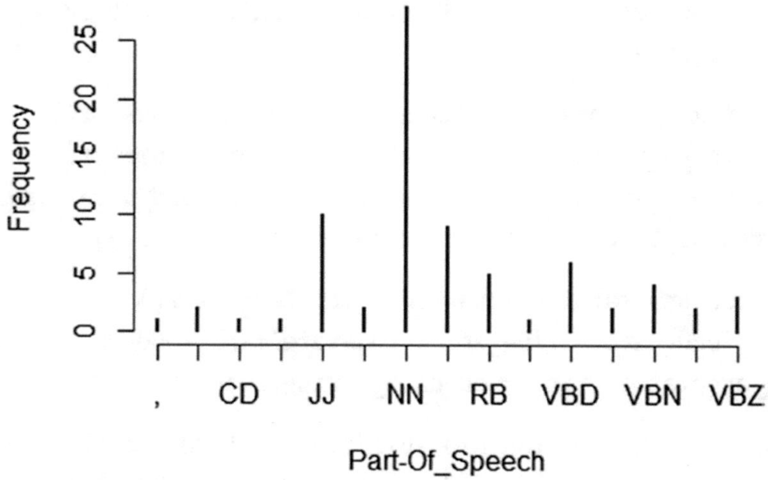

Figure 6-68. *Part-of-speech frequency*

```
 Extract token/POS pairs (all of them)
head(sprintf("%s/%s", fine_food_data_string[fine_food_data_string_
an2w], tags),15)
  [1] "twizzlers/NNS"     "strawberry/VBP"     "childhood/NN"
  [4] "favorite/JJ"       "candy/NN"           "made/VBD"
  [7] "lancaster/NN"      "pennsylvania/NN"    "y/RB"
 [10] "s/VBZ"             "candies/NNS"        "inc/CC"
 [13] "one/CD"            "oldest/JJS"         "confectionery/NN"
```

Nouns (NN) seem to be a frequently used part-of-speech, followed by adjectives (JJ) in this data. It makes a lot of intuitive sense, since in review related data, people talk about restaurants and food and their characteristics like "good," "bad," "awesome," and so on. Such POS identification could help in better understanding the reviews than reading the entire textual information.

6.12.5 Word Cloud

The word cloud helps in visualizing the words most frequently being used in the reviews (see Figure 6-69):

```
library(SnowballC)
library(wordcloud)
```

```
fine_food_data_corpus <-VCorpus(VectorSource(fine_food_data_selected$Text))

fine_food_data_text_tdm <-TermDocumentMatrix(fine_food_data_corpus, control
=list(
tolower =TRUE,
removeNumbers =TRUE,
stopwords =TRUE,
removePunctuation =TRUE,
stemming =TRUE
))
wc_tdm <- rollup(fine_food_data_text_tdm,2,na.rm=TRUE,FUN=sum)
matrix_c <-as.matrix(wc_tdm)
wc_freq <-sort(rowSums(matrix_c))
wc_tmdata <-data.frame(words=names(wc_freq), wc_freq)

wc_tmdata <-na.omit(wc_tmdata)
wordcloud (tail(wc_tmdata$words,100), tail(wc_tmdata$wc_freq,100), random.
order=FALSE, colors=brewer.pal(8, "Dark2"))
```

Figure 6-69. *Word cloud using Amazon Food Review dataset*

WordCloud is a simple exploratory tool to understand the general trend in the word usage, which could further help in building intuitions and insights.

6.12.6 Text Analysis: Microsoft Cognitive Services

In this section, we introduce you to the powerful world of text analytics by using a third-party API called from within R. We use the Microsoft Cognitive Services API to show some real-time analysis of text from the Twitter feed of a news agency.

Note Microsoft Cognitive Services are chosen to show some real-world examples of text analytics. We do not endorse any third-party tool or services.

Microsoft Cognitive Services is a machine intelligence service from Microsoft. It was previously known as Project Oxford. This service provide a cloud-based APIs for developers to do a lot of high-end functions like face recognition, speech recognition, text mining, video feed analysis, and many others. We use their free developer service to show some text analytics features, which include the following:

- *Sentiment analysis:* What is the sentiment of tweet? Is it positive or negative or neutral?
- *Topic detection:* What is the topic of discussion?
- *Language detection:* Can you provide written text and it shows you which language it is?
- *Summarization*: Can you automatically summarize a big document to make it manageable to read?

We will be using Twitter feeds for sentiment analysis and topic detection, some random text from a language for language detection, and an article to summarize it.

To start with this example, we need to set up an account with Microsoft cognitive service and get an API key to work with their REST API. The key can be obtained by registering at `https://www.microsoft.com/cognitive-services/`.

You will also need a Twitter developer account to set up application in R to extract tweets. You can get a Twitter API key from registering at `https://apps.twitter.com/`.

First we will set up the TwitterR package by using the API key we got from the Twitter apps. The `twitterR()` package provides an interface to the Twitter web API.

```
library("stringr")
library("dplyr")

library("twitteR")
#getTwitterOAuth(consumer_key, consumer_secret)
consumerKey <- "INSERT KEY"
consumerSecret <- "INSERT SECRET CODE"

#Below two tokens need to be used when you want to pull tweets from your
own account
accessToken <- "INSERT ACCESS TOKEN"
accessTokenSecret <- "INSERT SECRET CODE"

setup_twitter_oauth(consumerKey, consumerSecret,accessToken,accessTokenSec
ret)
 [1] "Using direct authentication"
kIgnoreTweet <- "update:|nobot:"

GetTweets <-function(handle, n =1000) {

    timeline <-userTimeline(handle, n = n)
    tweets <-sapply(timeline, function(x) {
c(x$getText(), x$getCreated())
    })
    tweets <-data.frame(t(tweets))
names(tweets) <-c("text.orig", "created.orig")

    tweets$text <-tolower(tweets$text.orig)
    tweets$created <-as.POSIXct(as.numeric(as.vector(tweets$created.orig)),
    origin="1970-01-01")

arrange(tweets, created)
}

handle <- "@TimesNow"
tweets <-GetTweets(handle, 100)

#Store the tweets as used in the book for future reproducibility
write.csv(tweets,"Dataset/Twitter Feed From TimesNow.csv",row.names =FALSE)
tweets[1:5,]
```

```
                                                                   text.orig
 1    Procedures for this are at DGMO level which have been activated:
Def Min Parrikar on soldier who inadvertently cros<U+0085> https://t.co/
dUx77VDXGj
 4                                          IN PICS: Union Minister Venkaiah
Naidu pays tribute to Mahatma Gandhi #GandhiJayanti https://t.co/7gbSV4hHTN
 5                                IN PICS:  Union Minister Venkaiah Naidu flags
off the 'Swachhta Rally' from India Gate, Delhi https://t.co/XOwOxJRoSG
   created.orig
 1   1475379487
 2   1475380198
 3   1475380803
 4   1475380922
 5   1475381398
```

Now we have set up our Twitter account to pull feeds to our system. Now similarly let's set up a Microsoft cognitive services account. The package used for calling Microsoft services is `mscstexta4r`. The R client is for the Microsoft Cognitive Services Text Analytics REST API, including Sentiment Analysis, Topic Detection, Language Detection, and Key Phrase Extraction. An account *must* be registered at the Microsoft Cognitive Services website `https://www.microsoft.com/cognitive-services/` in order to obtain a (free) API key. Without an API key, this package will not work properly.

```
#install.packages("mscstexta4r")
library(mscstexta4r)
 Warning: package 'mscstexta4r' was built under R version 3.2.5
#Put the authentication APi keys you got from Microsoft

Sys.setenv(MSCS_TEXTANALYTICS_URL ="https://westus.api.cognitive.microsoft.
com/text/analytics/v2.0/")
Sys.setenv(MSCS_TEXTANALYTICS_KEY ="YOUR KEY")

#Initialize the service
textaInit()
```

Now one more input we need is a news article to show summarization. We are using this article: `http://www.yourarticlelibrary.com/essay/essay-on-india-after-independence/41354/`.

```
# Load Packages
require(tm)
require(NLP)
require(openNLP)

#Read the Forbes article into R environment
y <-paste(scan("Dataset/india_after_independence.txt", what="character",
sep=" "),collapse=" ")

convert_text_to_sentences <-function(text, lang ="en") {
# Function to compute sentence annotations using the Apache OpenNLP Maxent
sentence detector employing the default model for language 'en'.
  sentence_token_annotator <-Maxent_Sent_Token_Annotator(language = lang)

# Convert text to class String from package NLP
  text <-as.String(text)

# Sentence boundaries in text
  sentence.boundaries <-annotate(text, sentence_token_annotator)

# Extract sentences
  sentences <-text[sentence.boundaries]

# return sentences
return(sentences)
}

# Convert the text into sentences
article_text =convert_text_to_sentences(y, lang ="en")
```

Now that we have all the inputs ready, we will show the four major analytics items as listed previously in our sample data.

1. Sentiment Analysis

   Sentiment analysis will tell us what kind of emotions the tweets are carrying. The Microsoft API returns a value between 0 and 1, where 1 means a highly positive sentiment while 0 means a highly negative sentiment.

   ```
   document_lang <-rep("en", length(tweets$text))
   ```

```
tryCatch({

# Perform sentiment analysis
output_1 <-textaSentiment(
documents = tweets$text,    # Input sentences or documents
languages = document_lang
# "en"(English, default)|"es"(Spanish)|"fr"(French)|"pt"(Portugue
se)
)

}, error = function(err) {

# Print error
geterrmessage()

})
merged <-output_1$results

#Order the tweets with sentiment score
ordered_tweets <-merged[order(merged$score),]

#Top 5 negative tweets
ordered_tweets[1:5,]
                                                                text
 7
pakistan has been completely cornered: shrikant sharma https://t.
co/ujdux8z3er
 99                                                  hillary clinton
says wave of shootings show need to protect children (pti)
https://t.co/hptj0v8eja
 6   southern california on heightened alert until tuesday
following increased possibility of major earthquake:guv's office
of emergency services
 10   china yet again blocks india's bid at the un to ban jaish-e-
mohammad chief masood azhar by putting a technical hold https://t.
co/yzomd77htr
 100                                                         #update
#baramulla terror attack- 1 bsf jawan martyred, 1 jawan injured:
reports
```

```
        score
7   0.1440058
99  0.1752440
6   0.1770731
10  0.1947241
100 0.2508526
#Top 5 Positive
ordered_tweets[95:100,]
                                                                text
73      the artists<U+0092> practice,the curator<U+0092>s
vision,the commerce of the auction house,the best of the indian
art world on<U+0085> https://t.co/gbxzgzydzt
37      the artists<U+0092> practice,the curator<U+0092>s
vision,the commerce of the auction house,the best of the indian
art world on<U+0085> https://t.co/tqx07ytmku
43                           prime minister narendra modi extends
new year greetings to jewish community around the world https://t.
co/xzpoqq4npd
54 china provides pak terror shield, stalls masood azhar<U+0092>s
entry to terror list. #chinatopakrescue\n\ntune in,join special
broadcast on @timesnow
90         founder of sulabh international bindeshwar pathak
presents a book 'mahatma gandhi's life in colour' to pm modi
https://t.co/r1zsqwt93r
9                                                    2nd test,
day 3: new zealand all out for 204 in 1st innings, india lead by
112 runs #indvsnz
       score
73 0.9468260
37 0.9484612
43 0.9579207
54 0.9739059
90 0.9759967
9  0.9879231
```

The sentiment analyzer has worked really well on the latest 100 tweets from the @TimesNow handle. You can do multiple things with this same application, for instance measure how many positive news and negative news ran on the leading news channel. This can give you a glimpse of the general sentiment in the country.

2. Topic Detection

For topic detection, let's try to see what @CNN official Twitter handle talked about in their last 100 tweets. The topic detection algorithm will try to read last 100 tweets as if it were a conversation and will bring the topic discussed in those transcripts (or tweets).

```
handle <- "@CNN"
topic_text <-GetTweets(handle, 150)
write.csv(topic_text,"Dataset/Twitter Feed from CNN.csv",row.
names=FALSE)

tryCatch({

# Detect top topics in group of documents
output_2 <-textaDetectTopics(
  topic_text$text,                   # At least 100 documents
(English only)
stopWords =NULL,           # Stop word list (optional)
topicsToExclude =NULL,     # Topics to exclude (optional)
minDocumentsPerWord =NULL, # Threshold to exclude rare topics
(optional)
maxDocumentsPerWord =NULL, # Threshold to exclude ubiquitous
topics (optional)
resultsPollInterval = 30L,  # Poll interval (in s, default: 30s,
use 0L for async)
resultsTimeout = 1200L,     # Give up timeout (in s, default:
1200s = 20mn)
verbose =FALSE# If set to TRUE, print every poll status to stdout
)
```

```
}, error = function(err) {

# Print error
geterrmessage()

})
output_2
 textatopics [https://westus.api.cognitive.microsoft.com/text/
 analytics/v2.0/topics?]
 status: Succeeded
 operationId: 726edfccabdd4acb87a90716d7165343
 operationType: topics
 topics (first 20):

 -----------------------------
       keyPhrase        score
 --------------------- -------
        clinton          17

         trump           15

     donald trump        10

         water            8

     rudy giuliani        8

    hillary clinton       7

       president          5

       trump tax          4

       reporter           4

 water monitor lizards    4

     famous parks         4

      beer corpse         4

  iconic talking bear     4
```

```
      teddy ruxpin        4
      daymond john        3
     police officer       3
    president obama       3
     bernie sanders       3
      defend trump        3
           tax            3
----------------------------
```

The topic detection in tweets list tells us that the CNN news channel was talking about the Donald Trump and Hilary Clinton during the 2016 US presidential election.

3. Language Detection

   Digital content nowadays is getting created in multiple languages. To broaden the scope of text mining, we need to automatically identify written languages and create collective senses out of them. Language detection methods helps us with identifying and translating languages. Here, I am creating five messages in five different languages using Google translator (see Figures 6-70 and 6-71). You can create your own examples.

```
<FONT ISSUE>
#1-ARABIC, 2-POTUGESE, 3- ENGLISH , 4- CHINESE AND 5 - HINDI

lang_detect<-c("Ø£Ù†Ø§ Ø¹Ø§Ù„Ù… Ø§Ù„Ø¨ÙŠØ§Ù†Ø§Øª","Eu sou um cientista de dados","I am a data scientist","æˆ'æ˜¯ä¸€ä¸ªç§'å-¦å®¶çš„æ•°æ&#x008D;®","
à¤®à¥ˆà¤‚ à¤•à¤• à¤¡à¥‡à¤Ÿà¤¾ à¤µà¥ˆà¤œà¥•à¤•à¤¾à¤¨à¤¿à¤• à¤¹à¥‚à¤•")
```

```
> #1-ARABIC, 2-POTUGESE, 3- ENGLISH , 4- CHINESE AND 5 - HINDI
>
> lang_detect<- c("أنا عالم البيانات","Eu sou um cientista de dados","I am a data scientist","我是一个科学家的数据","
+ मैं एक डेटा वैज्ञानिक हूँ")
```

***Figure 6-70.** Language detection input*

```
tryCatch({

# Detect top topics in group of documents
# Detect languages used in documents
output_3 <-textaDetectLanguages(
  lang_detect,                          # Input sentences or documents
numberOfLanguagesToDetect = 1L    # Default: 1L
)

}, error = function(err) {

# Print error
geterrmessage()

})
output_3
 texta [https://westus.api.cognitive.microsoft.com/text/analytics/
v2.0/languages?numberOfLanguagesToDetect=1]
```

```
> output_3
texta [https://westus.api.cognitive.microsoft.com/text/analytics/v2.0/languages?numberOfLanguagesToDetect=1]

-----------------------------------------------------------------------
           text                     name          iso6391Name   score
---------------------------- ------------------ ------------- -------
    أنا عالم البيانات              Arabic            ar          1

Eu sou um cientista de dados     Portuguese          pt          1

   I am a data scientist          English            en          1

    我是一个科学家的数据       Chinese_Simplified    zh_chs        1

         मैं एक डेटा                 Hindi             hi          1
         वैज्ञानिक
           हूँ
-----------------------------------------------------------------------
```

***Figure 6-71.** Language detection output*

Microsoft has been able to detect all the language correctly. This service is very powerful when we know content about the same topic gets created in different languages and how to bring them into the same platform.

4. Summarization

For summarization, we will use the article we loaded from the website. The algorithm will try to contextually mine the document sentence by sentence and then will create an ordered list of sentences from the document that summarizes them.

```
article_lang <-rep("en", length(article_text))
tryCatch({

# Get key talking points in documents
 output_4 <-textaKeyPhrases(
documents = article_text,    # Input sentences or documents
languages = article_lang
# "en"(English, default)|"de"(German)|"es"(Spanish)|"fr"(French)|"
ja"(Japanese)
  )

}, error = function(err) {

# Print error
geterrmessage()

})

#Print the top 5 summary
output_4$results[1:5,1]
 [1] "While some have a high opinion of Indiaâ<U+0080><U+0099>s
     growth story since its independence, some others think the
     countryâ<U+0080><U+0099>s performance in the six decades has
     been abysmal."
 [2] "Itâ<U+0080><U+0099>s arguably true that the Five-Year Plans
     did target specific sectors in order to quicken the pace of
     development, yet the outcome hasnâ<U+0080><U+0099>t been on
     expected lines."
```

```
[3] "And, the country is taking its own sweet time to catch up
    with the developed world."
[4] "All efforts are frustrated by lopsided strategies and inept
    implementation of policies."
[5] "India is the worldâ<U+0080><U+0099>s largest democracy."
```

The summarization states that the article talks about India and its way toward development. It also emphasizes the democracy in India.

In this chapter, we say how powerful the text analytics is for monitoring human behavior. We learned the basics in R and learned to use powerful APIs. You can explore more in the field of NLP.

6.12.7 Conclusion

We saw an opportunity to convert poorly structured set of character streams and batches of data into a meaningful set of information using text mining based preprocessing and NLP algorithm-based model building. Though text mining is most appropriately placed under Natural Language Processing (NLP), which itself is considered a subfield of machine learning. The algorithms used for text summarization, part-of-speech tagging, uses statistical techniques heavily.

We now move into the final topic of the chapter, where we discuss the most contemporary ideas of making machine learning algorithms more suitable to work on streams of data. In other words, algorithms that could learn from the continuous streams of data as they come into the system instead of using a batch of training data.

6.13 Online Machine Learning Algorithms

In many practical machine learning models, adapting to the changing data in the real world is a critical requirement. There are two possibilities for tackling such changing needs:

- Manually update the model frequently in a periodic manner (maybe once in a week, month or year) depending on how fast and how many changes take place in the business where the model is deployed once. Such as with medical diagnostics for cancer prediction. As you would expect, the type of cancer is not evolving very quickly with time. So, such a model could remain for a long time, even if there are no updates. However, when some new data from a cancer patient comes in, it's possible to manually update the model and deploy it back into the system.

- Updating the model in real time as the data is flowing in the system. For example, if Google completely moves to a machine learning model-based search engine, then the currently used heuristic algorithm might adapt on the go with search queries coming from the users. Figure 6-72 shows the process of online updates as the new data stream comes into the system.

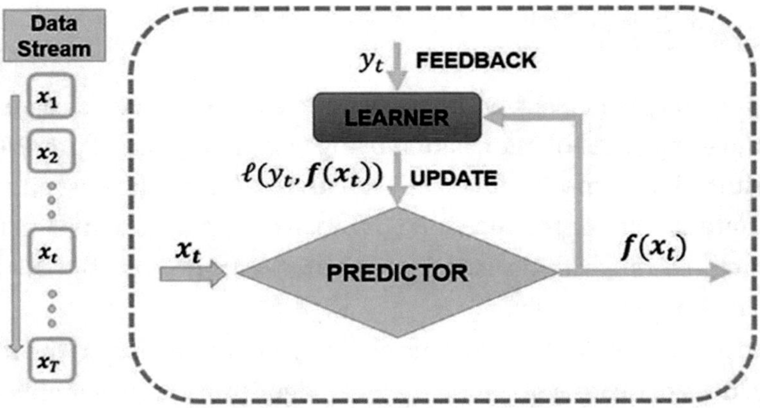

Figure 6-72. *Online machine learning algorithms (Source: `http://www.doyensahoo.com/introduction.html`)*

Figure 6-72 shows how the predictor takes the continuous input data stream and learns from it and the feedback update happens to the learning model.

There are many benefits and challenges that come with such online real-time-based learning methods, notably:

- *Efficient and space optimized:* Since there is no need to pass a large amount of data as a batch to the learning model, we could train the model with one observation as a time and update the model. This speeds up the model training and brings optimized storage. Discard the data if it doesn't improve the model performance.

- *Difficult to create a pipeline:* Creating such an online learning data pipeline is a challenging task. In one hand, if the volume and velocity of data is high, training the model could become a bottleneck. However, if the model pipeline is controlled, a lot of storage would be required.
- *Model evaluation is hard:* Unlike the batch processing where we had a controlled training and testing dataset, wherein testing data could be used to evaluate the model, here with the online data, it's not possible. At any given instance we don't know if the model has seen enough different types of observations to be able to truly perform as per the expectation.

Even with many such challenges, online machine learning is an emerging research as more and more systems are becoming real-time consumers of data and speed of adaptability is a top priority. We will use the `HouseWorth` dataset and apply the online update method of Unsupervised Fuzzy Competitive Learning. Although a detailed discussion of this topic is beyond the scope of this book, we demonstrate with the help of an example of how well this method works for clustering problems. This method works by performing an update directly after each input signal (i.e., for each single observation).

6.13.1 Fuzzy C-Means Clustering

This is the fuzzy version of the known k-means clustering algorithm as well as an online variant (Unsupervised Fuzzy Competitive learning). We will use the package e1071 in R, which has an implementation of the algorithm in a function named `cmeans`.

As the R documentation on the topic describes, the data given by *x* is clustered by generalized versions of the fuzzy c-means algorithm, which use either a fixed point or an online heuristic for minimizing the objective function.

$$\sum_{i=1}^{n}\sum_{j=1}^{c} w_i u_{ij}^{m} d_{ij}$$

where

w_i is weight of the observation *i*

u_{ij} is the membership of observation i in cluster j

d_{ij} is the distance between observation i and center of cluster j

1. Data Preparation

```
library(ggplot2)
 Warning: package 'ggplot2' was built under R version 3.2.5
library(e1071)
 Warning: package 'e1071' was built under R version 3.2.5
Data_House_Worth <-read.csv("Dataset/House Worth Data.
csv",header=TRUE);

str(Data_House_Worth)
 'data.frame':    316 obs. of  5 variables:
  $ HousePrice   : int  138800 155000 152000 160000 226000 275000
                   215000 392000 325000 151000 ...
  $ StoreArea    : num  29.9 44 46.2 46.2 48.7 56.4 47.1 56.7 84
                   49.2 ...
  $ BasementArea : int  75 504 493 510 445 1148 380 945 1572 506
                   ...
  $ LawnArea     : num  11.22 9.69 10.19 6.82 10.92 ...
  $ HouseNetWorth: Factor w/ 3 levels "High","Low","Medium": 2 3 3
                   3 3 1 3 1 1 3 ...
#remove the extra column that are not required for the model
Data_House_Worth$BasementArea <-NULL
```

2. Fuzzy C-Mean Clustering

Observe that we are passing the value `ucfl` to the parameter method, which does an online update of the model using Unsupervised Fuzzy Competitive Learning (UCFL).

```
online_cmean <-cmeans(Data_House_Worth[,2:3],3,20,verbose=TRUE,met
hod="ufcl",m=2)
 Iteration:   1, Error: 465.1579393478
 Iteration:   2, Error: 444.0414997086
 Iteration:   3, Error: 424.6549206588
 Iteration:   4, Error: 406.6721061449
 Iteration:   5, Error: 389.8788008700
 Iteration:   6, Error: 374.1842570779
 Iteration:   7, Error: 359.5913592120
```

```
 Iteration:   8, Error: 346.1483860876
 Iteration:   9, Error: 333.9078002276
 Iteration:  10, Error: 322.9024279730
 Iteration:  11, Error: 313.1374056984
 Iteration:  12, Error: 304.5921263137
 Iteration:  13, Error: 297.2268898905
 Iteration:  14, Error: 290.9907447391
 Iteration:  15, Error: 285.8286344099
 Iteration:  16, Error: 281.6870892396
 Iteration:  17, Error: 278.5183573747
 Iteration:  18, Error: 276.2831875877
 Iteration:  19, Error: 274.9525794936
 Iteration:  20, Error: 274.5088021136
print(online_cmean)
 Fuzzy c-means clustering with 3 clusters

 Cluster centers:
   StoreArea  LawnArea
 1  21.44992  9.584415
 2  43.59627  9.916090
 3  11.04677 11.214669

 Memberships:
                 1            2            3
   [1,] 0.6250584893 2.446492e-01 1.302923e-01
   [2,] 0.0004209086 9.993824e-01 1.966837e-04
   [3,] 0.0110012372 9.835467e-01 5.452043e-03
   [4,] 0.0254099375 9.620333e-01 1.255677e-02
   [5,] 0.0344305970 9.474942e-01 1.807525e-02

 Closest hard clustering:
   [1] 1 2 2 2 2 2 2 2 2 2 1 2 3 1 2 3 3 2 2 1 1 2 2 2 1 2 2 1 2 1
       3 2 2 2 2
  [36] 2 2 2 1 1 2 1 2 1 2 1 3 2 2 2 1 1 1 2 1 2 2 2 2 2 3 2 2 1 2
       2 2 1 2 1
  [71] 2 1 1 2 1 3 2 2 2 1 2 2 2 2 2 2 2 2 2 1 3 2 1 2 2 1 1 2 2 2
       1 2 2 2 2
```

```
[106] 1 2 2 2 2 2 1 2 2 1 1 2 1 3 2 2 1 2 2 1 2 1 1 2 2 1 2 2 2 1
      2 2 1 2 2
[141] 2 2 2 2 2 1 1 1 2 2 1 1 1 2 2 2 3 2 2 1 2 2 1 1 2 2 1 1 1 2
      1 1 2 3 1
[176] 2 2 2 2 2 1 2 2 2 2 2 2 1 1 1 1 2 2 2 2 1 2 1 1 2 2 2 2 2 2
      2 2 2 2 1
[211] 2 2 3 1 3 2 1 1 2 1 2 1 3 2 1 2 1 2 1 1 2 1 1 2 2 2 2 2 1 2
      2 1 1 1 1
[246] 2 2 2 2 2 2 2 3 2 2 3 3 2 1 2 1 2 2 2 2 1 1 1 2 2 2 2 2 2 2
      2 2 1 2 1
[281] 1 1 2 1 2 2 1 1 2 1 2 1 2 2 1 1 2 1 2 2 1 3 2 2 2 2 2 2 2 1
      2 2 2 2 2
[316] 3

Available components:
[1] "centers"     "size"        "cluster"     "membership"  "iter"
[6] "withinerror" "call"
```

3. Visual Evaluation of Cluster Accuracy

   The plot shows the overlap of cluster formed by online fuzzy c-means algorithm and the classification variable we created manually. The plot has a near perfect overlap, which indicates a good cluster.

```
ggplot(Data_House_Worth, aes(StoreArea, LawnArea, color =
HouseNetWorth)) + geom_point(alpha =0.4, size =3.5) + geom_
point(col = online_cmean$cluster) + scale_color_manual(values
=c('black', 'red', 'green'))
```

The plot in Figure 6-73 shows that the clusters substantially overlap on our prior classification. This is fair evidence of the power of online machine learning.

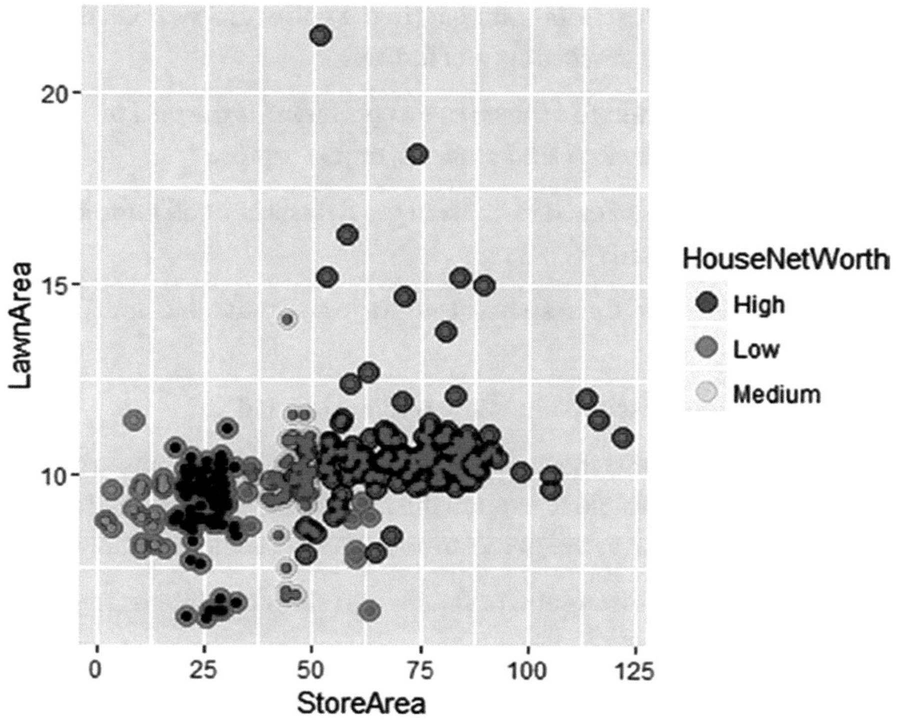

Figure 6-73. *Cluster plot with fuzzy C-means clustering*

6.13.2 Conclusion

In today's fast world, the time to decision is more important than the quality of decision. Partly it's driven by the competitive landscape and partly due to the cost of delay. Online machine learning tools and techniques are bound to rise in the machine learning world in the coming days. Our industry and researchers have to work together to create elegant algorithms as well as hardware/software that can implement those algorithms with high volume and high velocity of data flow.

6.14 Model Building Checklist

Before the chapter ends, we have complied a checklist of questions that you need to address before taking up any project in machine learning. Whenever it comes to choosing an ML algorithm or deciding to use ML on a new problem, an assessment of the available data is the most important part in the entire process. Ask this broad checklist of questions before proceeding any further:

- What is that you want to achieve in this problem? Is the goal to predict, estimate a value, find patterns, or just explore ?
- What are the types of each variable in the dataset? Is it all numeric, categorical, or mixed?
- Have you identified the response (output) and predictor (input) variables?
- Are there many missing values and outliers in the data?
- How would you solve the problem if, let's say, ML algorithms are not to be used. Is it possible to explore the data using simple statistics and visualization to arrive at the answers to the problem without ML?
- Does the boxplot, histogram, or scatter plot show any interesting insights in the data?
- Did you find the standard deviation, quartile, mean, and correlation measures for all numerical variables? Does it show anything interesting?
- How large is your dataset? Does your problem require the complete data to be used or is a small sample good enough?
- Are there enough computational resources (RAM, storage, and CPU) to run any ML algorithm?
- Do you think that the current data might soon become old and the ML model might require an update soon after it's built?
- Are there any plans to build a data product out of the final ML model?

This checklist might sound a little too big; however, if you figure out the answers to these questions before you jump into building an ML model, you will potentially have a savings of 40%-60% of your time.

6.15 Summary

A field like machine learning is vast because of the application it has found over the years in many academic disciplines and industries. The years of advancement in tools and technology has taken machine leaning a step closer to even the naïve user without much statistical background. This has given rise to the practical applicability of the methods found in machine learning and development of many ML-centric products and design. We are living in exciting times to be in the field of machine learning, which offers endless opportunities. Experts who are machine learning literate are in high demand in many industries. The time is not far away when machine learning will form the core of every industry and product, where it's not just coding the software with some set of logical statements, but infusing a learning algorithm within which it adapts to the changing needs.

CHAPTER 7

Machine Learning Model Evaluation

Model evaluation is the most important step in developing any machine learning solution. At this stage in model development we measure the model performance and decide whether to go ahead with the model or revisit all our previous steps as described in the PEBE, our machine learning process flow, in Chapter 1. In many cases, we may even discard the complete model based on the performance metrics. This phase of the PEBE plays a very critical role in the success of any ML-based project.

The central idea of model evaluation is minimizing the error on test data, where error can be defined in many ways. In the most intuitive sense, error is the difference between the actual value of the predictor variable in data and the value the ML model predicts. The error metrics are not always universal, and some specific problems require creative error metrics that suit the problem and the domain knowledge.

It is important to emphasize here that the error metric used to train the model might be different from evaluation error metric. For instance, for a classification model you might have used the `LogLoss` error metric, but for evaluating the model, you might want to see a classification rate using a confusion matrix.

In this chapter, we enumerate the basic idea behind evaluating a model and discuss some of the methods in detail.

The learning objectives of this chapter are as follows:

- Introduction to model performance and evaluation
- Population stability index
- Model evaluation for continuous output

K. Ramasubramanian and A. Singh, *Machine Learning Using R*, https://doi.org/10.1007/978-1-4842-4215-5_7

- Model evaluation for discrete output
- Probabilistic techniques
- Illustration of advanced metrics like the Kappa Error Metric

7.1 Dataset

The dataset for this chapter is the same as what we introduced in Chapter 6 to explain the machine learning techniques for regression-based methods and classification problems. Let's take a quick recap of them once and then we can jump into the concepts.

7.1.1 House Sale Prices

We will be using the house sale prices dataset detailed in Chapter 6. Let's have a quick look at the dataset.

```
library(data.table)

Data_House_Price <-fread("Dataset/House Sale Price Dataset.csv",header=T,
verbose =FALSE, showProgress =FALSE)

str(Data_House_Price)
 Classes 'data.table' and 'data.frame':   1300 obs. of 14 variables:
  $ HOUSE_ID         : chr  "0001" "0002" "0003" "0004" ...
  $ HousePrice       : int  163000 102000 265979 181900 252000 180000 115000
                            176000 192000 132500 ...
  $ StoreArea        : int  433 396 864 572 1043 440 336 486 430 264 ...
  $ BasementArea     : int  662 836 0 594 0 570 0 552 24 588 ...
  $ LawnArea         : int  9120 8877 11700 14585 10574 10335 21750 9900
                            3182 7758 ...
  $ StreetHouseFront: int  76 67 65 NA 85 78 100 NA 43 NA ...
  $ Location         : chr  "RK Puram" "Jama Masjid" "Burari" "RK Puram" ...
  $ ConnectivityType: chr  "Byway" "Byway" "Byway" "Byway" ...
  $ BuildingType     : chr  "IndividualHouse" "IndividualHouse"
                            "IndividualHouse" "IndividualHouse" ...
```

```
 $ ConstructionYear: int  1958 1951 1880 1960 2005 1968 1960 1968 2004 1962
                    ...
 $ EstateType       : chr  "Other" "Other" "Other" "Other" ...
 $ SellingYear      : int  2008 2006 2009 2007 2009 2006 2009 2008 2010 2007
                    ...
 $ Rating           : int  6 4 7 6 8 5 5 7 8 5 ...
 $ SaleType         : chr  "NewHouse" "NewHouse" "NewHouse" "NewHouse" ...
 - attr(*, ".internal.selfref")=<externalptr>
```

These are the variables and their types. It can be seen that the data is a mix of character and numeric data.

The following code and Figure 7-1 present a summary of `House Sale Price`. This is our dependent variable in all the modeling examples we built in this book.

```
dim(Data_House_Price)
 [1] 1300   14
```

```
Check the distribution of dependent variable ( House Price). We plot a
histogram to see how the House Price are spread in our dataset.
```

```
hist(Data_House_Price$HousePrice/1000000, breaks=20, col="blue", xlab="House
Sale Price(Million)",
main="Distribution of House Sale Price")
```

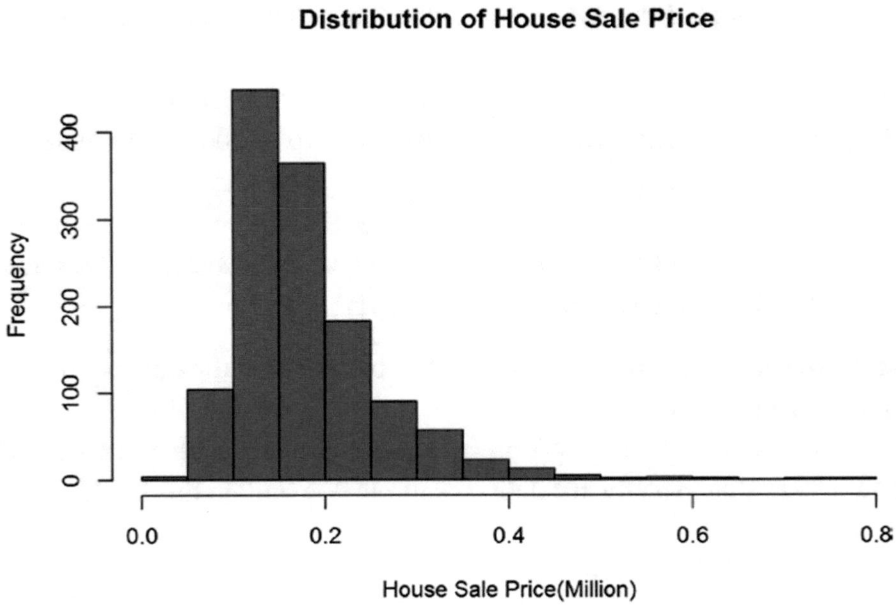

Figure 7-1. *Distribution of house sale price*

Here, we call the summary() function to see basic properties of the HousePrice data. The output gives us a minimum, first quantile, median, mean, third quantile, and maximum.

```
#Also look at the summary of the Dependent Variable
summary(Data_House_Price$HousePrice)
   Min. 1st Qu.  Median    Mean 3rd Qu.    Max.
  34900  129800  163000  181500  214000  755000
#Pulling out relevant columns and assigning required fields in the dataset
Data_House_Price <-Data_House_Price[,.(HOUSE_ID,HousePrice,StoreArea,StreetH
ouseFront,BasementArea,LawnArea,Rating,SaleType)]
```

The following code snippet removes the missing values from the dataset. This is important to make sure the data is consistent throughout.

```
#Omit Any missing value
Data_House_Price <-na.omit(Data_House_Price)

Data_House_Price$HOUSE_ID <-as.character(Data_House_Price$HOUSE_ID)
```

These statistics give us some idea of how the house price is distributed in the dataset. The average sale price is $181,500 and the highest sale price is $755,000.

7.1.2 Purchase Preference

This data contains transaction history for customers who bought a particular product. For each customer_ID, multiple data points are simulated to capture the purchase behavior. The data is originally set for solving multiple classes with four possible products of insurance industry. Here, we show a summary of the purchase prediction data.

```
Data_Purchase <-fread("Dataset/Purchase Prediction Dataset.csv",header=T,
verbose =FALSE, showProgress =FALSE)
str(Data_Purchase)
 Classes 'data.table' and 'data.frame':   500000 obs. of 12 variables:
  $ CUSTOMER_ID          : chr  "000001" "000002" "000003" "000004" ...
  $ ProductChoice        : int  2 3 2 3 2 3 2 2 2 3 ...
  $ MembershipPoints     : int  6 2 4 2 6 6 5 9 5 3 ...
  $ ModeOfPayment        : chr  "MoneyWallet" "CreditCard" "MoneyWallet"
                          "MoneyWallet"  ...
  $ ResidentCity         : chr  "Madurai" "Kolkata" "Vijayawada" "Meerut" ...
  $ PurchaseTenure       : int  4 4 10 6 3 3 13 1 9 8 ...
  $ Channel              : chr  "Online" "Online" "Online" "Online" ...
  $ IncomeClass          : chr  "4" "7" "5" "4" ...
  $ CustomerPropensity   : chr  "Medium" "VeryHigh" "Unknown" "Low" ...
  $ CustomerAge          : int  55 75 34 26 38 71 72 27 33 29 ...
  $ MartialStatus        : int  0 0 0 0 1 0 0 0 0 1 ...
  $ LastPurchaseDuration: int  4 15 15 6 6 10 5 4 15 6 ...
  - attr(*, ".internal.selfref")=<externalptr>
```

This data output shows a mixed bag of variables in the purchase prediction data. Carefully look at the dependent variable in this dataset, PurchaseChoice, which was loaded as an integer. We have to make sure before we use that for modeling that it's converted into factor.

Similar to the continuous dependent variable, we will create the dependent variable for a discrete case from the purchase prediction data. For simplicity and easy explanation, we will only be working with product preference ProductChoice as a dependent variable with four levels (i.e., 1, 2, 3, and 4). See Figure 7-2.

```
dim(Data_Purchase);
 [1] 500000     12
#Check the distribution of data before grouping
table(Data_Purchase$ProductChoice)

      1      2      3      4
 106603 199286 143893  50218
```

The barplot below shows the distribution of ProductChoice. The highest volume is in for ProductChoice = 2, then 3 followed by 1 and 4.

```
barplot(table(Data_Purchase$ProductChoice),main="Distribution of
ProductChoice", xlab="ProductChoice Options", col="Blue")
```

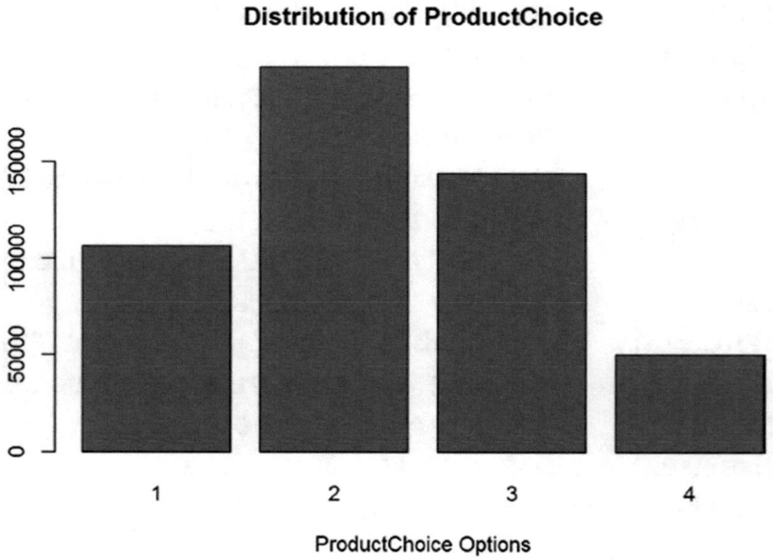

Figure 7-2. *Distribution of product choice options*

In the following code, we subset the data to select only the columns we will be using in this chapter. Also we remove all missing values (NA) to keep the data consistent across different options.

```
#Pulling out only the relevant data to this chapter

Data_Purchase  <- Data_Purchase[,.(CUSTOMER_ID,ProductChoice,MembershipPoints,
IncomeClass,CustomerPropensity,LastPurchaseDuration)]

#Delete NA from subset

Data_Purchase <-na.omit(Data_Purchase)

Data_Purchase$CUSTOMER_ID <-as.character(Data_Purchase$CUSTOMER_ID)
```

This subset of data will be used throughout this chapter to explain the various concepts.

7.2 Introduction to Model Performance and Evaluation

Model performance and evaluation is carried out once you have developed the model and want to understand how the model performs on the test data/validation data. Before the start of model development, you usually divide the data into three categories:

- *Training data*: This dataset is used to train the model/machine. At this stage, the focus of the machine learning algorithm is to optimize some well-defined metric reflecting the model fit. For instance, in Ordinary Least Square, we will be using the training data to train a linear regression model by minimizing squared errors.
- *Testing data*: Test dataset contain data points that the ML algorithm has not seen before. We apply this dataset to see how the model performs on the new data. Most of the model performance and evaluation are calculated and evaluated against thresholds in this step. Here, the modeler can decide if the model needs any improvement and can make the changes and tweaks accordingly.
- *Validation data*: In many cases, the modeler doesn't keep this dataset due to multiple reasons (e.g., limited data, short time period, larger test set, etc.). In essence, this dataset's purpose is to check for overfitting of the model and provide insights into calibration needs.

Once the modeler believes the ML model has done well on testing data and starts to use validation data, they can't go back and change the model. They rather have to try to calibrate the model and check for overfitting. If the model fails to set standards, we are forced to drop the model and start the process again.

Depending on the problem and other statistical constraints, the proportion of these datasets will be decided. In general, for sufficiently large data we may use the 60:20:20 ratio for our training, testing, and validation datasets.

Model performance is measured using test data and the modeler decides what thresholds are acceptable to validate the model. Performance metrics are in general generated using the basic criteria of model fit, i.e., how different the model output is from the actual. This error between actual and predicted will be the error that should be minimized for a good performance.

Within the scope of this book, we will be discussing how to use some commonly used performance and evaluation metrics on two types of model output (predictor) variables:

- *Continuous output*: The model or series of models that give a continuous predicted value against a continuous dependent variable in model. For instance, house prices are continuous and, when used to predict using a model, will be giving continuous predicted values.
- *Discrete output*: The model or series of models that gives a discrete predicted value against a discrete dependent variable in model. For instance, for a credit card application, the risk class of the borrower when used in predictive model for classification will give a discrete predicted value (i.e., predicted risk class).

We can expand this list based on other complicated modeling techniques and how we want to evaluate them. For instance, think about a logistic model; the dependent is a binomial distributed variable but the output is on the probability scale (0 to 1). Depending on what is the final purpose of the business, we have to decide what to evaluate and at what step of the process. For completeness purposes, you can use concordant-discordant ratios to evaluate the model separation power among 0s and 1s. Concordant-discordant ratios are discussed in Chapter 6. You are encouraged to pursue statistical underpinning of model performance measurement concepts.

7.3 Objectives of Model Performance Evaluation

Business stakeholders play an important role in defining the performance metrics. The models have direct implications on costs for business. Simply minimizing a complicated statistical measure might not always be the best model for a business. For illustration purposes, assume a credit risk model for credit scoring new applicants. A few of the input variables are internal and some are purchased from external sources. The model performs really well by having external data from multiple parties, which comes with a cost. In that case simply having a model with minimum classification error is not enough; the model output should also make economic sense to the business.

In general, we can classify the purpose of model performance and evaluation focus into three buckets. These three are part of general framework for using statistical methods and their interpretation.

- *Accuracy*: The accuracy of a model reflects the proportion of right predictions—in a continuous case, its minimum residual, and in discrete, the correct class prediction. A minimum residual in continuous cases or a few incorrect classifications in discrete case implies higher accuracy and a better model.
- *Gains*: The gains statistic gives us an idea about the performance of the model itself. The method is generalized to different modeling techniques and is very intuitive. This compares the model output with the result that we get without using a model (or a random model). So in essence, this will tell you how good the model is compared to a random model that has a random outcome. When comparing two models, the model having the higher gains statistics at a specified percentile is preferred.
- *Accreditation*: The model accreditation reflects the credibility of a model for actual use. This approach ensures that the data on which model is applied is similar to the training data. Population stability index is one of the measures to ensure accreditation before using the model. Population stability index is a measure to ascertain if the model training dataset is similar to the data where the model is used, or the population is stable with respect to the features used in the model. The index value varies from 0 to 1, with high values indicating greater similarity between the predictors in the two datasets. A stable population confirms the use of model for prediction.

More details about population stability index are in Section 7.4.

These kinds of scenarios are abundant in actual practice. In this book, we will discuss the basic statistical methods used to evaluate the model performance. We will also look at the intuitive way of thinking about model performance. Intuitive ways of thinking help create new error metrics and add business context while measuring model performance.

7.4 Population Stability Index

Population stability is seldom ignored by modelers while testing the model performance on various datasets. The idea here is to ensure that the testing dataset is the same as the train dataset. If this is the case, the model performance tested on this data will give you insights into how well the model performed; otherwise, your model performance results are of no use.

Consider an example. You developed a model for predicting mean income of U.S. consumers using a dataset from 2000 to 2009. You developed the model by training it on dataset from 2000 to 2007 and then kept the last two years for testing the model. What is going to happen with the test results? The trained model might be the best model but the model performance in the test results is still bad. Why? Because the population characteristics between train and test have changed. The U.S. economy went through a severe recession between Q4 2007 and Q4 2008. In statistical terms, the underlying population is not stable between the two periods.

Population stability is very important in time series data to keep following the underlying changes in the population to make sure that the model stays relevant. The financial services industry has been using this metric for a long time to make sure the financial models are relevant to the market.

Let's illustrate the concept of population stability for a continuous distribution. We will divide the population data into two portions, say `set_1` and `set_2`. In machine learning performance testing, think about `set_1` as the train data and `set_2` as the test data.

Note The concept of population stability is very important when the underlying relationship structure of dependent and independent variable is affected by external unseen factors.

```
#Create set 1 and set 2 : First 2/3 as set 1 and remaining 1/3 as set 2
summary(Data_House_Price$HousePrice)
   Min. 1st Qu.  Median    Mean 3rd Qu.    Max.
  34900  127500  159000  181300  213200  755000
set_1 <-Data_House_Price[1:floor(nrow(Data_House_Price)*(2/3)),]$HousePrice
summary(set_1)
   Min. 1st Qu.  Median    Mean 3rd Qu.    Max.
  34900  128800  160000  180800  208900  755000
set_2 <-Data_House_Price[floor(nrow(Data_House_Price)*(2/3) +1):nrow(Data_
House_Price),]$HousePrice
summary(set_2)
   Min. 1st Qu.  Median   Mean 3rd Qu.    Max.
  52500  127000  155000 182200  221000  745000
```

For the continuous case, we can check for stability using two sample Kolmogorov-Smirnov tests (KS test). KS testing is a non-parametric test for comparing the cumulative distribution of two samples.

The empirical distribution function Fn for n iid observations Xi is defined as:

$$F_n(x) = \frac{1}{n}\sum_{i=1}^{n} I_{[-\infty,x]}(X_i)$$

where $I_{[-\infty, x]}(X_i)$ is the indicator function, equal to 1 if $X_i \leq x$ and equal to 0 otherwise.

The Kolmogorov-Smirnov statistic for a given cumulative distribution function F(x) is

$$D_n = \sup_x \left| F_n(x) - F(x) \right|$$

where *sup x* is the maximum of the set of distances.

Essentially, the KS statistic will get the highest point of difference between the empirical distribution comparisons of two samples and, if that is too high, we say the two samples are different. In terms of population stability, it says your model performance can't be measured on new samples and the underlying sample is not from the same distribution on which the model was trained.

In following code first defines a function `ks_test()` that plots the Empirical Cumulative Distribution Function (ECDF) and displays the KS test result.

```
#Defining a function to give ks test result and ECDF plots on log scale
library(rgr)
ks_test <-function (xx1, xx2, xlab ="House Price", x1lab
=deparse(substitute(xx1)),x2lab =deparse(substitute(xx2)), ylab ="Empirical
Cumulative Distribution Function",log =TRUE, main ="Empirical EDF Plots -
K-S Test", pch1 =3, col1 =2, pch2 =4, col2 =4, cex =0.8, cexp =0.9, ...)
{
  temp.x <-remove.na(xx1)
  x1 <-sort(temp.x$x[1:temp.x$n])
  nx1 <-temp.x$n
  y1 <-((1:nx1) -0.5)/nx1
  temp.x <-remove.na(xx2)
  x2 <-sort(temp.x$x[1:temp.x$n])
  nx2 <-temp.x$n
  y2 <-((1:nx2) -0.5)/nx2
  xlim <-range(c(x1, x2))
  if (log) {
    logx <- "x"
    if (xlim[1] <=0)
stop("\n Values cannot be .le. zero for a log plot\n")
  }
  else logx <- ""
plot(x1, y1, log = logx, xlim = xlim, xlab = xlab, ylab = ylab,
main = main, type ="n", ...)
points(x1, y1, pch = pch1, col = col1, cex = cexp)
points(x2, y2, pch = pch2, col = col2, cex = cexp)
  temp <-ks.test(x1, x2)
print(temp)
}
```

Here, we call the custom function, which performs this KS test on `set_1` and `set_2` and displays the Empirical Cumulative Distribution Plots (ECDF)—see Figure 7-3:

```
#Perform K-S test on set_1 and set_2 and also display Empirical Cumulative
Distribution Plots
ks_test(set_1,set_2)
```

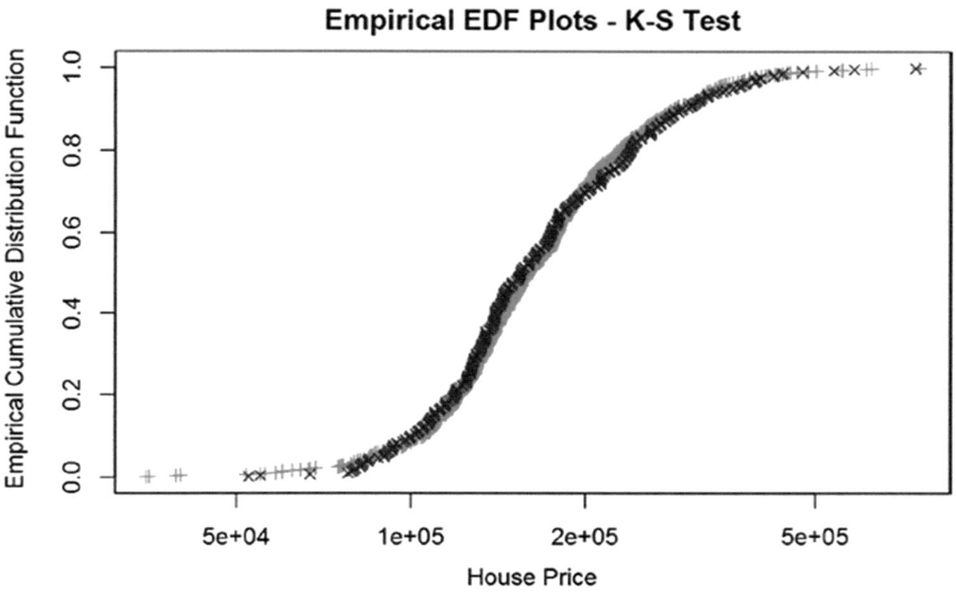

Figure 7-3. *ECDF plots for Set_1 and Set_2*

Here, we show the hypothesis test results for the KS test. This is the Kolmogorov-Smirnov test for the hypothesis that both distributions were drawn from the same underlying distribution.

```
  Two-sample Kolmogorov-Smirnov test

data:  x1 and x2
D = 0.050684, p-value = 0.5744
alternative hypothesis: two-sided
```

As you can see, the p-value is more than 0.05 and we fail to reject the null hypothesis. So we are good to go ahead and test model performance on test data. Also, looking at the Empirical Cumulative Distribution Function (ECDF) plot, we can see the ECDF for both the samples look the same, and hence they come from the same population distribution.

How do the results look when the population becomes unstable? Let's manipulate our set_2 to show that scenario.

Consider that set_2 was exposed to a new law, where the houses in set_2 were subjected to additional tax by a local body and hence the prices went up. The question we will have is, can the existing model still perform well on this new set?

```
#Manipulate the set 2
set_2_new <-set_2*exp(set_2/100000)

# Now do the k-s test again
ks_test(set_1,set_2_new)
```

Now let's again plot the ECDF for set_1 and set_2 and see how they look in comparison (see Figure 7-4).

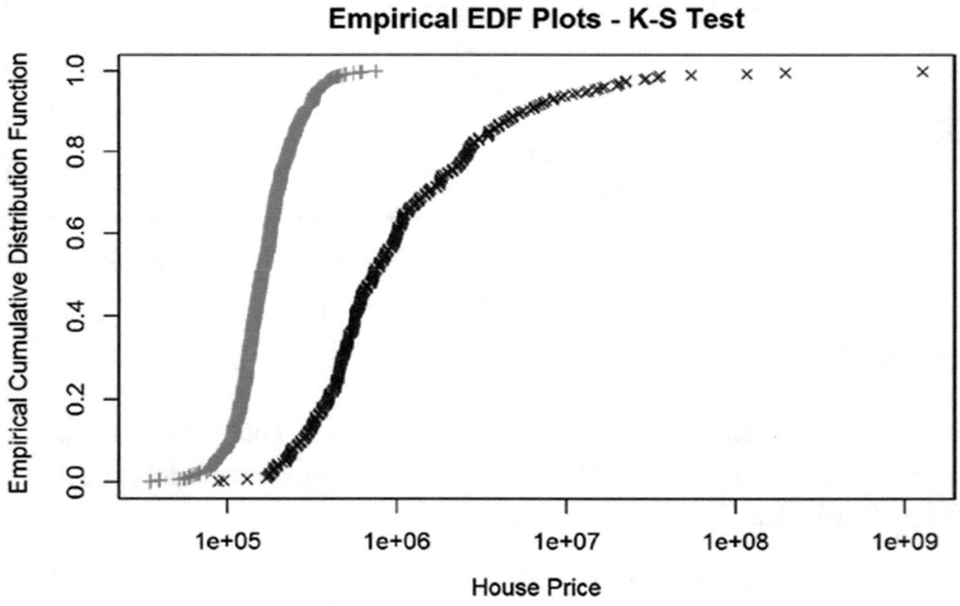

Figure 7-4. *ECDF plots for Set_1 and Set_2 (manipulated)*

We again perform the KS test to check the hypothesis results.

```
  Two-sample Kolmogorov-Smirnov test

data:  x1 and x2
D = 0.79957, p-value < 2.2e-16
alternative hypothesis: two-sided
```

The KS test's p-value is less than 0.05 and hence the test rejects the null hypothesis that both samples are from the same population. Visually the ECDF plots look way different from each other. Hence, the model can't be used on new dataset, although the dataset is of the same schema and business feed.

We can quickly show how to do population stability tests for discrete cases of purchase prediction for `ProductChoice`. The test is performed by calculating the statistic, Population Stability Index (PSI), defined as here:

$$PSI=\sum((n1i/N1)-(n2i/N2))*\ln((n1i/N1)/(n2i/N2))$$

where $n1i,n2i$ is the number of observations in bin i for populations 1 and 2, and N1,N2 is the total number of observations for populations 1 and 2.

As the Population Stability Index for the discrete case does not follow a distribution, we have threshold values. As a rule, values below thresholds can be used to interpret the population stability index:

- A PSI < 0.1 indicates a minimal change in the population.
- A PSI 0.1 to 0.2 indicates changes that require further investigation.
- A PSI > 0.2 indicates a significant change in the population.

This code snippet calculates the Population Stability Index using this formula.

```
#Let's create set 1 and set 2 from our Purchase Prediction Data
print("Distribution of ProductChoice values before partition")
 [1] "Distribution of ProductChoice values before partition"
table(Data_Purchase$ProductChoice)

      1      2      3      4
 104619 189351 142504  49470
set_1 <-Data_Purchase[1:floor(nrow(Data_Purchase)*(2/3)),]$ProductChoice
table(set_1)
 set_1
     1      2      3      4
 69402 126391  95157  33012
set_2 <-Data_Purchase[floor(nrow(Data_Purchase)*(2/3) +1):nrow(Data_
Purchase),]$ProductChoice
table(set_2)
```

```
set_2
    1      2      3      4
35217  62960  47347  16458
```

Now we will treat `set_1` as population 1 and `set_2` as population 2 and calculate the PSI. A similar exercise can be repeated with different parameters to see if the population remains stable with respect to other discrete distributions.

```
#PSI=Summation((n1i/N1)(n2i/N2))ln((n1i/N1)/(n2i/N2))

temp1 <-(table(set_1)/length(set_1) -table(set_2)/length(set_2))

temp2 <-log((table(set_1)/length(set_1))*(table(set_2)/length(set_2)))

psi <-abs(sum(temp1*temp2))

if(psi <0.1 ){
cat("The population is stable with a PSI of   " ,psi)
} else if (psi >=0.1&psi <=0.2) {
cat("The population need further investigation with a PSI of     "  ,psi)
} else {
cat("The population has gone through significant changes with a PSi of  " ,psi)
}
The population is stable with a PSI of 0.002147654
```

As you must have observed from these examples, essentially we are comparing two distributions and making sure the distributions are similar. This test helps us ascertain how credible the model would be on the new data.

7.5 Model Evaluation for Continuous Output

The distribution of dependent variables is an important consideration in choosing the methods for evaluating the models. Intuitively, we end up comparing the residual distribution (actual versus predicted value) with either normal distribution (i.e., random noise) or some other distribution based on the metrics we choose.

This section is dedicated to the cases where the residual error is on a continuous scale. Within the scope of this chapter, we will focus on the linear regression model and calculate some basic metrics. The metrics come with their own merits and demerits, and we will try to focus on some of them from a business interpretation perspective.

Let's fit a linear regression model with the variables subsetted to a forward selection on the house price data. Then, with this model, we will show different model performance metrics.

```
# Create a model on Set 1 = Train data

linear_reg_model <-lm(HousePrice ~StoreArea +StreetHouseFront +BasementArea
+LawnArea +Rating    +SaleType ,data=Data_House_Price[1:floor(nrow(Data_
House_Price)*(2/3)),])

summary(linear_reg_model)

 Call:
 lm(formula = HousePrice ~ StoreArea + StreetHouseFront + BasementArea +
     LawnArea + Rating + SaleType, data = Data_House_
Price[1:floor(nrow(Data_House_Price) *
     (2/3)), ])

 Residuals:
     Min       1Q  Median      3Q     Max
-432276   - 22901   -3239  17285  380300

 Coefficients:
                        Estimate Std. Error t value Pr(>|t|)
 (Intercept)          -8.003e+04 3.262e+04  -2.454 0.014387 *
 StoreArea             5.817e+01 9.851e+00   5.905 5.48e-09 ***
 StreetHouseFront      1.370e+02 8.083e+01   1.695 0.090578 .
 BasementArea          2.362e+01 3.722e+00   6.346 3.96e-10 ***
 LawnArea              7.746e-01 1.987e-01   3.897 0.000107 ***
 Rating                3.540e+04 1.519e+03  23.300  < 2e-16 ***
 SaleTypeFirstResale   1.012e+04 3.250e+04   0.311 0.755651
 SaleTypeFourthResale -3.221e+04 3.678e+04  -0.876 0.381511
 SaleTypeNewHouse     -1.298e+04 3.190e+04  -0.407 0.684268
 SaleTypeSecondResale -2.456e+04 3.248e+04  -0.756 0.449750
 SaleTypeThirdResale  -2.256e+04 3.485e+04  -0.647 0.517536
 ---
 Signif. codes:  0 '***'  0.001 '**' 0.01 '*' 0.05 '.' 0.1 ' ' 1
```

```
Residual standard error : 44860 on 701 degrees of freedom
Multiple R-squared: 0.7155, Adjusted R-squared: 0.7115
F-statistic: 176.3 on 10 and 701 DF, p-value: < 2.2e-16
```

The model summary shows a few things:

- The multiple R-square of the fitted model is 71.5%, which is a good fit model.
- The `SaleType` variable is insignificant at all levels (but we have kept that in model as we believe that it's an important element of `HousePrice`).
- The p-value for the F-test of the overall significance test is less than 0.05, so we can reject the null hypothesis and conclude that the model provides a better fit than the intercept-only model.

Now we will move on to the performance measures for a continuous dependent variable.

7.5.1 Mean Absolute Error

Mean absolute error or MAD is one of the most basic error metrics used to evaluate a model. MAD is directly derived from the residual error first norm. This is the average/mean of the absolute errors.

In statistics, the mean absolute error is an average of the absolute errors

$$\mathrm{MAE} = \frac{1}{n}\sum_{i=1}^{n}\left|f_i - y_i\right| = \frac{1}{n}\sum_{i=1}^{n}\left|e_i\right|.$$

where f_i is the prediction and y_i the true value.

There are other similar measures like Mean Absolute Scaled Error (MASE) and Mean Absolute Percentage Error (MAPE). In all these measures, the performance is summarized in a way that it treats both underprediction and overprediction the same, and mean signed difference is ignored. This is a specific demerit because of ignorance to over-prediction or under-prediction. In business problems we are usually fine with error in one direction but not the other. For instance, calculating credit loss on credit cards. The business should be fine if it is overpredicting the loss and hence keeping a little more in reserve. However, the other side is highly costly and may trigger bankruptcy in extreme cases.

```
#Create the test data which is set 2
test <-Data_House_Price[floor(nrow(Data_House_Price)*(2/3) +1):nrow(Data_
House_Price),]

#Fit the linear regression model on this and get predicted values

predicted_lm <-predict(linear_reg_model,test, type="response")

actual_predicted <-as.data.frame(cbind(as.numeric(test$HOUSE_ID),as.
numeric(test$HousePrice),as.numeric(predicted_lm)))

names(actual_predicted) <-c("HOUSE_ID","Actual","Predicted")

#Find the absolute residual and then take mean of that
library(ggplot2)

#Plot Actual vs Predicted values for Test Cases
ggplot(actual_predicted,aes(x = actual_predicted$HOUSE_ID,color=Series)) +
geom_line(data = actual_predicted, aes(x = actual_predicted$HOUSE_ID,
y =Actual, color ="Actual")) +
geom_line(data = actual_predicted, aes(x = actual_predicted$HOUSE_ID, y =
Predicted, color ="Predicted")) +xlab('HOUSE_ID') +ylab('House Sale Price')
```

It's clear from the plot in Figure 7-5 that the actual is very close to the predicted. Now let's find out how our model is performing on a Mean Square Error metric.

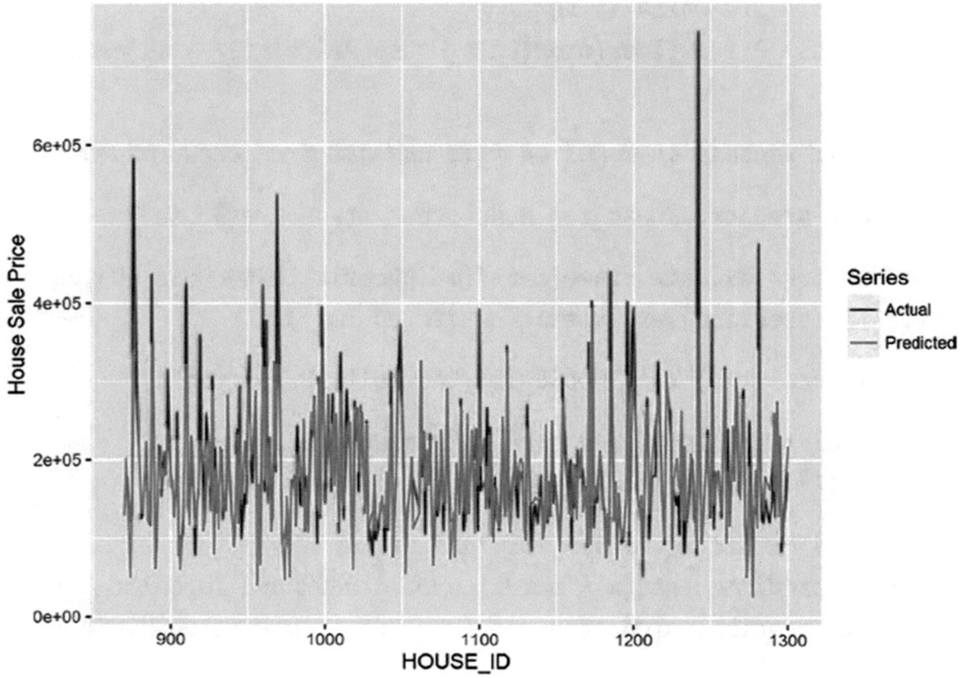

Figure 7-5. *Actual versus predicted plot*

```
#Remove NA from test, as we have not done any treatment for NA
actual_predicted <-na.omit(actual_predicted)

#First take Actual - Predicted, then take mean of absolute errors(residual)

mae <-sum(abs(actual_predicted$Actual -actual_predicted$Predicted))/nrow(ac
tual_predicted)

cat("Mean Absolute Error for the test case is  ", mae)
 Mean Absolute Error for the test case is   29570.3
```

The MAE says on average the error is $29,570. This is equivalent to saying on the dollar scale, that a 17% error is expected for a mean of $180,921.

This metric can also be used to fit linear model. Just as least square method is related to mean squared errors, mean absolute error is related to least absolute deviations.

7.5.2 Root Mean Square Error

Root mean square error or RMSE is one of the most popular metrics used to evaluate continuous error models. As the name suggests, it is the square root of mean of squared errors. The most important feature of this metric is that the errors are weighted by means of squaring them.

For example, suppose the predicted value is 5.5 while the actual value is 4.1. Then the error is 1.4 (5.5 - 4.1). The square of this error is 1.4 x 1.4 = 1.96. Assume another scenario, where the predicted value is 6.5, then the error is 2.4 (6.5 - 4.1), and the square of error is 2.4 x 2.4 = 5.76. As you can see, while the error only changed 2.4/1.4 = 1.7 times, the squared error changed 5.76/1.96 = 2.93 times. Hence, RMSE penalizes the far off error more strictly than any close by errors.

The RMSE of predicted values $\hat{y}_t$ for times t of a regression's dependent variable y_t is computed for n different predictions as the square root of the mean of the squares of the deviations:

$$\text{RMSE} = \sqrt{\frac{\sum_{t=1}^{n}\left(\hat{y}_t - y_t\right)^2}{n}}$$

It is important to understand how the operations in the metric change the interpretation of the metric. Suppose our dependent variable is house price, which is captured in dollar numbers. Let's see how the metric dimensions evolve to interpret the measure.

The predicted and actual value is in dollars, so their difference is error, again in dollars. Then you square the error, so the dimension becomes dollar squared. You can't compare a dollar square value to a dollar value. So, we square root that to bring back the dimension to dollars and can now interpret RMSE in dollar terms. It's important to note that generally, the metrics for model comparison are dimensionless, but for the model itself, we prefer metrics having some dimension to provide a business context to the metric.

```
#As we have already have actual and predicted value we can directly
calculate the RMSE value

rmse <-sqrt(sum((actual_predicted$Actual-

actual_predicted$Predicted)^2)/nrow(actual_predicted))

cat("Root Mean Square Error for the test case is  ", rmse)
 Root Mean Square Error for the test case is   44459.42
```

Now you can see that the error has scaled up to $44,459. This is due to the fact that we are penalizing the model for far away predictions by means of squaring the errors.

As mentioned earlier as well, if you want to use a metric to compare datasets or models with different scales, you need to bring the metric into a dimensionless form. We can do the same with RMSE by normalizing it. The most common way is by dividing the RMSE by range or mean:

$$\text{NRMSD} = \frac{\text{RMSD}}{y_{\max} - y_{\min}} \; or \; \text{NRMSD} = \frac{\text{RMSD}}{\overline{y}}$$

This value is referred to as the normalized root-mean-square deviation or error (NRMSD or NRMSE) and id usually expressed as a percentage. A low value indicates less residual variance and hence is a good model.

7.5.3 R-Square

R-square is a popular measure used for linear regression based techniques. The appropriate terminology used by statisticians for R-square is Coefficient of Determination. The Coefficient of Determination gives an indication of the relationship between the dependent variable (y) and a set of independent variables (x). In mathematical form, it is a ratio of residual sum of squares and total sum of squares. Again, note that this measure is also originating from residual (error metric) using actual and predicted values. Here, we explain how the R^2 metric gets calculated for a model, and then how we interpret the metric.

Note Capital R^2 and r^2 are loosely used interchangeably but they are not the same. R^2 is the multiple R^2 in a multiple regression model. In bivariate linear regression, there is no multiple R, and $R^2 = r^2$. So the key difference is applicability of the term (or notation): multiple R implies multiple regressors, whereas R^2 doesn't.

A dataset has n values marked *y1...yn* (collectively known as *yi* or as a vector y = [y1...yn]), each associated with a predicted (or modeled) value *f1...fn* (known as *fi*, or sometimes ŷi, as a vector f).

The residual (error in prediction) is defined as ei = yi - fi (forming a vector e).

If $\bar{y}$ is the mean of the observed data $\bar{y} = \frac{1}{n}\sum_{i=1}^{n} y_i$ then the variability of the dataset can be measured using three sums of squares formulas:

- The total sum of squares (proportional to the variance of the data):

$$SS_{tot} = \sum_i (y_i - \bar{y})^2,$$

- The regression sum of squares, also called the explained sum of squares:

$$SS_{\text{reg}} = \sum_i (f_i - \bar{y})^2$$

- The sum of squares of residuals, also called the residual sum of squares:

$$SS_{\text{reg}} = \sum_i (y_i - f_i)^2 = \sum_i e_i^2$$

- The general definition of the coefficient of determination or r^2 is

$$R^2 = 1 - \frac{SS_{\text{res}}}{SS_{tot}}$$

In Figure 7-6, we can see the interpetation of the sum of squares and how they come together to form the definition of the coefficient of determination.

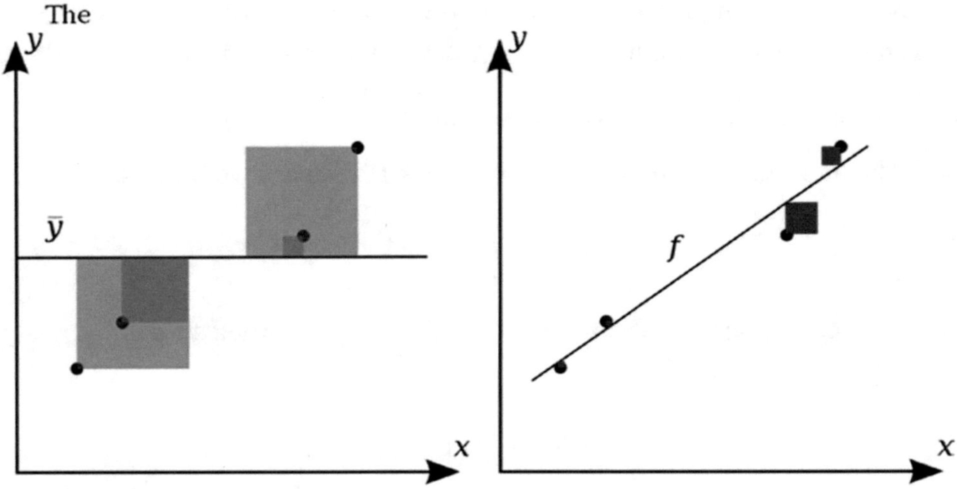

Figure 7-6. *Image explaining squared errors (taken from `https://en.wikipedia.org/wiki/Coefficient_of_determination`)*

R^2 = 1- Blue Color/Red Color

These small squares represent the squared residuals with respect to the linear regression. The areas of the larger squares represent the squared residuals with respect to the average value.

On left the linear regression fits the data in comparison to the simple average, while on the right it fits the actual value of data. R^2 is then a ratio between them, indicating if rather than taking a simple average, you use this model how much more you will be able to capture. Needless to say, a perfect value of 1 means all the variation is explained by the model.

Since R^2 is a proportion, it is always a number between 0 and 1.

- If $R^2 = 1$, all of the data points fall perfectly on the regression line (or the predictor x accounts for all the variation in y)
- If $R^2 = 0$, the estimated regression line is perfectly horizontal (or the predictor x accounts for none of the variation in y)
- If R^2 is between 0 and 1, it explains variance in y (using the model is better than not using the model)

Though R-square is the default output of all the standard linear regression packages, we will show you the calculations as well. Another term that you need to be aware is adjusted R-squared. It makes the correction for the number of predictors in the model. In other words it takes into account the overfitting of the model due to a high number of predictors, and it increases only if the new term improves the model more than would be expected by chance.

```
#Model training data ( we will show our analysis on this dataset)

train <-Data_House_Price[1:floor(nrow(Data_House_Price)*(2/3)),.(HousePrice
,StoreArea,StreetHouseFront,BasementArea,LawnArea,StreetHouseFront,LawnArea
,Rating,SaleType)];

#Omitting the NA from dataset

train <-na.omit(train)

# Get a linear regression model
linear_reg_model <-lm(HousePrice ~StoreArea +StreetHouseFront +BasementArea
+LawnArea +StreetHouseFront +LawnArea +Rating +SaleType ,data=train)

# Show the function call to identify what model we will be working on

print(linear_reg_model$call)
 lm(formula = HousePrice ~ StoreArea + StreetHouseFront + BasementArea +
     LawnArea + StreetHouseFront + LawnArea + Rating + SaleType,
     data = train)
#System generated Square value
cat("The system generated R square value is " , summary(linear_reg_model)$r.
squared)
 The system generated R square value is  0.7155461
```

You can see that the default model output calculated R-square for us. The current linear model has an R-square of 0.72. It can be interpreted as 72% percent of the variation in house price is "explained by" the variation in predictors `StoreArea`, `StreetHouseFront`, `BasementArea`, `LawnArea`, `StreetHouseFront`, `LawnArea`, `Rating`, and `SaleType`.

Here, we calculate the measure step by step to get the same R-square value.

```
#calculate Total Sum of Squares

SST <-sum((train$HousePrice -mean(train$HousePrice))^2);

#Calculate Regression Sum of Squares

SSR <-sum((linear_reg_model$fitted.values -mean(train$HousePrice))^2);

#Calculate residual(Error) Sum of Squares

SSE <-sum((train$HousePrice -linear_reg_model$fitted.values)^2);
```

One of the important relationships that these three sum of squares share is

```
SST = SSR + SSE
```

You can test that on your own. Now we will use these values and get the R-square Model evaluation: R-square for our model:

```
#calculate R-squared

R_Sqr <-1-(SSE/SST)

#Display the calculated R-Sqr

cat("The calculated R Square is  ", R_Sqr)
 The calculated R Square is   0.7155461
```

You can see that the calculated R-square is the same as the `lm()` function output. You can now see the calculations behind R-square.

In this section, you saw some of the basic metrics that we can create around the errors (residuals) and interpreted them as a measure of how well our model will do on the actual data. In the next section, we introduce techniques for discrete cases.

7.6 Model Evaluation for Discrete Output

In the previous section, we introduced metrics for models where the dependent variable and predicted values were of continuous types. In this section, we introduce some metrics for cases where the distribution is discrete.

For this section, we go back to our purchase prediction data and generate the metrics and discuss their interpretation. We leverage the setup we created for population stability.

7.6.1 Classification Matrix

A classification matrix is the most intuitive way of looking at the performance of a classifier. This is sometimes also called a confusion matrix. Visually, this is a two-way matrix with one axis showing the distribution of the actual class and the other axis showing a predicted class (see Figure 7-7).

Two Class Classification		Predicted Class	
		1	0
Actual Class	1	True Positive (TP)	False Negative(FN)
	0	False Positive(FP)	True Negative(TN)

Figure 7-7. *Two-class classification matrix*

The accuracy of the model is calculated by the diagonal elements of the classification matrix, as they represent the correct classification by the classifier, i.e., the actual and predicted values are the same.

```
Classification Rate = (True Positive + True Negative) / Total Cases
```

Now we will show you the classification matrix and calculate the classification rate for our purchase prediction data. The method we will use for modeling probabilities is a multinomial logistic and the classifier will pick the highest probability.

Note To avoid the class imbalance problem, we will be using stratified sampling to create equal size classes for illustration of model performance concepts. A class imbalance problem causes the probabilities to bias toward the high frequency classes, and hence the classifier fails to allocate classes to low frequency classes.

```
#Remove the data having NA. NA is ignored in modeling algorithms
Data_Purchase<-na.omit(Data_Purchase)

#Sample equal sizes from Data_Purchase to reduce class imbalance issue
library(splitstackshape)
Data_Purchase_Model<-stratified(Data_Purchase, group=c("ProductChoice"),size
=10000,replace=FALSE)

print("The Distribution of equal classes is as below")
 [1] "The Distribution of equal classes is as below"
table(Data_Purchase_Model$ProductChoice)

     1     2     3     4
 10000 10000 10000 10000
```

Build the multinomial model on Train Data (Set_1) and then test data (Set_2) will be used for performance testing

```
set.seed(917);
train <-Data_Purchase_Model[sample(nrow(Data_Purchase_Model),size=nrow(Data_
Purchase_Model)*(0.7), replace =TRUE, prob =NULL),]
dim(train)
 [1] 28000     6
test <-Data_Purchase_Model[!(Data_Purchase_Model$CUSTOMER_ID
%in%train$CUSTOMER_ID),]
dim(test)
 [1] 20002     6
```

Fit a multinomial logistic model

```
library(nnet)
mnl_model <-multinom (ProductChoice ~MembershipPoints +IncomeClass
+CustomerPropensity +LastPurchaseDuration, data = train)
 # weights:  68 (48 variable)
 initial  value 38816.242111
 iter  10 value 37672.163254
 iter  20 value 37574.198380
 iter  30 value 37413.360061
```

```
iter  40 value 37327.695046
iter  50 value 37263.280870
iter  60 value 37261.603993
final  value 37261.599306
converged
```

Display the summary of model statistics

```
mnl_model
 Call:
 multinom(formula = ProductChoice ~ MembershipPoints + IncomeClass +
     CustomerPropensity + LastPurchaseDuration, data = train)

 Coefficients:
   (Intercept) MembershipPoints IncomeClass1 IncomeClass2 IncomeClass3
 2   11.682714      -0.03332131  -11.4405637   -11.314417   -11.307691
 3   -1.967090       0.02730530    0.9855891     1.644233     2.224430
 4   -1.618001      -0.12008110    1.5710959     1.692566     2.062924
   IncomeClass4 IncomeClass5 IncomeClass6 IncomeClass7 IncomeClass8
 2   -11.547647   -11.465621   -11.447368   -11.388917   -11.367926
 3     2.023594     2.119750     2.201136     2.169300     2.241395
 4     1.911509     2.062195     2.296741     2.249285     2.509872
   IncomeClass9 CustomerPropensityLow CustomerPropensityMedium
 2   -12.047828            -0.4106025               -0.2580652
 3     1.997350            -0.8727976               -0.5184574
 4     2.027252            -0.6549446               -0.5105506
   CustomerPropensityUnknown CustomerPropensityVeryHigh
 2                -0.5689626                  0.1774420
 3                -1.1769285                  0.4646328
 4                -1.1494067                  0.5660523
   LastPurchaseDuration
 2           0.04809274
 3           0.05624992
 4           0.08436483

 Residual Deviance: 74523.2
 AIC: 74619.2
```

```
Predict the probabilities

predicted_test <-as.data.frame(predict(mnl_model, newdata = test,
type="probs"))

Display the predicted probabilities

head(predicted_test)
          1         2         3          4
 1 0.3423453 0.2468372 0.2252361 0.18558132
 2 0.2599605 0.2755778 0.2546863 0.20977542
 3 0.4096704 0.2429370 0.2482094 0.09918326
 4 0.2220821 0.2485851 0.3188838 0.21044894
 5 0.4163053 0.2689046 0.1763766 0.13841355
 6 0.4284514 0.2626000 0.1948703 0.11407836

Do the prediction based in highest probability

test_result <-apply(predicted_test,1,which.max)

table(test_result)
 test_result
    1    2    3    4
 8928 1265 3879  5930

Combine to get predicted and actuals at one place

result <-as.data.frame(cbind(test$ProductChoice,test_result))

colnames(result) <-c("Actual Class", "Predicted Class")

head(result)
   Actual Class Predicted Class
 1            1               1
 2            1               2
 3            1               1
 4            1               3
 5            1               1
 6            1               1
```

Now when we have the matrix of actual versus predicted, we will create the classification matrix. Now we will calculate some key features of the classification matrix:

- *Number of cases*: Total number of cases or number of rows in test (n)
- *Number of classes*: Total number of classes for which prediction is done (nc)
- *Number of correct classification*: This is the sum over the diagonal of classification matrix (diag)
- *Number of instances per class*: This is the sum of all the cases in actual (rowsums)
- *Number of instances per predicted class*: This is the sum of all the cases in predicted (colsums)
- *Distribution of actuals*: The total of rowsums divided by the total
- *Distribution of predicted*: Total of colsums divided by the total

```
Create the classification matrix

cmat <-as.matrix(table(Actual = result$`Actual Class`, Predicted =
result$`Predicted Class`))

Calculated above mentioned measures in order

n <-sum(cmat) ;
cat("Number of Cases  ", n);
 Number of Cases   20002
nclass <-nrow(cmat);
cat("Number of classes  ", nclass);
 Number of classes   4
correct_class <-diag(cmat);
cat("Number of Correct Classification  ", correct_class);
 Number of Correct Classification   3175 395 1320 2020
rowsums <-apply(cmat, 1, sum);
cat("Number of Instances per class  ", rowsums);
 Number of Instances per class   4998 4995 5035 4974
colsums <-apply(cmat, 2, sum);
```

```
cat("Number of Instances per predicted class  ", colsums);
 Number of Instances per predicted class   8928 1265 3879 5930
actual_dist  <-rowsums  /n;
cat("Distribution of actuals  ", actual_dist);
 Distribution of actuals   0.249875 0.249725 0.2517248 0.2486751
predict_dist <-colsums /n;
cat("Distribution of predicted  ", predict_dist);
 Distribution of predicted   0.4463554 0.06324368 0.1939306 0.2964704
```

These quantities are calculated from the classification matrix. You are encouraged to verify these numbers and get a good understanding of these quantities. Here is the classification matrix and classification rate for our classifier:

```
Print the classification matrix - on test data

print(cmat)
       Predicted
 Actual    1    2    3    4
      1 3175  312  609  902
      2 2407  395  825 1368
      3 1791  284 1320 1640
      4 1555  274 1125 2020

 Print Classification Rate

classification_rate <-sum(correct_class)/n;
print(classification_rate)
 [1] 0.3454655
```

The classification rate is low for this classifier. A classification rate of 35% means that the model is classifying the cases incorrectly more than 50% of the time. The modeler has to dig into the reasons for the low performance of the classifier. The reasons can be the predicted probabilities, underlying variables explanatory power, a sampling of imbalanced classes, or may be the method of picking the highest probability itself.

The model performance here is helping us find out if the model is actually performing up to our standards. Can we really use this in an actual environment? What might be causing the low performance? This step becomes important for any machine learning exercise.

7.6.2 Sensitivity and Specificity

Sensitivity and specificity are used to measure the model performance on positive and negative classes separately. These measures allow you to determine how the model is performing on the positive and negative populations separately. The mathematical notation helps clarify these measures in conjunction with the classification matrix:

- *Sensitivity*: The probability that the test will indicate the `True` class as `True` among actual true. Also called True Positive Rate (TPR) and in pattern recognition called the precision. Sensitivity can be calculated from classification matrix (see Figure 7-7).

  Sensitivity, True Positive Rate = Correctly Identified Positive/ Total Positives = TP/(TP+FN)

- *Specificity*: Probability that the test will indicate that the `False` class and `False` are among an actual False. Also called the True Negative Rate (TNR) and in pattern recognition, called recall. Specificity can be calculated from classification matrix (see Figure 7-7).

  Specificity, True Positive Rate = Correctly Rejected/Total Negatives = TN/(TN+FP)

Sensitivity and specificity are characteristics of the test. The underlying population does not affect the results. For a good model, we try to maximize both TPR and TNR, and the Receiver Operating Characteristic (ROC) helps in this process. Receiver Operating Curve is a plot between sensitivity and (1- specificity), and the highest point on this curve provides the cutoff which maximizes our classification rate. We will discuss the ROC curve in the next section and connect it back to optimizing sensitivity and specificity.

Note Sensitivity and specificity are calculated per class. For a multinomial class, we tend to average out the quantity over the classes to get a single number for the whole model. For illustration purposes, we will show the analysis by combining the classes into a two-class problem. You are encouraged to extend the concept to a full model.

```
The analysis is shown for ProductChoice == 1

Actual_Class <-ifelse(result$`Actual Class` ==1,"One","Rest");
Predicted_Class <-ifelse(result$`Predicted Class` ==1, "One", "Rest");

ss_analysis <-as.data.frame(cbind(Actual_Class,Predicted_Class));

Create classification matrix for ProductChoice == 1

cmat_ProductChoice1 <-as.matrix(table(Actual = ss_analysis$Actual_Class,
Predicted = ss_analysis$Predicted_Class));

print(cmat_ProductChoice1)
       Predicted
 Actual   One Rest
   One  3175 1823
   Rest 5753 9251
classification_rate_ProductChoice1 <-sum(diag(cmat_ProductChoice1))/n;

cat("Classification rate for ProductChoice 1 is  ", classification_rate_
ProductChoice1)
 Classification rate for ProductChoice 1 is   0.6212379

Calculate TPR and TNR

TPR <-cmat_ProductChoice1[1,1]/(cmat_ProductChoice1[1,1] +cmat_
ProductChoice1[1,2]);

cat(" Sensitivity or True Positive Rate is ", TPR);
  Sensitivity or True Positive Rate is  0.6352541
TNR <-cmat_ProductChoice1[2,2]/(cmat_ProductChoice1[2,1] +cmat_
ProductChoice1[2,2])

cat(" Specificity or True Negative Rate is ", TNR);
  Specificity or True Negative Rate is  0.6165689
```

The result shows that for `ProductChoice == 1` our model is able to correctly classify in total 63% of cases, among which it is able to identify 61% as "one" from a population of "one" and 62% as "rest" from a population of "rest". The model performance is better at predicting "rest" from the population.

7.6.3 Area Under ROC Curve

A receiver operating characteristic (ROC), or ROC curve, is a graphical representation of the performance of a binary classifier as the threshold or cutoff to classify changes. As you saw in the previous section, for a good model we want to maximize two interdependent measures—TPR and TNR—the ROC curve will show that relationship. The curve is created by plotting the true positive rate (TPR) against the false positive rate (FPR) at various cutoffs or threshold settings.

However, as we are using a multiclass classifier, we are not using a cutoff to classify. You are encouraged to rebuild the multiclass model as a binary model (one and rest) for other ProductChoices/classes, and then use the built-in functions of the ROCR package.

Here we show ROC curve and Area Under the Curve (AUC) value, assuming the model only had two classes: ProductChoice "One" and "Rest". This will give us a scale of cutoffs if we were to use only probability for class "One"/1. Observe in the following code we are recreating the model to change the multiclass problem into a binary classification problem. Essentially, the probability scale multinomial distributes the probabilities among classes in such a way that the sum is 1, while for ROC we need full range of probabilities for a class to play with the threshold/cutoff values of classification.

For illustration purposes, we will use our purchase prediction data with only two classes of choices—0 or 1—defined here:

- 1 if the customer chooses product 1 from a catalog of four products; this forms our positives
- 0 if the customer chooses any other product than 1; this forms our negatives

Here we create binary logistic model with this definition.

```
# create a the variable Choice_binom as above definition
train$ProductChoice_binom <-ifelse(train$ProductChoice ==1,1,0);
test$ProductChoice_binom <-ifelse(test$ProductChoice ==1,1,0);
```

```
Fit a binary logistic model on the modified dependent variable,
ProductChoice_binom.
```

```
glm_ProductChoice_binom <-glm( ProductChoice_binom ~MembershipPoints
+IncomeClass +CustomerPropensity +LastPurchaseDuration, data=train, family
=binomial(link="logit"))
```

```
Print the summary of binomial logistic model

summary(glm_ProductChoice_binom)

 Call:
 glm(formula = ProductChoice_binom ~ MembershipPoints + IncomeClass +
     CustomerPropensity + LastPurchaseDuration, family = binomial(link =
     "logit"),
     data = train)

 Deviance Residuals:
     Min       1Q   Median       3Q      Max
 -1.2213  -0.8317  -0.6088   1.2159   2.3976

 Coefficients:
                             Estimate Std. Error z value Pr(>|z|)
 (Intercept)               -13.360676  71.621773  -0.187    0.852
 MembershipPoints            0.038574   0.005830   6.616 3.68e-11 ***
 IncomeClass1               12.379912  71.622606   0.173    0.863
 IncomeClass2               12.142239  71.622424   0.170    0.865
 IncomeClass3               11.881615  71.621801   0.166    0.868
 IncomeClass4               12.086976  71.621763   0.169    0.866
 IncomeClass5               11.981304  71.621759   0.167    0.867
 IncomeClass6               11.874714  71.621761   0.166    0.868
 IncomeClass7               11.879708  71.621765   0.166    0.868
 IncomeClass8               11.759389  71.621792   0.164    0.870
 IncomeClass9               12.214044  71.622000   0.171    0.865
 CustomerPropensityLow       0.650186  0.054060   12.027  < 2e-16 ***
 CustomerPropensityMedium    0.435307  0.054828    7.939 2.03e-15 ***
 CustomerPropensityUnknown   0.952099  0.048078   19.803  < 2e-16 ***
 CustomerPropensityVeryHigh -0.430576  0.065156   -6.608 3.89e-11 ***
 LastPurchaseDuration       -0.062538  0.003409  -18.347  < 2e-16 ***
 ---
 Signif. codes:  0 '***' 0.001 '**' 0.01 '*' 0.05 '.' 0.1 ' ' 1

 (Dispersion parameter for binomial family taken to be 1)
```

```
    Null deviance: 31611  on 27999  degrees of freedom
Residual deviance: 29759  on 27984  degrees of freedom
AIC: 29791

Number of Fisher Scoring iterations: 11
```

We will be using RORC library in R to calculate the Area Under the Curve (AUC) and to create the Receiver Operating Curve (ROC) . The ROCR package helps to visualize the performance of scoring classifiers.

```
Now create the performance dataset to create AUC curve

library(ROCR)
test_binom <-predict(glm_ProductChoice_binom,newdata=test, type
="response")
pred <-prediction(test_binom, test$ProductChoice_binom)
perf <-performance(pred,"tpr","fpr")

Calculating AUC

auc <-unlist(slot(performance(pred,"auc"),"y.values"));

cat("The Area Under ROC curve for this model is  ",auc);
 The Area Under ROC curve for this model is   0.6699122

Plotting the ROCcurve

library(ggplot2)
library(plotROC)
debug <-as.data.frame(cbind(test_binom,test$ProductChoice_binom))
ggplot(debug, aes(d = V2, m = test_binom)) +geom_roc()
```

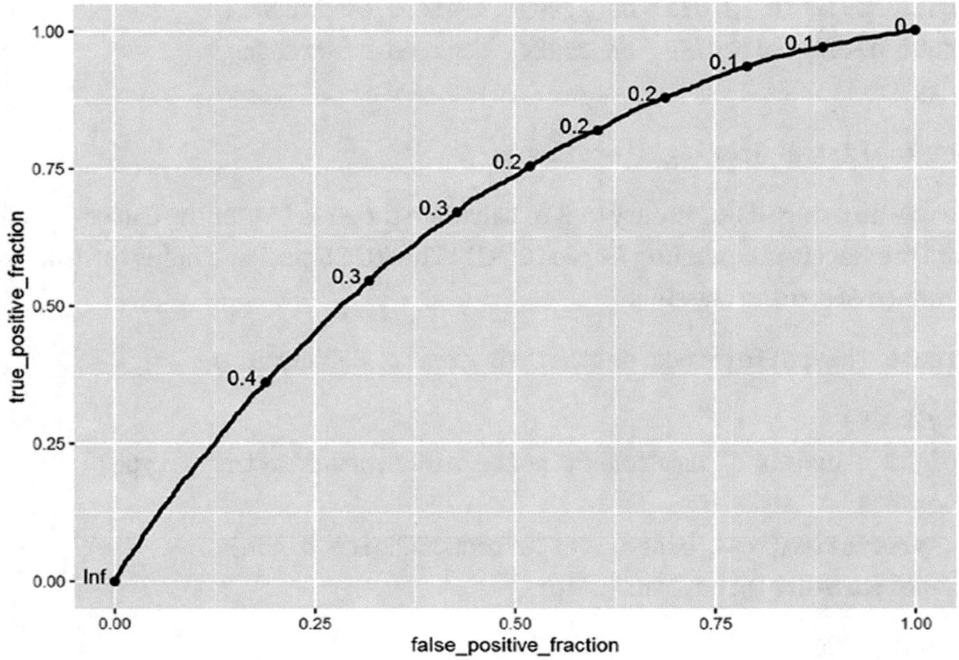

Figure 7-8. *ROC curve*

We used a `ggplot()` object and `plotROC` library to plot the ROC curve with cutoff values highlighted in the plot for easy reading (see Figure 7-8).

In the plot, we want to balance between true positive and false positive, and maximize the true positive while minimizing the false positive. This point will be the best cutoff/threshold value that you should use to create the classifier. Here, you can see that the value is close to 0.2—true positive is ~74% while false positive is ~48%.

Chapter 6 discussed the use of this optimal value, i.e., 0.2 to use as a cutoff for a binary classifier. Refer to that chapter's logistics regression discussion. The ROCR R package details are available at `https://cran.r-project.org/web/packages/ROCR/ROCR.pdf`.

7.7 Probabilistic Techniques

Generally, there is no such specific classification of model performance techniques into probabilistic and otherwise. However, it is helpful for you to understand how more complicated methods are emerging for model performance testing. Probabilistic techniques are those which are based on sampling and simulations. These techniques differ from what we discussed in previous sections; in previous sections we had residuals with us to create metrics. In probabilistic techniques, we will be simulating and sampling subsets to get a robust and stable model.

In this section, we touch at a very high level the two techniques corresponding to two major buckets of probabilistic tools that data scientists have at their disposal, although both are resampling based techniques:

- Simulation based: K-fold cross-validation
- Sampling based: Bootstrap sampling

A very good understanding of these concepts is provided by Ron Kohavi, Stanford in a much celebrated paper "A Study of Cross-Validation and Bootstrap for Accuracy Estimation and Model Selection," *International Joint Conference on Artificial Intelligence* (IJCAI), 1995. The readers interested in this topic should read this paper. In this section, we touch on these ideas from the perspective of using them in R.

7.7.1 K-Fold Cross-Validation

Cross-validation is one of the most used techniques for model evaluation and lately has been accepted as a better technique than residual-based metrics. The issue with residual-based methods is that you need to keep a test set, and just with one test set they don't exactly tell you how the model will behave on unseen data. So while train, test, and validate methods are good, probabilistic simulation and sampling provide us with more ways to test that.

K-fold cross-validation is very popular in the machine learning community. The greater the number of folds, the better the interpretation (recall the Law of Large Numbers). Steps to execute k-fold cross-validation include:

Step 1: Divide the dataset into k subsets.

Step 2: Train a model on k-1 subsets.

Step 3: Test the model on the remaining one subset and calculate the error.

Step 4: Repeat Steps 1-3 until all subsets are used exactly once for testing.

Step 5: Average out the errors by this scenario simulation exercise to get the cross-validation error.

The advantage of this method is that the method by which you create the k-subsets is not that important compared to the same situation in the train/test (or holdout cross-validation) method. Also, this method ensures that every data point gets to be in a test set exactly once, and gets to be in a training set k-1 times. The variance of the resulting estimate is reduced as k is increased.

The disadvantage of this method is that the model has be to estimated k-times and then testing done for k-times, which means a higher computation cost (computation cost is proportional to the number of folds). A variant randomly splits the data and controls each fold size. The advantage of doing this is that you can independently choose how large each test set is and how many trials you average over.

Note In cross-validation techniques, we don't keep train and test subsets. Usually, data scientists keep a validation set outside the cross-validation to test the model final model fit. In our example, we will treat our train as train set and test as validation dataset.

Let's show an example with our house sales price problem. You are encouraged to apply the same techniques on the classification problems as well.

```
library(caret)
library(randomForest)
set.seed(917);
```

```
Model training data (we will show our analysis on this dataset)
```

```
train <-Data_House_Price[1:floor(nrow(Data_House_Price)*(2/3)),.(HousePrice
,StoreArea,StreetHouseFront,BasementArea,LawnArea,StreetHouseFront,LawnArea
,Rating,SaleType)];
```

```
Create the test data which is set 2
```

```
test <-Data_House_Price[floor(nrow(Data_House_Price)*(2/3) +1):nrow(Data_
House_Price),.(HousePrice,StoreArea,StreetHouseFront,BasementArea,LawnArea,S
treetHouseFront,LawnArea,Rating,SaleType)]
```

```
Omitting the NA from dataset
```

```
train <-na.omit(train)
test <-na.omit(test)
```

```
Create the k subsets, let's take k as 10 (i.e., 10-fold cross validation)

k_10_fold <-trainControl(method ="repeatedcv", number =10, savePredictions
=TRUE)

Fit the model on folds and use rmse as metric to fit the model

model_fitted <-train(HousePrice ~StoreArea +StreetHouseFront +BasementArea
+LawnArea +StreetHouseFront +LawnArea +Rating +SaleType, data=train, family
= identity,trControl = k_10_fold, tuneLength =5)

Display the summary of the cross validation

model_fitted
 Random Forest

 712 samples
   6 predictor

 No  pre-processing
 Resampling: Cross-Validated (10 fold, repeated 1 times)
 Summary of sample sizes: 642, 640, 640, 641, 640, 641, ...
 Resampling results across tuning parameters:

  mtry  RMSE      Rsquared
   2    40235.04  0.7891003
   4    37938.62  0.7961153
   6    38049.31  0.7927441
   8    38132.67  0.7914360
  10    38697.45  0.7858166

RMSE was used to select the optimal model using the smallest value.
The final value used for the model was mtry = 4.
```

You can see from the summary that the model selected by cross-validation has a higher R^2 than the one we created previously. The new R-square is 80% and the old was 72%. Also, notice that the default metric to choose the best model is RMSE. You can change the metric and function type based on the need and the optimization function.

7.7.2 Bootstrap Sampling

We have already discussed the bootstrap sampling concepts in Chapter 3. We are just extending the idea to our problem here. Based on random samples from our data, we will try to estimate the model and see if we can reduce the error and get the high-performance model. When we use these techniques as a performance evaluation technique, you can see we already have fixed the model, i.e., the predictors, and trying to see probabilistically what gives the best performance and how much.

For showing the bootstrap example, we will extend what we showed for cross-validation.

```
Create the the boot experiment, let's take samples as as 10 (i.e., 10-sample
bootstrapped)

boot_10s <-trainControl(method ="boot", number =10, savePredictions =TRUE)

Fit the model on bootstraps and use rmse as metric to fit the model

model_fitted <-train(HousePrice ~StoreArea +StreetHouseFront +BasementArea
+LawnArea +StreetHouseFront +LawnArea +Rating  +SaleType, data=train,
family = identity,trControl = boot_10s, tuneLength =5)

Display the summary of the boost raped model

model_fitted
 Random Forest

 712 samples
   6  predictor

 No pre-processing
 Resampling: Bootstrapped (10 reps)

Summary of sample sizes: 712, 712, 712, 712, 712, 712, ...
Resampling results across tuning parameters:
```

```
  mtry  RMSE      Rsquared
   2    40865.52  0.7778754
   4    38474.68  0.7871019
   6    38818.70  0.7819608
   8    39540.90  0.7742633
  10    40130.45  0.7681462

RMSE was used to select the optimal model using the smallest value.
The final value used for the model was mtry = 4.
```

In the bootstrapped case, you can see that the best model is having a R^2 of 79%, which is still higher than the 72% in the previous case but less than the 10-fold cross-validation one. One important thing to note is that the bootstrap samples run again and again for model estimation, but cross-validation maintains exclusivity of subsets in each run.

The probabilistic methods are complex and difficult to understand. It is recommended that only experienced data scientist use them, as an in-depth understanding of the machine learning algorithm is required to set these experiments and interpret them properly. The next chapter on parameter tuning is an extension of the probabilistic techniques that we discussed here.

7.8 The Kappa Error Metric

In recent days, machine learning practitioners are trying a lot of new and complicated error metrics for evaluation as well as model creation. These new error metrics are important, as they solve for some specific business problems/objectives. With high computing power, we can frame our own optimization function and apply the iterative algorithm with data.

Kappa or Cohen's Kappa coefficient is a statistic that measures the relationship between observed accuracy and expected accuracy. Jacob Cohen introduced Kappa in a paper published in the *Journal Educational and Psychological Measurement* in 1960. A similar statistic, called Pi, was proposed by Scott (1955). Cohen's Kappa and Scott's Pi differ in terms of how the expected probability is calculated. This method found the first use case in inter-rater agreements, with different raters rating the same cases in different buckets.

In the machine learning world, the Kappa is adopted to compare a pure random chance with a model. This type of metric is very effective in cases of imbalanced classification. For example, suppose your training data has 80% "Yes" and 20% "No". Without a model, you can still achieve up to 80% accuracy in classification (diagonal) if you simply assign everyone a "Yes".

A more formal definition of Kappa is given here.

Cohen's Kappa measures the agreement between random approach and modeled approach, where each classify *N* items into *C* mutually exclusive categories.

The equation for κ is:

$$k = \frac{p_0 - p_e}{1 - p_e} = 1 - \frac{1 - p_0}{1 - p_e}$$

where *po* is the relative observed agreement among two approaches, and *pe* is the hypothetical probability of a chance overlap, using the observed data to calculate the probabilities of each approach randomly selecting each category. If the approaches are in complete agreement then κ = 1. In rare situations, Kappa can be negative. This is a sign that the two observers agreed less than would be expected just by chance.

For more detailed reading, refer to Fleiss, J. L. (1981) *Statistical Methods for Rates and Proportions*, 2nd ed. (New York: John Wiley) and Banerjee, M.; Capozzoli, Michelle; McSweeney, Laura; Sinha, Debajyoti (1999), "Beyond Kappa: A Review of Interrater Agreement Measures" from *The Canadian Journal of Statistics.*

We will use the purchase prediction data with a very simple model to illustrate the Kappa and accuracy measure. The `caret()` package is used to show this example. This package provides a unified way of training and evaluation of almost 270 different kinds of models. The details of this package are provided in Chapter 8.

```
library(caret)
library(mlbench)
```

```
Below we randomly sample 5000 cases to make the computation faster.
set.seed(917);
train_kappa <-Data_Purchase_Model[sample(nrow(Data_Purchase_
Model),size=5000, replace =TRUE, prob =NULL),]
```

```
train() function confuses between numeric levels, hence convert the
dependent into text i.e., 1->A, 2->B, 3-> C and 4->D
```

```
train_kappa$ProductChoice_multi <-ifelse(train_kappa$ProductChoice ==1,"A",
ifelse(train_kappa$ProductChoice ==2, "B",
ifelse(train_kappa$ProductChoice ==3,"C","D")));

train_kappa <-na.omit(train_kappa)

Set the experiment

cntrl <-trainControl(method="cv", number=5, classProbs =TRUE)

Below the distribution shows that number of cases with each purchase
history

Distribution of ProductChoices

table(train_kappa$ProductChoice_multi)

    A    B    C    D
 1271 1244 1260 1225

Making the column names as legitimate names

colnames(train_kappa) <-make.names(names(train_kappa), unique =TRUE,
allow_ =TRUE)

Convert all the factors into factors in R

train_kappa$ProductChoice_multi <-as.factor(train_kappa$ProductChoice_multi)
train_kappa$CustomerPropensity <-as.factor(train_kappa$CustomerPropensity)
train_kappa$LastPurchaseDuration <-as.factor(train_
kappa$LastPurchaseDuration)

Now, the following code will create a random forest model for our sample
data. Fit the model with method as RandomForest.

model_fitted <-train(ProductChoice_multi ~CustomerPropensity
+LastPurchaseDuration, data=train_kappa, method="rf", metric="Accuracy",
trControl=cntrl)

The result displayed the kappa metrics
```

```
print(model_fitted)
 Random Forest

 5000 samples
    2 predictor
    4 classes: 'A', 'B', 'C', 'D'

 No pre-processing
 Resampling: Cross-Validated (5 fold)
 Summary of sample sizes: 4000, 3999, 4000, 4001, 4000
 Resampling results across tuning parameters:

   mtry  Accuracy   Kappa
    2    0.3288009  0.1036580
   10    0.3274019  0.1024999
   19    0.3268065  0.1017419

Accuracy was used to select the optimal model using the largest value.

The final value used for the model was mtry = 2.
```

Create the predicted values and show that in classification matrix

```
pred <-predict(model_fitted, newdata=train_kappa)
confusionMatrix(data=pred, train_kappa$ProductChoice_multi)
 Confusion Matrix and Statistics

          Reference
Prediction   A   B   C   D
         A 830 653 475 427
         B  97 133 108  85
         C 134 179 304 210
         D 210 279 373 503

Overall Statistics

               Accuracy : 0.354
                 95% CI : (0.3407, 0.3674)
    No Information Rate : 0.2542
    p-Value [Acc > NIR] : < 2.2e-16
```

```
                 Kappa : 0.1377
 Mcnemar's Test P-Value : < 2.2e-16

Statistics by Class:

                     Class: A Class: B Class: C Class: D
Sensitivity            0.6530   0.1069   0.2413   0.4106
Specificity            0.5830   0.9228   0.8602   0.7717
Pos Pred Value         0.3480   0.3144   0.3676   0.3685
Neg Pred Value         0.8314   0.7573   0.7709   0.8014
Prevalence             0.2542   0.2488   0.2520   0.2450
Detection Rate         0.1660   0.0266   0.0608   0.1006
Detection Prevalence   0.4770   0.0846   0.1654   0.2730
Balanced Accuracy      0.6180   0.5149   0.5507   0.5911
```

From an interpretation point of view, the following guidelines can be used:

- Poor agreement when Kappa is 0.20 or less
- Fair agreement when Kappa is 0.20 to 0.40
- Moderate agreement when Kappa is 0.40 to 0.60
- Good agreement when Kappa is 0.60 to 0.80
- Very good agreement when Kappa is 0.80 to 1.00

In this model output, the Kappa value is 0.1377, which implies that there is poor agreement between a random model and our model. Our model results differ from the random model. Now, there can be two possibilities—the model is performing worse than the random model or it is performing exceptionally well. Looking at the accuracy measure—35.4% implies that our model did not do a good job in classification. We need more data and features to get a good model.

7.9 Summary

Model evaluation is a very intricate subject. This chapter just scratched the surface to get you started on the idea of model evaluation. The model evaluation subject brings a lot of depth to the measures we use to evaluate the performance. In this ever-changing analytics landscape, businesses are using models for different purposes, sometimes in custom ways to model a problem to help make business decisions. This trend in industry has given rise to the competitive nature of evaluation measures.

To solve a business problem in a real setting, you have to optimize two different objective functions:

- Statistical measure, the one we discussed in this chapter
- Business constraints, a problem/business specific measures

Let's try to understand these constraints on the model performance by an example. Suppose you have to build a model to classify customers into eight buckets. However, the cost of dealing with each bucket of customer is different. Serving a customer in bucket 8 is 10 times more costly than serving someone from bucket 1. Similar to this is the cost of each bucket varies with the bucket number and with some other factors.

Now if the business decides to use a model to classify the objects into these classes, how will you evaluate the performance of the mode? A pure statistical measure of performance might not fit the situations. How we can think about creating hybrid performance metrics, or a serial dependent matrix? The concept of evaluation is a very deep and fairly involved one. Data scientists have to come up with creative and statistically valid metrics to suit business problems.

This chapter introduced the concept of population stability index, which confirms if we can use use the model for prediction. Then we classified our evaluation metrics into continuous and discrete cases. The continuous metrics discussed were different functions of residuals, i.e., mean absolute error, root mean square error, and R-square. The discrete set of measures included classification rate, sensitivity and specificity, and area under the ROC curve. We used our house price data and purchase prediction data to show evaluation metrics examples.

These evaluation techniques are more suited to statistical learning models. The advanced machine learning models do not have any distribution constraints and cannot be evaluated and interpreted on conventional metrics. We introduced probability methods to evaluate machine learning models, i.e., cross-validation and bootstrap sampling. These two methods form the backbone of machine learning model performance evaluation.

In the end we discussed an important metric for multiclass problems, the Kappa metric. This metric is gaining in popularity as, in classification problems, each misclassification has a different cost associated with it. Hence, we need to measure performance in a relative manner.

The model performance and evaluation techniques are evolving quickly. The performance metrics are becoming multigoal optimization problems and hence are also helping the algorithms adopt new ways to fit data. We will continue with some more advanced topics in the next chapter, where we will introduce the difference between statistical learning and machine learning, including how this difference allows us to do more with the data and then how to go about improving the model performance using ensemble techniques. The next chapter introduces the tradeoff between bias and variance, to help us understand the limits of what can be achieved in performance with given constraints.

CHAPTER 8

Model Performance Improvement

Model performance is a broad term generally used to measure how the model performs on a new dataset, usually a test dataset. The performance metrics also play the role of thresholds to decide whether the model can be put into actual decision making systems or needs improvements. In the previous chapter, we discussed some performance metrics for our continuous and discrete cases. In this chapter, we discuss how changing the modeling process can help us improve model performance on the metrics.

Feature selection plays an important role in modeling development process. It is the features that have information to explain the dependent variable. Data scientists spend a lot of time selecting and creating features for fitting predictive models. The feature engineering process involves selection of a best set of features and their transformations. These sets of features are then fed into a algorithm to quantify the relationships. The algorithm learns from the data and creates a predictive model. Model performance improvement methods are then applied to boost the performance on the error metrics of interest. The higher levels properties of a model, e.g., complexity and speed of learning, also impact the model performance. These high-level parameters are known as hyper-parameters. We will discuss hyper-parameters more in the following sections. Broadly there are two ways to improve the model performance, specifically in machine learning algorithms:

- Add more features and improve the quality of data
- Optimize the hyper-parameters

This first point is what we have been discussing so far in the book. However, we also discussed some algorithms where the learning process is influenced by hyper-parameters, e.g., in decision trees, the depth of the tree, the number of folds in cross-validation, etc. Now these parameters are independent of the features and influence the

K. Ramasubramanian and A. Singh, *Machine Learning Using R*, https://doi.org/10.1007/978-1-4842-4215-5_8

model performance. For instance, you can have two different decision tree models using the same set of predictors but different hyper-parameters to train them. To understand the performance optimization process, we need to understand the tradeoff between bias and variance. Bias refers to the difference between the true and predicted values, while variance refers to the spread around the mean of predicted values. Bias and variance are the two vital components of imprecision/performance in predictive models, and in general there is a tradeoff between them. The tradeoff is nonlinear, which means normally reducing one leads to increasing the other.

This chapter will look at these issues and provide illustrations in R to equip you on how to implement some of the popular performance improvement techniques using R.

The dataset for this chapter is the same as the previous chapter (purchase prediction and house sale price), as we show you how the concepts from this chapter influence the results from previous metrics.

Note The R illustrations in this chapter are computationally heavy, so you are advised to check the machine configuration before running these examples.

While we try to balance out simplicity and completeness in this chapter, we expect the user of these techniques to have good understanding of numerical computing and the machine learning algorithm. References to research papers will be shared for detailed reading on statistical underpinnings.

The learning objectives for this chapter are as follows:

- Machine learning and statistical modeling
- Overview of the Caret package
- Introduction to hyper-parameters
- Hyper-parameter tuning illustrations
- Bias versus variance tradeoffs
- Introduction to ensemble learning
- Advanced methods in ensemble learning
- Advanced topic: Bayesian optimization

8.1 Overview of the Caret Package

The Caret package is one of the most powerful packages in R. This package allows users to explore the machine learning algorithms to their fullest potential. The Caret package (short for classification and regression training) contains functions for complex regression and classification problems. The package has a dedicated Git page and is one of the actively updated and documented packages of R. The Caret package is created and maintained by Max Kuhn from Pfizer.

The Caret package has numerous functions for model development and evaluation metrics for performance measurement. Being a comprehensive package, it can be used for other techniques in sampling and also for sophisticated feature selection processes. There are two of the most important function/tools in the Caret package:

- `trainControl()`
- `train()`

The `trainControl()` function is like a wrapper that defines the rule for model training and the conditions around how sampling and grid search is to be done. The `train()` function is very powerful function that can support 230 types of models available in the Caret package (see Figure 8-1). The primary function/tool, `train()`, can be used for:

- Model evaluation, using cross-validation, resampling, and other conventional metrics. It also can be used to measure the effect of tuning parameters in performance.
- Model selection by choosing the best model based on optimal parameters, so multiple metrics can be calculated to choose the final model.
- Model estimation using any of the 230 types of models listed in the train model list with default parameters or tuned ones.

By default, the function automatically chooses the tuning parameters associated with the best value, although different algorithms can be used to tune the parameters (Source: `http://topepo.github.io/caret/model-training-and-tuning.html`).

```
Define sets of model parameter values to evaluate
for each parameter set do
    for each resampling iteration do
        Hold–out specific samples
        [Optional] Pre–process the data
        Fit the model on the remainder
        Predict the hold–out samples
    end
    Calculate the average performance across hold–out predictions
end
Determine the optimal parameter set
Fit the final model to all the training data using the optimal parameter set
```

Figure 8-1. *The train() function algorithm in the Caret package*

In general, the basic use of the Caret package includes first defining `trainControl()` and then calling the `train()` function. Here we show the generic syntax of calling these two functions in order to use the Caret functionality.

Others are available, such as repeated K-fold cross-validation, leave-one-out, etc. The function train control can be used to specify the type of resampling. By default, a simple bootstrap resampling is used:

```
rfControl <-trainControl(# Example, 10-fold Cross Validation
method ="repeatedcv",    # Others are available, such as repeated K-fold
cross-validation, leave-one-out etc
number =10,              # Number of folds
repeats =10# repeated ten times
                              )
```

The first two arguments to train are the predictor and outcome data objects, respectively. The third argument, `method`, specifies the type of model (see train model list or train models by tag). Here is an example that fits a `randomForest` model via the `randomForest` package, which was tested with 10-fold cross-validation:

```
set.seed(917)
randomForectFit1 <-train(Class ~.,   # Define the model equation
data = training,                     # Define the modeling data
method ="rf",                        # List the model you want to use,
                                       caret provide list of options in
                                       train Model list
```

```
trControl = rfControl,           # This defines the conditions on how
                                   to control the training
                 ... )            # Other options specific to the
                                   modeling technique
randomForectFit1
```

More information about `trainControl` is given in a later section. Details can be found at `http://topepo.github.io/caret/model-training-and-tuning.html`.

As this is the core package in R, it deals with almost all of the machine learning techniques. Therefore, it's important to keep in mind its functionality.

Note In this chapter we will not be using the full dataset. The illustrations will be on smaller set of data to make sure you can replicate the results on less powerful machines.

8.2 Introduction to Hyper-Parameters

In machine learning, we deal with two kind of parameters, ones that are the standard model parameters and ones that are the hyper-parameters. The core difference between these two types of parameters is that model parameters can be directly learned from the underlying data and hyper-parameters cannot. The machine learning model training process is used to learn the data and then fit the model parameters.

However, the hyper-parameters are not directly learned from the data and are actually very influential in model performance. Hyper-parameters explain the "higher-level" properties of the model such as its complexity, how fast it should learn, and how much depth it should go into. Another important thing is that hyper-parameters are fixed before training starts, hence, the model standard parameters are learned. We can say that hyper-parameters decide the rules of model training by which model standard parameters are estimated.

Now, how are the hyper-parameter decided? What influences the hyper-parameter selection process? This area is summed up as *hyper-parameter optimization* and will be touched upon at a high level in an upcoming section.

Another way to look at hyper-parameters is as a prerequisite for a Bayesian approach to statistical learning, which involves finding the probability distribution of the model parameters given a training dataset. For instance, an artificial network training will require four preset hyper-parameters for learning from the data: selection of the model type with algorithm, selection of the architecture of the network, assignment of training parameters, and learning the model parameters. Generally, we can divide the hyper-parameters into four decision points before we train the model with data:

- *Model type:* Decide what type of model you choose in machine learning, like feed-forward or recurrent neural network, support vector machine, linear regression, etc.
- *Architecture:* Once you decide the model type, you give inputs on what the boundaries of the model learning process are, i.e., number of hidden layers, number of nodes per hidden layer, batch normalization and pooling layer, etc.
- *Training-parameter:* Once you decide on the model type and architecture, you decide how the model should learn, i.e., learning and momentum rate, batch size, etc. These parameters are sometimes called training parameters.
- *Model parameter:* Once you provide these inputs, the model training process starts and the model parameters are estimated, such as weights and biases in a neural network.

Some examples of hyper-parameters are:

- Depth of trees or number of leaves
- Latent factors in a matrix factorization
- Learning rate (in neural network based methods)
- Hidden layers in a deep neural network
- Number of clusters in a k-means clustering

To illustrate the effect of hyper-parameters on the model performance, we will create an example with different hyper-parameters and check the performance of the model. For this example, we will use a subset of the purchase prediction data.

In the following example, we are creating two random forest models with the same underlying data and the same predictor variables, but with two different values for the hyper-parameter (the number of trees):

- ntree = 20
- ntree = 50

Here are the accuracy results for both cases:

```
setwd("C:/Personal/Machine Learning/Run Chap 8");
library(caret)
library(randomForest)
set.seed(917);
# Load Dataset
Purchase_Data <-read.csv("Purchase Prediction Dataset.csv",header=TRUE)

#Remove the missing values
data <-na.omit(Purchase_Data)

#Pick a sample of records
Data <-data[sample(nrow(data),size=10000),]
```

- Model 1: with tree size = 20

Here are the results for the algorithm using 20 trees in the random forest algorithm.

```
fit_20 <-randomForest(factor(ProductChoice) ~MembershipPoints +CustomerAge
+PurchaseTenure +CustomerPropensity +LastPurchaseDuration,
data=Data,
importance=TRUE,
ntree=20)
#Print the result for  ntree=20
print(fit_20)
```

Here are the results for the algorithm using 20 trees in the random forest algorithm.

```
Call:
 randomForest(formula = factor(ProductChoice) ~ MembershipPoints
 +      CustomerAge + PurchaseTenure + CustomerPropensity
 + LastPurchaseDuration,  data = Data, importance = TRUE, ntree = 20)
               Type of random forest: classification
                     Number of trees: 20
No. of variables tried at each split: 2

        OOB estimate of  error rate: 64.27%
Confusion matrix:
    1    2    3   4 class.error
1 550 1035  495 104   0.7481685
2 730 1927 1051 199   0.5067827
3 449 1300 1005 165   0.6557040
4 149  450  300  91   0.9080808
```

- Model 1 with tree size = 50

Here are the results for the algorithm using 50 trees in the random forest algorithm.

```
fit_50 <-randomForest(factor(ProductChoice) ~MembershipPoints +CustomerAge
+PurchaseTenure +CustomerPropensity +LastPurchaseDuration,
data=Data,
importance=TRUE,
ntree=50)
#Print the result for  ntree=50
print(fit_50)
```

```
Call:
 randomForest(formula = factor(ProductChoice) ~ MembershipPoints
 +      CustomerAge + PurchaseTenure + CustomerPropensity
 + LastPurchaseDuration,   data = Data, importance = TRUE, ntree = 50)
               Type of random forest: classification
                     Number of trees: 50
No. of variables tried at each split: 2
```

```
        OOB estimate of  error rate: 63.35%
Confusion matrix:
    1    2    3   4 class.error
1 502 1153  472  57   0.7701465
2 712 2065  994 136   0.4714615
3 427 1329 1029 134   0.6474820
4 147  467  307  69   0.9303030
```

We can see by just changing the hyper-parameters that the results are different. The overall error rate in ntree=50 has come down to 63.35% from 64.27%. Among the classification in each class, the classification rate of classes 1 and 4 improved by approx. 3% while from classes 2 and 3, it decreased. Now the next important question to answer is what is the most cost- and time-effective way to find an optimal value of the hyper-parameters.

8.3 Hyper-Parameter Optimization

In machine learning, hyper-parameter optimization or model selection is the process of choosing a set of hyper-parameters for a machine learning algorithm. The set of hyper-parameters that maximize the model performance are then chosen for actual model training and testing. Cross-validation is generally used for measuring the performance of the model in terms of cross-validation error rate or some other user-defined method, e.g., bootstrap error, leave-one-out, etc.

In short, learning algorithms learn model parameters that model/fit the input data well, while hyper-parameter optimization is to ensure the model does not overfit its data by tuning, e.g., regularization. There are multiple algorithms suggested to optimize the hyper-parameters of any algorithm. There are multiple popular packages and paid services also available to optimize the parameters. Most of them are based on some or another variation of the Bayesian approach. We will illustrate the parameter tuning by different methods on the same model. This will help you get a comparative understanding of how the results change and what can be influencing them.

The most popular methods are listed here, with some context. We are not providing any direct comparison of these methods as the selection of method is influenced by many factors, including but not limited to type of model, computation power, time-space complexity, etc.

- *Manual search:* Create a set of parameters using best judgment/experience and test them on the model. Choose the one that works best for the model performance.
- *Manual grid search*: Create an equally spaced grid or custom grid of a combination of hyper-parameters. Evaluate the mode on each grid point and choose the ones with the best model performance.
- *Automatic grid search*: Let the program decide a grid for you and do the search in that space for the best hyper-parameters.
- *Optimal search*: In this method we generally don't freeze the grid beforehand, but allow the machine to expand the grid as and when needed.
- *Random search*: In general, choosing some random points in the hyper-parameter search space works faster and better. Although this saves a lot of spatial and time cost, it might not always give you the best/optimal set of hyper-parameters.
- *Custom search*: Users can define their own functions and guide the algorithm on how to find the best set of hyper-parameters.

Note Most of these parameter tuning/optimization techniques are search problems in high dimensional space. The searching is done on an iterative and guided basis, mostly numerical only. The following sections illustrate the popular optimization methods.

8.3.1 Manual Search

The details of the model for manual search optimization are discussed in this section.

Response Variable: `ProductChoice`

Predictors: `MembershipPoints`, `CustomerAge`, `PurchaseTenure`, `CustomerPropensity`, and `LastPurchaseDuration`

Error Calculation: Cross-Validation

Model Type: Random forest

```
# Manually search parameters
library(data.table)
# load the packages
library(randomForest)
library(mlbench)
library(caret)
# Load Dataset

dataset <-Data
metric <- "Accuracy"
```

Here, we set the `trainControl` function with the `method="repeatedCV"`, meaning use repeated cross-validation, and search `method = "grid"`, meaning search in the grid defined by `tunegrid`.

```
# Manual Search
trainControl <-trainControl(method="repeatedcv", number=10, repeats=3,
search="grid")
tunegrid <-expand.grid(.mtry=c(sqrt(ncol(dataset)-2)))
modellist <-list()
```

Here, we set the `train` function with `method="rf"`, meaning use the random forest algorithm to fit the model and the number of trees as `ntree` from the loop variables.

```
for (ntree in c(100, 150, 200, 250)) {
set.seed(917);
    fit <-train(factor(ProductChoice) ~MembershipPoints +CustomerAge
+PurchaseTenure +CustomerPropensity +LastPurchaseDuration, data=dataset,
method="rf", metric=metric, tuneGrid=tunegrid, trControl=trainControl,
ntree=ntree)
    key <-toString(ntree)
    modellist[[key]] <-fit
}
# compare results by resampling
results <-resamples(modellist)
#Summary of Results
summary(results)
```

```
Call:
summary.resamples(object = results)

Models: 100, 150, 200, 250
Number of resamples: 30

Accuracy
      Min. 1st Qu. Median   Mean 3rd Qu.   Max. NA's
100 0.3880  0.3990 0.4107 0.4081  0.4134 0.4364    0
150 0.3890  0.3996 0.4117 0.4094  0.4147 0.4390    0
200 0.3864  0.3974 0.4095 0.4081  0.4139 0.4360    0
250 0.3884  0.4013 0.4097 0.4090  0.4167 0.4390    0

Kappa
       Min. 1st Qu.  Median    Mean 3rd Qu.   Max. NA's
100 0.04385 0.06549 0.08044 0.07803 0.08661 0.1209    0
150 0.05301 0.06481 0.08014 0.07977 0.08831 0.1235    0
200 0.04243 0.06214 0.07847 0.07757 0.08953 0.1196    0
250 0.04427 0.06311 0.08145 0.07873 0.08884 0.1244    0
```

```
#Dot Plot of results
dotplot(results)
```

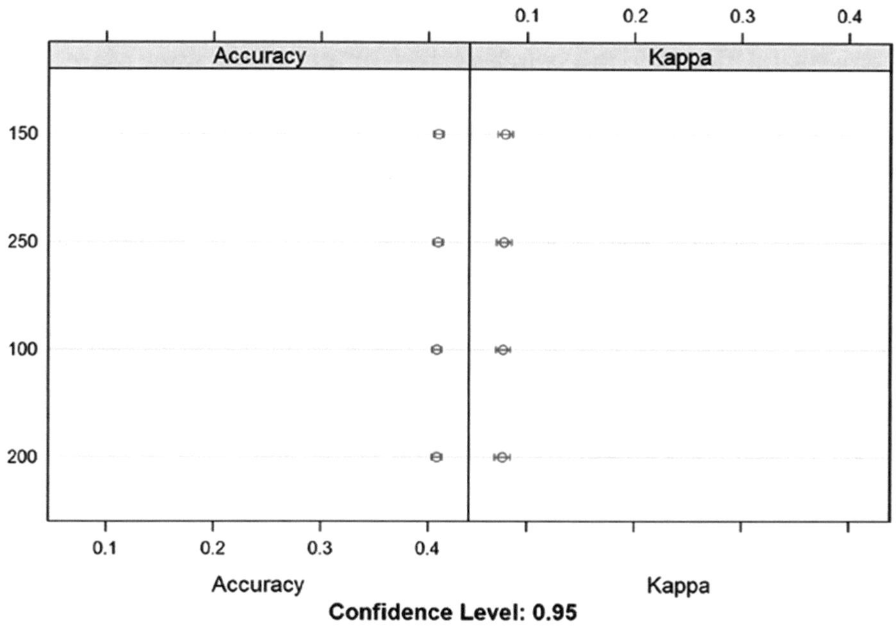

Figure 8-2. *Performance plot accuracy metrics*

You can see in Figure 8-2 that the accuracy doesn't vary much between the different parameter values. This can mean that our search is not comprehensive or the model is able to learn most of the features of data in less than the 100-tree random forest model. Also, the independent variables list should be increased.

8.3.2 Manual Grid Search

The details of the model for manual grid search optimization are discussed in this section.

Response Variable: `ProductChoice`

Predictors: `MembershipPoints`, `CustomerAge`, `PurchaseTenure`, `CustomerPropensity`, and `LastPurchaseDuration`

Error Calculation: Cross-Validation

Model Type: Learning Vector Quantization (LVQ)

```
# Tune algorithm parameters using a manual grid search.
seed <-917;
dataset <-Data
```

Here, we set the trainControl function with method="repeatedCV", meaning use repeated cross-validation, and the search method = "grid", meaning search in the grid defined by grid.

```
# prepare training scheme
control <-trainControl(method="repeatedcv", number=10, repeats=3)
# design the parameter tuning grid
grid <-expand.grid(size=c(5,10,20,50), k=c(1,2,3,4,5))
# train the model
model <-train(factor(ProductChoice) ~MembershipPoints +CustomerAge
+PurchaseTenure +CustomerPropensity +LastPurchaseDuration, data=dataset,
method="lvq", trControl=control, tuneGrid=grid)

# summarize the model

print(model)
 Learning Vector Quantization

 10000 samples
     5 predictor
     4 classes: '1', '2', '3', '4'

 No pre-processing
 Resampling: Cross-Validated (10 fold, repeated 3 times)
 Summary of sample sizes: 9001, 9000, 9000, 9001, 8999, 9000, ...
 Resampling results across tuning parameters:

   size  k  Accuracy   Kappa
    5    1  0.3403649  0.01508857
    5    2  0.3443983  0.02464750
    5    3  0.3582986  0.03118553
    5    4  0.3556306  0.02933887
    5    5  0.3510002  0.03342766
   10    1  0.3375292  0.02790863
   10    2  0.3387723  0.03024152
   10    3  0.3398577  0.03016096
   10    4  0.3484939  0.04030847
   10    5  0.3457038  0.04743415
```

```
  20     1  0.3403710  0.04013057
  20     2  0.3321322  0.02956459
  20     3  0.3380415  0.03934963
  20     4  0.3422641  0.04213952
  20     5  0.3449026  0.04611466
  50     1  0.3353654  0.03588394
  50     2  0.3358704  0.03255331
  50     3  0.3428662  0.04369310
  50     4  0.3421693  0.04713980
  50     5  0.3437377  0.04756819

Accuracy was used to select the optimal model using  the largest value.
The final values used for the model were size = 5 and k = 3.
```

```
# plot the effect of parameters on accuracy
plot(model)
```

The tuning algorithm shows the best tuning parameters. Figure 8-3 also shows the top line peaking on the accuracy plot, which corresponds to the best model.

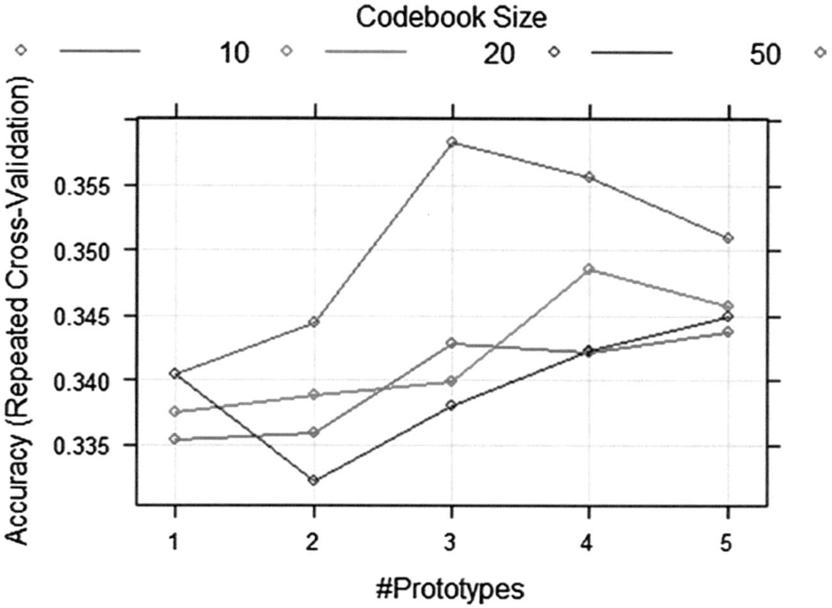

***Figure 8-3.** Accuracy across cross-validated samples*

8.3.3 Automatic Grid Search

The details of the model for automatic grid search optimization are discussed in this section.

> *Response Variable*: `ProductChoice`
>
> *Predictors*: `MembershipPoints`, `CustomerAge`, `PurchaseTenure`, `CustomerPropensity`, and `LastPurchaseDuration`
>
> *Error Calculation*: Cross-Validation
>
> *Model Type:* Learning Vector Quantization (LVQ)

```
# Tune algorithm parameters using an automatic grid search.
set.seed(917);
dataset <-Data
```

Here, we set the `trainControl` function with `method="repeatedCV"`, meaning use repeated cross-validation and the search method being `default`, i.e., an automatic grid search.

```
# prepare training scheme
control <-trainControl(method="repeatedcv", number=10, repeats=3)
# train the model
model <-train(factor(ProductChoice) ~MembershipPoints +CustomerAge
+PurchaseTenure +CustomerPropensity +LastPurchaseDuration, data=dataset,
method="lvq", trControl=control, tuneLength=5)
# summarize the model
```

```
print(model)
 Learning Vector Quantization

 10000 samples
     5 predictor
     4 classes: '1', '2', '3', '4'
```

```
No pre-processing
Resampling: Cross-Validated (10 fold, repeated 3 times)
Summary of sample sizes: 9000, 8999, 9001, 9001, 9000, 9000, ...
Resampling results across tuning parameters:

  size  k   Accuracy   Kappa
  11     1  0.3402322  0.03666635
  11     6  0.3402335  0.03518447
  11    11  0.3394009  0.04093310
  11    16  0.3499678  0.04415707
  11    21  0.3444298  0.04208990
  13     1  0.3379881  0.03523337
  13     6  0.3459702  0.04826571
  13    11  0.3464008  0.05010497
  13    16  0.3467346  0.05055072
  13    21  0.3497683  0.05600358
  16     1  0.3313684  0.03813657
  16     6  0.3460655  0.05013518
  16    11  0.3417672  0.04646887
  16    16  0.3502685  0.04977277
  16    21  0.3456003  0.04755585
  19     1  0.3299696  0.03229510
  19     6  0.3392352  0.04576555
  19    11  0.3361026  0.03859754
  19    16  0.3479016  0.05067015
  19    21  0.3451598  0.04997000
  22     1  0.3365661  0.03454596
  22     6  0.3459982  0.04399154
  22    11  0.3441293  0.04592163
  22    16  0.3506335  0.05187679
  22    21  0.3512329  0.05437707

Accuracy was used to select the optimal model using  the largest value.
The final values used for the model were size = 22 and k = 21.
```

```
# plot the effect of parameters on accuracy
plot(model)
```

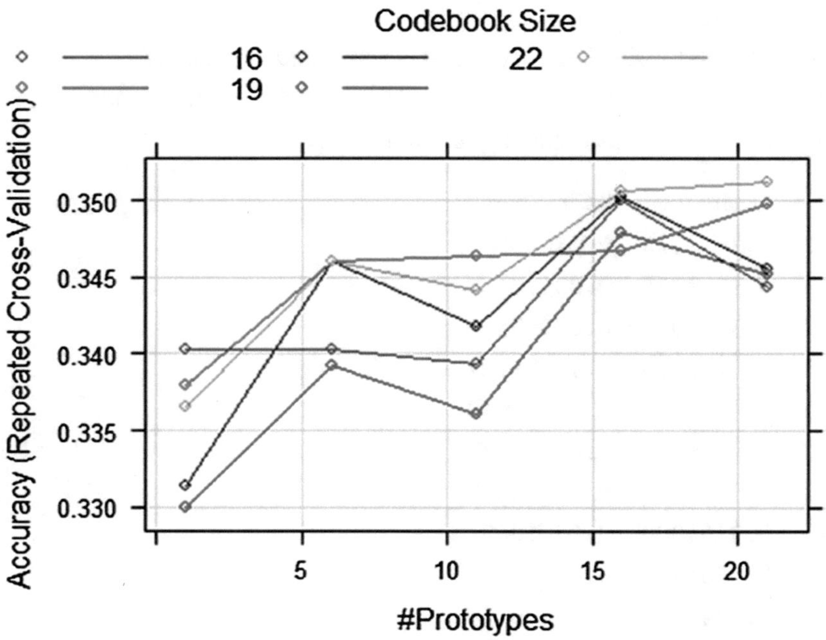

Figure 8-4. *Accuracy across cross-validated samples for an automatic grid search*

The automatic grid search optimization in Figure 8-4 shows the best model would be with parameters of size=22 and k= 21, which corresponds to an accuracy of 0.3512. This differs from our manual grid search, where the optimal parameters were size= 5 and k=3, with an accuracy of 0.3581.

8.3.4 Optimal Search

The details of the model for optimal search optimization are discussed in this section.

Response Variable: `ProductChoice`

Predictors: `MembershipPoints`, `CustomerAge`, `PurchaseTenure`, `CustomerPropensity`, and `LastPurchaseDuration`

Error Calculation: Cross-Validation

Model Type: Recursive Partitioning and Regression Trees

Observe the following three expand.grids we used for the tuneGrid parameter in the train function.

- *Manual search:* expand.grid(.mtry=c(sqrt(ncol(dataset)-2)))
- *Manual grid search:* expand.grid(size=c(5,10,20,50), k=c(1,2,3,4,5))
- *Optimal search:* expand.grid(.cp=seq(0,0.1,by=0.01))

In the optimal search, the parameters to expand.grid are more granular, which means the algorithm will be able to converge to a global optimum much better than the others. For example, by modifying the by = 0.01 in the seq function to have more decimal places, you can further increase the granularity. However, keep in mind that increasing the granularity will take computational effort.

```
# Select the best tuning configuration
dataset <-Data
```

Here, we set the trainControl function with the method="repeatedCV", meaning use repeated cross-validation, and parameter tuning is done on tunegrid.

```
# prepare training scheme
control <-trainControl(method="repeatedcv", number=10, repeats=3)
# CART
set.seed(917);
tunegrid <-expand.grid(.cp=seq(0,0.1,by=0.01))
fit.cart <-train(factor(ProductChoice) ~MembershipPoints +CustomerAge
+PurchaseTenure +CustomerPropensity +LastPurchaseDuration, data=dataset,
method="rpart", metric="Accuracy", tuneGrid=tunegrid, trControl=control)
 Loading required package: rpart

fit.cart

 CART

 10000 samples
     5 predictor
     4 classes: '1', '2', '3', '4'
```

```
No pre-processing
Resampling: Cross-Validated (10 fold, repeated 3 times)
Summary of sample sizes: 9000, 8999, 9001, 9001, 9000, 9000, ...
Resampling results across tuning parameters:

  cp    Accuracy   Kappa
  0.00  0.3557312  0.05943192
  0.01  0.4014336  0.04179296
  0.02  0.3966989  0.02481739
  0.03  0.3907000  0.00000000
  0.04  0.3907000  0.00000000
  0.05  0.3907000  0.00000000
  0.06  0.3907000  0.00000000
  0.07  0.3907000  0.00000000
  0.08  0.3907000  0.00000000
  0.09  0.3907000  0.00000000
  0.10  0.3907000  0.00000000

Accuracy was used to select the optimal model using  the largest value.
The final value used for the model was cp = 0.01.
# display the best configuration
print(fit.cart$bestTune)

    cp
2 0.01

plot(fit.cart)
```

The plot in Figure 8-5 clearly shows the peak of accuracy is at a cp value equal to 0.1, which corresponds to an accuracy of 0.41, which is higher than our previous optimized models. Also observe our model in this case is Recursive Partitioning and Regression Trees.

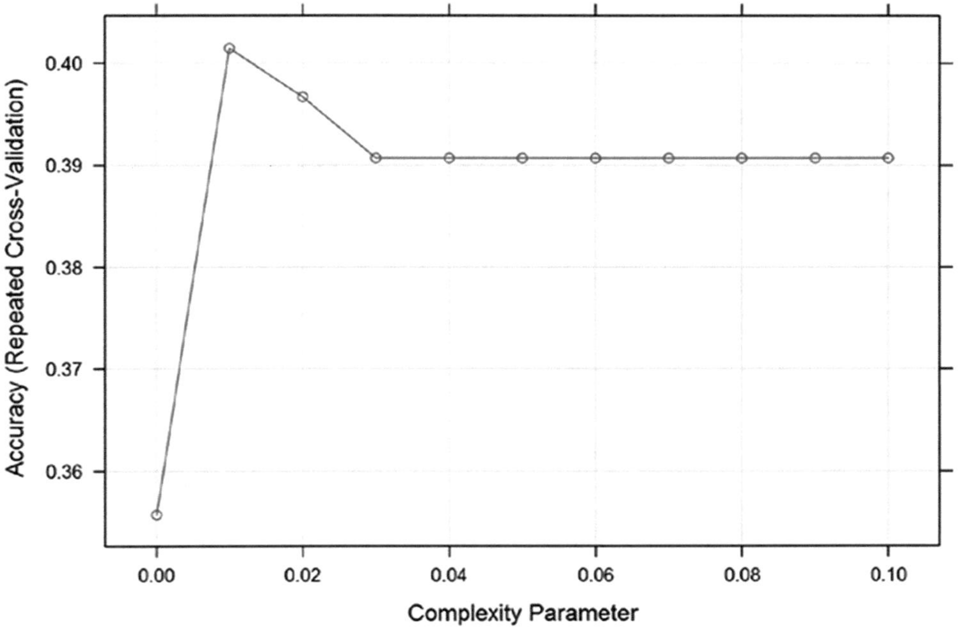

Figure 8-5. *Accuracy across cross-validated samples and complexity parameters*

8.3.5 Random Search

The details of the model for random search optimization are discussed in this section.

Response Variable: `ProductChoice`

Predictors: `MembershipPoints`, `CustomerAge`, `PurchaseTenure`, `CustomerPropensity`, and `LastPurchaseDuration`

Error Calculation: Cross-Validation

Model Type: Random forest

```
# Randomly search algorithm parameters

# Select the best tuning configuration
dataset <-Data
```

Here, we set the trainControl function with method="repeatedCV", meaning use repeated cross-validation, and the predictor search set to random.

```
# prepare training scheme
control <-trainControl(method="repeatedcv", number=10, repeats=3,
search="random")
# train the model
model <-train(factor(ProductChoice) ~MembershipPoints +CustomerAge
+PurchaseTenure +CustomerPropensity +LastPurchaseDuration, data=dataset,
method="rf", trControl=control)
# summarize the model
print(model)
```

```
Random Forest

10000 samples
    5 predictor
    4 classes: '1', '2', '3', '4'

No pre-processing
Resampling: Cross-Validated (10 fold, repeated 3 times)
Summary of sample sizes: 9000, 9000, 9002, 9000, 9000, 8999, ...
Resampling results across tuning parameters:

  mtry  Accuracy   Kappa
  3     0.4091006  0.07772332
  4     0.3863345  0.08039752
  6     0.3640687  0.06873901

Accuracy was used to select the optimal model using  the largest value.
The final value used for the model was mtry = 3.
```

```
# plot the effect of parameters on accuracy
plot(model)
```

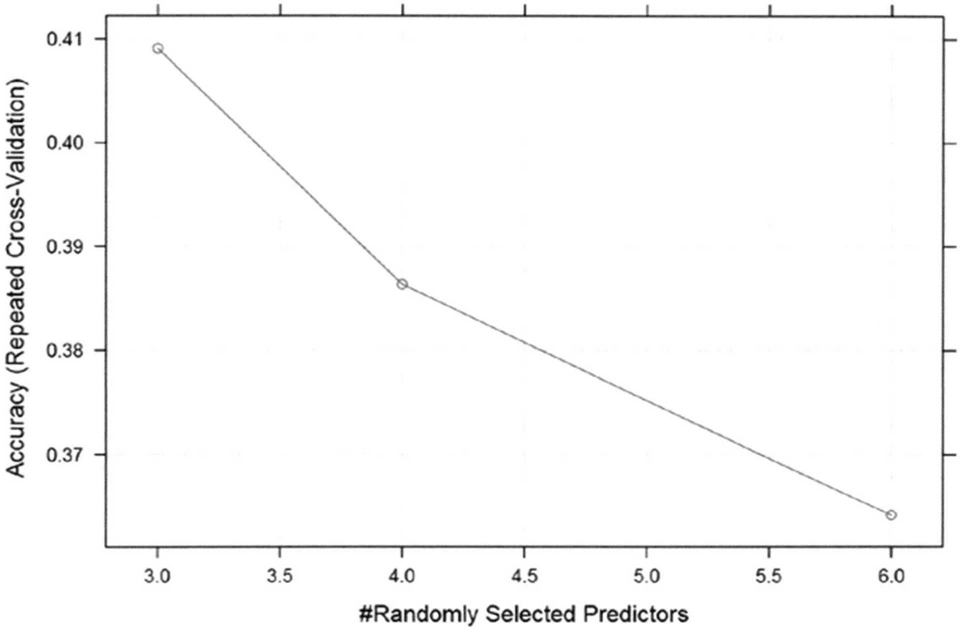

Figure 8-6. *Accuracy across cross-validated sets and randomly selected predictors*

Random search algorithms are usually faster and more efficient in tuning. In this case, the plot in Figure 8-6 shows that the algorithm was able to optimize the problem with fewer iterations. The random forest model is used in this example. Random forests are optimized quickly with random search. This saves a lot of time in tuning random forest models.

8.3.6 Custom Searching

Custom search algorithms provide advanced ways of guiding the algorithm to optimize tuning parameters. Advanced users of machine learning can create their own search algorithms to optimize hyper-parameters. In this example, we show one such search optimization.

> *Response Variable:* `ProductChoice`
>
> *Predictors:* `MembershipPoints`, `CustomerAge`, `PurchaseTenure`, `CustomerPropensity`, and `LastPurchaseDuration`
>
> *Error Calculation:* Cross-Validation
>
> *Model Type:* Custom random forest

```
setwd("C:/Personal/Machine Learning/Chapter 8/");
library(caret)
library(randomForest)
library(class)
# Load Dataset
Purchase_Data <-read.csv("Purchase Prediction Dataset.csv",header=TRUE)

data <-na.omit(Purchase_Data)

#Create a sample of 10K records
set.seed(917);
Data <-data[sample(nrow(data),size=10000),]
# Select the best tuning configuration
dataset <-Data

# Customer Parameter Search

# load the packages
library(randomForest)
library(mlbench)
library(caret)
```

In this example, we have come up with a custom function for evaluation. The algorithm of randomForest is inherited for a classification problem. This is an advanced way of creating your own search functions.

```
# define the custom caret algorithm (wrapper for Random Forest)
customRF <-list(type="Classification", library="randomForest", loop=NULL)
customRF$parameters <-data.frame(parameter=c("mtry", "ntree"),
class=rep("numeric", 2), label=c("mtry", "ntree"))
customRF$grid <-function(x, y, len=NULL, search="grid") {}
customRF$fit <-function(x, y, wts, param, lev, last, weights, classProbs, ...) {
randomForest(x, y, mtry=param$mtry, ntree=param$ntree, ...)
}
customRF$predict <-function(modelFit, newdata, preProc=NULL, submodels=NULL)
{  predict(modelFit, newdata)}
```

```
customRF$prob <-function(modelFit, newdata, preProc=NULL, submodels=NULL)
{   predict(modelFit, newdata, type ="prob")}
customRF$sort <-function(x){ x[order(x[,1]),]}
customRF$levels <-function(x) {x$classes}

# Load Dataset

dataset <-Data

metric <- "Accuracy"

# train model
trainControl <-trainControl(method="repeatedcv", number=10, repeats=3)
tunegrid <-expand.grid(.mtry=c(1:4), .ntree=c(100, 150, 200, 250))
set.seed(917)
custom <-train(factor(ProductChoice) ~MembershipPoints +CustomerAge
+PurchaseTenure +CustomerPropensity +LastPurchaseDuration, data=dataset,
method=customRF, metric=metric, tuneGrid=tunegrid, trControl=trainControl)
print(custom)

 10000 samples
     5 predictor
     4 classes: '1', '2', '3', '4'

 No pre-processing
 Resampling: Cross-Validated (10 fold, repeated 3 times)
 Summary of sample sizes: 9000, 8999, 9001, 9001, 9000, 9000, ...
 Resampling results across tuning parameters:

   mtry  ntree  Accuracy   Kappa
   1     100    0.4091336  0.05088226
   1     150    0.4078343  0.04944209
   1     200    0.4082998  0.04973571
   1     250    0.4076663  0.04861050
   2     100    0.4141003  0.07256969
   2     150    0.4145340  0.07306897
   2     200    0.4142334  0.07232983
   2     250    0.4144336  0.07289516
   3     100    0.4090333  0.07980804
```

```
  3      150     0.4081328  0.07744357
  3      200     0.4079661  0.07782225
  3      250     0.4086323  0.07818017
  4      100     0.3797990  0.07244785
  4      150     0.3804304  0.07231228
  4      200     0.3826303  0.07566550
  4      250     0.3838646  0.07796204

 Accuracy was used to select the optimal model using  the largest value.
 The final values used for the model were mtry = 2 and ntree = 150.
```

```
plot(custom)
```

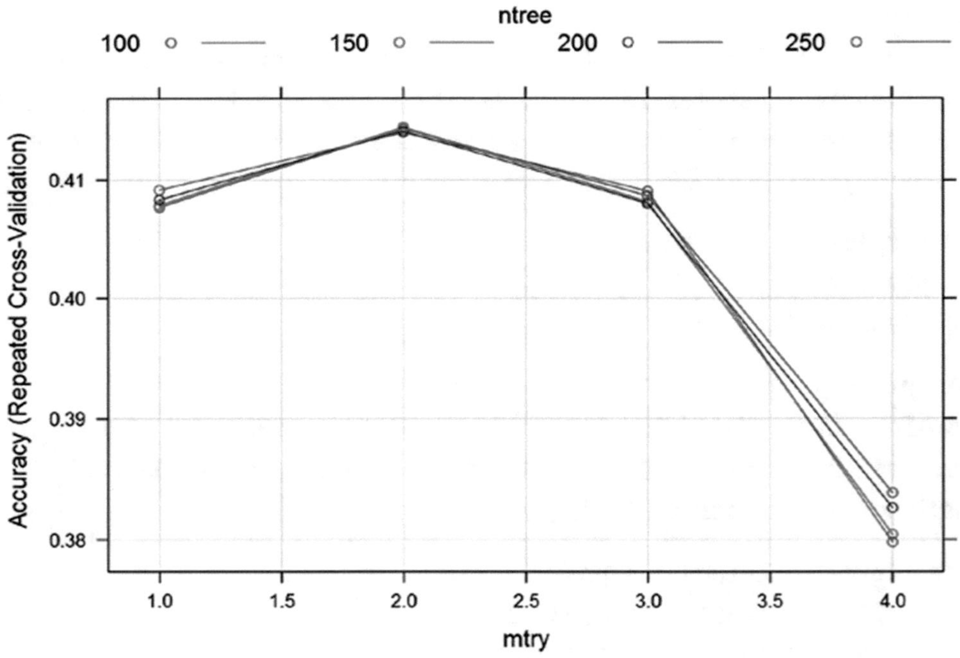

***Figure 8-7.** Accuracy across cross-validated samples and parameter mtry*

Custom search optimization gives us the highest accuracy of 0.415 so far. For this problem this seems to be the best accuracy. Again, to emphasize, we were using the same data and the same variable and saw how performance kept on varying. The next section discusses a very important concept in model performance, bias, and variance.

8.4 The Bias and Variance Tradeoff

The errors in any machine learning algorithm can be attributed to bias, variance, and an irreducible error. The tradeoff or dilemma of bias and variance is the problem of minimizing bias and variance simultaneously in any machine learning algorithm. In general, reducing one tends to increase the other.

In performance measurement, we say bias causes underfitting, while variance causes overfitting. Figure 8-8 shows a very good graphical representation, provided by Scott Fortmann-Roe, in his blog using a bull's eye diagram.

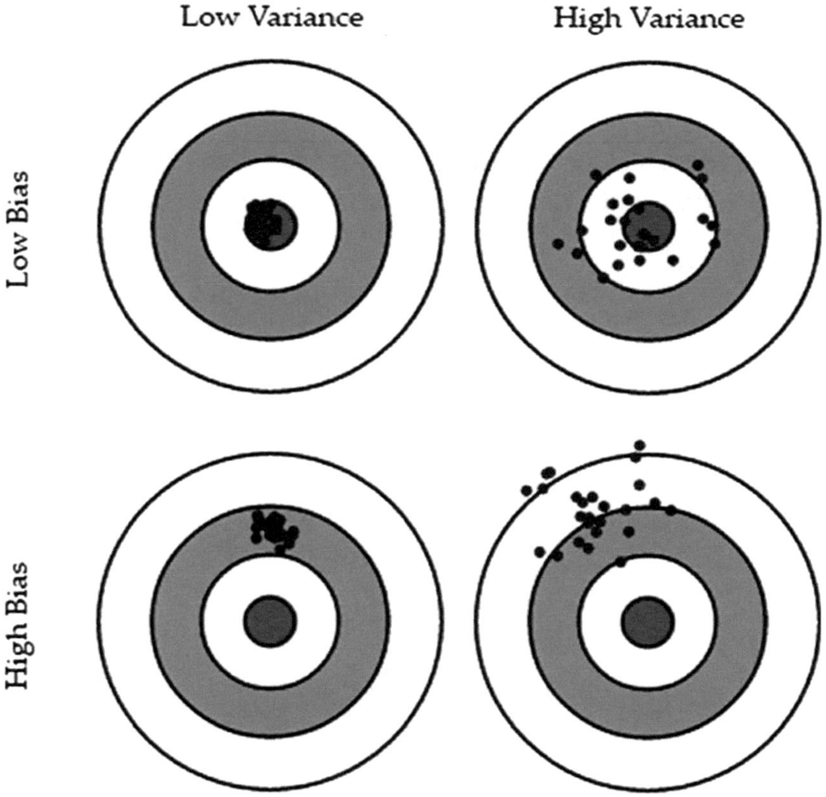

Figure 8-8. *Bias and variance Illustration using the bull's eye plot*

Fortmann further provides a conceptual definition of errors due to bias and variance. Looking at the image in Figure 8-8, it becomes easy to visualize how errors due to bias and variance impact results. The simple definition is provided by Fortmann-Roe:

- *Error due to bias:* The error due to bias is taken as the difference between the expected (or average) prediction of our model and the correct value that we are trying to predict.
- *Error due to variance:* The error due to variance is taken as the variability of a model prediction for a given data point. Again, imagine that you can repeat the entire model building process multiple times. The variance is how much the predictions for a given point vary between different realizations of the model (Source: `http://scott.fortmann-roe.com/docs/BiasVariance.html`).

The breaking of generalization errors in machine learning algorithms is called bias-variance decomposition, and it reduces the errors into three components:

- *Square of bias*
- *Variance*
- *Irreducible error*

Mathematically, the decomposed equation looks like this:

$$\mathrm{E}\left[\left(y-\hat{f}(x)\right)^2\right]=\mathrm{Bias}\left[\hat{f}(x)\right]^2+\mathrm{Var}\left[\hat{f}(x)\right]+\sigma^2$$

where

$$\mathrm{Bias}\left[\hat{f}(x)\right]=\mathrm{E}\left[\hat{f}(x)-f(x)\right]$$

and

$$\mathrm{Var}\left[\hat{f}(x)\right]=\mathrm{E}\left[\hat{f}(x)^2\right]-\mathrm{E}\left[\hat{f}(x)\right]^2$$

The derivation of this equation is also easy and can be done for generalized cases, as follows.

For any random variable, variance is defined as

$$\mathrm{Var}[X] = \mathrm{E}\left[X^2\right] - \mathrm{E}[X]^2$$

Equivalently

$$\mathrm{E}\left[X^2\right] = \mathrm{Var}[X] + \mathrm{E}[X]^2$$

assume, $f = f(x)$ and $\hat{f} = \hat{f}(x)$, as f is deterministic.

$$\mathrm{E}[f] = f$$

Hence,

$$y = f + \epsilon \text{ and } \mathrm{E}[\epsilon] = 0$$

imply

$$\mathrm{E}[y] = \mathrm{E}[f + \epsilon] = \mathrm{E}[f] = f.$$

Also,

$$\mathrm{Var}[\epsilon] = \sigma^2$$

Hence,

$$\mathrm{Var}[y] = \mathrm{E}\left[(y - \mathrm{E}[y])^2\right] = \mathrm{E}[(y-f)^2] = \mathrm{E}[(f + \epsilon - f)^2] = \mathrm{E}[\epsilon^2] = \mathrm{Var}[\epsilon] + \mathrm{E}\left[\epsilon\right]^2 = \sigma^2$$

Since, ϵ and $\hat{f}$ are independent, we have

$$\begin{aligned}
\mathrm{E}\left[\left(y - \hat{f}\right)^2\right] &= \mathrm{E}\left[y^2 + \hat{f}^2 - 2y\hat{f}\right] \\
&= \mathrm{E}\left[y^2\right] + \mathrm{E}\left[\hat{f}^2\right] - \mathrm{E}\left[2y\hat{f}\right] \\
&= \mathrm{Var}[y] + \mathrm{E}[y]^2 + \mathrm{Var}\left[\hat{f}\right] + \mathrm{E}\left[\hat{f}\right]^2 - 2f\mathrm{E}\left[\hat{f}\right] \\
&= \mathrm{Var}[y] + \mathrm{Var}\left[\hat{f}\right] + \left(f - \mathrm{E}\left[\hat{f}\right]\right)^2 \\
&= \mathrm{Var}[y] + \mathrm{Var}\left[\hat{f}\right] + \mathrm{E}\left[f - \hat{f}\right]^2 \\
&= \sigma^2 + \mathrm{Var}\left[\hat{f}\right] + \mathrm{Bias}\left[\hat{f}\right]^2
\end{aligned}$$

The irreducible error is the noise term in the true relationship that cannot fundamentally be reduced by any model. This derivation in the linear regression setup is explained in "Notes on Derivation of Bias-Variance Decomposition in Linear Regression," by Shakhnarovich, Greg (2011). A similar decomposition is possible in other machine learning algorithms.

Further, the tradeoff is shown here. The graphical representation of this tradeoff also gives us an idea as to how to tweak our machine learning algorithms to reach that sweet spot where the variance and bias are minimum given this tradeoff constraint.

The following code snippet shows this tradeoff on a real model prototype. In the following example, we calculate mean square error, bias, and variance for hypothetical data, and then plot how varying the value of `shrink`, a number vector, changes these quantities.

```
mu <-2
Z <-rnorm(20000, mu)

MSE <-function(estimate, mu) {
return(sum((estimate -mu)^2) /length(estimate))
 }

n <-100
shrink <-seq(0,0.5, length=n)
mse <-numeric(n)
bias <-numeric(n)
variance <-numeric(n)

for (i in 1:n) {
 mse[i] <-MSE((1 -shrink[i]) *Z, mu)
 bias[i] <-mu *shrink[i]
 variance[i] <-(1 -shrink[i])^2
}
```

Now let's the plot the Bias-Variance tradeoff using the plot function; we can use the `ggplot` function as well.

```
# Bias-Variance tradeoff plot

plot(shrink, mse, xlab='Shrinkage', ylab='MSE', type='l', col='pink',
lwd=3, lty=1, ylim=c(0,1.2))
lines(shrink, bias^2, col='green', lwd=3, lty=2)
```

```
lines(shrink, variance, col='red', lwd=3, lty=2)
legend(0.02,0.6, c('Bias^2', 'Variance', 'MSE'), col=c('green', 'red',
'pink'), lwd=rep(3,3), lty=c(2,2,1))
```

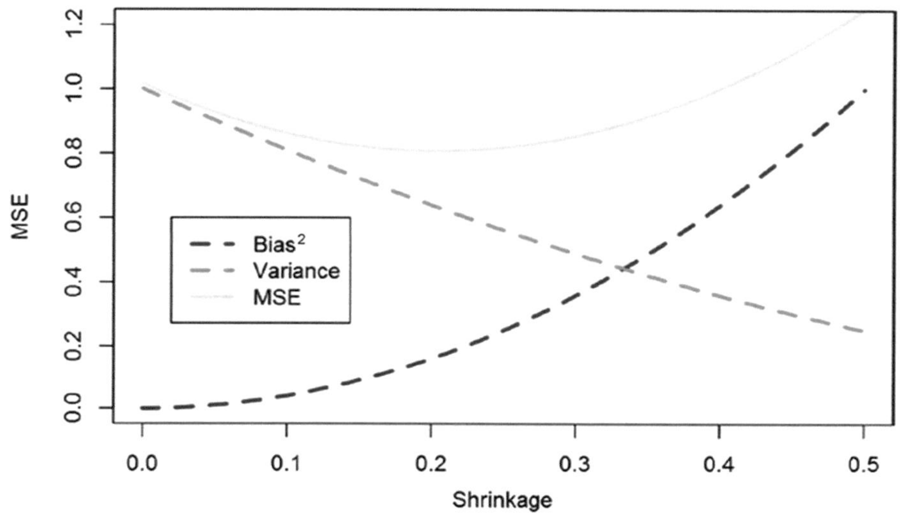

Figure 8-9. *Bias versus variance tradeoff plot*

You can see in the plot in Figure 8-9 that the variance and bias have the opposite behavior. The best optimal point for a model exists where the bias and variance meet. And this is the point that we try to use for the final model. The early indications of the model performance suffering from bias or variance can be seen by fitting the model on the test data. Test data is not seen by the model and hence we can measure its true performance or error on test data/hold out data.

- *Model suffering from variance:* When the model fits well on the train data but poorly fits on the test data. This shows that the variability of prediction is high and high variance error is dominating.
- *Model suffering from bias:* When the model fits poorly on both train and test data. The error due to bias is driving the bad performance of the model.

Having a good understanding of the bias-variance tradeoff helps you decide which methods can be applied to correct for bias or variance issues in the model. But before we jump to the main methods of performance improvements by dealing with bias and variance, we list a few common steps that might be taken to improvement the model performance:

- Bring more data into the model
- Bring in more features
- Revisit feature selection and create stronger features
- Use regularization methods of feature selection to help
- Explore sampling (upsample/downsample/resample)
- Try other learning algorithms

Once you are satisfied with these steps, you can think of applying them to improve model performance.

8.5 Introduction to Ensemble Learning

The general idea of ensemble learning is better decision making with collective intelligence. The ensemble techniques are certainly a game changer in machine learning. In statistics and machine learning, ensemble learning means learning from multiple algorithms to improve the model performance.

Generally, the supervised algorithms perform the task of searching for a solution in hypothesis/parameter space and finding a suitable hypothesis/parameter that fits the problem at hand. As with any search problem, we can't always find the best solution in limited iterations. In such situations, ensembles can be used to combine multiple hypotheses to form a (generally) better hypothesis.

As more than one model is involved in the process of ensemble, they are obviously computationally heavy as well as difficult to evaluate on a single parameter. In general, fast algorithms are recommended to be used in ensemble methods, e.g., decision tree ensembles (`randomForest`); however, slower algorithms benefit from ensemble methods equally. Similarly, you can apply ensemble learning to unsupervised learning algorithms. An ensemble learns from underlying models, hence it is itself a supervised learning algorithm.

We will use an example to understand the benefits of ensemble learning by voting ensembles.

8.5.1 Voting Ensembles

Voting ensembles are the most popular ensemble method in classification problems. This ensemble combines the final class results from multiple models and chooses the one with the majority vote. It need not be only majority votes; you can weigh them based on multiple other factors, e.g., individual model performance, complexity, etc. For explaining an example of an ensemble, Figure 8-10 is an illustration of majority votes.

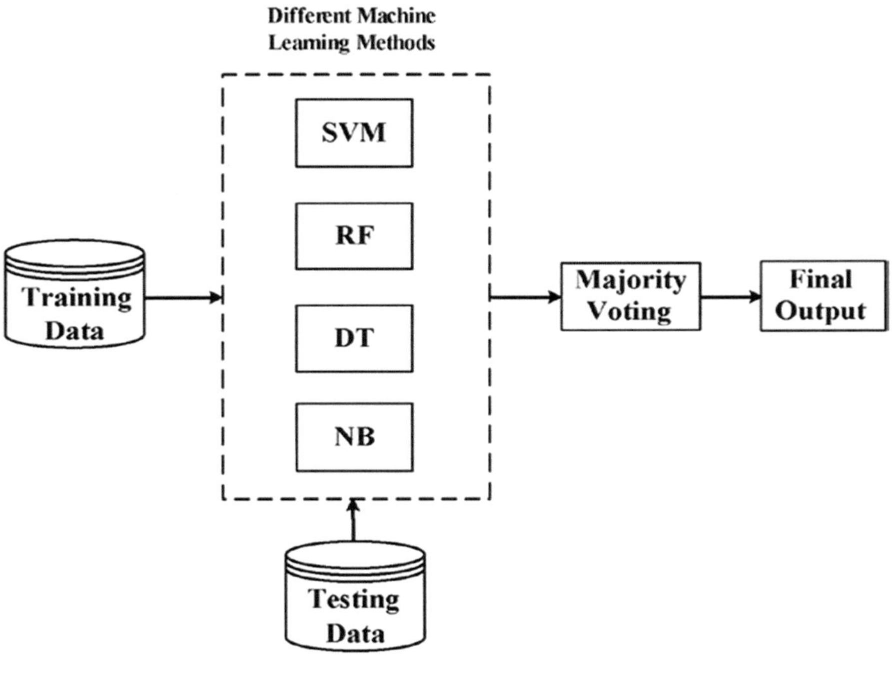

Figure 8-10. *Voting ensemble learning for a classification problem*

(Source: *Ensemble learning prediction of protein "protein interactions using proteins functional annotations",* by Saha, Zubek et al.)

Now to help internalize the idea of voting ensembles, let's understand from a hypothetical example, as illustrated here.

> *Problem*: Finding defective bulbs (=1) in a manufactured lot of bulbs.
>
> *Ensemble models*: We have three inspection experts (read models)—A, B, and C—to identify defective pieces. You can use any one of them or all of them.

Additional information: Accuracy of A is 0.7, accuracy of B is 0.6, and accuracy of C is 0.65. Their decision is independent of any other decision.

We have three binary classifiers models (A, B, and C) with 0.7, 0.6, and 0.65 accuracy, respectively. We will now show what happens if all of these models are used together in an ensemble model with the majority vote.

For a majority vote with three models, we can expect four outcomes:

- *All three are correct*
    a. *0.7 * 0.68 * 0.65 = 0.3094*
- Two are correct
    a. *0.7 * 0.68 * 0.35*
    b. *0.7 * 0.32 * 0.65*
    c. *0.3 * 0.68 * 0.65 = 0.4448*
- Two are wrong
    a. *0.3 * 0.32 * 0.65*
    b. *0.3 * 0.68 * 0.35*
    c. *0.7 * 0.32 * 0.35 = 0.2122*
- All three are wrong
    a. *0.3 * 0.32 * 0.35 = 0.0336*

In scenario 2 (two are correct), we can see that on average, the majority vote ensemble corrects for ~44% of the cases. This ensemble of three models will give us an average accuracy of ~75.4% (0.4448 + 0.3094), which is more than any individual model. However, the important consideration to see this kind of increase is the assumption that the models were independent of each other and their prediction was independent of each other. This independence condition generally doesn't hold and hence sometimes you might struggle to see improvements in model performance, even with a high dimensional ensemble.

8.5.2 Advanced Methods in Ensemble Learning

Broadly, there are two types of ensemble helping in variance and bias reduction. There are some variants around the same idea like blending, stacking, and custom ensembles, but the core idea can be explained by the two methods of bagging and boosting.

8.5.2.1 Bagging

Bootstrap aggregation, also called *bagging*, is an ensemble meta-algorithm. This algorithm improves the stability and accuracy of the model and reduces the overfitting issue. This method can be used with any method; in cases of continuous functions, it takes the weighed average of the output of the models, in classification, it weighs the output to ensemble into one single output.

Bagging was proposed by Leo Breiman in 1994 for improving results of a classification problem. Details of his original work can be found in his technical paper, "Bagging Predictors" Technical Report No. 421, 1994, Department of Statistics.

Figure 8-11 shows a bagging ensemble flow. The steps in bagging are broadly divided into four parts:

1. Creating samples from training data; number of samples should be of appropriate numbers (not too many or too few).
2. Train the model on individual samples.
3. Create classifiers from each model and store the results.
4. Based on the type of ensemble, weighted or majority vote or some custom way. Combine the results to predict the test data.

The image in Figure 8-11 illustrates the four steps in bagging mentioned earlier (Source: `http://cse-wiki.unl.edu/`).

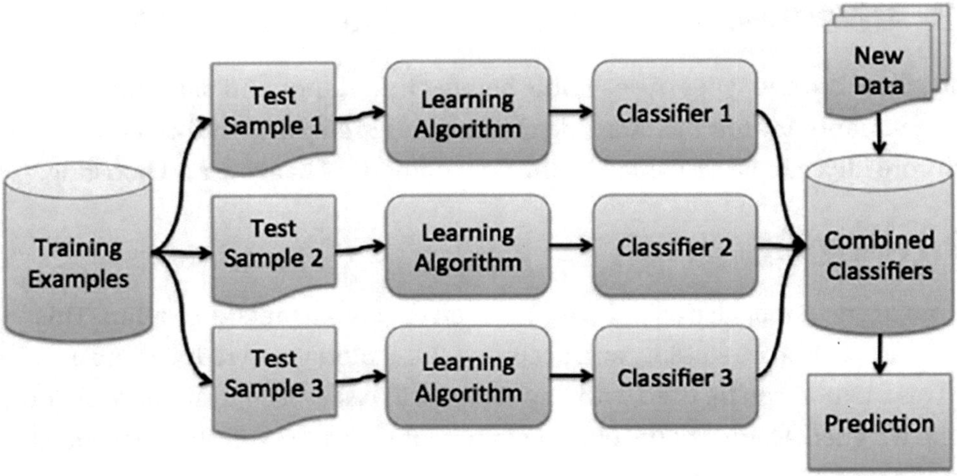

Figure 8-11. *Bagging ensemble flow*

Consider these important features of bagging:

- Each model is developed in parallel and independent of each other
- Helps decrease the variance but ineffective in reducing bias
- Best suited for high variance, low bias models (complex models)
- RandomForest is a good example (the `randomForest` algorithm prunes the tree to reduce correlation)

8.5.2.2 Boosting

Similar to bagging, boosting is also an ensemble meta-algorithm meant to reduce bias in supervised learning models. Historically, boosting tries to answer the question, suppose we have a classifier that always gives a classification less than 50% (weak classifier). Can we build a sequence of models to reach zero error (minimal error)? Theoretically, this is possible by successively passing the residual to successive models. In general, the successive models create so many convoluted relationships in final models that it becomes difficult to explain the models; hence, boosting sometimes is known to create a black box, something very hard to explain and understand.

For instance, if you design three-pass boosting, and suppose the classifier is always 40% correct, then for a set of 100 objects in first pass, you will have 60 misclassified. In the second pass, it only pass the misclassified objects, so 36% will be misclassified (60% of 60). Again in the third pass, you pass the misclassified and get 22% misclassified. So essentially, by using a classifier with only 40% accuracy, you can create an ensemble with an error equal to 22% (22/100) only, or a model with 78% accuracy.

However, in reality the theoretical underpinnings remain the same, but the improvements are not that dramatic, as many other factors come in to play, e.g., with each pass the model becomes weak, reweighing, correlation etc.

Figure 8-12 shows a boosting ensemble flow. The steps in boosting are described here:

1. First fit a model on a full training dataset. In Figure 8-12, you get 42% accuracy in the first model.
2. Fit another classifier to get 65% accuracy.
3. Fit the third model to get 92% accuracy.
4. Now you combine these different classifiers to form a strong classifier.

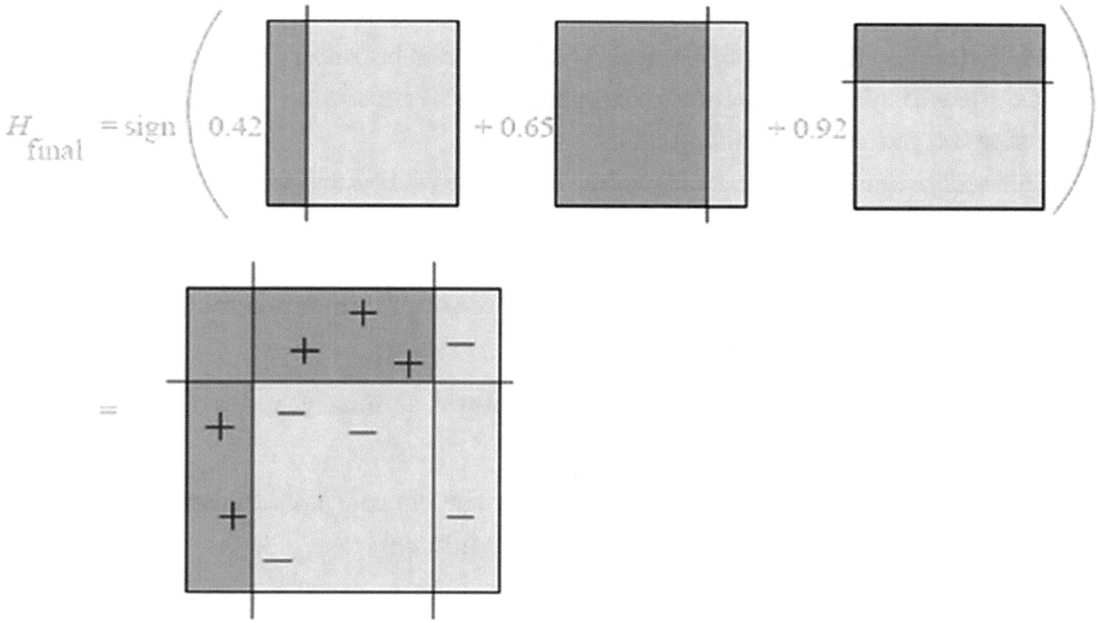

***Figure 8-12.** Boosting ensemble flow*

(Source: `https://alliance.seas.upenn.edu`.) You can see here that the boosted machine. i.e., the combined classifier, is performing far better than individual classifiers.

A few important features of boosting are listed here:

- Each model is developed sequentially, so each successive model is built on the previous model-lacking area.
- Helps decrease the bias, but is ineffective in reducing variance.
- Best suited for low variance, high bias models.
- Gradient boosting machine is a powerful algorithm using boosting ensemble.

In the following sections, we show one example each of bagging, boosting, blending, and stacking on our purchase prediction data. The output tables are easy to read and the plot will make the process of model improvement clear.

Note that the parameters are not tuned for the examples.

8.6 Ensemble Techniques Illustration in R

Ensemble training is broadly of two types—bagging and boosting. However, there are many other variants researchers have proposed. In this section, we show some examples in R using our purchase prediction data.

This section shows a chunk of R codes, which are reproducible for any dataset you want to use. The specific function calls and their options can be accessed in the documentation of the Caret package and other dependencies.

For all of the following examples, there are three important functions to calibrate for each of the techniques:

- `trainControl()`: Sets the sampling method, summary, and other training parameters.
- `train()`: Trains the models with the `trainControl()` parameters; the modeling method is also defined in this function.
- Ensemble method: Combines the results from different models using custom functions, resample, or `caretEnsemble` functions.

Let's now start building ensemble models using the R environment.

8.6.1 Bagging Trees

The two most popular bagging algorithms are used here:

- Bagged CART (regression tree)
- Random forest

The following code creates two models based on these techniques and shows the comparison between these two tree methods.

```
library(caret)
library(randomForest)
library(class)
library(ipred)
# Load Dataset
Purchase_Data <-read.csv("Purchase Prediction Dataset.csv",header=TRUE)

data <-na.omit(Purchase_Data)

# Create a sample of 10K records
set.seed(917);
Data <-data[sample(nrow(data),size=10000),]
# Select the best tuning configuration
dataset <-Data
# Example of Bagging algorithms
control <-trainControl(method="repeatedcv", number=10, repeats=3)
metric <- "Accuracy"
```

The following code snippet fits a bagged tree model.

```
# Bagged CART
set.seed(917)
fit.treebag <-train(factor(ProductChoice) ~MembershipPoints +CustomerAge
+PurchaseTenure +CustomerPropensity +LastPurchaseDuration, data=dataset,
method="treebag", metric=metric, trControl=control)

 Loading required package: plyr

 Loading required package: e1071
```

The following code snippet fits a random forest model.

```
# Random Forest
set.seed(917)
fit.rf <-train(factor(ProductChoice) ~MembershipPoints +CustomerAge
+PurchaseTenure +CustomerPropensity +LastPurchaseDuration, data=dataset,
method="rf", metric=metric, trControl=control)
```

This summarizes the bagged results from the two methods using the `resamples()` function in the Caret package.

```
# summarize results
bagging_results <-resamples(list(treebag=fit.treebag, rf=fit.rf))
summary(bagging_results)
```

```
Call:
summary.resamples(object = bagging_results)

Models: treebag, rf
Number of resamples: 30

Accuracy
         Min. 1st Qu. Median   Mean 3rd Qu.  Max. NA's
treebag 0.327  0.3444 0.3505 0.3518  0.3583 0.384    0
rf      0.395  0.4095 0.4167 0.4151  0.4216 0.435    0

Kappa
           Min. 1st Qu.  Median    Mean 3rd Qu.   Max. NA's
treebag 0.02242 0.04812 0.05498 0.05786 0.06759 0.1044    0
rf      0.04252 0.06536 0.07513 0.07387 0.08290 0.1032    0
```

```
dotplot(bagging_results)
```

The accuracy for the random forest is better than the bagged CART. The plot in Figure 8-13 shows the comparison of both algorithms on Kappa and accuracy.

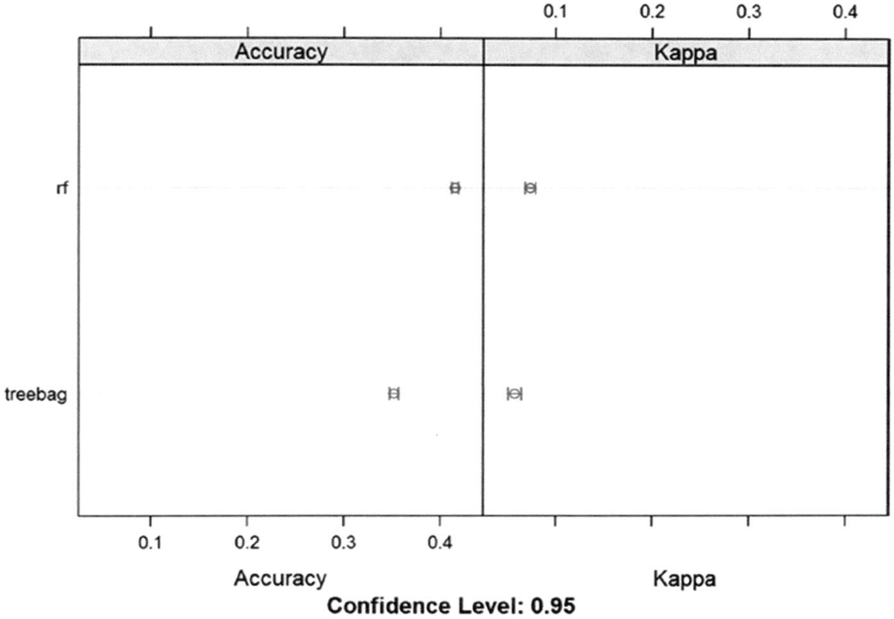

Figure 8-13. *Accuracy and Kappa of bagged tree*

8.6.2 Gradient Boosting with a Decision Tree

For boosting, we will see the two most popular algorithms:

- C5.0: Decision tree developed by Ross Quinlan
- Gradient Boosting Machine

The following code first creates a C5.0 decision tree model and then a GBM model. Once we have both models ready, we create a boosting ensemble with these two models combined.

```
library(C50)
library(gbm)

dataset <-Data;
# Example of Boosting Algorithms
control <-trainControl(method="repeatedcv", number=10, repeats=3)
metric <- "Accuracy"
```

Here, we are fitting a C5.0 decision tree model.

```
# C5.0
set.seed(917)
fit.c50 <-train(factor(ProductChoice) ~MembershipPoints +CustomerAge
+PurchaseTenure +CustomerPropensity +LastPurchaseDuration, data=dataset,
method="C5.0", metric=metric, trControl=control)
fit.c50
```

```
C5.0

10000 samples
    5 predictor
    4 classes: '1', '2', '3', '4'

No pre-processing
Resampling: Cross-Validated (10 fold, repeated 3 times)
Summary of sample sizes: 9000, 8999, 9001, 9001, 9000, 9000, ...
Resampling results across tuning parameters:

  model  winnow  trials  Accuracy   Kappa
  rules  FALSE    1      0.3924345  0.07807159
  rules  FALSE   10      0.3924345  0.07807159
  rules  FALSE   20      0.3924345  0.07807159
  rules   TRUE    1      0.4003660  0.03854515
  rules   TRUE   10      0.4003660  0.03854515
  rules   TRUE   20      0.4003660  0.03854515
  tree   FALSE    1      0.3786998  0.06855999
  tree   FALSE   10      0.3786998  0.06855999
  tree   FALSE   20      0.3786998  0.06855999
  tree    TRUE    1      0.3999658  0.03799627
  tree    TRUE   10      0.3999658  0.03799627
  tree    TRUE   20      0.3999658  0.03799627

Accuracy was used to select the optimal model using  the largest value.
The final values used for the model were trials = 1, model = rules
 and winnow = TRUE.
```

```
plot(fit.c50)
```

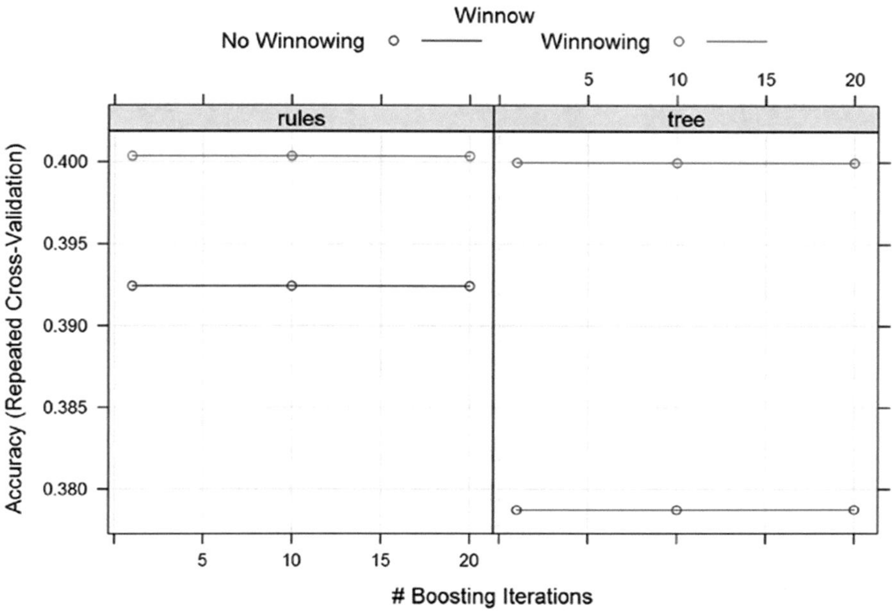

Figure 8-14. *Accuracy across boosting iterations: C5.0*

The model selects the optimal model using the largest value of accuracy. See Figure 8-14.

Here, we create a Gradient Boosting Machine (GBM) with the same dataset. See Figure 8-15.

```
# Stochastic Gradient Boosting
set.seed(917)
fit.gbm <-train(factor(ProductChoice) ~MembershipPoints +CustomerAge
+PurchaseTenure +CustomerPropensity +LastPurchaseDuration, data=dataset,
method="gbm", metric=metric, trControl=control, verbose=FALSE)
fit.gbm
```

```
 Stochastic Gradient Boosting

 10000 samples
     5 predictor
     4 classes: '1', '2', '3', '4'
```

```
No pre-processing
Resampling: Cross-Validated (10 fold, repeated 3 times)
Summary of sample sizes: 9000, 8999, 9001, 9001, 9000, 9000, ...
Resampling results across tuning parameters:

  interaction.depth  n.trees  Accuracy   Kappa
  1                   50      0.4133000  0.07395657
  1                  100      0.4112656  0.07721806
  1                  150      0.4104981  0.07825744
  2                   50      0.4157985  0.08170535
  2                  100      0.4138310  0.08341336
  2                  150      0.4136634  0.08690728
  3                   50      0.4133309  0.08146098
  3                  100      0.4117326  0.08628274
  3                  150      0.4108320  0.08948114

Tuning parameter 'shrinkage' was held constant at a value of 0.1

Tuning parameter 'n.minobsinnode' was held constant at a value of 10
Accuracy was used to select the optimal model using  the largest value.
The final values used for the model were n.trees = 50, interaction.depth
 = 2, shrinkage = 0.1 and n.minobsinnode = 10.
```

```
plot(fit.gbm)
```

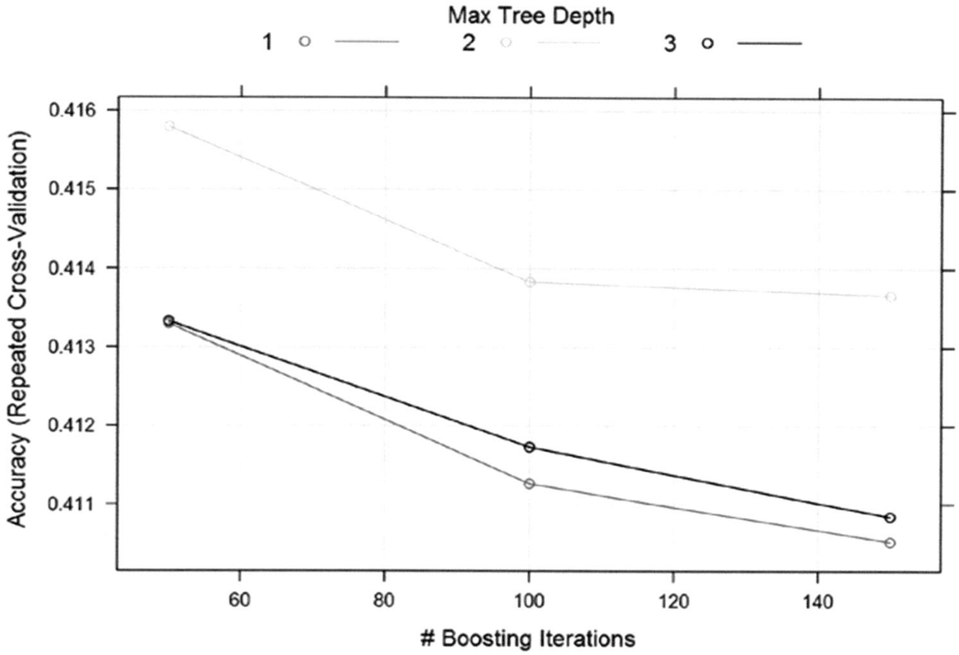

Figure 8-15. *Accuracy across boosting iterations: GBM*

Now we summarize the results by combining the GBM and C5.0 models using the `resamples()` function in the Caret package.

```
# summarize results
boosting_results <-resamples(list(c5.0=fit.c50, gbm=fit.gbm))
summary(boosting_results)
```

```
Call:
summary.resamples(object = boosting_results)

Models: c5.0, gbm
Number of resamples: 30

Accuracy
      Min. 1st Qu. Median   Mean 3rd Qu.   Max. NA's
c5.0 0.376  0.3917 0.4008 0.4004  0.4088 0.4226    0
gbm  0.398  0.4112 0.4153 0.4158  0.4209 0.4286    0
```

```
Kappa
          Min. 1st Qu.  Median    Mean 3rd Qu.    Max. NA's
c5.0 0.00000 0.02886 0.04001 0.03855 0.05701 0.07496    0
gbm  0.05248 0.07366 0.08241 0.08171 0.08875 0.10530    0
```

```
dotplot(boosting_results)
```

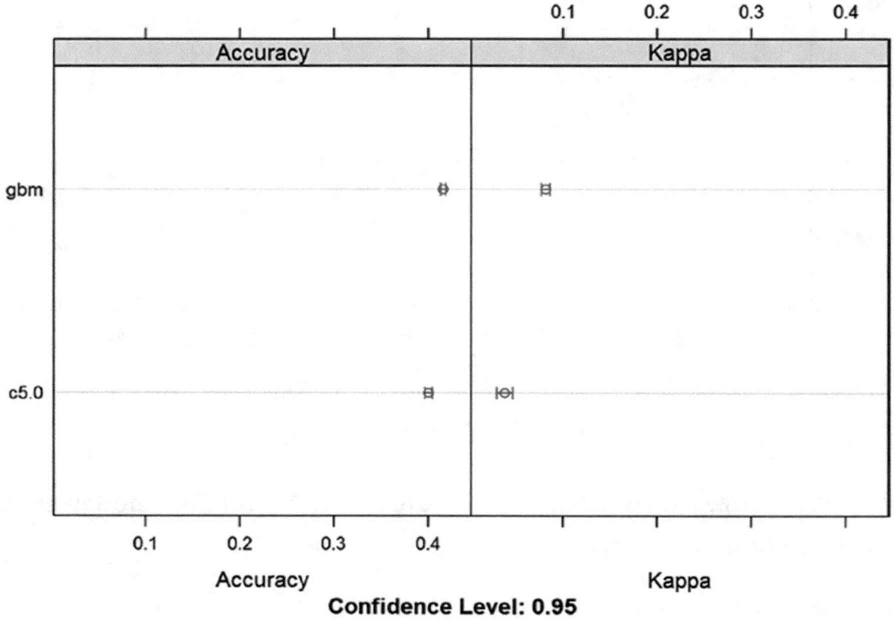

Figure 8-16. *Accuracy across the boosting ensemble*

We can see that the C5.0 algorithm produces an accuracy of 40.5% for the best model, while GBM gives a model with 41.5% accuracy (see Figure 8-16). Gradient boosting seems to be fitting the data better with the boosting algorithm.

8.6.3 Blending KNN and Rpart

Blending is an ensemble where the output of different models is combined with some weights, and all the model output is not treated equally. The following example uses two techniques to blend:

- knn
- rpart

In this example, we will be blending the knn and rpart methods as a linear combination of models. The models will be combined by using the caretEmseble() function.

caretEnsemble is a package for making ensembles of Caret models. The details of this package can be accessed at https://cran.r-project.org/web/packages/caretEnsemble/vignettes/caretEnsemble-intro.html.

Blending (linear combination of models)

```
# load libraries
library(caret)
library(caretEnsemble)

library(MASS)

set.seed(917);
Data <-data[sample(nrow(data),size=10000),];

dataset <-Data;

dataset$choice <-ifelse(dataset$ProductChoice ==1 |dataset$ProductChoice
==2 ,"A","B")

dataset$choice <-as.factor(dataset$choice)
# define training control
train_control <-trainControl(method="cv", number=4, savePredictions=TRUE,
classProbs=TRUE)
# train a list of models
methodList <-c('knn','rpart')
models <-caretList(choice ~MembershipPoints +CustomerAge +PurchaseTenure
+CustomerPropensity +LastPurchaseDuration, data=dataset, trControl=train_
control, methodList=methodList)
# create ensemble of trained models
ensemble <-caretEnsemble(models)
# summarize ensemble
summary(ensemble)
```

```
The following models were ensembled: knn, rpart
They were weighted:
-1.9876 0.4849 3.4433
The resulting Accuracy is: 0.6416
The fit for each individual model on the Accuracy is:
 method  Accuracy  AccuracySD
    knn 0.5924004 0.007451753
  rpart 0.6397990 0.005863011
```

This output shows that knn and rpart are individually accurate with 59% and 63% accuracy, while the blending model is 64% accurate. This shows that blending allows us to marginally improve the classification results. In general, the improvementsEnsemble techniques, R:KNN and Rpart, blending can be even in the order of 10%.

The next methods of stacking are very similar to blending. The only difference is that in stacking, we will stack models one after another and then weigh output from each model to create an ensemble.

8.6.4 Stacking Using caretEnsemble

Stacking is similar to blending, the only difference is the way the data is extracted for successive models. The general principle is to not use the training data itself for boosting.

Therefore, we apply rules like using cross-fold validation (the out-of-fold is used to train the next layer)—*stacking*—and/or use a holdout validation (part of the train is used in the first layer, part in the second)—*blending*.

For example, let's take the previous example of the knn and rpart models fit for ensemble. Assume that the training set had 100 cases to classify. Then in blending:

1. knn *built on 100 cases.*

2. rpart *built on 100 cases.*

3. Ensemble model = c1*Knn + c2*Rpart, *where* c1 *and* c2 *are some* weights given to each model before combining. This was how we blended these two methods.

The example for stacking will look something like this:

1. knn built on 100 cases, it classifies 60 correctly.
2. Build rpart *on the 40 misclassified* cases from previous model, which allows you to classify 20 more correctly. (This is an ideal situation. In reality the training 100 cases will be weighted in a way that the misclassified cases get more weight in training than the correctly classified case in the previous mode of the stack.)
3. *Now combine the results of the two model runs in ensemble. In other words, you stack results from one model to other.*

This example is a simplistic view of how the process of blending and stacking differ in principle. In general, both the methods give multiple models, which we weigh to combine them into a single ensemble model.

We can combine (or stack) the predictions of multiple Caret models using the caretEnsemble package. In this example, we will stack five different algorithms on our purchase prediction data:

- Linear Discriminate Analysis (LDA)
- Classification and Regression Trees (CART)
- Logistic regression (via Generalized Linear Model or GLM)
- k-Nearest Neighbors (KNN)
- Support Vector Machine with a Radial Basis Kernel Function (SVM)

```
# Example of Stacking algorithms
library(kernlab);

# create submodels
control <-trainControl(method="repeatedcv", number=10, repeats=3,
savePredictions=TRUE, classProbs=TRUE)
```

Here are the settings the algorithm lists for stacking. The five algorithms are stored in the algorithmList variable, which will be used as a parameter in the training function.

```
algorithmList <-c('lda', 'rpart', 'glm', 'knn', 'svmRadial')
set.seed(917)
models <-caretList(choice ~MembershipPoints +CustomerAge +PurchaseTenure
+CustomerPropensity +LastPurchaseDuration, data=dataset, trControl=control,
methodList=algorithmList)
results <-resamples(models)
summary(results)

 Call:
 summary.resamples(object = results)

 Models: lda, rpart, glm, knn, svmRadial
 Number of resamples: 30

 Accuracy
             Min. 1st Qu. Median   Mean 3rd Qu.   Max. NA's
 lda       0.6240  0.6330 0.6443 0.6424  0.6510 0.6600    0
 rpart     0.6260  0.6315 0.6383 0.6403  0.6470 0.6640    0
 glm       0.6270  0.6336 0.6447 0.6432  0.6518 0.6580    0
 knn       0.5710  0.5825 0.5940 0.5908  0.5990 0.6070    0
 svmRadial 0.6226  0.6381 0.6470 0.6462  0.6558 0.6683    0

 Kappa
              Min. 1st Qu.  Median    Mean 3rd Qu.   Max. NA's
 lda       0.14170 0.16630 0.18680 0.18430  0.2038 0.2357    0
 rpart     0.12510 0.15430 0.16750 0.17140  0.1859 0.2319    0
 glm       0.14290 0.16440 0.18650 0.18430  0.2010 0.2282    0
 knn       0.03609 0.06526 0.09152 0.08519  0.1047 0.1255    0
 svmRadial 0.13230 0.16290 0.18680 0.18370  0.2019 0.2319    0

dotplot(results)
```

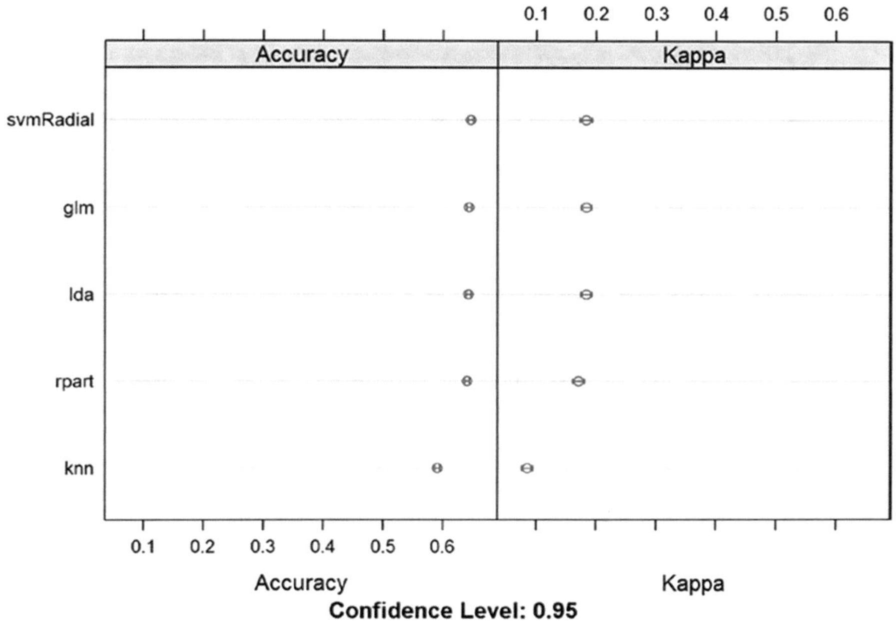

Figure 8-17. *Accuracy and Kappa of individual models*

We can see from the dot plot in Figure 8-17 that the performance has gone up to 60% by stacking multiple algorithms together. Also note that the model training was very resource intensive and model complexity is not suitable for a production environment.

Now let's see following the correlation between the results for each of the stacking models. The correlation will show how many results were the same across the models. If the number of predictions overlapping is high, we might not see any improvement in results due to stacking.

```
# correlation between results
modelCor(results)

                  lda        rpart         glm          knn     svmRadial
lda        1.00000000  0.65576463 0.974747749 -0.0145770069  0.7366291336
rpart      0.65576463  1.00000000 0.675976986 -0.0350947255  0.6936118174
glm        0.97474775  0.67597699 1.000000000  0.0039610564  0.7336378830
knn       -0.01457701 -0.03509473 0.003961056  1.0000000000 -0.0008377878
svmRadial  0.73662913  0.69361182 0.733637883 -0.0008377878  1.0000000000

splom(results)
```

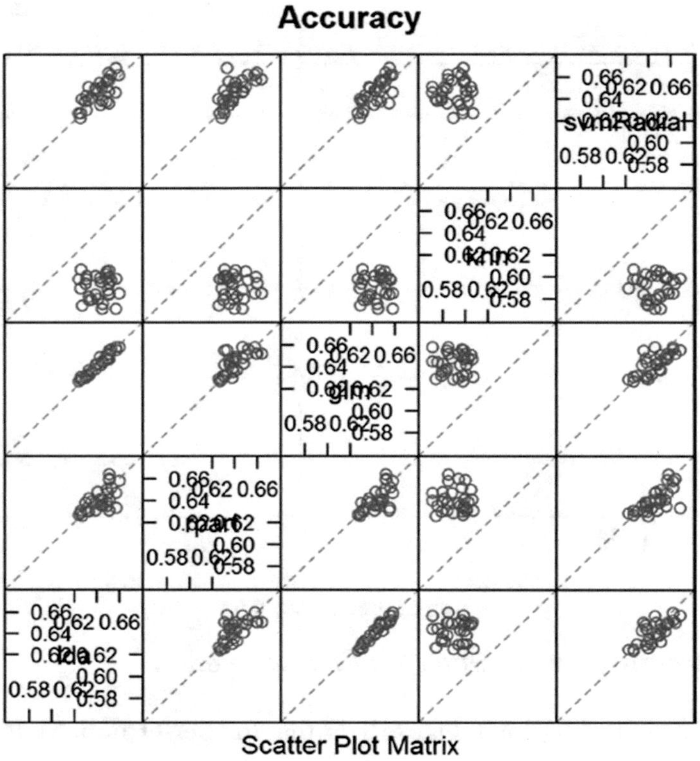

Figure 8-18. *Scatter plot to list correlations among results from stacked models*

Model correlations seem to be high for a few of the models—for instance `lda` and `glm`, `lda` and `svmradial`, etc. This impacts the ensemble power as discussed in the previous sections.

In the previous example, knn was the base model and other models were stacked on that. We can actually change the stacking order by using the `caretStack()` function. Here we show the same example by rearranging the stack. In the first case we start with the `glm` model and in second we start with a random forest and then will compare results if stacking improved the results.

Stacking using GLM:

```
# stack using glm
stackControl <-trainControl(method="repeatedcv", number=10, repeats=3,
savePredictions=TRUE, classProbs=TRUE)
set.seed(917)
```

```
stack.glm <-caretStack(models, method="glm", metric="Accuracy",
trControl=stackControl)
print(stack.glm)

 A glm ensemble of 2 base models: lda, rpart, glm, knn, svmRadial

 Ensemble results:
 Generalized Linear Model

 30000 samples
     5 predictor
     2 classes: 'A', 'B'

 No pre-processing
 Resampling: Cross-Validated (10 fold, repeated 3 times)
 Summary of sample sizes: 27000, 26999, 27000, 27000, 27000, 27001, ...
 Resampling results:

   Accuracy   Kappa
   0.6441887  0.1845648
```

Using glm to stack has given an accuracy of 64%. In the next section, we did the same stacking with randomForest.

```
# stack using random forest
set.seed(917)
stack.rf <-caretStack(models, method="rf", metric="Accuracy",
trControl=stackControl)
print(stack.rf)

 A rf ensemble of 2 base models: lda, rpart, glm, knn, svmRadial

 Ensemble results:
 Random Forest

 30000 samples
     5 predictor
     2 classes: 'A', 'B'
```

```
No pre-processing
Resampling: Cross-Validated (10 fold, repeated 3 times)
Summary of sample sizes: 27000, 26999, 27000, 27000, 27000, 27001, ...
Resampling results across tuning parameters:

  mtry  Accuracy   Kappa
  2     0.6372440  0.1944063
  3     0.6356217  0.1927612
  5     0.6335549  0.1885745

Accuracy was used to select the optimal model using  the largest value.
The final value used for the model was mtry = 2.
```

Using `randomForest`, we get an accuracy close to 63.7% which is close to the `glm` accuracy but a little lower. Hence for this experiment, stacking using `glm` works the best. Again, we can re-emphasize that the correlation among some methods is high, so adding them to the stack will not benefit the model's accuracy.

8.7 Advanced Topic: Bayesian Optimization of Machine Learning Models

In machine learning, hyper-parameter tuning plays an important role. Data scientists are now paying attention to tuning the parameters before putting the final model in production. Hence it is important to touch briefly on one of the most important optimization techniques, called Bayesian optimization. Yachen Yan released a new package for Bayesian optimization in R very recently. We will show you how to use this package on the house price data.

Bayesian optimization is a way to find global optimal point for a black box function (model evaluation metric as a function of hyper-parameters) without requiring derivatives. The work done by Jonas Mockus was well received in the academic community; a comprehensive introduction to this topic can be found in "Bayesian Approach to Global Optimization: Theory and Applications," Jonas Mockus, Kluwer Academic (2013).

For this example, we will first get an initial set of hyper-parameters by using random tuning. This will give us multiple values generated across a wide range. Here we are creating 20 random parameters. The example has been inspired by the article by Max

Kuhn, director at Pfizer on revolutions. The article can be accessed at http://blog.revolutionanalytics.com/2016/06/bayesian-optimization-of-machine-learning-models.html.

```
setwd("C:/Personal/Machine Learning/Chapter 8/");
library(caret)
library(randomForest)
library(class)
library(ipred)
library(GPfit)
# Load Dataset
House_price <-read.csv("House Sale Price Dataset.csv",header=TRUE)

dataset <-na.omit(House_price)

#Create a sample of 10K records
set.seed(917);

rand_ctrl <-trainControl(method ="repeatedcv", repeats =5, search ="random")

rand_search <-train(HousePrice ~StoreArea +BasementArea +SellingYear
+SaleType +ConstructionYear +Rating, data = dataset, method ="svmRadial",
 Create 20 random parameter values
tuneLength =20,
metric ="RMSE",
preProc =c("center", "scale"),
trControl = rand_ctrl)
rand_search

 Support Vector Machines with Radial Basis Function Kernel

 1069 samples
    6 predictor

 Pre-processing: centered (10), scaled (10)
 Resampling: Cross-Validated (10 fold, repeated 5 times)
 Summary of sample sizes: 961, 962, 963, 962, 963, 962, ...
 Resampling results across tuning parameters:
```

```
    sigma        C           RMSE      Rsquared
    0.005245534  22.6530619  43909.17  0.7456410
    0.013918538   0.9927528  42284.81  0.7655819
... 0.730177279  90.8484676  57009.90  0.5687722
    1.858138939   0.5329669  63431.60  0.4909382
```

RMSE was used to select the optimal model using the smallest value. The final values used for the model were sigma = 0.04674319 and C = 3.112494.

```
ggplot(rand_search) +scale_x_log10() +scale_y_log10()
```

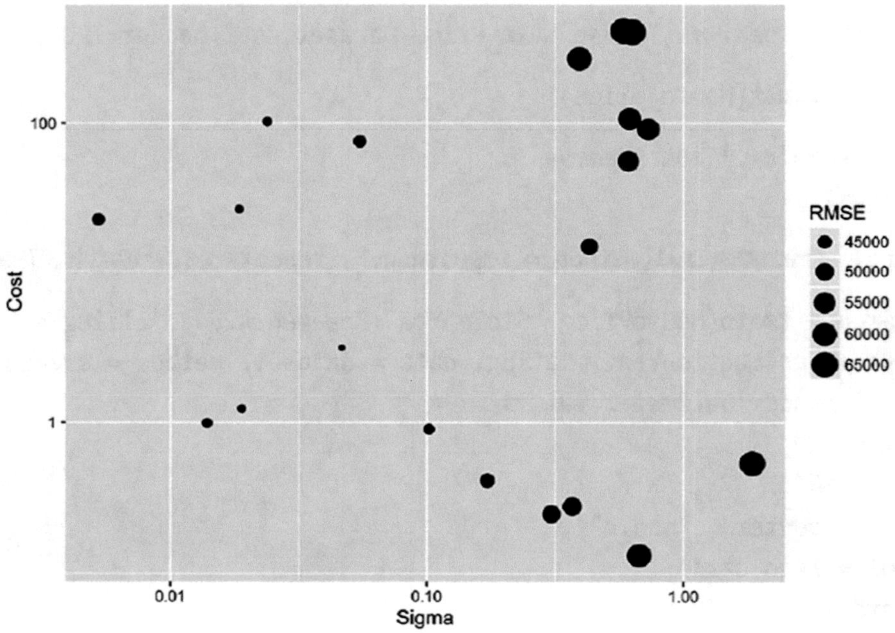

***Figure 8-19.** RMSE in cost and Sigma space*

```
getTrainPerf(rand_search)
```

```
  TrainRMSE TrainRsquared    method
1  41480.77     0.7706348 svmRadial
```

This example is an optimization that assumes the Bayesian model is based on Gaussian processes to predict good tuning parameters. Hence, a linear regression type of framework is used for this Bayesian analysis.

For a combination of cost and Sigma, we can calculate the bounds of the predicted RMSE. Due to the uncertainty of prediction, it is possible to find a better direction for optimization.

```
# Define the resampling method
ctrl <-trainControl(method ="repeatedcv", repeats =5)
```

Use this function to optimize the model. The two parameters are evaluated on the log scale given their range and scope.

```
svm_fit_bayes <-function(logC, logSigma) {
  Use the same model code but for a single (C, sigma) pair.
   txt <-capture.output(
     mod <-train(HousePrice ~StoreArea +BasementArea +SellingYear +SaleType
     +ConstructionYear +Rating , data = dataset,
method ="svmRadial",
preProc =c("center", "scale"),
metric ="RMSE",
trControl = ctrl,
tuneGrid =data.frame(C =exp(logC), sigma =exp(logSigma)))
   )
    The function wants to _maximize_ the outcome so we return
    the negative of the resampled RMSE value. `Pred` can be used
    to return predicted values but we'll avoid that and use zero
list(Score = -getTrainPerf(mod)[, "TrainRMSE"], Pred =0)
 }
```

Define the bounds of the search.

```
 lower_bounds <-c(logC = -5, logSigma = -9)
 upper_bounds <-c(logC =20, logSigma = -0.75)
 bounds <-list(logC =c(lower_bounds[1], upper_bounds[1]),
logSigma =c(lower_bounds[2], upper_bounds[2]))
```

```
 Create a grid of values as the input into the BO code
initial_grid <-rand_search$results[, c("C", "sigma", "RMSE")]
initial_grid$C <-log(initial_grid$C)
initial_grid$sigma <-log(initial_grid$sigma)
initial_grid$RMSE <--initial_grid$RMSE
names(initial_grid) <-c("logC", "logSigma", "Value")
```

Run the optimization with the initial grid and with 30.

```
library(rBayesianOptimization)

set.seed(917)
 ba_search <-BayesianOptimization(svm_fit_bayes,
bounds = bounds,
init_grid_dt = initial_grid,
init_points =0,
n_iter =30,
acq ="ucb",
kappa =1,
eps =0.0,
verbose =TRUE)

 20 points in hyperparameter space were pre-sampled
 elapsed = 7.02   Round = 21  logC = -0.6296  logSigma = -3.2325  Value = -
4.260364e+04

  Best Parameters Found:
 Round = 43   logC = 3.5271   logSigma = -3.3272  Value = -4.106852e+04

ba_search
 $Best_Par
     logC  logSigma
  3.527062 -3.327152

 $Best_Value
 [1] -41068.52
```

```
$History
    Round        logC   logSigma     Value
 1:     1  3.120295026 -5.2503783 -43909.17
 2:     2 -0.007273577 -4.2745337 -42284.81
49:    49  1.765610990 -2.6130250 -41510.91
50:    50  3.286583098 -3.4811229 -41876.16
    Round        logC   logSigma     Value

$Pred
   V1 V2 V3 V4 V5 V6 V7 V8 V9 V10 V11 V12 V13 V14 V15 V16 V17 V18 V19 V20
1:  0  0  0  0  0  0  0  0  0   0   0   0   0   0   0   0   0   0   0   0
   V21 V22 V23 V24 V25 V26 V27 V28 V29 V30
1:   0   0   0   0   0   0   0   0   0   0
```

The best values are found as follows:

Round = 43
logC = 3.5271
logSigma = -3.3272
Value = -4.106852e+04

Let's now develop a model with these parameters to see if the optimization did actually work.

```
final_search <-train(HousePrice ~StoreArea +BasementArea +SellingYear
+SaleType +ConstructionYear +Rating, data = dataset,
method ="svmRadial",
tuneGrid =data.frame(C =exp(ba_search$Best_Par["logC"]),
sigma =exp(ba_search$Best_Par["logSigma"])),
metric ="RMSE",
preProc =c("center", "scale"),
trControl = ctrl)

final_search

 Support Vector Machines with Radial Basis Function Kernel

 1069 samples
    6 predictor
```

```
Pre-processing: centered (10), scaled (10)
Resampling: Cross-Validated (10 fold, repeated 5 times)
Summary of sample sizes: 962, 961, 964, 961, 964, 963, ...
Resampling results:

  RMSE      Rsquared
  41595.45  0.7671211

Tuning parameter 'sigma' was held constant at a value of 0.0358952

Tuning parameter 'C' was held constant at a value of 34.02386
```

The following command will provide the comparison across the models. The comparison is done using one sample t-test.

```
compare_models(final_search, rand_search)

  One Sample t-test

data:  x
t = 0.061836, df = 49, p-value = 0.9509
alternative hypothesis: true mean is not equal to 0
95 percent confidence interval:
 -3612.507  3841.883
sample estimates:
mean of x
 114.6878
```

The model fit on the new configuration is comparable to random searches in terms of the resampled RMSE and the RMSE on the test set. This shows that the optimization did work well.

8.8 Summary

Machine learning models are very complicated when compared to statistical models. The machine learning models, along with ensemble, have increased the complexity of models. The models have become difficult to explain and far more difficult to segregate a component-wise contribution of features. The ensemble model further adds to complexity in relationships of dependent variables and predictor variables quantified by the machine learning model. On the other hand, the machine learning algorithm makes it possible to use any data in any volume without any assumptions. This makes machine learning stand apart from statistical learning and opens up bag of opportunities to model virtually any data problem.

One of the major contrasts between statistical learning and machine learning is the way both models extract/learn from the given dataset. Machine learning algorithms are iterative in nature and depend on some "high-level parameters," which define the complexity of model, learning rate, etc. These parameters are commonly known as hyper-parameters. Hyper-parameters impact the model performance to a large extent as they define the higher dimension parameters of how the model should learn from the data. We learned some methods to optimize these hyper-parameters. All the optimization model fitting in this chapter is done using a very power package in R, named Caret, which stands for classification and regression training. It can accommodate close to 230+ models in a single function call.

In this chapter, after introducing various types of hyper-parameter optimizations methods, we introduced the very important topic of bias and variance tradeoff. This tradeoff is a limitation applicable to all statistical models and lies at the heart of any model performance optimization problem. The tradeoff states that you cannot decrease bias and variance simultaneously. Ensemble methods were then introduced to create models that can reduce bias, boosting ensemble, and reduce variance bagging ensembles. Bagging and boosting are both powerful techniques, and they have become very popular in recent years.

This chapter also illustrated four very popular ensembles examples using R code, bagging, boosting, blending, and stacking. The results are compared and issues like correlation in results were also discussed. In the end, we introduced a very advanced technique in hyper-parameter optimization, called Bayesian optimization. This is a hot topic of research, as the machine learning models have become so huge that a grid search is a not feasible solution for hyper-parameter optimization.

In recent times, the machine learning methods have become computationally demanding as well. You can sense the enormity of computational power we require by noting the fact that for this chapter we just used a sample of data. Adding more data and expanding the search grids can enhance the results. To be able to cater to the demand of machine learning algorithms, both with respect to volume of data and computational power, we need to explore scalable machine learning infrastructure and algorithms.

The next chapter introduces time series analysis, which is a classic forecasting technique with a heavy influence of statistics. In many practical business use cases, time series analysis is being widely used and has found wide acceptance.

CHAPTER 9

Time Series Modeling

Recording data indexed by time is an old way of collecting data for analysis. The time index data primarily serves the purpose of observing events that have high correlation with time and considerable part of the variance is due to changing times. The introduction to time series analysis will help you understand how to count time-dependent variations.

Time series analyses have wide applicability in the financial, economical, and surveys fields. While time series methods are embraced by fields studying natural process including meteorology, oceanography, and astronomy, there are many other fields that find it useful as well. This chapter introduces the basics of time series and explains how to analyze the underlying data.

The core tenants covered in this chapter are:

- Components of time series
- Test of stationarity
- ACF and AR model
- PACF and MA model
- ARIMA model
- Linear regression with AR errors

To discuss these concepts, we will be using the hourly power consumption dataset in this chapter.

The hourly power consumption data comes from PJM's website and is in megawatts (MW). PJM Interconnection LLC (PJM) is a regional transmission organization (RTO) in the United States. It is part of the Eastern Interconnection grid operating an electric transmission system serving all or parts of Delaware, Illinois, Indiana, Kentucky, Maryland, Michigan, New Jersey, North Carolina, Ohio, Pennsylvania, Tennessee, Virginia, West Virginia, and the District of Columbia.

The dataset is loaded and skimmed to suit the purpose of explaining the concepts. All assumptions, if applied, will be stated in the appropriate sections.

K. Ramasubramanian and A. Singh, *Machine Learning Using R*, https://doi.org/10.1007/978-1-4842-4215-5_9

9.1 Components of Time Series

Time series data is collected over a period of time with generally fixed time intervals. The *univariate time series* is defined as equally spaced time measurement of same variable. This feature makes the very nature of data different from what we see in linear regression models. The key differences are that the data is not necessarily independent and identically distributed and the ordering of data is very important.

The models that we build in a time domain mostly relate to predicting values of series based on past values and past prediction errors. In some cases, the time component is also used as an ordinary x-variable for regression.

It is important to understand the time series data before we propose a modeling methodology. A few key things that one should look at are:

- Trends—Does the time series on average increase or decrease
- Seasonality—Does the series show seasonal changes of a similar scale
- Are there abrupt changes in the time series
- Are there clear outliers without any significant explanation in the time dimension
- Cyclicity—Can you spot long-term patterns that repeat

Let's now look at the dataset.

Note The series has been reduced to monthly aggregations, however, you can do the analysis at different time steps, e.g., daily, quarterly, etc.

```
library(reshape)
library(ggplot2)
library(dplyr)
library(lubridate)

Power_Consumption <- read.csv("Dataset/DOM_hourly.csv", header=TRUE)

# Reformat the datetime field into timestamp in R
Power_Consumption$Datetime <- as.Date(strptime(as.character(Power_
Consumption$Datetime),format="%Y-%m-%d %H:%M:%OS"))
```

```
Power_Consumption$Datetime <- floor_date(Power_Consumption$Datetime,"month")

#Aggregate the Data by Month Now
Power_Consumption <- Power_Consumption %>% group_by(Datetime)
%>%  summarise(Average_Consumption=mean(DOM_MW))

#The descriptive elements of time series are good to know before starting
the visualization.

#Number of records
dim(Power_Consumption)

## [1] 160   2

#Start Date & Time of Series
min(Power_Consumption$Datetime)

## [1] "2005-05-01"

#End Data & Time of Series
max(Power_Consumption$Datetime)

## [1] "2018-08-01"

#Interval of Recording Consumption - assuming all are equally spaced
Power_Consumption$Datetime[3]-Power_Consumption$Datetime[2]

## Time difference of 30 days

#Highest Consumption recorded
max(Power_Consumption$Average_Consumption)

## [1] 14236.33

#Lowest Consumption recorded
min(Power_Consumption$Average_Consumption)

## [1] 8681.653

#Average Consumption in The Series
mean(Power_Consumption$Average_Consumption)

## [1] 10962.52

start_Date <- as.Date("2006-01-01")
end_Date <- as.Date("2018-01-01")
```

```
#Simple Line Chart

ggplot(data = Power_Consumption, aes(x = Datetime, y = Average_Consumption)) +
  geom_line(color = 'red', size = 1) +
  scale_x_date(limits = c(start_Date, end_Date))+
  theme(legend.title=element_text(family="Times",size=20),
        legend.text=element_text(family="Times",face = "italic",size=15),
        plot.title=element_text(family="Times", face="bold", size=20),
        axis.title.x=element_text(family="Times", face="bold", size=12),
        axis.title.y=element_text(family="Times", face="bold", size=12)) +
    xlab("Time") +
    ylab("Power Consumption (in Mega Watt)") +
    ggtitle("Power Consumption Over Time by Month - 2005 to 2018")
```

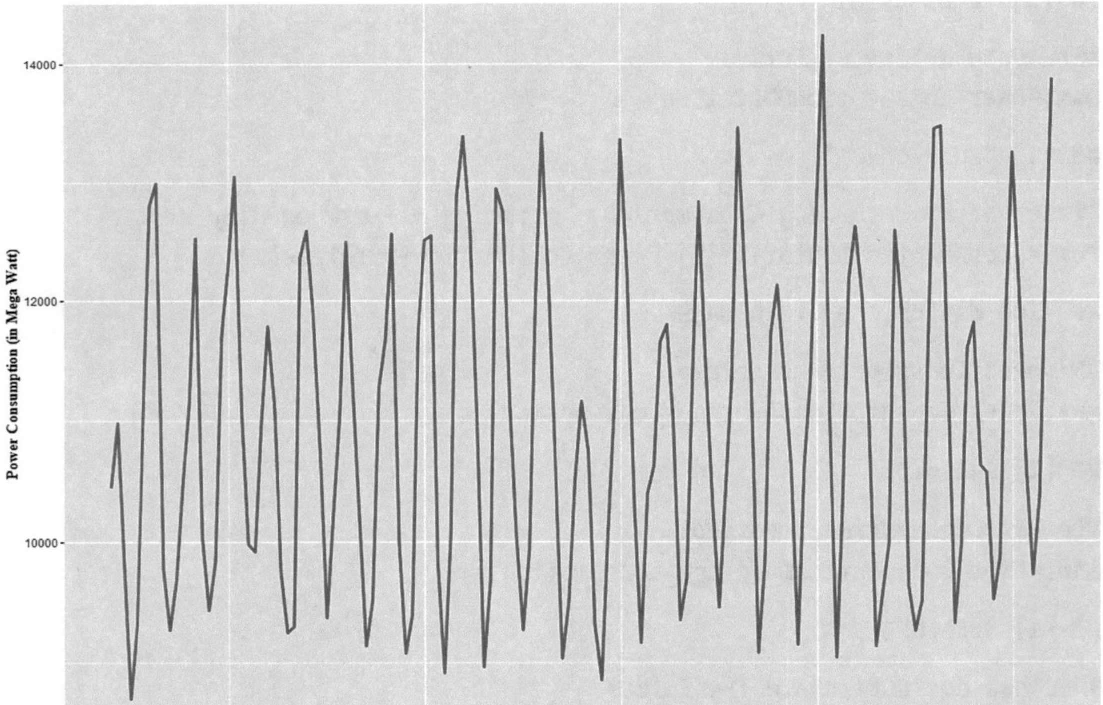

***Figure 9-1.** Power consumption over time by month, 2005 to 2018*

Some highlights from Figure 9-1:

- There seems to be no trend. The average consumption hovers around the mean.
- A cycle can be observed, with a cycle being a year.
- Seasonal patterns are visible in each cycle.

For further analysis, we will only look at the power consumption for the year 2015 to 2017 and try to bring the time series features to build time dependent univariate models. The following code analyzes the smooth curve superimposed on the trend for the 2015 to 2017 times series data.

```
#Let's only focus on time series analysis on 2015 onwards by setting axis
limits

start_Date <- as.Date("2015-01-01")
end_Date <- as.Date("2017-12-31")

Power_Consumption = Power_Consumption[as.Date(Power_Consumption$Datetime)
>= start_Date & as.Date(Power_Consumption$Datetime) <= end_Date,]

ggplot(data = Power_Consumption, aes(x = Datetime, y = Average_Consumption)) +
  geom_line(color = "red", size = 1) +
  stat_smooth(  color = "blue", fill = "yellow", method = "loess" )
```

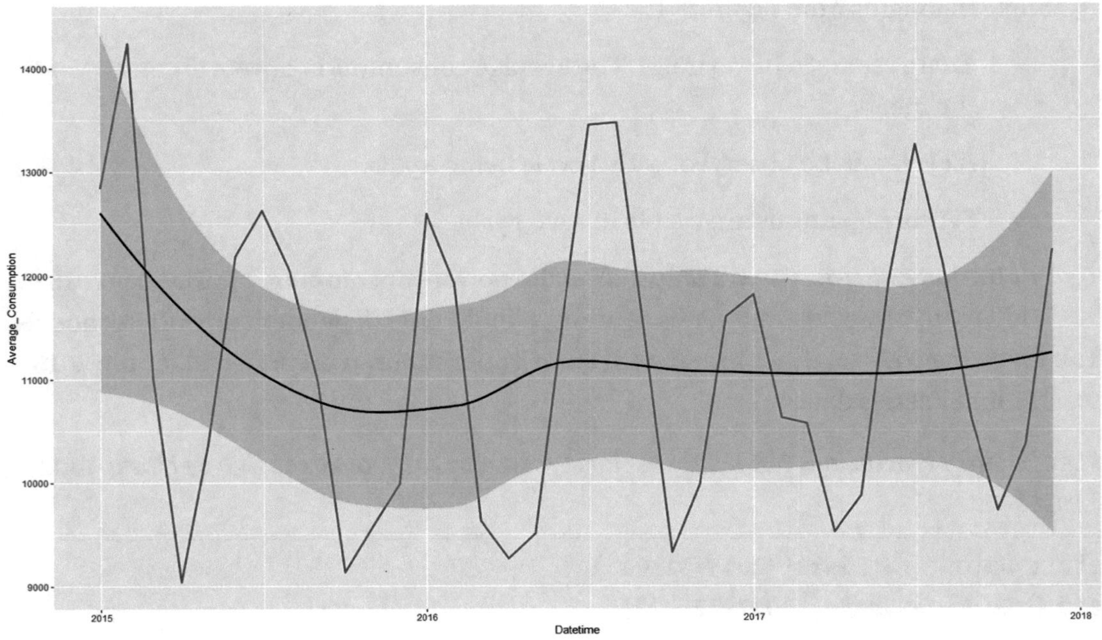

Figure 9-2. *Trend for 2015 to 2017 Time Series Data*

The smoothing in Figure 9-2 shows us that the data has a strong time varying dependence. You can see that the levels of average consumption are not monotonic in nature; they more or less remain the same as of the start of 2015 to the end of 2017. The average movement of consumption is a good use case for time series analysis.

9.2 Test of Stationarity

Stationarity of a time series is an important assumption for times series to make inferences from the autocorrelation function (ACF). Stationarity means that the autocorrelation for any particular lag remains the same regardless of time.

Autocorrelation of a random process is the correlation between values of time series at different times.

Let X be a random process and t be any point in time (t may be an integer for a discrete-time process or a real number for a continuous-time process). Then Xt is the value (or realization) produced by a given run of the process at time, t. Suppose that the process has mean μ_t and variance σ_t^2 at time t, for each t. Then the definition of the autocorrelation between times s and t is

$$R(s,t) = \frac{\mathrm{E}[(X_t - \mu_t)(X_s - \mu_s)]}{\sigma_t \sigma_s},$$

where E is the expected value operator.

More formally, a series X_t is said to be (weakly) stationary if it satisfies the following properties:

1. The mean $\mathrm{E}(x_t)$ is the same for all t.
2. The variance of x_t is the same for all t.
3. The covariance (and correlation) between x_t and x_{t-h} is the same for all t.

Let x_t denote the value of a time series at time t. The ACF of the series gives correlations between x_t and x_{t-h} for h = 1, 2, 3, and so on. Theoretically, the autocorrelation between x_t and x_{t-h} equals

$$\frac{\text{Covariance}(x_t, x_{t-h})}{\text{Std. Dev.}(x_t)\,\text{Std. Dev.}(x_{t-h})} = \frac{\text{Covariance}(x_t, x_{t-h})}{\text{Variance}(x_t)}$$

The denominator in the second formula occurs because the standard deviation of a stationary series is the same at all times.

We will now introduce the Dickey-Fuller test for stationarity and apply that to our dataset. Time series must be checked for stationarity before applying any of the time series modeling techniques.

A simple AR(1) model is

$$y_t = \rho y_{t-1} + u_t\, y_t = \rho y_{t-1} + u_t$$

where y_t is the variable of interest, t is the time index, ρ is a coefficient, and u_t is the error term. A unit root is present if $\rho = 1$. The model would be non-stationary in this case.

The Dickey-Fuller test checks the null hypothesis to see if a unit root is present in an auto-regressive model.

There are three main versions of the test:

1. Test for a unit root:

$$\Delta y_t = \delta y_{t-1} + u_t$$

2. Test for a unit root with drift:

$$\Delta y_t = a_0 + \delta y_{t-1} + u_t$$

3. Test for a unit root with drift and a deterministic time trend:

$$\Delta y_t = a_0 + a_1 t + \delta y_{t-1} + u_t$$

There are other statistical tests as well for testing stationarity. The popular ones are the Kwiatkowski-Phillips-Schmidt-Shin (KPSS) tests and the Phillips-Perron test.

```
# we will apply all three tests on our dataset and see how the results come
up for all three
library(aTSA)

#Augmented Dickey-Fuller test
stationary.test(Power_Consumption$Average_Consumption, method = c("adf"),
nlag = 12, type = c("Z_rho", "Z_tau"), lag.short = TRUE, output = TRUE)

## Augmented Dickey-Fuller Test
## alternative: stationary
##
## Type 1: no drift no trend
##       lag      ADF p.value
##  [1,]   0 -0.46154   0.505
##  [2,]   1 -0.69338   0.423
##  [3,]   2  0.00634   0.639
##  [4,]   3 -0.02059   0.631
##  [5,]   4 -0.19808   0.580
##  [6,]   5 -0.18173   0.585
##  [7,]   6 -0.01851   0.632
##  [8,]   7  0.10667   0.668
##  [9,]   8  0.09127   0.663
## [10,]   9  0.15219   0.681
```

```
## [11,]  10 -0.17595   0.587
## [12,]  11  0.40941   0.755
## Type 2: with drift no trend
##        lag   ADF p.value
##  [1,]    0 -3.59  0.0136
##  [2,]    1 -9.39  0.0100
##  [3,]    2 -5.09  0.0100
##  [4,]    3 -3.63  0.0121
##  [5,]    4 -2.55  0.1269
##  [6,]    5 -2.06  0.3076
##  [7,]    6 -1.97  0.3401
##  [8,]    7 -3.10  0.0397
##  [9,]    8 -3.80  0.0100
## [10,]    9 -3.46  0.0184
## [11,]   10 -2.26  0.2347
## [12,]   11 -1.64  0.4638
## Type 3: with drift and trend
##        lag   ADF p.value
##  [1,]    0 -3.48  0.0616
##  [2,]    1 -9.15  0.0100
##  [3,]    2 -5.01  0.0100
##  [4,]    3 -3.56  0.0499
##  [5,]    4 -2.51  0.3650
##  [6,]    5 -2.05  0.5380
##  [7,]    6 -1.98  0.5666
##  [8,]    7 -3.09  0.1474
##  [9,]    8 -3.83  0.0292
## [10,]    9 -3.59  0.0481
## [11,]   10 -2.82  0.2480
## [12,]   11 -1.97  0.5717
## ----
## Note: in fact, p.value = 0.01 means p.value <= 0.01
```

The test shows that the power consumption series passes the type 2 and type 3 test of stationarity, while the test is insignificant for type 1, the Dickey-Fuller test. We can consider this series good for applying time series models with drift and trend components.

9.3 ACF and AR Model

Suppose that the process has a mean μ_t and a variance σ_t^2 at time t, for each t. Then the definition of the autocorrelation between times s and t is

$$R(s, t) = \frac{\mathrm{E}\left[(X_t - \mu_t)(X_s - \mu_s)\right]}{\sigma_t \sigma_s},$$

The ACF can be presented in the ACF plot. The ACF plot quantifies autocorrelation at different lags.

```
# ACF

acf_values <- acf(Power_Consumption$Average_Consumption,type =
c("correlation"))

print(acf_values)

##
## Autocorrelations of series 'Power_Consumption$Average_Consumption',
by lag
##
##      0      1      2      3      4      5      6      7      8      9
##  1.000  0.443 -0.390 -0.659 -0.272  0.318  0.544  0.221 -0.368 -0.614
##     10     11     12     13     14     15
## -0.263  0.368  0.542  0.155 -0.311 -0.465
```

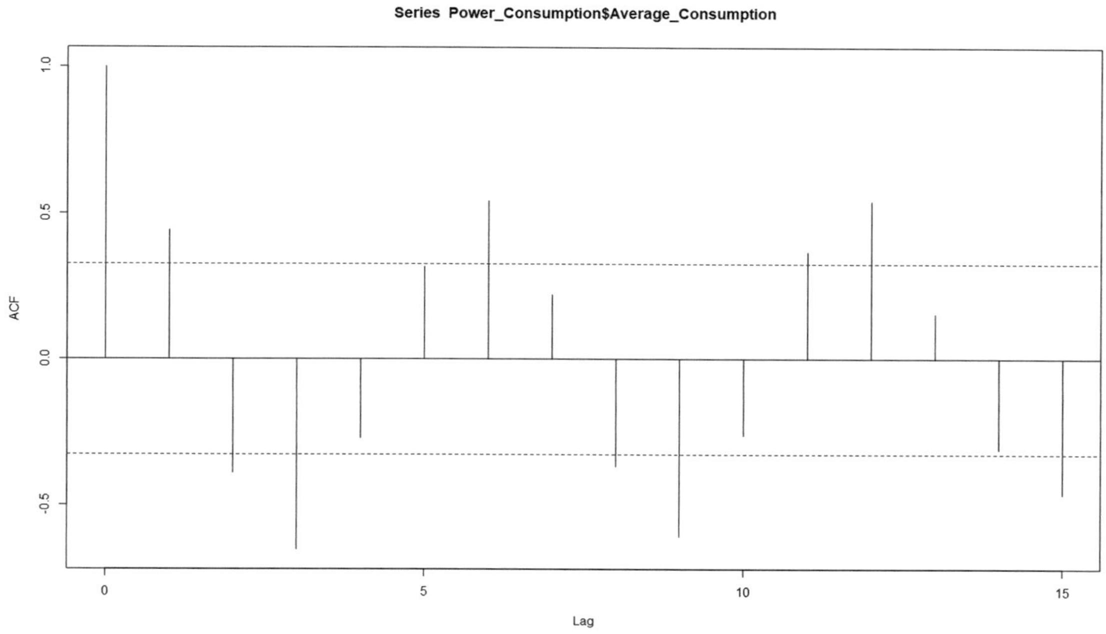

Figure 9-3. *ACF plot*

The ACF plot (see Figure 9-3) shows a pattern in the correlation at different lags of time. We will now try to fit a Auto-Regressive (AR) model to the series. By exploratory data analysis we know the data is aggregated at the month level and the pattern looks to be repeating each year. We can create an AR model with an order of 12; however, we will use AIC criteria to find the best order for our AR model.

The notation *AR*(*p*) indicates an auto-regressive model of order p. The AR(p) model is defined as

$$X_t = c + \sum_{i=1}^{p} \varphi_i X_{t-i} + \varepsilon_t$$

where $\varphi_1,\ldots,\varphi_p$ are the parameters of the model, c is a constant, and ε_t is any white noise.

White noise is noise that's independent and identically distributed with a mean of zero. In white noise, all the variables have the same variance and are not correlated with all other values in the series.

Any time series can contain two components, signal and white noise:

y(t) = signal(t) + noise(t)

The purpose of time series modeling is to reduce the signal part using modeling, so the residual is then white noise. White noise cannot be modeled, and hence it's important to test that residuals are actually white noise.

Now we will fit an AR model to the power consumption time series. See Figures 9-4 and 9-5.

```
library(stats)

ar_model <- ar(Power_Consumption$Average_Consumption, aic = TRUE,
order.max = NULL,method=c("yule-walker"))

print(ar_model)

##
## Call:
## ar(x = Power_Consumption$Average_Consumption, aic = TRUE,
order.max = NULL,     method = c("yule-walker"))
##
## Coefficients:
##       1        2
##  0.7669  -0.7297
##
## Order selected 2  sigma^2 estimated as  816100
library(forecast)

fit <- Arima(Power_Consumption$Average_Consumption,order=c(ar_
model$order,0,0))

#Plot acf plot for the residual to see if the AR model is able to handle
time variations
resid <- na.omit(ar_model$resid)

acf(resid,type = c("correlation"))
```

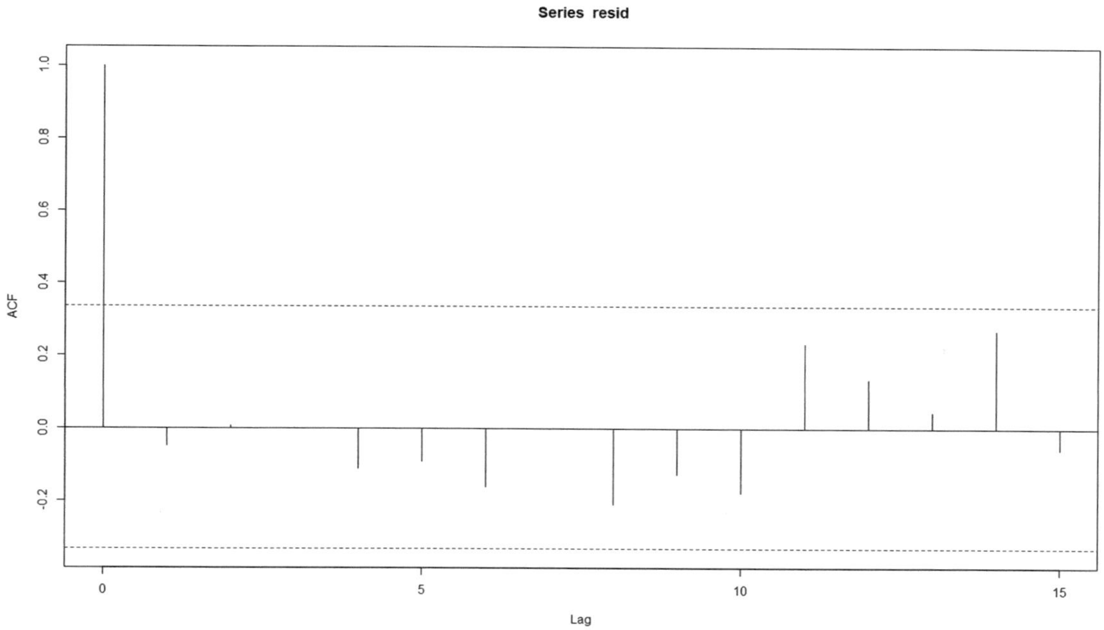

Figure 9-4. *ACF plot for the residual*

```
#Plot the fit of Ar(12) process

plot(fit$x,col="red", type="l")
lines(fitted(fit),col="blue")
```

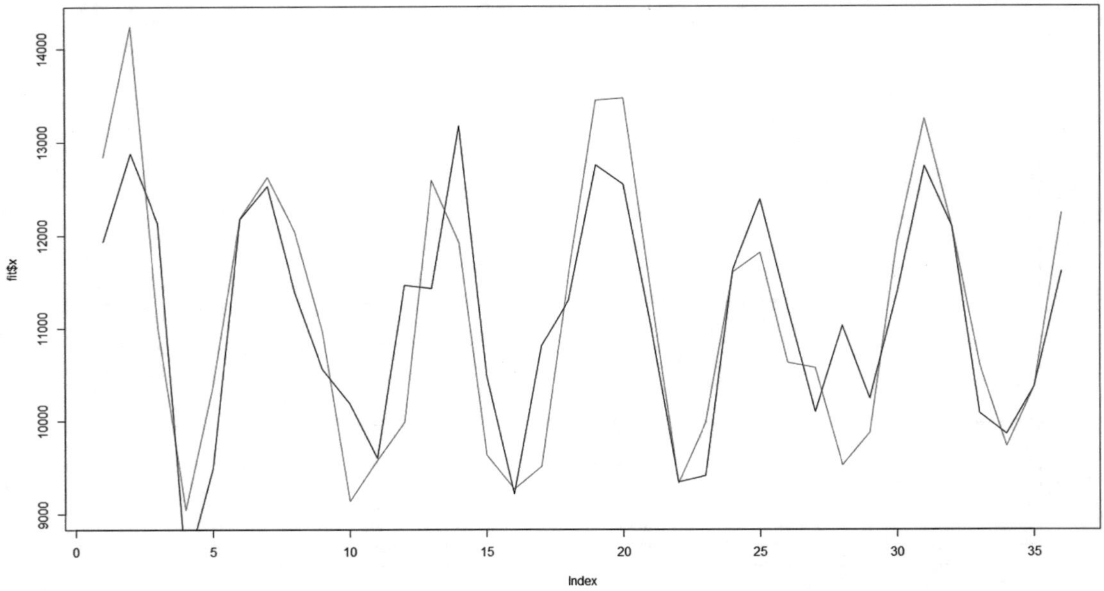

Figure 9-5. *Fitting AR of order 12*

You can observe the best AR process is chosen with an order of 12, which indicates that the time series is best represented as a 12 time lag process. This is equivalent to a repeat cycle of a year. The ACF plot also shows the reduction in ACF values and therefore signifies that the AR process explains the ACF spikes.

9.4 PACF and MA Model

In time series analysis, the autocorrelation function does not control other lags, while the partial autocorrelation function (PACF) gives the partial correlation of a time series with its own lagged values, controlling for the values of the time series at all shorter lags.

Given a time series z_t, the partial autocorrelation of lag k, denoted by $\alpha(k)$, is the autocorrelation between z_t and z_{t+k} with the linear dependence of z_t on z_{t+1} through z_{t+k-1} removed. Equivalently, it is the autocorrelation between z_t and z_{t+k} that is not accounted for by lags 1 to k, 1 inclusive.

$$\alpha(1) = \mathrm{Cor}(z_{t+1}, z_t),$$

$$\alpha(k) = \mathrm{Cor}\left(z_{t+k} - P_{t,k}(z_{t+k}), z_t - P_{t,k}(z_t)\right), \text{ for } k \geq 2,$$

where $P_{t,k}(x)$ denotes the projection of x onto the space spanned by $x_{t+1}, \ldots, x_{t+k-1}$.

Partial autocorrelation plots are a commonly used tool for identifying the order of an auto-regressive model. See Figure 9-6.

```
#Pacf(x, lag.max = NULL, plot = TRUE, na.action = na.contiguous,demean =
TRUE, ...)
pacf_values <- pacf(Power_Consumption$Average_Consumption)
```

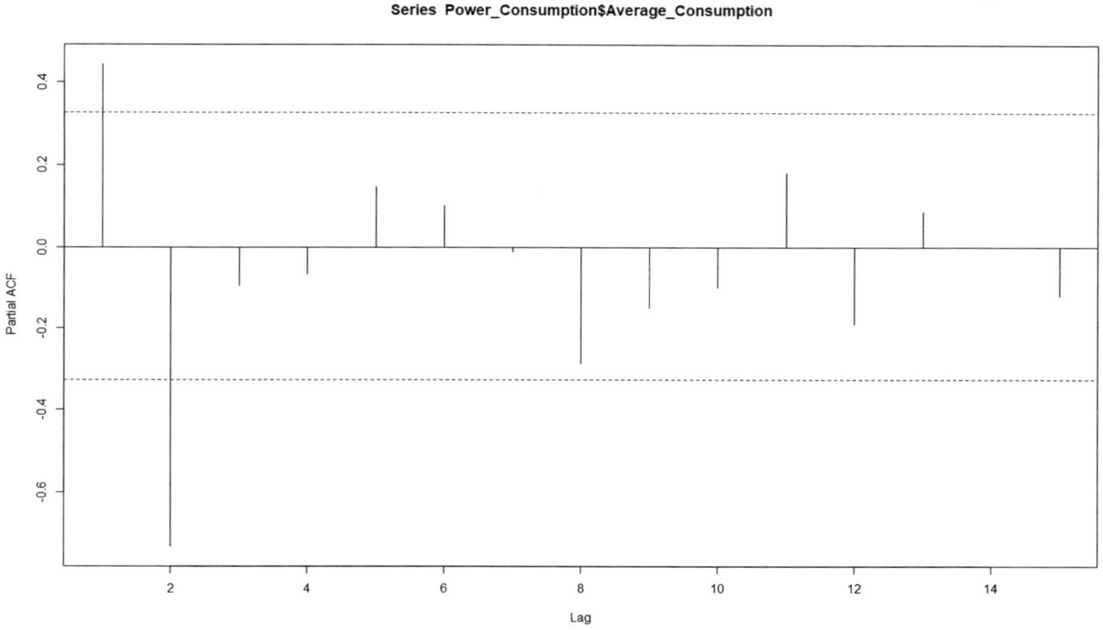

Figure 9-6. *PACF plot*

```
print(pacf_values)

##
## Partial autocorrelations of series
'Power_Consumption$Average_Consumption', by lag
##
##      1      2      3      4      5      6      7      8      9     10
##  0.443 -0.730 -0.097 -0.068  0.147  0.103 -0.011 -0.285 -0.151 -0.102
##     11     12     13     14     15
##  0.181 -0.191  0.087  0.001 -0.122
```

In the Figure 9-6, you can see why the AR model in the previous section chose an order of 12 for fitting an auto-regression model. The PACF factor is insignificant after 12 lags in the power consumption time series.

A moving average term in a time series model is a past error (multiplied by a coefficient). Moving average is also used to smooth the series. It does this be removing noise from the time series by successively averaging terms together.

Let $w_t \overset{iid}{\sim} N\left(0, \sigma_w^2\right)$, meaning that the w_t are identically, independently distributed, each with a normal distribution having mean 0 and the same variance.

The qth order moving average model, denoted by MA(q), is

$$x_t = \mu + w_t + \theta_1 w_{t-1} + \theta_2 w_{t-2} + \ldots + \theta_q w_{t-q}$$

The *invertability of MA models* states that an MA model is algebraically equivalent to a converging infinite order AR model. By converging, we mean that the AR coefficients decrease to 0 as we move back in time. See Figures 9-7 and 9-8.

```
library(forecast)

fit_ma <- Arima(Power_Consumption$Average_Consumption,order=c(12,0,1),
method="ML")

#Plot acf plot for the residual to see if the AR model is able to handle
time variations
resid <- na.omit(fit_ma$residuals)

acf(resid,type = c("correlation"))
```

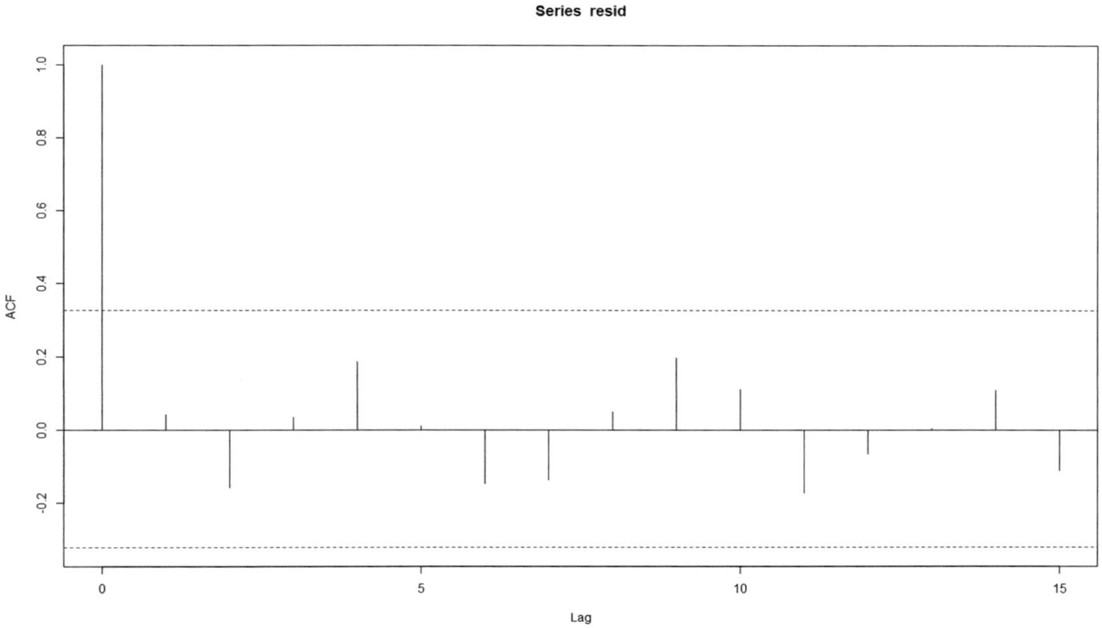

Figure 9-7. *ACF plot for the residual of an MA model*

```
pacf(resid,type = c("correlation"))
```

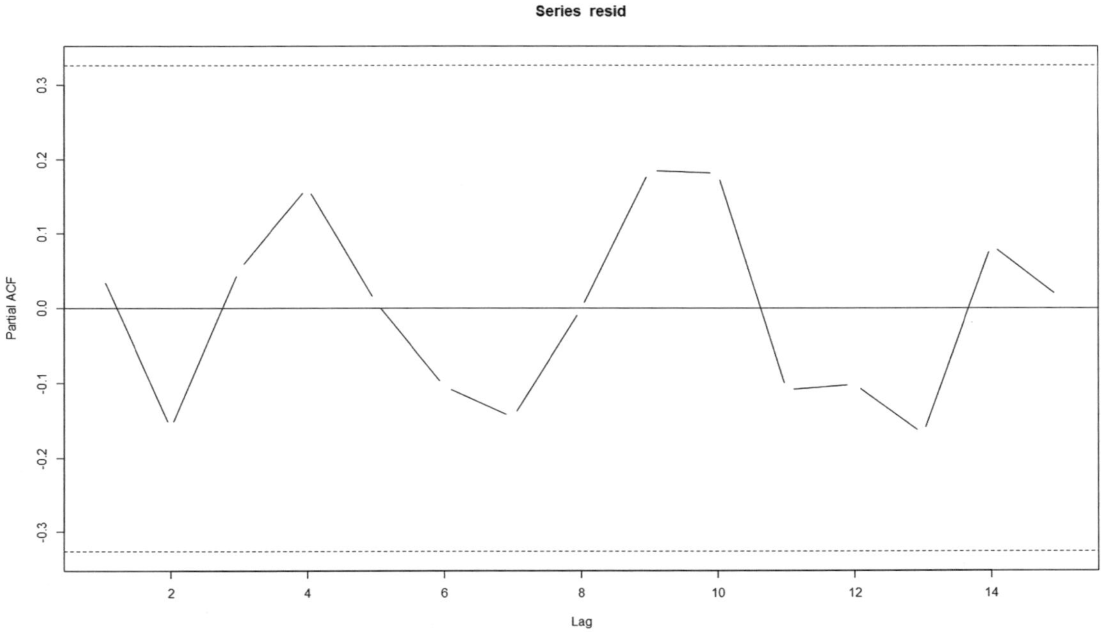

Figure 9-8. *PACF plot for the residual of an MA Model*

```
#Plot the fit AR(12) process

plot(fit_ma$x,col="red", type="l")
lines(fitted(fit_ma),col="blue")
```

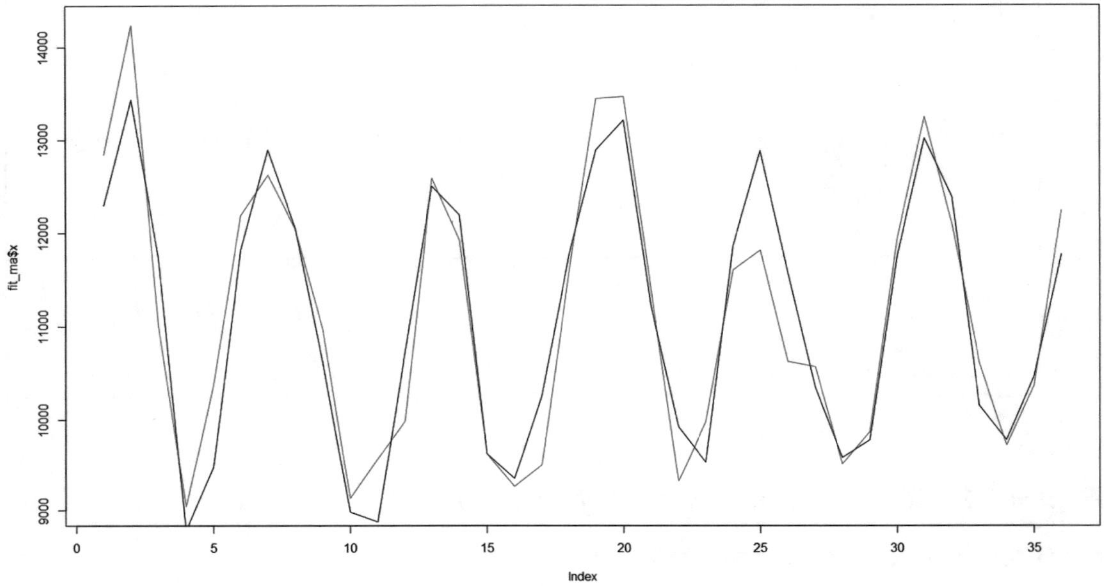

Figure 9-9. *Fitting MA model of order 12*

In the model shown in Figure 9-9, we added the moving average (MA) component to the AR(12) model. The MA component now is also correcting for the error terms in the time series. The PACF plot is now within statistical limits (see the dotted blue lines above and below); however, you can experiment with other orders to get more variations of the same models.

9.5 ARIMA Model

ARIMA stands for Auto-Regressive Integrated Moving Average. ARIMA models are the class of models applied to time series problems. They combine three key types of modeling processes into one modeling framework.

- *Differencing*: The differenced series is the change between consecutive observations in the original series and can be written as

$$y'_t = y_t - y_{t-1}.$$

We have shown first order differencing here. The second order differencing can be done as follows

$$\begin{aligned} y''_t &= y'_t - y'_{t-1} \\ &= (y_t - y_{t-1}) - (y_{t-1} - y_{t-2}) \\ &= y_t - 2y_{t-1} + y_{t-2}. \end{aligned}$$

Differencing reduces the non-stationary series to a stationary series. Stationary series are then used to develop ARIMA models. The order of differencing is the integration factor for the series, denoted as d in ARIMA model.

- *AR*: The auto-regressive order is denoted by p and tells us the number of lags required to fit an AR process to the stationary series. ACF and PACF help us identify the best set of parameters for the AR process.
- *MA*: The moving average order is denoted by q and tells us the number of error terms in a series to be regressed to reduce the differenced AR process residual to white noise.

9.5.1 Box-Jenkins Approach

Box-Jenkins is a set of approaches for time series analysis and for finding out the best fit for ARIMA models. This includes a step-by-step approach and a set of statistical methods:

- Testing and correcting for stationarity and seasonality using the ADF test
- Model fitting and testing using the ACF, PACF, and variance analyses (test for the ARCH effect)
- Finding the best p, d, and q parameters for ARIMA, with plots and ACF/PACF values
- Residual analysis to ensure the residual is white noise

ARCH stands for Auto-Regressive Conditional Heteroscedastic effects, which if present, means the time series exhibits autocorrelation in a squared series. This means that the variances of the error terms vary with time.

Let's run these steps on our dataset, which we have already been testing for some orders of ARIMA separately. See Figures 9-10 through 9-15.

```
library(tseries)
library(rugarch)
library(forecast)
#analysis
adf.test(Power_Consumption$Average_Consumption) #perform stationarity test
```

```
##
##  Augmented Dickey-Fuller Test
##
## data:  Power_Consumption$Average_Consumption
## Dickey-Fuller = -3.5612, Lag order = 3, p-value = 0.04991
## alternative hypothesis: stationary
```

```
#model identification
acf(Power_Consumption$Average_Consumption) # lag checking and model
identification
```

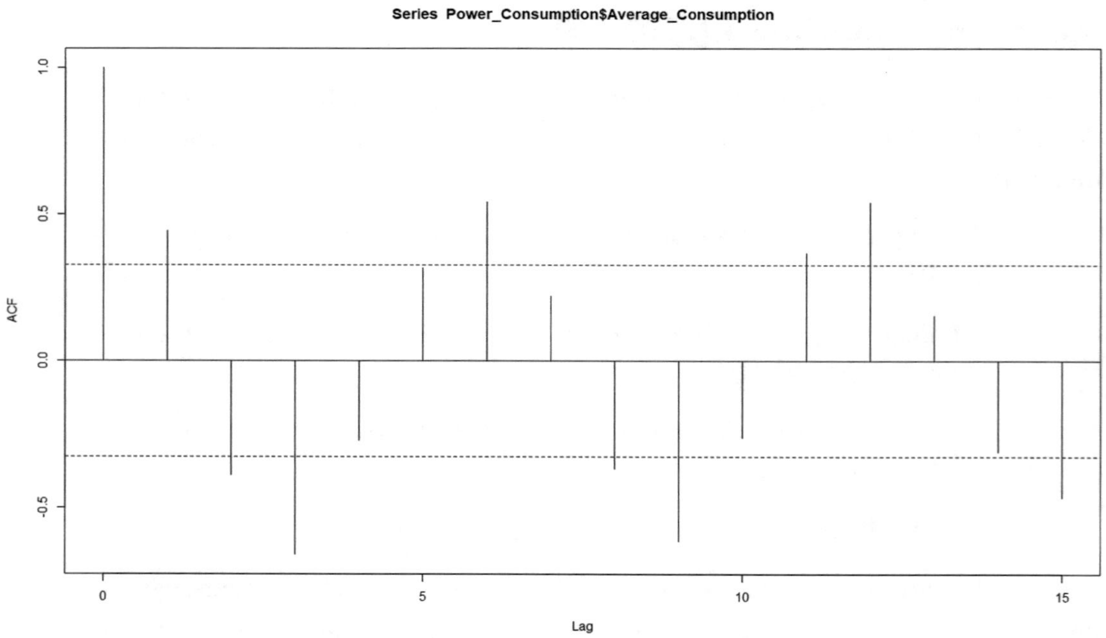

Figure 9-10. *ACF plot for checking the lag*

```
pacf(Power_Consumption$Average_Consumption) # lag checking and model
identification
```

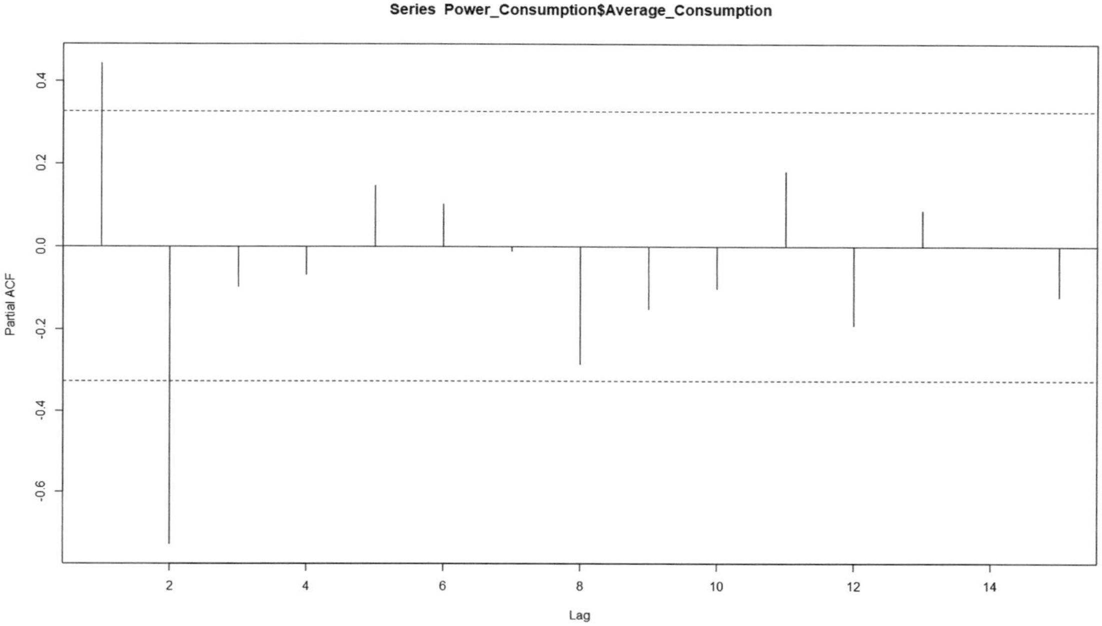

***Figure 9-11.** PACF for checking the lag*

```
Box.test(Power_Consumption$Average_Consumption,lag=12,type="Ljung-Box")
#check autocorrelation

##
##  Box-Ljung test
##
## data:  Power_Consumption$Average_Consumption
## X-squared = 108.68, df = 12, p-value < 2.2e-16

Box.test(Power_Consumption$Average_Consumption^2,lag=12,type="Ljung-Box")
# check arch effect

##
##  Box-Ljung test
##
## data:  Power_Consumption$Average_Consumption^2
## X-squared = 101.4, df = 12, p-value = 3.331e-16
```

```
fit_arima <- arima(Power_Consumption$Average_Consumption,order=c(12,0,1),
method="ML") #perform lot of preceding task automatically
fit_arima

##
## Call:
## arima(x = Power_Consumption$Average_Consumption, order = c(12, 0, 1),
method = "ML")
##
## Coefficients:
##          ar1      ar2     ar3      ar4     ar5      ar6     ar7      ar8
##       1.1580  -0.6210  0.2081  -0.2377  0.1606  -0.1819  0.1244  -0.3554
## s.e.  0.1581   0.2559  0.2927   0.2965  0.2815   0.2981  0.2747   0.2711
##          ar9     ar10    ar11     ar12      ma1   intercept
##       0.0446  -0.2771  0.6703  -0.4458  -0.9888  11012.5211
## s.e.  0.2789   0.2704  0.2484   0.1828   0.1291     17.7354
##
## sigma^2 estimated as 226188:  log likelihood = -279.72,  aic = 589.44

###Residuals Analysis
rest<-residuals(fit_arima,standardize=TRUE)
acf(rest)
```

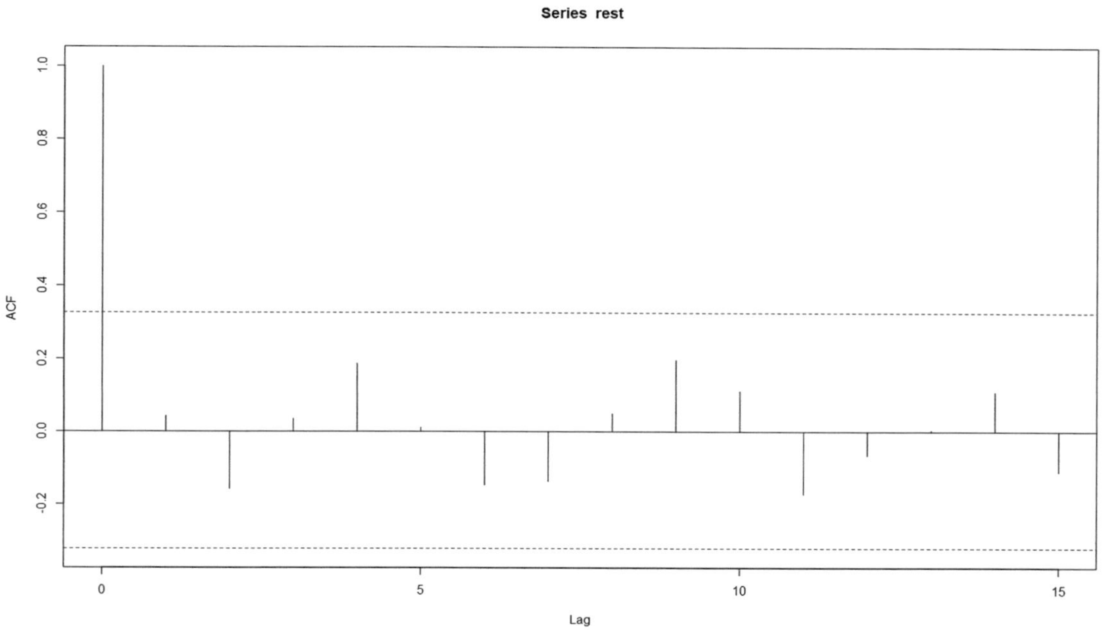

Figure 9-12. *ACF plot for residual analysis*

```
acf(rest^2)
```

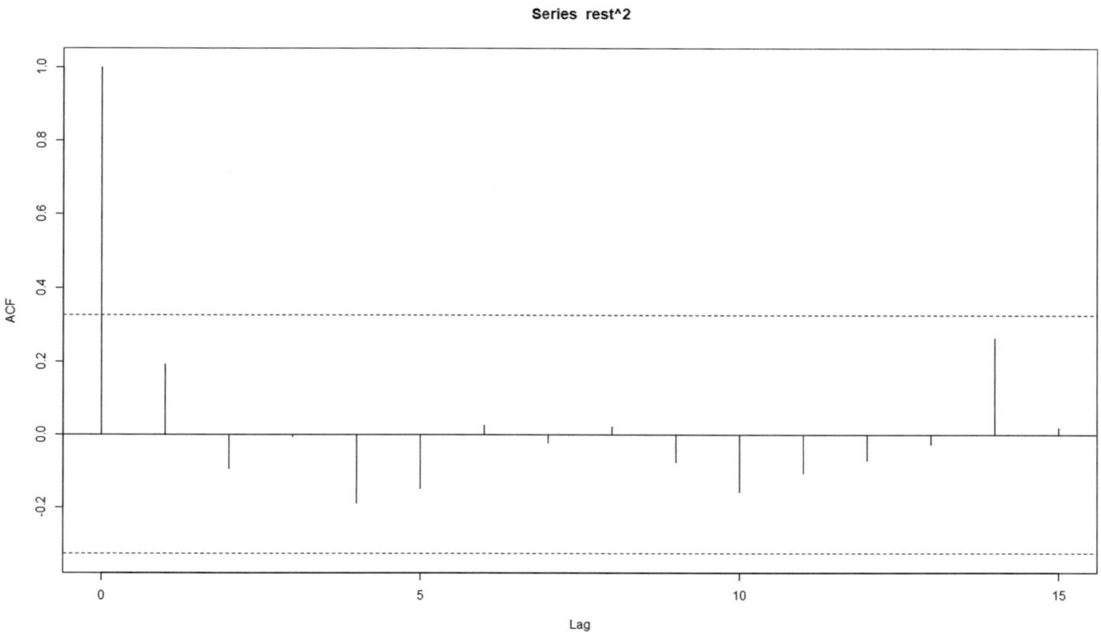

Figure 9-13. *ACF plot of the square of the residuals*

```
pacf(rest)
```

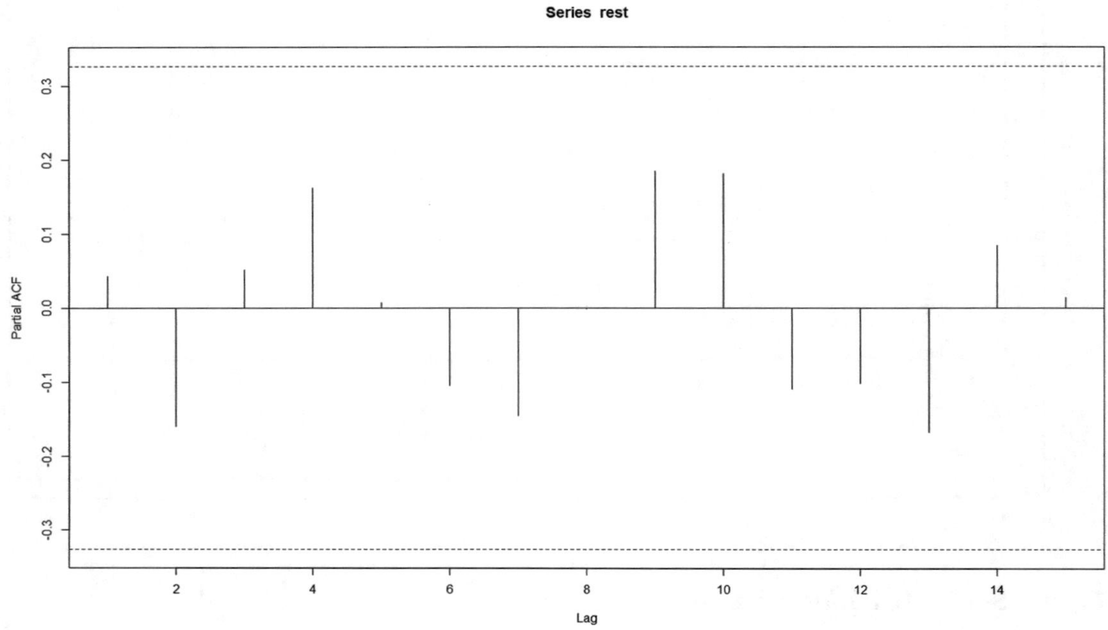

***Figure 9-14.** Boxplot showing the population (in billions) for the top 10 countries*

```
pacf(rest^2)
```

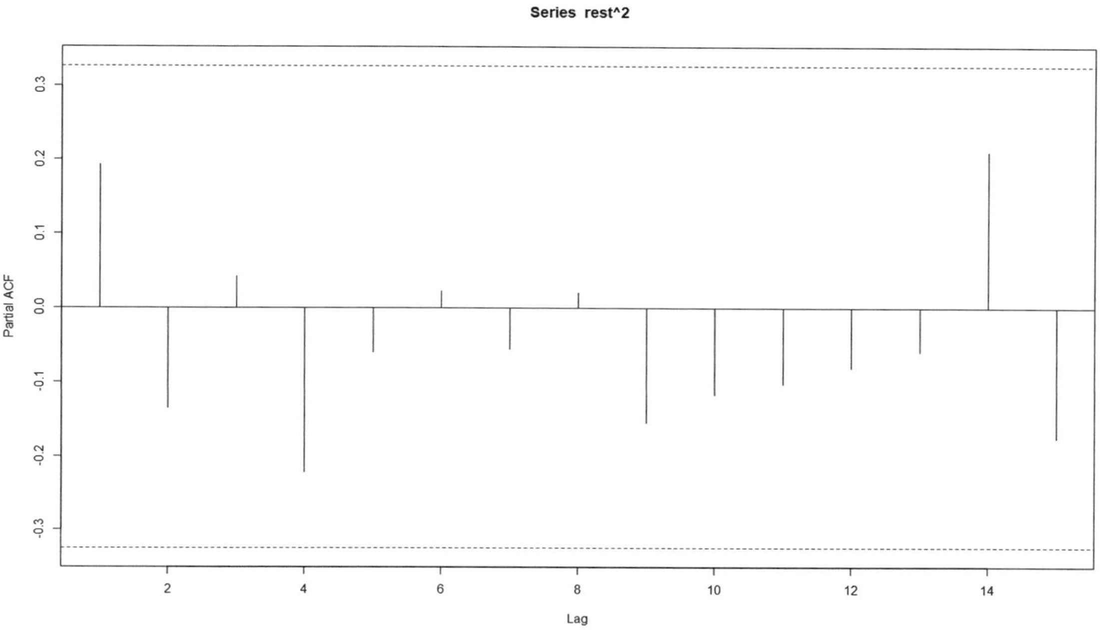

Figure 9-15. *PACF for residual analysis*

```
Box.test(rest,lag=12,type="Ljung-Box")

##
##  Box-Ljung test
##
## data:  rest
## X-squared = 9.1281, df = 12, p-value = 0.6919

Box.test(rest^2,lag=12,type="Ljung-Box")

##
##  Box-Ljung test
##
## data:  rest^2
## X-squared = 6.8569, df = 12, p-value = 0.8669
```

These steps can be applied to any univariate time series to analyze and fit a good ARIMA model. Fitting an ARIMA model involves finding the right order of differencing (d), the Auto-regressive order (p), and a moving average order(q).

Now let's use the ARIMA fit model to forecast the next 12 months of consumption and compare that with the actual. The testing window in a time series is always a continuous ordered set of actuals. This is in contrary to the machine learning random sampling approach.

For our power consumption dataset, let's see how much accuracy a time alone model can bring to the forecast for the Jan 2018 to Dec 2018 prediction. See Figure 9-16.

```
par(mfrow = c(1,2))
fit1 <-  Arima(Power_Consumption$Average_Consumption, order = c(12,0,1),
            include.drift = T,method="ML")
future <-  forecast(fit1, h = 12)
plot(future)
fit2 <- Arima(Power_Consumption$Average_Consumption, order = c(12,0,1),
            include.drift = F,method="ML")
future2 <- forecast(fit2, h = 12)
plot(future2)
```

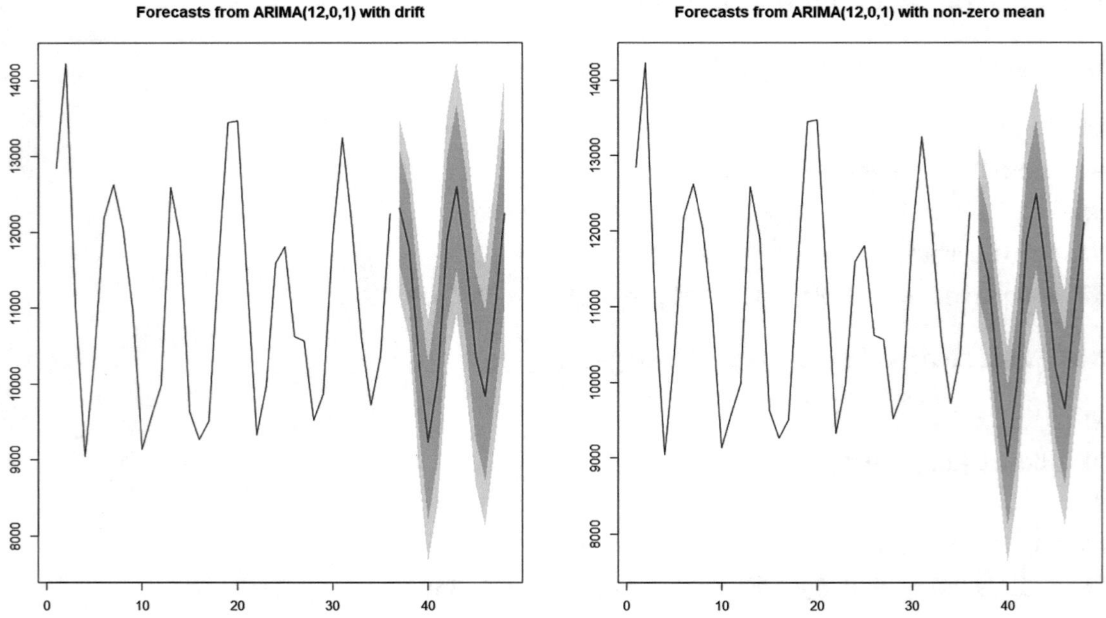

Figure 9-16. *Forecast for the period Jan 2018 to Dec 2018*

This prediction for the year 2018 is within the assumption that the time dependence of the series is the only reason for the variance and our model has captured those variances by modeling auto-regressive and moving average components.

However, the models have more than time components in the variance. We need to see how to model the combined effects of independent variables and time variance. One of the methods to incorporate these two effects are the auto-regression models discussed in the next section.

9.6 Linear Regression with AR Errors

When we try to fit a linear regression model for observations having time series structures, the residual shows a high degree of autocorrelation. This results in residuals not following the linear regression assumptions of the independent errors.

Modeling the error, called an error process, helps us adjust the estimated regression coefficients and standard errors. More generally, we can model the error as ARIMA structure as well.

Suppose that x_t and y_t are time series variables. A simple linear regression model with auto-regressive errors can be written as

$$y_t = \beta_0 + \beta_1 x_t + \epsilon_t$$

with $\epsilon_t = \phi_1\epsilon_{t-1} + \phi_2\epsilon_{t-2} + \cdots + w_t$ and $w_t \sim$ iid $N(0, \sigma^2)$

If we let $\Phi(B) = 1 - \phi_1 B - \phi_2 B^2 - \cdots$, then we can write the AR model for the errors as

$$\Phi(B)t = w_t$$

If we assume that an inverse operator, $\Phi^{-1}(B)$, exists, then $\epsilon_t = \Phi^{-1}(B)w_t$.

So, the model can be written as

$$y_t = \beta_0 + \beta_1 x_t + \Phi^{-1}(B)w_t,$$

where w_t is the usual white noise series.

Follow these steps to fit an auto-regression model:

1. Start by doing an ordinary regression. Store the residuals.
2. Analyze the time series structure of the residuals to determine if they have an AR structure.

3. If the residuals from the ordinary regression appear to have an AR structure, estimate this model and diagnose whether the model is appropriate.

Now, let's apply these steps to another simulated dataset and see if introducing the AR structure helps improve the model. See Figures 9-17 through 9-19.

```
deposit_rate <- read.csv("Dataset/dow_jones_index.csv",header=TRUE)
deposit_rate <- na.omit(deposit_rate)

deposit_rate$time <- as.Date(deposit_rate$time,format="%d-%m-%Y")

#Let's plot the time series to too how the sales trend
library(ggplot2)

ggplot(data = deposit_rate, aes(x = time, y = y)) +
  geom_line(color = 'red', size = 1) +
  theme(legend.title=element_text(family="Times",size=20),
        legend.text=element_text(family="Times",face = "italic",size=15),
        plot.title=element_text(family="Times", face="bold", size=20),
        axis.title.x=element_text(family="Times", face="bold", size=12),
        axis.title.y=element_text(family="Times", face="bold", size=12)) +
  xlab("Time") +
  ylab("Bank Deposit") +
  ggtitle("Quarterly Deposit in Bank")
```

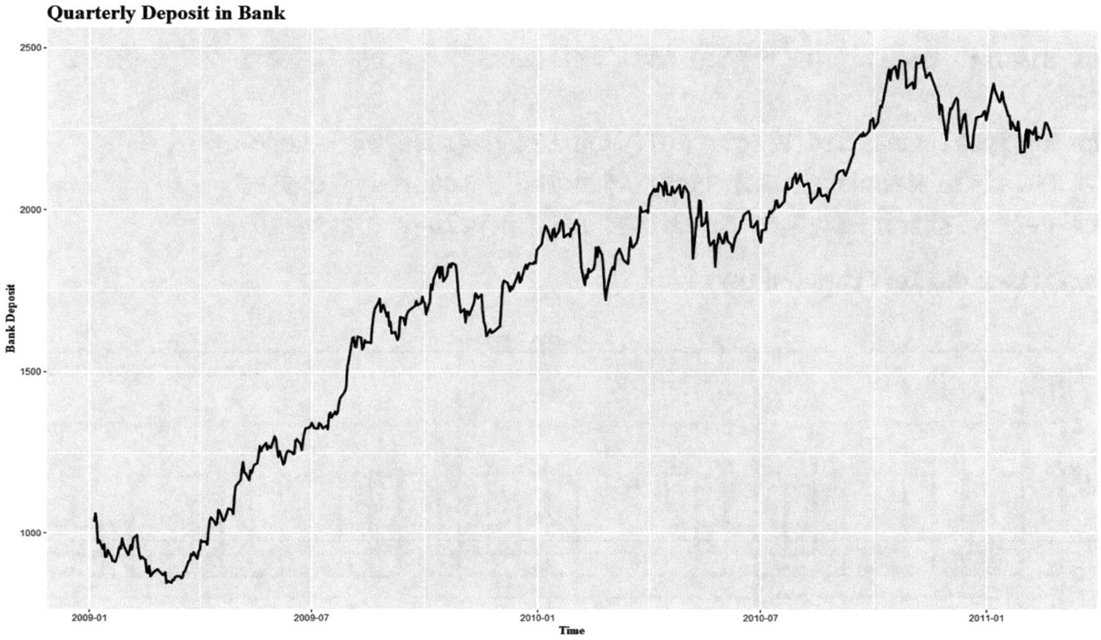

Figure 9-17. *Quarterly deposits in the bank from the Dow Jones dataset*

```
# Fit a linear regression model and analyze the residuals for AR structure
by acf plot test
library(astsa)

fit_linear <- lm(y ~ x_prime,data=deposit_rate)
summary(fit_linear)

##
## Call:
## lm(formula = y ~ x_prime, data = deposit_rate)
##
## Residuals:
##      Min       1Q   Median       3Q      Max
## -1115.99  -193.28    30.77   223.04   751.42
##
## Coefficients:
##             Estimate Std. Error t value Pr(>|t|)
## (Intercept)  2691.40      38.79   69.39   <2e-16 ***
## x_prime      -193.88       7.52  -25.78   <2e-16 ***
```

```
## ---
## Signif. codes:  0 '***' 0.001 '**' 0.01 '*' 0.05 '.' 0.1 ' ' 1
##
## Residual standard error: 307.9 on 534 degrees of freedom
## Multiple R-squared:  0.5545, Adjusted R-squared:  0.5537
## F-statistic: 664.7 on 1 and 534 DF,  p-value: < 2.2e-16
```

```
acf2(residuals(fit_linear))
```

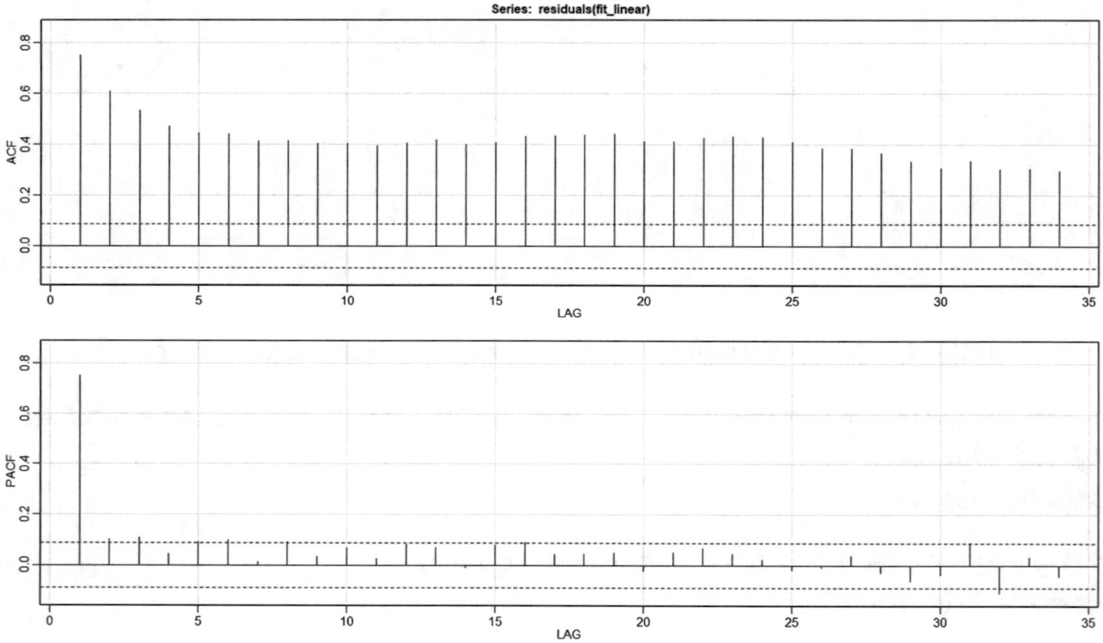

***Figure 9-18.** Histogram and density plot showing GDP and population for developed and developing countries*

```
##          ACF  PACF
##   [1,] 0.75  0.75
##   [2,] 0.61  0.10
##   [3,] 0.53  0.11
##   [4,] 0.47  0.04
##   [5,] 0.44  0.09
##   [6,] 0.44  0.10
##   [7,] 0.41  0.01
##   [8,] 0.41  0.09
```

```
##  [9,] 0.40  0.03
## [10,] 0.40  0.07
## [11,] 0.40  0.03
## [12,] 0.41  0.08
## [13,] 0.42  0.07
## [14,] 0.40 -0.01
## [15,] 0.41  0.08
## [16,] 0.43  0.09
## [17,] 0.43  0.04
## [18,] 0.44  0.04
## [19,] 0.44  0.05
## [20,] 0.41 -0.02
## [21,] 0.41  0.05
## [22,] 0.43  0.07
## [23,] 0.43  0.04
## [24,] 0.43  0.02
## [25,] 0.41 -0.02
## [26,] 0.39 -0.01
## [27,] 0.38  0.04
## [28,] 0.37 -0.03
## [29,] 0.33 -0.06
## [30,] 0.31 -0.04
## [31,] 0.34  0.09
## [32,] 0.30 -0.11
## [33,] 0.30  0.03
## [34,] 0.30 -0.04
```

```
ar1res = sarima (residuals (fit_linear), 1,0,0, no.constant=T) #AR(1)
```

```
## initial  value 5.728871
## iter   2 value 5.307745
## iter   3 value 5.307727
## iter   4 value 5.307720
## iter   4 value 5.307720
## final  value 5.307720
## converged
## initial  value 5.307628
```

```
## iter   2 value 5.307627
## iter   3 value 5.307626
## iter   3 value 5.307626
## iter   3 value 5.307626
## final  value 5.307626
## converged
```

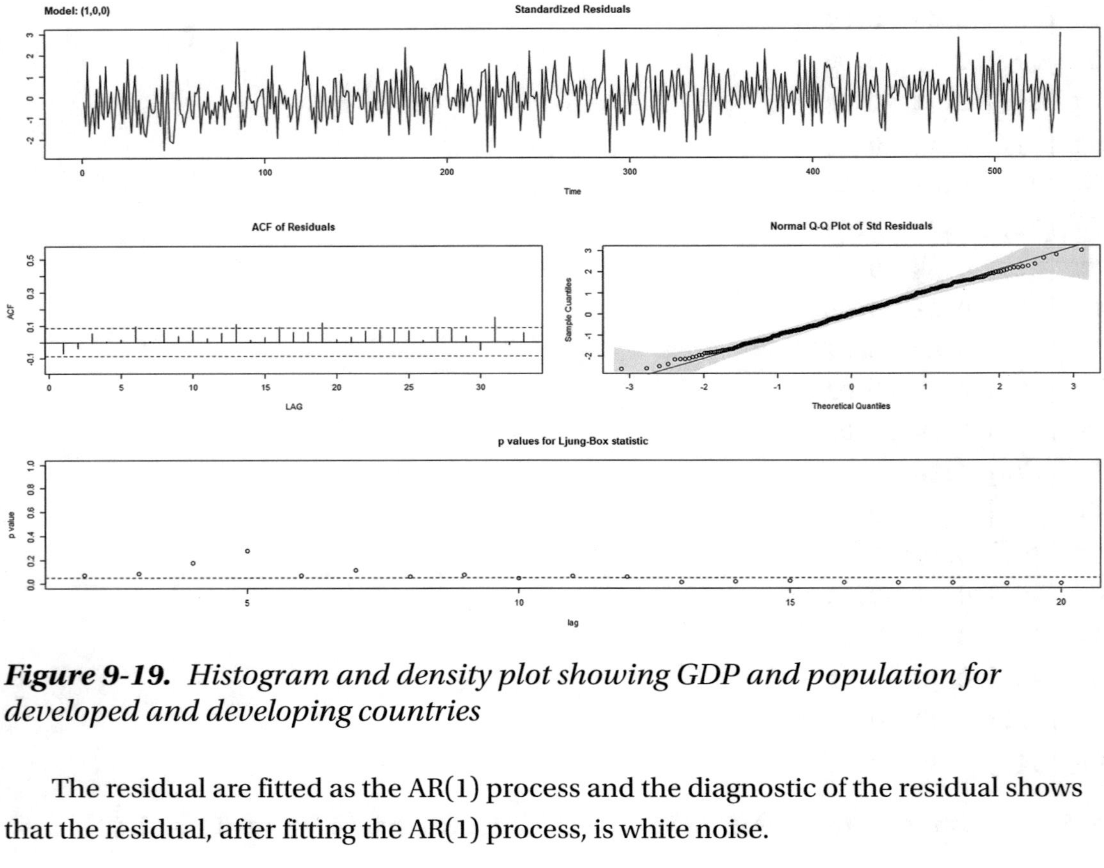

Figure 9-19. *Histogram and density plot showing GDP and population for developed and developing countries*

The residual are fitted as the AR(1) process and the diagnostic of the residual shows that the residual, after fitting the AR(1) process, is white noise.

9.7 Summary

This chapter introduced the key components of time series modeling at a high level and explained how R packages help us do the analysis of time series. We started by looking at the time series plot of a univariate time series. The visual inspection of a time series tell us about the trend, seasonality, outliers, and other features of the time series. Then we also looked at the autocorrelation and partial autocorrelation functions, which help us test time series validity before we apply any modeling techniques.

We also introduced the AR and MA processes for fitting a model. The concept of stationary time series was also introduced along with differencing. We discussed the Box-Jenkins approach to fitting an ARIMA model to univariate time series. Toward the end of the chapter, we introduced the concept of linear regression with an AR error structure.

CHAPTER 10

Scalable Machine Learning and Related Technologies

A few years back, you would have not heard the word "scalable" in machine learning parlance. The reason was mainly attributed to the lack of infrastructure, data, and real-world application. Machine learning was being much talked about in the research community of academia or in well-funded industry research labs. A prototype of any real-world application using machine learning was considered a big feat and a demonstration of breakthrough research. However, time has changed ever since the availability of powerful commodity hardware at a reduced cost and big data technology's widespread adaption. As a result, the data has become easily accessible and software developments are becoming more and more data savvy. Every single byte of data is being captured even if its use is not clear in the near future.

As you witnessed in Chapter 6, the machine learning algorithm has a lot of statistical and mathematical depth, but that's not sufficient for it to become scalable. The veracity of such statistical techniques is only enough to work on a small dataset that wholly resides in one machine. However, when the data size grows big enough to challenge the storage capabilities of a single machine, the world of distributed computing and algorithmic complexities starts to take over. And in this world, questions like the following start to emerge:

- Does the algorithm run in linear or quadratic time?
- Do we have a distributed (parallel) version of the algorithm?
- Do we have enough machines with required storage and computing power?

K. Ramasubramanian and A. Singh, *Machine Learning Using R*, https://doi.org/10.1007/978-1-4842-4215-5_10

If the answers to these questions are yes, you are ready to think big. A very recent notion of building data products, which we emphasized in our PEBE machine learning process flow, originates from our ability to scale things that can cater to the demand of ever-changing technology, data, and increasing number of users of the product. We are continuously learning from the incremental addition of new data.

In this chapter of the book, we take you through the exciting journey of big data technologies like Apache Hadoop, Hive, Pig, and Spark, with special focus on scalable machine learning using real-world examples. We present an introduction to these technologies.

10.1 Distributed Processing and Storage

Imagine a program that uses the most optimized algorithm with the best running time (time complexity) and it's designed for efficient storage as well. However, the notion of best running time for a company like Google is a few microseconds or even less (for its search program) and a company involved in DNA sequencing might be willing to spend even a few days or weeks for the program to complete. Parallel and distributed computing, before the big data revolution started, was solving the problem of execution time. The same programs were ported to run on multiple machines (servers) at the same time. In other words, the program was divided into many subtasks and assigned to multiple machines executing it at the same time. The paradigm shift big data brought this way of distributed computing was to design a mechanism that efficiently divides the data as well as the program that processes it. The type of problems people thought about in the distributed computing era and the big data generation have also had a big makeover. For example, problems like the vertex graph coloring problem (finding a way to color the vertices of a graph so that no two adjacent vertices share the same color) is considered a computationally challenging task even for a small graph with a few vertices. There is lot of literature available to designing such distributed programs like the one described in the references at the end of the chapter.

On the other hand, when enormous volumes of data are involved, for example, sorting an array of a billion numbers, the big data technologies have found their way through the solution. Our focus in this chapter is to highlight some of the technologies in this domain using a real-world example.

Although the evolution of distributed and parallel computing began many decades ago, its widespread use has been made possible by two breakthrough works, which led to an entire application development and further state-of-the-art technologies. The first such breakthrough came from Google in 2003, with their "Google File System" followed by "MapReduce: Simplified Data Processing on Large Clusters" in 2004. The former provided a scalable distributed file system for large distributed data-intensive applications and the latter designed a programming model and an associated implementation for processing and generating large datasets. They provide an architecture for dividing and storing a lot of data in smaller chunks across thousands of machines (nodes) and taking computations locally to the machines with smaller chunks of data than running on the entire data.

The second breakthrough, which took this technology to the masses, was in 2006, with Apache Hadoop, a complete open source framework for distributed storage and processing. Hadoop successfully demonstrated that, by using large computer clusters built from commodity hardware, it's possible to achieve reduced computation time and automatically handle hardware failures.

10.1.1 Google File System (GFS)

The design principle behind GFS was done keeping in mind the demand of data-intensive applications. GFS provided the scalable distributed file system (for storage) for large data.

Handling terabytes of data using thousands of disk over thousands of machines speaks to the humongous tasks such systems are designed to process.

As shown in Figure 10-1, which was originally published in the paper "Google File System," a GFS master stores the metadata about every data chunk stored in a GFS chunk server.

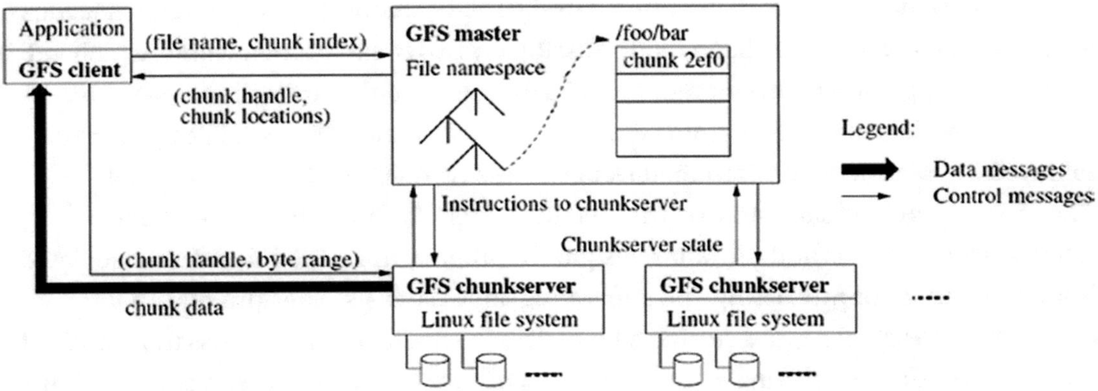

Figure 10-1. *A Google file system*

The metadata contains the file and chunk namespace (an abstract container holding unique name or identifier), file to chunk mappings, and the location of each chunk's replica for fault tolerance. In the initial design, there was only a single master; however, the most contemporary distributed architectures have much more complex settings even around the master. The GFS client interacts with the master for metadata requests and all the data requests go to the chunk servers.

10.1.2 MapReduce

The distributed processing using MapReduce is at the core of how a task on a big dataset is divided according to the distributed storage. MapReduce was designed as a programming model applying a certain logic, which could range from a sorting operation to running a machine leaning algorithm on a large volume of data.

In a nutshell, as the paper, "MapReduce: Simplified Data Processing on Large Clusters," explains, users specify a map function that processes a key-value pair to generate a set of intermediate key-value pairs, and a reduce function that merges all intermediate values associated with the same intermediate key. In simpler terms, you break the data into smaller chunks and write a map function to process a key-value pair from each of the smaller chunks simultaneously in the different nodes. This in turn generates an intermediate key-value pair, which travels over the network to a central node to get merged by certain logic defined by reduce function. The combination of these two is called the MapReduce program. We will see a simple example of this in the Hadoop ecosystem section.

Figure 10-2, from the classic paper, "MapReduce: Simplified Data Processing on Large Clusters," shows how the input file that's split into smaller chunks is placed on workers (chunk server) where the map program executes.

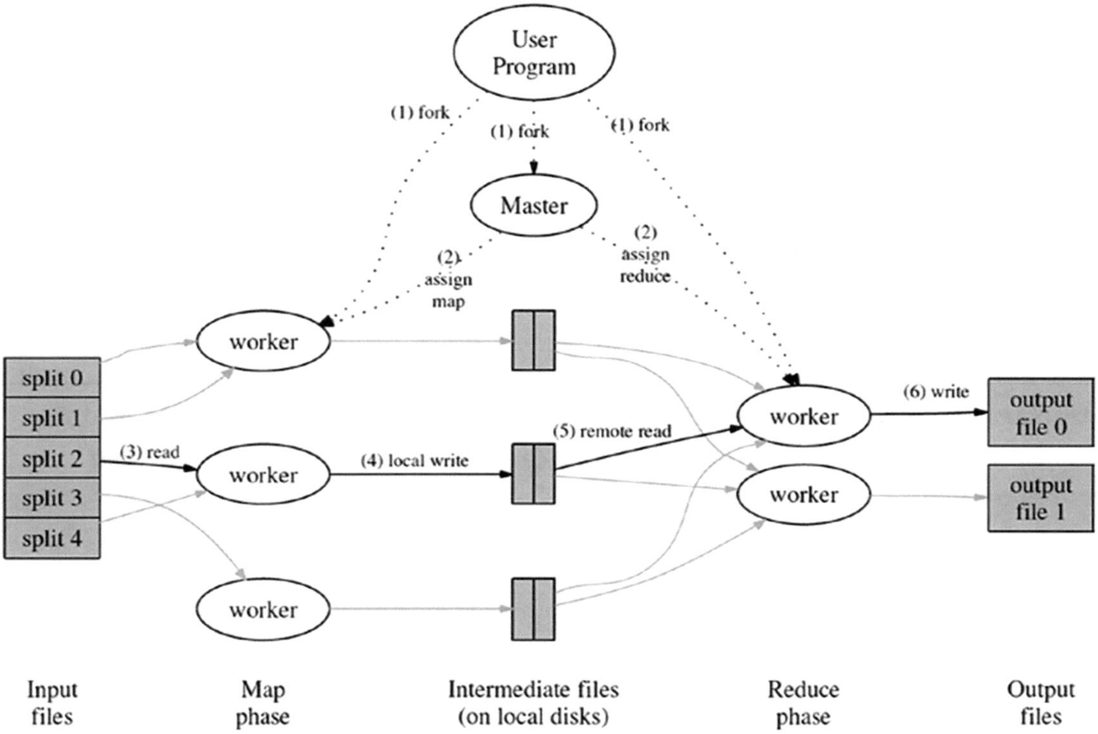

Figure 10-2. *MapReduce execution flow*

Once the map phase has completed its assigned task, it writes the data back into the local disk on the chunk servers, which is then picked up by the Reduce program to finally output the results. This entire process executes seamlessly even if there are hardware failures. We will explain MapReduce in greater detail later in the next section.

10.1.3 Parallel Execution in R

In the CRAN documentation titled, "Getting Started with doParallel and foreach," by Steve Weston and Rich Callaway, the creators of the package `doParallel`, they explain, "The doParallel package is a "parallel backend" for the foreach package. It provides a mechanism needed to execute foreach loops in parallel. The foreach package must be used in conjunction with a package such as doParallel in order to execute code in parallel."

Foreach is an idiom that allows for iterating over elements in a collection, without the use of an explicit loop counter.

Before we go into some examples of MapReduce and discuss the Hadoop ecosystem, let's see some ways to simulate the random forest algorithm (explained in Chapter 6) using parallel execution in multi-core CPUs of a single machine. We use the credit score dataset.

10.1.3.1 Setting the Cores

Using the `doParallel` library in R, we can set the number of cores of the CPU, which you want your machine to use in while running the model. There are algorithmic ways to decide (beyond the scope of this book) how many cores you should be using if a dedicated machine for such processing is available. However, if it's your personal machine, don't overkill the system by using many cores. Keep in mind that assigning all the cores to this process could crash your other processes due to insufficient resources. To be safer, we used the c-2 cores, where c is the number of cores available in your machine.

```
library(doParallel)

# Find out how many cores are available (if you don't already know)
c =detectCores()
c
 [1] 4
# Find out how many cores are currently being used
getDoParWorkers()
 [1] 1
# Create cluster with c-2 cores
cl <-makeCluster(c-2)

# Register cluster
registerDoParallel(cl)

# Find out how many cores are being used
getDoParWorkers()
 [1] 2
```

10.1.3.2 Problem Statement

The data being used here builds a model, which can predict whether a customer would default in repaying the bank loan or not (a binary classifier) using random forest. For this demonstration, we are simply looking for the time that it takes to build the model when executed in serial versus parallel manners.

```
Problem : Identifying Risky Bank Loans

setwd("C:\\Users\\Karthik\\Dropbox\\Book Writing - Drafts\\Chapter Drafts\\
Chapter 9 - Scalable Machine Learning and related technology\\Datasets")
credit <-read.csv("credit.csv")
str(credit)
 'data.frame':    1000 obs. of  17 variables:
  $ checking_balance    : Factor w/ 4 levels "< 0 DM","> 200 DM",..: 1 3 4
  1 1 4 4 3 4 3 ...
  $ months_loan_duration: int  6 48 12 42 24 36 24 36 12 30 ...
  $ credit_history      : Factor w/ 5 levels "critical","good",..: 1 2 1 2
  4 2 2 2 2 1 ...
  $ purpose             : Factor w/ 6 levels "business","car",..: 5 5 4 5 2
  4 5 2 5 2 ...
  $ amount              : int  1169 5951 2096 7882 4870 9055 2835 6948 3059
  5234 ...
  $ savings_balance     : Factor w/ 5 levels "< 100 DM","> 1000 DM",..:
  5 1 1 1 1 5 4 1 2 1 ...
  $ employment_duration : Factor w/ 5 levels "< 1 year","> 7 years",..:
  2 3 4 4 3 3 2 3 4 5 ...
  $ percent_of_income   : int  4 2 2 2 3 2 3 2 2 4 ...
  $ years_at_residence  : int  4 2 3 4 4 4 4 2 4 2 ...
  $ age                 : int  67 22 49 45 53 35 53 35 61 28 ...
  $ other_credit        : Factor w/ 3 levels "bank","none",..: 2 2 2 2 2 2
  2 2 2 2 ...
  $ housing             : Factor w/ 3 levels "other","own",..: 2 2 2 1 1 1
  2 3 2 2 ...
  $ existing_loans_count: int  2 1 1 1 2 1 1 1 1 2 ...
  $ job                 : Factor w/ 4 levels "management","skilled",..:
  2 2 4 2 2 4 2 1 4 1 ...
```

```
 $ dependents          : int  1 1 2 2 2 2 1 1 1 1 ...
 $ phone               : Factor w/ 2 levels "no","yes": 2 1 1 1 1 2 1 2 1 1 ...
 $ default             : Factor w/ 2 levels "no","yes": 1 2 1 1 2 1 1 1 1 2 ...
# create a random sample for training and test data
# use set.seed to use the same random number sequence as the tutorial
set.seed(123)
train_sample <-sample(1000, 900)

str(train_sample)
 int [1:900] 288 788 409 881 937 46 525 887 548 453 ...
# split the data frames
credit_train <-credit[train_sample, ]
credit_test  <-credit[-train_sample, ]
```

10.1.3.3 Building the Model: Serial

Note the time it takes to execute the random forest model in a serial fashion on the training data created.

```
Training a model on the data

library(randomForest)

#Sequential Execution
system.time(rf_credit_model <-randomForest(credit_train[-17],
                                            credit_train$default,
ntree =1000))
   user  system elapsed
    1.8     0.0     1.8
```

10.1.3.4 Building the Model: Parallel

In the parallel version of the code, instead of directly using the random forest model with `ntree` = 1000 parameters (which means build 1000 decision trees), we are going to use the `foreach` function with `%dopar%`, so we can split the 1000-decision tree building process into four processes. Each part builds 250 decision trees using the `randomForest` function.

```
#Parallel Execution
system.time(
  rf_credit_model_parallel <-foreach(nt =rep(250,4),
.combine = combine ,
.packages ='randomForest')
                                    %dopar%
randomForest(
                                      credit_train[-17],
                                      credit_train$default,
ntree = nt))
    user  system elapsed
    0.33    0.09    1.73
```

10.1.3.5 Stopping the Clusters

Stop all the clusters and resume the execution in a serial fashion.

```
#Shutting down cluster - when you're done, be sure to close #the parallel
backend using
stopCluster(cl)
```

Observe here, approximately, that the parallel execution is 80% faster (it might differ based on your system) than the sequential one. If a single machine using multi-cores could bring such a huge improvement, imagine the time and resources you'd save when using a large computing cluster.

Notes:

- The "user time" is the CPU time charged for the execution of user instructions of the calling process.
- The "system time" is the CPU time charged for execution by the system on behalf of the calling process.

In the next section, we go a little deeper into the Hadoop ecosystem and demonstrate the first "hello world" example using Hadoop and R.

10.2 The Hadoop Ecosystem

There are plenty of resources on Hadoop due to is popularity. Taking a broad view, the Hadoop framework consists of the following three modules (the technical details of the framework are beyond the scope of this book):

- *Hadoop Distributed File System:* This is the storage part of Hadoop, the core where the data chunks really reside. Dividing data into smaller segments means you need a meticulous way of storing the references in the form of metadata and making them available to all the processes requiring it.
- *Hadoop YARN:* Yet Another Resource Negotiator, this is also known as the data operating system. Starting with Hadoop 2.0, YARN has become the core engine driving the processes efficiently by a prudent resource management framework.
- *Hadoop MapReduce:* MapReduce decides the execution logic of what needs to be done with the data. The logic should be designed in such a way that it can execute in parallel with smaller chunks of data residing in a distributed cluster of machines.

On top of this, there are many additional software packages specially designed to work on the Hadoop framework, namely Apache Pig, Hive, HBase, Mahout, Spark, Sqoop, Flume, Oozie, Storm, Solr, and more. All this software is necessary because of the paradigm shift Hadoop brought in the traditional scheme of relational and small-scale data. We will take a brief look of Apache Pig, Hive, HBase, and Spark in this chapter, as they are the three main pillars of the Hadoop ecosystem. Figure 10-3 shows these tools organized in the Hadoop ecosystem.

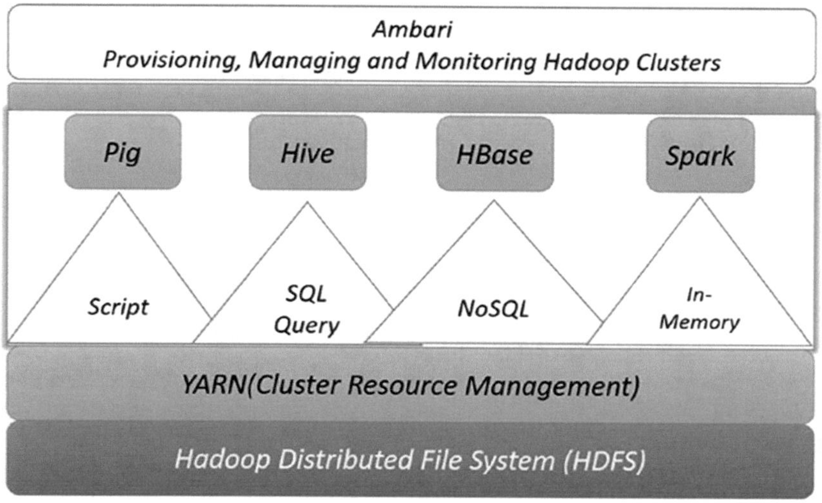

Figure 10-3. *Hadoop components and tools*

We first discuss the MapReduce, which sits in the YARN layer of Hadoop, the processing super-head.

10.2.1 MapReduce

MapReduce is a programming model for designing parallel and distributed algorithms on a cluster of machines. At a broad level, it consists of two procedures. There is *Map*, which performs operations like filtering and sorting. It processes the key-value pair and generates a intermediate key-value pair. Then there is *Reduce*, which merges all the intermediate values with the same key. If a problem could be expressed this way, then it's possible to use a MapReduce to break the problem into smaller parts. Over the years, this model has been successfully used in many real-world problems. In order to understand this model, let's look at a simple example of word count.

10.2.1.1 MapReduce Example: Word Count

Imagine there is a news aggregator application trying to build an automatic topic generator for all their articles in the web. The first step in the topic generator algorithm is to build a bag-of-word with their frequencies or, in other words, count the number of occurrences of each word in an article. Since there are an enormous number of articles on the web, it definitely requires huge computational power to be able to build this topic generator.

Figure 10-4 shows the MapReduce execution flow as the article is split into many key-value pairs, processed by the Map function, which generates the intermediate key-value pair of word and a value of 1. Another process called *shuffle* moves the output of map to the Reducer, where finally the values are added for each keyword.

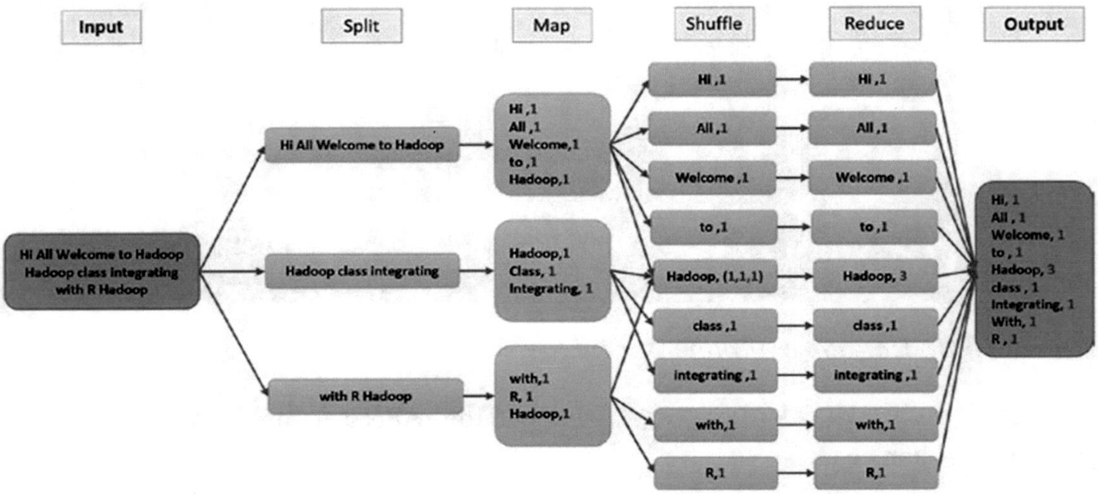

Figure 10-4. *Word count example using MapReduce*

Notes:

- The example needs a Linux/UNIX machine to run.
- Appropriate system paths need to be defined by the administrators.
- Here is the system information in which the code was executed.

    a. `platform`: `i686-redhat-linux-gnu`

    b. `arch`: i686

    c. `os`: Linux-gnu

    d. `system`: i686, Linux-gnu

    e. `major`: 3

    f. `minor`: 1.2

    g. `year`: 2014

    h. `month`: 10

i. `day`: 31

j. `svn rev`: 66913

k. `language`: R

l. `version.string`: R version 3.1.2 (2014-10-31)

- The appropriate Hadoop version is required to run the code. This code runs on Hadoop version 2.2.0, build 1529768. Comparability of this code with the latest version of Hadoop is not checked.

You must set the environment variable with the location of the Hadoop `bin` folder and the Hadoop streaming JAR.

```
Sys.setenv(HADOOP_CMD="/usr/lib/hadoop-2.2.0/bin/hadoop")
Sys.setenv(HADOOP_STREAMING="/usr/lib/hadoop-2.2.0/share/hadoop/tools/lib/
hadoop-streaming-2.2.0.jar")
```

Then you install and call the `rmr2` and `rhdfs` libraries. Once they are successful, you initialize the HDFS to read or write data from HDFS.

```
library(rmr2)
library(rhdfs)

# Hadoop File Operations

#initialize File HDFS
hdfs.init()
```

Then you put some sample data into the HDFS using the `put()` function in the `rhdfs` library.

```
#Put File into HDFS
hdfs.put("/home/sample.txt","/hadoop_practice")
 [1] TRUE
```

Then you define the Map and Reduce function. This code snippet defines the way the Map and Reduce function are going to scan the text file and *tokenize* (a term generally given to splitting a given sentence or doc by a separator like a space) into key-value pairs for counting.

```
# Reads a bunch of lines at a time
#Map Phase
map <-function(k,lines) {
  words.list <-strsplit(lines, '\\s+')
  words <-unlist(words.list)
return( keyval(words, 1) )
}

#Reduce Phase
reduce <-function(word, counts) {
keyval(word, sum(counts))
}

#MapReduce Function
wordcount <-function (input, output=NULL) {
mapreduce(input=input, output=output, input.format="text", map=map,
reduce=reduce)
}
```

Then you run the wordcount. The `wordcount` function we defined is now ready to be executed on Hadoop. Before calling the function, ensure that you have set the base directory where the input file exists and where you want to put the output generated by the `wordcount` function:

```
 read text files from folder input on HDFS
 save result in folder output on HDFS
 Submit job

basedir <- '/hadoop_practice'
infile  <-file.path(basedir, 'sample.txt')
outfile <-file.path(basedir, 'output')
ret <-wordcount(infile, outfile)
```

Fetch the results. Once the execution of the `wordcount` function is complete, you can fetch the results back into R and convert that into a data frame and sort the results, as shown in this code snippet.

```
 Fetch results from HDFS
result <-from.dfs(outfile)
```

```
results.df <-as.data.frame(result, stringsAsFactors=F)
colnames(results.df) <-c('word', 'count')
tail(results.df,100)

         word count
1           R     1
2          Hi     1
3          to     1
4         All     1
5        with     1
6       class     1
7      hadoop     3
8     Welcome     1
9 integrating     1

head(results.df[order(results.df$count, decreasing =TRUE),])

    word count
7 hadoop     3
1      R     1
2     Hi     1
3     to     1
4    All     1
5   with     1
```

Since the entire book is written in R, we have presented this example of word count where R integrates with Hadoop using its Hadoop streaming library, which is built in the packages `rhdfc` and `rmr2`. For demonstration sake, such an integration might be fine but in a real production system, it might not be a robust solution. Other programming languages like Java, Scala, and Python have a robust production-level code integrity and a tight coupling with the Hadoop framework. In the coming sections, we introduce the basics of Hive, Pig, and HBase, and conclude with a real-world example using Spark.

10.2.2 Hive

The most critical paradigm shift required in terms of adapting to a big data technology like Hadoop was the ability to read, write, and transform data as one is familiar doing in the Relational Database Management Systems (RDBMS) using SQL (Structured Query Language). RDBMS has a well-structured design of tables grouped into databases that follow a predefined schema. Querying any table is easy if you follow the SQL syntax, logic, and schema properly. The databases are well managed in a data warehouse.

Now, in order to facilitate such ease of querying the data stored in HDFS, there was a need for a data warehouse tool that's strongly coupled with the HDFS and, at the same time, provide the same capabilities of querying like the traditional RDBMS. Apache Hive was developed keeping this thought at the center of its design principles. Although the underlying storage is HDFS, the data could be structured in a well-defined schema. Among all the other tools in the Hadoop ecosystem, Hive is the most used component across the industry. The advanced technical discussion on the Hive architecture and design is beyond the scope of this book; however, we will present introductory material here in order for you to connect with the larger scheme of things when it comes to big data.

There are many tools in the market that help with large-scale data processing from various sources in a company and put it into a common data platform (Hive is a must data processing engine in such data platforms), which is then made available across companies to analysts, product managers, developers, operations analysts, and so on. Qubole Data Service is one such platform offering such a processing service. It also provides a GUI for writing SQL queries that run on Hive.

Notes:

- In the following demonstrations, we used a Linux virtual machine from Cloudera. However, if you have an instance of Linux OS installed in your personal systems, you can follow the link `https://cwiki.apache.org/confluence/display/Hive/GettingStarted` to set up Hive.
- Alternatively, you could download a virtual machine (also called Sandbox) from Cloudera, Hortonworks, or MapR. These virtual machines are prebuilt with all the necessary tools and components of Hadoop to get you started quickly. Here are couple of options. Horton

VM: `http://hortonworks.com/products/sandbox/` and Cloudera VM: `http://www.cloudera.com/downloads/quickstart_vms/5-8.html`. For the demonstrations in this chapter on Pig, Hive, HBase, we used a VM from Cloudera.

- We will use the native command-line interface to show some basics of Hive.

10.2.2.1 Creating Tables

The query looks very similar to the traditional SQL query; however, what happens in the background is a lot different in Hive. Upon successful execution of this query, a new file is created in the HDFS in the default database of Hive warehouse (see Figure 10-5).

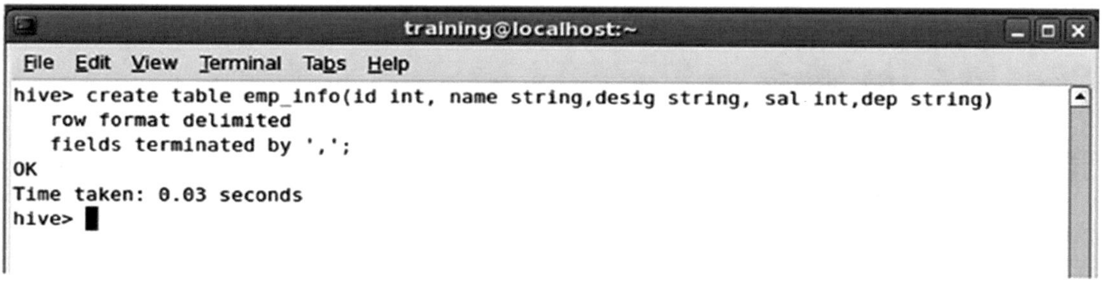

Figure 10-5. *The Hive create table command*

Figure 10-6 shows the `emp_info` table in the folder structure `/user/hive/warehouse/` of HDFS.

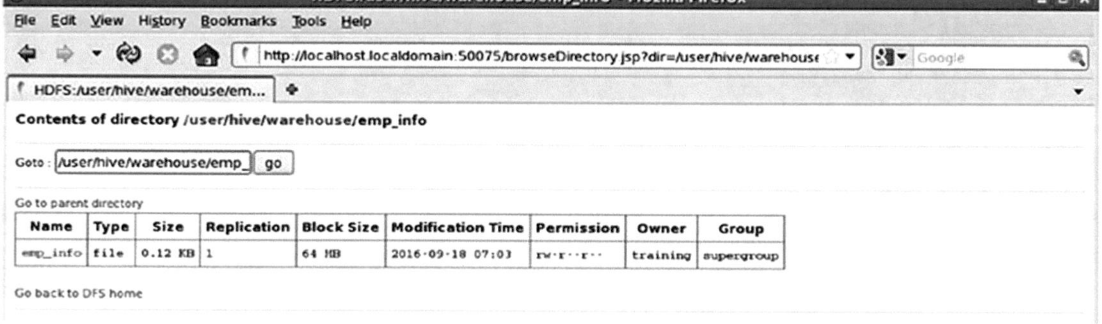

Figure 10-6. *Hive table in HDFS*

10.2.2.2 Describing Tables

Once the table is created, you can use the `describe formatted emp_info;` command to see the structure of the table matching the one we used during creation. Along with column name, it also shows the data type of the column (see Figure 10-7).

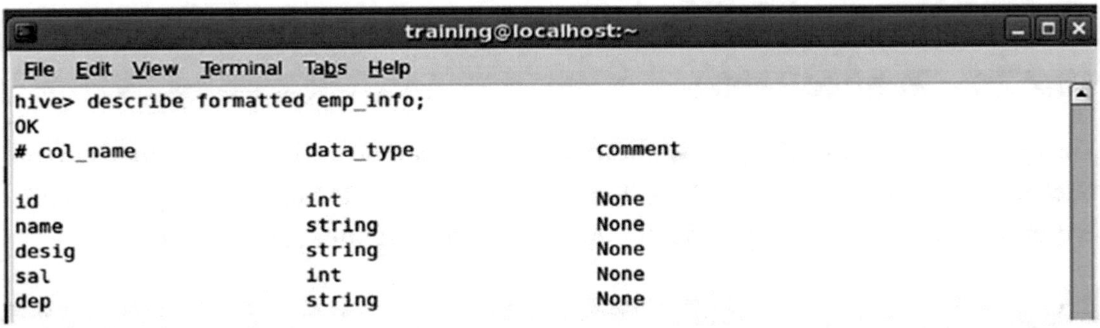
training@localhost:~
File Edit View Terminal Tabs Help
hive> describe formatted emp_info;
OK
col_name data_type comment
id int None
name string None
desig string None
sal int None
dep string None

Figure 10-7. *The describe table command*

10.2.2.3 Generating Data and Storing it in a Local File

The table is now ready to be loaded with some data. We have shown in Figure 10-8 the generation of some dummy data and storing it in the local directory in a file named `emp_info`.

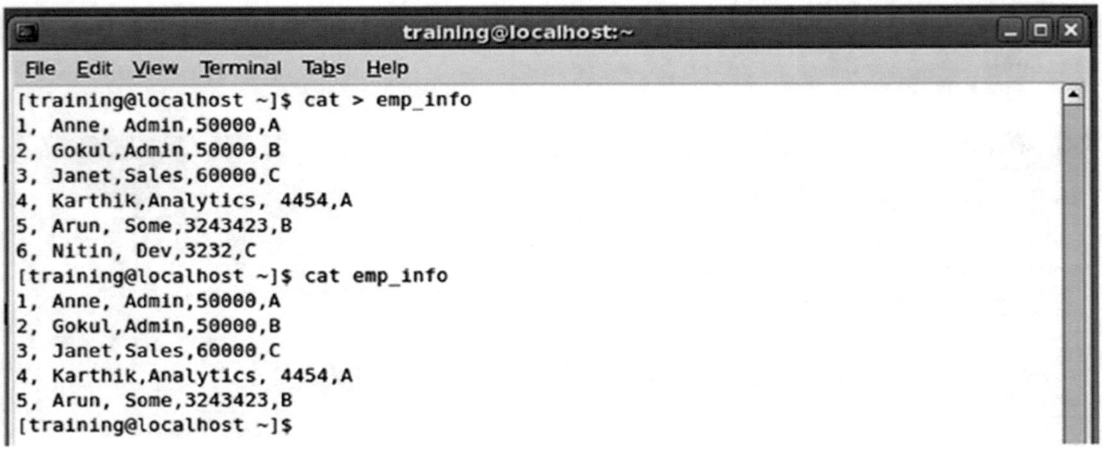
training@localhost:~
File Edit View Terminal Tabs Help
[training@localhost ~]$ cat > emp_info
1, Anne, Admin,50000,A
2, Gokul,Admin,50000,B
3, Janet,Sales,60000,C
4, Karthik,Analytics, 4454,A
5, Arun, Some,3243423,B
6, Nitin, Dev,3232,C
[training@localhost ~]$ cat emp_info
1, Anne, Admin,50000,A
2, Gokul,Admin,50000,B
3, Janet,Sales,60000,C
4, Karthik,Analytics, 4454,A
5, Arun, Some,3243423,B
[training@localhost ~]$

Figure 10-8. *Generate data and store in local file*

10.2.2.4 Loading the Data into the Hive Table

Once we have the data in a local file, using the command `load data local inpath '/home/training/emp_info' into table emp_info;` we will load the data into the Hive table `emp_info` in HDFS (see Figure 10-9).

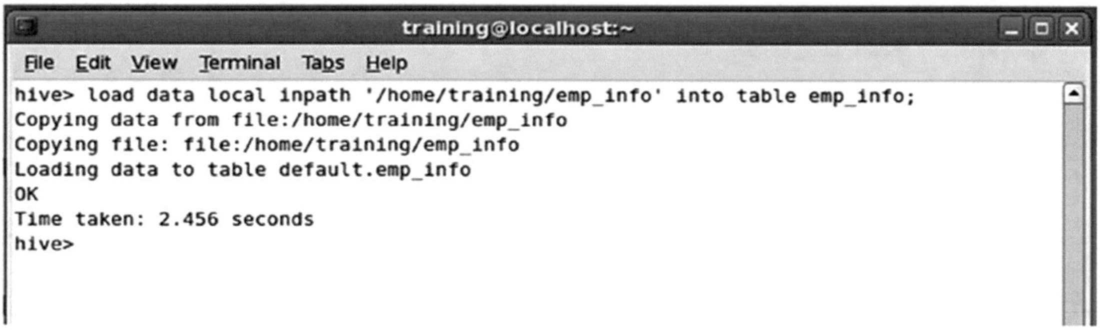

Figure 10-9. *Load the data into a Hive table*

Figure 10-10 shows the data in the HDFS file that we loaded from the local file system.

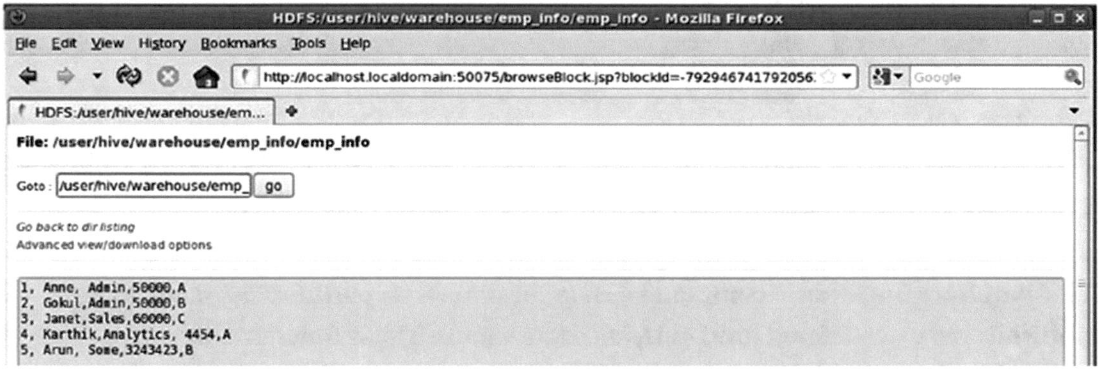

Figure 10-10. *Data in the HDFS file*

10.2.2.5 Selecting a Query

Figure 10-11 shows two varieties of the `select` query. The first one is without a `where` clause and the second one uses `where dep = 'A'`. Notice how the MapReduce framework built into Hadoop comes into play in the Hive query. This is the exact reason why we associate tools like Hive with the Hadoop ecosystem. The only difference here, unlike with the Word count example, is that we don't have to explicitly define any Map or Reduce methods; instead Hive automatically does that for us.

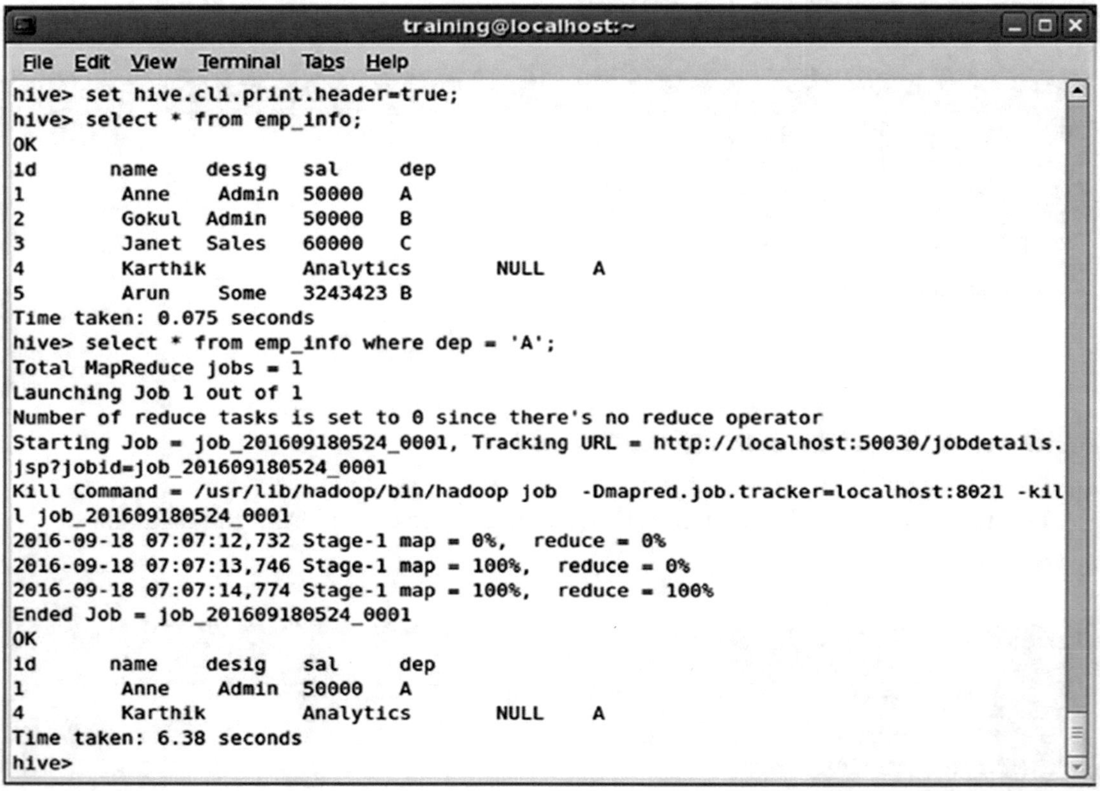
training@localhost:~
File Edit View Terminal Tabs Help
hive> set hive.cli.print.header=true;
hive> select * from emp_info;
OK
id   name   desig   sal   dep
1   Anne   Admin   50000   A
2   Gokul   Admin   50000   B
3   Janet   Sales   60000   C
4   Karthik   Analytics   NULL   A
5   Arun   Some   3243423 B
Time taken: 0.075 seconds
hive> select * from emp_info where dep = 'A';
Total MapReduce jobs = 1
Launching Job 1 out of 1
Number of reduce tasks is set to 0 since there's no reduce operator
Starting Job = job_201609180524_0001, Tracking URL = http://localhost:50030/jobdetails.
jsp?jobid=job_201609180524_0001
Kill Command = /usr/lib/hadoop/bin/hadoop job -Dmapred.job.tracker=localhost:8021 -kil
l job_201609180524_0001
2016-09-18 07:07:12,732 Stage-1 map = 0%, reduce = 0%
2016-09-18 07:07:13,746 Stage-1 map = 100%, reduce = 0%
2016-09-18 07:07:14,774 Stage-1 map = 100%, reduce = 100%
Ended Job = job_201609180524_0001
OK
id   name   desig   sal   dep
1   Anne   Admin   50000   A
4   Karthik   Analytics   NULL   A
Time taken: 6.38 seconds
hive>

Figure 10-11. *Select query with and without a where clause*

Apart from these basic commands, Hive supports data partitioning, table joins, multi-inserts, user-defined functions, and data export. These functionality are comprehensive enough for analytical databases to be migrated into Hive.

10.2.3 Apache Pig

Apache Pig is an analytical platform for large datasets. Pig programs, which are written in Pig Latin, are compiled by Pig's infrastructure layer to produce a sequence of MapReduce programs, thus achieving parallelism. Its strong coupling with Hadoop provides the storage structure of HDFS and process handling by YARN.

Let's revisit our word count example from the MapReduce section and see how we write the same example in a series of Pig Latin commands. For the detailed documentation on Pig set and usage, refer to `http://pig.apache.org/docs/r0.16.0/start.html`.

10.2.3.1 Connecting to Pig

The `pig -x local` command connects to a local file system. Simply using the `pig` command in the terminal will connect to the HDFS. For our word count example, we will stick with the local file system, as shown in Figure 10-12.

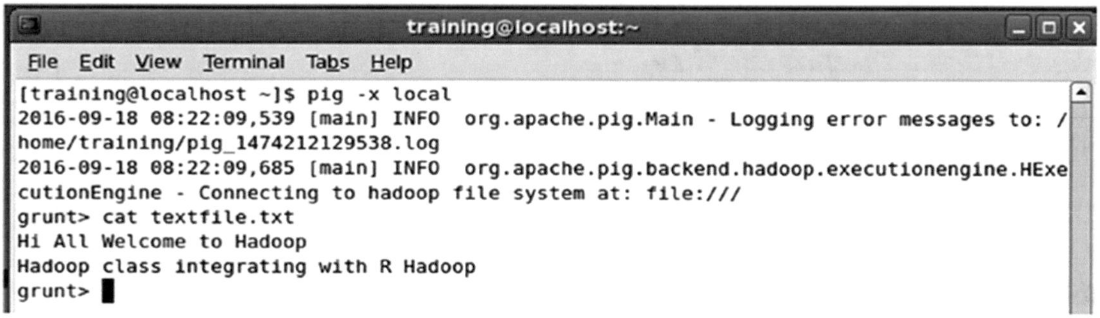

Figure 10-12. *Connecting to Pig using the local file system*

10.2.3.2 Loading the Data

The command `A1 = load '/home/training/wc.txt' as (line:chararray);` will scan the file and store each line and character array. The `dump A1` command will output the following (see Figure 10-13):

```
(Hi All Welcome to Hadoop )
(Hadoop class integrating with R Hadoop)
```

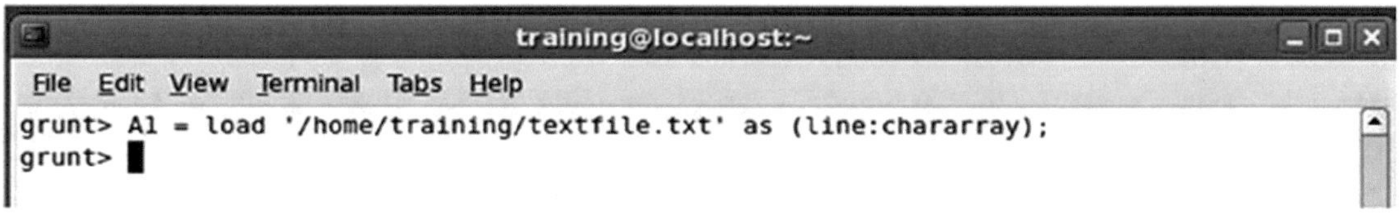

Figure 10-13. *Load data into A1*

10.2.3.3 Tokenizing Each Line

Tokenize each line into a word and store it as a list. The `dump A2` command will output the following (see Figure 10-14):

```
({(Hi),(All),(Welcome),(to),(Hadoop)})
({(Hadoop),(class),(integrating),(with),(R),(Hadoop)})
```

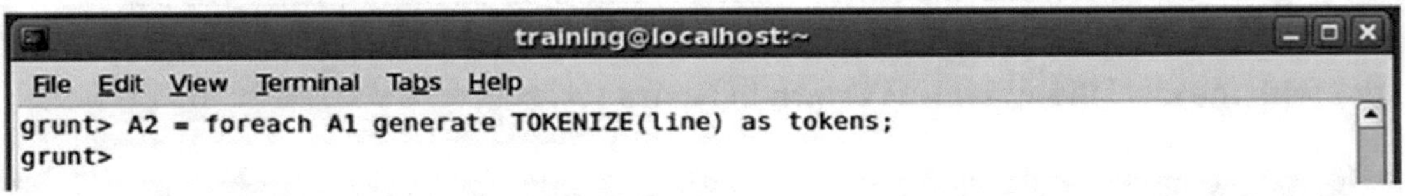
training@localhost:~
File Edit View Terminal Tabs Help
grunt> A2 = foreach A1 generate TOKENIZE(line) as tokens;
grunt>

Figure 10-14. *Tokenize each line*

10.2.3.4 Flattening the Tokens

The `A3 = foreach A2 generate flatten(tokens) as words;` command will further break each tokenized line into a token of words. The `dump A3` command will output the following (see Figure 10-15):

```
(Hi)
(All)
(Welcome)
(to)
(Hadoop)
(Hadoop)
(class)
(integrating)
(with)
(R)
(Hadoop)
```

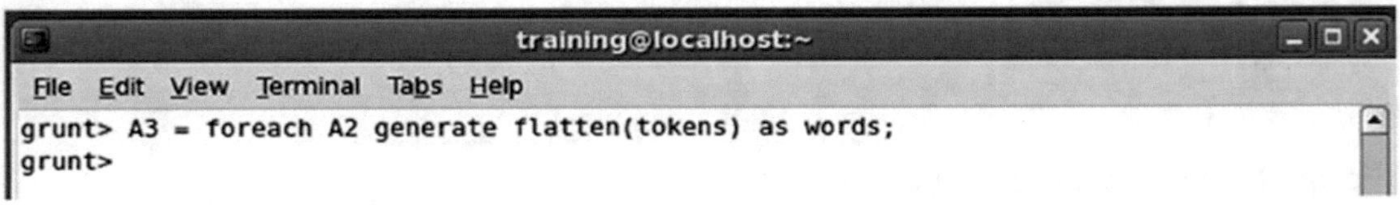
training@localhost:~
File Edit View Terminal Tabs Help
grunt> A3 = foreach A2 generate flatten(tokens) as words;
grunt>

Figure 10-15. *Flattening the tokens*

10.2.3.5 Grouping the Words

Using the command `A4 = group A3 by words;` will create a key-value pair of words and the list of the word repeated as many times as it is contained in the tokenized list. The `dump A4` command will output the following (see Figure 10-16):

```
(R,{(R)})
(Hi,{(Hi)})
(to,{(to)})
(All,{(All)})
(with,{(with)})
(class,{(class)})
(Hadoop,{(Hadoop),(Hadoop),(Hadoop)})
(Welcome,{(Welcome)})
(integrating,{(integrating)})
```

training@localhost:~
File Edit View Terminal Tabs Help
grunt> A4 = group A3 by words;
grunt>

Figure 10-16. *Grouping words*

10.2.3.6 Counting and Sorting

The following two commands will generate the key-value pair of a word and the number of its occurrence in the document and subsequently sort by count.

- A5 = `foreach A4 generate group,COUNT(A3);`
- A6 = `order A5 by $1 desc;`

The `dump A6` command will output the following:

```
(Hadoop,3)
(R,1)
(Hi,1)
(to,1)
(All,1)
```

```
(with,1)
(class,1)
(Welcome,1)
(integrating,1)
```

Using Pig, many such analytical workflows involving selection, filter, join, union, sorting, grouping, and transformation could be created with ease on large datasets.

10.2.4 HBase

So far we have been discussing representing data in a structured format of rows and columns with predefined schema, which once it's made, is difficult to tweak for changing requirements. In other words, though Hive offered a distributed version of RDBMS on large datasets, it still requires you to follow a fixed database schema and store the data in warehouse based on it. However, with rapidly changing data we need random, real-time read/writes on large distributed data. In such a scenario, the database can't be relational anymore; it has to be what people in the big data world call NoSQL. HBase was modeled after Google's big table: a distributed storage system for structured data on Google file system (GFS).

Contrary to a traditional RDBMS system, which stores every row of data with all its columns even if there are many null values and redundant data across tables due to normalization, HBase is a columnar store. This means that each row of data is stored by column family. For example, if you have an employee table with column family called `details`, you could store columns like `name`, `age`, and `qualification` under the `details` column family. So if there is a new column called `address`, it could be added under `details` in real-time.

10.2.4.1 Starting HBase

Start the HBase using the shell script `start-hbase.sh`. Run the following three commands (see Figure 10-17):

1. `cd /usr/lib/hbase/`
2. `sudo bin/start-hbase.sh`
3. `hbase shell`

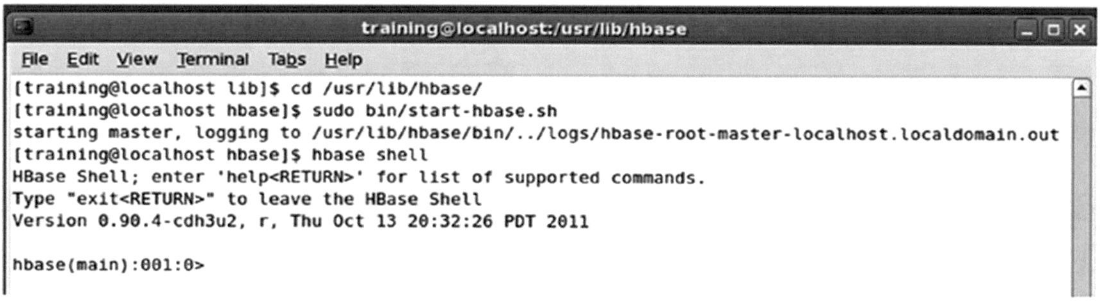

Figure 10-17. *Starting HBase*

10.2.4.2 Creating the Table and Put Data

The following commands will create a table named `employee` with two columns called `details` and `salary`. And in the `details` column family, it will put the data under the `name` and `gender` column (see Figure 10-18).

1. `create 'employee','details','salary'`
2. `put 'employee','e1','details:name','karthik'`
3. `put 'employee','e1','details:gender','m'`
4. `put 'employee','e1','salary:sal','20000'`

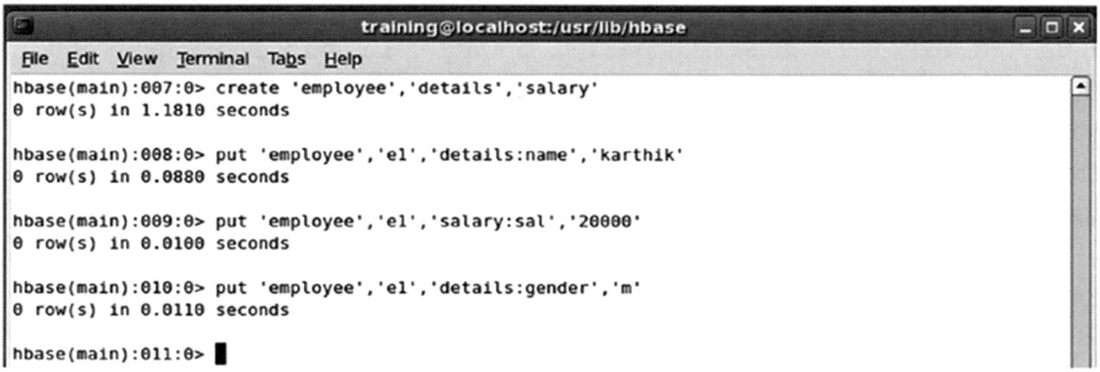

training@localhost:/usr/lib/hbase
File Edit View Terminal Tabs Help
hbase(main):007:0> create 'employee','details','salary'
0 row(s) in 1.1810 seconds
hbase(main):008:0> put 'employee','el','details:name','karthik'
0 row(s) in 0.0880 seconds
hbase(main):009:0> put 'employee','el','salary:sal','20000'
0 row(s) in 0.0100 seconds
hbase(main):010:0> put 'employee','el','details:gender','m'
0 row(s) in 0.0110 seconds
hbase(main):011:0>

Figure 10-18. *Create and put data*

10.2.4.3 Scanning the Data

Using the command `scan 'employee'`, you can see how the data is stored in HBase. Each row corresponds to the column values under a column family (see Figure 10-19).

Figure 10-19. *Scan the data*

A comprehensive reference guide on HBase can be found at `http://hbase.apache.org/book.html#arch.overview`.

10.2.5 Spark

Spark provides lightning-fast cluster computing (similar to distributed computing with multiple nodes working together). Spark has an advanced Directed Acyclic Graph (DAG)-based execution engine, which makes it 100 times faster than Hadoop MapReduce in RAM or memory and 10 times faster on disk. Contrary to Hadoop, which supports only Java, in Spark, you can write applications using Java, Scala, Python, and R. If this was not sufficient, Spark also offers SQL, streaming, machine learning, and graph libraries that could be combined in any fashion to create an application pipeline. Apart from accessing data from HDFS, in Spark, you can connect to HBase, Cassandra, S3, and many more.

In this chapter, we use SparkR, which is a lightweight frontend offering to use Apache Spark from R. It's light but very rich in functionality. In a nutshell, SparkR provides the following functionality:

- You can create SparkDataFrames from the local data frames or hive tables.
- On SparkDataFrames, operations like selecting, grouping, and aggregation as offered by `dplyr` package in R are possible.

- You can run SQL queries directly on the hive from R.
- It provides some set of machine learning algorithms from the MLlib library of Spark.

This powerful offering is definitely taking the industry by storm. However, we will keep our focus on machine learning library of Spark, MLlib.

For interested readers, more details on Spark can be found at `http://spark.apache.org/docs/latest/index.html`.

10.3 Machine Learning in R with Spark

MLlib is Spark's machine learning (ML) library. Its goal is to make practical machine learning scalable and easy. At a high level, it provides tools such as:

- *ML algorithms:* Common learning algorithms such as classification, regression, clustering, and collaborative filtering
- *Featurization*: Feature extraction, transformation, dimensionality reduction, and selection
- *Pipelines*: Tools for constructing, evaluating, and tuning ML pipelines
- *Persistence*: Saving and loading algorithms, models, and pipelines
- *Utilities*: Linear algebra, statistics, data handling, etc.

Currently, SparkR supports the following machine learning algorithms:

- Generalized Linear Model
- Accelerated Failure Time (AFT) Survival Regression Model
- Naive Bayes Model and KMeans Model

Under the hood, SparkR uses MLlib to train the model. The following code in R is taken from our earlier example of housing price predictions, but this is a scalable version of the model using SparkR.

Note (for Windows users) before running the code, follow these steps:

1. Download pre-built for Hadoop 2.7 and later Spark release from `http://spark.apache.org/downloads.html`.
2. Extract the files into the `C:-2.0.0-bin-hadoop2.7` folder (you can choose your own location).

3. Create a symbolic link for the SparkR library using the following command in the cmd prompt: `mklink /D "C:Files-3.2.2" "C:-2.0.0-bin-hadoop2.7"`.
4. Using RStudio or the R command line, test using library (SparkR).

Let's go into the R code that follows and understand how SparkR helps build a scalable machine learning model with a Spark engine. Keep in mind that the code is executed in a standalone Spark cluster with only one node. The true potential of Spark could only be seen if the same code runs on a large enterprise cluster of computing nodes with Spark.

10.3.1 Setting the Environment Variable

The following command will let R know the location where Spark and Hadoop binaries are installed in your machine. Remember, both of these are the same environment variable as you would have set in your system properties (for Windows machines).

```
#Set environment variable
Sys.setenv(SPARK_HOME='C:/Spark/spark-2.0.0-bin-hadoop2.7',HADOOP_HOME=
'C:/Hadoop-2.3.0')
.libPaths(c(file.path(Sys.getenv('SPARK_HOME'), 'R', 'lib'),.libPaths()))
Sys.setenv('SPARKR_SUBMIT_ARGS'='"sparkr-shell"')
```

10.3.2 Initializing the Spark Session

Once the environment variables are set, initialize the SparkR session with parameters like `spark.driver.memory`, `spark.sql.warehouse.dir`, and so on, as shown in the following code snippet. This initialization is required in order for the R environment to connect with Spark running in the local machine.

```
library(SparkR)
library(rJava)

#The entry point into SparkR is the SparkSession which connects your R
program to a Spark cluster
```

```
sparkR.session(enableHiveSupport =FALSE, appName ="SparkR-ML",master
="local[*]", sparkConfig =list(spark.driver.memory ="1g",spark.sql.
warehouse.dir="C:/Hadoop-2.3.0"))
 Launching java with spark-submit command C:/Spark/spark-2.0.0-bin-
hadoop2.7/bin/spark-submit2.cmd   --driver-memory "1g" "sparkr-shell"
C:\Users\Karthik\AppData\Local\Temp\Rtmpuoqh3M\backend_port1030727b704d
Java ref type org.apache.spark.sql.SparkSession id 1
```

10.3.3 Loading Data and the Running Preprocess

Load the housing data introduced in Chapter 6 and perform the same set of preprocessing steps as shown in the following code snippet:

```
library(data.table)

#Read the housing data
Data_House_Price <-fread("/Users/karthik/Dropbox/Book Writing - Drafts/
Chapter Drafts/Chapter 7 - Machine Learning Model Evaluation/tosend/House
Sale Price Dataset.csv",header=T, verbose =FALSE, showProgress =FALSE)

str(Data_House_Price)
 Classes 'data.table' and 'data.frame':   1300 obs. of  14 variables:
  $ HOUSE_ID          : chr  "0001" "0002" "0003" "0004" ...
  $ HousePrice        : int  163000 102000 265979 181900 252000 180000 115000
  176000 192000 132500 ...
  $ StoreArea         : int  433 396 864 572 1043 440 336 486 430 264 ...
  $ BasementArea      : int  662 836 0 594 0 570 0 552 24 588 ...
  $ LawnArea          : int  9120 8877 11700 14585 10574 10335 21750 9900 3182
  7758 ...
  $ StreetHouseFront: int  76 67 65 NA 85 78 100 NA 43 NA ...
  $ Location          : chr  "RK Puram" "Jama Masjid" "Burari" "RK Puram" ...
  $ ConnectivityType: chr  "Byway" "Byway" "Byway" "Byway" ...
  $ BuildingType      : chr  "IndividualHouse" "IndividualHouse" "IndividualHouse"
  "IndividualHouse" ...
  $ ConstructionYear: int  1958 1951 1880 1960 2005 1968 1960 1968 2004 1962 ...
  $ EstateType        : chr  "Other" "Other" "Other" "Other" ...
  $ SellingYear       : int  2008 2006 2009 2007 2009 2006 2009 2008 2010 2007 ...
```

```
 $ Rating          : int  6 4 7 6 8 5 5 7 8 5 ...
 $ SaleType        : chr  "NewHouse" "NewHouse" "NewHouse" "NewHouse" ...
 - attr(*, ".internal.selfref")=<externalptr>
#Pulling out relevant columns and assigning required fields in the dataset
Data_House_Price <-Data_House_Price[,.(HOUSE_ID,HousePrice,StoreArea,Street
HouseFront,BasementArea,LawnArea,Rating,SaleType)]

#Omit any missing value
Data_House_Price <-na.omit(Data_House_Price)

Data_House_Price$HOUSE_ID <-as.character(Data_House_Price$HOUSE_ID)
```

10.3.4 Creating SparkDataFrame

Now, create the training and testing SparkDataFrame by splitting the original dataset `Data_House_Price` into the first two-thirds and the rest (the final third) for training and testing, respectively. It's similar to the data frame in R, which helps store any tabular data of rows and column, but in Spark its implementation is much more efficient to handle network transfers and process thousands of computing nodes.

```
#Spark Data Frame - Train
gaussianDF_train <-createDataFrame(Data_House_Price[1:floor(nrow(Data_
House_Price)*(2/3)),])

#Spark Data Frame - Test
gaussianDF_test <-createDataFrame(Data_House_Price[floor(nrow(Data_House_
Price)*(2/3) +1):nrow(Data_House_Price),])

class(gaussianDF_train)
 [1] "SparkDataFrame"
 attr(,"package")
 [1] "SparkR"
class(gaussianDF_test)
 [1] "SparkDataFrame"
 attr(,"package")
 [1] "SparkR"
```

10.3.5 Building the ML Model

Essentially this is the core of this chapter. The first machine learning model built to scale to work with large datasets. spark.glm is a function in the MLlib library of Spark with a scalable implementation of Generalized Linear Model (GLM). Ideally, nothing changes as far as the syntax goes (except for the function name), but under the hood, there could be large army of nodes working together, automatically running the MapReduce program and many other operations supported by Spark to achieve the final outcome.

```
# Fit a generalized linear model of family "gaussian" with spark.glm
gaussianGLM <-spark.glm(gaussianDF_train, HousePrice ~StoreArea
+StreetHouseFront +BasementArea +LawnArea +Rating  +SaleType, family
="gaussian")

# Model summary
summary(gaussianGLM)
```

```
Deviance Residuals:
(Note: These are approximate quantiles with relative error <= 0.01)
    Min       1Q   Median       3Q      Max
-432276   -23923    -4236    16522   380300

Coefficients:
                         Estimate  Std. Error  t value   Pr(>|t|)
(Intercept)              -80034    32619       -2.4536   0.014387
StoreArea                58.172    9.8507      5.9054    5.4833e-09
StreetHouseFront         136.98    80.828      1.6947    0.090578
BasementArea             23.623    3.7224      6.3461    3.9629e-10
LawnArea                 0.77459   0.19875     3.8973    0.0001066
Rating                   35402     1519.4      23.3      0
SaleType_NewHouse        -12979    31904       -0.40681  0.68427
SaleType_FirstResale     10117     32497       0.31132   0.75565
SaleType_SecondResale    -24563    32480       -0.75626  0.44975
SaleType_ThirdResale     -22562    34847       -0.64748  0.51754
SaleType_FourthResale    -32205    36778       -0.87567  0.38151

(Dispersion parameter for gaussian family taken to be 2012650630)
```

```
    Null deviance: 4.9599e+12  on 711  degrees of freedom
Residual deviance: 1.4109e+12  on 701  degrees of freedom
AIC: 17286

Number of Fisher Scoring iterations: 1
```

10.3.6 Predicting the Test Data

In the final step, you can now predict the house prices on the test dataset using the ML model built in the previous step. Refer to Chapter 6 to understand the evaluation criteria for this model.

```
#Prediction on the gaussianModel
gaussianPredictions <-predict(gaussianGLM, gaussianDF_test)
names(gaussianPredictions) <-c('HOUSE_ID','HousePrice','StoreArea','Street
HouseFront','BasementArea','LawnArea','Rating','SaleType','ActualPrice',
'PredictedPrice')
gaussianPredictions$PredictedPrice <-round(gaussianPredictions$Predicted
Price,2.0)
showDF(gaussianPredictions[,9:10])
 +-----------+--------------+
 |ActualPrice|PredictedPrice|
 +-----------+--------------+
 |   139400.0|      128582.0|
 |   157000.0|      202101.0|
 |   178000.0|      164765.0|
 |   120000.0|       50425.0|
 |   130000.0|      155841.0|
 |   582933.0|      333450.0|
 |   309000.0|      255584.0|
 |   176000.0|      192695.0|
 |   125000.0|      132784.0|
 |   130000.0|      140085.0|
 |   169990.0|      183082.0|
 |   213000.0|      222965.0|
 |   144000.0|      122123.0|
 |   118500.0|      158940.0|
```

```
|   138000.0|      116004.0|
|   437154.0|      346572.0|
|   230000.0|      261396.0|
|    82000.0|       61949.0|
|    85000.0|      119914.0|
|   214900.0|      218930.0|
+-----------+-------------+
only showing top 20 rows
```

10.3.7 Stopping the SparkR Session

In the end, when the job is done, execute the following code to free all the resources being held for this process, like CPU and memory.

```
sparkR.stop()
```

While this code is running, you can fire up `http://localhost:4040/jobs/` in your browser and see the progress of your Spark jobs. For every job that is generated automatically upon the execution of this code, you could look at the DAG visualization and see how the Spark engine actually carries out the job.

In order to understand how visualization is built to understand what your application is actually doing on the Spark cluster, follow these blog post from databricks:

`https://databricks.com/blog/2015/06/22/understanding-your-spark-application-through-visualization.html`

10.4 Machine Learning in R with H2O

As we are ending this journey of machine learning in this book, we want to introduce one more powerful platform for R users, called H2O. We have been discussing some powerful techniques in machine learning like deep learning, text analysis, ensembles, etc.. These techniques are not feasible to be executed on individual machines and need high-power computing.

R is a popular language and remarkably adaptable to different platforms and it has provided options for integrating itself to powerful high-performance computing environments. In previous chapters and sections, we showed some examples, like

Microsoft Cognitive Serves, Spark, and other Apache products. In this last section, we introduce H2O, which is an open source high performance cluster for big data analysis.

H2O was developed and maintained by H2O.ai, formerly Oxdata, a startup founded in 2011. H2O is marketed as "The Open Source In-Memory, Prediction Engine for Big Data Science." It offers an impressive array of machine learning algorithms. The H2O R package provides functions for building GLM, GBM, K-means, Naive Bayes, Principal Components Analysis, random forests, and deep learning (multi-layer neural net models).

H2O is a Java Virtual Machine that is optimized for doing "in-memory" processing of distributed, parallel machine learning algorithms on clusters. A "cluster" is a software construct that can be fired up on your laptop, on a server, or across the multiple nodes of a cluster of real machines, including computers that form a Hadoop cluster. According to the latest documentation, the H2O software can be run on conventional operating systems like Microsoft Windows (7 or later), MacOS X (10.9 or later), and Linux (Ubuntu 12.04; RHEL/CentOS 6 or later). It also runs on big data systems, particularly Apache Hadoop Distributed File System (HDFS), and is available on several popular virtual machines like Cloudera (5.1 or later), MapR (3.0 or later), and Hortonworks (HDP 2.1 or later). It also operates on cloud computing environments, for example using Amazon EC2, Google Compute Engine, and Microsoft Azure. The H2O Sparkling Water software is databricks-certified on Apache Spark.

For R, the H20 package is available on CRAN. Before you proceed to the demo of H20, we recommend you follow these URLs, which have some well documented materials:

- Complete documentation on the H20 package: `https://cran.r-project.org/web/packages/h2o/h2o.pdf`
- Another documentation on H2O is available at the h2o.ai: `http://docs.h2o.ai/h2o/latest-stable/h2o-docs/index.html`
- More implementation of ML algorithms for H2O: `https://github.com/h2oai/h2o-3/tree/master/h2o-r/demos`
- Installation of H2O: A user-friendly and easy-to-follow description of installation is provided here: `http://h2o-release.s3.amazonaws.com/h2o/master/1735/docs-website/Ruser/Rinstall.html`

- A presentation on high-performance Machine Learning in R with H2O: `http://www.stat.berkeley.edu/~ledell/docs/h2o_hpccon_oct2015.pdf`

10.4.1 Installation of Packages

Once you are done installing the prerequisites, the following code will fetch the latest release of the H20 package for R and install that in the local system.

Notes:

- A good Internet connection is recommended before you try this code. All computations are performed (in highly optimized Java code) in the H2O cluster and initiated by REST calls from R.
- It's advisable not to experiment with these codes in your local machines with large volumes of data (it's safe to run the demos shown in the following code on your local machines).

```
# The following two commands remove any previously installed H2O packages for R.
if ("package:h2o" %in%search()) { detach("package:h2o", unload=TRUE) }
if ("h2o" %in%rownames(installed.packages())) { remove.packages("h2o") }

# Next, we download, install, and initialize the H2O package for R.
install.packages("h2o", repos=(c("http://s3.amazonaws.com/h2o-release/h2o/
rel-kahan/5/R", getOption("repos"))))

#Alternatively you can install the package h2o from CRAN as below
install.packages("h2o")
```

10.4.2 Initialization of H2O Clusters

Once the installation is done, you can fire an instance of clusters for the computation by calling the `init()` function.

```
# Load the h2o library in R
library(h2o);
#Initiate a cluster in your machine
localH2O =h2o.init()
The above function will return an output saying Connection successful as shown below:
 Starting H2O JVM and connecting: .... Connection successful!

 R is connected to the H2O cluster:
     H2O cluster uptime:          4 seconds 188 milliseconds
     H2O cluster version:         3.10.0.6
     H2O cluster version age:     1 month and 9 days
     H2O cluster name:            H2O_started_from_R_abhisheksingh_zve484
     H2O cluster total nodes:     1
     H2O cluster total memory:    0.89 GB
     H2O cluster total cores:     4
     H2O cluster allowed cores:   2
     H2O cluster healthy:         TRUE
     H2O Connection ip:           localhost
     H2O Connection port:         54321
     H2O Connection proxy:        NA
     R Version:                   R version 3.2.3 (2015-12-10)

 Note:  As started, H2O is limited to the CRAN default of 2 CPUs.
        Shut down and restart H2O as shown below to use all your CPUs.
            > h2o.shutdown()
            > h2o.init(nthreads = -1)
```

Once you have initiated a cluster into your local machine, you are ready to run your computations on high-power clusters of H2O. There are lot of other examples to get you started with Gradient Boosting Machine (GBM), Generalized Linear Models (GLM), ensemble tress, and many more.

10.5 Summary

In the days to come, as the cost of infrastructure goes down and data volume increases, the need for scaling up will become the first priority in the machine learning process flow. Every single application built on machine learning first has to start with the thinking of scalable implementation. Most of the traditional RDBMS systems will soon become obsolete as the data starts to explode in its size. The giants in the industry have already started to take the first step toward migrating to systems that support large scales and the agility to change as per business needs. In the not-so-far future, a greater emphasis on efficient algorithmic designs and a focus on subjects like quantum computing will start to appear when answers to the growing data volume issue are addressed by another wave of disruptive technology.

We have taken a comprehensive journey into the world of machine learning by drawing the inspiration from the fast growing data science methodology and techniques. Though a vast majority of the ML model building process flow exists and is explained with much elegance in the classic literature, we felt a need to stich the ML model building process flow with the modern world thinking emerging from data science.

We have also simplified the statistics and mathematics wherever possible to make the study of ML more practical and give plenty of additional resources for further reading. The depth of topics like sampling, regression models, and deep learning is so deep and diverse that each of these topics could produce a book of equal size. However, practical applicability of such algorithms were made possible because of the plethora of R packages available in CRAN.

Since R is the preferred programming language for beginners as well as advanced users for building quick ML prototypes around a real-world problem, we chose R to demonstrate all the examples in the book. If you want to pursue machine learning for you career or research work, a fine balance of skillsets in computer science, statistics, and domain knowledge will prove to be useful.

CHAPTER 11

Deep Learning Using Keras and TensorFlow

There was time when data and computing resources were so scarce that every data point generated by a business application or IT infrastructure was not stored, and application design had no data-driven thinking. The times have indeed changed, with the abundance of computing and storage resources, where we have the "data first" thinking and increasing volumes of data are now available from every business application. Large enterprises are now built with a business model involving revenue generation from inferences coming out from data. The most promising advancement in this surge in data and availability of computing power is how differently we are looking at solving complex problems.

Deep learning, which has its roots in traditional machine learning algorithms like neural networks, has been in existence for many decades now, however, the time couldn't be more appropriate for its return. This chapter has been included as a last chapter in the second edition of the book, as it's natural to think of deep learning as a scalable machine learning algorithm, which could work on large volumes of data. Frameworks like TensorFlow are suitably designed to run these algorithms.

More formally, deep learning algorithms are inspired by human cognitive systems that are capable of learning complex data representations. Deep learning can be supervised, semi-supervised, and unsupervised. Like neural networks, deep learning architectures are built with multiple layers of neurons, for better feature extraction. They therefore create many levels of abstraction, often referred to as a hierarchy of concepts.

In this chapter, we focus on developing an understanding of various deep learning architectures—libraries like Keras, frameworks like TensorFlow, and problems where deep learning algorithms have created a disruptive movement of research and leapfrog development.

K. Ramasubramanian and A. Singh, *Machine Learning Using R*, https://doi.org/10.1007/978-1-4842-4215-5_11

11.1 Introduction to Deep Learning

Deep leaning is a sub-field of machine learning and it draws its roots from neural network models. Figure 11-1 illustrates the overlapping relationship between artificial intelligence (AI), machine learning (ML), and deep learning (DL).

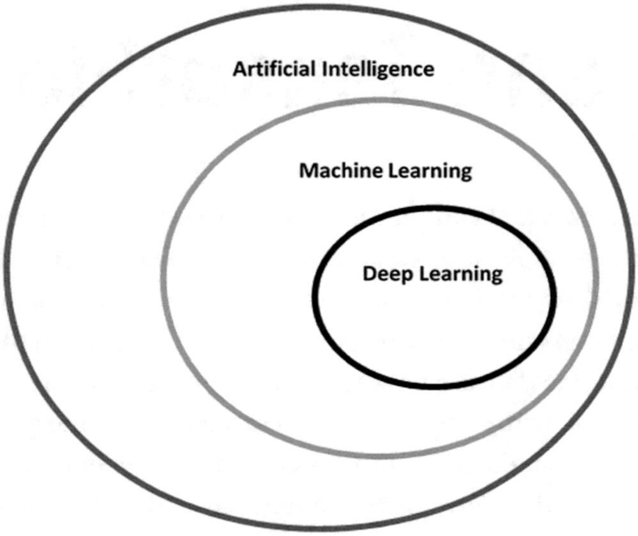

Figure 11-1. *Overlap of AI, ML, and DL*

For image classification, machine learning models are only designed to use linear classifiers on a given feature set. However, linear classifiers can only create simple regions like spaces separated by hyperplanes. Such linear classifiers are not good at detecting variations in position, orientation, or light. A similar argument could be made for video, speech, and audio. On the other hand, deep learning architecture contains multilayer stacks of modules that learn by computing non-linear input-output mappings. For this reason, such architecture is capable of learning from the representations of high-level of abstractions in text, video, audio, speech, and images. Section 11.2 will walk you through the popular deep learning architectures and their applications in various domains.

11.2 Deep Learning Architectures

In this section, we discuss some popular deep learning architectures being used widely in real-world applications. However, keeping in mind the scope of this book, we will limit the details to the minimum and refer to the appropriate materials wherever required. Deep learning architectures are rapidly evolving with a lot of research interest from various fields.

11.2.1 Convolutional Neural Networks (CNN)

Compared to a traditional neural network, Convolutional Neural Networks (CNN) structures its neurons in 3D (width, height, and depth), as shown in Figure 11-2. Every layer of CNN transforms the 3D input to 3D output. In the Figure 11-2, the red input layer represents the image, so its width and height would be the dimensions of the image, and the depth would be three, each corresponding to the red, green, blue channels.

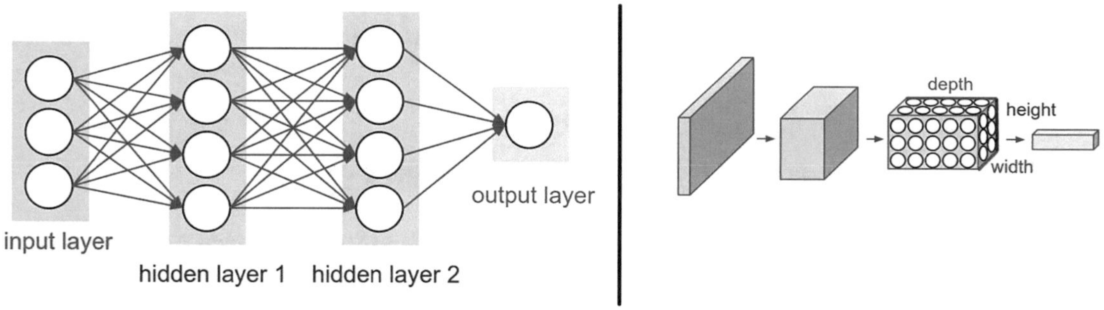

Figure 11-2. *Neural networks versus convolutional neural networks. Source:* `http://cs231n.github.io/convolutional-networks/`

Figure 11-3 provides a basic architecture of CNN, which extends to more sophisticated architectures like LeNet, AlexNet, ZF Net, GoogLeNet, VGGNet, and ResNet, to name a few. Using all the layers between the input to the output softmax layer, the network learns various features of the given data, no matter how complex the patterns. In many ways, it truly mimics the human mind. More details on these architectures could be found in "CS231n Convolutional Neural Networks for Visual Recognition Provides" [7].

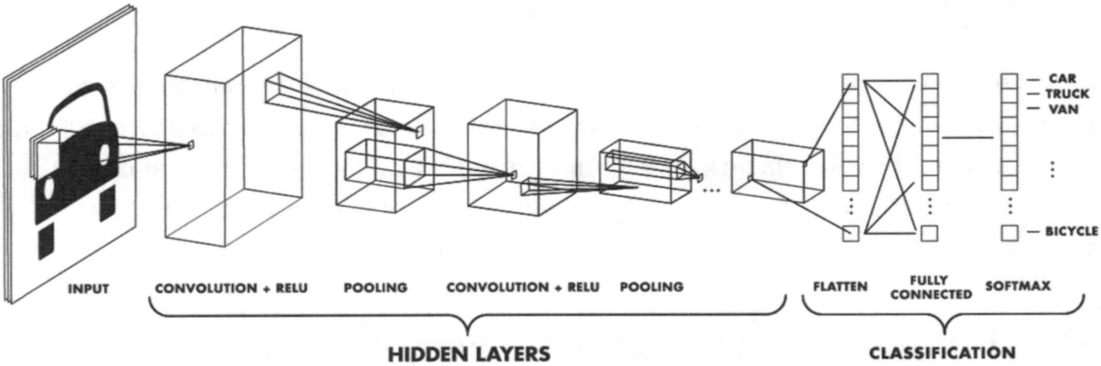

Figure 11-3. *Convolutional neural networks. Source:* *`https://www.mathworks.com/videos/introduction-to-deep-learning-what-are-convolutional-neural-networks--1489512765771.html`*

CNN's architectures are suitable for object classification and detection in images or video frames. It's popular among the computer vision practitioners. CNN architectures are widely being used in security surveillance using CCTV feeds, detection of abnormality in MRIs and CT Scans, face recognition-based applications and many other computer vision use cases.

11.2.2 Recurrent Neural Networks (RNN)

Recurrent Neural Networks (RNN) is fast becoming popular for its neural network-based architecture with a built-in internal memory. The history of RNN dates back to the 1980s; however, like the other deep learning architectures, its potential is being realized in recent days with the availability of affordable and abundant computing power.

Figure 11-4 shows the difference between RNN and the feed-forward neural network. RNN typically processes the current input and remembers what it has learned from previous input.

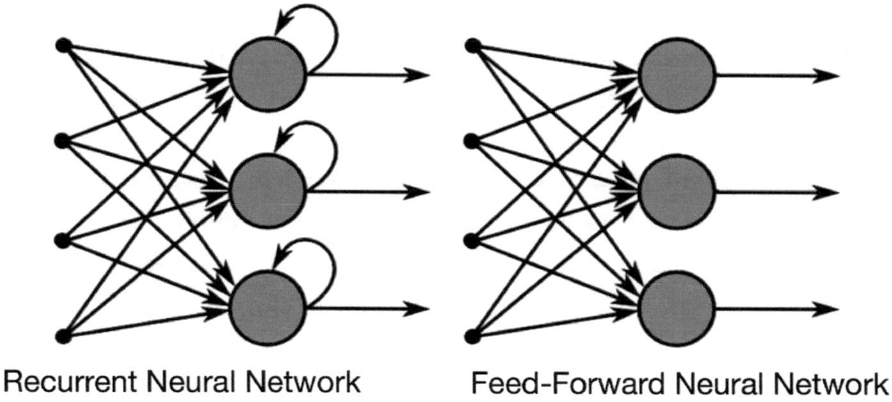

Figure 11-4. *Feed-forward neural networks versus convolutional neural networks. Source:* `https://towardsdatascience.com/recurrent-neural-networks-and-lstm-4b601dd822a5`

Also note that while feed-forward neural networks map one input to one output, RNNs can map one to many, many to many (translation), and many to one (classifying a voice). Figure 11-5 shows the different types of mapping in RNN.

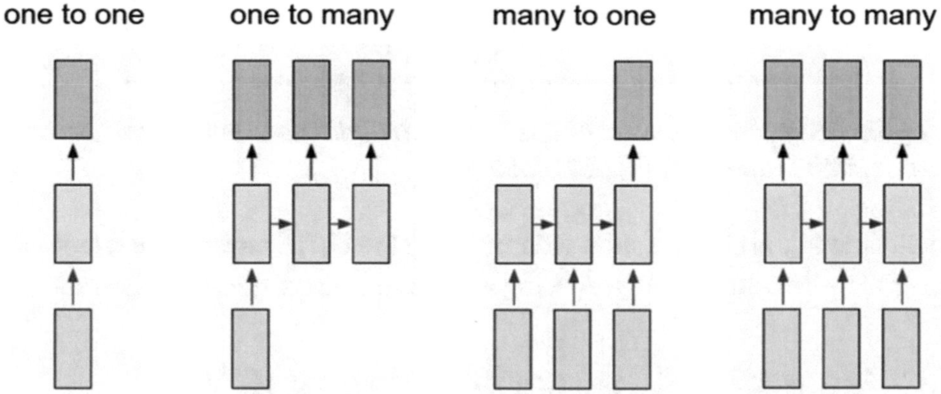

Figure 11-5. *RNN mappings. Source:* `https://towardsdatascience.com/recurrent-neural-networks-and-lstm-4b601dd822a5`

RNN's capability to remember the important parts of the input makes it perform well with sequential data like speech, text, time series, audio, and video.

One limitation of RNN is its short-term memory. In order to work around this limitation, RNN could be combined with Long-Short Term Memory (LSTM) cells, which effectively make it capable of storing long-term memory as well. These are often called LSTM networks. LSTMs enable RNNs to remember their inputs over a long period of time. The memory is designed as a gated cell (gate could be open or close), which can decide to store (open gate) or delete (close gate) the information based on the importance of the information. Figure 11-6 shows a typical LSTM cell.

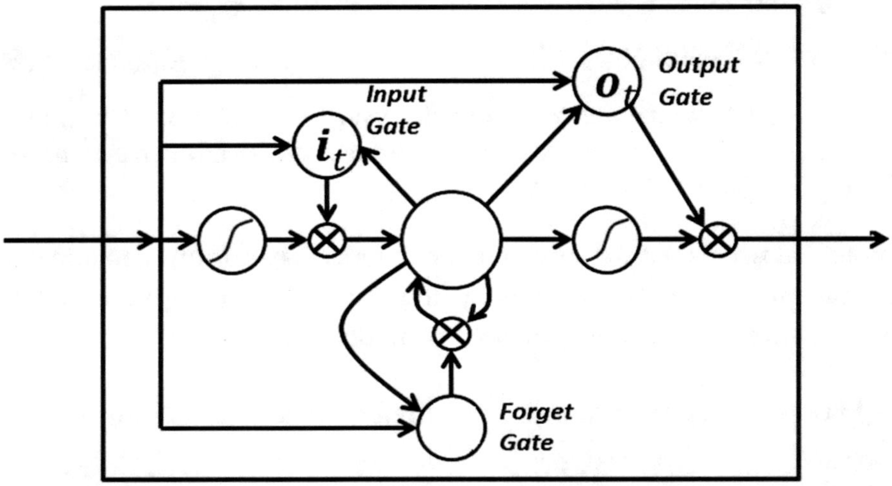

Figure 11-6. *LSTM cell. Source:* `https://towardsdatascience.com/recurrent-neural-networks-and-lstm-4b601dd822a5`

We will later in the chapter show a demo using the LSTM network for a real-world problem of identifying duplicate text using a Quora duplicate questions dataset.

11.2.3 Generative Adversarial Network (GAN)

Apart from the popular AlexNet, VGG Net, GoogleNet, ResNet, and SegNet architectures mentioned in Section 11.2.1, we will briefly explain the Generative Adversarial Network (GAN), one of the most interesting ideas evolved from the field of machine learning in the last decade.

As articulated in the article, "A Beginner's Guide to Generative Adversarial Networks (GANs)"[8], GANs potential is huge, because they can learn to mimic any distribution of data. That is, GANs can be taught to create worlds eerily similar to our own in any domain: images, music, speech, and prose. They are robot artists in a sense, and their output is impressive—poignant even.

GAN is based on a generative algorithm. In Chapter 6, we show multiple examples of discriminative algorithm, where it tries to classify inputs based on input features. For example, given a patient record in a diabetic dataset, classify whether the patient is diabetic or not. Mathematically this could be represented as P(Y|X), where Y is the class (Yes or No) and X in the input feature vector. In a generative algorithm, we flip this relationship and ask, "Can we generate all the features of a diabetic patient?" In other words, assuming a person is diabetic, how likely are we to observe the given input feature?

So, in GAN, one neural network, which we call generator, generates new data instances, while the other, the discriminator, decides whether each instance of data it reviews belongs to the actual training dataset.

The discriminator model is a classifier that determines whether a given image looks like a real image from the dataset or like an artificially created image. This is basically a binary classifier that will take the form of a normal CNN. The generator model takes random input values and transforms them into images through a deconvolutional neural network. Figure 11-7 shows the architecture.

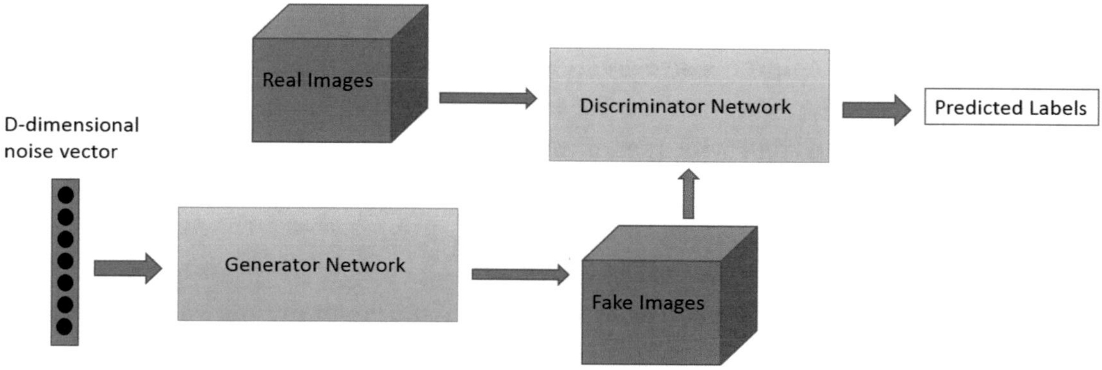

***Figure 11-7.** GAN architecture. Source: `https://www.oreilly.com/learning/generative-adversarial-networks-for-beginners`*

GANs are powerful concepts in many ways, and they could truly put into perspective a capability only a human being could think of doing. Imagine a GAN model generating plausible images of birds and flowers from detailed text descriptions. The research paper, "Generative Adversarial Text to Image Synthesis," [10] demonstrates this idea. The possibilities of this network is immense in various fields like assistance to a disabled person, interior decoration, generating creative art-forms, and so on.

11.3 Deep Learning Toolset

There are numerous tools and software stacks available for building deep learning models on top of CPU or GPU hardware. Since deep learning models are computationally resource intensive, more and more GPU usage is seen in recent days. The various software being designed for deep learning are designed keeping in mind the complexity of the algorithm and the computation needs. In this section, we explore various available toolsets for building a deep learning model on real-world, large datasets.

11.3.1 High-Level Library

Keras is the undisputed choice for open source high-level neural network API originally written in Python. Keras soon became the de-facto standard for building the deep learning architectures on top of many backend engines (discussed in the next section), like TensorFlow, CNTK, and Theano. It supports both CNNs and RNNs and runs on CPU as well as GPU machines.

Detailed documentation of using Keras could be found at `https://keras.io/`.

Apart from Keras, we also have Apache MXNet, a library designed for deep learning. Although MXNet is a comprehensive and flexible Python API, it has not gained enough interest from the developer community for widespread usage. In our demos in this chapter, we use Keras, as it provides seamless usage with R.

11.3.2 Backend Engine or Frameworks

Backend engines like TensorFlow, Theano, and CNTK are generally known as software libraries for dataflow programming. Certain references also describe these engines as machine learning frameworks. These backend engines provide the platform for operations that neural network like architectures perform on multidimensional data arrays like matrix multiplication. In frameworks like TensorFlow, computations are expressed as stateful dataflow graphs, which makes it very efficient when working on large volumes of data and makes it easy to deploy the computation across a variety of platforms like CPU, GPU, or TPU.

In our demo, we will use the TensorFlow framework, which is the most popular among these engines.

11.3.3 Hardware Capability

As the various deep learning libraries and frameworks evolved, the need for more powerful and specialized processing hardware also started picking up. Starting from the general purpose CPUs to the latest Tensor Processing Units (TPUs) from Google, these specialized hardware designs are intricately built by keeping in mind the kind of operations deep learning networks entail. Google's TPU has been designed for efficient and faster IOs to bring down the amount of time it takes to train a model.

The Graphical Processing Unit (GPU), which is widely used in high-definition animation rendering and gaming systems, was repurposed for performing high-speed computations. In the current work on deep learning, GPUs are the most preferred choice of processing unit for their faster model training.

11.3.4 Programming Language Choice

The choice of programming language for building a machine learning and deep learning model has been over the years slowly drifting toward Python. This popularity of Python is mostly attributed to the readiness of Python code for production deployments. It's robust and widely regarded as at-par with traditional programming languages like C/C++, which are built for speed and with elegance.

In order to keep the consistency throughout the book, for all the demos in the chapter, we have adopted using R.

11.3.5 Cloud Infrastructure

Since a deep learning model requires a lot of computational power, the commodity hardware in one's private infrastructure like laptops or desktops are not equipped with the required capability. There are many choices available in the public cloud, like Amazon AWS, Google Cloud, and Microsoft Azure. For the purpose of our demos in the book, readers can choose one of these options in the rstudio blog: `https://blog.rstudio.com/2018/09/12/getting-started-with-deep-learning-in-r/`.

However, we have chosen an example dataset and problem that can pretty much work in a modest capacity desktop or laptop system. Keep in mind that all cloud platforms have a cost associated with them. Read the pricing structure carefully before using any cloud platforms.

11.4 Use Case: Identify Duplicate Questions in Quora

Quora in the year 2017 had offered an extensive Quora Question Pairs dataset, containing 404,000 question pairs in a Kaggle (an online platform for many data science projects) competition. The objective of the competition was to get the most accurate model for predicting which pair of questions is a duplicate. For a platform like Quora, this will hugely help them in question categorization, assignment, and so on. The problem sounds very trivial for the human mind, but when it comes to machine's understanding the semantic meaning of a pair of questions, it involves a complex learning process. So, what better suits deep learning when it comes to a complex problem?

In the following demonstration in R, we walk you through a implementation called the Siamese Recurrent Architecture. We would like to credit Daniel Falbel with the post, "Classifying Duplicate Questions from Quora with Keras" at `https://blogs.rstudio.com/tensorflow/posts/2018-01-09-keras-duplicate-questions-quora/`[6].

11.4.1 Environment Setup

First we need to install Keras and TensorFlow as the backend. They provide all the library we need for data preprocessing and model building:

```
#Installing Keras

install.packages("keras")
library(keras)
install_keras()

#Install TensorFlow as a Backend for Keras. By default it takes CPU but you could also mention, "tensorflow = "gpu"

install_keras(tensorflow)
```

11.4.2 Data Preprocessing

In order to run our model, we need to prepare the data in an appropriate format. The following code tokenizes the words into integers using the `text_tokenizer` and `fit_text_tokenizer` methods from the keras library:

```
#loading keras
library(keras)

#Data can be downloaded from
#https://www.kaggle.com/c/quora-question-pairs/data

quora_data <- read.csv("train.csv")
quora_data <- quora_data[1:1000,]

quora_data$question1 = as.character(quora_data$question1)
quora_data$question2 = as.character(quora_data$question2)

# Example Question Pairs
quora_data$question1[1]

 [1] "What is the step by step guide to invest in share market in india?"

quora_data$question2[1]

 [1] "What is the step by step guide to invest in share market?"

#Keras tokenizer

tokenizer <- text_tokenizer(num_words = 50000)
tokenizer %>% fit_text_tokenizer(unique(c(quora_data$question1,
quora_data$question2)))

#Text tokenizer to transform each question1 and question2 into a list of
integers

question1 <- texts_to_sequences(tokenizer, quora_data$question1)
question2 <- texts_to_sequences(tokenizer, quora_data$question2)
```

In the following code, we compute the length of each question (number of words). Since all the questions are not equal in length, we need to pad the word list with additional integers starting from 50001 (we have used the integer 1 to 50000 during tokenization). Padding normalizes the sequences to the same size so that we can feed them to the model.

```
library(purrr)
questions_length <- c(
  map_int(question1, length),
  map_int(question2, length)
)
```

From the quantiles, we can observe that 99% of questions have at most length 31 so we can choose a padding length between 15 and 30. We can pick 20 to begin with (we can also tune this parameter later).

```
#80th, 90th, 95th and 99th Quantiles

quantile(questions_length, c(0.8, 0.9, 0.95, 0.99))

  80%   90%   95%   99%
14.00 18.00 23.00 30.01

# Padding Length = 20
question1_padded <- pad_sequences(question1, maxlen = 20, value = 50000 + 1)
question2_padded <- pad_sequences(question2, maxlen = 20, value = 50000 + 1)
```

11.4.3 Benchmark Model

In order to appreciate the goodness of this deep learning model, let's build a very crude benchmarking model using logistic regression and discuss its limitations.

We will create two predictors (input variables): percentage of words from question1 that appear in question2 and vice versa. Then we will use a logistic regression to predict if the questions are duplicates (Yes or No).

```
percentage_words_question1 <- map2_dbl(question1, question2,
~mean(.x %in% .y))
percentage_words_question2 <- map2_dbl(question2, question1,
~mean(.x %in% .y))

quora_logit_model <- data.frame(
  percentage_words_question1 = percentage_words_question1,
  percentage_words_question2 = percentage_words_question2,
  is_duplicate = quora_data$is_duplicate
) %>%
  na.omit()
```

```
#With this input variables, we'll create the logistic model. We will take
10% of the data as a sample for validation.

val_sample <- sample.int(nrow(quora_logit_model), 0.1*nrow(quora_logit_model))
quora_logistic_regression <- glm(
  is_duplicate ~ percentage_words_question1 + percentage_words_question2,
  family = "binomial",
  data = quora_logit_model[-val_sample,]
)
summary(quora_logistic_regression)

Call:
glm(formula = is_duplicate ~ percentage_words_question1 + percentage_words_
question2,
    family = "binomial", data = quora_logit_model[-val_sample,
        ])

Deviance Residuals:
    Min       1Q   Median       3Q      Max
-1.5921  -0.9099  -0.6120   1.1451   2.0271

Coefficients:
                            Estimate Std. Error z value
(Intercept)                -2.253465   0.009658 -233.32
percentage_words_question1  1.523784   0.023031   66.16
percentage_words_question2  1.666304   0.022780   73.15
                           Pr(>|z|)
(Intercept)                  <2e-16 ***
percentage_words_question1   <2e-16 ***
percentage_words_question2   <2e-16 ***
---
Signif. codes:  0 '***' 0.001 '**' 0.01 '*' 0.05 '.' 0.1 ' ' 1

(Dispersion parameter for binomial family taken to be 1)

    Null deviance: 479144  on 363842  degrees of freedom
Residual deviance: 431873  on 363840  degrees of freedom
AIC: 431879
```

```
Number of Fisher Scoring iterations: 3

#Calculate the accuracy on our validation set

pred <- predict(quora_logistic_regression, quora_logit_model[val_sample,],
type = "response")
pred <- pred > mean(quora_logit_model$is_duplicate[-val_sample])
accuracy <- table(pred, quora_logit_model$is_duplicate[val_sample]) %>%
  prop.table() %>%
  diag() %>%
  sum()
accuracy
## [1] 0.75
```

We get an accuracy of around 65%. This is slightly better than a random guess. Now let's see how the deep leaning model performs.

11.4.4 Siamese Recurrent Architectures

We will use a Siamese Network based on the research paper, "Siamese Recurrent Architectures for Learning Sentence Similarity," to predict whether the pair of questions is duplicated. It's a special type of neural network where instead of model learning to classify its inputs, the neural network learns to differentiate between two inputs.

11.4.4.1 Siamese Adaptation of the Long Short-Term

The memory (LSTM) network for labeled data comprised of pairs of variable-length sequences is applied to assess semantic similarity between questions (unlike the logistic regression we saw in the previous section where we took the word-to-word similarity).

Figure 11-8 shows the Siamese Network consisting of two similar neural networks, each taking one of the two input questions. The last layers of the two networks are then fed to a contrastive loss function (unlike the classification problem where we typically take a cross entropy loss function). The two sister networks are identical with the exact same weights.

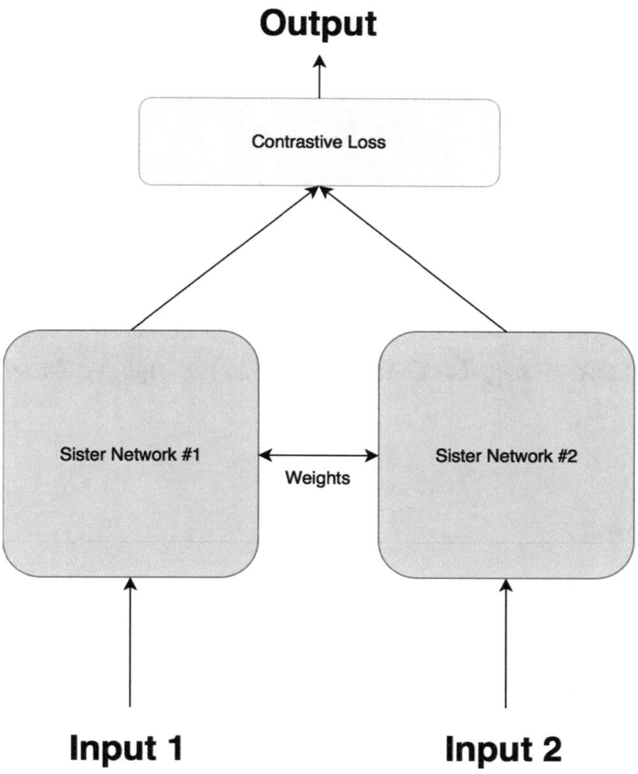

Figure 11-8. *Siamese Architecture. Source:* *https://hackernoon.com/one-shot-learning-with-siamese-networks-in-pytorch-8ddaab10340e*

11.4.4.2 Building the Siamese Architecture

The following code will construct the various layers of the Siamese Architecture.

Inputs of the Model

```
input1 <- layer_input(shape = c(20), name = "input_question1")
input2 <- layer_input(shape = c(20), name = "input_question2")
```

Embed the Questions in a Vector

```
word_embedder <- layer_embedding(
  input_dim = 50000 + 2, # vocab size + UNK token + padding value
  output_dim = 128,      # hyperparameter - embedding size
```

```
  input_length = 20,      # padding size,
  embeddings_regularizer = regularizer_l2(0.0001) # hyperparameter -
  regularization
)
```

LSTM Layer

```
seq_embedder <- layer_lstm(
  units = 128, # hyperparameter -- sequence embedding size
  kernel_regularizer = regularizer_l2(0.0001) # hyperparameter -
regularization
)
```

Embeddings Layers

Define the relationship between the input vectors and the embeddings layers. Here we use the same layers and weights on both inputs—the Siamese Network. Even if we switch question1 and question2, the architecture makes sure that we don't get two different outputs:

```
vector1 <- input1 %>% word_embedder() %>% seq_embedder()
vector2 <- input2 %>% word_embedder() %>% seq_embedder()
```

Cosine Similarity

Cosine similarity is used. The syntax shows that it's a dot product of the two vectors without the normalization part.

```
cosine_similarity <- layer_dot(list(vector1, vector2), axes = 1)
```

Sigmoid Layer

The final sigmoid layer to output the probability of both questions:

```
output <- cosine_similarity %>%
  layer_dense(units = 1, activation = "sigmoid")
```

11.4.5 The Keras Model

The Keras model defined in terms of its inputs and outputs. The model minimizes the *logloss*, which is equivalent to minimizing the binary cross entropy using the Adam optimizer.

```
model <- keras_model(list(input1, input2), output)
model %>% compile(
  optimizer = "adam",
  metrics = list(acc = metric_binary_accuracy),
  loss = "binary_crossentropy"
)
```

11.4.6 The Model Summary

```
summary(model)
```

```
________________________________________________________________
Layer (type)          Output Shape  Param  Connected to
================================================================
input_question1 (In (None, 20)    0
________________________________________________________________
input_question2 (In (None, 20)    0
________________________________________________________________
embedding_3 (Embedd (None, 20, 12 640025 input_question1[0][0]
                                          input_question2[0][0]
________________________________________________________________
lstm_3 (LSTM)         (None, 128)   131584 embedding_3[0][0]
                                          embedding_3[1][0]
________________________________________________________________
dot_3 (Dot)           (None, 1)     0      lstm_3[0][0]
                                          lstm_3[1][0]
________________________________________________________________
dense_4 (Dense)       (None, 1)     2      dot_3[0][0]
================================================================
Total params: 6,531,842
Trainable params: 6,531,842
Non-trainable params: 0
________________________________________________________________
```

11.4.7 The Validation Sample

Sample for validation before model fitting:

```
set.seed(1817328)
val_sample <- sample.int(nrow(question1_padded),
size = 0.1*nrow(question1_padded))

train_question1_padded <- question1_padded[-val_sample,]
train_question2_padded <- question2_padded[-val_sample,]
train_for_duplicate <- quora_data$is_duplicate[-val_sample]

val_question1_padded <- question1_padded[val_sample,]
val_question2_padded <- question2_padded[val_sample,]
val_is_duplicate <- quora_data$is_duplicate[val_sample]
```

11.4.8 Train the Model

We use the `fit()` function to train the model. The function takes the padded question1 and question2 along with parameters like batch size, number of epochs, and validation dataset.

```
model %>% fit(
  list(train_question1_padded, train_question2_padded),
  train_for_duplicate,
  batch_size = 64,
  epochs = 10,
  validation_data = list(
    list(val_question1_padded, val_question2_padded),
    val_is_duplicate
  )
)
```

```
Train on 363861 samples, validate on 40429 samples
Epoch 1/10
363861/363861 [==============================] - 2010s 6ms/step - loss:
0.5807 - acc: 0.7447 - val_loss: 0.5424 - val_acc: 0.7732
```

```
Epoch 2/10
363861/363861 [==============================] - 1894s 5ms/step -
loss: 0.5254 - acc: 0.7835 - val_loss: 0.5150 - val_acc: 0.7900
Epoch 3/10
363861/363861 [==============================] - 1845s 5ms/step -
loss: 0.4999 - acc: 0.7986 - val_loss: 0.5015 - val_acc: 0.7960
Epoch 4/10
363861/363861 [==============================] - 1841s 5ms/step -
loss: 0.4812 - acc: 0.8099 - val_loss: 0.4882 - val_acc: 0.8044
Epoch 5/10
363861/363861 [==============================] - 1838s 5ms/step -
loss: 0.4672 - acc: 0.8175 - val_loss: 0.4844 - val_acc: 0.8069
Epoch 6/10
363861/363861 [==============================] - 1851s 5ms/step -
loss: 0.4565 - acc: 0.8233 - val_loss: 0.4804 - val_acc: 0.8105
Epoch 7/10
363861/363861 [==============================] - 1859s 5ms/step -
loss: 0.4481 - acc: 0.8291 - val_loss: 0.4762 - val_acc: 0.8116
Epoch 8/10
363861/363861 [==============================] - 1855s 5ms/step -
loss: 0.4413 - acc: 0.8338 - val_loss: 0.4767 - val_acc: 0.8147
Epoch 9/10
363861/363861 [==============================] - 1840s 5ms/step -
loss: 0.4343 - acc: 0.8385 - val_loss: 0.4726 - val_acc: 0.8173
Epoch 10/10
363861/363861 [==============================] - 1847s 5ms/step -
loss: 0.4278 - acc: 0.8420 - val_loss: 0.4695 - val_acc: 0.8189
```

11.4.9 Save the Model

We could save our model for inference with the save_model_hdf5() function.

```
save_model_hdf5(model, "model-question-pairs.hdf5")
```

11.4.10 Model Performance

We could observe that the LSTM based deep learning performed far better than our benchmark logistic regression model. Although we have stopped at nine epochs, it seems possible that if we run `fit()` for a few more epochs, the accuracy will further increase with the drop in the loss. The closeness of the two lines in Figure 11-9 of training data loss and validation loss show no sign of overfitting or underfitting, which is a good sign. The same argument could be made by looking at the training and validation accuracy, in the bottom plot of Figure 11-9.

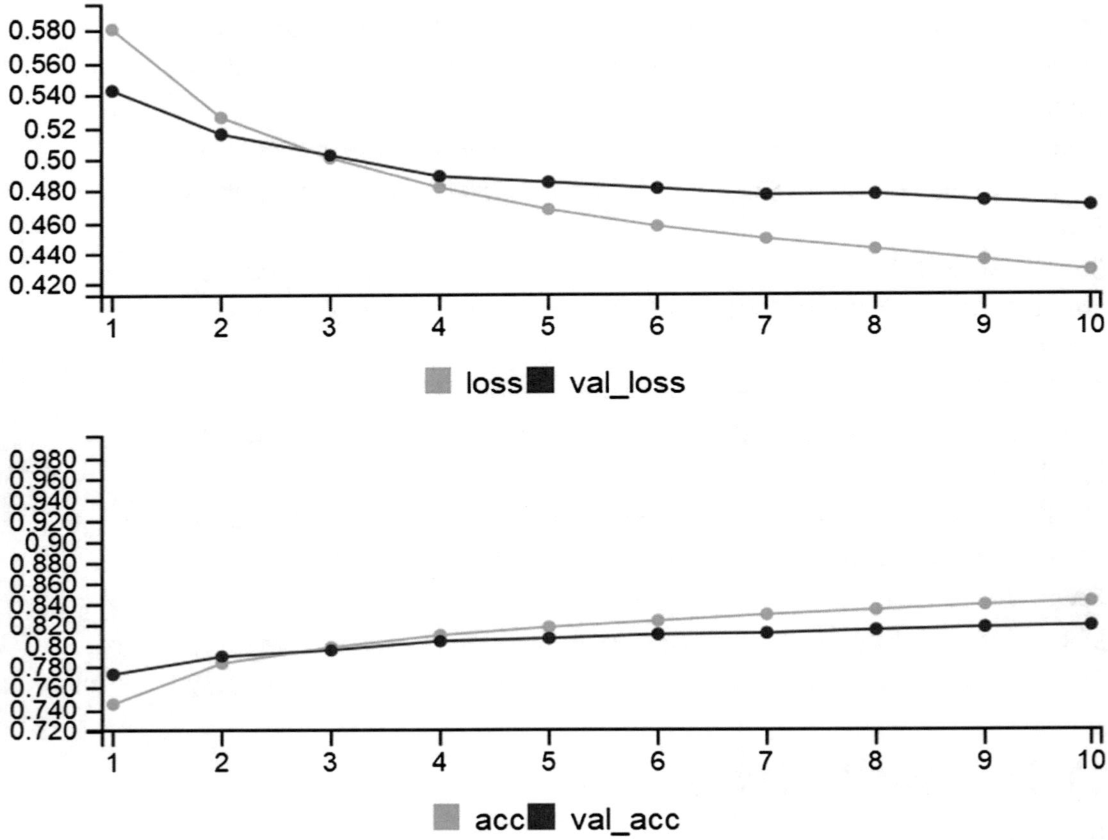

Figure 11-9. *Model performance during the model fitting*

11.4.11 Make Predictions

Once the model is trained, we can use it for predictions. We need to perform the same preprocessing that we did during the training before we can use the model for prediction. The score tells the probability of similarity.

```
library(keras)
model <- load_model_hdf5("model-question-pairs.hdf5", compile = FALSE)
tokenizer <- load_text_tokenizer("tokenizer-question-pairs")

predict_question_pairs <- function(model, tokenizer, question1, question2) {
  question1 <- texts_to_sequences(tokenizer, list(question1))
  question2 <- texts_to_sequences(tokenizer, list(question2))

  question1 <- pad_sequences(question1, 20)
  question2 <- pad_sequences(question2, 20)

  as.numeric(predict(model, list(question1, question2)))
}
```

11.4.12 Example Predictions

We can pass different pairs of questions to see how the model performs:

```
predict_question_pairs(
  model,
  tokenizer,
  "What is Machine Learning?",
  "What is Deep Learning?"
)

[1] 0.475016

#Example 2
predict_question_pairs(
  model,
  tokenizer,
  "What is Machine Learning",
  "What are Machine Learning algorithms"
)
```

```
[1] 0.499557

#Example 2
predict_question_pairs(
  model,
  tokenizer,
  "What is a Machine Learning",
  "What is a Machine Learning algorithm"
)

[1] 0.5062091
```

We could observe that the score improves as we bring the textual likeliness of questions closer to one another. This algorithm performs well with even the semantic meaning of the questions. However, to increase the accuracy of this model further, we need to perform either a greater number of epochs or tune the hyperparameters. The entire exercise of improving the model, as we discussed in our PEBE model building flow, requires a trial-and-error approach before we could finally determine the best model.

We also encourage readers to explore the model hyperparameter tuning, which would further improve the model accuracy. You can further refer to the code by Daniel Falbel [11] for hyperparameter tuning. Keep in mind that the hyperparameter tuning may require considerable computation resources. Consider using some of the cloud platform as mentioned earlier in the chapter.

11.5 Summary

In this concluding chapter of the book, we provided a brief introduction to various deep learning architecture and showed one real-world use case using a custom LSTM-based deep learning architecture. The modular way of experimenting with deep learning architecture has made the field of deep learning interesting and it's leading to a new wave of solutions to complex problems. Researchers around the world are coming out with numerous innovative architectures and they are ever growing in number. We also hope in the coming years that the implementation of various deep learning models will be equally adapted for R and Python.

Index

A

B

K. Ramasubramanian and A. Singh, *Machine Learning Using R*, https://doi.org/10.1007/978-1-4842-4215-5

C

D

E

I

J

K

L

M

N

T

U

V

W, X, Y, Z

Printed in the United States
By Bookmasters